THE IMPERFECT UNION

THE IMPERFECT UNION

*A History of Corruption
in American Trade Unions*

by John Hutchinson

E. P. Dutton & Co., Inc.
NEW YORK   1970

First Edition
Copyright © 1970 by John Hutchinson
All rights reserved. Printed in the U.S.A.

Published simultaneously in Canada by Clarke, Irwin & Company Limited, Toronto and Vancouver

Library of Congress Catalog Card Number: 71-95467

In Tribute
to my Mother
Dorothy Marshall Hutchinson
and
to my Father
John Edward Hutchinson

Preface

In the spring of 1957 the United States Senate authorized an investigation of improper practices in American labor-management relations. Conducted under the chairmanship of Senator John L. McClellan of Arkansas, the inquiry lasted over three years, involved 1,526 witnesses, and produced 46,-510 pages of testimony. It revealed conflicts of interest, breaches of faith, bribery, extortion, theft and violence on the part of union officials and others in the pursuit of private gain. It attracted world-wide attention, moved the American labor movement to unprecedented disciplinary action against some of its constituent unions, and resulted in an Act of Congress which imposed stringent and most unwelcome restrictions on the activities of American unions. It was the most devastating indictment of American trade union behavior ever compiled.

But if the evidence was damning, it was also incomplete. The problem was an old one, dating back to the nineteenth century; but few attempts were made to explain its origins and persistence. The scale of present wrong-doing was a surprise to trade unionist and layman alike; but little was done to apportion the blame. As with almost all previous inquiries into trade union corruption, the McClellan investigation was directed overwhelmingly at the imperfections of union leaders alone, at the fact of misbehavior but not the cause, at the need for the reform of labor organizations but not of the conditions which surround them. The charges of corruption were in most cases valid enough. It is not so clear that the sources of the trouble were adequately understood, or that the Congress took proper care to make the punishment fit the crimes.

Trade union corruption is a complex matter. Whatever the inducements or compulsions, there is always the personal decision to corrupt or be corrupted; no analysis of corrupt trade union behavior can bypass the matter of the philosophical equipment of the trade unionist who betrays his calling. It is also a problem of union government; the incidence of error usually bears some relationship to the abuse or indifference of the union member.

These are the most obvious factors, but they are not the only ones. Corruption owes little more to immoral union leaders than it does to predatory employers who, throughout the history of American business, have sought by cheating and violence to circumvent the strictures of competition, union-

7

ization, and the law. It is a companion of the corruption in politics and law enforcement which for generations has characterized some of the major cities of the nation, sheltering the guilty and embroiling the innocent in crime. It owes a debt to the insanity of Prohibition and its enduring legacy of organized defiance of the law. It thrives in the procedural jungle of the American criminal law. It stems from the social conditions of the cities— from the tensions of an immigrant society, the customs of racial discrimination and ethnic isolation, the miseries of the slums and the frustrations of the underprivileged, the ignorance of the poor and the indifference of the rich. It has, finally, drawn strength from a public philosophy which, in electing for the competitive society, has tended to trumpet only its virtues, according either praise or tolerance to the victors in a battle lightly burdened with rules.

Corruption is neither simple in origin nor easy to repair. The revelations of the McClellan Committee and its forbears brought about an interest in change and the passing of new laws to effect it. Those laws have in important ways been salutary, disciplining the internal processes of unions and the behavior of their officials, raising the standards of fiscal responsibility and increasing the sensitivity of leaders to the interests of their members. But in some ways they have also been irrelevant, if not punitive; a feature of the most recent labor legislation is the restrictions it imposes, in the name of morality, on economic activities of unions which bear no essential relationship to immorality. It is probably too much to expect the early disappearance of all the major factors which produce trade union corruption; but if patience is required, the labor movement should not in the interim be selected for punishment irrelevant to conditions for which, in any case, it bears only a most limited responsibility. If the aim is understanding rather than accusation and remedy rather than retribution, there is a duty to look beyond the institution of trade unionism to the forces which influence its ways. Trade union corruption, such as it is, is fundamentally a problem of the society in which it exists. It should be solved by the many, not left to the few.

This, at any rate, is the thesis here. It is open to challenge, if only because of the inadequacy of its documentation.

Corruption is an elusive subject. It is, first of all, a matter of standards. There are many aspects of trade union behavior which, depending on the disposition of the observer, can be regarded as admirable or base, dishonest or realistic, destructive or statesmanlike; the field for debate is immense. One principle, however, is hopefully beyond dispute: that trade unionism should not be employed as an instrument of commercial profit. I have therefore chosen to regard corruption as the use of union power for private enrichment by anyone. There are other forms of the disease, but I am concerned with them here only as they contribute to the unsanctioned pursuit of money. This is a selective standard; but it seems to be a pertinent one, quite sufficient for one volume.

The great problem is evidence. Some corruption is undetectable, or obscure in nature and extent. Some of it, in the zone between slander and proof, is a matter for conjecture, fine material for the scavenger but a nightmare for the scholar. Equally exasperating are those charges of misbehavior which, through folklore or personal inquiry, are believed true by the investigator but—because of the demands of evidence, the dangers of libel, or the vulnerability of those involved—are unprintable. Even where corruption is established by investigation or confession, the detail is often blurred, the responsibility diffuse, the balance of causes unclear.

The truth is seldom easy to establish. The corrupt have their own reasons for silence. Loyalty to the organization, legitimate or mistaken, often curbs the tongues of those close to the guilty. Fear, whether of organizational discipline or underworld reprisals, is an effective mute. The apologetics of union leaders, the extravagances of business and other critics, and the pieties of public officials, are poor materials. Private records of unsavory episodes are seldom available, and definitive public documentation is rare. The writer on corruption is accordingly denied the precision of evidence and conclusion enjoyed by commentators on healthier subjects, compelled to modesty in theory and restraint in his judgments on men.

But documents do exist, confessions have been made, trials and investigations have been held, and men of experience and responsibility have had their say. There may even be, in the mass of careless comment on the subject, a limited but real persuasiveness in sheer volume; not all of the charges can be untrue, and there seems to run through all but the most venomous of speculations a vein of fact which cannot be ignored. It might not be impossible, that is, to construct with care a case which reasonable men can believe.

The aim is justice; the problem is proportion; the danger is exaggeration. Corruption is a colorful subject, and it is easy for the imagination to enlarge upon the importance of the evidence. Further, any student with a decade and a fortune at his disposal could no doubt uncover more corruption than has been recorded. But it would be infamous to infer that where there is silence there is abounding sin, that corruption—like the iceberg—lies largely below the surface. Few subjects have been investigated so lengthily in modern times; few subjects attract the light so quickly. There cannot be much more to tell; two generations of ethical respectability on the part of the vast majority of union officials is a safe assumption. I have found it necessary, furthermore, to discriminate among the evidence. There are some instances—not cited here—where corruption has been charged, but where the usable evidence is poor or debatable. Other cases are minor, hardly of consequence in character or impact; their inclusion, even if they could be properly documented, would contribute little but saturation to the account. I have, therefore, chosen those examples of corruption which represent the major themes, or have been most in the public eye, and for which the fullest documentation is available. I hope it is not too much to claim that they represent the heart and most of the scale of the problem.

This is a history of corrupt practices in American trade unionism and labor-management relations from about 1890 to the early 1960's, and a commentary on causes and remedies. Whatever the imperfections of the book, the lessons of the period and the problem should inform the judgment of every citizen concerned with the free society and the proper contribution of free trade unionism to its preservation.

John Hutchinson
Los Angeles

Acknowledgments

I am not sure that everyone mentioned here will be happy about it. They have all been helpful in one way or another, and it would seem churlish not to acknowledge their contribution. But the subject is a sensitive one, and mine by no means the only point of view. It is therefore particularly important for me to say that I alone am responsible for what is written here. Indeed, my relations with those listed below have ranged from fraternal concord to downright disagreement. I apologize if the recording of any names has caused offense. There are others who have helped, but who must remain anonymous. I am equally grateful to them.

This book has been prepared largely in association with the Institute of Industrial Relations on the Berkeley campus of the University of California, and the Institute of Industrial Relations and the Graduate School of Business Administration on the Los Angeles campus of the University. It has taken a long time to write. I am indebted to Benjamin Aaron, Irving Bernstein, Earl Cheit, Frederic Meyers, Arthur M. Ross and Lloyd Ulman for their friendship and patience with a slow colleague. An earlier version of the manuscript was accepted some years ago by the University of London as a Ph.D. thesis. I am grateful to Ben Roberts of the London School of Economics and Allen Flanders of Oxford University for their consideration and advice.

Philip Taft has read the entire manuscript and freely offered me the benefit of his immense knowledge of American labor history. Walter Galenson, the late Joseph Lohman, and the late Peter Odegard were generous in their time and suggestions.

I have sought the help or criticism of many trade union officials. I am particularly grateful to President Paul Hall of the Seafarers International Union of North America who, whatever our respective points of view, has been prepared to discuss with characteristic candor the issues involved. Others to whom I am grateful for comments or assistance include the late Vice-President Anthony Anastasio, International Longshoremen's Association; Herb Brand, Editor, *The Seafarers Log;* President Russell Crowell, AFL-CIO Laundry and Dry Cleaning International Union; President Emeritus David Dubinsky, International Ladies Garment Workers Union; Ted Ellsworth, formerly of the International Association of Theatrical and Stage Employees and now of the Institute of Industrial Relations, UCLA;

the late Secretary-Treasurer John F. English, International Brotherhood of Teamsters; Nat Goldfinger, Director of Research, AFL-CIO; Vice-President George Hardy, Service Employees International Union; President Ralph Helstein, United Packinghouse Workers of America; President Sal Hoffman, Upholsterers International Union; Logan Kimmel, Records Administrator, AFL-CIO; Lane Kirkland, Secretary-Treasurer, AFL-CIO; the late President Emeritus John L. Lewis, United Mine Workers of America; Gene Mailes, formerly of the IATSE; Peter McGavin, Executive Secretary-Treasurer, Maritime Trades Department, AFL-CIO and former Special Assistant to President Meany; President Ed Miller, Hotel and Restaurant Employees and Bartenders International Union; President Jacob Potofsky, Amalgamated Clothing Workers of America; President Alex Rose, United Hatters, Cap and Millinery Workers International Union; Leon Stein, Editor, *Justice;* former President James A. Suffridge, Retail Clerks International Association; President David Sullivan, Service Employees International Union; Assistant President Gus Tyler, ILGWU; Secretary-Treasurer Morris Weisberger, Sailors Union of the Pacific; President Jerry Wurf, American Federation of State, County and Municipal Employees; and Vice-President Charles Zimmerman, ILGWU. However, I feel bound to note that I have solicited the comments of various other union leaders, but without response.

A number of government officials and private citizens were helpful. They include Myles Ambrose, former Executive Director, Waterfront Commission of New York Harbor; Congressman Jeffery Cohelan of California; the late Commissioner John Holcombe, Bureau of Labor-Management Affairs, United States Department of Labor; J. Edgar Hoover, Director, Federal Bureau of Investigation; Harold Huxley, Regional Director, Office of Labor-Management and Welfare Fund Reports, United States Department of Labor; the late Senator Robert F. Kennedy; Frank Hogan, District Attorney, New York City; Virgil Peterson, Operating Director, Chicago Crime Commission; John Siegenthaler, former assistant to Attorney General Robert F. Kennedy; and Mathew O. Tobriner, Associate Justice, Supreme Court of California.

Nancy Fujita, the most perfect of secretaries, bore for years the administrative and typing burden. Margaret Mould and Hazelle Van Gorder helped in a variety of ways. Ray Goodman, Shirley Matthews, Barbara Palmer, Rose Price, Helen Scroggs and Barbara Stempel helped with the typing. Rose Price and Helen Scroggs alone typed the entire final version of the manuscript. Trevor Bain, Glen Cain, Lester Rosenthal, Frank Rush, Jeffrey Schevitz, Dennis Scott and Edgar Vermeesch assisted with bibliographical and other research.

John Neale, Town Clerk of Salisbury, Rhodesia, gave me—during long hours and out of an old friendship brightly renewed—the benefit of his rich experience in local government, and other wise counsel besides.

The late Sam Eubanks contributed more than he knew to whatever is valuable in this book. He was a distinguished trade union official and public servant, the best of friends, and gave all the time and wisdom that he had.

My wife and children have suffered long and patiently in the writing of this book. I hope it was worth it.

John Hutchinson
Los Angeles

Contents

Part I
The Prologue

In the closing years of the nineteenth century, the American labor movement came to a turning point in its commitments and fortunes. For nearly a hundred years it had known little but defeat. Impatient with the hardships and felt inequities of early American life, many labor organizations had cast about for ideas which would bring them greater strength and security—experimenting with political unionism, socialism, syndicalism, anarchism, cooperation, and the One Big Union. Inexperienced in organization, unrealistic in expectations, harried by a hostile society, addicted to schemes too visionary for their members, their occasional heady successes were never more than preludes to oblivion.

By the end of the century, however, one strain had prevailed. In business unionism—the pursuit of improvements in wages, hours and working conditions primarily through collective bargaining with private employers —had been found a philosophy more finely attuned to circumstance, much more realistic and productive, than its competitors. It accepted the mores and institutions of capitalist America, in R. F. Hoxie's phrase, "as inevitable, if not as just." It was primarily an economic idea, seeking its rewards in the legislatures, suspicious of politics and public authority. It regarded the trade union not as an instrument for social reform but as a bargaining agent concerned with early and tangible gains. If, in practice, it permitted the championship of broader causes, its motives were essentially utilitarian; and if it lacked the glory of more cosmic philosophies, it suited the dispositions of an increasing number of people. By 1900 it was without a serious rival.

The bearer of the now dominant tradition was the American Federation of Labor. Founded in 1886, and based on craft unions of skilled workers limited in their expectations of trade unionism, it was committed to business unionism from the outset.

The times, it seemed to the leaders of the AFL, were unpropitious for a labor movement with broad ambitions. This was, after all, the Gilded Age, the high tide of American capitalism. The mounting power of corporate enterprise had grafted upon the public conscience a philosophy of acquisition. Economic gain was the proper goal of every citizen; the market was the only reliable testing ground of ability and contribution; wealth was the true mark of success and even of virtue; and the unsuccessful should accept

19

their fate. It was the best of all possible systems, sanctioned by results and even the Almighty. "The good Lord," said John D. Rockefeller, "gave me my money."

The morals of the business community spread to the legislatures and the courts. Politics was regarded by many of its practitioners as a means of personal enrichment, bribery as a proper source of power and income. "If you have to pay money to have the right thing done," said Collis P. Huntington, the founder of the Southern Pacific Railroad, "it is only right and just to do it." The judiciary was also proper quarry for the spoilsman. "I think the time well spent," Huntington commented, "when it is a man's duty to go up and bribe the judge."

Prompted by bribery or not, the courts came to read the gospel of wealth into the laws of the land. "The Supreme Court," Ralph Henry Gabriel wrote, "abandoned its ancient policy of self-restraint. It transformed the old due-process clause into an instrument with which it built the individualism of the gospel of wealth into the constitutional law of the nation. It called a corporation a person so that no property would go unprotected. It created in the doctrine of the freedom of contract a weapon with which to meet the challenge of organized labor to the absolute authority of the employer within his shop." The lower courts followed suit. In the last twenty-five years of the century, statutes requiring a statement of cause for the discharge of an employee, forbidding the use of scrip or payment in kind, outlawing or regulating company stores, fixing the hours of work in private employment, and protecting the right of workmen to join unions, were all struck down as unconstitutional.

Then, to confirm the worst fears of the establishment, came the spectre of trade union violence. The bombings and killings in the anthracite fields during the 1870's, attributed to the Molly Maguires; the anarcho-syndicalist overtones of the Haymarket riot in 1886; and the violence of the various railroad and steel industry strikes of the times—all pressed upon the public mind an image of the labor movement as a threat to property, peace, and the liberty of the citizen. Particularly after the Haymarket affair, the legislatures, the courts and the employers joined in an unprecedented effort to place fresh curbs on the activities of unions. "I am tired of hearing about laws for the benefit of men who work in the shops," said William Jennings Bryan. Legislatures dominated by business interests passed a spate of laws placing new restrictions on union rights. Court records showed a sharp increase in the number of trade unionists convicted of conspiracy, coercion and breaches of the peace. Employers launched open shop campaigns, fought unions with lockouts and private police, made free with the blacklist and the yellow dog contract. It was an age of danger for organized labor, and a time to take stock. The success of trade unionism, it seemed to AFL President Samuel Gompers and those who followed him, depended upon a realistic adaptation to the conditions of the times.

"We are practical men," Adolph Strasser told a committee of the United States Senate in 1885. "We have no ultimate ends. We are going on from day to day. We are fighting only for immediate objects—objects that can be realized in a few years." Strasser, president of the Cigar Makers and one of Gompers' closest associates, spoke for the AFL.

The federation's position was clear. Intellectuals, prone to panaceas, were not to be trusted. The association of trade unionism with revolutionary movements was self-contradictory and always disastrous. Producers' or workers' cooperatives were impractical and in any event incompatible with the institution of trade unionism. Independent political action was foolish; the existing major parties were too strong and flexible to be seriously challenged, and should be bargained with rather than fought. In any case, a minority such as organized labor should avoid dependence on legislation for strength and stability. Good laws were hard to get and uncertain in their implementation. Collective bargaining was more productive and reliable and should be the basic weapon of all unions, with the strike used only as the last resort. Unions should work primarily for stronger collective bargaining agreements, control over the job, and cooperation with the employers to enforce mutually acceptable rules of the trade. The corollary to the acceptance of a union was its respect for the rights of the employer and of private property. The creed of the AFL was thus a commitment to private enterprise, a suspicion of public authority, and a reliance on independent economic power in the pursuit of limited ends.

The AFL's suspicion of authority embraced its own. Throughout his life Gompers insisted on independence of action as the key to effective trade unionism. He and his associates always had more respect for an organization able to stand on its own feet than for one which leaned upon the federation or sister unions. The solidarity of trade unions was important, but less so than self-reliance. The first loyalty of the trade unionist was to his own organization. "I look first," Strasser said, "to the trade I represent; I look first to cigars, to the interests of men who employ me to represent their interests." The result was a spirit of confederation in the affairs of the AFL. The affiliation of individual unions with the federation was in any case voluntary, involving little surrender of autonomy. The only powers of the AFL were those delegated to it by its constituent unions, and they were sparingly endowed.

The looseness of federation government had its counterpart—if an increasingly qualified one—in the government of individual unions. The development of national union organization and authority was a major feature of American trade unionism in the late nineteenth and early twentieth centuries; the growth of national markets, the advent of large-scale corporations, the desire of unions to equalize bargaining power and union conditions from area to area, the dangers of non-union competition, the general objective of job control and the growing importance of federal legislation in trade union matters, all contributed to the centralization of authority in national unions.* But the process, for reasons of geography and habit, was slow and uneven. Further, the essentially local character of some industries —such as the building trades—required the vesting of considerable autonomy in the local affiliates of the national unions involved. As a result the disciplinary powers of some unions hardly exceeded those of the federation.

This combination of philosophy and structure was the leading characteristic of the American labor movement until recent times. It was a responsive system, deriving its forms and attitudes from the nature of the society with which it bargained. It was successful, if durability and economic advance are the yardsticks of success. It dominated the American labor movement until the great schism of 1935, achieved much for its members, survived the recessions and open shop campaigns of both centuries, and entrenched itself firmly in its chosen jurisdictions. It was, quite possibly, the system best suited to the times.

But it had its flaws. If craft unionism was the most practicable means of organization, it lent itself to insular action, encouraging division among those who in partnership might have protected their standards. If autonomy was the condition of association or effective bargaining, it often left free from retribution those who did violence to their trust. And if business unionism was the creed for the day, it made few demands on the social conscience of its adherents. The logic which created the AFL made it vulnerable to dishonest servants and predatory enemies. There was a price to be paid.

* National unions based in the United States which have members in Canada are referred to as international unions.

Part II
The Building Trades

1: The Industry

The building industry, declared Judge Kenesaw Mountain Landis in 1921, "is a thing diseased." It had been for a long time.

Building was a large industry, a bellwether of the economy. Traditionally highly speculative, rigorous in competition between small local firms, easy to enter and heavy in business casualties, it was also inefficient. It had never been much affected by technological change, and most of the work was done with simple tools. There was little outside competition—a fact which tended to harden into custom the technological deficiencies of the industry. And in time the absence of external challenge permitted the development of collusive practices among employers—including price-fixing and the rigging of bids—which reduced the discomforts of local competition and passed the burden of inflated costs on to the customer. Sometimes unions were involved.

Trade unionism in the construction industry became important after the Civil War. The unions were craft organizations, localized in operation and authority. Once firmly established, as they were in many major urban centers by 1900, they were more than a match for most employers. Employers' organizations were generally weak. In particular, since so much of the work was done by specialist subcontractors, employers tended to organize themselves and bargain with unions on a single craft basis. There were, in the late 1890's, virtually no city-wide employers' associations in existence.

The unions, on the other hand, enjoyed a number of advantages. In response to anti-union activities by the employers, they had begun in the last quarter of the century to employ full-time officials known as walking delegates * to protect their interests. And the need for full-time representatives was imperative. The violent opposition of some employers, the development of complex work rules, the geographical dispersion of work and the short duration of most construction projects, required the engagement of full-time officials, impervious to the threats of the employers, expert in the trade, with a roving commission and ample authority.

The job was rarely a sinecure. Anti-union sentiment in the early years was formidable and widespread; the walking delegate often suffered the antagonism, not only of employers, but of police and public officials. He was,

* Later to be known as business agents.

25

as Gompers once complained, a common object of ridicule, usually represented in the press as an illiterate bully, interested only in his own prosperity. He was often the victim of violence from outside, and of suspicion on the part of his constituents. He was seldom well-paid, and sometimes enjoyed less job security than those he represented.

But his position was inherently powerful. He was usually the chief executive of his local union, vested with considerable personal authority. He was the employment agent of his members and, if his local union was well organized, controlled the labor supply of the employers. He supervised the work of his craft and was the chief interpreter of labor-management agreements. Most important of all, he was empowered to call strikes. A time-consuming grievance procedure was useless in an industry where firms went quickly out of business, where workers were highly mobile, where the protection of jurisdictional rights was essential to survival, and where the short duration and scattered location of jobs made time the most crucial factor of all. The walking delegate was therefore given the right—unknown in unions with a more stable and physically concentrated membership—to call instantaneous strikes without seeking the consent of his members or the sanction of higher authorities. It was a powerful weapon and a tempting one, as events were to show.

Further, the building trade unions were usually affiliated with city-wide building trades councils. The power of the councils varied, but at a minimum they organized support for striking affiliates, and sometimes assumed great influence or control over organizing, bargaining and striking activities. Again, the employers were at a disadvantage. If they were not always concerned about price levels, they nevertheless often worked under terminal contracts which left them open to heavy fines if their projects were not finished on time. The high costs and speculative nature of the industry also made owners anxious to begin reaping a return on their investments as soon as possible.

A strike was thus the event most to be feared by contractors and owners alike. Rather than provoke a work stoppage, many of them were willing to meet the cost of a small wage increase or—at times and sometimes preferably—of a bribe to a union official. In turn, some union officials collected "strike insurance" from compliant or fearful employers in return for a promise of labor peace.

The relationship was not always uncordial. Few employers retained a permanent work force, preferring to depend on unions to supply labor when needed; naturally they wanted the best men available, and often cultivated friendly relationships with the union officials concerned. There was even an element of fraternity involved. Many contractors were former craftsmen themselves, usually—because of the uncertainties of the industry —retaining membership in their old unions, often returning to the trade in poorer times. Union leaders were usually close in ideology to the employers. Business unionism found its most advanced expression in the building trades. The union was regarded as a business institution, an agent for the economic interests of its members. The affairs of the craft came first, well before the claims of inter-union cooperation or the labor movement as a whole. Trade unionism was a matter of organized self-interest, not much concerned with larger issues or the general welfare. The building industry was, in some fashion, a philosophical community. If self-interest meant an occasional clash between labor and management, it was not inconsistent with a deep understanding of the meaning of the game. Better still, self-interests could coincide. They sometimes did, to the profit of the parties and at a cost to the community.

The conditions of the industry, in sum, conspired to make dishonesty an easy and profitable indulgence. Competition, when undisciplined, made some employers eager to bribe and some union officials happy to extort. Even when the absence of external competition and the ease of local collusion enabled employers to fix prices and rig bids, there were always employers anxious to bribe, and union officials strong enough to extort.

There was a third factor. Local government in the United States during the latter half of the nineteenth century and much of the twentieth was not noted for its honesty. "Those were the days," wrote Austin MacDonald, "of utter inefficiency, of complete indifference to public opinion . . . Virtually everywhere it was the same." Those were the great days of the party bosses, of corrupt political machines, of partisan and pecuniary law enforcement, of an organized sacking of the public purse. Public contracts were an especially lucrative source of graft, when the absence of effective control permitted the erection and maintenance of public facilities at grossly inflated prices, to the financial benefit of employers, union officials and political incumbents. In private building, tolerance for inferior standards was not hard to purchase. The law was often a party to systems of bribery and extortion. Political corruption, if it did not cause industrial corruption, was scarcely a hindrance to it. A segment of the construction industry, therefore, was governed from time to time and place to place by a quadrumvirate of grafters, rich in power and resources. But there was a limit to public tolerance, and each of the major conspiracies came under the scrutiny of the legislatures and the law. The first of these was uncovered in New York.

2: New York

"Tammany is Tammany," wrote Lincoln Steffens in 1903, "the embodiment of corruption." Tammany Hall, the headquarters of the Democratic Party in New York City, was temporarily out of favor when Steffens wrote of it, but for a generation it had been the major influence in city politics, earning for New York the reputation for being the worst-governed city in the country.

Tammany was not altogether corrupt. It was a service organization, most solicitous of its friends and potential supporters. Its agents at the ward and precinct levels performed many services of importance to the citizens of New York, not least to newly arrived immigrants who—ignorant of language, laws and customs—needed the help of experienced hands to meet their immediate and usually distressing problems. Tammany protected the ignorant from the inconveniences of the law, helped the poor and indigent, settled new Americans in gainful occupations, protected the jobs of those already at work and, with sure political touch, remembered birthdays and other anniversaries. "Tammany kindness," Steffens also said, "is real kindness, and will go far, remember long, and take infinite trouble for a friend."

All Tammany demanded was a vote. The great principle was loyalty. Violence was also a tradition in Tammany politics, used unsparingly to crush any opposition. Successive leaders of the Tammany machine rose to power through the use of their fists or more lethal weapons; there were few survivors of factional disputes. The treatment of external disloyalty or opposition was equally ruthless. Voters of dubious disposition were threatened or molested at the polls. Dissidents and Republicans within the reach of Tammany influence in public or private employment were likely to find themselves out of work. Businessmen who failed to pay proper tribute to Tammany were denied access to municipal contracts and harried in other matters by an unfriendly bureaucracy.

Such a system of intimidation and enforcement, of course, needed the cooperation of the police. Tammany was able to requisition it. The Board of Police Commissioners was elective, and it was dominated by Tammany Hall. The Board in turn controlled all appointments, transfers and promotions in the police force. The result was an organization not only tolerant of the nether side of Tammany operations but an active party to it.

28

In 1895 the New York State Senate appointed a special committee under Senator Clarence Lexow to investigate the New York City Police Department. "It has been shown," the Committee reported, "that in a very large number of election districts in the City of New York, almost every conceivable crime against the elective franchise was either committed or permitted by the police, invariably in the interest of the dominant Democratic organization of the city . . ." Republican voters, poll-watchers and anti-Tammany election workers were falsely arrested or physically attacked by policemen. Patrolmen acted as canvassers for Tammany, sometimes entering election booths to check on voting behavior. Police officers at all levels cooperated in the illegal registration of voters and the provision of "repeat" voters at the polls.

The police department was also a part of the machinery of graft. Patrolmen paid up to $300 for first appointments and further installments for desired assignments and promotions. Every police captain was associated with a Tammany wardman. The latter, in return for undisturbed operations, collected tribute from saloons, brothels, criminals, gamblers and businessmen, retaining an established proportion of the revenue and turning the remainder over to the captain. The captain took his share, giving the rest to his divisional inspector. Inspectors paid agreed amounts to police commissioners and Tammany district leaders. Policemen at all levels, in turn, engaged in their own rackets unmolested by Tammany Hall. "It seemed, in fact," the Lexow Committee said, "as though every interest, every occupation, almost every citizen, was dominated by an all-controlling and overshadowing dread of the police department." Even the lone Tammany representative on the Committee was driven to admit that the department should be reorganized.

One of the most fruitful fields of corruption was the construction industry. New York was growing rapidly, spending some $100,000,000 a year on new construction alone. The industry was regulated by the city's Department of Buildings, whose officials were legally vested with a great deal of discretion in the interpretation and enforcement of the rules. Most of these officials were Tammany appointees.

In 1900 the New York State Assembly appointed a special committee under Assemblyman Robert Mazet to study New York City politics. The Committee paid some attention to the building industry. "Here . . . ," the Committee said, "we find the dominant theory of the present government corrupt." The building inspectors of the Department were poorly paid and thus susceptible to bribery. Enforcement of the Department's rules varied widely, depending on the financial arrangements made between builders, the inspectorate, and higher officials. Some rules were ignored, inferior or dangerous construction was overlooked, and uncompetitive bids for public works were accepted. Contractors unacceptable to Tammany found their bids rejected, approval of their projects subjected to unexplained delays, or work in progress hampered by excessive inspection and literal interpretation of the rules. The building commissioner himself was allowed and used so much discretion that for all practical purposes, the Mazet Committee said, "there are no fixed and determined building laws in the City of New York."

The decisions of the commissioner could be appealed to a Board of Examiners. The Board, however, was composed mainly of employer representatives who showed little interest in changing the system. Bribery was regarded as standard procedure in the industry. For the rest, competition was discouraged and collusion in price-fixing and pre-arranged bidding was the general practice. "Corruption," according to the 1903 New York *Real Estate Record and Builders' Guide,* "was deep-seated and permeated the trades." But Tammany and the employers were not the only partners. Trade unionists were also involved.

In 1902 the building trades unions in New York City combined to form the United Board of Building Trades. It was a powerful organization, the Bricklayers being the only large union to remain unaffiliated. The Board was empowered to arbitrate inter-union jurisdictional disputes and to suspend local unions which refused to comply with its decisions. It also assumed strong influence over labor-management relations throughout the industry. An affiliated union might proceed independently against an employer, but in so doing it forfeited the support of the Board. Once a grievance against an employer was brought in, it became the property of the Board. The final arbiter of all grievances, the architect of unity and the dominant figure in the New York building trades, was Samuel J. Parks.

Parks was the chief business agent of the Housesmiths', Bridgemen's and Structural Iron Workers' Union. For many years he had been an itinerant laborer, working as a lumberman, river-driver, coal-heaver, sailor, railroad brakeman and bridgeworker before entering the employ of the George A. Fuller Construction Company in Chicago. Fuller, impressed by Parks's ability in both oratory and violence, brought him to New York in 1896 to restore orderly relations with the Housesmiths in that city. Parks became active in the Housesmiths upon his arrival, remaining on the payroll of both the union and the company until his death.

His impact on the union—which had virtually disintegrated after an unsuccessful strike in 1886—was immediate and formidable. In a matter of weeks, through a mixture of cajolery and violence, he had fully revived the Housesmiths' local in Manhattan. He then became involved in city-wide building trades affairs, finally engineering the reunification of almost all building trades locals in the city. During Parks's entire stay in New York, a period of general turmoil in the industry, the Fuller Construction Company evidently suffered not a single strike.

Parks found a natural outlet for his talents in the Housesmiths. The International Association of Bridge and Structural Iron Workers, with which Parks's local was affiliated, was a young union, formed in 1896 when the use of structural steel was in its infancy. Its members were largely unskilled, undergoing an apprenticeship period of only six to eighteen months. The trade was hazardous, and involved a disabling and fatal accident rate much higher than in other building trades. It was an itinerant calling, attracting what Luke Grant called "roving and irresponsible workmen, more noted for strength and physical courage than for trained skill and intelligence." The requirements of the trade, John R. Commons wrote early in this century, "are not so much mechanical skill as recklessness and daring. The men say they do not die, but are jerked over the river. The strength of the union is the danger of the trade and the rivet that drops on the head of the non-union man."

For such men Parks was a natural leader. Impressive in physique and proficient in the trade, he was a bully who once said he would rather fight than eat. He had a simple solution for riveters who were reluctant to join the union. "Some did not believe unions would be good for them," he said, "and I gave them a belt on the jaw. That changed their minds." He would not only knock down a dissenter but stand on the man's face, and for those to whom he could not give his personal attention there was a standing "entertainment committee" to administer justice.

Parks was not, however, wholly dependent upon violence for results. "Only a fool," remarked New York District Attorney William Travers Jerome, "would underestimate his power . . . He has personal magnetism and power to convince others his word is law. He has physical bravery, daring and a dashing style of leadership . . . his shrewdness is beyond question." Parks was an effective union leader, and succeeded during his stewardship in raising the daily wage of ironworkers from $2.50 to $4.50—to a level, that is, with the highest paid craftsmen in the industry. He was rewarded with the loyalty of most of his 4,500 members who—despite repeated charges of graft—tended to regard him as a martyr until almost the end of his career. Parks, however, served not only his members but himself.

The United Board of Building Trades, with Parks as president, had particularly cordial relations with the large employers in the industry, about six of whom dominated half the industry. These employers had, for the unions they dealt with, a number of advantages. They employed large numbers of men for relatively long periods of time. Their buildings were usually assured of rental upon completion, their business comparatively free from the high risks encountered by the small employers in the field. They paid wages higher than union scale, employed none but union members, and were careful to maintain good relations with union representatives. In return they got the best craftsmen and were relatively free from strikes. "We favor these companies," a Board delegate said, "because they're fair . . . they don't try to sneak out of union agreements . . . they do straight business. They don't keep us waiting for wages, nor hanker after scabs."

There was more to the relationship, however, than the statesmanship of the builders. Even for the largest companies there were expensive uncertainties in the industry. Owners still wanted to collect rents on time, and contractors were still subject to penalty payments. Strikes were still a problem, and some employers insured against them by the direct bribery of business agents.

The system was evidently introduced to New York by Parks's sponsor, the Fuller Construction Company. It was the largest company in the industry, a nationwide operation, directly employing its own craftsmen rather than leasing specialty work to subcontractors. It was a profitable concern, building faster and cheaper than most contractors, and protected itself well. "It is known," Commons wrote, "that this company paid considerable sums to [Board] delegates for services . . . It is certainly true that the Fuller Company suffered little or nothing from strikes during the reign of the United Board, while other builders were continually troubled." Fuller was not the only company, of course, to bribe union officials; it was simply more systematic and ambitious than others. "The Fuller Company," a union official said, ". . . went the older companies one better . . . Instead of buying delegates occasionally, they were able to own a supply outright."

If some union officials were happy to accept bribes from the larger, friendlier and more reliable companies, they were equally ready to insist on payments from the less reliable, more evasive and more vulnerable smaller companies. In 1902 the largest painters' union in New York City was the Amalgamated Association of Painters and Decorators. A smaller union, the International Brotherhood of Painters, had only a few hundred members in the city but a considerable membership outside. It had already been refused affiliation with the United Board. However, when the Amalgamated demanded a wage increase from a subcontracting employers' association—the Association of Interior Decorators and Cabinet Makers—the latter opened secret negotiations with the Brotherhood. The Brotherhood thereafter struck painting employers with work outside the city, obtaining from these firms an agreement to employ only Brotherhood men inside the city.

At first the Amalgamated received the support of the United Board, which called out on strike the other trades where Brotherhood men were employed. "But the ring in control of the Board," Commons wrote, "offered to seat the Brotherhood on payment of a large sum of money." The Brotherhood said it was unable to raise the funds, whereupon the Board demanded and received $17,000 from the employers' association as an initiation fee for the Brotherhood. The latter organization was then admitted to the Board, which remained officially neutral in the contest between the rival unions. But the employers were not wholly out of pocket. They recognized the Brotherhood and negotiated a secret agreement which provided almost a dollar less a day in wages than had been demanded by the Amalgamated.

Extortion was most commonly practiced, however, by individuals. It was presented in some cases as a demand for "waiting time," that is, as payment for wages lost in strike action. Sometimes it was a condition for the return to work of men on strike. In its crudest form it was simply strike insurance, a payment to avoid future trouble on the job. It was a common practice of Parks and some of his associates, and finally came to public attention.

Rumors of graft in the building trades began to appear with increasing frequency in the New York newspapers in the early months of 1903, moving the New York Central Labor Union to a denial of such practices. But the rumors persisted and the evidence grew, and in June of that year public charges were made by District Attorney William Travers Jerome. "Not only has Mr. Jerome heard that blackmail is frequently extorted from builders and contractors by walking delegates," said the *New York Times,* "but . . . that building concerns are systematically corrupting organized labor by buying up walking delegates, whom they manipulate for the purpose of hampering rival concerns and in other ways furthering their own interests."

On June 5, 1903 Parks was arrested on a charge of extortion brought by the Hecla Iron Works. The Hecla affidavit claimed that Parks had demanded $1,000 as his price for industrial peace, although no dispute existed at the time. "You've never done anything for the walking delegates," Parks evidently said. "Ain't it about time? One thousand dollars from Hecla Iron Works would make things easy over here." Hecla refused to pay, and Parks brought the firm's 1,200 building trades employees out on strike, at a cost of $50,000 to the company. In due course a conference was arranged between Parks and the president of Hecla Iron Works, who asked what he must do. "I'm it," proclaimed Parks, "you pay me. I don't care a damn for the union, the president of the union, or the laws of the country. You can go back to work when you pay Sam Parks $2,000."

The company paid, but complained to the District Attorney. Parks was arrested. He was bailed out the following day for $5,000 provided by William Devery, a former New York chief of police. The Housesmiths then passed a vote of confidence in their leader and authorized the expenditure of $1,000 in his defense. At the same meeting Assemblyman Richard Butler, a member of the union, called for a resolution condemning Jerome for prosecuting Parks. The resolution carried without debate. Parks was borne shoulder-high out of the union hall to a nearby saloon.

The following week, however, Parks was arrested several times and indicted on a total of five charges involving extortions from the construction firms of Brandt Brothers, Lobel-Andrews, Josephus Plenty, and Tiffany as well as the Hecla Iron Works. Each of the four additional firms charged in affidavit that Parks had demanded $300 as the price of calling off strikes in progress. Parks said the money was for waiting time; but according to the Lobel-Andrews affidavit, when Parks was asked about settling the grievances which caused the strike, he replied: "If you pay the money you may do what you like; employ union men or not." Tiffany charged that when Parks was asked if the money would go to the union, he said: "Union nothing. This money goes to Sam Parks, and then you can employ union men or non-union men just as long as you please, as long as you don't get caught at it." Similar statements were made by the other plaintiffs.

About this time Lawrence Murphy, an ex-treasurer of the Journeymen Stonecutters Association, was arrested for appropriating $12,000 in union funds for himself and others. The prosecution charged, and the defense admitted, that it was the practice of a small group of Stonecutters' officials to meet regularly in a barroom to plan the demanding of money from employers in return for preventing or calling off strikes; the payments ranged from $10,000 to $50,000. Once received, the money was divided among some six officials. The same group had also misappropriated about $27,000 in union funds.

Murphy himself admitted taking $10,000 from employers, basing his defense in part on the principle that the union had no claim on the money since it was obtained by extortion. The prosecution also produced a letter from John Mitchell, president of the United Mine Workers of America, stating that among the monies Murphy had stolen from the union was the sum of $1,000 donated by the Stonecutters' membership to help the miners in a strike in the Pennsylvania anthracite fields. Murphy's wife confirmed the prosecution's charges, and Murphy was sentenced to five years in prison. But Murphy evidently thought he was a victim of discrimination.

As the judge pronounced the sentence, Murphy shouted: "This is a put-up job. The others got as much as I did. They are trying to do me." His anxiety was misplaced; five of his associates also went to jail.

Parks was brought to trial on August 14, together with Timothy McCarthy of the same union and Richard Carvel of the Derrickmen. Parks was finally found guilty of extorting $200 from Josephus Plenty in order to end a strike on a Hoboken pier, and was sentenced to two years in Sing Sing prison. The Housesmiths voted to pay Parks's salary while he was in there. The United Board voted confidence in him, and recommended that in his honor a draped riderless horse be led in the annual Labor Day parade. The precaution proved unnecessary. Parks was soon released on a certificate of reasonable doubt, his bond of $16,000 provided by John J. Byrne, a nephew of former police chief Devery. Parks rode with Devery in a carriage at the head of a welcoming parade through the 9th Assembly District, and announced that he and Devery—who was a candidate for mayor—would lead the Labor Day parade. They did so, Parks riding a white horse and wearing a white sash trimmed with gold lace.

He also defeated an attempt by a reform faction in his local union to assume control by driving them physically from the hall. Shortly afterwards the United Board sent a delegation to the convention of the Iron Workers in Kansas City to promote Parks for the presidency of the union, which had suspended the New York Housesmiths. Parks was defeated, but failed by only three votes to elect his own nominee and have the suspension of his local union raised.

He was now re-arrested and committed to trial on the Tiffany charge, his local union depleting its treasury in his defense. A bail of $23,000 was offered by former police captain Daniel C. Moynihan but refused by the court. Parks was convicted of extortion, sentenced to a further two and a half years in prison, and resigned from his local union office. Now his resignation was accepted with wild enthusiasm. The reform faction had by this time assumed control of the Housesmiths and was able to inform the membership that Parks, far from being a martyr for the union, had disposed of some $150,000 in union funds without an accounting and held a personal account in the Garfield National Bank of $11,000. Parks soon left for Sing Sing, never to return. He died of a cardiac condition in May, 1904.

The decline of Parks was accompanied by a marked change in labor-management relations in the New York building trades. The revelations of extortion, accompanied by two unsuccessful strikes, brought about a weakening of the United Board and a strengthening of the employers. The latter now transformed an informal group, the Building Trades Club, into the more official New York Building Trades Employers Association (BTEA).

With a stronger organization, Manhattan employers were able to stage a completely effective lockout of building materials drivers, laying off some 70,000 employees in all. The lockout divided the United Board. Parks led the unskilled workers in an internal fight, maintaining a majority on the Board of one vote. Most of the skilled trades then seceded, forming a Board of Skilled Mechanics; they revoked their support of the Teamsters, the materials dealers opened their yards, and the strike was broken.

During the strike the employers had reinforced their new organization. Formerly, employers in the several trades, while maintaining their own organizations, had affiliated with the employers' central group only as individuals. Now the central organization was based on the trade associations themselves, assuring the affiliation of every individual employer belonging to such associations. The powers of the BTEA were broad, including the authority to "determine, regulate and control the conduct of the members of this association and the employers' associations represented on the board in all matters pertaining to their relations with their employees." Each employer was bonded to ensure compliance with the Association's decisions and prohibited from resigning during a temporary suspension of business. Membership in the Association was virtually compulsory, since the constitutional provisions of the BTEA, and the affiliation of the powerful Mason Builders Association, in effect required members of the Association to trade only with each other.

It was a strong combination, and with the unfavorable publicity now surrounding the United Board, succeeded in forcing the building trades unions to accept its terms. These included an arbitration plan which almost completely eliminated the sympathetic strike, the jurisdictional strike, and the power of a walking delegate to call strikes on his own. It was enforced where necessary by the formation of dual unions by the employers. With the collapse of the Parks regime it became effective throughout the New York building trades, and presaged more than a decade of relative peace in the industry.

The arbitration plan itself lasted until 1910. It broke down mainly because of the restrictions it placed on the power of the walking delegates. The plan provided that delegates could not be members of the Board of Arbitration, although the BTEA was allowed direct representation. The restriction was resented and finally eliminated. Other factors contributed to the formal demise of the plan. The Board of Arbitration took up a great deal of the time of its members; it became involved in labor-management politics, thus weakening its authority; and its existence was in any event resented by the international unions since it contributed to the strength of a localist sentiment. The plan was officially dropped in 1910, and the power of the business agents revived. As before, one of them became the leading figure among the building trades unions in New York City. His name was Robert P. Brindell, and he became the most successful extortionist the building trades were ever to know.

Brindell was a semi-illiterate Canadian who had worked in New York as a longshoreman and drugstore clerk before becoming a dock builder's helper in 1905. He joined the Independent Dock Union which, in 1907, was granted a federal charter by the AFL.* In 1910 the IDU lost its charter for non-payment of *per capita* taxes to the AFL, but remained active as an independent union. Within a few months two-thirds of the IDU's members broke away, formed the Municipal Dock Builders Union, and received an AFL charter.

Brindell stayed with the IDU, becoming its business agent in 1912. In 1914 he agreed to participate in unity negotiations with the United Brotherhood of Carpenters—the largest union in the field—and representatives of the AFL. Both Gompers and President William Hutcheson of the Carpenters appear to have regarded Brindell as a strong man capable of helping them in their respective aims. Gompers wanted to bring about the affiliation of all New York building trades unions, through the United Board, with the Building Trades Department of the AFL. Hutcheson wanted control over the almost-autonomous New York City District Council of Carpenters. At the 1914 convention of the New York State Federation of Labor, Hutcheson was awarded the IDU, chartering it as Local 1456 of the Carpenters. Gompers then revoked the charter of the MDBU, which soon affiliated with the Iron Workers as Local 177. The Iron Workers strongly resented Gompers' action, fearing that it would open the way to a revival of corrupt practices in the building trades.

Their fears were justified. The Carpenters now exerted pressure on the employers both within and outside the city, forcing them one by one to sign with Carpenters Local 1456. The position of Local 177 slowly declined, relations between the Iron Workers and the AFL became worse, and in 1916 the international union was expelled from the federation. Thus by the end of 1917 the Carpenters were unchallenged on the docks. Hutcheson then moved to gain control of the Carpenters' District Council, rescinding an agreement it had with the New York employers. His action was rejected by a vote of the Council, whereupon he suspended all sixty-three affiliated local unions. The next union convention upheld Hutcheson's action;

* "Federal" charters are issued to local unions which do not have an affiliation with an international union, thus permitting direct affiliation with the parent federation. Most federal locals attach themselves in time to an individual international union.

the employers supported the international union; and Brindell completed the rout by use of violence. Hutcheson then reassigned the New York membership into 1,000-member locals, appointing each of the local union presidents.

Brindell's reward was the leadership of the New York building trades. He had already consolidated his hold on Local 1456, suspending or expelling the few who opposed him. He awarded himself a salary of fifty cents per member a month—the local now had 5,000 members—making himself the highest-paid union official in the United States. In October, 1919 he reorganized the Board of Business Agents—the controlling element in the old United Board—into the Building Trades Council, becoming its president at $14,000 a year and affiliating it with the AFL Building Trades Department. His regime was strict, although beneficial to his friends. No rank and file members were admitted as delegates. All delegates were elected for three-year terms at a minimum stipend of $75 a week. Only one copy of the Council's minutes was kept, and no accounting was made of the Council's finances. The Council's offices were maintained, at a rent of $1,000 a month, in a building owned by Mrs. Brindell. As additional security Brindell had himself elected—in violation of the Council's constitution—president for life.

Nor did Brindell suffer much from external opposition. A few of the older crafts had stayed outside the Council, but usually they were left alone. One unaffiliated local union, however, was deemed essential to Brindell's extortionary activities. The Housewreckers' Union, an AFL affiliate popularly called the Zaranko Union after its president, had refused to join the Council despite intimidatory action by Brindell. Brindell obtained a new housewreckers' charter from the AFL. The employers were at first reluctant to hire Brindell's men—most of whom were quite inexperienced at the trade—but soon found themselves with strikes on their hands, or denied contracts by builders and owners. The Zaranko Union rapidly went out of business, its members being forced by Brindell to pay an initiation fee of fifty dollars and a permit fee of ten dollars a week for the privilege of working. Brindell was now secure, and ready to turn his power into profit.

In 1919 the New York State legislature authorized an investigation of the building industry in New York City and elsewhere. There were ample general grounds for concern. An acute housing shortage in New York City had resulted in an abnormally low incidence of moving, a steeply rising level of rents, overcrowding, unsanitary conditions, a marked increase in infant mortality, and a rapid spread of contagious diseases. For some time, also, there had been rumors of illegal combinations and practices in the industry which, according to one estimate, contributed a full twenty percent to the costs of construction. The Committee, under the chairmanship of State Senator Charles C. Lockwood, held exhaustive hearings. It was soon evident, as the *New York Times* observed, that the Committee had on its hands "a scandal of major proportions."

Combination, the Lockwood Committee said, was the primary fact of the building industry. The Committee found "that throughout the length and breadth of the country producers are combined with producers; manufacturers with manufacturers; dealers with dealers; workingmen with workingmen. Not only do these combinations extend horizontally between members of the same class, but vertically from the members of one class to another . . . so that the whole industrial and commercial system in the industries connected with building construction is riveted in an interwoven and interlocking criss-cross of combination and obligatory arrangements." The Committee concluded that the employers were mainly to blame for the decline of the industry in New York. "The Employers' Association and the constituent associations entering into its membership," the Committee said, "are more largely than any other single factor responsible for the acts that have done so much to cripple the building operations in the City of New York . . . It was largely through the assistance and encouragement of this Association by reason of the character of its contacts with the [Building Trades] Council and with other labor unions that these constituent associations were able to force unwilling members into their fold and impose upon them unlawful restraints upon competition . . . Many of such constituent associations were a mere cover for price-fixing, restriction of output or division of territory and for the practice of many other devices that had for their purposes the exaction of tribute from owners, builders and contractors."

The building trades associations used various means to achieve and maintain their authority. General contractors affiliated with the BTEA could subcontract only with other affiliates. Many of the specialist associations, in turn, controlled the practice of bidding for contracts. In one instance, all bids in the limestone, plumbing, heating and ventilating trades were first submitted to James T. Hettrick, the attorney for the associations involved. Hettrick then raised the level of all bids, arranging for one subcontractor to submit a bid lower than the new level but still well in excess of the original minimum bid; the choice of the low bidder was based on his average annual business over the previous seven years. The builders then had no choice but to accept the new minimum bid. In return for his services Hettrick received from one to three percent of the successful bid, while another three percent was distributed among the remaining members of the association involved. In another area, control over materials prices was maintained by a system of quotation cards circulated among associations and at public functions of the industry, leading to a uniform price for similar products.

Additional disciplines were provided in cooperation with the Building Trades Council. The Council dealt initially with BTEA members, meeting their demands for labor before those of any non-members. It struck builders who were slow in meeting their financial obligations to the Association, becoming in effect a collection agency for the BTEA. Contractors who were not members of the BTEA were particularly afflicted with labor troubles; some specialist associations, in fact, paid regular salaries to business agents who in return forced employers to join the associations under threat of a strike.

The system was effective. The BTEA employers enjoyed a relative immunity from competition and in many cases a trouble-free relationship with the building trades unions. "Your Committee," the Lockwood Committee reported, "has been unable to discover a single instance in which a prominent member of the Employers' Association was a victim of Brindell's extortions." Brindell occasionally clashed with minor Association members, but there was ample scope outside the Association for his irregular activities. The BTEA was not a monopoly, for some one-third of all New York employers remained outside the Association. It was to these non-members that Brindell usually turned for his reward.

The housewrecking trade came quickly under his influence. His control over the labor force, virtually complete since his destruction of the Zaranko Union, converted his office into a bivouac for employers seeking his favor. A "kosher list" of boss housewreckers was drawn up, naming those employers who agreed to work exclusively with Brindell. Almost all owners, builders and contractors consulted with Brindell before any housewrecking contracts were let; in turn, Brindell awarded the best contracts to those housewreckers who paid him the largest bribes. Sometimes the bribe was a percentage of the fee paid by the housewrecker to an owner for permission to wreck the building; on other occasions it was represented as a fee for the supply of labor. Wreckers refusing to cooperate with Brindell were refused contracts by owners and builders; some were driven out of business altogether, often returning to Brindell for permission to resume activities in the industry on a smaller scale. The price varied with the size of the job. In 1920 the Albert J. Volk Company offered Brindell $2,000 for permission to continue a job already begun. "Do you think I am a piker?" Brindell asked. He finally accepted $2,500, with a promise of larger sums in the future.

In other cases it was a simple matter of strike insurance. In 1919 the Todd, Iron and Robertson Company paid Brindell $50,000 to guarantee peaceful labor conditions during the construction of the new Cunard docks. The Tench Construction Company, about to undertake the building of five piers on Staten Island, agreed to pay Brindell one-half of one percent of the estimated construction cost of $3,252,673. A variation of strike insurance was imposed on open shop operations. Some of the major steel producers had embarked on a nation-wide open shop campaign, and among other things forbade the employment of union workmen on steel construction jobs. Brindell then began pulling workmen in other crafts off the building sites, allowing them to return to work in return for a bribe; no effort was made to organize the non-union iron workers. In other non-union situations Brindell often charged the employers a fee for each non-union workman employed, or collected payments from non-union workmen themselves in return for temporary work permits.

Brindell's sources of illegitimate income were not confined to employers and non-union workmen. Each of the 115,000 individual members of the unions affiliated with the Building Trades Council paid $1 a year into the Council's Compensation Department. Every affiliated local union paid ten dollars a month for each initial delegate and five dollars for each additional delegate. There were other revenues from the sale of dues cards and souvenir brochures, from fines for violating Council rules, and from injured workmen who were persuaded to sign over their compensation rights to the Fund in return for a lump sum considerably below the total compensation demanded by the Fund from the affected employers. Roswell D. Tompkins, secretary and treasurer of the Council, was unable to give the Lockwood Committee an accounting of the disposal of the Council's income. The Committee itself concluded that in less than a year Brindell had made over $1,000,000. Parks, by comparison, became an object of nostalgia. "Today," said George Balker, a builder and real estate operator later indicted for his intermediary role in the building trades extortions, "he would be only a cheap grafter . . . I wish he was here today."

Brindell succeeded by court action in avoiding any appearances before the Lockwood Committee, but he was soon brought to trial on charges of extortion. Early in 1921 he was found guilty and sentenced to five to ten years in prison. Hettrick was also indicted for conspiracy and sent to jail. Altogether 529 individuals were indicted for extortion or conspiracy, of whom eighty-one were union officials, the rest employers or public officials.

Brindell went to Sing Sing, where he was well treated. He received special meals, and was allowed to meet with his family and union associates outside of the prison. When news of this leaked out to the press he was transferred temporarily to the much stricter Dannemora prison, but after public indignation subsided he was sent to Great Meadows—perhaps the most lenient of New York penal institutions—to complete his sentence.

He was released in December, 1924. Neither the district attorney nor Lockwood Committee Counsel Samuel Untermyer was invited to his parole hearing, and he was given an unconditional parole. Subsequent press criticism caused the parole board to prohibit him from holding union office. Brindell thereupon attempted to resume control over Local 1456, but his return was resented and he was expelled from membership. The parole board then exiled him to his Schroon Lake estate in upstate New York, where he died in January, 1927.

The success of the Lockwood Committee in ridding the industry of corrupt practices was limited. Tammany was opposed to the investigation from the outset. Indeed, shortly before the hearings started, Mayor John ("Honest John") Hylan's Committee on Building and Building Materials issued a report claiming that the price of building materials, far from being artificially boosted, were determined solely by the laws of supply and demand; the principal factor in increased building costs was wages, it said. Brindell was a close friend of Hylan, by whom he had been appointed to the city's Housing Commission. William P. Kenneally, the chairman of Tammany Hall's executive committee and vice president of the Board of Aldermen, was a walking delegate for the Steam Fitters and an official of the Building Trades Council; he doubtless had a personal interest in the investigation, since he had once obtained a contract for a friend for limestone work on the County Court House; the contract was let to the sole, pre-arranged bidder for $2,327,000, or approximately double the market price. Other building trades officials held positions at Tammany Hall.

The first revelations of the Lockwood Committee brought a flurry of activity at Tammany Hall. A Tammany emissary left for Washington, D.C. to consult with government officials; despite promises of cooperation in prosecutions from U.S. Attorney General J. Mitchell Palmer, the Lockwood Committee later reported that almost no federal assistance had been received. Tammany officials and New York building contractors also cooperated in three attempts to halt by injunction the examination of certain of the city's books by the Committee. The employers opposed the Committee's work, the BTEA denouncing its inquiry as a "Russian-Polish-Turkish inquisition." Finally, when Untermyer announced the Committee's intent to investigate banks, insurance companies and other lending institutions active in the construction industry, the New York State General Assembly threatened to curb the Committee's activities. No action was taken to implement the Committee's recommendations for new legislation to curb corrupt practices in the building industry.

The Committee did have some temporary effect on industrial relations in the construction field. Employers abandoned some of their associations—fourteen of which had been indicted for conspiratorial practices—abrogated the BTEA agreement with the Building Trades Council, engaged in the unilateral lowering of wages, and maintained at least one company union for the purpose of weakening the bargaining power of the building trades unions. On the other hand, they stopped the practice of working to estimates, adopting instead a cost-plus formula which contributed to a further rise in building costs.

With the breakdown of the industry's arbitration plan, the Committee proposed a new settlement between the BTEA and the Building Trades Council. It suggested the maintenance of existing wages, subject to arbitration by a standing joint Board of Arbitration; if the Board found "inefficiency" in any craft it would order a reduction of one dollar in daily wage rates. The Building Trades Council accepted the plan but the employers did not, the latter insisting on the right to have separate contracts with individual unions. "While shouting loudly for collective bargaining on their side," the Committee said of the employers, "they do not seem to want collective bargaining on the side of the men, and the purpose is quite evident. They want to be able to play off one Union against another Union in controversies, and create perhaps a different scale for skilled labor in each industry which will lead to nothing but running discontent and demoralization."

The Committee declared itself satisfied with the response of the unions. "The Unions have on the whole," it said, "with a few conspicuous exceptions, shown a commendable spirit in meeting the suggestions of the Committee . . . at all times amenable to reason, their attitude in this respect being in pleasing contrast with the insincere and defiant position of many of the business lawbreakers with whom the Committee has had to deal." Aside from its arbitration plan, the Committee had recommended the democratization of internal union procedures, the limitation of initiation fees and restrictions on entry into the building trades unions, the adoption of proper accounting and auditing procedures, the ending of union discrimination against non-association employers, and the prohibition of union intervention in the realm of Art.* The Building Trades Council seemed anx-

* The Lockwood Committee had reported that the owner of the new Ambassador Hotel was forced to tear down part of a wall because a business agent of the Painters, presumably a thwarted artist, had decided that the color and style of the Travertine

ious to comply, and offered no resistance when, in September, 1921, Gompers sent in President John Donlin of the AFL Building Trades Department to supervise the reform of the Building Trades Council.

The relief was short-lived. One immediate effect of the Lockwood Committee's investigation was an upturn in construction activity, but the conditions and institutions which contributed to earlier abuses remained. The penalties visited on the convicted were for the most part light or nonexistent; the employers retained the substance if not the form of many of their former malpractices; and the reforms imposed upon the Building Trades Council were insufficient to prevent the revival of extortionary practices. "From some of the testimony before us," the New York Industrial Survey Commission said in 1927, ". . . it is evident that promises made to the Lockwood Housing Committee and to Mr. Untermyer, their counsel, have been forgotten or disregarded." The spirit of Brindell was still alive.

In 1928 President Arthur Huddell of the International Union of Operating Engineers became disturbed with the internal politics of New York City Local 403, placed it in receivership, and appointed as trustee Patrick J. Commerford, business agent of IUOE Local 125 and a vice president of both the New York State Building Trade Council and the New York State Federation of Labor.

In 1931 Commerford expelled twenty-five dissenters from the local without trial, warning employers not to hire them. The rebels sought an injunction against their expulsion, whereupon the international union disbanded Local 403 and merged it with Local 125, refusing membership in Local 125 to the dissidents. However, the court ordered the reinstatement of the rebels and the payment by Local 125 of $24,250 in damages to them.

The following year 630 members of Local 125 filed suit to obtain an accounting of finances, charging that the officers of the local were governing it arbitrarily and for their personal profit. Commerford responded with threats of violence. Owen S. M. Tierney, counsel for the plaintiffs, was warned to stop the proceedings or find himself "at the bottom of a river." An undertaker called at the home of John Irwin, leader of the rebels, and asked Mrs. Irwin for "the corpse"; she was later called by telephone and told that this was not a mistake but a serious warning. Commerford himself shot at process servers and refused to testify properly at the trial. The financial secretary of Local 125 said at the trial that $13,000 had disappeared

marble used did not suit his taste, even though the work was acceptable to the owner and his nationally known architect. The Painters, as it happened, had jurisdiction over the work.

without an accounting during 1931 and that the local's books had been destroyed. The court granted full relief to the plaintiffs and ordered a new election in the local. All the insurgent candidates were elected. On the day of the court's decision, however, President John Possehl of the IUOE—Huddell had recently been murdered—revoked the charter of Local 125 and set up a new Local 130 with Commerford as supervisor.

In June, 1932, Commerford was indicted for income tax evasion. Edward A. White, treasurer of the United Hoisting Company, testified in court that he had paid Commerford a salary of $50 a week in 1929, and $75 a week in 1930 and 1931, for permission to employ non-union men. James Fee, the owner of the Carlton Hoisting Company and an open shop employer, said he gave Commerford $25 a week in 1927, and $50 a week in 1928 and 1929, for the same purpose. Commerford apparently also received $2,500 from the Grenmal Construction Company, $5,000 from the R. J. Murphy Company, $5,000 from the P. J. Carlin Company, and $7,000 from the W. F. Gahagan Company to call off strikes. Two officers of the Hod Carriers and Common Laborers—Angelo Virga of Local 706 and Luciano Abruzzo of Local 763—testified that they each paid a $500 bribe to Commerford to obtain the affiliation of their locals to the New York Building Trades Council. A parade of employers testified to Commerford's good character but in vain, and he was sentenced to a year and a day in jail. Christian G. Norman, the executive officer of the BTEA, offered to act as Commerford's guardian if he were paroled.

Commerford later returned to union affairs. At the 1937 convention of the Mine, Mill and Smelter Workers—a CIO union later expelled on grounds of Communist domination—President Reid Robinson reported that Commerford had been appointed during the past year as international organizer for the New York area. Commerford arranged for the issuance of several local union charters, but the international union later discovered that the locals had virtually no members, and that they were being used "as a job-selling agency whereby the heads of the locals were selling permits for the men to work and not taking them into the organization at all." The union investigated Commerford, discovered his criminal past, and expelled him.

Meanwhile, the members of Local 125 had continued their protest activities and obtained fifteen successful court decisions, leading to the restoration of their charter in late 1935. Shortly afterwards the international union removed all the local's officers and appointed as the new supervisor one Joseph Fay.

Fay was the business agent of Local 805 in Newark, New Jersey, and a vice president of the international union. He was a convivial man, a lavish spender, a gambler who was reputed to have lost more than $50,000 in Newark gambling houses. Prominent in New Jersey labor and political circles, he was described in 1933 by Acting Governor E. L. Richards as "one of the real forces in American life." He was a partner with Theodore Brandle, the leading building trades union official in New Jersey, in banking and other business activities, and together with two fellow officers in Local 805 owned the International Excavating Company of Newark. He was expelled from office by the international union in 1932 for his business activities, but reinstated two months later with the support of his local union after promising to divest himself of his business interests.

After his appointment as receiver for Local 125, Fay consolidated all New York City locals of the Operating Engineers into one. He then turned to the Hod Carriers and, in cooperation with Hod Carriers' International Vice-President James Bove, took control over Locals 45, 250, 266 and 731 of the latter union. Only Local 102 held out. Norman Redwood, the business agent of the local, insisted upon autonomy of operation and resisted various attempts at bribery and intimidation.

A jurisdictional dispute now arose between Fay and Redwood, and Local 102 struck a construction project on the New York subways. Samuel Rosoff, the contractor for the project and one of Fay's friends, threatened Redwood with violence if the strike were not called off. Redwood appealed to his international union and received its official support, but got no help at all from other Hod Carriers' locals in the city. Fay accused Redwood of "dickering with the CIO" and asked the Building Trades Council to obtain the revocation of Local 102's license to do business in New York. Redwood kept Local 102 on strike, saying his men would not go back to work "with a gun stuck in their backs." The following day he was shot dead.

Fay and Bove met no further opposition and began a career of widespread extortion. In 1937, AFL President William Green * approached Possehl about Fay, but was told his misgivings were unfounded. The decline of public and private construction during World War II reduced but did not eliminate the criminal activities of Fay and Bove, and in May, 1943, both were indicted for extortion and conspiracy to extort from contractors. The court proceedings showed that they had embarked on their career of extortion in 1936 with the beginning of tunnel work on the $300,000,000 Delaware River water supply project. The prosecution devel-

* Green, former Secretary-Treasurer of the United Mine Workers, had succeeded Gompers as President of the AFL in 1924.

oped ample private testimony against both defendants, but experienced some difficulty in persuading witnesses to take the stand. "They won't testify at the trial," Fay told United States District Attorney Frank S. Hogan. "I'll see to that."

Several witnesses refused to appear, but enough testimony was given to satisfy the jury of the defendants' guilt. The two chief officers of the Walsh Construction Company stated that Fay and Bove had originally demanded $250,000, but had settled, between 1938 and 1942, for a total of $212,000, all of which was entered on the company's books as bonuses to executives and other employees. A representative of B. Perini and Sons, Inc., said that the company paid Fay and Bove $25,000 on a Delaware River contract and $50,000 on a contract on the Lincoln Tunnel under the Hudson River. It became apparent that the defendants had extorted a total of at least $368,000 on the water supply project alone. Hogan personally estimated that the total was more than a million dollars.

Fay and Bove, like Commerford, relied mainly on character witnesses, some of the latter professing high regard for the defendants while admitting giving money to them. Counsel for the defense did not deny the payments, but argued that they were voluntary offerings—perhaps even bribes—for the purpose of ensuring the good will of the defendants. The jury was unpersuaded. In March, 1945, Fay and Bove were found guilty of extortion and given sentences of eight and a half years.

Fay was also indicted in December, 1946, for income tax evasion. Various witnesses attested to giving him a total of at least $186,000. Fay admitted receiving $40,000, saying he did not keep the money but turned it over to others as part of a "labor relations deal." He was acquitted. A formal inquiry was launched into the conduct of the trial, but with no results.

Bove was less fortunate. After his conviction for extortion it was discovered that some $250,000 was missing from Bove's Local 60 of the Hod Carriers. He was indicted in May, 1945, for grand larceny and found guilty on seventy-four counts. He received a sentence of ten to twenty years, and after pleading guilty to income tax evasion got another five years. Shortly afterwards several locals of the Hod Carriers filed damage suits for $3,-400,000 against the international union, charging that their members had been forced to work at substandard wages and under dangerous working conditions because of Bove's collusion with the employers.

Two of Bove's union associates were also convicted of attempting to extort $100,000 from a contractor. When the company offered to pay that sum in wage increases to union members the offer was refused.

3: New Jersey

Across the Hudson River from New York lies Jersey City, a sister community. For many years it was the barony of Frank Hague, the Democratic mayor of the city. "I," he once declared, "am the law."

He was indeed. Elected Director of Public Safety for the city in 1917, he destroyed the policemen's and firemen's unions and set up a system of political spies, assuring himself control over Jersey City law enforcement for as long as he held office. He became mayor the same year, and reigned over the city and surrounding Hudson County for thirty-one years. In 1919 he challenged the Democratic leadership of the state and engineered the election of his own choice, State Senator Edward I. Edwards, to the governorship. Edwards was the first of a procession of Hague nominees to the gubernatorial chair, all of whom helped to ensure, through appointments to the judiciary and other public offices, the immunity of the Hague machine to the attentions of the law.*

There were the usual appurtenances of machine politics. The public payroll was inflated, the *per capita* cost of government in Jersey City increasing 300 percent in the first ten years of Hague's regime. The loyal and enormous majorities Hague rolled up year after year in municipal and other elections were buttressed by the votes of the dead, the insane, and former residents long since gone. There were expensive public services, and lucrative public contracts for Hague's best friends.

Nor did the mayor neglect his own welfare. "Politics," he said, "is a business." Hague never received more than $8,000 a year in salary, but in 1929 a joint committee of the State legislature reported that he had made cash investments of $392,910.50 between 1918 and 1927. Hague refused to answer any of the committee's questions. The United States Treasury also investigated his assets and ordered him to pay $1,800,000 in delinquent taxes and penalties.

But graft was not the only problem. "The Hague organization," wrote

* Hague's special achievement in the field of judicial appointments was the elevation in 1939, by Governor A. Harry Moore, of Hague's son Frank Jr. to the New Jersey State Supreme Court. Frank Jr. had failed in several attempts to obtain a law degree, but succeeded in passing the State Bar examination on his first try—a remarkable performance, since in those days only one-third of all candidates for the State Bar succeeded in passing on their first attempts.

Dayton David McKean, "alone among American city machines, has systematically and successfully used the methods of terrorism, the infiltration of groups and associations, the suppression of criticism, and the hierarchical principle of leadership that has characterized the fascist regimes of Europe." An army of spies reported on dissenters; political opponents often found their mail had been opened or did not receive it at all; telephone wires were tapped; property owners opposed to Hague were harassed by building department officials, had their licenses revoked and their property unfavorably reassessed.

For social dissenters there were special measures. "Whenever I hear a discussion of civil rights and the rights of free speech and the rights of the Constitution," Hague said, "always remember you will find him [*sic*] with the Russian flag under his coat; you never miss." Dissenters, particularly trade unionists, were denied access to public halls, molested by the police and, very often, thrown bodily out of Jersey City.

Jersey City was for the most part a non-union town. As late as 1936 the local Chamber of Commerce was able to report that "the industries of this city are more than eighty percent open shop." This condition was largely Hague's doing, although he tolerated the building trades unions in return for their political support. They probably had little choice in the matter, since they depended a good deal on public contracts for work, and Hague's other weapons were formidable. But not all building trades support was reluctant. In particular, Hague enjoyed for many years the close friendship of Theodore Brandle.

Brandle, during the early years of Hague's administration, was the business agent of Local 45 of the Iron Workers in Jersey City. Later he became president of the Hudson County Building Trades Council, president of the state body of the Iron Workers, president of the New Jersey State Building Trades Council, and a powerful influence in the Jersey City Central Labor Union and the State Federation of Labor.

He was also a businessman. In 1926 he founded the Labor National Bank of Jersey City, installing himself as president. Also in the 1920's he formed, in partnership with former State Assemblyman Joseph Hurley, the Branleygran Company, a bonding and insurance firm specializing in the construction industry. In 1927 he became president of the New Jersey Iron League, the principal employers' organization in the iron and steel construction trade; it was his intention, he said, "to serve both sides." He was, finally, Hague's most valued labor supporter. He first came into political prominence in 1924 when he led the opposition to the drive within the state labor movement to endorse, as did the AFL Executive Council, the presidential candidacy of U.S. Senator Robert M. LaFollette. Brandle won, on Hague's behalf, the labor endorsement of Democratic candidate John W. Davis. "I will," he said, "bring every labor union man in the state to the support of Hague's leadership."

He helped in other ways. When Hague was charged with income tax evasion, Brandle eased the burden of repayment with a personal check for $60,000. He was to regret his generosity, but for the moment he was a rich and powerful man. He was the most influential union official in New Jersey, and his association with Hague was well publicized, bringing handsome rewards. Builders found it difficult to obtain public contracts without his approval. He helped engineer the familiar trade conspiracies betwen unions and employers, and enjoyed a pleasant immunity from the attentions of the Jersey City police during labor disturbances.

His wealth increased, and in due course he ran afoul of the United States Treasury Department. He was indicted for income tax evasion in 1931, pleaded guilty, and paid $88,000 in back taxes. John E. Delaney, another official of Local 45, testified at Brandle's trial that between 1927 and 1930 he had collected more than $200,000 for Brandle from employers seeking to avoid labor disputes. There was other evidence that Brandle had received $10,000 from the Iron League. President Green of the AFL asked President P. J. Morrin of the Iron Workers to take action to protect "the integrity, the good name and the standing" of both the union and the labor movement. It was some time before disciplinary action was taken, but another, ironic retribution was at hand.

Jersey City, because of Hague's largesse to his friends and supporters, was the most heavily taxed city in the United States. With the arrival of the depression it became increasingly difficult to obtain public funds to stimulate economic activity in the area. Businesses went bankrupt or left the city, and since the public payroll could not be decreased without weakening the Hague machine, Hague turned to a policy of labor peace, low wages and employer supremacy.

In December, 1931, the Iron Workers struck the open shop McClintic-Marshall contract on the Pulaski Skyway in Hudson County. Hague asked Brandle to call off the strike. There had been rumors of friction between the two men over an Iron Workers' strike at the Jersey City Medical Center—Hague's personal creation and greatest pride—but they were denied. Now Brandle evidently considered himself a rival to Hague and refused to call off the Skyway strike. In the subsequent pitched battles between company guards and iron workers, one of the guards was killed. The Jersey City police intervened and broke the strike. "We simply cleaned the place out," Hague later testified. "We didn't allow pickets. We didn't allow anything then."

The strike ruined Brandle. He was forced to close his labor bank, and he allegedly spent his entire fortune—in an admirable but belated act of loyalty—on strike benefits, hospital benefits for injured iron workers, and legal fees for the successful defense of the twenty or so of his members who were accused of murder. Now the union intervened. In March, 1933, Local 45 voted 359-1 to accept Brandle's resignation, and three months later he was expelled from the International union for "misuse of powers." He was refused credentials at the 1933 convention of the State Federation of Labor, and in 1934 resigned as president of the State Building Trades Council. He later tried to return to power in Local 45, but failed after Hague warned that he would not tolerate "gorilla labor leaders" in Jersey City. Brandle then sued Hague for return of the $60,000 he had provided in 1931. Hague claimed the debt had been paid, and the case was settled out of court.

Hague went on, as he said, to "disorganize" the labor movement in Jersey City. By court actions he bankrupted a number of local unions. Injunctions were issued promptly and in great quantities against picketing, handbilling, and even the holding of union meetings. With the advent of CIO organizers in Jersey City the battle was intensified. The police were authorized to seize anyone "who cannot give a good account of himself." Pickets were arrested and kept in jail on prohibitive bail until strikes were broken. In the seamen's strike of 1936–37 all meeting places were closed and sources of food were closed to the strikers. "In addition to outright physical violence," McKean wrote, "unions found their halls closed for violations of the building codes; union leaders were deported from Jersey City, offered the choice of jail or exile; and signs, pamphlets, handbills and other union property were seized. Newspaper men, photographers, writers, and representatives of civil rights groups were arbitrarily barred from locations where the strikes were in progress. . . . There appears to be in the record no instance of a strike being won in Jersey City by the workers during the years 1931 to 1937."

Opposed to the CIO *, the State Federation of Labor now gave Hague its support and Robert Lynch, the president of the Hudson County Building Trades Council, called him "the protector of the people." But the CIO filed suit to prevent the enforcement of Jersey City ordinances and was upheld

---

* The CIO—founded by John L. Lewis in 1935 as the Committee on Industrial Organization—became the Congress of Industrial Organizations in 1938 in a breakaway movement from the AFL. It was based on the organization of union members by industry, rather than by craft as was the case with the AFL. The two federations competed fiercely with each other until 1955, when they merged to form the AFL-CIO.

by the United States Supreme Court. The odds had changed. Hague now allied himself with the CIO, thereby losing the support of the State Federation of Labor and many business groups. It was not a serious loss. Hague remained in power for another ten years.

4: *Chicago*

"First in violence," Lincoln Steffens wrote of Chicago, "deepest in dirt; loud, lawless, unlovely, ill-smelling, irreverent, new; an over-grown gawk of a village . . ."

Chicago was a growing town. From 1870 to 1900 its population rose from less than 300,000 to nearly 1,750,000. It was now a great railroad and shipping center, a bustling industrial community, home of 200 millionaires and the nation's worst sweatshop system. Like New York, it was a port of entry for immigrants, a "mosaic of foreign language cities." It was an unhealthy place, primitive in public services, ravaged by contagious diseases, with the death rate from typhoid twice that of New York. It was also an open town, with over 2,000 gambling houses, the largest red-light district in the United States, and ten saloons for every church. "Criminally," Steffens wrote, "it was wide open; commercially it was brazen; socially it was thoughtless and raw; it was a settlement of individuals and groups and interests with no common city sense and no political conscience."

The Tammany Hall of Chicago was known as the Cook County Democracy. It yielded nothing in turpitude to its eastern counterpart. After the mayoralty election of 1897, the reformist Civic Federation of Chicago named fifty-seven out of sixty-eight aldermen as grafters and succeeded in obtaining convictions of twenty-one of them for vote stealing. The control of Chicago politics lay in the hands of ward bosses and aldermen who dispensed jobs, awarded public franchises and liquor licenses, counted the votes, and cooperated with the police in mutually beneficial enterprises. The bribery of public officials was commonplace, and police extortion from both shady and legitimate enterprises was said to be even more extensive than in New York. The saloon trade was owned mainly by aldermen and other public officials, the premises often being operated as combined drinking, gambling and wenching resorts.

City ordinances in all three fields of relaxation were generally ignored. "After all," Superintendent of Police Joseph Kipley complained, "it isn't right to expect me to know everything that is going on in town." Mayor Carter J. Harrison, Sr., was more forthright. "I don't believe in closing saloons on Sunday," he said. "I do believe in lowering the blinds and closing the front doors." In later years his standards changed. The Chicago of his incumbency, he wrote, was "the exclusive appanage of a low-browed, dull-witted, base-minded gang of plug-uglies, with no outstanding characteristic beyond an unquenchable thirst for money." Nor were conditions to improve. Chicago's reputation as the wickedest city in America, based on a lurid half-century of lawlessness and vice, rose steadily in the twentieth century to become a legend of civic corruption. Not the least of the victims was the Chicago labor movement.

"Early in the nineties," Eugene Staley wrote, "the Chicago Trade and Labor Assembly fell into the hands of a group of self-seeking men who for a time made the name 'labor leader' synonymous with 'crook' and 'grafter' . . . There was a labor directory graft, which yielded profits from the advertising . . . Labor Day picnics and souvenir programs could be made to pay handsome returns. The lobby graft and the committee graft were means of tapping the treasury of the central body itself. Then, of course, there were innumerable ways for sharing the funds of political parties in return for maneuvers in the Trade Assembly or for leading a fake labor political movement calculated to cut into the votes of the opposition party. 'Aldermanic nominations' at the hands of various personally-conducted labor parties were sold like radishes—so much a bunch with a discount for cash customers." The fruits of graft, according to one estimate, amounted in the three or four years prior to 1892 to at least $100,000, none of which was evidently used for legitimate trade union purposes.

The central figure in these operations was William C. Pomeroy, a business representative of the Chicago waiters' union. He became financial secretary of the Labor Assembly in 1886, and by the early 1890's dominated both the Assembly and the Illinois State Federation of Labor. He was a talented man. " 'He might have made a wonderful record in Congress or in the labor movement,' " Staley reported, "is the unanimous opinion of those who knew him in his prime—if only he had been honest. 'He would sooner make five dollars in a crooked way than ten dollars honestly, because the one involved scheming and the other didn't so much. And he had brains enough to make it either way.' " Pomeroy was particularly accomplished in the labor paper advertising racket, first gaining control of it in Chicago, then running the *Official Annual Labor Gazette* of the State Federation of Labor. He also gained a reputation for breaking strikes in return for bribes from the employers. "The condition here," a Chicago union leader wrote to Gompers, "is enough for one to lose heart in the labor movement." It was 1895 before the downstate element in the State Federation succeeded in ousting Pomeroy from power, after which Gompers brought about his expulsion from trade union office.

On the employers' side, Secretary John C. Driscoll of the Coal Teaming

Interests struck up an alliance in the early 1900's with Albert Young, a teamsters' business agent. Young then withdrew from the AFL International Teamsters' Union, formed the Teamsters' National Union, and signed an agreement with Driscoll for a thirty percent increase in wages and cartage. Driscoll, in cooperation with Young, organized the employers into associations. The combined power of the TNU and the associations enabled Driscoll to embark on a lucrative career in the settlement of industrial disputes. He bribed union officials to settle strikes, employed "wrecking crews" to molest disobedient workmen, and broke the strikes of the unbribable with TNU support. Tried in 1905 for extortion, he admitted having paid out $50,000 in employer funds in five years to settle some 400 strikes.

As in New York, the Chicago building trades unions were more strongly organized than the employers. The Chicago Building Trades Council, established in 1890, assumed powers comparable to those of the New York body. Every prospective strike had to be approved by the Board of Business Agents of the Council, whose actions in such matters were binding on all affiliates. Further, while the Council itself did not negotiate agreements, it denied support in the event of strike action if it had not previously endorsed an agreement by a two-thirds majority. The Council, dominated by the Board, was for years the controlling force in the industry. As in New York, its power was abused.

The architect of abuse was Martin B. ("Skinny") Madden. A former hobo, Martin became business agent of the Steamfitters' Helpers in 1896. Ruling "by gun and blackjack," a guard of thugs always at his side, he conducted local union elections by inviting his supporters to line one side of the hall, his opponents the other; he was soon elected president, treasurer and business agent for life. He then became *de facto* leader of the Building Trades Council, dominated the Chicago Federation of Labor, and in 1903 was powerful enough to choose the president of the Illinois State Federation of Labor.

He was a colorful man, "flashily dressed. His trousers were fresh from the ironing board of the tailor, and his coat was the latest cut," wrote Harold Seidman. "He sported a fancy lavender-colored waistcoat and in his shirt front a diamond sparkled. Patent leather shoes adorned his feet. His whole appearance indicated he had no lack of money and spent much of it on himself." He enjoyed the luxury of a chauffeur-driven limousine, lived in expensive apartments, ran several saloons and various other enterprises. "Show me an honest man," he said, "and I'll show you a fool." Madden was an extortionist, and by his misdeeds succeeded in unifying the employers and destroying the Building Trades Council.

Before 1899 the Chicago building trades employers were organized mainly into trade associations, negotiating agreements with individual unions. The system was generally satisfactory, extortion by business agents being easily absorbed through the price-fixing and bid-rigging practices of the employers. But by 1899 the over-production of the previous six years, the long upward movement of prices and the slackness of business induced by a coming presidential election presented some employers with the threat of bankruptcy. The employers then formed the Chicago Building Contractors Council, vested it with full powers in labor-management relations, and turned to the attack. The Council demanded the elimination of all restrictions on work, machinery and the admission of apprentices, and also the abolition of the sympathetic strike. The Building Trades Council, meanwhile, had demanded the right to negotiate with non-members of the trade associations in order to increase the jobs available. The result was a deadlock. In December, 1900 the employers declared a lockout.

Madden felt he was in a strong position. Most building tradesmen in Chicago were organized and affiliated, and several unions had recently struck successfully to abrogate their exclusive agreements. Madden also enjoyed close relations with the city administration. Several building trades union officials were on the city payroll. Mayor Harrison, in what was interpreted as a gesture of support, had recently appointed Edward Carroll—a former Pomeroy supporter and Madden's puppet president of the Building Trades Council—as president of the Chicago Civil Service Board. Harrison had no desire to antagonize Madden with the approach of city elections, and the employers were later to claim that during the course of the lockout the city administration supported the unions and that the police had refused to protect non-strikers and the property of the employers. In any event, Madden felt free to take an uncompromising stand, uttered vain threats of a coast-to-coast building trades strike, and undertook a campaign of violence against workers who crossed the building trades picket lines. There were 150 cases of violence and five deaths during the lockout.

The employers were adamant. "The cause of the dispute," the United States Industrial Commission reported, "was the determination of the employers to destroy the building trades council . . . The contractors admit that they are unwilling to abandon their central organization, while they intend to compel the workingmen to abandon theirs." They were also supported by the banking community—more skillfully led, more temperate in their public deeds and utterances, more solicitous of public opinion than the bragging Madden. In midsummer, the Bricklayers defected and signed a capitulation agreement with their employers. Other surrenders followed quickly, and by the end of the year the Building Trades Council began to break up. In April, 1901, it voted to disband. It was succeeded by the Chicago Building Trades League, which agreed to the employers' terms—the abolition of the sympathetic strike, the settlement of disputes by arbitration, and the abandonment of the right to refuse to work with non-union men.

Madden had suffered a severe reverse, but made his way back. In 1903 he organized the Associated Building Trades of Chicago in competition with the League. In 1905 he was ousted from power in the Chicago Federation of Labor and the Illinois State Federation, but the following year succeeded in capturing the presidency of the League. The League never developed the power of the former Building Trades Council, but its weakness was more than countered by the decline of the Building Contractors Council. Evidently satisfied that their objectives had been permanently won, many employers and trade associations disaffiliated from the parent body, which increasingly lost control over working conditions.

One result was a revival of corruption. "More 'graft money,'" wrote Royal Montgomery, "was paid during 1907, probably, than at any time since the dark ages before 1899."

Madden got his share. In one case, brought to light at his subsequent trial, he demanded $20,000 from the builders of the twenty-story Insurance Exchange Building; when he received only $10,000, work on the site stopped at the tenth floor. Madden was arrested for extortion in 1909; his bond of $50,000 was posted by State Senator John Broderick, and he escaped with a fine of $500. It was his only conviction. Thereafter his power declined, but never vanished. A victim of tuberculosis, he continued to call strikes from his bed in the Grand Pacific Hotel until his death in 1912.

The decade following the debacle of 1901 was one of chaos. The disintegration of the central organizations of both unions and employers meant the end of city-wide bargaining, a rise in jurisdictional disputes, a decreased ability on the part of the unions to strike effectively, a loss of influence by the employers over the conditions of work, and a revival of graft. In time, both sides came to see the need for central organization. In 1909 the Building Trades Council was re-established. In 1911 the employers set up the Building Construction Employers' Association, and something like a balance of power was restored. After a four-week lockout in 1913 over an attempt by the employers to reassert the principles of 1901, the Council and the Association signed an agreement providing for the arbitration of disputes by a Joint Conference Board, and for the prohibition of strikes and lockouts for periods of three years. Life was now more sedate, the new stability lasting until the 1920's.

But the new order had its drawbacks. "Protected by strong organization on both sides," Montgomery wrote, "a range of monopolistic combinations between organized employers and organized workers had emerged in certain trades." In 1914 the Chicago *Herald* printed a series of articles alleging wholesale corruption among building trades unions. Indictments were returned against fifty-four business agents and six employers. Two business agents were shot, one by an angry employer, the other by union members in self-defense. Death threats were sent to the State's Attorney and two members of the grand jury, and two witnesses for the prosecution were physically attacked. The Building Trades Council took action against those indicted, expelling from membership representatives of the Sheet Metal Workers, the Upholsterers, the Boilermakers, and the Glaziers. In the midst of the trials, however, the District Attorney for Cook County resigned from office. Most of the indictments were not pursued, only a few light sentences resulted, and the extortions continued. Illegal activities, however, were not confined to business agents. By now the employers had developed criminal combinations and practices to an unprecedented extent. The consequent increase in prices and decline in building activities finally brought about a major legislative investigation into the industry.

In February, 1921, the General Assembly of Illinois created a joint legislative commission to inquire into "combinations and agreements" in the construction industry. The Commission, under the chairmanship of State Senator John T. Dailey, experienced some difficulty in pursuing its task. "Every species of pressure and intimidation," the Commission said, "was exerted by the representatives of those various groups frequently linked arm in arm in the same conspiracy . . . So entrenched and secure, and so confident had this conspiracy become, that it defied with impunity all the prosecuting agencies of the State and of the Federal Government. Witnesses were intimidated by threat not merely of injury to person and property, and of discharge from employment, boycott, ostracism, and isolation, but also of the loss of their very lives." But the investigation continued, and produced a damaging verdict.

"[S]carcely any building," the Commission reported, "large or small, erected in Chicago in the last two years, has been immune from the imposition of graft . . . union labor was betrayed, disgraced, and brought into thorough disrepute by many criminal agents . . . [Graft] ran into millions of dollars every year, was imposed upon builders by business agents, who in notable instances were not even members of the craft . . . The principle of collective bargaining was so buried beneath a maze of crooked practices and crime that its fundamental purpose could not be recognized. Union labor was exploited in the interests of dishonest leaders who amassed fortunes for themselves, and who employed murderers, sluggers, and bomb throwers in their nefarious war upon society. Graft was not the exception but was the general rule in building construction."

The details were familiar. Simon O'Donnell, a former president of the Building Trades Council, evidently received $40,000 in strike insurance from the Longacre Construction Company, $4,000 from the North Shore Hotel for settling a strike, $13,750 in strike insurance on the Bunte Building, and other payments in connection with the construction of the Webster Hotel. A Mr. Schardt, business agent for the Carpenters, extracted $1,200 from the Liquid Carbonic Company in return for permission to install certain equipment in the company's buildings. The builders of the Sovereign Hotel paid $7,500 in all to Charles Wright of the Carpenters, Al Young of the Iron Workers, Michael Artery of the Machinery Movers, and others; the architect for the hotel testified that the cost estimates for construction included one percent for graft. William G. Krieg, architect for the Stratford Theatre, stated that he paid Patrick Kane of the Sheet Metal Workers $3,-000, Al Young of the Iron Workers between $1,800 and $3,000, and an unspecified amount to Roy Shields of the Painters. Joseph Trinz, a theatre owner, said that he paid $3,500 to the structural steel workers, $5,000 to Michael J. Boyle of the Electrical Workers and $9,500 to the Painters to end various strikes.

The Commission emphasized an unhappy trend in union leadership. "Many important unions in the city of Chicago," it said, "are controlled by convicts and professional criminals . . . gunmen and convicts have seized hold of the offices of these unions for the sole purpose of increasing conspiracy that they might get money from the citizens of Chicago by a reign of terror . . ." This was not a novel development, professional criminals having infiltrated the Chicago labor movement a quarter of a century before; but the proportions were new. It was a foretaste of things to come.

There were alliances between union officials and employers. "The general building conspiracy," the Commission said, "could not exist without the aid of the contractors. Behind every crooked business agent there was a crooked contractor. Some contractors through choice, others through fear, and others through intimidation became a part of this corrupt system, and either by active aid, tolerance or passive acquiescence aided, abetted, and assisted the criminal business agents. Contractors aided this system in many instances by maintaining these business agents on their payrolls, requiring no labor whatsoever of them in return. In many instances, contractors entered the domain of labor politics and financed the campaigns of business agents favorable to their interests. In some cases contractors even financed the trips of labor agents to conventions in distant cities."

The Commission also condemned the corrupt practices of employers' associations. "Associations of materials men have been guilty of practices as hurtful to building operations as the criminal practices of crooked business agents," it said. "The associations, by cunningly devised schemes, have endeavored to avoid the conspiracy laws of the State. Exchange of cost information, pooling of bids, exchange of bids and of price lists, reporting to each other of bids and contracts, average cost systems, restrictive agreements with labor unions, agreements with dishonest labor leaders, and many forms of 'cooperative competition' and other euphemisms, have served as devices for the restraint of trade and the inflation of prices . . . The financial burdens imposed upon the building industry by these associations are greater even than [those] imposed by grafting business agents. The opinion expressed by many witnesses is that the artificial burden placed upon building by crooked business agents and criminal associations connected with the building industry have increased the cost of building at least thirty percent. These agencies are responsible for the housing shortage in Chicago, the almost complete cessation of building, and increased rentals."

The Commission levelled a final charge against the employers: "Such evil practices as super-speculative loans, fictitious values, exorbitant rates of interest, excessive money charges, fraudulent representations, false advertising and other disreputable practices, have been very frequently indulged in . . . Concerns guilty of [these practices] have been indirectly responsible for a large amount paid for labor graft . . . By reason of expensive money charges, builders, in the expeditious settlement of unjustified strikes, did not hesitate to meet the demands of dishonest labor leaders, at almost any cost, rather than face delay in the completion of building projects involved."

The Dailey Commission report led to the indictment of 124 defendants, most of them business agents. Few of the cases ever reached the courts. Only eighteen defendants were sentenced to prison terms, and of these only a handful served time. Governor Len Small of Illinois pardoned the rest.

The consequences for the Chicago building trades unions, however, were severe. Many employers blamed the current housing shortage on high wages, demanded a twenty percent cut, and staged a six-week lockout in 1921. Then both unions and employers agreed on Federal Judge Kenesaw Mountain Landis as the arbitrator for the dispute. His decision, strongly influenced by the Dailey Commission disclosures, was catastrophic for the unions.

Going beyond the formal agreement to arbitrate only wages, Landis ordered the abandonment of all sympathetic strikes, the removal of restrictions on materials, and the abolition of work rules which inconvenienced the employers. He also ordered the restoration of old wage differentials, imposing wage reductions in many cases to levels below those which even the employers were willing to accept. Most of the unions and many employers refused to go along with his decision, prompting the formation of the Citizens' Committee to Enforce the Landis Award. The Committee raised and spent $3,000,000, recruited a mobile guard of 700 men to protect non-union workmen, imported 21,000 strikebreakers, and shut off construction loans to firms which worked with unions refusing to comply with the Landis award.

In the ensuing violence, a number of buildings were bombed and many workmen injured. Two policemen were shot dead, whereupon the police raided scores of union offices and made wholesale arrests of business agents. The Building Trades Council split into two factions, one for and one against the award. Not even the personal intervention of Gompers succeeded in preventing a long series of internecine battles and the consequent operation of much of the Chicago construction industry under open shop conditions. Not until 1927 was the Building Trades Council reunited and a reversion to pre-1921 wages and working conditions achieved.

These were the major cases of corruption in the building trades. Extortion continued but never with the flamboyance of the past. In general, the advance of municipal reform and the growing sensitivity of the labor movement to adverse publicity contributed to the disappearance of the empires of Parks, Brindell and Madden. But corruption in the building trades unions before World War II was notable for something other than its scale. It was practiced, by and large, by men who originated in the industry, who could at least claim to be trade unionists, and who could often point away from their failings to considerable services rendered on behalf of their members. But alongside men like Parks and Fay there had come to prominence a different breed, with few claims to legitimacy or service. Particularly since Prohibition, the American labor movement had suffered the attentions of an intruder far more malicious and dangerous than the fallen building tradesman: the professional racketeer.

Part III
The Racketeers

5: The Rise of the Gangs

Gangsterism was a prominent feature of American city life during much of the nineteenth century. The enormous growth in population, the chaos of the cities, the prejudice against and among immigrant groups, the absence of civic sense and tradition, the casual morals of machine politics, the heritage of frontier justice and the acquisitive ethics of the age, all helped to create in many cities a custom of violence and an indifference to the law.

City gangs, for much of the century, were poorly organized and not very ambitious, largely content with casual violence and petty crime. In time, however, they grew in strength and jurisdiction. Conditions in the industrial slums drove many of its inhabitants to seek an escape in crime. Racial prejudice encouraged ethnic isolation among the immigrants and a distrust of the established order; the impatience of second-generation immigrants with the occupational and cultural barriers of race then brought into being the ethnic gangs, with great power in particular industries—the Irish in the building trades, the Irish and Italians on the waterfront, the Italians in the service trades, and the Jews in the garment industry.

Now the political machines, bent on graft and impatient of opposition, enlisted the aid of the gangs in molesting political opponents, exacting tribute and delivering the vote. The reward was immunity. In many areas the police and the judiciary, subject to political rule and privy to the practices of their masters, were less concerned with law and order than with a share of the spoils. The gangs thus received official protection for their expanding activities. "Policemen dare not arrest them," wrote Austin MacDonald, "district attorneys as a rule have not the courage to prosecute them, and few judges will pronounce a sentence upon them." The principal fields of gang activity became gambling, prostitution and the liquor trade; the general practice—except in the case of establishments owned or favored by political incumbents—was the extortion of regular payments from gaming rooms, houses of leisure and saloons in return for an absence of harassment.

Ambition grew with prosperity. Observing the opportunities for service in the turbulent field of industrial relations, some gangs entered the field as strikebreakers, but this was not, until the twentieth century, an important extension of extortionary jurisdiction. Unions in the meantime seldom responded violently with the use of mercenaries. The gangs were well-entrenched and prosperous, but they concerned themselves in the main with the traditional vices. Their leap to new power was yet to come. Prohibition paved the way.

On January 16, 1920, the Eighteenth Amendment to the Constitution of the United States came into effect. The Amendment prohibited "the manufacture, sale or transportation of intoxicating liquors . . . for beverage purposes" within the United States. Then followed the enactment of the National Prohibition Enforcement Act, commonly known as the Volstead Act, which defined intoxicating liquors, prescribed the conditions under which they might or might not be used, and provided penalties for violations of the law.

The hopes of the abolitionists were high. "Now for an era of clear thinking and clean living," declared the Anti-Saloon League of New York. Supporters of the new law claimed it would end drunkenness, empty the jails, lower the crime rate, uplift the young and elevate the "moral grandeur" of America. "This law," declared John F. Kramer, the first Prohibition Commissioner, "will be obeyed in cities, large and small, and in villages, and where it is not obeyed it will be enforced . . . The law says that liquor to be used as a beverage must not be manufactured. We shall see that it is not manufactured. Nor sold, nor given away, nor hauled in anything on the surface of the earth or under the earth or in the air."

It was the idlest of boasts. Seldom was law so honored in the breach or so contrary in its effect. The production of grapes and corn sugar multiplied, millions of gallons of industrial alcohol were diverted annually for illicit purposes, smuggling became a major industry, brewing and distilling equipment was sold openly in the stores, and the manufacture of home-brews became a flourishing family occupation. By 1927 the drinking of high-proof beverages had passed the 1917 historic peak of 172 million gallons, the estimates of victory ranging from eight to 135 million gallons. Prohibition, as John McConaughy noted, was a burlesque.

With such heroic disobedience of the law, there were few signs of moral grandeur. In the first decade of Prohibition, the annual rate of arrests for drunkeness in 365 major cities—excluding Chicago, for which no credible statistics are available—climbed from seventy-one per 10,000 persons to 146. There was a great increase in juvenile drunk arrests—sixfold in Washington, D.C.—moving Colonel William Baker of the Salvation Army to state that the experiment of Prohibition "has diverted the attention of the Salvation Army from the drunkard in the gutter to the girls and boys in their teens." Deaths from alcoholism quadrupled throughout the country, increasing more than eightfold in thirsty New York City. The federal jail population almost tripled, the proportion of jail sentences for liquor law violations multiplying tenfold. Even President Warren Harding, a tolerant and tippling man himself, conceded that the state of liquor law enforcement was "the most demoralizing factor in public life." It was hard thereafter to claim much for the Great Experiment.

The most gruesome result was crime. If the flouting of the law by resentful citizens seemed to them harmless and even droll, their indulgence brought unprecedented power and affluence to the professionals in crime. The trade in contraband liquor before federal Prohibition was substantial, owing to the widespread adoption of state and local dry laws; but now the market expanded greatly, state and local governments tended to relax their enforcement activities with the advent of federal responsibility, and the power of the gangs increased.

The conditions for success in bootlegging were control over the distribution and sale of alcoholic beverages; a readiness for violence; and a working immunity from the law. Racketeers now assumed almost complete control over the trade in potable liquor, their operational requirements producing a lasting underworld influence in the trucking, hotel and restaurant trades; the rivalries and depredations of the bootleggers produced a murder rate unrivalled in modern times and a terror of the private justice of the gangs; while the law was corrupted. By 1922 more than forty Coast Guard officers and men had been convicted of working with smugglers, while many others were dishonorably discharged. During Prohibition almost one-tenth of all federal enforcement officials were discharged for malfeasance in office. In the cities the police departments were corrupted, many officers becoming rich in the process, and the underworld intensified its political activities.

Services performed by the racketeers were varied, including the augmentation of voter registration lists, the intimidation or kidnaping of election officials, the faking of election returns, the molesting of voters and, where necessary, the murder of awkward politicians. The result, in many cities, was a virtual suspension of the law on Prohibition and an immunity for bootleggers in their various criminal activities. "Trying to enforce the law in Philadelphia," wrote the famous Marine General Smedley D. Butler, who had been recruited by the city with great flouish to enforce Prohibition, "was worse than any battle I was ever in." As the National Commission of Law Observance and Law Enforcement, itself in favor of Prohibition, reported to President Herbert Hoover in 1932:

When conspiracies are discovered from time to time, they disclose combinations of illicit distributors, illicit producers, local politicians, corrupt police and enforcement agencies, making lavish payments for protection and conducting an elaborate system of individual producers and distributors . . . Organized distribution has outstripped organized enforcement . . .

As to corruption it is sufficient to refer to the reported decisions of the courts during the past decade in all parts of the country, which reveal a succession of prosecutions for conspiracies, sometimes involving the police, prosecuting and administrative agencies of whole communities; to the flagrant corruption disclosed in connection with the diversion of industrial alcohol and unlawful production of beer; to the record of federal prohibition administration as to which cases of corruption have been continuous and corruption has appeared in services which in the past had been above suspicion; to the records of state police organizations; to the revelations as to police corruption revealed in surveys of criminal justice in many parts of the land; to the evidence of connection between corrupt local politics and gangs and the organized unlawful liquor traffic and of systematic collection of tribute from that traffic for corrupt political purposes.

There were, finally, the temptations of power. With the law in league and the public quiescent, the leaders of organized crime now sought to expand their jurisdictions. They moved into the ownership of hotels and restaurants, and became active in such ancillary trades as linen, tobacco, mineral waters, laundry, light foods and condiments. The special sensitivity of the perishable food industry to interruptions of work encouraged extortion in the fruit, vegetable, fish and poultry trades. In some highly competitive industries, such as the garment trades, employers engaged the services of gangsters to discipline the industry, mitigate the rigors of competition, and stave off the organizing efforts of unions; the result in some areas was the establishment of "protective associations," supported by employers' contributions and administered by racketeers, which enforced membership, fixed prices, and restricted entry into the trade. Some unions, in turn, solicited the help of gangsters in defense against predatory employers and rival unions. The racketeers themselves provided services impartially in most cases, sometimes serving both sides simultaneously. The 1920's were lucrative years for the gangs, although industrial racketeering remained a poor substitute for bootlegging. The decease of Prohibition in 1933, however, created a new demand for sources of illegitimate income. With old markets gone, but with the law not yet recovered and political protection still available, more gangs now turned to industrial racketeering. They succeeded, in the years following Repeal, in achieving an unparallelled influence in labor-management relations. The principal theatres of victory, not surprisingly, were New York and Chicago.

6: The Gangs in New York

The gangs of New York in the earlier years of the nineteenth century were street organizations, known by such exotic names as the Roach Guards, the Plug Uglies, and the Dead Rabbits. They were not essentially criminal organizations although, as Collinson Owens observed, "their habits were terrible." They were occasionally involved in political issues, as in the Draft Riots of 1865, but seldom engaged in organized criminal activities. During the latter part of the century they became more ambitious, practicing minor extortion in various fields of entertainment under such names as the Hudson Dusters, the Whyos, the Gophers, the Fourth Avenue Tunnel Gang, and the Five Pointers.

They now claimed the attention of Tammany Hall, which organized a series of "social clubs" as recruiting centers for old and new gangs. "It was usually through these organizations," Herbert Asbury wrote, ". . . that arrangements were made with the gang leaders for thugs to blackjack voters at the polls, act as repeaters and, on occasion, to remove opponents who had made themselves obnoxious or dangerous." Tammany, in return, provided political protection, legal counsel, and bail bond financing. The gangs became stronger, sometimes provided Tammany leaders from their ranks, and in time explored new fields.

Their first important incursion into industrial relations came in the 1890's. Monk Eastman, perhaps the most prominent New York gangster of the time, was the first major recruit of the employers, and was regularly engaged to attack pickets and union officials. He was followed by other gang leaders such as John ("Big Jack") Zelig, Jacob ("Little Augie") Orgen, Joseph ("Joe the Greaser") Rosenzweig, Pincus ("Pinchy") Paul, and Benjamin ("Dopey Benny") Fein. Their duties were specialized. Because of a general distaste for manual labor, these men and their followers seldom entered industrial plants to become strikebreakers as such, but limited themselves to picket-line violence and personal assaults. They worked initially and mainly for the employers, but in time were hired by some unions. This was particularly true in the needle trades, where the high proportion of women workers in the industry created a special need for outside reinforcements. Some gangsters, indeed, preferred to work for unions, since they came from working-class homes and felt some ideological affinity for labor organizations. However, most of them were quite impartial, readily switching paymasters or even working simultaneously for opposing sides.

Fein was one of the most successful. He began his criminal career at the age of ten on the East Side of Manhattan, rising through the ranks as petty thief, lush worker * and pickpocket to become a gang organizer of unusual system and skill. Concentrating geographically on lower Manhattan and industrially on the garment trades, he divided the area into districts, assigning subordinate gangs to each district and, at least towards the end of his career, seldom engaging in violence himself, acting mainly as an entrepreneur.

Testimony varies as to his choice of customer. According to Benjamin Stolberg, he provided strike-breaking services to employers in the garment trades during the great strikes of 1909 and 1910. Evidence produced at his trial for extortion in 1915, however, indicated that at least by that time he preferred working for unions. The prosecution stated at the trial that on one occasion Fein had rejected an employer's offer of $15,000 just to stay neutral in a strike, on the grounds that his sympathies were with the union. "The man really had a conviction," said Assistant District Attorney Lucien S. Breckinridge, "that he was helping in his own way in a cause in which he believed . . . He tried to convince me that he would have made the raids for the union leaders for nothing, except that he found it easier to get pay for them."

Whatever Fein's motives, his services were systematic and not overpriced. He charged $150 for raiding and wrecking a small plant, $600 for a similar attack on a large plant, $200 for throwing a manager or foreman down an elevator shaft or breaking his thumb or arm, $200 for a "complete knock-out" of a person of "average importance," and $60 to $600—depending upon the eminence of the victim—for shooting a man in the leg or removing his ear. These prices included fees for Fein's subordinates, who received a flat rate of $7.50 a day with a varying per diem allowance for out-of-town operations. At the time of his trial Fein was enjoying a personal income of some $15,000 a year. He was convicted of extortion, but received only a light sentence in return for a full confession. His notoriety, however, prevented a return to his trade.

The gangs remained, and during the tolerant 1920's became more influential. Tammany was still the dominant political force, but now more sophisticated. "The new Tammany," wrote Norman Thomas and Paul Blanchard, "is the old Tammany with the wisdom of age and experience added . . . a notable shift in tactics has occurred. The votes of aldermen and other city officials are almost never sold directly and the city treasury itself

* One who robs drunks.

is safe from theft. The real fortunes of the new Tammany are gathered through brokerage services." Tammany officials in private business attracted customers by promising them friendly treatment at Tammany Hall. City officials accepted private payments for awarding franchises, leases and other licenses, or for condoning the violation of city ordinances and regulations. Both politicans and policemen collected graft from the city's estimated 32,000 speakeasies.

The evidence was abundant. A state legislative investigation under the chairmanship of Assemblyman Schuyler M. Meyer disclosed the existence of graft in a number of city departments, Tammany influence with Police Commission appointments and police assignments, and the holding of inexplicably large bank accounts by police officials. In 1931 a committee chaired by Judge Samuel Seabury charged that New York District Attorney Thomas B. Crain had consistently associated with the underworld and engaged in the manipulation of bogus stocks; that businessmen had paid $50,000 in political kickbacks for the lease of city piers and other facilities; that the city's Magistrate's Court was dominated by patronage and honeycombed with graft; and that both the New York County Sheriff Thomas M. Farley and Mayor James J. Walker had enriched themselves in public office. Walker, in particular, had apparently accepted money from contractors interested in municipal legislation, held stock in companies with city contracts, and had banked close to a million dollars in his first five years in office. Sheriff Farley banked $360,000 in seven years on a total salary of $90,000. Kings County Sheriff James A. McQuade saved $52,000 in six years on a net official income of less than $50,000. Also within a period of six years, Tammany leader James T. McCormick of the 22nd Manhattan District banked $384,788, largely composed of illegal marriage fees he collected as a deputy city clerk. The average annual income of a Tammany leader during these years, according to Dr. Joseph McGoldrick of Columbia University, was about $100,000.

Law enforcement was clearly imperfect. "The courts," declared the National Commission on Law Observance and Law Enforcement, "know that some of the prosecutors are crooked and the prosecutors know that some of the courts are crooked, and both know that some of the police are crooked, and the police are equally well informed as to them." In 1926, the Commission said, "only 4% of all felony cases in New York City resulted in convictions for the offenses originally charged, compared to 4.9% in Chicago, 17% in Cincinnati, 38.3% in rural New York State, and 60.7 in Milwaukee."

All three reports brought demands for reform and the traditional promises from City Hall, but to slight effect. "The evidence before me," Seabury said in 1932, "compels the conclusion that the much-heralded warfare on racketeers ended in complete and abject surrender by the law-enforcing authorities in New York City."

Meanwhile the racketeers prospered. The most prominent of them after Fein was Arnold Rothstein, the son of a rich and highly respected garment manufacturer. He posted bail for each of the eleven gangsters and twenty-three union officials who were indicted following Fein's confession. None was convicted. Rothstein went on to finance at one time or another such celebrated racketeers as Irving ("Waxey Gordon") Wexler, Charles ("Lucky") Luciano, Jack ("Legs") Diamond, Frank Costello, Phillip ("Dandy Phil") Kastel, Abner ("Longy") Zwillman, Arthur ("Dutch Schultz") Flegenheimer, Louis ("Lepke") Buchalter and Charles ("Charley the Gurrah") Shapiro. Rothstein was, according to Daniel Bell, "the short term commercial banker for half the underworld of the United States." But he has a specialty. "His main interest," said Bell, "was industrial racketeering, and his entry was through labor disputes." Under his guidance racketeers moved into a number of industries—including the needle trades, trucking, entertainment, longshoring and the culinary trades. By 1930, the New York *World* estimated, some twenty-five industries in New York were controlled or influenced by the underworld.

Rothstein was murdered in 1928. His chief successors were Buchalter and Shapiro, who had been collaborating in racketeering for some years. In 1929 both were arrested for throwing acid on the stocks of clothing manufacturers, but were released without prosecution. They then became active in various industries in New York and New Jersey—principally flour, baking and the garment industry. They first got control of trucking operations, then extorted from the primary employers. "They offered 'protection' to the employers against labor trouble," Benjamin Stolberg has written, "and some firms paid as much as $10,000 not to have . . . stink bomb squads ruin their goods or wreck their premises. Then the racketeers would offer their services to local union officials for the settlement of any difficulties with the employers, whom they claimed, with some justice, to control. Business agents and other officials who couldn't see the light were beaten within an inch of their lives. 'Control' of the union could then be sold in turn to the employers." It was a large and profitable enterprise, Buchalter and Shapiro employing as many as 250 collectors and enforcers, and extracting between $5,000,000 and $10,000,000 a year from employers and unions. "The magnitude of the operations of these racketeers," District Attorney Frank S. Hogan said in 1944, "and the brutal power they exercised over legitimate business was unprecedented in criminal annals."

From 1929 on, the two gangsters underwent a series of trials for offenses ranging from industrial extortion to traffic in narcotics, but managed through acquittals, delays and fugitive action to avoid imprisonment until 1940. In that year both men received life sentences for extortion. Shapiro went to jail to serve out his term. Buchalter was turned over to the New York State authorities to face a charge of murdering a minor garment industry employer. He had killed in a fit of pique unrelated to his extortionary activities, and was unfortunate in that no one took the trouble to intimidate the witnesses. He was executed in 1944, in the sole example of the capital punishment of a major underworld figure in modern times.

Buchalter and Shapiro were among the leaders of their kind; there would be few like them again in the brazenness, if not the scale, of their extortions. But they owed less to their adventurousness and ability than to an unfortunate set of social circumstances. Their chief success was in the New York needle trades—the history of that industry illustrating as well as any the entrée that a proper combination of circumstances will give to the professional criminal. Though Buchalter and Shapiro had no true successors, the conditions which produced them remained. New York politics was still prone to graft in civic and police administration, and always noted for what New York Judge John M. Murtagh called the "turnstile justice" of the courts. The reputation of Tammany Hall, briefly rehabilitated after World War II, was re-tarnished by charges of fealty to Frank Costello, the alleged "prime minister" of the American underworld. The needle trades, while considerably civilized by the efforts of unions and the best of employers, retained enough of their primeval habits and bad connections to ensure—in one section at least—the survival of the gangs. And on the New York waterfront the environment of the industry, the greed of the employers, the adjustability of union leaders, the interests of politicians and the ineffectiveness of the law, combined to produce the classic case in American labor history of the domination of a trade union by the forces of crime.

7: The Needle Trades

The New York garment industry—centered around the manufacture of hats, furs and clothing—has always shared some of the characteristics of the building trades, with added complications of its own. The average business unit is small, competition is intense, profits are generally low, and business failures are frequent. Entry into the industry is even easier than in the building trades, requiring little capital. Since equipment is cheap, wages are the most important cost. Competition tends to be at the expense of labor.

It was a hard industry to organize. Until recent times it was populated mainly by immigrants of Jewish and Italian origin, people unused to the language or the culture, even less welcome than the Irish, and in many cases desperate enough to work under almost any conditions. Unionization was made more difficult by the practice of "home work" performed singly or in small groups in private houses for low piece rates, and by the subcontracting system known as "jobbing," whereby primary manufacturers or "jobbers"—save those running large "inside" shops where all operations were conducted under one roof, or those making luxury items requiring the highest quality work—contracted out the cut cloth to myriads of smaller firms for sewing, finishing and pressing. Most small contractors worked for long hours at low return. Some migrated out of the city to small communities which offered them low rents, low taxes, and the cooperation of the police in resisting the needle trades' unions. Some turned to the underworld for protection, and some of the unions followed suit. "The discovery was then made," Joel Seidman noted, ". . . that it was easier to hire hoodlums than get rid of them afterward."

The Men's Clothing Industry

The United Garment Workers of America was one of the first of the modern needle trade unions. Founded in 1891, it was a combination of native American members—mainly of Irish and German descent—and Jewish socialists in the men's clothing industry. The UGWA affiliated with the AFL, and for some years conducted a militant and successful policy in New York. After an unsuccessful strike in 1896, however, the leadership of the union became more conservative, discouraged striking, advocated coop-

74

eration with the employers, and confined its activities mainly to the work-clothes trade and the promotion of the union label.

Discontent with the leadership grew, reaching a high point in the successful strikes of 1910 in Chicago and 1912 in New York, both of which were led by socialists and established the union in new sections of the industry. In 1914 the UGWA denied credentials to a number of rebel delegates, most of whom later left the UGWA to form the Amalgamated Clothing Workers of America under Sidney Hillman. The AFL affiliation of the UGWA caused the Amalgamated to withdraw from the federation, and it remained independent until the 1930's. After a series of organizational battles with the UGWA, it soon became the foremost union in the men's clothing industry.

The rise of the Amalgamated moved some employers to desperate measures. Although less competitive than the ladies' garment industry, the men's clothing industry also used the jobbing system. The highly skilled cutters in the jobber establishments were usually organized; the less-skilled workers in the contract shops were not. The contractors brought in the racketeers. The union, according to some sources, responded in kind.

"The most that can be said in mitigation of the Amalgamated's part in the entente of racketeers and labor," *Business Week* stated in 1957, "is that it used them in self-defense. Employers used them first." Thomas E. Dewey, in his days as a special prosecutor for the State of New York, had already made the same point. "The Amalgamated," *Business Week* said, "still in its organizational phase, would send delegates to an open shop to recruit for the union. The employer would buy protection from the Jewish Mob. Amalgamated delegates would be beaten up, employers who showed an interest in the union terrorized . . . It [the union] began to do business on its own with the Jewish Mob."

The Amalgamated has always denied the charges. As early as 1922, indeed, it complained to the New York District Attorney of the use of racketeers by the employers. "The simple truth," wrote President Jacob Potofsky of the Amalgamated in 1957, "is that neither Hillman nor the Amalgamated Clothing Workers of America ever trafficked or dealt with any underworld figure . . . Hillman and his associates, at considerable personal risk, moved vigorously and effectively to eliminate them. They remain eliminated to this very day." The charges against Hillman are still in dispute. There is more substantial evidence, however, of links between the underworld and some secondary leaders in the union.

"A clothing shop in the Bronx," *Business Week* reported, "making a 'contract' with [Arnold] Rothstein, would announce a wage cut and declare it no longer recognized the Amalgamated. Disgruntled employees, Amalgamated members, would strike and set up a picket line. Rothstein thugs would appear and drive the pickets away with threats, if that was sufficient. If not, a few beatings would do the trick. The police were bribed not to interfere."

Buchalter now entered the scene as the agent for minor Amalgamated officials. His men performed as regular pickets and, when Rothstein forces appeared, attacked the invaders with fists or sticks; later, as the numbers on both sides grew, knives and guns were used. Buchalter allegedly provided additional services—arson in the shops, tampering with elevator cables in loft buildings, destroying clothing stocks with acid, forcing trucks off the road, and beating or murdering opponents. His power increased after Rothstein's death, and he assumed—in cooperation with Shapiro—virtual control of the Jewish gangs in New York. He organized truck owners and self-employed drivers into a truckmen's association, raising the cartage prices for men's clothing and dividing the proceeds with the members of the association. He developed a proprietary interest in the industry, buying into a number of firms, and also became influential in the clothing drivers' local of the Amalgamated. Like other gangsters, he now served both sides.

In 1931 Buchalter moved to gain control of the strategic cutters' Local 4 of the Amalgamated. It was a natural corollary to his power in trucking, and would enable him to direct work to non-union contract shops. Philip Orlofsky, the leader of Local 4 and one of Hillman's opponents, struck up an alliance with Buchalter and ceded effective control of the local to him. Buchalter then tried to take over other Amalgamated locals, threatening a number of officials with death unless they sided with him, and establishing for a brief period—in cooperation with Orlofsky—the Independent Clothing Workers Union.

The Amalgamated intervened. Hillman had been unable to glean much information from the intimidated officers and members of Local 4 and now, after talks with some trusted employers on the timing of his action, brought the issue into the open. In May, 1930, he instituted a routine inspection of the books of Local 4, uncovering huge irregularities. He then called a meeting of all New York City local union executive board members. "We might as well be frank and outspoken here," he told them, "and say out in the open what we have been saying to each other in private. What the New York market is suffering from more than anything else is the racketeering evil . . . [It] is a struggle to determine whether the racketeers are going to control the working conditions and wage rates of the clothing workers in New York, or whether the workers are to do that themselves through their own organization. As far as the organization is concerned, we are here to serve notice that we will fight the underworld to a finish."

Shortly afterwards, Hillman—now under a twenty-four-hour armed guard—led a march of 300 union officials, industry representatives and prominent citizens to the steps of City Hall, there to petition Mayor Walker for help against the racketeers. He publicly recited to Walker the effects of underworld penetration of the industry, noting the widespread unemployment of Amalgamated members because of the racket-protected shops in and around the city, the assaulting of union pickets and the shooting of union officials, the cooperation given by some employers to the racketeers, and the refusal of most witnesses to violence and racketeering to testify in court. "The gangsters boast," Hillman said, "that they are as strong as the government of the city . . . we believe it is mere cowardly bluff. But they have issued their challenge . . ."

The Mayor was suitably surprised. "You mean," he said, "that they claim to have political influence? . . . that cannot be done."

Before his own malodorous departure from public office, Walker did in fact provide some support to the Amalgamated. The union called a general strike the following month, ostensibly against the industry as a whole but essentially against the racket-protected shops. At Hillman's request, policemen from the Homicide Squad rather than the suspect Industrial Squad were dispatched into the clothing district to protect the strikers. The newspapers also supported the strike. "In such times," the New York *Herald-Tribune* said editorially, "it is nothing short of criminal that thirty-odd thousand workers, as poor as this city's garment workers are, should have been forced out on strike by a number of unscrupulous employers . . . some exploiters saw in the depression an opportunity to re-impose the sweatshop conditions of the last generation . . . This situation is not criminal in the figurative sense only, for it has been made possible by an actual league between some employers and an underworld 'gorilla' organization which league recently took on the aspect of a criminal racket . . ." The strike was partially successful, having brought a number of runaway shops under union contract.

Hillman now moved against the cutters' local. On August 24, 1931, the General Executive Board of the Amalgamated met and filed charges against the officers of the local, charging that $89,000 in special assessments had disappeared during the past year, as well as $60,000 in dues over a period of two years. It also accused the officers of "scabbing" and coming to terms with open shop employers. Amalgamated officers and members subsequently submitted affidavits in a court trial stating that Orlofsky had stolen the local's books and threatened members with death.

The accused officers refused to meet with the General Executive Board, whereupon the Board ordered the local to be put into trusteeship.

In the early morning of August 29 the then Vice-President Jacob Potofsky, in company with other union officials and some Homicide Squad men, camped outside the offices of Local 4. At a prearranged time a motion for trusteeship was presented to and adopted by the Board. Potofsky was informed of the action, opened the offices of Local 4 with a duplicate key, showed the occupants the trusteeship documents, and barricaded himself and his companions inside. Orlofsky supporters attacked the premises in the afternoon but were held off until reinforcements from the international union arrived. The ousted leaders of Local 4 sought an injunction against the Amalgamated but failed. All resistance soon ended, and the international union remained in control.

With this, the influence of the underworld in the Amalgamated and the industry ceased to be a major problem. As late as 1940, Hillman asked for amendments to the Amalgamated's constitution to provide safeguards against possible racketeer infiltration; but he also said at the time that he knew of no corruption in the union, and there have been no references to it since. During the 1930's and 1940's the men's clothing industry became almost wholly organized and labor-management relations in it notable for their cordiality. The public record, at least, seems to be devoid of evidence of racketeering in the industry since 1931.

The Fur Industry

"The fur business," *Fortune* said in 1936, "is almost completely irrational from the trap to the shop window. It is a business of little candor, less security, and no statistics. It is a playground for speculators and individualists."

The industry was vulnerable to the predatory and the corrupt. Fur manufacturing was a skilled trade, performed largely by hand and resistant to mechanization. Thus entry into the business was easy, the capital equipment for a small business costing less than $100. Most shops were small: one-quarter had only one or two employees; one-half employed four workers, or less. The industry was highly susceptible to changes in fashion, season and economic conditions, unstable in prices, prodigious in business failures, and desperate in its ethics.

"The small shops do not keep books, shift rapidly from place to place, and lock their doors against inspection," a 1936 report of the National Recovery Administration noted. The many employers in the industry were fiercely competitive, secretive and suspicious of each other, uncooperative in facing common problems. As a result, wrote Victor Fuchs, the industry was "ridden with internal disputes, complacent in good years, despairing in bad ones, and ill-equipped to meet the competition of other industries for the customer's favor." The erratic demand for fur clothes provided only four months' work a year for the average fur worker, so many of them took in home work, competing with the shops at low rates of pay. The depression hit the fur industry hardest of all the needle trades, the imports of fur dropping by 1932 to one-quarter, and exports to one-third, of 1929 levels. The industry's lowest ebb coincided with, and perhaps invited, a bold intervention by racketeers.

The fur workers were the slowest of the garment industry crafts to establish a permanent organization. They were mainly German and Jewish in origin, and maintained separate and quarrelling organizations until they came together in 1912 with the founding of the International Fur Workers Union.

The IFWU remained the dominant union in the industry until the 1920's, but it had a violent history, complicated by internal disputes between Communist and other ideological elements in the union. A general strike in the industry in 1912, according to Philip S. Foner, was accompanied by the systematic use of gangsters by the employers. "Hired gangsters and gunmen," he says, "brutally attacked and slugged strikers on the picket lines, making no exceptions of women strikers, whom they beat cruelly. Young girls walked the picket lines and gathered in the strike halls with bandaged heads and mutilated faces . . . A newspaperman at the strike hall reported strikers being brought in 'whose clothes were hanging in tatters on them, the skin cut and horribly bruised from the bottles and iron bars with which they were attacked' . . . That the police authorities interfered openly on behalf of the bosses was common knowledge." The *New York Times* was more restrained. The fur employers, it reported three days after the strike had begun, "will open their shops with strikebreakers without protection tomorrow. If any attempt is made to annoy the workers the Police Department will be called upon to protect them." The police were brought in and there were reports of violence, particularly against women fur workers.

The IFWU, again according to Foner, itself resorted to professional violence not only against the employers but against the Communist and other opponents of the conservative leadership of the union. "The gangsters did very well for themselves," Foner writes. "They collected huge sums from the union for keeping the workers in check. And they exacted tribute from the employers for protecting their shops against militant workers . . . Another source of income for the strong-arm men was the money they extracted from the non-union workers who paid weekly for permission to work in the shops. When these workers wanted to become members of the union they were forced to pay graft in order to get a book." Gangsters were allegedly used freely in the 1920 strike of the IFWU, working for both the union and the employers, manning picket lines for the former and supplying strikebreakers for the latter. The strike lasted thirty weeks and failed, leading to internal rebellion in the union and the eventual emergence of the Communist rebels as the dominant force in the New York area.

The IFWU's third major strike took place in 1926 in New York. Gangsters evidently now found a new employer. "In 1925," wrote Benjamin Gitlow, a former high official in the Communist party of the United States, "we Communists took over the New York Furriers Union, through an alliance with leading gangsters and racketeers that had broken away from the notorious Kaufman machine, centering around Morris Kaufman, then the International President of the International Fur Workers Union . . . The very gangsters who formerly had used knives and blackjacks against the Communists now protected them instead of protecting Kaufman . . . Communists, who had made the fight against gangsterism the main issue among the Furriers, had no qualms about making a deal with the gangsters, accepting their protection and services, including the most nefarious gangster activities, just as long as they controlled the union and dominated its affairs."

"It appears," said Judge Francis X. Mancuso when ordering a grand jury investigation of the strike, "that a group of strong-arm men and gangsters has been engaged by the union to commit assaults on workingmen who refuse to join their unions or refuse to sympathize with them by joining their strike. These strong-arm men are ready to render services to either side." An AFL committee under the chairmanship of Vice-President Matthew Woll reported charges of wholesale bribery of the New York police by the IFWU New York Joint Board through an attorney "whose duty it was to buy members of the Police Department, the District Attorney's staff, the Industrial Squad and even all the officers in two stations so that the authorities would be on the side of the strikers." Woll stated at a court inquiry that Isadore Shapiro, the chairman of the Joint Board, had told him that the union had paid $3,800 to policemen during the strike on a sliding scale ranging from $20 a week for sergeants to $250 a week for inspectors. Ben Gold, the Communist leader of the New York Furriers, was frank about the use of police to beat up non-strikers. "If a man said he was going to scab," he evidently told Woll, "he got his. We made no secret of it." In 1939 Maurice L. Malkin, a former Communist official of the IFWU, told a Congressional committee that the Communists borrowed $1,750,000 from

Arnold Rothstein to finance the 1926 strike, that Jack Diamond and other gangsters had worked for the union, and that some $110,000 was paid in bribes to the police.

The Joint Board won the strike, greatly enhancing the prestige of its Communist leadership. The AFL and the IFWU then set up a new Furriers Joint Council to compete with the Joint Board. In 1928 the Joint Board seceded from the union and helped to found—in cooperation with Communist elements in the International Ladies Garment Workers Union—the Needle Trades Workers Industrial Union. The NTWIU made almost no headway in the ladies' garment industry, but it dominated the New York fur market by 1932. By 1937 it represented almost all fur workers in the New York area.

Meanwhile, however, a major policy change had taken place. In 1927 the Moscow-directed Red International of Labor Unions had adopted a policy of dual unionism—Communist-led unions would compete with non-Communist-led unions—and the New York Furriers followed suit. But in 1934 the RILU policy changed to one of "boring from within," whereupon the NTWIU opened unity negotiations with the IFWU and re-affiliated in the same year against the protests of the AFL. Gold was elected manager of the New York Joint Council, becoming president of the international union in 1937. Thus it was the Communist leadership of the union which had to deal with the entry of Buchalter and Shapiro into the New York fur industry at the invitation of the employers.

Prior to 1932 the fur dressing trade was perhaps the most competitive section of the fur industry, the dressers competing sharply for the attentions of the raw fur suppliers on the one hand and of the manufacturers and dealers on the other. In 1932, after three years of depression and desperate competition, the dressers formed two associations for the protection of their interests. These were the Protective Fur Dressers Corporation (PFDC), representing seventeen of the largest rabbit skin dressing companies, and the Fur Dressers Factor Corporation (FDFC), representing forty-six of the principal dressers of fur other than rabbit skin.

"The purposes and functions of these two combinations," the Federal Bureau of Investigation reported, "were to drive out of existence all non-member dressing firms; to persuade all dealers to deal exclusively with members of their combinations . . . to eliminate competition; to fix uniform prices by agreement; to set up a quota system whereby each of the different members received a certain percentage of the entire business handled by the members of the combination; to provide a credit system enforcing frequent periodic settlements and effectively blacklisting any dealer who for any reason would not pay on settlement day. The objectives of this combination . . . were effected by intimidation and violence of the most vicious character . . ."

All dealers and manufacturers were notified by the associations that their business in fur dressing should now be conducted solely with association members designated in advance, that certain price increases would take effect immediately, and that all accounts must be settled in full at the end of each week. Non-conformists were disciplined. The associations set up a system of observers to detect shipments of furs to and from non-members of either association. Reprisals began with threatening telephone calls, followed if necessary by physical assault by squads armed with lead pipes and blackjacks, or by stink-bomb and acid attacks on fur stocks, or by murder. Within two years the two associations controlled between eighty and ninety percent of the trade.

Buchalter and Shapiro were the enforcers. They were approached in April, 1932, by Abraham Beckerman, formerly of the Amalgamated Clothing Workers and now general manager for the Fur Dressers Factor Corporation. "I had been personally acquainted with them," he told the FBI, "and accordingly I called one of them on the telephone and went up to see them . . . I explained what the situation was; that there was a certain amount of organization work, meaning rough stuff, that would have to be done and inquired whether they were in a position to undertake it . . . They told me they would take care of me." The FDFC had already concluded a protective agreement with Owney Madden, another gang leader, but wished to get out of it. Buchalter and Shapiro consulted with Madden and agreed, in return for jurisdiction, to take only half of the initial fees the latter had received from the dressers. They then told Beckerman they would work at first on a piece-rate basis, but wished to be retained eventually on an annual salary of about $50,000 a year. In practice they were paid in lump sums of $2,000 to $2,500 at a time. The money was paid directly by the FDFC or indirectly through the device of over-payments by the FDFC to the National Fur Skin Dressing Company. The two gangsters received in all some $30,000 for their services to the FDFC. Similar arrangements were made with the PFDC.

Conflict now arose between the associations and the NTWIU. Morris Kaufman, the former president of the IFWU, now worked for the FDFC. The corporation subsequently tried to sign labor agreements only with AFL unions, prompting violence between itself and the NTWIU.

The break between the PFDC and the fur workers came during a meeting between PFDC President Samuel Mittelman and Irving Potash, the secretary-treasurer of the NTWIU. Relations had hitherto been cordial.

PFDC officials later testified that Gold and Potash had reached an agreement with the corporation to eliminate competition in the industry; the union was to receive a substantial improvement in wages, and in return— with the help of a $30,000 "organizing fund" provided by the employers— would force non-member firms into the corporation through stink-bombs and threats. Mittelman now introduced Potash to Shapiro, saying "You will have to deal with Mr. Gurrah, because Mr. Gurrah is the Protective."

Potash refused to talk with Shapiro and left. Morris Langer, an organizer for the PFDC, later attended a meeting with officers of the corporation; he was told that the union must cooperate with the corporation, and was asked to strike three firms which had refused to join the PFDC. Langer, like Potash, spoke strongly against the corporation's enforcement policy, and a few weeks later he was murdered. Gold, Potash and other NTWIU officials then received threats to their safety. On April 24, 1933, a group of Buchalter's agents staged an armed attack on the NTWIU's headquarters. One gangster and two fur workers were killed and fifteen fur workers wounded. Seven of Buchalter's men went to jail for the attack.

In November, 1933, a federal grand jury handed down three indictments for collusive activities in the fur industry. The first two charged the two associations and some 120 firms with anti-trust activities. Buchalter and Shapiro were named in both indictments. Officers of the FDFC and PDFC were found guilty and sent to jail or fined. Buchalter and Shapiro received prison sentences in both cases, forfeited their bail and became fugitives, and were not imprisoned until later and on other charges.

The third indictment was against the NTWIU and its officers on anti-trust grounds. The indictment was left on file for seven years, then reactivated by the Department of Justice. A verdict of guilty was reversed on appeal. The IFWU, meanwhile, had affiliated with the Congress of Industrial Organizations. It was expelled from the CIO in 1949, went into decline, and in 1955 merged with the Amalgamated Meat Cutters and Butcher Workmen, losing its Communist leadership in the process.

The Headwear Industry

"For sheer cut-throat competition," *Fortune* said in 1936, "the ladies' millinery manufacturers almost make the automobile dealers look like a pack of Quakers . . ." Some twenty-six percent of annual production had to be sold in the two peak months around Easter and Labor Day, and demand was decreasing. One business in four failed every year. Probably half of all companies lost money every year. Dollar sales in the industry dropped from $209,000,000 in 1927 to $77,000,000 in 1933; total wages fell from $47,000,000 to $24,000,000. Mechanization cut the work force

and increased productivity, but had little effect on sales. A movement towards bulk buying sharply reduced prices but stimulated business hardly at
all. A survey of 200 millinery firms showed that their average annual profit
was $534 in 1935 and $149 in 1936. "The millinery industry," *Fortune* observed, ". . . is entering its second decade of a seemingly permanent state
of collapse."

The first union in the headwear industry was the United Hatters of
North America, founded in 1896. In 1899 the Hatters absorbed the United
Hat Makers, a Jewish organization, and soon represented most employees
in the men's felt hat trade in New York. The United Cloth Cap and Hat
Makers was established in 1901, organizing almost all cap makers in New
York during the next few years. Both unions later moved into the millinery
field and engaged in bitter jurisdictional rivalry for many years. In 1924
they agreed to retain their basic jurisdictions but to cooperate in organizing
millinery and other workers in the industry. The Hat Makers were the
more successful of the two unions in millinery. In 1934 the two unions
merged into the United Hatters, Cap and Millinery Workers International
Union. Prior to that event, however, racketeers had entered the millinery
field. The Hat Makers group was thus the organization most concerned.

Headwear employers had hired gangsters as early as 1904, but not in important numbers until the 1920's. In most cases gangsters were hired by
employers as a protection against unionization, but on occasion they were
retained by local unions, and sometimes set up independent unions themselves. Because of the special turbulence of the millinery industry, they
concentrated most of their efforts there.

In 1927 the wife and children of Nathaniel Spector, the manager of Hat
Makers Local 24, were threatened because of Spector's attempt to organize
a non-union shop. Spector appealed to the police, but received no help. In
the same year Alex Rose, secretary-treasurer of Local 24, received a visit
in his office from Jacob ("Little Augie") Orgen and Jack Diamond. Orgen
said that his organization was about to supply protection to some thirty-five
manufacturers and had guaranteed to prevent any strikes or wage increases
in return for a fee of $100,000 a year. The millinery workers were at that
time on strike against one of the protected employers. Rose was ordered to
call off the strike or face the consequences. He refused, his life being saved
—according to the Seabury report—only because Orgen was murdered
soon afterwards. Orgen, against the wishes of Buchalter and Shapiro, had
evidently taken $2,000 from the Chelsea Hat Company in return for protec-
tion, and $50,000 from a group of painting contractors during a strike in
1927. On October 15, 1927, he was ambushed by Buchalter and Shapiro
and killed.

In 1930, alarmed at the continuing decline in the economic condition and ethical standards of the industry, a group of millinery manufacturers combined into the Women's Headwear Group and asked the Hat Makers for an industry-wide contract. The union was in favor of the proposal, at least in principle. The racketeers were opposed. They had become an influence in the key hat-blockers' Local 42, and had also set up two independent unions—the Amalgamated Millinery Workers of America and the Millinery Workers of America. "It was clear to them," Charles Green has written, "that a collective agreement would greatly circumscribe their possible field of activity, for it would set up relatively uniform labor standards which would have behind them the collective strength of the manufacturers as well as the collective strength of the union."

The Hat Makers now asked District Attorney Thomas A. Crain for help, but received unexpected treatment. Spector was called to Crain's office, ostensibly to arrange for him to testify before a grand jury, but was told informally that his demand for a wage increase from a West Side manufacturer was in fact an attempt at extortion. The Hat Makers thereupon called a mass protest meeting and transmitted a resolution to Crain. "Should your office at any time decide," the resolution said, "to make a really sincere effort to rid the city of extortionists and criminals, we stand ready to assist you in every way possible."

No more was heard of the charge, but Crain's office came under fire in the Seabury report on the millinery industry the following year. The report said that a number of millinery manufacturers had accepted underworld protection against unionization; that the chief protector of the non-union shops after Orgen's death was Jacob ("Tough Jake") Kurzman, who received $10,000 a year for his services; that the New York City police had given Crain ample information on racketeering in the industry—including a list of millinery firms whose books had shown payments to Kurzman; but that the District Attorney had taken no effective action, and had indeed "thrown up his hands . . ."

The Hat Makers soon signed an industry-wide agreement with the Women's Headwear Group, and embarked on an anti-racketeer campaign throughout the industry. President Max Zaritsky sought the help of the police, who had previously abstained from intervening in disputes between the union and the racketeers. "Manufacturers are terrorized and harassed," Zaritsky wrote, "workers intimidated and threatened with bodily harm, officers of the union are shadowed by racketeers and their agents, and their homes visited by unknown persons . . . I take the liberty of asking you to lend your assistance to our men and women who are willing and ready to combat the growing evil of racketeering and gangsterism in the millinery industry." Lieutenant-Governor Herbert H. Lehman also asked the police to help, and they agreed.

The campaign began in March, 1932. A "Committee of 700" from Local 24 volunteered for picket-line duties. The hat blockers had stayed out of the industry-wide agreement, but friendly members of the local formed a "Unity Club" for picketing purposes. Shortly after dawn on March 10, a picket line of 150 union members assembled outside the Chelsea Hat Company, one of the larger protected shops. Kurzman and the officers of the independent Amalgamated were warned to stay away from the picket line. The police provided protection for the pickets, the news of their intervention spread rapidly throughout the garment district, and by nightfall the Chelsea Hat Company and several other employers had come to terms with the union. On March 17 the union declared a general strike throughout the industry, received the support of nearly all employers, and within a few days negotiated contracts with all the thirty-one shops said to have been receiving racketeer protection. "There is no longer," Zaritsky told the press, "a single shop in the industry under the influence of racketeers . . ."

The independent racket unions soon dissolved, leaving Local 42 as the only underworld redoubt. Max Golden, the leader of Local 42, had ordered all unionized blockers working in twelve shops employing non-union women trimmers to stay at work during the general strike. After the strike the Hat Makers formally charged him with disloyalty and revoked the charter of the local. Golden then approached Buchalter and Shapiro and offered them $25,000 for protection against the union. Vice-President Abraham Mendelowitz of the Hat Makers obtained an interview with one of Buchalter's assistants, reporting afterwards only that he had persuaded the Buchalter organization that "it would not be worth its while to move in on the millinery field. The members would fight too hard." Deprived of Buchalter's help, Golden led his remaining members into the United Hatters, but lost office when the 1934 merger took place.

The Ladies Garment Industry

The International Ladies Garment Workers Union was founded in 1900, with its few thousand members concentrated mainly in New York City. The skilled trades were manned largely by conservative native Americans, the more numerous semi-skilled trades by socialist Jewish immigrants. The union was ostensibly socialist in its ideology yet followed conservative trade union methods. The effective leadership of the union was in the hands of the conservative minority, many of whom had close links with

Tammany Hall and little taste for the more militant policies of the socialists.

Weak leadership and the depression of 1904 brought about a decline in union membership, followed by an increase in the influence of the militants. The union ran its first successful strike in 1907 among the children's cloakmakers and reefermakers. Then in 1909 came the walkout to be known as "The Uprising of the Twenty Thousand," a near-spontaneous strike among women employees in waist-making and dress-making, followed in 1910 by "the Great Revolt" among the cloakmakers. By 1912 the union claimed 50,000 members in New York City alone.

In 1920 the socialists were firmly in control of the ILGWU, but the Russian Revolution divided the union. The sympathizers, or "left-wing" socialists as they were called, welcomed the partnership of native Communists in union affairs and helped the Trade Union Educational League—a Communist-led rival to the AFL—to win control over the New York Joint Board of the ILGWU. The Board was already at odds with the international union on the grounds that it was underrepresented at ILGWU conventions; now, with the Communists in control, it made an open break with the "right-wing" socialist leadership of the union.

With the lifting of the depression of the early 1920's, the ILGWU proposed a "New Program" calling for greater efficiency in the industry, higher competitive standards, a forty-hour week, a minimum work-year of thirty-two weeks and—most important of all—the assumption by the jobbers of the responsibility for maintaining union conditions in contract shops. The last demand was intended to limit the number of contractors any one jobber could employ, thus eliminating runaway contractors and sweat-shop conditions. A Special Advisory Committee appointed by Governor Al Smith reported in favor of the union's program in both 1925 and 1926, with the one reservation that the managerial prerogative be protected by allowing any employer to discharge up to ten percent of his employees in any one year. President Morris Sigman of the ILGWU recommended that the Committee's report be accepted as a basis for negotiations. The inside manufacturers agreed, but—for their own reasons—the jobbers and the Communists did not. On July 1, 1926, the New York Joint Board called a general strike in the New York cloak market.

The strike was a disaster for the union. It lasted twenty-six weeks, cost some $3,500,000 in union funds of which $1,000,000 was never accounted for, resulted in an unfavorable settlement for the union and the loss of half the ILGWU cloak trade membership, and split the union. It also marked a major intervention by the underworld in the industrial relations of the industry.

Professional violence was already a mark of the industry. In 1914 a private detective named Max Sulkes organized an independent union known as the International Ladies Garment Workers of the World, later described by Stolberg as "an outright racket designed to provoke violence and corruption." The rapid growth of the industry's labor force—increasingly composed of Italian and Latin American immigrants—and the spread of the industry into unorganized areas, prompted some employers to make use of Sulkes and other enforcers. Elements in the ILGWU responded in kind. Five ILGWU officials were indicted "for hiring thugs to terrorize employers and workers"; they were acquitted, but other evidence was available.

"We attacked the entrenched trade union officials," Benjamin Gitlow wrote later, "for resorting to the service of professional gangsters and drew a bitter moral that this was the morass into which reactionary leadership was leading the host trade unionists, but when we hired gangsters and resorted to gangster methods, we pointed with pride to the heroic achievements of the rank and file, glorying in the revolutionary upsurge of the class-conscious masses."

ILGWU Vice-President Charles S. Zimmerman, in 1926 the leading Communist on the Joint Board, has denied the use of professional enforcers by the Communists in the ILGWU. "We did not need them," he has said. "We had our own." The violent activities of indigenous militants, and their subsequent careers, have been recorded. "As could have been expected," said Melech Epstein, "some of the young men, used as shock troops in the strikes, preferred to continue living on their nerves and knives . . . A number of the gangsters who later terrorized the unions and employers were sons of honest garment workers who were either demoralized by the easy money of the Prohibition era or by living off the unions during the strikes or drives."

"The employers," wrote Stolberg of the 1926 strike, ". . . had their full complements of gangsters, and the Joint Board fought back with professional gorillas. Employers hired the Legs Diamond gang and the Joint Board hired Little Augie. Later it was discovered that both gangsters were working for Arnold Rothstein . . . But the inexperienced [Joint Board] leadership finally lost control over its strong-arm men, who engaged ultimately in factional warfare. The Right met gangsters with gangsters."

The Joint Board now sought the services of Rothstein to end the strike. "In their efforts to get together with the employers to settle the strike," Stolberg said, "the leaders of the Joint Board soon discovered that many manufacturers and jobbers were doing business directly with Arnold Rothstein . . . Rothstein in turn was in touch with the Communist party, which dealt with him precisely because of his great power in the industrial underworld. In short, since the Communist party leaders wished to settle with the employers over the heads of the International [union] administration, the whole set-up forced them to deal through underworld channels." Rothstein's role in the strike was affirmed by District Attorney Joab H. Banton in 1929 after examining the late gangster's private papers.

With the intervention of Rothstein as arbitrator, the gangsters disappeared from the picket lines. The Joint Board then signed an agreement with the manufacturers, but on terms less favorable than those recommended by the Mayor's Special Advisory Committee. The international union put the Joint Board into trusteeship, removed its Communist officers and, early in 1927, settled with the contractors and jobbers on terms only slightly better than those acceded to by the manufacturers. It was a hollow victory. The strike had stripped the union of its financial reserves and severely reduced its numbers, morale, and influence in the industry. It was poorly equipped for the adversities to come.

The gangsters remained, and became more powerful with the simplification in style of women's clothing. The resultant economies of production and the multiplication of shops increased competitive pressure among the employers and intensified their open shop activities; they also strained the policing resources of the ILGWU and led to disciplinary measures against employers by some ILGWU officials which did not "look well on the books." The depression brought new problems. Still weak from the reverses of 1926, the ILGWU sank to one-third of its pre-strike membership and suffered a decline in wages and working conditions among those still employed. The weakness of the union and the increasing migration of employers out of New York in search of cheap labor produced a general deterioration in the labor-management relations of the industry. Such collective agreements as were in existence, Max Danish noted, tended to be honored "less in observance than in breach."

Only the racketeers prospered. In July, 1930, ILGWU Secretary-Treasurer David Dubinsky asked local law enforcement officers for help in eliminating gangster activities which, he said, had taken on impetus after a successful dress strike earlier in the year. Dubinsky charged that racketeers were taking some $2,000,000 a year from employers, either for protection against unionization or by posing as ILGWU representatives and extorting under threat of harassment. The union then submitted to the District Attorney the names of twenty employers who had allegedly paid $100,000 during the past year to one or another of the twelve gangs said to be active in the industry. Some employers' organizations denied the charges, saying that the union was trying to discredit them for organizing purposes. "It is very plain," the ILGWU replied, "that these employers have been easily intimidated. They would rather accuse the union than the racketeers . . . As a matter of fact, the list . . . was equally divided between union and non-union employers." The Association of Dress Manufacturers, alone among the employers' organizations, conceded that it had received complaints of racketeering from some of its members, but claimed that the amount of money paid over had not been large. The efforts of the ILGWU and friendly employers brought about no appreciable change in the situation. The racketeering continued, and the strength of the union declined. "Our union, the newly elected ILGWU President Dubinsky told his General Executive Board in 1932, "is at a low ebb, its very life may be uncertain . . ."

The New Deal saved the union. The National Industrial Recovery Act of 1933, which affirmed the right of unions to organize under the protection of the federal law, prompted a major organizing drive by the ILGWU which raised its membership from 40,000 in 1932 to 200,000 in 1934. The NIRA was declared unconstitutional in 1935, and its administrative arm, the National Recovery Administration, ceased to exist; but the industry codes developed by the NRA had brought a welcome measure of stability to wages, prices and working conditions in the industry, and their provisions were largely retained in the industry by new collective bargaining agreements. The employers also became less tolerant of the racketeers. As Daniel Bell wrote, the latter had "played a stabilizing role by regulating competition and fixing prices. When the NRA came in and assumed this function, the businessman found that what had once been a quasi-economic service was now pure extortion, and he began to demand police action."

The result was an unprecedented degree of labor-management cooperation against racketeering, but it was not altogether successful. In 1934 the NRA charged that eight large manufacturers and jobbers "were employing racketeers in a program of intimidation and violence" against other employers and union members to enforce violations of the dress industry code. Buchalter and Shapiro were named in the charge, but continued their depredations unharmed. In 1937 racketeers James Plumeri and John ("Johnny Dio") Dioguardi were arrested for extortion from garment industry truck owners and for forcing them into employer associations, but escaped punishment. A number of employers were arrested at the same time for violence against union representatives—one of the defendants being named as the chief collector for Buchalter and Shapiro—but received only light punishment or none at all. In 1944 the United States Department of Justice accused two garment industry trucking associations of "conspiracies to control and restrict and monopolize" their section of the industry through "violence and threats of violence." A similar suit was brought in

1951. In both cases the accused escaped with light fines or promises of good behavior.

But the violence continued. In 1948 a number of ILGWU officers were assaulted, and the union charged that open shop employers were responsible; some manufacturers conceded at the time that there had been a "pronounced rise" in racketeering since World War II. The ILGWU began a series of stop-work protest meetings, Dubinsky charging that the current challenge to the industry was as serious as that presented fifteen years before by Buchalter and Shapiro. Union pickets were attacked, for which the ILGWU blamed "non-union truckers seeking to protect open shop manufacturers against organization." Some employers alleged in turn that the ILGWU itself was responsible for bringing professional enforcers into the industry. In 1949 William Lurye, an ILGWU organizer active in the campaign against the open shops, was murdered. At a mass stop-work meeting of 65,000 garment workers, Dubinsky openly charged a number of dress manufacturers with hiring three gangsters to kill Lurye. Two men, Benedict Macri and John Guisto, were identified as Lurye's assassins, but Guisto disappeared and Macri was acquitted for lack of corroborative evidence. "Lurye's associates," District Attorney Frank S. Hogan said, "would not or could not shed any light on the murder, although they were in the immediate vicinity when the crime was committed."

"The first choice a New York dress manufacturer has to make, outside the high fashion field," the New York *Herald-Tribune* reported in 1958, "is whether he wants a racketeer as partner, creditor or competitor. No matter which way he turns, he will probably have a racketeer as his trucker." Underworld activities in the industry included dividing business among favored employers, demanding interest-free "loans" from businessmen, keeping double sets of accounts to conceal income not only from the garment industry but also from shadier enterprises, paying wages on one garment price but selling the garment at another, cutting wages—particularly those of Negro and Puerto Rican workers—in protected shops, stealing styles, destroying competitive stocks, and feeding contract work out to shops in Pennsylvania allegedly protected by the Mafia.

Convictions on any count were almost non-existent. Racketeers were safe not only because of the severe shortage of witnesses but also because of their links with major underworld figures through blood, marriage, or business partnership. Five men with criminal backgrounds, the *Herald-Tribune* said, had a direct interest in trucking firms representing at least ten percent of the billion-dollar annual business in dress trucking, and an indirect interest in firms controlling twenty percent of the garment industry as a whole. The ILGWU, the paper noted, faced enormous problems in enforcement of union conditions since—because of the mercurial nature of enterprise and employment in the industry—it had to organize 200,000 new members and 600 new shops a year simply to maintain its strength; but both the union and the employers were attacked for lethargy in fighting the racketeers and for failing to cooperate fully with law enforcement agencies. "Experience teaches us," D.A. Hogan said, "that racketeers cannot exist if businessmen and labor leaders will cooperate with law enforcement officials. Apathy, fear and self-interest have deprived us of that cooperation."

"All we can do," Dubinsky maintained, "is strike them. It is up to the government to put them in jail." There were, however, other factors complicating the problem. The ILGWU had long been troubled with the acceptance or solicitation of bribes from employers by some of its accountants and minor officials, in return for the concealment of payments due the ILGWU's welfare fund or for lax enforcement of the labor-management agreement, and the union had taken disciplinary action; but it sometimes felt it necessary to regard its sources of intelligence on such practices as privileged, believing that to reveal them in court proceedings would be to cut them off. In yet another matter it found intervention difficult. The garment truck drivers' Local 102 remained under corrupt influence for years because the union was convinced that any ILGWU official sent in to reform the local would be murdered. There were some, indeed, who said that the ILGWU was paying the price for the underworld protection it hired a generation before, and was now being forced to tolerate inferior conditions imposed by marginal operators who had graduated from enforcement to management.

The union, however, continued its attacks on the open shops. In 1959 it conducted a general strike in the industry, bringing under contract a number of racket-controlled shops, particularly in Pennsylvania. The strike was followed by a nation-wide union label campaign and an appeal to federal and state authorities for help in ridding the industry of underworld influence. The *New York Times* praised the "exceptional influence" of the union and the "ethical leadership" of Dubinsky in an industry "which has given notorious racketeers a high yield area in which to operate."

The weight of the evidence was that racketeering in the ladies' garment industry was an enduring problem, remediable only by degrees. There have at least been no reports of its demise.

8: The Waterfront

The Port of New York is rich in assets. It has a great natural harbor and deep water. It is relatively free from maritime hazards, fed by navigable rivers and by a conflux of railroads and highways. It has some 900 piers, quays and wharves on a waterfront over 700 miles long. It is surrounded by the heaviest urban concentration in the United States and served by the country's chief banking and commercial institutions. It is host to more ocean, coastal and inland maritime traffic than almost all other American ports combined, and is probably the leading trading center of the world.

The natural advantages of the port, however, have never been matched by its man-made facilities. Piers are old, often too narrow to accommodate the heavy trucks used in waterfront cartage. They are often isolated from railroad terminals, and have few direct or close connections with the main trunk lines feeding the port. Trucks arriving at the waterfront, often unable to use the piers, choke the streets around them.

Such congestion is costly, involving the uneconomic use of men and equipment. As a result, longshoring has long been the single most expensive item for shipping and other companies using the piers. For shippers it exceeds the cost of maintaining vessels in harbor. For truckers the crowding of the streets is a major financial burden, lengthening delivery schedules and raising the wage bills for drivers and helpers. Profits for shipowners depend on a cheap turn-round of ships, for truckers on a good position in the line. The problem is time, the incentive is to minimize the cost of the waterfront labor force. The history of longshore unionism in New York has been largely one of the accommodation of employers by union officials at the expense of the working longshoreman.

Longshoring is primarily a manual occupation, modest in its demand for skill, harsh in its physical toll, second in danger only to mining. It is basically a casual occupation, highly sensitive to shipping schedules, the weather, seasonal variations in business and the vagaries of international trade and politics. The industry therefore tends to attract men accustomed to menial work, low wages and uncertain working conditions. For a hundred years the New York waterfront has been a haven for immigrants —from legal entrees to ship jumpers—who are anxious for work, willing to please, and often at arm's length from the law. The Irish were the first, comprising as late as the 1880's some ninety-five percent of the longshore

93

work force. They were a clannish group, detested by the native born and barred by prejudice from more congenial occupations, rough in their ways and jealous of intruders. "The West Side [of Manhattan] was a community," Daniel Bell related, "with the men living near the piers, in Chelsea and in the brownstone strip between the Tenderloin and the river. The saloons and parish houses bounded their lives. They rarely moved away. They lived as an isolated mass against the other ethnic masses of the city."

The Italians came next, most of them to Brooklyn, comprising by 1912 one-third of all New York longshoremen. Resented as much by the Irish as by the older stock, they were first used as strikebreakers, then recruited in large numbers to discourage the outbreak of labor disturbances. "The tremendous increase of unskilled labor by immigration," said Charles B. Barnes, "the eagerness of the Italians for work, their willingness to submit to deductions from their wages, leaving a neat little commission to be divided among foremen, saloon keepers, and native bosses—all these considerations insured the permanence of the Italian in longshore work." Then, in successive if smaller contingents, came the Yugoslavs, the Poles, the Negroes and other minorities. Many of them were illiterate, most of them unskilled, all of them poor and desperate for work. They were easy prey for the powerful and dishonest on the waterfront.

Trade unionism in New York longshoring dates from the formation in the 1880's of the Longshoremen's Union Protective Association. After the turn of the century the LUPA came under the control of Richard Butler, a longshoreman and Democratic politician. Butler, a protégé of Devery and sometime associate of Parks and Brandle, was a versatile man who claimed to have invented the "ten-to-one" voting system in his race for the New York State Assembly in 1902. "Up till then," he told his biographer, "repeaters were content to drop two ballots at a time, but I realized I had to do something drastic to win . . . We folded the ballots in sets of ten, dampened them with water . . . [and] . . . pressed the bundles of ten until they were thin enough to slip through the slit in the ballot boxes." Butler was an innovator in another matter, launching the tradition of personal bargaining with employers and politicians which was to distinguish longshore industrial relations for more than a generation.

Earlier, in 1892, a lumber handlers' union was started on the Great Lakes, assuming in 1894 the title of International Longshoremen's Association. In 1914 the ILA absorbed most of the LUPA. T. V. O'Connor of the ILA was elected president. Butler became vice president in charge of the Atlantic district of the union. For a time, O'Connor and Butler shared control of the union with Paul Vacarelli, otherwise known as Paul Kelly, a former prize fighter become minor criminal. Vacarelli was the leader of the garbage scow trimmers and, like Butler, a local politician and saloon keeper. He contributed to the early influx of criminals on to the waterfront, his saloon becoming the haunt of Zelig, Monk Eastman and others. In later years he became involved in the violent affairs of other unions and evidently engaged, through his control of the garbage scows, in rum-running during Prohibition.

The triumvirate was an unstable one, and in 1917 Butler ran against O'Connor for the presidency of the union. He was supported by Vacarelli, Mayor Hylan, Arnold Rothstein and various underworld figures, but lost narrowly after Vacarelli switched sides. He ran and lost again in 1919, then led a strike in protest against the 1919 ILA agreement with the employers. Both Hague and Hylan supported him, but he lost. It was the last longshore strike in New York for twenty-six years. Butler returned to politics, later being appointed superintendent of the Bronx Terminal by Mayor Walker. O'Connor stayed in office until his retirement in 1927. The new president of the ILA was Joseph P. Ryan.

His reign was a disaster. "This was the period," stated Charles P. Larrowe, "when the corruption of the union was accomplished." Ryan was a longshoreman by trade, big and heavy-fisted in his youth, wordy and lachrymose in public all his life. He was also a Tammany man, well-versed in its traditions. "He broke in under me in 1913," Butler recalled, "and if he hasn't forgotten the tricks I taught him he ought to get along . . ." Ryan's talents and training served him well. He satisfied the Irish by his presence, and prudently left the Italians alone. His influence with Tammany and other centers of power grew with time, serving to protect the union and the employers from the attentions of the law. He was tolerant of poor morals and the evils of the industry, light in his claims on the employers, casual in his concern for longshoremen. He remained in office for twenty-five years.

New York was the center of the union, and Ryan controlled it after a fashion by chartering excessive numbers of local unions, some of them only paper organizations, but all of them with votes. In general, however, the ILA was a loose-knit institution, in Bell's phrase a "collection of Chinese warlords," an alliance of relatively independent units under the control of various individuals or gangs. Local union democracy was a casual affair, few locals voting in secret, some of them not voting at all. The smallness of many locals also encouraged their domination by underworld cabals through intimidation and force.

But perhaps the main source of autocratic control and other abuses was the archaic system of hiring. Longshoring can be largely decasualized, as it has been on the Pacific Coast and in some European countries, by the registration of longshoremen, the centralization of job information, and some form of seniority or rotation in hiring. In New York, however, the employers believed that speed and economy of operation were best achieved through low wages and intensive job competition among a surplus labor force. The ILA agreed, to the cost of its members and the community.

The oldest system of hiring was the shape-up, the arbitrary selection of men by a hiring boss from crowds grouped loosely around him at the piers. The open shape-up was later modified by the hiring of regular work gangs on some of the piers, with additional men chosen as needed from the shape-up. But the regular gangs were not actually stable groups, their composition changing from day to day by voluntary or involuntary action. The work force as a whole was kept at a size far in excess of real needs. The surplus was local as well as port-wide. Longshoremen were encouraged to shape up at individual piers, seldom moved to other parts of the harbor, and were usually heavily dependent for work on the whim of the hiring boss. The leadership of the ILA also often intensified job competition and their own control by hiring, in preference to ILA members and in defiance of the agreement between the ILA and the New York Shipping Association, off-duty policemen, taxi drivers, and others interested in a little extra money for a few hours' work each week. The system vested enormous power in the hiring bosses, created a pliable labor force, and brought about wholesale corruption.

The kickback in return for work was common, sometimes amounting to twenty percent of wages. Sometimes the payments were tendered as dues to "hiring clubs" run by hiring bosses or their friends. On other occasions the payments were made directly on the docks, a system of signals—typically involving the display of toothpicks in the hatband—having been developed to inform the hiring boss of the amounts he could expect to get. Some bosses took up regular collections for imaginary charities. Others stationed bookmakers on the piers and instituted virtually compulsory betting.

Theft was a problem, amounting in the salad years to perhaps three times the annual rate of all other ports combined. Individual pilferage was frequent, but not a great financial burden for shippers and their customers. Organized theft was much more serious. Imported goods were stolen by the truckload from the piers, or "hijacked" between the piers and the inland terminals. The procedure for stealing exported goods was both simpler and safer. The loading boss indicated to the checker the amount to be stolen, the checker gave the truck-driver a false receipt, and the booty was hauled away from the piers at the convenience of the parties. Since many consignments were destined for faraway countries, their loss remained undiscovered for weeks at a time. When insurance investigators finally reached the piers, they found that the signature on the receipt was fraudulent, met with silence from implicated officials and job-conscious longshoremen, and wrote off the loss.

Payroll padding—the sharing of unearned wages between the hiring boss, the payroll clerk, and the rulers of the pier or the ILA local involved —was another abuse. Uniquely in the United States, the brass check system of payment survived on the waterfront until recent years. Longshoremen received on hiring a numbered brass check relating to the work to be done; on pay day they surrendered the brass check in return for cash wages. However, the checks were transferable and could be tendered for payment by anyone. Thus was devised the simple system of dispatching less than a full gang for a particular job, but submitting brass checks for a full complement when the work was done, then dividing the surplus wages between the controlling parties. The system was temporarily frustrated by the introduction and compulsory tendering of Social Security cards after 1935; but many longshoremen soon obtained two cards, working a minimum number of hours on one, then collecting unemployment insurance on the first while working additional hours on the second. Hiring bosses and others also obtained extra cards, using them to add fictitious work gangs to the roster.

The brass check was also involved in another racket. Being transferable, the check could be turned over to a money-lender by a longshoreman in need of ready money. Accordingly there developed, with the complicity of employers and union officials, the practice of loan-sharking—the charging of extortionate rates of interest on loans. Those rates usually ranged from ten cents to twenty-five cents a week on the dollar, the loan-shark often collecting the longshoremen's pay and deducting the interest before handing back the remainder, and sometimes charging a service fee as well as interest. On some piers it was almost impossible for a longshoreman to obtain work unless he promised the hiring boss to borrow money from the resident usurer. In 1949 District Attorney Hogan estimated that the annual income of waterfront loan-sharks was some $200,000 a year. Several loan-sharking cases were prosecuted that year, but because of the difficulty in obtaining longshoremen as witnesses, only one conviction resulted. The defendant in that case was Frank Savio, a boss checker and strong-arm man for the ILA, for whom Ryan served as a character witness.

Probably the most lucrative racket was in loading. Shippers took no responsibility for the on- and off-loading of goods to and from their trucks. As a result there developed the institution of "public loading," the transmission of goods between the floor of the pier and the tailboard of the truck. Performed at first by casual labor, it later became professionally organized and, since time was the most important element of all, highly profitable. What began as a cheap service ended as an extortionary monopoly; the public loaders charged all the traffic would bear, including the imposition of "hurry-up" fees on truckers who wanted a privileged place in the line, and even of charges where no loaders were required. It was an enviable business, a magnet for the underworld, and the cause of several successive murders during the 1920's and the 1930's. It was, in fact, the principal source of access for criminals into positions of power in the ILA. Public loaders often seized control of entire pier operations, thence of local unions and their treasuries, enjoying dual status as both the employers and the union representatives of the men on the piers.

The evidence was plentiful. In 1939 the "Bowers Mob," under the leadership of Michael ("Mickey") Bowers, assumed control over the North River piers serving the European passenger lines. Two murders had occurred in a fight for control, and the Bowers organization filled the vacuum. As Dominick Genova, then a working longshoreman, said:

> After the Bandit [Richard Gregory] was knocked off there was a fight for power on the upper West Side. Suddenly a new mob walked in. This was the Bowers mob, and I started paying dues to those boys. We got a membership book for $26, a cut rate. The official rate was $50. The mob never put stamps in our book. I guess 2,000 men paid off in this way. The collector was Harold Bowers, Mickey's cousin.

Resistance was dangerous. In 1937, six ILA locals in Brooklyn—once controlled by the Camarda family—came under the control of Albert Anastasia, the alleged executioner for *Murder, Inc.,* chief enforcement agency of the American underworld. A young longshoreman by the name of Pete Panto led an insurgent movement against the locals and its leader, claiming in due course 1,000 supporters among the members of the new local. In 1939 he disappeared; his body was found a year later in a lime pit in Ohio.

The infiltration continued, the public loaders forming their own port-wide collection and enforcement agency—Varick Enterprises—in the 1930's. The agency was dissolved in the 1940's after an investigation by the District Attorney's office, but the criminal elements remained. In 1951 a New York State Board of Inquiry reported that a number of public loaders and ILA officials had "substantial" criminal records, that they were organized for enforcement purposes, and that both the ILA and the employers condoned their activities.

Some employers were frank and explicit. "Yes," one of them said, "our labor policy is tough. It has to be . . . because it is a rough, rough business. Now about criminals on the dock; this may sound terrible to you, but

I don't care whether they are criminals or not, just so long as they don't hurt me. In fact, to be perfectly frank, if I had a choice of hiring a tough ex-convict or a man without a criminal record I am more inclined to take the ex-con. Know why? Because if he is in a boss job he'll keep the men in line and get the maximum work out of them. They'll be afraid of him."

In 1951 a New York probation officer asked an official of the Standard Fruit and Steamship Company why the company had employed Albert Ackalitis, a well-known former convict, as a foreman. "We would like to have twenty Ackalitises," the official said. "We get more work out of the man than anybody else. We're not interested in his personal affairs." The recruitment of ex-convicts was not occasional. "At least one stevedore," wrote George Cable Wright, "is known to have assured himself of a sufficient number of muscle men by pleading with state parole officers to release 200 men from prison so that they could go to work for him. Through collusion with union officials such men were provided with union books as soon as they were released."

Ryan cooperated. He was for years a member of the New York State Parole Board, and was an enthusiastic rehabilitator. "They talk about us giving jobs to men who've gone wrong and have served time," he said. "Where are these poor devils to go? Because a man has done wrong once, it don't show he's a criminal. Why, a man can't get paroled unless somebody'll give him a job, and these are the very men who stop other men from stealing. Many times, we've heard of a fellow who's got a record stopping men who are broaching cargo. Lay off, boys, he'll say. That'll go against me." Ryan also appointed a number of ex-convicts as organizers for the ILA.

Both the union and the employers liked the system, and paid for its protection. For a generation the waterfront was, in Bell's phrase, "a political enclave." "Neither the ILA nor the companies," the *New York Times* reported in 1953, "could perpetuate the system without at least the tacit consent of officials in New York and New Jersey. Many of these officials accept campaign contributions from ILA racketeers and stevedore executives, give them political jobs, keep up social contacts with them."

Ryan was the central figure. The emblem of his political stature was the Joseph P. Ryan Association, an organization designed primarily to promote the prestige of its founder. The Association's principal annual activity was a banquet, whose honorary chairmen and leading guests over the years included virtually every important public official in New York and New Jersey, among them Mayor Walker, Mayor Hague, Mayor Vincent Impelliteri, Governor Alfred E. Smith, Governor Thomas E. Dewey, and Governor Franklin D. Roosevelt, while the banquet officials each year usually included a contingent of ex-convict ILA officials. Membership in the Association was ostensibly confined to working longshoremen, but policemen were welcome, and for a purpose. "It is a well-known fact," the Senate Committee on Commerce was told in 1938, ". . . that Mr. Ryan still has sufficient influence in certain police precincts to pack his local meetings with plain-clothes men who participate in the union meetings, even to the extent of voting."

Ryan's troubles began after World War II. Control by the United States Navy over the docks during the war had kept down racketeering and, by increasing the number and stability of regular work gangs, had produced a measure of unity and heightened expectations among longshoremen. Veterans returning from the services were less patient with the old ways, more insistent on effective and honest leadership. On the other hand, with the departure of the Navy from the waterfront, racketeering elements were ready to wrest more spoils from the industry, while Communist elements—aware of the much superior bargaining record of West Coast longshoremen—prepared to challenge the authority of Ryan.

In 1945 a wildcat strike shut down the port. Virtually leaderless, and opposed by both the ILA and the New York labor movement, the strikers nevertheless stayed out for eight days and won better terms from the employers than the ILA had originally asked for. But the shape-up remained. "[We] are in basic agreement," the New York Shipping Association and the ILA stated in a joint release, "that the shape-up system of hiring should be maintained . . . [We] agree that the inconveniences of the system are more than offset by its advantages." Another wildcat strike took place in 1947, Ryan disappearing from the scene to sign a private agreement with the employers. The following year he signed a second modest agreement with the NYSA, and provoked a third wildcat strike. This time, however, Ryan declared the strike official and increased his terms. It was the first official strike in the history of the ILA, and produced significant wage and welfare benefits. Ryan nevertheless blamed the strike on the Communists, and dulled its triumph by joining with the employers to obtain the exemption of longshoring from the premium pay provisions of the federal wage and hour law, thus depriving longshoremen of millions of dollars in back pay.

The underworld expanded its control, particularly in New Jersey. In 1948 Edward J. Kenny overthrew the Hague machine and became Mayor of Jersey City. Ryan stayed loyal to Hague, rejected Kenny's demands for jobs on the waterfront for the faithful, and struck Piers D and F. The strike was settled by compromise after a month: Kenny kept Pier D;

Hague and Ryan shared Pier F. Elsewhere others were in control. In 1952 the Senate Armed Services Committee found that hiring at the Claremont Terminal was in the hands of Anthony ("Tony Cheese") Marchitto; recruitment was from a list of 500 job-hunting politicians, indexed by wards, and unrelated to waterfront experience. Anthony ("Tony Bender") Strollo, an ex-convict and a former associate of Luciano, controlled the United States Army Linden Pier in New Jersey. Kenny had once branded Strollo as a New York gangster, but later surrendered his claim to patronage on the pier at a secret hotel meeting described by District Attorney Hogan as "an appalling demonstration of underworld domination of the waterfront."

The truckers also became restive. In 1948 the New York Motor Carriers Association rebelled against arbitrary loading rates. Ryan arranged a meeting between the truckers and the loaders, but despite a formal agreement on rates the imposition of erratic charges continued. The city then asked the shippers to designate officially the loaders they wanted on the piers. The shippers did so, naming the individuals already in control, many of whom had criminal records. Official municipal approval was thus given to the public loaders, who now became members of the ILA, although they were in fact private contractors.

In 1951 another wildcat strike took place. Ryan blamed it on the Communists, and tried but failed to persuade the National Labor Relations Board to seek an injunction against it; in New Jersey, however, ILA organizer Ed Florio helped the employers to obtain an injunction against the striking locals there. A Board of Inquiry appointed by Governor Dewey reported that the ILA had not given its members proper notice of the proposed agreement with the NYSA before asking them to vote on it; that many members of the ILA negotiating committee were self-appointed; and that ballot-box stuffing and other irregularities had taken place during the voting on the agreement. The Board persuaded the strikers to go back to work in return for a few immediate benefits, but public concern remained. Mayor William O'Dwyer of New York City appointed a Joint Committee on Port Industry, a subcommittee of which reported to him on waterfront conditions. The subcommittee, which included McCormack and Ryan, saw no cause for concern. "We have found," it said, "that the labor situation on the waterfront . . . is generally satisfactory from the standpoint of the worker, the employer, the industry and the government . . . The morale of the men has been good." But the report was unpersuasive. On November 20, 1951, Governor Dewey asked the New York State Crime Commission to conduct a major investigation of the New York waterfront.

It was not an easy task. "Many longshoremen," the Commission reported, "recalling the long series of unsolved murders on the docks, were deterred by fear from testifying." Some claimed ignorance or simply refused to testify, while others, with something to hide, invoked the Fifth Amendment. The difficulties were great, but the Commission was industrious. The evidence, collected in over 4,000 interviews and 30,000 pages of testimony, was conclusive.

The Commission noted the steady deterioration in the competitive position of the port, blaming it in part on inadequate facilities, but attributing most of it to "criminal or quasi-criminal" practices. It found widespread collusion between shipping and stevedoring companies on the one hand and ILA officials on the other "to the serious detriment of the dock worker and the public." Stevedoring companies made cash payments to union officials at all levels to keep down wage rates. Daniels and Kennedy, a major stevedoring and trucking company, gave $1,500 a year for five years to Ryan himself. Ryan claimed that this and other payments were contributions to an anti-Communist fund he had set up to fight the infiltration of the West Coast International Longshoremen's and Warehousemen's Union under Harry Bridges; but the fund was a secret to ILA members. It was kept in Ryan's private bank account, which showed no record of anti-Communist disbursements, and had been depleted of $31,651 for such non-political items as a cruise in the Caribbean, golf club dues, health insurance premiums and expensive clothes. The Jarka Corporation, the largest stevedoring company in the United States, paid over $58,000 to ILA officials from 1947 to 1951. The John W. McGrath Company made secret payments of undisclosed amounts to Patrick ("Packy") Connolly, executive vice president of the ILA, on the understanding that the money was to go to Harold Bowers. The Naciroma Company paid $2,000 to Edward Florio for overlooking irregular working conditions. The Pittston Stevedoring Corporation paid a total of $1,250 in 1951 to Vincent ("Barney Cockeye") Brown and Anthony ("Tony Cheese") Marchitto, business agents of Locals 1478 and 1247 respectively, for supplying labor gangs at $50 a ship. The Jarka Corporation paid $100 a month to Anthony ("Joe the Gent") Giantomasi for good service. "That's one thing I'll say about Joe the Gent," Jarka Vice-President N. J. Palihnich testified, "he was always available. He came down there and settled the matter."

The Commission investigated the "phantom" system—the practice of placing fictitious names on payrolls. Timothy ("Timmy") O'Mara, a convicted felon who worked as a boss loader on various piers, was carried on the Huron Stevedoring Corporation payroll for eight years as Edward Joseph Ross, receiving more than $25,000 for imaginary services. The Commission questioned T. Maher, a superintendent for Huron.

Q. What do you mean by a phantom?

A. Somebody on your payroll not by that name, not by their real name.

. . .

Q. What does O'Mara do to earn all this money?

A. Well, O'Mara was to keep labor—that they wouldn't be going out on strike—that was my understanding.

. . .

Q. Was O'Mara fairly successful in preventing strikes?

A. Yes, sir; yes, sir.

There were other occasions for payment. Michael Castellana, vice president of the Jules S. Sottnek Company, a stevedoring concern, gave some $11,000 to Michael Clemente, financial secretary and business agent of ILA Local 856, when the latter's daughter was married; he also financed a vacation for Mr. and Mrs. Clemente at the Casablanca Hotel in Miami Beach. Ryan testified that the acceptance of Christmas gifts from employers was "the practice" among ILA officials; he was himself a frequent beneficiary. The Commission also traced massive payments—amounting to hundreds of thousands of dollars over a five-year period—by stevedoring companies to shipping firms, evidently to buy business or good will. Bookkeeping on the matter was casual, if not downright deceptive, particularly when union officials were also rewarded. William J. McCormack disclosed that his four principal companies spent more than $980,000 in unexplained cash payments between 1947 and 1951. Between 1947 and 1952 the Jarka Corporation spent nearly half a million dollars in petty cash; about $160,-000 went to shipping company representatives, but no accounting was made of the rest. During the same period the Sottnek organization spent $278,973 for undisclosed purposes, destroying all vouchers made out prior to 1952. John T. Clark and Son, Inc., made unexplained cash payments of $289,487, altering the books to conceal their destination. President Harold J. Beardell of the Clark company testified.

Q. And did you know that the reason why they made the changes was to eliminate all entries showing payments to union officers and delegates?

A. That's correct.

"It was established," the Commission said, "that at least thirty percent of the officials of the ILA longshore locals have police records. Waterfront criminals know that the control of the local is a prerequisite to conducting racket operations on the piers. Through their powers as union officials, they place their confederates in key positions on the docks, shake down steamship and stevedoring companies by threats of work stoppages, operate the lucrative public loading business, and carry on such activities as pilferage, loan-sharking and gambling." The Commission cited as examples the control of the North River waterfront from Pier 84 to Pier 97 by the Bowers group, some of whom had criminal records; the domination of the East River section by Clemente, a convicted extortioner; the former hegemony of Albert Anastasia over the six Camarda locals in Brooklyn in cooperation with such ex-convicts as Vincent Mangano, Gioacchino ("Dandy Jack") Parisi and Anthony ("Tony Spring") Romeo; and the control of the New Jersey docks by Marchitto, Vincent ("Barney Cockeye") Brown and the late Frank ("Biffo") DeLorenzo. "The unfortunate conditions continue today," the Commission said, "substantially as they have existed for the past thirty years."

Ryan was partly to blame, having appointed a series of ILA organizers with criminal records. One of these was Edward J. McGrath, who had a record of twelve arrests on charges ranging from petty larceny to murder, and who had served time for robbery and felonious assault. Without previous longshoring experience, he became an ILA organizer shortly after completing in 1936 a burglary sentence in Sing Sing and remained with the ILA until 1951, controlling the rackets on the lower West Side in cooperation with his brother-in-law, John M. ("Cockeye") Dunn.* Harold Bowers, alias Frank Donald, was appointed ILA organizer for the North River area in 1951, although he had a record of arrests for robbery, grand larceny, possession of a gun and congregating with known criminals. As already noted, he was a member of the Bowers Mob which controlled the upper North River piers, and also served as financial secretary for "Pistol Local" 824—so known because of the number of successional murders it had witnessed—although he testified that he had no knowledge of the duties of a financial secretary. Alex Di Brizzi, alias Al Britton, had been arrested fifteen times on charges including grand larceny, felonious assault and violations of the liquor and gambling laws. He was appointed organizer for Staten Island in 1946, later becoming president of Local 920 and an international vice president of the ILA. Florio, a convicted bootlegger, served as organizer for New Jersey from 1946 and controlled the Hoboken piers—noted for payroll padding—until his conviction for perjury in 1952 after denying that he had received money from a stevedoring company; from 1948 to 1952 he also earned close to $25,000 from a loading concession in Hoboken, employing members of his own union.

The Commission looked into the financial affairs of thirty-four New

---

* Dunn controlled various piers in Manhattan. "We believe," said former Assistant District Attorney William J. Keating, "Dunn was responsible for at least fifteen murders." He was electrocuted in 1948 for shooting Andrew Hintz, a hiring boss on Pier 51 who refused to obey his orders.

York ILA locals, concluding that only eleven of them kept records that were in any way acceptable. Many ILA officials, the Commission said, had been guilty of "flagrant infidelity in administering the financial affairs of their locals. Financial records are often so badly kept and financial procedures and safeguards are so inadequate as to justify suspicions of appropriations of union funds . . ." The abuses listed by the Commission included payments to relatives of ILA officials for unspecified services; the mysterious disappearance or "theft" of union records; the commingling of union and personal bank accounts; and the almost complete absence of adequate auditing procedures. The Commission questioned Anthony V. Camarda, the financial secretary of Local 1199.

> Q. Now . . . there was shortage in funds in your local union of $3,281.42, on the first day of January of this year . . . You can't account for it, can you?
> A. No, sir.

ILA International Vice-President Constantine ("Gus") Scannavino was asked about payments made to Michael Cosenza, his nephew and allegedly a business agent for Local 327-1.

> Q. He's been in Arizona for three years, hasn't he?
> A. Yes.
> Q. And has he continued to be the business agent of that local?
> A. He is the business agent of that local.
>
> . . .
>
> Q. He hasn't performed any services for the local in the last three years, has he?
> A. That's right.
> Q. And he has been getting $75 a week and expenses for three years without doing any work for that local?
> A. The local can answer what they send that money for.
> Q. But you know, though, they do send him money?
> A. Of course.

Charles Spencer, financial secretary, Local 866, discussed his work.

> Q. Did you keep any disbursement books?
> A. No, sir.
> Q. Did you keep any record of any expenditures that were made?
> A. No, sir.
> Q. Did you keep any records of any receipts that you took in?
> A. No, sir.
> Q. Did you keep any daily records of receipts of dues . . . ?
> A. No, sir.
>
> . . .

Q. As a matter of fact, Mr. Spencer, to be brutally frank about it, what you did with the money of that union that was left over after paying expenses was to put it in your own pocket, isn't that right?

A. That's right.

Anthony P. Guistra was financial secretary of one of the Camarda locals when Anthony Romeo took over for Albert Anastasia in the 1930's.

Q. And did you have a talk with Romeo when he took over that local?

A. No, sir. He came over and he told me, "I'm the boss here."

Q. What did you say to him?

A. What could I say? I was scared to death . . .

. . .

Q. And did he demand money from the treasury of that local?

A. Always . . . When the money comes in from the dues, he used to take it away . . . Maybe it runs about $20,000, something like that.

Mario Frullano of Local 1277 once tried to get service from his union.

Q. Tell us what the argument was about.

A. Well, I happened to see the business agent on the pier, and I went over to him. I wanted to find out why we were being charged three dollars a month and weren't getting any benefits for it.

. . .

Q. That is all you remember?

A. No. I remember that I got in an argument with him and two other men . . . the first thing you know, I got kicked by someone . . .

Q. You got kicked in the groin?

A. Yes, sir.

Q. And badly hurt?

A. Yes, sir.

Q. You went to the hospital?

A. Yes, sir.

"Many ILA locals," the Commission said, "have never employed democratic procedures in conducting their internal affairs. The officers exercise a free hand in running their locals. A virtually disenfranchised membership has been unable to participate effectively in the conduct of union business." Union meetings were held without proper notice. Some locals dispensed with both meetings and elections for years at a time. Some locals re-elected officials by simple motion, others put defeated candidates into office anyway, and some—such as the Camarda locals—came under the domination of single families. Salvatore Camarda, the financial secretary of Local 327, was asked about the frequency of local union mettings.

Q. Now, how many meetings has Local 327 had in the last three years?

A. We have been having a meeting every quarter and most of the time we haven't got a quorum and only the officers show up and we can't have any.

. . .

Q. So how many meetings have you actually been able to hold then in the past three years . . . ?

A. About three or four.

Many ILA officials engaged in private business on the waterfront. Florio and John Moody, a member of Local 306, sold equipment to stevedores and contracted to move garbage from the piers. Connie Noonan, the president of the platform workers' local, was for a time president of Varick Enterprises, the public loaders' collection agency. Danial Gentile, a longshoreman sentenced to life imprisonment for complicity in the Hintz murder, was a controller in the waterfront numbers racket run by Dunn, McGrath and Noonan. Thomas W. ("Teddy") Gleason, a holder of several offices in the ILA and later its international president, allegedly engaged in a number of enterprises with Noonan, including the importation of bananas, the export of sulphur and nickel, and the sale of armed airplanes to the Dominican Republic.

The Commission also investigated the recruitment of hiring bosses. Steamship and stevedoring companies had the right, under the ILA-NYSA collective bargaining agreement, to select their own hiring bosses. In practice the ILA chose almost all of them. Some of its selections were unsurprising. One McNay, the hiring boss on the "Queen Mary" and "Queen Elizabeth" piers, had been arrested for attempted burglary, robbery and assault, had been convicted of unlawful entry and robbery, and was still on parole when appointed as a hiring boss. Albert Ackalitis, the hiring boss on Pier 18 on the North River, was a former member of the Arsenal Mob with a long record of arrests and convictions. Daniel St. John, the hiring boss on Pier 84, had been arrested for larceny, burglary, assault, robbery, possession of dangerous weapons and for murder, and had been convicted once for possessing a gun and four times for petty larceny. James ("Teddy") O'Rourke, the hiring boss on Pier 88, had been convicted of petty larceny and grand larceny. All of the above refused to testify. In all, the Commission listed twenty-two hiring bosses with police records, who through their control of hiring participated in or encouraged "assault, organized theft, pilferage, extortion, kickbacks, loan-sharking, gambling, payroll padding, other criminal activities and even murder . . ."

Public loading, the Commission declared, was controlled by loaders "whom truckmen must employ and pay to load trucks regardless of whether the loaders do any work, are needed, or are unwanted." The loaders also had their own local union, which had no constitution or by-laws or defined jurisdiction, but which included many employers as members. The steamship and stevedoring companies refused to accept responsibility for public loading, offering no resistance to the influx of functionless criminals. L. F. O'Meara, the terminal manager of the A. H. Bull Steamship Company, commented on four public loaders with criminal records.

> Q. Now, is it or is it not a fact that those four men just forced their way into that situation?
> A. That is correct, sir.
>
> • • •
>
> Q. They have free access to the pier?
> A. They have, sir.
> Q. They do no physical labor?
> A. The four men in question do not, sir.
>
> • • •
>
> Q. Why don't you put them off the pier?
> A. Well . . . for fear of a strike . . .

The dual status of many public loaders as businessmen and ILA members enabled them to avoid signing union contracts and paying union wages and benefits, and to use union influence to obtain business. The five brothers and a brother-in-law who constituted the India Wharf Loaders, Inc., were all ILA members; when they wanted to control the loading of newsprint for the New York *Daily News,* they banned the paper handlers' local from the Brooklyn piers, set up a picket line and eventually drove the *Daily News* trade to Portland, Maine. All the thirty-one stockholders of George Sellenthin, Inc., the company in control of all public loading on Staten Island, were members of the ILA. Salvatore Trapani of King's Loaders, Inc., was an ILA shop steward in Brooklyn, as was Ralph Schettino, president of the company. None of these men worked as longshoremen, but received pay as shop stewards. The net result of the public loading system, the Commission said, was a substantial diversion of traffic to other ports, the growth of organized theft and other criminal activities, the repetition of serious work stoppages, and a substantial loss of income to shipping interests.

"The evidence," the Commission concluded, "demonstrates that the Port of New York is in danger of losing its position of supremacy to which its natural advantages entitle it . . . the time has come for drastic action. What we do now may well be decisive of the future of the Port."

The Commission advocated legislation providing for effective public control of the waterfront, abolishing the shape-up, instituting a port-wide registration and licensing system, and requiring minimum standards of behavior from the ILA. Both New York and New Jersey swiftly passed a law, ratified by the Congress, establishing the Waterfront Commissions of New York Harbor with broad powers to regulate the longshoring industry. The AFL was also moved to novel disciplinary action. The passing of William Green in 1952 had brought to the presidency of the AFL a man with untraditional views of the powers and obligations of the federation. President George Meany demanded from the ILA a series of reforms as the condition of continued affiliation. The ILA refused to comply and was expelled. The AFL then chartered a new union, the International Brotherhood of Longshoremen, and embarked on a campaign to oust the ILA from the waterfront.

The portents for both the Waterfront Commission and the AFL were favorable. The unprecedented publicity given to waterfront conditions, the enormity of the abuses revealed, the overwhelming public support for reform and the evident discontent of the longshoremen themselves, all pointed to a new order in the Port of New York. But the conditions were complex, the remedies imperfect, and allies unpredictable or weak. Both change and disappointment lay ahead.

9: The Gangs in Chicago

Chicago lies at the southern tip of Lake Michigan. At the time of its incorporation in 1833 its population was 200, but its proximity to water and the midwestern farmlands soon made it—with the exception of New York— the fastest growing city and most important railroad, trading and financial center in the United States.

With the settlers came the parasites. From its earliest days Chicago enjoyed an unsavory reputation. "As the Civil War came to a close," wrote Virgil Peterson, "no city had a more formidable underworld than Chicago." From the beginning the gamblers, the saloon-keepers and the brothel-owners were the welcome partners—when they were not the unwelcome masters—of the political leaders of the city. "It was a system," Peterson said, "which was to become a permanent fixture in Chicago and to give the city its reputation as the crime capital of the nation."

The alliance prospered, never disturbed for long by criticism. "You are gigantic in your virtues," the British evangelist William T. Stead told a Chicago audience, "and gigantic in your vices. I don't know in which you glory the most." The Chicago Vice Commission of 1910 reported the making of fortunes in prostitution, but omitted any mention of Everleigh House —perhaps the most famous brothel in America—and many other favored establishments. In 1911 the Chicago Civil Service Commission made known the existence of a conspiracy between gamblers, policemen and politicians to drive uncooperative gamblers out of the city. "Professional criminals," the Chicago City Council Committee on Crime said in 1915, "have built up a system which may be called a 'crime trust,' with roots running through the police force, the bar, the bondsmen, the prosecutor's office, and political officials . . . members of the police force, and particularly the plainclothes staff, are hand in glove with criminals. Instead of punishing the criminal, they protect him. Instead of using the power of the law for the protection of society, they use it for their own personal profit . . . The exact extent of this system it is impossible to determine, but there is no doubt that its ramifications are so wide as to cripple the machinery for the enforcement of the law."

There was worse to come. "Once upon a time," Lloyd Wendt and Herman Kogan relate, "there really was a Big Bill Thompson." A brawler and a cowboy in his youth, an athlete by choice and a politician by accident, a

110

Republican isolationist who earned the nickname of "Kaiser Bill," an Anglophobe who made a major campaign promise to "punch King George in the snoot," Thompson was elected mayor of Chicago in 1915 and brought to the city's politics a buffoonery, duplicity, skill and amorality unique even for Chicago. While promising reform to the alarmed, he opened the saloons on Sunday, curtailed the powers of the police morals squad, publicly associated with gamblers and criminals, and ran a wide-open city. "Gamblers and vice lords," Peterson states, ". . . entered into alliances with officials at almost every level of government."

Prohibition cemented the relationship. As early as 1921, Chief of Police Charles C. Fitzmorris complained publicly that "a large percentage" of Chicago's policemen were engaged in bootlegging. "To all intents and purposes," Peterson writes, "organized gunmen were in control of City Hall." Democrat William E. Dever, a reformer, succeeded Thompson in 1923, but the new administration made little difference. The major gangs continued their operations within the city or from hospitable suburbs, their wars for control producing over 200 gang murders during Dever's term of office. The electorate retired Dever in 1927 and brought back Thompson, who had campaigned on an anti-crime platform. "I want them out," he said of the gangsters, "in ninety days." But he did not. He had accepted campaign contributions from the underworld, and now appointed its friends to public office, allowed the gangs to resume their activities unhindered, and watched the law decline.

In 1929 the Illinois Association for Criminal Justice returned an indictment of law enforcement in Chicago. The evidence was conclusive, the Association reported, "that crime was organized on a scale and with resources unprecedented in the history of Chicago . . . that the leading gangsters were practically immune from punishment; and . . . that the position of power and affluence achieved by gangsters and their immunity from punishment was due to an unholy alliance between organized crime and politics." The entire judicial system, the Association said, was subject to political influence in the disposition of cases. Appointments to the state's attorney's staff were made on political grounds, most appointees being ignorant of the criminal law and in any case spending most of their time on political activities. A high proportion of cases was stricken for want of prosecution, or simply removed from the court docket, while the reduction of charges from grave to petty offenses through political influence had become so prevalent "that the criminal population has become contemptuous of the law and fear of punishment is no longer a deterrent of crime . . ." Many municipal judges were active political partisans, taking orders from political machines; as a result, delays in trials were easily obtained through continuances or harmless bond forfeitures, while the practice of one judge reviewing the acts of another ostensibly on grounds of *habeas corpus* had led to "intolerable confusion and abuse."

The Chicago police department, the Association said, was both demoralized and inefficient. Poor administration was partly to blame, but the main cause was the influence on law enforcement wielded by politicians and gangsters in league with each other. The underworld provided money and manpower in city elections, and was rewarded by the fixing of criminal cases. "Honest policemen," the report said, "discover that the machinery is against them and the demoralization of the department begins . . . the city is at the mercy of the crooks."

The findings of the Association were supplemented in 1931 by those of the Chicago Citizen's Police Committee. From 1920 to 1929, the Committee said, there were 2,722 murders and manslaughters in Chicago, excluding homicides due to criminal negligence. From 1923 to 1929, by conservative estimate, there were 257 gang murders—including the assassination of twenty-five union officials—of which 230 were unsolved; not one of the murders resulted in a conviction. Many criminal lawyers had developed permanent relationships with the underworld, negotiated bargains with the police for their clients, bribed juries, and furnished professional witnesses and fabricated alibis. Professional bondsmen acted as general "fixers" around the courts. Court clerks and bailiffs were usually partisan political appointees. Elected judges were sensitive to political considerations and sometimes received direct financial support from the underworld. "Probations are granted defendants," the Committee found, "who under the law are not entitled to probation. Felonies are waived in cases not warranting such action . . . The clerk's office and the state's attorney's office continue to lose files . . . the failure of prosecution witnesses to appear continues to result in a wastebasket disposition . . . Criminal justice in Chicago has come to be a symbol. By common consent it stands as a perfect example of civic failure and corruption."

The publicity was bad, and Thompson lost office in 1931 to Democrat Anton J. Cermak. The improvement was undiscernible. Cermak was secretary of the United Society—the principal organization of brewers, distillers and saloon-keepers in Chicago—and was the creator of a powerful ward organization which for years had collaborated with syndicated gambling in the city. The main result of Cermak's election was a shift in municipal favors from one gang to another. The change was unpopular, and produced an outbreak in gang warfare. In February, 1933, Cermak went to Miami to participate in a reception for President-elect Franklin D. Roosevelt and was fatally wounded at Roosevelt's side. At least two Chicago citizens prominent in the opposition to organized crime have since attributed the slaying to offended gangsters.

Cermak was succeeded by Edward J. Kelly who, in cooperation with Patrick A. Nash, chairman of the Cook County Democratic Central Committee, created the political machine which ruled Chicago for the next fourteen years. The times had changed. Prohibition was gone, and the depression had engendered greater political awareness and activity on the part of the citizenry, alleviating some of the traditional electoral abuses and raising somewhat the standards of the professional politician. But the difference was marginal. "The depression has brought some improvement in the ethical standards of the party workers in the city," Harold F. Gosnell wrote, "but these standards are pitched at a very low level." Vote frauds, violence at the polls, the appointment of criminals as election judges, the murder of political opponents, the underworld financing of political campaigns and the fixing of court cases remained, and the underworld prospered.

Now dominant in the liquor industry, gangsters became even more active in politics, anxious to promote business and to stop any attempts to enact local-option prohibition ordinances. The principal gambling operations enjoyed full political protection, flourishing openly by 1934 in some 7,500 establishments in and around Chicago. Crime became more highly organized and centralized; the gradual resolution of underworld jurisdictional problems brought about a decline in intramural violence and a more systematic relationship with the political order. "It is doubtful," noted Peterson, "if any city has ever been the sanctuary for a greater number of professional criminals than Chicago in the early and middle 1930's."

In 1941 the Chicago *Tribune* obtained a set of underworld bookkeeping records for the area of Cook County outside of Chicago. The records showed a gross profit of $320,966 for the month of July, 1941, of which $26,980 was paid in graft to politicians and public officials. Peterson recorded an earlier estimate which put the graft paid to politicians at some $20,000,000 a year in metropolitan Chicago. The wartime tax trials of underworld bondsmen William R. Skidmore and William R. Johnson showed that they acted as intermediaries between the political and criminal machines, graft being collected at regular parades at the Lawndale Scrap Iron and Metal Company on the South Side, with a former investigator for the state's attorney's office acting as cashier.

The police usually stood aside. "Everybody knows," the Kelly-supported county clerk testified before a grand jury in 1943, "how promotions are made in the police department. Most captains are appointed by the Mayor on recommendations of the ward committeemen. Every ward committeeman knows that Civil Service examinations are mostly a sham—it's all handled through the Mayor.'" It was a stable system, surviving the war and re-peated investigations and even the departure of the discredited Kelly from office in 1947. It was also a pervasive system, reaching out in its peak years beyond the fields of bootlegging, vice and gambling into the commer-cial and industrial life of Chicago and beyond. The power over business and trade unionism it brought to its chief underworld practitioners was as spectacular as it was unprecedented.

The Chicago underworld of the earlier part of the century was a collec-tion of geographical or occupational fiefs. In gambling, Mont Tennes con-trolled the North Side, James O'Leary the South Side, Alderman John Rogers the West Side, and Alderman Michael ("Hinky Dink") Kenna and John ("Bathhouse John") Coughlin the prosperous downtown Loop dis-trict. Mont Tennes was the most important of these, and after a series of bombing wars from 1907 to 1909 came to control all handbook and race-track gambling in Chicago. In prostitution the leading entrepreneur was James ("Big Jim") Colosimo, aided by such local lieutenants as Michael ("Mike De Pike") Heitler, Frank ("Dago") Lewis and the brothers Harry and Jake ("Greasy Thumb") Guzik. Prohibition multiplied the number of gangs—the O'Banions, the Genna Brothers, the Aiello Brothers, the George ("Bugs") Moran gang and others—some of whom joined forces during the 1920's.

The chief cause of amalgamation was the remarkable ability of the suc-cessors to Colosimo. Early in the century Colosimo recruited New York gangster John Torrio as his chief assistant. Torrio, as the pleasures of wine and flesh increasingly distracted Colosimo, gradually took charge of opera-tions. His power increased with the advent of Mayor Thompson and Prohi-bition, and he expanded into bootlegging and gambling. Colosimo was now an obstacle. On May 11, 1920, he was shot to death, evidently by Frank ("Frankie Yale") Uale, whom Torrio was said to have imported from New York for that purpose. Torrio then brought about a number of gang alliances, and within a year or so was the most powerful gangster in Chi-cago. He was, however, more attached to life than some of his peers. In 1925 he barely survived gunshot wounds inflicted by his enemies, where-upon he abdicated in favor of his principal lieutenant, a former music hall bouncer by the name of Alphonso Capone.

Capone was braver than Torrio, an even more capable organizer, and ut-terly ruthless. "Al Capone," said Peterson, "marshaled the forces of the underworld as they had seldom been marshaled before." He was responsi-ble for the violent invasion of Cicero after Dever's election, which brought that suburb under the control of the Torrio organization. After 1925 he consolidated his power with a series of gang murders, particularly the St.

Valentine's Day Massacre of 1929. He gave an estimated $250,000 to Thompson's 1927 campaign, and manned crucial polling stations with his gunmen. After the election he moved his headquarters from Cicero to the Hotel Metropole in Chicago, setting up his gambling operations at Clark and Madison Streets, one block from City Hall. Undisturbed by the law, he reaped thereafter from his various enterprises an income estimated by federal authorities at $110,000,000 a year. He was so powerful that, according to Chicago Crime Commission President Frank J. Loesch, he once offered to police the entire city of Chicago in return for protection in the labor, liquor and gambling rackets.

In 1931 Capone was convicted of income tax evasion and sent to Alcatraz prison, but the organization he had built—now known as the "syndicate"—was a durable one. Under the leadership of Frank ("The Enforcer") Nitti, together with Jake Guzik, Murray ("The Camel") Humphreys, Sam ("Golf Bag") Hunt, Paul ("The Waiter") Ricca and others, it maintained its hold on the nether life of Chicago. One of its assumed jurisdictions was the field of industrial relations.

"Gangsterised industry," declared Gordon L. Hostetter, the executive director of the Employers' Association of Chicago, in 1932, "is not a mere possibility. It is an established fact." "The 'association' business," the Association's 1927 report had stated, "has come to be a most profitable racket . . . Certain business men, desiring to create a monopoly in their particular field, engage men whose very names strike terror in the hearts of the timid to organize an association of proprietors in their line. In soliciting members the organizers make vague reference to the possibility of damage to property and persons, and to prevent which the association is being organized. If the proprietor does not join quickly his plant is bombed, windows broken, stench bombs exploded on his premises, employees assaulted, or perhaps called on strike. If employees are not union, then his store or business place is picketed and commodity deliveries in and out are stopped." Some union leaders, the Association said, had "conspired with certain employers and employer groups, and set up organizations under harmless-sounding names, through which the two are enriching themselves at the expense of a credulous public . . . The union uses the employer to drive all workmen into its folds, discipline recalcitrant union members, extort money and special privileges . . . The employer uses the union to eliminate competition, fix prices, discipline the employer who shows the least sign of independence, and to generally 'stabilize' his business."

The Association claimed that labor-management combinations involving the use of professional coercion were active in the laundry and dry cleaning, window washing, industrial waste, pulp and paper, machinery moving, fish marketing, poultry, light foods, dental supplies, candy manufacturing, automobile supplies and repairs, pharmacy, soft drink, building materials, garbage disposal, milk distribution, tire repairs, florist, shoe repairing, restaurant, furniture moving, art glass, carpet and linoleum laying, window shade and drapery, wire fencing, electrical supplies, haircutting, interior decorating and photographic trades. Not all the partnerships were voluntary. "The gang," the Illinois Association for Criminal Justice said, "is more powerful than the police. The natural result of this is that the law of force should be extended to legitimate lines of business as a substitute for the law of the land. Over ninety legitimate businesses are dominated by gangsters."

Inevitably this meant an underworld invasion of the labor movement. "Organized labor in Chicago," declared the *Tribune* in 1930, "stands in peril of being delivered into the hands of gangsters, according to labor leaders who expressed their fears today. Already several unions, rated as the most powerful and active in the city, have been taken over completely by Alphonso ("Scarface Al") Capone . . . Other leading unions are being forced to pay monthly tribute to stave off the gangsters . . . the labor men feel themselves helpless to stem the inroads being made by the racketeers on their organizations. Some of the union heads, in fact, have gone to Capone seeking his help in meeting the demands of other gangsters."

An approach to Capone made some sense. His organization was by far the most powerful of its kind, but it was not the only one. Extortion was a competitive business. The Chicago teamsters were troubled by both the Tuohy gang and Murray ("The Camel") Humphreys. Capone himself drove out competitive extortioners from the laundry and dry cleaning trades, and fought the Moran gang for influence in the building trades. John ("Machine Gun Jack") McGurn fought the Dead Shots for control of the automobile repair and bill posting trades.

The effect of gang rivalry was the imposition of double or variable extortionary rates. Some union and business leaders thus went to Capone with the request that he drive out the competition and bring a measure of stability to extortionary activities. There was—if the late gangster Roger Tuohy can be believed—an attempt by a number of union leaders to create a defense fund, hire bodyguards, and resist by all available means the invasion of any gang; certainly special precautions were taken by some organizations. But resistance was sporadic and in many cases futile. By 1932, according to Crime Commission President Loesch, the Capone organization controlled or exacted tribute from "fully two-thirds" of all trade unions in Chicago. Even the AFL, not disposed to exaggerate the extent of gangster influence in the labor movement, evidently conceded that twenty-eight of its local affiliates in Chicago were under the domination of racketeers.

The true extent of underworld influence in the Chicago labor movement during these years is no doubt impossible to document. As in other places, it was a condition replete with allegations but spare in proof, marked then by the silences of fear, today by genuine or convenient amnesia. A combination of circumstances—the ecology of the city, the legacy of Prohibition, the distaste for commercial competition, the partnership of the law and the underworld, and the tolerant ethics of the time—had produced a criminal lodgement in the Chicago labor movement of major proportions. It was a shared responsibility. Some union leaders fought back against high odds and often with mortal consequences. Others did not; but with the law corrupted, the politicians compromised, the underworld protected and murder among the easiest of crimes, their quiescence was not altogether surprising.

Repeal brought a change for the worse. The activities of gangsters in the Chicago labor movement during Prohibition, while substantial, were confined essentially to local operations. Legalization of the liquor trade, however, sharply reduced the revenues of the underworld and caused it to seek new sources of income. The leading gangs had small cause for timidity. Their successes during Prohibition had endowed them with a legend of invulnerability and a powerful machine. The advent of Repeal, if it lowered their income, did little to reduce their political influence or to sharpen the scruples of the community. They now took aim at a new level of influence: the international union.

10: The Culinary Trades

"In many respects," Jere L. Sullivan told his members in 1917, "our union occupies the least secure of any field in the economic world. . . ."

Sullivan was the international secretary-treasurer of the Hotel and Restaurant Employees. Founded in 1892, the HRE represented cooks, waiters, waitresses, bartenders, dishwashers and kindred employees. The hotel and restaurant industry was intensely competitive, noted for poor working conditions, an unstable labor force and—at least in the restaurant sector—low profit margins and a high rate of business failures. In 1917 Sullivan could claim only 65,000 members in an industry employing hundreds of thousands of people. During the next two years the union lost 5,000 members with the passage of new state and local prohibition laws. The Volstead Act hastened the decline of the union. Twenty thousand bartenders surrendered their union cards, many of them going to work in non-union speakeasies. Scores of long-established locals died, or maintained only a nominal existence with a handful of loyal members. By 1923 the HRE had only 37,000 members.

The union attempted to retrieve some of its losses by organizing the speakeasies. It was a difficult task. The bootleggers were often violent in response and usually immune to police reprisal. The union also received little help from public officials who were reluctant to recognize in public the existence of establishments they patronized in private, and who sometimes actively opposed picketing and other union organizing tactics. But the campaign met with some success, and in due course there developed an unwelcome but inevitable association between the HRE and the underworld. It was a useful link for HRE members otherwise condemned to work under non-union conditions, but it brought trouble to the organization.

The bartenders themselves were partly to blame. Some of them converted the premises of their local unions into speakeasies, gambling rooms or bootleg supply centers. Disciplinary actions of the international union were unavailing. The underworld found that bartenders could be used to push individual brands, and according to two officers of the HRE, "deliberately set out to capture bartenders' locals and use their membership."

Repeal was accompanied by a substantial increase in HRE membership, but also by a more determined effort by racketeers to increase their influence in the union. In 1932 a number of newspapers claimed that the Capone organization planned to take control of the liquor industry, the Brewery Workers, the HRE, and elements of the Teamsters. The charges of gangster infiltration were denied by President Edward J. Flore of the HRE; but shortly after the presidential election of 1932 he conferred in Chicago with Secretary-Treasurer Joseph Obergfell of the Brewery Workers, who then told newspaper reporters that "Our union has understood for some time that Chicago's gangland had plans to get its clutches on our industry . . . We ask the cooperation of all concerned to keep this industry out of the hands of gangsters."

Privately, Flore himself was disturbed. "The racketeers are creeping into some of our local unions," he confided to a friend at the 1934 HRE convention. "I really don't know what we should do."

He had ample grounds for concern, both in New York and Chicago. Most unionized culinary workers in New York belonged to independent locals under aggressive left-wing leadership. The employers, after an establishment had been organized by the independents, would wherever possible sign an agreement with the HRE. "Workers employed in such places," wrote Matthew Josephson in an approved history of the HRE, "found that nothing resembling a union shop was established; that conditions remained as intolerable as before; and that when workers protested they were beaten up by hoodlums, discharged, and placed on an employers' association blacklist."

In September, 1933, three New York officials of the HRE—Paul N. Coulcher and Alexander Retek of Local 16 and Abraham Borson of Local 302—were indicted with twenty-two other persons for extortion from restaurant owners. The indictment was largely the result of protests by members of Locals 16 and 302 and by Benjamin Gottesman, the secretary-treasurer of New York Local 1.

Gottesman had repeatedly sought the help of local law enforcement officials in resisting extortionary activities, but he had received none, nor was he called to testify at the trial. "Without a vestige of investigation," Thomas E. Dewey said later, "the case was brought to trial resting only on the testimony of those poor workers who had taken their lives in their hands to complain and during three days the case was so badly presented that every defendant was freed."

A group of rank-and-file members of Local 16 then protested to Flore, complaining of dictatorial government in the local and of a conspiracy between the leadership of the local and the employers to repress protest and maintain "miserable conditions, long hours, low wages, indecent treatment. . . . The uniform racket is blooming. We are forced to spend twenty-two dollars for uniforms for miserable jobs that don't bring us a living. . . .

There is no auditing committee or trustees to check up on financial affairs. The officials call strikes and settle them without consulting the membership. They remove duly elected shop chairmen at will, replacing them with their henchmen. They keep any member who is opposed to their tactics out of Union headquarters; they refuse to accept dues from members in good standing."

The HRE General Executive Board tried four New York officials—Coulcher, Retek, Charles Baum of Local 16 and Charles Koenig of Local 302—just prior to the 1934 convention of the union. The trial was inconclusive, Flore being authorized to conduct further investigations. He then left for England as an AFL fraternal delegate to the annual conference of the British Trades Union Congress. During his absence HRE International Vice-President John J. Kearney suspended Local 302 for refusing to sign a legitimate agreement with the United Restaurant Association of New York. When Flore returned to New York he was met in the outer harbor by a boatload of officials from Locals 16 and 302. "The racketeering union officers," Kearney later testified, "took Flore off to a hotel in mid-town New York, and what happened there was that he might have been intimidated."

Flore contended that Kearney had exceeded his authority, that the union might lose the suit Local 302 had brought against it, and that in any case he had other plans for reform. The 1934 convention gave the General Executive Board increased authority to deal with internal wrongdoing, but Coulcher and the others were cleared of the charges against them. Then, in March, 1935, one Jules Martin, an accomplice of New York bootleg chief Dutch Schultz, was murdered in Troy, New York. An investigation by District Attorney Thomas E. Dewey indicated that Schultz had long been working with Coulcher and others in extorting huge sums from New York restaurant owners. The case went to trial in 1936.

The trial showed that Coulcher went to work for Schultz and Martin in 1926 in one of their speakeasies. In 1932, evidently with their support, he ran for the secretary-treasurership of Local 16. The first vote count was faked on Coulcher's behalf, and when a recount was demanded he brought in armed guards to supervise the second tabulation. Coulcher was elected with Baum and Retek—both former employees of Schultz and Martin—who became president and delegate respectively of Local 16. All three now joined with Schultz in a plan to shake down the entire restaurant industry in New York City. Louis Koenig of Local 16 and Borson and Max Pincus of Local 302 were made accomplices. Gottesman was approached and told "We have all the unions in your line. You are the one that is the missing link . . . the boys have decided to take you over." Gottesman balked, and for years later he was in danger of mob retaliation.

Schultz and his associates now organized some ninety percent of all New York restaurant owners into the Metropolitan Restaurant and Cafeteria Owners Association, charging a minimum initiation fee of $250, five dollars a week in dues, and additional levies for not calling strikes—some owners paying as much as $25,000 a year to the Association. Collective bargaining involved the presentation of extravagant demands to an employer, accompanied where necessary by picketing and stink-bombing; the Association's collector would then settle for the regular initiation fee and dues, or a special assessment; in return no bargaining demands were made and the employer continued to impose his own wages and working conditions. Dewey estimated that the total amount extorted or willingly paid exceeded $1,000,000. Some fifteen percent of the revenues went to the participating officials of Locals 16 and 302, the remainder to Schultz.

The trial ended in March, 1937. Pincus, at the opening of the trial, had jumped or been pushed to his death from a hotel window. Schultz was dead, killed by fellow racketeers because of his threat to assassinate Dewey. Martin, Koenig and Borson had all been murdered by persons and for reasons unknown. Coulcher received a sentence of fifteen to twenty years; other HRE officials were imprisoned for varying terms. The HRE suspended Locals 16 and 302 and later negotiated mergers with the independents. The books of the suspended locals showed an untraceable deficit of $100,000. The membership of both locals turned in disgust to left-wing leadership.

An even more serious situation had arisen in Chicago. In 1928 the HRE revoked the charter of Bartenders' Local 278 for consorting with bootleggers. The leader of a newly chartered Local 278 was George B. McLane, once said to own a speakeasy, but now apparently divorced from bootlegging. For some time McLane seemed to keep the local free from unnecessary entanglements with the Chicago syndicate while enjoying some success in organizing the speakeasies, and in 1934 became an international vice president of the HRE.

After Repeal, however, he began to encounter violent opposition from the Capone interests. Pickets were assaulted, but received no protection from the police. In March, 1935, according to his own affidavit, McLane received a telephone call from a syndicate representative who demanded a payment of $500. When McLane refused to pay he was told that the Capone organization would take over Local 278. A week later McLane accepted an invitation to lunch from the same caller. At the restaurant he was confronted by Frank Nitti, Capone's accepted successor. Nitti demanded that McLane put one Louis Romano on the payroll of Local 278, and when McLane objected placed a gun on the table and politely asked how Mrs. McLane would look in black. Romano joined Local 278, the picket line violence ceased, and the local rapidly became the largest bartenders' organization in the HRE.

In 1938—again according to his own testimony—McLane was summoned to a meeting attended by Nitti and other gangsters, President George Browne of the International Alliance of Theatrical and Stage Employees, and Browne's special assistant William Bioff. The group proposed to McLane that he run for the presidency of the HRE at the next convention, stating that a two-year stint in office by McLane would give them time to "parcel out different parts of the country." McLane showed reluctance and again was threatened at gun-point by Nitti, who told him to run for office or find himself "in an alley." Accompanied by racketeers and bodyguards, McLane embarked on a nation-wide campaign to capture the presidency from Flore. Financed with $100,000 in underworld funds, he visited local unions throughout the country, dispensing funds and accumulating an impressive number of allies.

The 1938 convention took place in San Francisco. The McLane delegation, some of its members armed with guns and blackjacks, roamed the convention in search of supporters, dispensing unlimited hospitality at the Whitcomb Hotel. They secured one important ally in Robert Hesketh, the respected secretary-treasurer of the union, who unexpectedly joined McLane and denounced Flore as a co-conspirator with Communists in the East Coast locals. For a time McLane seemed in a strong position, but the incumbents were firm. International Vice-President Hugo Ernst, leader of the largest delegation and later to become international president, arranged with the San Francisco Labor Council and the police department for reinforcements to protect Flore's supporters. When several of the latter were assaulted, police took away twenty-six revolvers, and other weapons, from McLane delegates. But the tension remained. Flore had refused a police offer of bodyguards; one of his supporters had been kidnapped and told to leave the city on pain of his life; and there was fear of violence if the vote went against McLane.

The opposition provided some relief. "We come in here with clean hands," said John Staggenburg of Local 278 in nominating McLane. "If it could be written in the records—and it is not—what this man has done in the last four years since he has been vice president, it would make fine reading. . . ." Delegate Ben Parker of Chicago Local 25 rose to second the nomination.

Delegate Parker: I have worked in every millionaire's house in Chicago . . . I used to wait on Sam Insull. . . . I came in contact with a wonderful character by the name of Al Brown, afterwards they hung on him the name of Al Capone. What crime did he commit? . . . Mr. Insull—I liked him too, because he was a wonderful character and a generous gentleman, but no more than Scarface Al Brown. He was a gentleman, and he wasn't a thug; he is a victim of the bankers' racket.

Chairman Ernst: The gentleman is evidently seconding the nomination of Al Capone. The nomination of Al Capone is not before the convention. . . .

Delegate Parker: If I lived in San Francisco, I would start a movement to move that disgraceful rock from this community.

Chairman Ernst: I do not think that Alcatraz Island is before the convention. If you desire to second the nomination of a candidate, all right.

Delegate Parker: I am very willing to do that. . . . I take great pleasure now, after having been disturbed both by the insane people and those who want to stop progress, in seconding the nomination of George McLane.

McLane lost. Romano seized the microphone and called upon the McLane delegates to leave the hall and hold another convention. Some of them followed, but no rump convention took place.

On syndicate orders Romano was appointed president of Local 278 and given full control over the local's finances, and on Romano's instructions McLane left for a three-month vacation out of the state. When he came back he was told his services were no longer required. McLane then brought suit against Nitti, Romano and others, describing in his affidavit his experiences since the intervention of the underworld in the affairs of Local 278. Just before the trial, however, he revoked his affidavit, dropped the suit, and went back to tending bar in Chicago. Romano stayed in office.

11: The Building Service Employees

George Scalise was a former pimp who, during the 1920's and 1930's, associated with such New York gangsters as Luciano, Uale, Louis ("Pretty Boy") Amberg, Buchalter, Shapiro and others. During that time he engaged in racketeering activities in local unions of garage employees, automobile washers, retail clerks, beauty shop workers, Italian butchers and laundry employees, and was for some time a vice president of Local 272 of the Teamsters. He also owned a strikebreaking agency called the Sentinel Service Company. In July, 1934, Scalise was appointed chief international representative for the eastern region of the Building Service Employees International Union.* The announcement of the appointment was made by BSEIU President Jerry J. Horan in the offices of the Sentinel Service Company.

The appointment of Scalise was the first step towards implementing the decision of Frank Nitti and his associates to take over the international union. The BSEIU was a young organization, founded in 1921 to represent custodial and other service employees in office, apartment, hotel, hospital, public and other buildings. It was also a small organization, most of its 18,000 members being in Chicago, where the union's headquarters were maintained.

Scalise, working under the supervision of New York gangster Anthony ("Little Augie Pisano") Carfano, soon made his influence felt. In the fall of 1934, Local 32B of the BSEIU was on the verge of a major organizing campaign in New York City. James J. Bambrick, the president of the local, had selected the garment district as the locus of the campaign, and quickly discovered the strength of Buchalter and Shapiro in the industry. Shortly before a contemplated strike, he was called to a meeting in a loft building near Fifth Avenue and 22nd Street where he was instructed by Shapiro not to call the strike. Bambrick protested but was further informed that he would be contacted by Scalise and Isidore ("Izzy") Schwartz. Schwartz later told Bambrick that he and Scalise were working with Buchalter and Shapiro, that they intended to extort money from building owners in the garment industry, and that if Bambrick cooperated his share of the proceeds would be at least $300,000. As for the members of Local 32B, Bambrick was advised to "throw the crumbs a crust."

* Now the Service Employees International Union.

124

Bambrick refused the bribe and called the strike. The employers were enraged, having assumed that they had already bought their way out of the strike. They answered with violence and sent thousands of strikebreakers against Local 32B. But the local won the strike and went on to become the largest affiliate of the BSEIU, representing about one-third of the entire membership of the union.

The 1935 BSEIU convention was held in Chicago at the Hotel Bismarck where, for associated purposes, Nitti, Francis Mariote, Ricca, Louis ("Little New York") Campagna, Pisano, McGurn, William ("Baby Face") Nelson, Joseph Adonis and other members of the syndicate were staying. Bambrick, an unwelcome recruit to the union, was refused financial assistance to liquidate the debts incurred by Local 32B during the strike, and was ordered to bring his *per capita* payments up to date. The following year Scalise—by now an international vice president—urged Bambrick to join him and Schwartz in one of their business enterprises, and when Bambrick refused, organized a "strike" of Local 32B organizers just prior to the expiration of a city-wide contract. Shortly afterwards he told Bambrick that an attempt was to be made on the latter's life by "The Boilermaker," a Chicago gunman. From that time, Bambrick wrote, he lived "in an atmosphere of stark terror." Soon, he said, he was forced to pay Scalise $10,000 for protection against assassination. He took the money from union funds, an act which later sent him to jail.

Horan died in April, 1937. Scalise then allegedly met with syndicate representatives Frank Diamond, Charles Fiaschetti and Michael Carozza at the Hotel Bismarck. Scalise was informed—Schwartz later testified—that First Vice-President William L. McFetridge was uncooperative and therefore ineligible for the presidency; that Scalise, the junior vice president, would be the candidate; and that once in office he would donate half of his union income to the syndicate in return for its support. Scalise was thereafter appointed to the presidency of the union by the BSEIU's executive board.

In 1941 Bambrick was convicted of misappropriating $10,000 from the funds of Local 32B. It was established at the trial that he gave $7,500 to Scalise, but no satisfactory accounting was made of the remainder. "Bambrick," Thomas E. Dewey later said of the case, "for many years apparently was a legitimate labor leader with a long record on behalf of labor. . . . Thereafter this international union brazenly made a professional criminal, George Scalise, its president. Forced to take orders from the Capone mob and Scalise, Bambrick at first resisted and then succumbed. Eventually . . . he became a coconspirator with Scalise." Bambrick received a short sentence in jail, claiming at the time that his conviction was the result of a conspiracy between David Sullivan, the secretary-treasurer of Local 32B, and Victor Herwitz, an assistant district attorney under Dewey who later became legal counsel of the local. In 1949, however, Bambrick wrote an apology to Sullivan for this and other charges of malfeasance in office, saying that "anything I have ever said reflecting upon your honor and integrity, I must in all truth, withdraw . . . [the accusations were] inspired by bitterness." Sullivan had defeated Bambrick for the presidency of the local and went on to become president of the international union. "Mr. Bambrick," he wrote to the author in 1962, "was basically a trade unionist, was by no stretch of the imagination a hoodlum or a racketeer, but unfortunately because of the pressures of that time became involved." Bambrick was never returned to union office.

Meanwhile, a determined resistance to Scalise had developed in California. Charles Hardy, the international vice president for the West Coast, became publicly critical of Scalise's methods and friends, opposed his attempt to dominate the West Coast region of the union, and defied his orders. Scalise once told Hardy to get rid of a subordinate officer he disliked. "You," Hardy said, "go jump in the lake."

Hardy charged specifically that Scalise had failed to account for the *per capita* contributions made by locals to the international union; that Scalise's own salary was unknown; and that Hardy's requests at various executive board meetings for an accounting had been refused. In return, Scalise threatened Hardy's life on a number of occasions, and suspended him from his vice presidency in December, 1939.

The international union then brought court action against Hardy in a move to take control of the San Francisco locals. Hardy filed a counter-complaint to prevent further *per capita* payments until a satisfactory accounting of previous payments had been made; to prevent his own removal from office by enjoining his forthcoming trial before the BSEIU executive board; and to prohibit Scalise from commandeering the records and property of the San Francisco locals. In affidavit Hardy charged—as was shown at Scalise's trial in 1940—that the latter received as salary half of all membership initiation fees and *per capita* payments from BSEIU locals in the eastern region—between $8,000 and $10,000 a month; that Scalise also received some $25,000 a year in expenses *; that he retained a number of gunmen on the BSEIU payroll for coercive purposes; and that several BSEIU executive board members had been threatened with death and went in continual fear of their lives. The other members of the board submitted affidavits stating that Hardy's charges on the last score were "a figment of

* Scalise was probably, by a comfortable margin, the highest-paid union official in the United States at that time.

his own imagination," and in identical letters to Scalise upheld Hardy's suspension from office. A San Francisco local court enjoined the BSEIU from taking over the property and assets of Local 9, the local at suit, but considered itself unable to offer further relief except to insist that Hardy's trial board not include Scalise or International Vice-President Thomas J. Burke. Scalise lost an appeal against the decision. By subsequent agreement among the parties Hardy was tried by a board of San Francisco Bay Area union officials and—except on minor procedural matters—exonerated of the charges levelled against him by Scalise.

The court action, together with attacks on Scalise by journalist Westbrook Pegler, paved the way for Scalise's downfall. In April, 1940, he was indicted for extorting $97,150 from Chicago property owners; the prosecution claimed that the actual amount extorted was about $1,000,000. He was also put on trial shortly afterwards by Dewey in New York City for stealing $60,087 from the union; in this case the prosecution believed Scalise had taken more than $200,000. There was a further indictment for income tax evasion, the federal government collecting $307,947 in taxes, interest and penalties.

Schwartz testified at the second trial, stating that Scalise had indeed been put in office by the Chicago syndicate and confirming the financial conditions imposed. Kenneth Ashley, the union's bookkeeper, testified that he falsified union records to hide various payments to Scalise, and that a regular account was kept for Frank Diamond, Capone's brother-in-law. Harry Altschuler, the union's auditor, said that he was told by Scalise to prepare a statement which would be a "financial picture" of the union, but that he was not allowed to check expenses nor given access to some of the union's books. One of the secret items, the court learned, was a free vacation in Cuba for Scalise, Burke, Carfano and Fiaschetti.

The finances of the BSEIU were evidently not under careful supervision. McFetridge, who succeeded Scalise at the 1940 convention of the union, was questioned in court about Scalise's income.

Q. Did you ever hear any resolution proposed at any meeting of the executive board at which you were present confirming, adopting or ratifying any arrangement with George Scalise whereunder he was to receive a fixed percentage of the per capita tax of any local union affiliated with the international?

A. No. . . . I heard in the office there was some arrangement made with Scalise, but never in executive board meetings was it discussed, to my memory.

A parole board report submitted to the trial judge said that as early as 1932 a Chicago group under Nitti had moved into the BSEIU—a charge formerly denied by Horan; that as a vice president, Scalise had shared offices with Carfano; and that as a subsidiary activity Scalise and Carfano had employed a gang of thugs, supplying them with fake police badges and using them to engage in petty extortion. A death-bed affidavit by Matthew Taylor, the president of an elevator operator's local in Chicago, stated that Horan and Campagna had offered him a bribe of $50,000 to step out of the leadership of the local, then affiliated with the International Union of Elevator Constructors; that Scalise—with the help of AFL President William Green—had forced him to affiliate his local with the BSEIU; that he had paid $30,415 in tribute to the syndicate from his local's treasury; and that he had once determined to kill both Scalise and Burke, but that "something went wrong."

Scalise, having already been suspended by the BSEIU executive board, resigned in April, 1940. In a statement read to the convention the following month, he claimed a clean police record since his conviction, while a minor, for white slavery; pointed to the growth of the union during his time in office from 20,000 to 70,000 members; and protested against the "despicable attacks" made on him by his critics. "My election as President to this International Union," he said, "came about as a recognition of my accomplishments. . . . These attacks on me together with those conceived by a District Attorney, a presidential aspirant, are responsible for the unfortunate position I find myself in tonight. This unholy alliance of venom and unselfishness, you will agree, is formidable." He also claimed he had made efforts "to weed out any corruption" in the union, and charged "the Hardy clan" in San Francisco with a variety of misdeeds and collaboration with the enemies of the union.

The convention resolved "to accord to George Scalise the full presumption of innocence until proven guilty" and to "extend aid to get a fair trial and fraternal aid"; elected McFetridge, who promised to fight against "waste, graft and corruption"; and acted to require more careful supervision of the union's finances and ethics. Otherwise it took little notice of the passing of Scalise, and dwelt not at all on the misfortunes he had brought to the union.

Hardy, the single rebel, regained his vice presidency in 1942, retaining it until his premature death in 1948; but little was ever said of the past. The reflections came later. "You know," McFetridge told the 1960 convention, "we inherited the darndest racket in the United States. . . . One of the terrible actions that was taken was to move on one of the great trade unionists and the one person who made our organization possible on the West Coast, Charles Hardy." It was tardy recognition.

Scalise spent ten years in prison for theft, forgery and income tax evasion. He was released in July, 1950. In February, 1955, he pleaded guilty to charges of conspiracy and bribery in dealings with the welfare fund of the Distillery Workers and was given another year in jail.

12: The Theatrical Employees

In 1933 George Browne was the business agent for Stagehands Local 2 of the International Alliance of Theatrical and Stage Employees in Chicago. The IATSE was and is the principal union representing production workers in the legitimate theatre and the motion picture industry. Browne had run for the presidency of the union in 1932 without success. Now he made the acquaintance of William ("Willie") Bioff, a former procurer with a record of arrests for burglary and vagrancy, a suspect in more than one murder case, and for some time a minor figure in the Capone organization.

Browne and Bioff conceived the idea, admirable during the depression, of organizing a soup kitchen for unemployed members of Local 2. Employed members were required to buy two meal tickets at a time for thirty-five cents, one of which was given to an unemployed member. Funds for less altruistic purposes were available from other sources. Bioff allegedly received money from local politicians in return for votes. He and Browne also demanded from Barney Balaban, owner of a large motion picture circuit, the restitution of a twenty percent cut in stagehand pay imposed in 1929; when Balaban protested that this would oblige him to restore all other pay cuts, Browne and Bioff settled for a $20,000 gift to the soup kitchen. Soup was cheap. Browne and Bioff were able to keep a substantial surplus of funds for themselves.

They celebrated their new wealth in a drunken party at the restaurant of Nicholas ("Nick") Circella, or Nick Dean, a Capone man. Circella and Frank Rone, one of Capone's former bodyguards, reported the evident prosperity of Browne and Bioff to their syndicate superiors. Browne and Bioff were summoned to two meetings in suburban Riverside attended by Nitti, Campagna, Charles ("Cherry Nose") Gioe, Philip d'Andrea, Ricca and—on the second occasion—by Buchalter. Nitti told Browne he should run again in 1934 for the IATSE presidency, and asked him to name the territories in which his support had been weakest in 1932. Nitti then listed the underworld leaders who would bring the appropriate pressure to bear in 1934, naming Luciano and Buchalter in New York, Zwillman in New Jersey, Al Palizzi in Cleveland and John Dougherty in St. Louis. Nitti assured Browne of victory, adding that the syndicate would consider itself entitled to fifty percent of all extorted moneys thereafter.

The 1934 convention of the IATSE took place in Louisville, Kentucky.
130

Underworld representatives attended in force, openly supporting Browne for the presidency. Incumbent President William C. Elliott chose for unannounced reasons not to run, his departure unmarked by farewells of his own or any of the traditional praises offered by a convention to a retiring president. An attempt was made to persuade former President William E. Canavan to run; at first he agreed, then withdrew after threats to his safety. Browne was elected without opposition. One of his first acts was to appoint Bioff as his personal representative.

A wider prospect was now open. In New York, Browne and Bioff threatened cinema owners with a strike, collected $150,000 for not calling it, and allowed a ten percent cut in projectionists' wages. In Chicago, they pressed the Chicago Exhibitors' Association for a second projectionist in every booth, but settled for a personal donation of $100,000. Bioff took $25,000 from Nathaniel Barger, owner of the Rialto Theatre in Chicago, later claiming half the theatre's profits and sending Isidor Zevin—the syndicate-appointed bookkeeper of the IATSE—to audit the Rialto's books as a precaution against cheating. Gangster Frank Maritote was put on Barger's payroll at $200 a week for no duties at all, later being replaced by d'Andrea. Barger was forced to sell another property—the Star and Garter burlesque house—to offset his losses on the Rialto. Bioff collected half the proceeds.

But Hollywood was the prize. The IATSE had found it hard to organize. Dominated by five companies and concentrated in a relatively compact area, the film production industry was nevertheless noted for casual employment conditions. The glamor of the industry had attracted a surplus labor force; employment was largely on a short-term basis, with workers moving continuously from one employer or location to another according to the schedule of films in production. However, with the entry into the industry of eastern capital and of management accustomed—unlike employers in the traditionally open shop Los Angeles area—to negotiating with the unions, the IATSE managed to secure a foothold in Hollywood by the mid-1920's.

Unfortunately for the IATSE, the industry was also beset by jurisdictional problems. The IATSE was organized on a multi-craft basis, most crafts having separate locals but coming under the discipline of the international union. This brought the IATSE into conflict with the single-craft Painters, Carpenters and Electrical Workers. In 1933 a dispute with the Electrical Workers over sound technicians brought about the almost complete defeat of the IATSE, reducing its Hollywood members in a few weeks from some 9,000 to less than 200.

Now, however, there developed a close and nation-wide financial relationship between production in Hollywood and the distribution of films throughout the country, with a much greater monetary investment in the latter. The IATSE controlled most of the labor force in distribution. It was the dependence of the employers on undisturbed distribution, and on freedom from the stink-bombing of theatres, that contributed most of all to the resurgence of the IATSE in Hollywood and the holding of the industry to ransom by Browne and Bioff.

They opened negotiations with the studios in 1936. The talks deadlocked, and the IATSE struck the Paramount theatres in Chicago. The effect was immediate and the warning sufficient. The IATSE was readmitted to the basic agreement between employers and unions in Hollywood, and negotiated a wage increase and a union shop. IATSE membership in Hollywood jumped to 12,000 almost overnight.

The consolidation of the union brought handsome rewards to Browne and Bioff. Bioff was the spokesman. "Now look . . . ," he told Nicholas Schenck, president of Loew's Incorporated and chief negotiator for the employers in 1936, "I want you to know I elected Browne president and I am his boss. He is to do whatever I want him to do. Now your industry is a prosperous industry and I must get $2,000,000 out of it." Bioff later confirmed the exchange. "I told Nicholas Schenck," he said at a grand jury hearing in 1943, "to get together with other producers and get a couple of million together. Schenck threw up his hands in the air and raved. I told him if he didn't get the others together we would close every theatre in the country." In time the extortions were not always unwelcome, since they were often accompanied by muted collective bargaining demands, but for the moment the producers were concerned with mitigating the burden. Bioff finally accepted an offer of $50,000 a year from each of four major companies, with $25,000 from a smaller company. The first instalment was paid the following day by Schenck and President Sidney R. Kent of 20th-Century-Fox, who deposited $75,000 in cash on a bed in the hotel suite occupied by Browne and Bioff. Subsequent court proceedings showed that between 1936 and 1940 the two IATSE officials received more than $1,-100,000 from the employers.

Unchallenged by the employers, Browne and Bioff now affirmed their control over the union. They had good news to offer: the IATSE had become the dominant union in the industry and had obtained substantial benefits. Browne, by now a vice president of the AFL, was greeted at the IATSE convention in 1938 with high praise and protestations of loyalty, and had his term of office extended from two to four years. "At present," he told the convention, "we are riding the crest of power and stability." He took the opportunity to levy a special assessment of two percent of the earnings of all IATSE members; the ostensible purpose of the assessment was to create a defense fund against "unethical" employers who were trying to undermine union conditions. Browne was given full control over the fund and instructed to take action against any local union failing to pay its quota. The assessment yielded some $60,000 a month, but no accounting of it was ever made.

Browne also acknowledged his debt to Bioff. "I would be greatly remiss in my duty," he said, "if I did not call attention to the splendid and successful efforts of my personal Representative . . . No man ever worked harder and accomplished as much as he did, fighting the producers tooth and nail."

Sidney Kent also appeared at the convention. The record would show, he said, that "we have had less interruption of employment, less hard feeling, less recrimination, and have built more good will than any industry I know of in the country." Browne thanked him for his comments. "The appearance of President Kent, I do believe," he added, "shows indication of a new era in the relationship between the employer and the employee . . . I think it is going to do great things for us and the country in general . . . As we sow, so shall we reap."

Retribution had already begun. In 1936 a number of dissident members of Local 37, under receivership at Bioff's suggestion, engaged Los Angeles attorney Carey McWilliams and filed suit to obtain an accounting of the defense fund. The suit came to nothing, but the publicity it gained and the widespread unrest among the IATSE Hollywood locals prompted an investigation by the Committee on Capital and Labor of the California State Assembly. The inquiry lasted only forty-eight hours, did not involve the questioning of Browne or Bioff, and produced a report favorable to Bioff and the IATSE. The speed, dubious procedure and bland conclusions of the report aroused some curiosity and produced, the following year, a report on the investigation itself.

The second report stated that Assembly Speaker William J. Jones of Los Angeles, who controlled the purse strings of Assembly committees, had shown no initial interest in a proposal by McWilliams that there should be a public investigation of the IATSE. Then he reversed himself and funded the investigation. About this time Jones's law associate, Colonel William H. Neblett, allegedly told Louis B. Mayer, the head of Metro-Goldwyn-Mayer, that it would be possible to get rid of the IATSE if Mayer wished. Mayer disclaimed interest, referring the matter to Nicholas Schenck, but the rumor spread that Mayer and Jones were planning an investigation of the IATSE. The union, according to a Treasury agent, then made out checks to Neblett and Jones. The Assembly committee report—evidently typed by

IATSE stenographers—was issued the day after the signing of the IATSE checks. Neblett now asked Mayer for help in subduing the unfavorable publicity on Bioff. Bioff himself later said that he had paid $5,000 to Neblett to quash the Assembly investigation; that he had asked Mayer, Spitz and the Schenck brothers to divert the Assembly committee's attention from him; that the committee then "let up on me"; and that on Joseph Schenck's advice he left for a trip to Europe and South America at Schenck's expense.

But the embarrassments continued. Open opposition to Browne and Bioff now flourished in the Hollywood IATSE locals. Robert Montgomery, the actor-president of the Screen Actors' Guild persuaded the executive board of the union to hire two ex-FBI agents to look into the charges of corruption in the IATSE; the agents' report brought about the income tax indictment of Joseph Schenck and shed more light on Bioff's past and present activities.

In 1938 Nitti evidently ordered Bioff to resign from the IATSE for a year to allow the bad publicity to subside. Bioff did so, with a eulogium from the General Executive Board of the union. "Your work for this organization in years gone by," the Board wrote to Bioff, "has been outstanding not only in the results obtained, but also in the quiet, business-like and effective manner in which you have gone about your work, and the high integrity and honesty you have displayed in all your dealings . . . Should you find, however, that it is not possible to comply with our request and withdraw your resignation, the General Executive Board has unanimously . . . voted you one year's salary."

Bioff returned to the payroll the following year. Soon, however, Westbrook Pegler published an account of a prison sentence Bioff had received for pimping in Illinois which he had never served. Bioff was extradited to Chicago for court proceedings, his departure from the chairmanship of the IATSE Hollywood negotiating committee producing a flood of telegrams from local unions protesting their faith in him and demanding his return. Early in 1940 he was committed to Bridewell jail to serve his sentence. While there he received a warning. During a visit from Gioe he indicated that he wanted to retire from labor racketeering. The next day Campagna came to see him and asked for confirmation. "Yes, sir," Bioff said, "I want to resign." "Well, Willie," Campagna said, "anybody who resigns, resigns feet first. Do you understand what that means?" Bioff understood and did not resign.

For the moment he had troubles enough. Bioff returned again to the IATSE payroll in September, 1940; but during his absence Joseph Schenck —in return for an easement of his three-year income tax sentence—had given testimony on the extortionary activities of Browne and Bioff. Browne received eight years and Bioff ten, but for the present neither man implicated his underworld associates.

The 1942 IATSE convention took note of their departure. "Inasmuch as our former President has served the International in a wholly satisfactory manner in various official capacities for many years," said the newly elected President Richard Walsh, "it must be assumed that he had become the victim of circumstances beyond his control. If he was cognizant of the acts being perpetrated by his appointees, possibly he was left with the alternative of remaining silent or paying the supreme penalty . . . As the legal prosecution started outside our ranks, it was left entirely to the courts to establish the innocence or guilt of the accused. Every aid and assistance was extended to preclude the possibility of anyone working on behalf of the Alliance being unjustly prosecuted and punished for promoting its advancement . . . Despite the fact that our actions were unproductive, under the circumstances they were wholly justified." The convention took precautions against the recurrence of similar episodes, shortening the presidential term from four to two years, adopting stricter accounting methods and formalizing the procedure for the calling of meetings.

Then, on February 2, 1943, an unusually brutal murder took place in Chicago. Estelle Carey, the paramour of Circella, was severely beaten, doused with gasoline and burned to death in her apartment. The murder was never solved, but Circella was now in jail for extortion, and rumor attributed the crime to the desire of the underworld to silence a possible witness to its connections with the IATSE. About the same time Browne's wife also received threats to her safety. Browne and Bioff thereupon agreed to appear before a grand jury. Browne was a reluctant witness, collapsing at the end of his brief testimony. Bioff testified with relish for nine days.

"I lied and I lied and I lied," he said of his previous claims to innocence. "I am just a low uncouth person. I'm a low type sort of man. People of my caliber don't do nice things." The jury believed what he said, and returned indictments for extortion on Nitti, Campagna, d'Andrea, Ricca, Gioe, Maritote and others. Nitti committed suicide on the day of the indictment. His lieutenants each received ten years in jail and a fine of $10,000. Campagna, Ricca and d'Andrea went to the federal penitentiary in Atlanta, Georgia. Gioe and the others joined Nick Circella in Leavenworth, Kansas. A second charge of mail fraud was not brought to trial.

Under ordinary circumstances the defendants could have hoped for parole in 1947. Given their records and the latent charge, however, the expectation was that they would serve all or most of their sentences. "It was believed," Virgil Peterson stated, ". . . that this outstanding indictment would act as a detainer which would prevent the premature release of the Capone gangsters from prison." It did not, the subsequent history of the case adding credence to the underworld's reputation of political influence and special exemption from the claims of the law.

Campagna and Ricca first asked for a transfer to Leavenworth, retaining as their lawyer Paul Dillon, a former campaign manager for the then Senator Harry Truman. Despite the objections of Leavenworth officials and the formal rejection of the request by the Federal Bureau of Prisons, both men were transferred in August, 1945. In Leavenworth the reunited gangsters received visits from attorney Eugene Bernstein and Anthony Accardo, Nitti's accepted successor. Since prison regulations limited visits to lawyers and relatives, Accardo posed as Joseph I. Bulger, a Chicago attorney.

Two initial obstacles had to be overcome: tax claims against the defendants amounting to half a million dollars, and the mail fraud indictment. The tax bill was settled by the Treasury for $126,000 with interest; the money was provided by unidentified persons who brought it in cash to Bernstein's office. Dismissal of the mail fraud indictment was more difficult, requiring the permission of the Attorney General of the United States. The prisoners selected as their attorney Maury Hughes of Texas, a long-time political associate of Attorney General Thomas Clark. Hughes apparently talked to officials in the U.S. Attorney's office in New York and to staff members of the Department of Justice, after which the indictment was dismissed.

There remained the problem of parole. The prisoners, it might have seemed, had little reason to expect generous treatment. In 1946 the Attorney General of the United States received a memorandum from the federal prosecutor in the original trial stating that the defendants were "notorious as successors to the underworld power of Al Capone. They are vicious criminals who would stop at nothing to achieve their ends. The investigation and prosecution were attended by murder, gun play, threatening of witnesses, perjury." At the appropriate time, however, Dillon went to Washington and requested parole for Campagna, Ricca, d'Andrea and Gioe. The parole board in Chicago received telephoned instructions from Washington to cable its approval of parole. The usual written report was not required; nor was the extended consultation with parole advisers, customary in such cases, undertaken. On August 13, 1947, one week after Dillon's visit to Washington, the prisoners were released.

The case prompted a congressional investigation, after which proceedings were instituted against all the parolees except d'Andrea. Campagna and Gioe went back to jail, but after legal maneuvers were permanently released. Ricca never returned to jail. Accardo and Bernstein were indicted for misrepresentation but were acquitted. All four parolees returned to racketeering.

Browne and Bioff were released after serving three years and a month of their sentences. Some IATSE locals were concerned lest the two men return to office, but the IATSE had changed its mind about them. "William Bioff is not now and never has been," the General Executive Board announced, "a member of this Alliance . . . This record which is now available to us proves that former President Browne betrayed the trust which the officers and members of the Alliance placed in him." The Board noted, however, "that one of the most clever parts of this conspiracy was so to conduct the affairs of the Alliance to make certain that the membership would be solidly behind Browne in the conduct of its affairs. The record which Browne presented to the Board was most impressive . . ." In support of its exegesis the Board citied a government brief which had been presented to the court during the appeals of the underworld accomplices of Browne and Bioff.

From the labor point of view the IATSE had created an enviable labor record in the past twenty-five years with regard to hours, wages and working conditions. As indicated below it was maintained and even improved during Browne's reign . . . Factually, the record shows that repeatedly these confederates did things to further the legitimate aims of their union in a manner utterly inconsistent with any theory that they were acting to the detriment of union members . . . Raises and union recognition were even obtained by Bioff for unions not a part of the IATSE . . . Bioff became the leader of all the unions dealing with the motion picture industry in California . . . and apparently without knowledge on the part of labor leaders in California of his illegal activities secured their adulation. Even a defense witness called to contradict portions of Bioff's testimony had to observe that Bioff did a good job for the IATSE.

"In view of such a record," the Board said, "it is not surprising that the delegates to the Convention in Louisville in 1940, voted unanimously to support Browne. It is true that at that time rumors were being circulated alleging certain illegal conduct on the part of Bioff and intimating that perhaps Browne was involved. However, as the sources of these rumors were known to be hostile to the labor movement as a whole, no recognition was given to them either by the delegates or the officers of the IA . . ." This was hardly the whole tale. There were, no doubt, extenuating circumstances surrounding the union's partial recall of the past. Progress had been substantial, if not maximal, under Browne and Bioff; in a time of schism the bonds of loyalty are strong; and the underworld embrace—

imposed from without, tolerated or encouraged by the employers, savage in reprisal and carefree of the law—was not the easiest subject for open communion. But not all the sources of rumor were hostile. Both the literature of the time and the folklore of the union were replete with alarming information. More was privately known than was publicly conceded.

The two parolees were now at large, but it was a precarious freedom. Both had violated the law of the underworld in testifying against their partners in crime. Browne, perhaps, had less to fear, since his testimony was halting and he had never been a full-fledged member of the criminal tribe. Bioff, on the other hand, was one of them, and knew well the price of betrayal.

Both men disappeared from sight. Bioff eventually settled in Phoenix, Arizona, living under the name of William Nelson. On November 4, 1955, he was blown to death by a bomb attached to the starter of his pick-up truck. The whereabouts of Browne are obscure.

The departure of Scalise and Bioff marked the end of a phenomenon. They were the first and last professional criminals ever to run an international union. But the conditions which thrust them into prominence—while the results were never again so bizarre—lingered within the labor movement and the surrounding society. The leadership of the underworld became more sophisticated and restrained in its tactics, but it never lost its grip on some sources of union power, and there were charges to come of criminal influence in high places. The activities of lesser criminals in union affairs continued, and local redoubts of corruption endured and developed. After World War II the rise of negotiated welfare funds provided, for the amateur and professional thief alike, a massive new source of plunder. The labor movement itself, grown more staid and secure, rich in resources but lacking in discipline, provided further temptations for its weaker servants. Corruption was a lasting problem, limited but persistent, sometimes stark but usually obscure in detail, easy to charge but hard to cure.

It was always, for reasons of both origin and impact, a problem as much for the nation as for the labor movement. Thus it came, from time to time, under the scrutiny of the Congress of the United States.

Part IV
The Intervention of Congress

13: The Preliminaries

"While I am on the stand," General Secretary Peter J. McGuire of the Carpenters told the Senate Committee on Education and Labor in 1885, "I may mention the fact to show how far some of the brutality has gone, that during the strike of the iron molders in Troy . . . a man named Schleicher armed the men in his employ—the men that we call 'scabs'—armed them with revolvers, and told them he would pay them fifteen dollars each for every union man that they shot . . . his action resulted in the shooting of several union men . . . Both of the men that were shot [dead] were unarmed . . ." The Committee was conducting the first major Congressional investigation of labor-management relations in the United States. It was not formally concerned with violence, but it was the first to document the tradition.

In 1898 the Congress created the United States Industrial Commission to report on relations between labor, management and agriculture in the United States. "It is a well-known fact," the Commission said, ". . . that too often labor disputes are accompanied by intimidation and violence . . . Threats and intimidation on the part of strikers sometimes give place to more overt acts . . . In some extreme and rare instances armed conflicts occur, or even secret assassinations . . . Resort to violence is especially likely to occur where employers endeavor to import considerable bodies of men from other parts of the country to take the place of the strikers . . . Men of foreign birth or negroes are frequently employed, confessedly as strikebreakers." There was also some evidence, the Commission said, "that employers had instigated violence with a view to influencing public opinion in their favor, and also in certain cases for the sake of injuring prominent labor union men, against whom they had a spite . . . the evidence was not altogether clear."

Violence and graft were among the subjects considered by the United States Commission on Industrial Relations, established by the Congress in 1912. "No testimony," the Commission said, ". . . has left a deeper impression than the evidence that there exists among the workers an almost universal conviction that they, both as individuals and as a class, are denied justice in the enactment, adjudication, and administration of law . . . that such beneficient measures as become laws are largely nullifed by the unwarranted decisions of the courts; that the laws which stand upon the statute books are not equally enforced, and that the whole machinery of government has frequently been placed at the disposal of the employers for the oppression of the workers . . ."

"The entire problem of policing industrial disputes," the Commission declared, *"grows out of the problem of the strikebreaker and the attitude of the State toward him."* * The law was on the employers' side, the courts and government officials usually holding that "the entire machinery of the State should be put behind the strikebreaker." Public institutions in almost every industrial state were placed at the service of the employers. State and local police were joined by the militia, private guards and detectives, and vigilante organizations "which usurp and exercise the functions of the police." Public authorities were guilty in many strikes of establishing "a military despotism under so-called martial law," the suspension of *habeas corpus,* wholesale arrests, mass imprisonment in bull pens, and the deportation of strikers from the state. In many cases the police power was turned over to employers "or arrogantly assumed by them." Criminals employed by detective agencies were clothed, by the process of deputization, "with arbitrary power and relieved of criminal liability for their acts." These and other private enforcers were openly partisan, broke strikes by any means, and were guilty of "endless crimes" and "wanton killings." The courts complied, often being controlled by employers "to give legal sanction to lawlessness," in general recognizing only two rights in an industrial dispute: the right of the employer to do business, and the right of the strikebreaker to work.

"Physical force," the Commission said, "may be and is used by both employers and employees . . . Such physical aggression is seldom used by employees, as they are strategically the weaker party . . . The use of force by workers is normally directed not against the person or the property of the employer, but against strikebreakers and guards." Union violence in these early days was typically of the responsive sort, directed almost exclusively at strikebreakers, and essentially non-professional. It was not always to be so.

In 1933 the Senate Committee on Commerce began an investigation of racketeering in the United States. It was concerned mainly with racketeering not involving unions, but it did conduct hearings on salary kickbacks by building tradesmen and orchestra musicians to their union officials in New York City, and heard Stephen Summer, the octogenarian leader of a

* Italics in original.

Chicago milk drivers' local, describe how, with the end of Prohibition, the gangs took a greater interest in union affairs.

A. They came to our place and they politely said, "We are coming in, and when we do you are going out." . . . They told us plainly that the milk business looked to them like a good business for their boys to engage in after prohibition. . . . I said, "All right, but I think you have come to the wrong place." . . . So in time they offered $100,000 for us to step out and them to step in. To that we told them nothing doing. Finally we said, "All right if it is a fight you want, we will give it to you." . . . It got so bad that we had to fortify our office. . . . We have prepared to take care of ourselves. We are going to do it. . . . We are not out hunting them, but if they come our way we are going to take care of ourselves, and them, too, if we can.

The Committee held further hearings in 1937, finding evidence of extortion and kickbacks in several industries, mainly by "wildcat" or racket unions. Racketeers were particularly strong in the New York poultry industry, where they charged excessive fees for delivery services, chicken coops and feed. "Domination," the Committee said, "has been enforced by a vicious system of intimidation by violence, arson and murder. Places of business have been bombed, thousands of chickens have been destroyed by gas bombs, poison, or fire; trucks have been wrecked. Gangs in high-powered cars patrolled highways and interrupted deliveries and kidnapped or killed the victims. Those who resisted or defied the leaders were broken by the ring, and persecuted by the crooked politicians protecting the rackets and obviously sharing in the spoils." The Committee blamed police corruption, weak courts, embroiled politicians, and a timid business community for what it described as "decadent social organization . . ." It was the first Senate committee to investigate and report on organized crime. Congress passed a law designed to limit kickbacks in public contracts, and another allowing the Secretary of Agriculture to require licenses of poultry dealers, but otherwise took no action.

Professional violence again engaged the attention of the Congress during the 1930's. The Senate Committee on Education and Labor, under the chairmanship of Senator Robert M. LaFollette of Wisconsin, conducted the most prolonged public inquiry on the subject ever held in the United States.

"Evidence of the use of strikebreakers and guards," the Committee reported, "is found in the records of almost every State and Federal investigation of a major industrial dispute." During the nineteenth century the strikebreaker was often recruited from the ranks of illiterates eager for work;

but in time he became a professional. "Thus by 1914," the Committee noted, "it is apparent that the strikebreaker had no status as a bona fide employee, but was simply one of an industrial mercenary army." The strikebreaker, in fact, was seldom used to maintain plant operations, if only because of his industrial incompetence, and was usually discharged at the end of a strike. The strike guard was his companion, ostensibly recruited to protect him. Both were usually employed on a regular basis by private detective agencies—among others the Pinkerton National Detective Agency, the Burns Agency, the George Williams Agency, Baldwin-Felts, the Waddell-Mahan Corporation, the Asher Detective Agency, and the Bergoff Service Bureau—specializing in such work. About one-third of all identified strikebreakers and guards, the Committee estimated conservatively, were professional criminals or had criminal records, showing "how closely the strikebreaking business approaches a gangland racket." Together they were responsible for most of the violence in industrial disputes.

Business was good. Strikebreakers were employed in a high percentage of disputes. Many employers' associations furnished strikebreakers as a normal service to their members. Industrial espionage was common, the Committee charging that the Pinkerton Agency alone "operated in practically every union in the country." "Senator," a senior officer of the Burns Agency testified, ". . . there is stools in every organization." There was also a thriving trade in industrial munitions such as baseball bats, ax handles, blackjacks, billies, steel bars, steam lines, charged wires, and "firearms of all types short of field pieces." One-half of total national gas-weapon sales went to private employers; from 1933 to 1937 Republic Steel alone bought ten times as many gas guns and twenty-six times as many gas shells and projectiles as embattled Chicago.

The Committee questioned J. F. McDade, a professional strikebreaker, on the skills of his trade.

Q. Can you tell us in a general way about the technique of strikebreaking agencies for whom you have worked?

A. If it is quiet sometimes at night some of the regular men will get out and cruise around in an automobile and hurl a piece of brick or possibly throw a piece of dynamite, or travel by in a car at fifty or sixty miles an hour and fire a few shots at some of our own guards. This is usually followed by a request for more guards . . . sometimes we have our own wrecking crew and, if two or three of the union officials were too violent and hurt some of the loyal workers, why we would go out at night, ring their door-bells and put two or three men there to beat them up and put them in hospital. That's a common occurrence on any job. The men usually employed for this work are ex-convicts, thieves, gangsters.

The Associated Industries of Cleveland supplied strikebreakers to the Statler Hotel during a strike in 1935 by the Hotel and Restaurant Employees. Paul Meggart, one of the strikebreakers, testified.

> A. Mr. Wright [the head strikebreaker] called me down . . . he gave me a drink. So there was a picket out there that was singing strike songs, some fellow from either the cooks or the waiters union. Wright says, "That Greek out there is a little bit too noisy . . . when that truck comes in, naturally those pickets are going to rush in after it, and I want you boys to go there and if you get a chance break that Greek's jaw." They did.
>
> . . .
>
> Q. Are guards usually armed on these jobs?
> A. They are . . . with whatever they can get hold of. Brass knucks or black-jacks . . . they usually have a gun.

In 1936 the International Ladies Garment Workers Union struck a number of Southern California employers for recognition. The Los Angeles Merchant and Manufacturers Association urged the employers to retain the Rodell Detective Agency and helped to obtain the assistance of the Los Angeles Police Department. Payments were evidently turned over periodically by employers to William F. Hynes, the chief of the Department's "Red Squad." No accounting of the money was ever made. Executive Secretary Nelson R. Wolfe of the Southern California Garment Manufacturers Association told the Committee that the money was provided because the employers thought "it would be the right thing to do . . . the nice thing to do . . . a nice gesture." He claimed the support of custom, citing the payment of $145,000 to police by shipowners during the 1934 West Coast waterfront strike. There was also a touch of conscience. The Los Angeles police, it seemed, worked for the employers mainly during their off-hours.

The law was weak. The first general federal law prohibiting the interstate transportation of strikebreakers was passed in 1936, but it made no provision for the regulation of strikebreaking agencies. Some states had laws against the importation of armed guards, but they too were generally ineffective. No states had laws prohibiting the use of strikebreakers or their employment agencies. Strikebreaking by violence was a national institution, a major industry, producing on occasion a response in kind.

After World War II the Congress turned once more to the problem of simple racketeering in industrial relations. In 1947 a subcommittee of the House Committee on Expenditures in the Executive Department issued a report on the Dock Street produce market in Philadelphia.

In 1947 Abraham Goldberg was president and Harry ("Turk") Daniels was financial secretary of Teamster Local 929 in Philadelphia. Both men solicited paid advertisements from employers for a labor newspaper, the *Pennsylvania Federationist;* sixty percent of the fees collected went to an independent agent, Benjamin Lapensohn, who was in the habit of giving Goldberg and Daniels Christmas presents "of generous proportions." Emerson Custis, a real estate broker, testified that he had wanted to build a new terminal market in Philadelphia; that Goldberg had said that his permission was required; that Lapensohn told him—Custis—that the matter could be settled by paying $36,000 to Goldberg and Lapensohn; but that the sum was never paid and the terminal never built.

Louis Segal, a Dock Street employee, left one job and sought another. He tried to get Goldberg's approval for the change, but Goldberg was out of the city. Segal obtained clearance from two other officials of Local 929; but when Goldberg returned he fined Segal $500—later reduced on compassionate grounds to $400—for making an unauthorized arrangement with an employer. Segal claimed he was ordered to deliver the money to Goldberg's office in used bills of five, ten and twenty dollar denominations, and never to disclose the payment.

In May, 1946, a number of railroad cars in the Philadelphia yards were immobilized in anticipation of a railroad strike. "The evidence is overwhelming," the Subcommittee found, ". . . that Goldberg issued the order for the tie-up of these cars . . . [and] attempted to extort approximately $6,000 or $100 per car from the anxious carlot receivers, claiming that amount was to be given to the railroad brotherhoods." The employers said they gave Goldberg $1,000. Goldberg claimed he received only $500, and was embarrassed because the amount was so small. The railroad unions denied receiving any money at all from Goldberg.

George L. Berry was president of the Printing Pressmen from 1907 to 1948. He was widely admired in the union and led it to unprecedented strength, but he also made money out of it while running it with an iron hand. He owned stock in the Clinchfield Hydro Electric Company, which supplied electricity to the Pressmen's Home in Tennessee; when Chicago Local 3 brought suit to end the arrangement Berry placed it in receivership. Berry also held thirty percent of the stock in the International Playing Card and Label Company, a privately owned firm which received some $893,000 in financial aid from the Pressmen; from 1932 to 1943 Berry's income from the firm was $152,420.31. The Pressmen's Board of Directors knew of the arrangement, Secretary-Treasurer William H. McHugh testifying that Berry assumed the presidency of the playing card company "to protect our interests."

In 1921 a federal court in Tennessee ordered Berry and others to return $165,000 in union funds used to develop the Clinchfield Company, but the international union forgave the debt. In 1939 Berry was given a one-year suspended sentence for federal income tax evasion; the union subsequently paid $29,930.37 in back taxes owed by Berry, although most of the money was recovered. Berry also had a farm, on which he spent $61,069.28 in union funds. The union sued his estate for the money after he died, as it sued for $69,623.22 owed by its late Secretary-Treasurer Joseph C. Orr.

Berry was an autocrat. Only one convention of the union was held between 1928 and 1948. The board of directors never met between 1941 and 1947. Berry's successor, J. H. De La Rosa, was asked about the dearth of board meetings.

Q. Were there ever any protests to Mr. Berry over the fact that there had been no board meetings?
A. Not that I know of . . . we did not have time to protest, because our minds were taken up with our work. . . . I will say this, the way Mr. Berry conducted the international union . . . it was just useless to protest to him . . . whatever matter he wanted to take up, he would send it to the board. And any matter he did not want to take up with the board, he did not take up with the board.

De La Rosa conceded in principle the need for protective legislation against autocratic presidents, noting also that members of the Pressmen could change their union's laws by secret referendum ballot.

Q. Who appoints the tellers?
A. The president.

In 1953 a Special Subcommittee of the House Committees on Government Operations and on Education and Labor investigated strikes and racketeering in the Kansas City area. Oscar R. Burden, the owner of a pipeline construction company, testified that he had paid $500 to Otto Bowles of the Laborers as a protection against featherbedding. Robert D. Sheehan, also engaged in pipeline construction, said his foreman had paid "somewhere between $400 and $500" to Nelson Price and Willard Wilkinson of Local 663 of the Laborers in Kansas City for permission to employ certain individuals as foremen, despite the fact that the labor-management agreement then in force gave the employer absolute discretion in the choice of foremen. Both Price and Wilkinson denied receiving any bribes, although they admitted receiving Christmas presents—including money—from various employers.

Later that year the Subcommittee held hearings in Michigan on the jukebox industry. Roy Clason, the business manager and president of the Michigan Automatic Phonograph Owners, was questioned.

Q. What is Local 985 of the Teamsters union?

A. . . . That is an alleged labor organization belonging to the Teamsters organization that is comprised of . . . virtually all the operators in Wayne, Oakland, and McComb counties, and their employees . . . They collect from each operator and from each employee of each operator twenty dollars dues per month.

The union and the operators ran a joint clearance system under which employers were given or refused permission to install a jukebox in any particular location. Clason suggested that employers on the "inside track" with the union could dispense with clearance, and cited the Meltone Music Company as an example.

Q. And who owns that?

A. Vincent Meli. I understand . . . a brother-in-law of William Bufalino, the head of the Teamsters Union . .

Q. Has Mr. Bufalino always been the president of [Local 985]?

A. No; prior to him was Gene James, Jimmy James.

·   ·   ·

Q. You know anything of the circumstances under which Jimmy James was replaced by Bufalino?

A. That was a mystery to everyone in the industry . . . [Bufalino] was, I believe, the president of the Bilvin Distributing Co. . . . at which time the so-called Italian Syndicate, or whatever you want to call it, went out and jumped, so to speak, about a thousand locations in Detroit. Jimmy James told the operators he was more or less on the spot with the Italian Syndicate, he had more or less to take him [Bufalino] in . . . Bufalino became more active. Eventually Jimmy said, "Well, boys, I'm going to shove off. I've got a better job in Chicago with the laundry workers union," and so he just departed.

Clason then alleged that intimidation was used to bring operators into a recently formed rival employer's organization, the Michigan Music Guild, with which Local 985 had better relations. He said that there had been eight to ten bombings, including stink-bombings, and that location owners wishing to throw out operators in favor with the Teamsters "can kind of figure that they are liable to have their windows broken or a stench-bomb or something."

The Subcommittee tried to obtain the records of Local 985. It was apparently forestalled by James Riddle Hoffa, president of Detroit Local 299 of the Teamsters, the most influential Teamster official in the Midwest, then a vice president and later the president of the international union, soon to become one of the most celebrated of all Congressional witnesses. Hoffa told the Subcommittee's representative that the local's records up to the present year had been destroyed. He testified that he had no business interest in the jukebox industry, but refused to discuss his other business activities or to say whether his wife was on the payroll of Local 985. He had an edifying exchange with an old foe, Republican Representative Clare Hoffman of Michigan.

Q. Are you a Democrat?
A. What do you think I am?
Q. I don't know. There is a gentleman who told me you were a Republican.
A. I am not. I go by the individual. I wouldn't vote for you. . . . I vote for somebody who is up-to-date.

. . .

Q. Just one question . . . are you an Italian?
A. I am not. I am Irish and Dutch.
Q. All right.
A. You don't want the truth. You would rather have it look like a syndicate.
Q. Don't worry.
A. I don't worry.

This was the end of the prelude, the last minor incursion into the matter of trade union corruption. Prior to World War II, most of the Congressional investigating committees had gone to work with other priorities in mind. The trade unions' record of violence and dishonesty seemed modest compared with that of the employers', and caused only passing concern. There was, at least during the 1930's, a strong sympathy for the labor movement and a ready suspicion of the motives of its Congressional critics. There was no sense of crisis, and the Congress was unmoved.

But the tide did turn. The postwar wave of strikes produced a new mistrust of union power and a sense of abuse. The Congressional investigations after 1946, while not always distinguished for style or judiciousness, were more deliberate in aim and disturbing in discovery. From one quarter or another the reports and rumors of malfeasance increased. Now there was a new mood. In 1953 the Congress began a major inquiry into possible misconduct in a special field: the administration of labor-management welfare funds.

14: The Welfare Funds

On April 1, 1946 the United Mine Workers of America struck the soft coal industry of the United States. Their main grievance was the refusal of the owners to finance a welfare fund. After seven weeks President Harry S Truman seized the mines. Thereafter UMWA President John L. Lewis and Secretary of the Interior James A. Krug signed an agreement providing for a welfare fund to be financed out of a royalty of five cents on each ton of coal.

The agreement was a landmark. Unions had provided welfare benefits for their members since the early nineteenth century, but only on a limited scale, seldom in the field of health, and almost never with the employer's money. The UMWA Welfare Fund—which in time provided comprehensive medical, surgical and hospital care to miners and their families—was extremely popular, and stimulated a rapid postwar growth of negotiated plans. The government helped. In 1947 the Taft-Hartley Act prescribed conditions for the joint administration of negotiated plans. In 1949 the federal courts ruled that group health insurance plans were a form of compensation and that employers affected by the Taft-Hartley Act were required to bargain about them. Negotiated plans continued to proliferate during the Korean War, once the federal Wage Stabilization Board had ruled that such benefits were not in conflict with its program. By 1954 some eleven million out of sixteen million workers covered by labor-management contracts—and a large proportion of dependents—were eligible for benefits under a negotiated welfare plan.

But there was no effective control. Federal and state insurance laws were uneven in administrative requirements and undemanding in ethical standards. The insurance industry, traditionally opposed to government intervention in its affairs, was without any viable code of conduct or disciplinary powers. The Taft-Hartley Act required audits of funds and banned improper payments by employers to union officials; but it did not require effective disclosure of welfare fund operations, prescribe any standards of operation, or define conflicts of interest. The only other federal statute applicable to negotiated welfare funds—the Internal Revenue Code—contained no provision for their supervision; violations of tax exemption rules were simply inconsistent with tax exempt status. "In seeing that the taxes levied by

150

Congress are paid," a Treasury official told a Senate subcommittee, "the Revenue Service does not seek to act as a regulatory agency."

The law was ineffective, the standards flexible, and the temptations great. Not all of the many millions of dollars now available to welfare funds were wisely or honestly spent. Most conspicuously in the field of health insurance there was avarice and theft on the part of custodians and entrepreneurs alike. In 1953 the Congress intervened.

"Information obtained," a Special Subcommittee of the House Committee on Education and Labor reported, "indicates a wide range of questionable practices by union officials, employers, insurance companies, administrators, and trustees connected with health and welfare funds. . . ." The Committee accused employers of abdicating their responsibilities as welfare fund trustees, union officials of using intimidation to dominate boards of trustees, insurance companies of levying excessive charges and acting collusively with brokers and union officials to their mutual advantage, and brokers and administrators of squandering welfare fund assets.

The Subcommittee asked Henry B. Ely, an attorney for sheetmetal contractors in the Los Angeles area, how he accounted for employer indifference to welfare fund operations.

A. I account for it in a number of ways . . . First of all, we didn't want the welfare fund . . . Second, our contractors said, in effect, the union forced it on us, we are paying it in there instead of wages, it is union money, so far as we are concerned. Let them do what they want with it.
Q. Could you tell us why you objected to this in the first place?

· · ·

A. Well, we thought it was creeping socialism.

Some employer representatives said that their lack of interest in welfare fund administration was due to union tactics: that they were forced by strikes and violence to accept welfare fund proposals or specific insurance policies which they did not want, to pay contributions for employees who were actually ineligible for benefits to accept union nominees as administrators, and to pay for insurance policies bought at above-market rates. Others said they were simply not interested in how their contributions were spent.

"The insurance industry," the Subcommittee said, "has no reason to be proud of the performance of some of the companies whose activities have come under subcommittee scrutiny. In some companies we have found a marked tendency to get business at any price." These companies made payments to union officials for good will, charged excessive retention fees, granted a high percentage of premium rebates to brokers assumed to have influence with union officials, and conspired with the latter to rig insurance bids. Brokers demanded high fees, paid commissions to helpful union officials, and cooperated with each other in the reduction of competition between insurance carriers.

Earl Liever, an insurance broker for two HRE locals in Atlantic City, received a commission of seventeen and one-half percent from the American Casualty Company, while the industry average was between three and four percent; he also shared with the company the difference between premium income and claims expenditures which most companies chose to return to policyholders as dividends. Over a period of five years the total premium income was $139,433.26. Liever's share was $24,334.31 in commissions and $13,868.35 classified in the account as dividends or refunds. The arrangement was apparently a secret.

Q. Did the trustees of the fund ever know what your arrangements were . . . ?
A. I would say not to my knowledge . . .

Some funds hired full-time administrators. The subcommittee criticized the handpicking of administrators by union officials, administrators acting as insurance consultants and brokers to their own funds, the wholesale payment of benefits to ineligible individuals, the keeping of unintelligible records, and improper payments by administrators to union officials.

Sometimes union officials acted as administrators. The Subcommittee questioned Eugene Williams, recording secretary of Teamster Local 544 in Minneapolis.

Q. Who keeps the fund's books?
A. I have three different persons working on these books; the first two were my stepdaughters. In fact, they were all my stepdaughters.

The local's pension fund had never been audited. Williams got a loan of $10,000 from the fund.

Q. Who used the money? Who used the $10,000?
A. I did.
Q. In what?
A. In a cafe and bar.

Williams had also borrowed money to buy a Cadillac from Jack Skimbo, a tavern owner. The Subcommittee said that Williams borrowed the money during a long Teamster strike against Skimbo's establishment.

Q. . . . Do you dispute that?

A. I don't dispute any of it. What the hell, if that is what your staff says it must be right.

Paul Dorfman was the secretary-treasurer of AFL Federal Local 20467, a waste material handlers' local in Chicago. He was friendly with Hoffa, and allegedly an intimate of underworld leaders in Chicago.

In 1946 Dorfman bought a sickness and accident policy for his members from Leo Perlman, head of the Union Casualty and Life Insurance Company. In 1949 Perlman persuaded Allen Dorfman, the son of Paul, to set up the Union Insurance Agency to handle Union Casualty's business. Allen Dorfman had no experience in the insurance industry, but borrowed $5,000 from his mother, Rose Dorfman, and went into business. He handled accounts principally for the Central States Conference of Teamsters, the Michigan Conference of Teamsters, and Local 1031 of the International Brotherhood of Electrical Workers in Chicago. Perlman apparently did most of the work.

Both the company and the agency prospered. Between 1948 and 1953 the gross direct premium income of the company increased from $1,-460,000 to $8,900,000 a year, while the agency received above-average commissions. In four years Rose Dorfman alone received a return of almost a quarter of a million dollars on her original investment. It later came to light that Paul Dorfman had solicited business from the Teamsters for the Union Insurance Agency, and that the welfare fund of the Michigan Conference of Teamsters—unknown to the employer trustees—owned stock in Union Casualty. Dorfman was expelled from union office by the AFL-CIO for unethical practices, principally on the ground that, in violation of the federation's rules, he had drawn salaries from both his local union and its welfare fund.

An employer trustee of the Central States Drivers Welfare Fund charged that Hoffa had been "trying to throw" business to Union Casualty, which finally obtained the fund's insurance at excessive rates. Hoffa denied any improper relationship between himself and the company, but he was asked about his private business activities.

Q. Do you have any real or personal property . . . Mr. Hoffa?

A. I have an interest in the Northwestern Oil Company, N. Dak., Bismarck.

Q. Who have other interests in that . . . ?

A. Dr. Lee Perlman and his wife, Dorfman, Hoffa . . . We each put up $10,000 . . . then we got involved in the question of Jack-O-Lantern Lodge . . . Eagle River, Wis. . . .

Q. Who was in that with you?

A. I have to tell you . . . Allen Dorfman, Rose Dorfman, Hoffa . . .

. . .

Q. Has the Union Insurance Agency itself put any money into this?

A. Yes, there is a note signed for a loan, $11,500 borrowed by Jack-O-Lantern Lodge from Union Insurance Agency . . .

"The assigned task," the Subcommittee said, "is far from completion. Because of the scope and complexity of the subject matter involved, it has been impossible, in the time available, to assemble adequate data on which legislative recommendations can be based . . ." The subcommittee recommended that further hearings be held, but there were none, and no final report was issued. However, a second, much longer, and more influential investigation was conducted by the United States Senate.

In April, 1954, the Senate authorized the Committee on Labor and Public Welfare to conduct a full-scale inquiry into welfare funds established by collective bargaining agreements. A subcommittee—briefly under the chairmanship of Senator Irving M. Ives of New York, but led for the most part by Senator Paul H. Douglas of Illinois—was assigned to the task, and conducted hearings in Philadelphia, Chicago and San Francisco. The Subcommittee on Welfare and Pension Funds, as it was known, did not publish the hearings but submitted an interim report to the Senate in January, 1955.

The Subcommittee examined twenty-nine group pension and welfare plans. It found seven of them well-managed, fourteen of them marked by "questionable practices," and six of them "grossly mismanaged," offering no conclusions about the remainder. The abuses were familiar: retention rates as high as thirty-nine percent; unilateral union control and employer indifference; the changing of welfare fund policies by brokers with a financial interest in the change; high administrative costs; poor or non-existent accounting; and low insurance benefits—amounting in one case to thirteen cents on the premium dollar—paid by insurance companies. One plan was under the exclusive control of a single union official. Some brokers simply arranged to be paid a service fee in addition to their commissions, while performing no administrative functions at all. The deliberate, premature changing of insurance carriers brought excessively large commissions to brokers and agents. Insurance companies paid high, flat commissions, far above normal levels, to brokers who controlled one welfare fund or another. The "irresponsible activities by some insurance companies, insurance agents and insurance brokers," the Subcommittee declared, "have reduced welfare fund income, drained off fund assets, and deprived employee beneficiaries of benefits they should rightly have received . . ."

Ignorance was a problem. "The average American," the Subcommittee found, "and the average union member and the average employer know little about insurance . . . Yet since 1949 thousands of union members and employers have become trustees of welfare funds . . . In making their decisions they have been handicapped frequently by lack of knowledge about insurance, particularly commission and acquisition practices in group insurance, and company underwriting customs, especially those involving retention and dividends. The Subcommittee marvels that so many of them bought so well."

The Subcommittee concluded, however, that existing state and federal laws were inadequate to regulate effectively the administration of welfare funds, and accused labor, management and the insurance industry of being "equally remiss in failing to take preventative action against abuse and mismanagement."

The Subcommittee issued its final report in April, 1956, after investigating a wide range of plans in various manufacturing and service industries. "It is not surprising," it said, "that in such an unsupervised environment . . . an unscrupulous minority has preyed upon such funds . . ." It noted that the AFL-CIO had adopted a code of ethics for the administration of welfare funds, but doubted that the objectives of the code would be quickly achieved. It accused employers of frequently abdicating their welfare fund responsibilities—although sometimes as a result of coercion—and of contributing in various ways to welfare fund maladministration, and also accused the insurance industry of involvement in most cases of wrongdoing, of opposition to the effective regulation of the industry, and of neglecting to adopt its own code of ethical behavior.

The Subcommittee came upon a very small number of plans, financed wholly by employer contributions but—contrary to the law—administered solely by union officials. One of these was the welfare fund of Local 286 of the United Automobile Workers (AFL) in Chicago.*

Local 286 was a general organization, its membership of 5,000 scattered around Chicago among some thirty-six employers in varying industries. No general membership meetings were ever held; meetings were convened according to shop or employer units; and delegate assemblies of shop stewards only rarely took place. The union leadership was very much in control, with its own special notions of stewardship.

Local 286 set up its welfare fund in 1951. The carrier was the Continental Assurance Company of Chicago, which for a time administered the fund as well. In 1952 the local assumed administrative responsibility, receiving an advance premium discount from the company for that purpose.

* Not to be confused with the United Automobile Workers headed by Walter Reuther and formerly of the CIO.

Until 1953 the employers paid their premiums directly to the insurance company; afterwards the premiums went directly to the union. The union justified the absence of a trust fund under joint management by arguing that the insurance premiums were in fact increases in dues, reflecting an identical increase in wages, and collected by the employers under a check-off system for remission to the union. In 1954 the insurance business of Local 286 was transferred to the American Continental Insurance Company of Chicago.

Angelo Inciso was the president of Local 286. He was also chairman of the board of directors of American Continental.

Q. Do you feel there was any possible conflict of interest between your operating the union and thus being the policy-holder, in effect, and also directing as the chairman of the board the active management of the insurance company?

A. It didn't interfere with my union business . . . all I did was to come in and had a right to look at their books and ask questions.

. . .

Q. You did not receive any salary for your position with the insurance company?

A. Nobody receives any salary . . .

. . .

Q. I think your son is employed at the insurance company part time?

A. Yes, he is. He goes to school and in his spare time he comes in and he fixes up the vouchers for them and files the vouchers away for them.

. . .

Q. I want to know who is running the insurance company.

A. Let's say I am.

The Subcommittee thought that Inciso's dual role was "highly irregular." It found that the welfare fund was commingled with the general funds of the local; that group policies were sold to Inciso's business acquaintances without benefit of actuarial advice; that records were incomplete and inaccurate; that a four percent administrative discount was taken from the company on Inciso's sole authority; that Local 286's legal counsel, Salvatore Oddo, received a flat two percent commission on the local's insurance policy on Inciso's orders; and that no outside audits were ever made. From 1951 to 1955 the local's general funds were enriched by $94,030.12 in insurance contributions. Some of the money was used for unusual purposes.

During 1953 and 1954, for example, Inciso spent $42,000 for "organizing," but no general accounting of expenditures was available. However, Inciso did specify some of the organizational costs, which included:

2 diamond dial watches and 2 diamond watch bands	$1,050.00
1 "gents" diamond ring	1,200.00
1 "gents" ring	1,100.00
3 cases of whisky	180.00
150 billfolds for committee and stewards	918.00
3 [money] clips	1,080.00
1 money clip	360.00
1 pen and pencil set and 2 pairs of cuff links	385.00
4 pairs of cuff links	460.00

Inciso was questioned about his largesse.

Q. What was the purpose of buying a $1,200 ring out of union funds, Mr. Inciso?

A. We have different local unions that do not belong to this local and at various times they do me favors . . .

Q. Do you get the consent of the dues-paying members for this?

A. No, because it would take me so long to get all my dues-paying members together, that before I get it done, it would be out of style.

. . .

Q. There is a disbursement of L. R. Sohn & Company, for "organizational expenses" and attached to that is a bill for "one gent's ring, $1,100."

A. Right . . . I may use the word, "organizational expense," when we are organizing a shop, where other unions help us out and we get some advice from them where we think it does a lot of good . . . It was actually a gift.

Q. These were pretty flashy rings, weren't they?

A. I get some pretty flashy information for it.

Inciso also travelled widely, seeking knowledge.

A. We talked about it with our membership, we should get into some of these foreign countries, see how they are operating . . . I went around to all these countries to find out what the living conditions were, what the working man was being paid and how he was living.

. . .

Q. What other places did you go beside the island of Curaçao and Venezuela . . . Now, can't you remember any of the countries besides Venezuela?

A. I don't recall.

. . .

Q. You must have been in a haze when you went to Vera Cruz.

A. That is the best way to go into these countries.

Q. Caracas, Venezuela, Dutch West Indies, and to Panama.

A. That is right.

Q. Do you remember Panama?
A. Not too much.
Q. And Kingston, Jamaica?
A. Right.

. . .

Q. What was the purpose of the trip to Europe?
A. I went to Europe to see how the living conditions were, and also to see how the situation was.
Q. In other words, you were conducting a—
A. Good will tour.
Q. To whom were you spreading good will?
A. Myself.

In company with his nephew, Inciso also went to Turkey, Lebanon, the French Riviera and Italy.

Q. The view of Vesuvius from Naples is very fine; isn't that right?
A. I don't know. I don't think that any of those countries are comparable with these countries here.
Q. Where besides Naples did you go?
A. I went to Rome.
Q. The Eternal City.
A. That's right.
Q. Did you see the Colosseum by moonlight . . . the Via dell'Impero from the Piazza Venezia . . . ?
A. I don't know. I didn't see any of these things.
Q. What did you see in Rome?
A. All I saw was what I thought was a lot of bad taste. Poor country.

. . .

Q. Do you really think this is a proper charge against a commingled fund which has both union dues and insurance contributions in it?
A. Well, Senator, I would say it is an appropriate bill as such. As far as the money coming from insurance or dues, that is where the difference arises here, as far as I am concerned.

Inciso was clearer on a related issue.

Q. I don't believe in reading moral lessons to other people, but I would like to ask you this: Do you think it is proper for a man who is representing low-paid workers to live on such a lavish scale when you go out?
A. Well, Senator, for one I don't believe our people are too low paid in our local union, and I fight for them to get them the best of everything, and I am sure that when I travel they should give me the best of everything.

Inciso's sentiments were endorsed by Anthony Doria, the treasurer of Local 286 and also the international secretary-treasurer of the UAW-AFL.

Q. Now . . . You have heard the testimony on Mr. Inciso's expenditures, and so forth. Do you regard these expenditures as proper, and indicating a proper sense of trusteeship and stewardship?

A. It is awful difficult for me to give you an answer: they are all attributable to organizational work generally . . . when we see an opportunity to come alive with individuals who might be influential . . . we will take them . . . It is just like other business people do . . . We learned all these things from business. We are following in their footsteps but not spending as much money, yet.

Q. Mr. Doria . . . I have been an attorney and represented business for a great number of years—in fact twenty-six—and I have never seen anything anywhere in business that even compared with the activities of this union.

A. You didn't?

Doria thought it was a matter of comparative standards.

A. It is not only done in labor. I know of a Senator who took one of these jaunts and I think they have very hazy ideas, too, of what they saw . . . again I don't agree with you because the day of the labor organization being next to the gashouse and the labor leader dressing like a turtle-necked-sweater bum used many times in caricature—that day is over . . . If the man sitting across the table from me wears a diamond ring, I think I am entitled to the same thing. I represent my people on the same level.

. . .

Q. Mr. Doria, what distresses me is that . . . you don't seem to realize that what you are doing is taking money out of the pockets of the workers . . . a sense of stewardship, a sense of trusteeship, would require a much more simple scale of living. You are not representing huge corporations. You are representing hard-pressed men . . . You can represent labor in a blue-serge suit from a nine-dollar room just as adequately, with more support from your rank and file.

A. No Senator . . . I don't think the scale is lavish. I can show you thousands and thousands of people in this country who wouldn't even stoop to this scale that we call lavish, here . . . But in labor organizations you do the same thing and it gets the spotlight of public opinion: "Is this thing right? Is this thing morally correct?"

Q. That statement is not correct, sir.

A. In what way is it wrong?

Chicago Local 52 of the Bricklayers set up a welfare fund in 1950. The employers contributed seven and a half cents an hour per employee; the employees themselves contributed another five cents an hour through a check-off system. According to the Subcommittee, there was no contractual recognition of the arrangement, no trust fund, no financial reporting, no employer participation, and no schedule of benefits. President Edward J. Gallagher of the local was the only person entitled to draw upon the fund; he alone determined the admissibility of claims and the scale of compensation. There seemed to be no record of any welfare or health insurance payments at all, but only of transfers of money from the welfare fund to three general bank accounts of the local. Over $200,000 were transferred between October, 1950, and November, 1954. The disposal of the money, once transferred, was not recorded. Much of it, in fact, had been transferred in direct cash payments to Gallagher.

Q. What disposition did you make of the cash . . . ?

. . .

A. It went for the members of our organization . . . There is many a thing that comes up in the organization that must be paid in cash . . . There was no reason for anybody to have any disposition as to who was getting the funds or otherwise, because they were given to those who were deserving of it, and in return, those that got it know it . . . I am more than liberal in giving the payments out . . . there is not a complaint in our organization by anybody.

. . .

Q. And so all of this discrepancy of these figures which amounts to $245,000, most of which was payable in cash, were dispensed by you without any control by any person . . . ?
A. Yes, sir.

. . .

Q. Can you tell me what the total in round figures was of the claims that you paid in any one of the last four years?
A. The total?
Q. Yes.
A. No, sir.

"On the basis of the evidence," the Subcommittee said, ". . . a great portion of the welfare fund and for that matter the other fund created by deductions from employees' wages went to the benefit of Mr. Gallagher." The employers were implicated. "Regardless of their contention that this fund was established at the union's insistence," the Subcommittee stated, "the fact that these employers knowingly agreed to such an arrangement without taking steps to comply with the law, or insisting on participating in a businesslike administration, renders them responsible, with the union, for the deplorable experiences which ensued."

The welfare fund of the Laundry Workers International Union was what the Subcommittee called "a good example of non-feasance on the part of trustees." The LWIU then represented some 65,000 employees in the laundry, cleaning, dyeing and associated trades. Its welfare fund, set up in 1950, was a nation-wide plan administered officially by a joint board of trustees through the LWIU Social Security Department at the union's headquarters in Indianapolis. LWIU President Samuel J. Byers was chairman of the welfare fund board of trustees. Matthew Dooley, attorney for the San Francisco Laundry Owners Association, was secretary-treasurer of the fund. The secretary-treasurer of the LWIU was Eugene C. ("Jimmy") James, late of Detroit. The broker for the fund was Louis J. Saperstein of Newark, New Jersey.

Despite the testimony of LWIU officials to the contrary, the Subcommittee found "considerable indications" that Saperstein controlled the placing of LWIU insurance, and that he gave it on a non-competitive basis to the Security Mutual Life Insurance Company of Binghamton, New York, "with ulterior purposes in mind."

It was a happy arrangement for Saperstein. Security Mutual was the carrier from April, 1950, to September, 1953, and gave Saperstein a flat ten and a half percent commission on premiums. Under a normal decremental arrangement, his total income from premiums would have been about $35,-000. In fact he received $262,507.59.

Saperstein evidently augmented this income by deceit. The California Life Insurance Company of Oakland, California, succeeded Security Mutual as the LWIU's carrier in October, 1953. Saperstein was the intermediary with both carriers from March, 1951, to April, 1954. All premiums were sent to him for remission to the insurance companies. The total premium remission was $3,948,563.09. Saperstein kept $913,885.53. He accomplished this diversion of funds by postdating the coverage of various contributing local unions, by holding on to late payments, and by reporting fewer members than those for whom he received payments. He then personally met outstanding claims, paid some of the administrative costs of the funds, and pocketed the rest of the money. The Subcommittee estimated that his net income from this source was $900,307.87. The regular internal audits of the funds did not reveal the embezzlements. Security Mutual, aided by Saperstein, conducted an audit in 1954. No discrepancies were discovered.

Saperstein apparently shared a substantial part of his illegitimate income with James. Saperstein's bookkeeper told the Subcommittee that on Saperstein's instructions she often returned between ten and twenty of the premiums "to take care of unemployment turnover."

Q. But to whom were the checks mailed?
A. Mailed to Mr. James . . . close to $10,000 or $20,000 a month.

. . .

Q. Where are these records . . . ?

. . .

A. I don't know. I assumed they had been lost or stolen. Someone had broken into the . . . office . . .

Saperstein, Myers and James invoked the Fifth Amendment. The Subcommittee claimed, however, that in 1951 James asked Security Mutual for a service fee for administering the welfare fund. The company agreed to pay $2,500 a month. Between January, 1951, and September, 1953, James received directly from this source a total of $85,000. The money disappeared.

The Subcommittee also found that the LWIU kept a bank account in Chicago, from which James was the only person allowed to make withdrawals. A total of $776,917.37 was deposited during the life of the account. Of this amount a sum of $573,269.47 tallied with checks drawn on two of Saperstein's accounts elsewhere—allegedly representing James's share of the diverted premiums; none of it ever reached the LWIU or its Social Security Department. A further sum of $92,110.96 was never accounted for.

James had another source of income, this from the welfare fund of LWIU Local 46 in Chicago. The fund was created in 1951 with James and Byers as trustees. The trust agreement provided that any dividends or surpluses would be passed on to the LWIU's Social Security Department. When the administration of Local 46's welfare fund was transferred to the international union in 1953 a sum of $26,536.97 in dividends and other resources never reached Indianapolis. Two deposits exactly equal to this amount were later traced to James's other union account in Chicago.

William J. Wilson, executive vice president and treasurer of the Greater Chicago Hotel Association, one of the contributors to Local 46's welfare fund, told the Subcommittee that as a small group the Association did not feel entitled to a trustee, and that he did not know who the incumbent trustees were.

Q. Have you people asked for a report concerning the operations?
A. We have not.
Q. Have your people participated . . . in the operation of the program?
A. No, sir.

James then claimed that he had given Wilson a complete financial report at the conclusion of the last contract negotiations, and the Subcommittee asked Wilson for confirmation.

A. He had some papers and documents we did not inspect. What they consisted of, I don't know.

In 1953 Security Mutual reduced Saperstein's commission to six percent and discontinued the $2,500 monthly payments to James, whereupon California Life became the carrier. Prior to the change, Saperstein, Byers, James, Dooley, legal counsel Jacob Friedlander of LWIU 284 in Jersey City, LWIU International Vice-President Charles Naddeo * and International Vice-President and Trustee Charles Goldstein all bought shares in California Life. They were joined by Vice-President Haines B. Wicks of Security Mutual, who left that company to become an actuary for California Life and consulting actuary for the LWIU welfare fund.

Dooley and Friedlander, in cooperation with three California Life officials, also set up the Founders Syndicate, a holding company, in Nevada. A sum of $450,000 from the LWIU welfare fund was then invested in Founders, which used the money to buy a controlling interest in California Life. The trustees of the welfare fund, without being informed that the Security Mutual policy had been cancelled or that the company had insisted upon the reduction of Saperstein's commission, then voted to transfer the welfare fund's business to California Life. After Saperstein was accused in 1954 of irregular practices in connection with another of his accounts, the Distillery Workers' welfare fund, the LWIU private stockholders in California Life surrendered their shares to the welfare fund, and Founders Syndicate was dissolved. All the individuals involved, the Subcommittee said, "placed themselves in a position to profit personally at the expense of the welfare fund . . . it was a most fortuitous circumstance that involved Saperstein in other insurance irregularities and adverse publicity in 1954 . . . [we are] inclined to attribute to that the fact that the LWIU fund suffered no greater losses. . . ." The Subcommittee laid to James and Saperstein the embezzlement of $1,008,500 in union funds.

Saperstein prospered for a while. From October, 1953, to April, 1954, the LWIU welfare fund remitted to California Life, either through Saperstein or directly, $680,237.16 in premiums. Saperstein's commission was ostensibly eight and a half percent. However, his total commission was an estimated $159,000, or about twenty-three and a half percent of premiums.

His brokerage with the LWIU was cancelled as a result of the Subcommittee's hearings. Soon afterwards he was seriously wounded in an attempt on his life, but recovered and went to jail with James for embezzlement.

James also stood trial in a Chicago federal court for income tax evasion. His defense, based on a 1946 decision of the United States Supreme Court, was that income from embezzlement was not subject to taxation. He was

---

* Naddeo was also the secretary-treasurer of an AFL–CIO federal local of can workers in Philadelphia. He was dismissed from office by the federation in 1957 for violating the AFL–CIO's Codes of Ethical Practices, particularly in financial matters.

convicted, and appealed to the Supreme Court. The Court held that thenceforward embezzled money would be taxable, but that its 1946 decision prevailed in James's case.

The Distillery, Rectifying, Wine and Allied Workers International Union negotiated a welfare fund in 1948. Called the Social Security Fund, and administered by three management and three union trustees, the plan provided benefits for some 23,000 members in sixty-five local unions. By 1955 its assets were slightly under $3,000,000. The carrier was Security Mutual, the broker was Saperstein. He had been introduced to Distillery Workers' Secretary-Treasurer Sol Cilento by Joseph ("Doc Rosen") Stacher, a convicted gambler and an associate of New Jersey racketeer Abner ("Longy") Zwillman.

In 1954 Cilento and Saperstein were tried for diverting some $540,000 in premium income from the Social Security Fund. Saperstein was convicted and went to jail. The charges against Cilento and two associates were dismissed on a technicality. When the Subcommittee investigated the Distillery Workers in 1955, Cilento had already resigned as secretary-treasurer of the union and trustee of the welfare fund, but he was still executive vice president of the union's large Local 2 in New York City. He was succeeded as trustee by Mortimer Brandenburg, the president of Local 2. The manager of the fund was Melvin Dykes, Cilento's nephew by marriage, who had been appointed in 1950 without previous insurance experience. The fund also employed two sons of Joseph D. O'Neill, president of the international union.

No dividends had been paid during the life of the Security Mutual policy. However, the company paid Cilento some $107,000 in administrative fees at the rate of $2,500 a month—the same rate of payments that it made to James. Security Mutual cancelled payments to both men simultaneously. At the end of 1955, evidently under pressure from the trustees, the company declared a dividend of $500,000. Van Schaick, chairman of the governing board of Security Mutual, personally thanked the Subcommittee for helping the company to start "on the cleanup road."

The Subcommittee estimated that Saperstein received some $900,000 in flat ten percent commissions between 1951 and 1952, kicking back about $290,000 to Cilento and others. Dykes told the Subcommittee that neither he nor the trustees were aware of Saperstein's commissions. Victor Feingold, legal counsel for both Local 2 and the international union, testified that to his amazement Security Mutual never discussed retentions, commissions or dividends with the trustees. "It is not too amazing," Senator Paul H. Douglas, Subcommittee chairman, told him. "If you had been here a couple of days ago you would have heard an insurance company testify that they didn't pay . . . dividends . . . unless there was a certain demand, and the old expression that the squeaking wheel gets the grease was used."

Harry Epstein was a broker in New Jersey. One of his clients was Local 306 of the Retail, Wholesale and Department Store Union, for which he obtained a health insurance policy from the Washington National Insurance Company in 1953. Epstein received a twenty percent commission from the local for the first year, and arranged for an annual five percent commission on renewals of the policy. He also received a contingent commission of ten percent of dividends, evidently in return for administrative duties. Torsion Balance Company, the employer involved, was unaware of the latter arrangement.

An additional administration fee of five percent of premiums was paid by Washington National, initially to one James Grafagnino, thereafter to RWDSU International Representative Dominic Tripode. Tripode had joined in Local 306's request for a change in carrier to Washington National. Grafagnino was unknown to the employer, and did not seem to perform any welfare fund duties. He was, however, Tripode's son-in-law and a former official of Local 306 before it affiliated with the RWDSU.

Tripode received administration fees from the welfare funds of nine local unions of the RWDSU. He claimed he spent considerable time helping the members of Local 306—many of whom apparently were illiterate—to process their claims on the welfare fund. The arrangement was personal, not part of his official duties for the international union.

Q. . . . Does the international president know you are getting a bonus for doing this other work?
A. I don't think so.
Q. Do the people in your union know you are getting this?
A. No, sir.

. . .

Q. I want to ask you this: how did you get in on this five percent in the first place? Whom did you talk with?
A. Mr. Epstein.

"True," the Subcommittee said, "the employees at Torsion Balance received the benefits guaranteed them in the contract, and the company as policyholder received some dividends. Nevertheless, sizeable proportions of the premiums were made away with without the knowledge or authorization of either the insured or the beneficiaries and paid to the broker. The situation is even worse in that the broker completely and deliberately con-

cealed such arrangements from the employer policyholder and the beneficiaries. The insurance company, in accepting verbal assurance from the
broker, took no steps to verify that the arrangements had actually been approved by the policyholder . . .''

The abuse most frequently uncovered by the Subcommittee was the
collection by insurance companies of high retention fees and the payment
by them of excessive commissions to brokers. The Subcommittee conducted field investigations of various companies suspected of such practices. One of these was the Continental Assurance Company of Chicago.

"There is strong indication," the Subcommittee noted, "that the Company's own home office, branch office and field representative organizations
do a substantial amount of the work necessary to obtain, install, service
and hold a case." Nevertheless, between 1951 and 1953 the company paid
out $208,000 in bonuses—in addition to regular commissions and fees—ev-
idently as administration fees. In some cases administration fees were paid
to both agents and policyholders, although the amount of administrative
work done by either was, in the Subcommittee's opinion, "subject to question."

The C. J. Simons Corporation was a general agent for Continental Assurance. "The Simons case," the Subcommittee declared, "is replete with instances in which the accumulations of payments such as those cited above
found their way to individuals who had no part in the administration of
welfare funds, but who were paid administration fees; to individuals without insurance broker's licenses, who had no part in 'selling' the insurance
but who were paid commissions; and to individuals with broker's licenses
who did no selling, furnished an occasional lead, but received commissions.
The amounts paid, in some instances, amounted to as much as $40,000."

The confessed purpose of such payments was to retain business. William
H. Croland of C. J. Simons conceded that he had withheld $164,000 in re-
fundable premiums, retaining none for his personal use by paying it out in
"administrative" fees. Large sums were paid to individuals who had no
part in the writing of insurance policies. Some were licensed, but others
were not. One was a plumber, one was an attorney, one was a municipal
judge, and two were union officials. The latter payments were made at the
behest of an employer representative.

Q. So . . . you know that in effect you were making a pay-off for the business,
didn't you?

A. . . . mine was not to question, mine was just to pay.

·   ·   ·

Q. Did you ever inquire as to what services these people were performing?

A. No, sir . . . after three years, I became convinced that something was wrong, but I didn't know what.

The Department of Banking and Insurance of the State of New Jersey was informed of the activities of the C. J. Simons Corporation, but apparently took no action.

The Washington National Insurance Company, the Subcommittee said, "had commission arrangements . . . which were decidedly out of the ordinary." Harry Epstein, and Dash and Love of Philadelphia, were the brokers involved. Both firms received additional commissions which were deducted from dividends or bonuses normally paid to policy holders. From 1951 to 1955 Epstein's income from additional commissions was $61,151.46, or 12 percent of premiums; over a period of three years Dash and Love received $65,008.84, or 13.5 percent of premiums. The insurance company said that the special fees were for administrative duties normally performed by itself, but reported the fees as expenses and contingency reserves rather than as additional commissions.

Epstein, in each case for which he was the broker, designated a union official who was to receive an administration fee of five percent of premiums; the premium rate was increased to absorb the cost. The company made no attempt to verify whether any administrative duties were performed. It was, however, more careful of other costs. It agreed to contribute to souvenir publications of three locals of the Hotel and Restaurant Employees, the Bakers, and the Shoe Workers, but deducted the cost from bonus payments to the welfare funds of the unions involved.

Standards were flexible. A policy written by Continental Casualty through Dash and Love for Local 195 of the Meat Cutters in Philadelphia levied a retention of 27.5 percent of premiums; despite a favorable claims experience, the local cancelled the policy, whereupon Dash and Love obtained a series of eight policies from Washington Life which paid between 60 and 80 percent of premiums in commissions; the local did not know of the commission arrangements, nor was it ever given any information on policy experience by Dash and Love. The Eastern Casualty Company wrote a policy for HRE Local 1115 in New York City, the average gross retention on which was 51.7 percent of premiums; on a policy it wrote for New York Teamster Local 816 the retention varied between 17.8 and 38.7 percent over a period of four years, while no dividends were paid nor accounting made; on a policy issued to New York Local 318 of the Pulp, Sulphite and Paper Workers, the company charged a gross retention rate of 65 percent in 1952 and 53.5 percent in 1953 and paid no dividends.

Nor was protection available. "There is no adequate legislation at either the Federal or State level," the Subcommittee reported, "to safeguard these welfare and pension funds or the rights of the employee-beneficiaries . . . a Federal disclosure act would bring a great measure of order to the operation of private employee welfare and pension plans . . . It cannot be assumed that the States will act uniformly or speedily, or that the problem can be met on a piecemeal basis." The Congress acted, passing the Welfare and Pension Plans Disclosure Act. The new law went into effect on January 1, 1959.

Meanwhile there had begun a routine investigation by the Permanent Subcommittee on Investigations of the Senate Committee on Government Operations of the procurement of textiles and uniforms by the armed services. The inquiry found "collusion between certain dishonest management and union officials that had the effect of increasing the cost to the government of goods and commodities it purchased and the supplying of inferior quality." The investigation continued, exploring unexpected byways.

In 1952 the International Chemical Workers Union revoked the charter of New York Local 496 because of alleged extortionary activities by officers of the local, and it then became Local 227 of the UAW-AFL. The Subcommittee charged the local's officers with forging checks, deceiving the members and making false statements to government authorities. One of the organizers for the local, and evidently its *eminence grise,* was New York gangster Johnny Dio. The Subcommittee questioned a former office employee of the local.

Q. Is it true that Johnny Dio had this charter granted to the local?
A. Yes.

. . .

Q. During 1954, Mr. Dio withdrew from the union . . . Did the union officials . . . keep in touch with Mr. Dio?
A. Well, it was more or less, I think, Mr. Dio kept in touch with them, I think.

. . .

Q. After Mr. Dio left the position of organizer, was there any money sent to Mr. Dio?
A. I think so . . .

. . .

Q. Did you not make a remark after the acid was thrown in [Victor] Reisel's eyes, regarding the kind of conversation you had heard in the office?
A. Well, I commented to my husband that in some way it could have been connected, but I wasn't positively sure.

. . .

Q. Are you under any fear at the moment or any apprehension for your personal safety?

A. Yes.

In 1955, Local 227 became Local 284 of the Teamsters, most of the original officers of Local 496 continuing their voyage. Five of them refused to testify before the Subcommittee.

Interest then turned to the Teamsters in general. Teamsters President Dave Beck refused to appear before the Subcommittee. Other Teamster officials declined to testify when they were subpoenaed.

By now the Subcommittee had come to suspect a scale of wrongdoing much larger than it had imagined at the outset. Its custodian was a determined man. "I anticipate that there will be further proceedings," said Chairman John L. McClellan of Arkansas.

There were indeed. In 1957 the Senate established a Select Committee on Improper Activities in the Labor or Management Field. McClellan became its chairman.* For three years the Committee presided over the most exhaustive and damaging examination of American trade union behavior ever conducted.

---

* The Committee came to be known informally as the McClellan Committee. Its original members were McClellan (Democrat, Arkansas), Irving M. Ives (Republican, New York), John F. Kennedy (Democrat, Massachusetts), Joseph R. McCarthy (Republican, Wisconsin), Sam J. Ervin (Democrat, North Carolina), Karl E. Mundt (Republican, South Dakota), Pat McNamara (Democrat, Michigan), and Barry Goldwater (Republican, Arizona). McCarthy soon died and was replaced by Republican Carl T. Curtis of Nebraska. McNamara resigned in 1958 in protest against what he thought were the labor-baiting tactics of the Republican members of the Committee, and was replaced by Democrat Frank Church of Idaho. Ives resigned because of ill health in late 1958 and was replaced by Republican Homer T. Capehart of Indiana. The chief counsel for the Committee during its entire tenure was Robert F. Kennedy.

15: The Butchers, the Bakers and the Entrepreneur

The Butchers

The Great Atlantic and Pacific Tea Company (A & P) is the largest private retail organization in the world. Until the 1950's it was unreceptive to the notion of collective bargaining, resisting all attempts to organize the meat cutters and retail clerks it employed, compiling a lengthy record of unfair labor practices in the process.* In particular, it always refused to bargain with a union which had not won representational rights through an election conducted by the National Labor Relations Board.

In 1952, however, after a series of unsuccessful organizing drives put on by the AFL Retail Clerks and the CIO Retail, Wholesale and Department Store Union, the eastern division of the A & P reversed its policy and recognized—without an NLRB election and after a dubious card count—the AFL Amalgamated Meat Cutters and Butcher Workmen as the exclusive representative of its meat cutters and retail clerks. It then brought pressure on its employees to join the Meat Cutters, and signed a substandard agreement with the union which was never discussed or ratified by the employees. It also reached a secret understanding with the union to retain the forty-five-hour week, although both the Retail Clerks and the RWDSU had won the forty-hour week elsewhere and had demanded it of the A & P. The retention of the forty-five-hour week saved the company, by its own reckoning, anywhere from $2,000,000 to $10,000,000 a year. The chief negotiator for the Meat Cutters was Max Block.

Block was president of New York Local 342 of the Meat Cutters and president of the Butchers District Council of New York and New Jersey. The A & P negotiations brought him a vice presidency of the international union. In 1953, when his brother Louis resigned from the presidency of New York Local 640, Max Block took his place while retaining his previous post. Louis Block became the administrator of the locals' welfare funds and the Labor Health Institute supported by them.

The Block family was prosperous. Mrs. Max Block and other members

* The federal labor law proscribes as "unfair" and enjoins a number of acts—such as intimidation and coercion—which interfere with the rights of employers, employees and unions under that law.

of the family owned the Black Angus restaurant in New York, retaining Max Block on the payroll for some years. Union staff and automobiles were used on restaurant business. Bohack, a major Long Island grocery chain under contract to the Meat Cutters, sold meat supplies directly from its warehouse to the Black Angus—a concession not granted to any other restaurant. Local union funds were invested without the sanction of the membership in the *Trade Union Courier,* a publication condemned by the labor movement in general as a racket and which evidently bought $15,000 worth of its own bonds for the Block family. Louis Block gave welfare fund business to one Max Singer, who reciprocated with a gift of $5,000, later becoming a business agent for Local 640 and forming an insurance company with Max Block's brother-in-law Harold Lippel. The Block brothers, Lippel and another union official spent more than $95,000 in union funds on annuities for themselves; union members were not informed of the investment, and records were falsified to show their approval. Max Block used most of the insurance on a union-owned car wrecked by his son to buy stocks in Food Fair, a grocery under contract to the union; the remainder of the insurance was deposited in his wife's bank account, although Block claimed to have replaced the car. Another union-bought car became the property of a business owned by the Blocks.

Max Block received free preferential rights to buy 4,800 stocks and debentures worth $3,600 from Louis Stein, the president of Food Fair. "Block," the Committee said, "received the rights as a gift." In all, Block's total investment of $14,000 in Food Fair stocks and bonds brought him $24,000; the $14,000 came from Local 640 as an "advance on salary." Block's payments were made over to Nathan Math, the attorney for Food Fair with whom Block negotiated on behalf of the union.

Max Block also asked the industrial relations representatives of various companies under contract to the union—including the A & P, Bohack, Grand Union and Food Fair—to develop business for the paper products firm of his son-in-law Martin Zeitler. Food Fair gave Zeitler $500,000 worth of orders over a period of two to three years; a labor-management contract negotiated between the Meat Cutters and the grocery chain during this period gave Zeitler a two-year grace period on pension contributions not accorded to any other firms at that time. The insurer, Connecticut General Life, was not required to honor the claims of Meat Cutters' members for the period involved.

The financial affairs of the two locals were less than exemplary. During 1955 and 1956 Max Block received $26,705 in expenses for which no accounting was made. He spent, without union authorization, $500 on a wedding present for his daughter and $500 on Israeli bonds for Nathan Math.

He billed the joint Teamsters-Butchers Organizing Committee for $10,-013.19 in connection with a strike estimated by a former officer of Local 640 to have cost no more than $2,500. He also spent $9,372.65 on four' trips to Florida for his wife and himself. On one three-week trip he spent $4,402.52. He said he went on business, although he admitted to some relaxation.

> Q. You got $2,607 from the international as advances to go, and another $1,007 from Local 342, and then above and beyond that your hotel rooms, pool, the solarium, the masseur-oil boy and the cabana were all charged to the union. Do you have any comment on that . . . ?
>
> A. In most cases this was business trips. In all the cases. I say I have had a little pleasure with it for a few days.
>
> Q. You must have had a good deal of pleasure on that last one.
>
> A. Very little . . . you don't have pleasure with money . . . I have more pleasure when I don't spend money.
>
> Q. You were able to fight it off this time . . . you spent over $4,000; it is around $165 a day.
>
> A. I must have been—you know.

The Block brothers were the main owners of a combined country club and real estate venture in Connecticut. A number of employers under contract to the Block locals—principally the Breslau Packing and Unloading Company, and Daitch-Crystal Dairies—were exempted from pension fund payments in return for investments in the country club; some of the Breslau employees were also allowed to remain non-union. Connecticut General Life, the sole insurer for Locals 342 and 640, invested $350,000 in a first mortgage on the club. The Meat Cutters' international office lent $25,000. Patrick E. Gorman, the international secretary-treasurer of the union, was asked about the loan.

> Q. How many country clubs has your union invested in?
>
> A. None.
>
> Q. That is the only country club?
>
> A. Yes . . . as Max told me, it was running down a little bit, and they needed some money to make repairs.
>
> • • •
>
> Q. Did you take it up with the board prior to the time that you made the loan? . . . Under your constitution, you must have the approval of the executive board . . . Did the executive board know that you were making this loan?
>
> A. No, not at the time; they all know it now.

Gorman was the guest of honor at a testimonial dinner in 1955 sponsored by Locals 342 and 640. The formal purpose of the dinner was to raise money for Israeli bonds. Gorman received a gift of $15,000 from one of the locals but returned it. The dinner realized a surplus of at least $25,-000. What Israel got was not made clear, but William Casale and Harold Lippel, the secretary-treasurers of the two locals, received $5,000 each from Max Block for their help in organizing the affair. Block was asked about Casale's honorarium.

Q. Why did you give him $5,000?
A. Well, what else are you going to do with the money? . . . I mean I would really like your opinion, if you have one.

Claude Hausserman of the Van Ilderstine Company was another investor in the country club. Daniel Beatson, a former business agent for Locals 342 and 640, commented on Block's negotiations with the company.

A. The contract was up on February 17, and the negotiations were dragging out through the summer . . . the agreement was this, that they would sign a contract, predated to February 17 . . . but the following year, on February 17, they would drag out the negotiations and get an arbitrator who would make an award around November of 1957 because the industry was unable to pay the money, the back pay, to February 17 . . . I told them I was sickened by it, and it was going to throw the membership into a turmoil, because they had rotten deals in the past, and this was the topper . . . I uncovered many shady deals, employers without contracts . . . I was taken off the job or they found something very busy for me to do someplace else and at a great distance away from where these deals were going on.

Democracy in Local 342, according to Beatson, was a perfunctory affair. No notices of union elections were sent out to members. The announcement of one meeting where an election was to be held simply stated that the agenda would consist of "new business, old business, and a financial report." Many members did not hear of the meeting until it was over. Nonetheless, the election took place.

Q. Did everybody have ample opportunity to nominate opposition?
A. No, there was none. It was open and close . . . The nominations were opened and somebody quickly stood up and made a motion that all incumbent officers be elected for another four years. Mr. Block closed the nomination and said, "All in favor, 'Aye,'" and they said "Aye," and didn't bother to ask who was against it . . .

Beatson said that in his experience vouchers were never verified, that local union checks were often signed in blank, that minutes were written of meetings that were never held, and that financial statements required by law were never made available to members. He was also familiar with Block's daily habits, having been his bodyguard for a while.

Q. Did he spend a great deal of time at the office . . . ?

A. Well, . . . he went to the office on occasions, during the racing seasons he would get up about eleven, drive out to the track, and go from the track to the Black Angus, and be at the Black Angus until maybe one or two o'clock in the morning and then he would go home again.

· · ·

Q. What about the union?

A. That was done mostly by telephone; there were many times we would go from the track to the office. A few times I remember we even skipped going to the track.

· · ·

Q. Did he have very high expenses . . . was he spending a lot of money on behalf of the union?

A. Not on behalf of the union; no.

Q. Was he spending large sums of money?

A. Yes . . . At the track.

Q. When you talk of large sums, how much are you speaking of?

A. Daily? Between $1,500 to $2,500.

The Committee concluded that Max Block and his relatives treated Locals 342 and 640 "as their own personal property and engaged in unconscionable exploitation of the rank-and-file union members . . . The testimony established that they milked the treasuries of more than $241,000 in salaries and expenses for the three-year period 1955–57 alone, and that they manipulated another $293,000 in questionable items in the same period, of which $11,000 was directly chargeable to the Block family."

Shortly after the hearings Max Block was summoned to the international union headquarters, where he submitted his resignation. Louis Block left his welfare fund jobs. Lippel, Casale and Singer resigned. The two Block locals were put into trusteeship. "The Amalgamated Meat Cutters . . . ," the Committee stated, "has enjoyed the reputation of being an honorable and responsible labor organization for many years . . . The Committee applauds the prompt action of the international union to remedy the shocking conditions that were exposed."

The Bakers

"A cardinal principle of our way of life," declared the Committee, "holds that men in positions of responsibility be strictly accountable for their stewardships."

It had investigated the Bakery and Confectionery Workers International

Union of America, a 160,000-member organization involved in the manufacture, shipping and sale of bakery products. The union was founded in 1886, and for virtually all of its life—under a leadership of predominantly German social-democratic lineage—had enjoyed a reputation for financial probity and democratic government. Now it had evidently fallen on poorer days.

James G. Cross became president of the Bakers in 1952 upon the elevation of William F. Schnitzler to the secretary-treasurership of the AFL. At the union's 1956 convention Cross made a number of constitutional changes which greatly enhanced his personal authority. The election of international union officers by secret referendum ballot of the membership—described at the convention as "an outmoded and outdated procedure . . . a definite waste of the membership funds"—was abandoned for an open ballot election by convention delegates. The convention committee which controlled the order of business, delegate credentials, auditing rules and other matters, once appointed by the president with the assent of the executive board, was now appointed by Cross alone. The practice of publishing the names of delegates in the union journal ahead of the convention—permitting the challenge of delegate credentials—was dropped.

The convention also transferred its right to set the salaries of the union's chief officers to the union's executive board; the board, as it happened, was composed of eighteen vice presidents, thirteen of whom were salaried international union representatives appointed at the pleasure of the president. Cross was also given the power to select and remove all international union representatives without the previously required consent of the executive board. The traditional detailed quarterly financial report to all local unions was dropped in favor of a bi-annual summary report. Checks once prepared by the secretary-treasurer for countersigning by the president were now to be prepared "at the direction" of the president. The power of the executive board to approve the banks in which union money was deposited was transferred to the president.

One of the dissidents at the convention was Joseph G. Kane, president of New York Local 525. He showed the McClellan Committee an article written by Cross for the union's journal in 1952. "Our organization," Cross had declared, "retains the basis of pure democracy, even more so than that of the Nation itself. We vote directly for the candidates, where in the Nation we vote for electors . . ." Kane was questioned.

Q. Tell me this. You were at the convention in San Francisco . . . Was there an altercation out there?

A. Yes; yes, sir, there was trouble. President Cross . . . came to my room in the Olympic Hotel . . . accompanied by [Vice President] George Stuart and Frank Gardone . . . and Frank Mykalo . . . Cross decided to give me a working over, which he did . . . He left the room with the other two. George Stuart, as I was dressing, put the gun in my back and told me to move . . .

Kane charged that other officials were also beaten up in their hotels. A San Francisco grand jury investigated the matter. It took no further action, but concluded that while the allegations of beatings were somewhat exaggerated, the case was "rampant with perjury"; and that Cross, contrary to his testimony, was in Kane's room "when the argument and alleged beating took place."

One of Cross's allies was International Vice-President Max Kralstein of New York. In June, 1956, Kralstein's friends in the union gave him a banquet, at which he received a gift of $57,818.94. Some of the money was raised by soliciting paid advertisements from employers for a union souvenir journal. The Committee questioned Joseph Kramer, a Manhattan employer who had had his problems with the union.

A. Mr. Hart [a union representative] approached me in the bakery shop and he was very nice, and he did not threaten me in any way, and he said, "We are having a dinner for Mr. Kralstein. I said, "Who is Mr. Kralstein; I never heard of Mr. Kralstein." He said, "Well, he is with us and he did a good job by merging the union, and we want to give him a dinner." "Well," I said, "that is all right, but I am not interested in that." He said, "Well, look, do you want to give us an ad, about $50?" And I said, "I will give you $25," and he said, "Well, no, $50 is the minimum" . . . and I gave him a check for $100. I said, "The reason I give you $100 is that I feel if I don't give you anything, I am afraid something would happen again . . . ," and he said, "Oh, no, whether you give anything or not, that doesn't make any difference . . . nothing will happen to you." But I personally was afraid that it might happen because I had a rough time with the union, with disagreements.

Kramer's advertisement in the journal, which he had no hand in composing, said "Best wishes to Max, whom we love and respect."

In Chicago, George Stuart was the trustee of Locals 100 and 300, which contributed $10,500 to an organizing drive in 1955 against the Salerno Biscuit Company, the largest cookie manufacturer in the Chicago area. Because of the failure of previous campaigns, this was planned to be a quiet one, and in fact was quite subdued. No reports were made to contributing locals on the expenditure of campaign funds. George Salerno, the president of the company, stated in affidavit that he was completely unaware of any attempt to organize his plant. Stuart's own reports to the international union made no reference to the campaign. The $10,500 was deposited in a special account and used at his discretion. Only $3,750 remained at the time of the Committee's investigation.

Again in 1955, Local 100 appropriated $13,100.18 for another organizing drive, but the money was used to buy Cadillacs for Cross and Stuart. Shortly afterwards more union money was used to buy a second Cadillac for Stuart, who then traded it in for a Corvette and pocketed the difference in price; it was his fourth union-bought car in less than two years. A check for $3,500 to be drawn on union funds was made out to him in 1955; the ostensible purpose of the check was to cancel an attorney's contract; according to other testimony no such contract existed. Stuart also promised Gilbert Mann, a former president of Local 100, that the union would take over the mortgage on Mann's house at a reduced rate; the monthly payments of fifty dollars—out of Mann's total monthly income of $98.50 —were paid into Stuart's personal savings account. Union funds were also used to buy Stuart an air-conditioner, a bed, jewelry, clothing, camera equipment and a high-fidelity phonograph. Stuart refused to testify before the Committee.

In 1955 Stuart fired two international union representatives who were working with Local 37 in Los Angeles on an organizing campaign against Van de Kamp's bakery, and suggested to the trustees of the local that they hire Kay Lower—a woman with a record of arrests for grand theft and prostitution—as their replacement. Cross told the Senate Committee that Miss Lower had obtained the names of thirty Van de Kamp employees for the union, justifying the $1,000 she was paid for her services. Miss Lower was less sure of her achievements.

Q. How many times have you been to [Van de Kamp's bakery] . . . ?
A. I can't remember.
Q. Once?
A. Perhaps.
Q. Twice?
A. Maybe . . . [an employee at] Van de Kamp's is a very good friend of mine.

. . .

Q. Did you get names of people from him . . . ?
A. Yes, I got names from him.

. . .

Q. We find that you attended quite a number of the bakers' conventions. What were you doing there?
A. I refuse to answer on the grounds that my testimony may incriminate me.
Q. For instance, on March 5, 1956, you were with the bakers down in Miami Beach.

. . .

A. I was there once with a girl friend on vacation.
Q. Were you there any other time?
A. Yes.
Q. With whom?
A. I refuse to answer on the grounds it might—you know.

Testimony was more conclusive on another matter. In 1948 Cross obtained a $16,000 mortgage on his Chicago home from the H. F. Philipsborn Mortgage Company; the firm was owned by the brother of Martin Philipsborn, Jr., a major figure in Zion Industries, Inc., a company which had contractual relations with the Bakers. Subsequently Cross borrowed $96,700 directly from Martin Philipsborn to buy two houses, one in Washington and the other in Florida.

In September, 1956, Local 1 of the Bakers in Chicago was granted strike sanction by Cross against Zion Industries. Cross then rescinded permission to stike and asked the local to accept a substandard contract for an extended period. The contract was never signed, the onset of the Committee's investigation being followed by new negotiations resulting in an improved agreement. Cross told the Committee he had advocated the adoption of the substandard contract after Philipsborn had agreed to allow the organization of his open shop candy plant; the agreement was made two months after Cross had borrowed $40,000 from Philipsborn. Cross testified that a contract with the candy plant had been signed for a number of months. Both John Klansek, an international representative for the Bakers, and Robert F. Kennedy, Committee Counsel, stated that they knew of no such contract.

Some weeks before the Committee's hearings on the Bakers, Secretary-Treasurer Curtis Sims filed charges with the union against Cross and Stuart, accusing them of maintaining improper relations with the employers and using the union for personal financial gain. The Bakers' hearing board cleared both Cross and Stuart, then suspended Sims from office for preferring charges in bad faith, resorting to the press on an internal union matter, and causing the hearing board the unnecessary expense of a special meeting. The letter informing Sims of his suspension was apparently typed the day before charges were preferred against him. Herman Cooper, the counsel for the union, conceded before the Committee that he had prepared in advance of the trial a letter assuming Sims' suspension, but none for another outcome. Senator Ervin recited to Cooper an old verse.

> I oft have heard of Lidford's law
> How in the morn they hang and draw
> And sit in judgement after.

The Committee described Cooper's act as "a shameful breach of the honorable traditions of the American legal profession." It also charged Stuart and Kralstein with enriching themselves by dubious means, and accused Cross of secretly conniving with the management to impose and extend a substandard contract, falsifying his expense accounts, spending union funds for his own pleasure, casting ignominy on the union by hiring a prostitute as an organizer, suppressing dissent in the union by violence, and perverting the democratic traditions of the Bakers. Retribution was not far away.

The Entrepreneur

Nathan Shefferman was a labor relations consultant in Chicago. He founded his firm, Labor Relations Associates, Inc., in 1939. Sears, Roebuck, for whom Shefferman worked at the time, provided the original working capital and most of Shefferman's early business; but by 1954 Shefferman had a nation-wide clientele of 400 individuals or organizations, branch offices in New York and Detroit, a staff of thirty-five, and had over the preceding seven years earned a gross income of $2,500,000.

Shefferman was a "union-buster." For a fee from employers he conducted "morale" surveys under one guise or another to assess employee attitudes toward unions; set up employee committees and encouraged antiemployer criticism within them to uncover pro-union employees; established "anti-union" committees in shops subjected to union organizing campaigns; and drove out established unions or supplanted them—sometimes with the cooperation of competitive union leaders—with company-oriented organizations. Some of his activities, according to the testimony of Raymond J. Compton, then the chief legal assistant to the chairman of the National Labor Relations Board, were probably illegal.

Shefferman was not averse to pitting one union against another. In 1955 the Packinghouse Workers attempted to organize the Morton Frozen Food Company in Webster, Iowa. The campaign failed in part because of the formation, with Shefferman's assistance, of an anti-union employees' committee. Within a year the company became a division of the Continental Baking Company of New York, which was under contract to the Bakers. Shortly afterwards the Bakers organized Morton Frozen Food, apparently with the approval of the employer and the assistance of Shefferman. The contract was drawn up in Shefferman's office; no union representatives were present. Vice-President Stuart of the Bakers later signed the contract, insisting on only minor modifications. Merle Smith, a field organizer for the Bakers, testified.

Q. That is what is generally termed a "sweetheart" contract, is it not?

A. That is right . . . Shefferman called me at home on November 23 or 24, and right before Thanksgiving and he was trying to give me heck because I hadn't elected all his officers on the list, and I had elected anti-company officers . . . I asked Mr. Stuart about it and he said to go along as far as possible with the list, but that he didn't think Shefferman was supposed to pick the officers . . .

. . .

Q. What was your reaction when you did read the contract?

A. It was one of disgust, disappointment . . . I was almost ready to blow my top . . .

The contract provided for a basic wage of $1.14 an hour, or only fourteen cents above the federal minimum wage; gave the company a free hand on wage increases; and left the "administration, modification or discontinuance" of the wage incentive system to the discretion of the company. The contract was not discussed with the membership of the union, nor submitted to them for ratification. Cross admitted to discussing the contract with the company, but denied any dealings with Shefferman. Stuart invoked the Fifth Amendment.

Shefferman had a special relationship with Dave Beck of the Teamsters. During their friendship Beck was at one time or another chairman of the Western Conference of Teamsters, executive vice president of the union, and international president. "A source of a great deal of Shefferman's power," the Committee found, "was his close association with Dave Beck. . . . The relationship was mutually profitable. Beck on a number of occasions received cash gifts from Shefferman. Beck's son was involved in a profitable business transaction with Shefferman's son. In addition, the Chicago labor consultant was used by Beck as a conduit through which he funnelled $85,000 of teamster union funds for the payment of his personal bills. Shefferman, on the other hand, was able to sell to employers his friendship with Beck and was able to rely on Beck's teamsters for effective resistance in efforts to defeat union organizing drives. While Shefferman was exuding soothing platitudes in speeches at union conventions, and while he was in almost daily telephonic communication with Beck, his large staff of agents, many operating under aliases, mounted vicious anti-union drives in all parts of the country."

The personal items that Shefferman bought for Beck with union money included a radio, golf equipment, sheets and pillow cases, football game tickets, nylon stockings, diapers, shorts, outboard motors, binoculars, furniture, boats, a deep freeze, a vacuum cleaner, a gun, and a biscuit box. The service, however, left something to be desired. "Tell them," Beck once wrote to Shefferman, "their socks I purchased are terrible, full of holes."

In 1949 the Teamsters decided to buy property in Washington, D.C. for a new headquarters building. A lot of 23,500 square feet on Louisiana Avenue was available at fifteen dollars a square foot. Shefferman represented Beck in the negotiations with the owner, the American Legion. He proposed to two other men that an intermediate corporation be set up to buy the property at the available price, then sell it to the Teamsters at eighteen dollars a square foot, yielding a profit of $75,000.

Shefferman's proposal fell through largely because of the misgivings of his associates, and the land was sold to the Teamsters for fifteen dollars a square foot. Beck told Teamster President Dan Tobin that negotiations with the American Legion had been prolonged and almost terminated because of the refusal of the Legion to sell the property at less than eighteen dollars a square foot. "Executive Vice President Beck," Tobin told the union's General Executive Board on June 10, 1949, "secured the services of an agent . . . He stated that this agent through diligent work and painstaking effort finally succeeded in having the American Legion agree to sell this property at a price of fifteen dollars a square foot . . . A saving to the [union] of approximately sixty-five to seventy-five thousand dollars."

Shefferman received a commission of $12,000 from the Teamsters. Five weeks later he made out a check to Beck for $8,000; six months later he sent Beck a second check for $4,000. The Committee asked him why.

A. As I started to say, I have known Mr. Beck for more than twenty years. Mr. Beck has been a friend and a very good friend. Mr. Beck, if you will permit me, is a terrific personality . . . Now, this is no laughing matter . . . I say in all sincerity that Mr. Beck is a generous man and a terrific personality and a very fine gentleman . . .

Q. Mr. Shefferman, could I suggest you answer the question about the checks?

A. This is part of the background . . . I talked it over with my boy, and I remembered that because it was Mr. Beck's taking me by the hand and introducing me to a good many people all over the nation, and helping me with my speeches, and I in turn doing the same, and we were fighting— and please, this is in all seriousness—together, and we put up a terrific fight on the matter of anti-Communism and the key of the free market place . . . I asked him to accept this money, whatever it was, that I gave him at that time because I have benefitted as a result of his help and constant companionship.

. . .

Q. You liked him so you gave him the money?

A. Sure. I thought he was entitled to it.

. . .

Q. The records show that from 1949 to 1950, and just for those two years, that you paid Mr. Beck some $24,500, of which these two checks are a part . . . You thought he was entitled to it?

A. Yes sir . . . I just thought I had done pretty well, and I was up in the higher tax brackets, and I thought I could well afford to give him some money.

. . .

Q. Did you charge it off as expense to your business?
A. Yes; I think we charged it off.

At the time of the $12,000 gift, Beck owed Shefferman $22,500.

The Committee investigated several cases where Shefferman had prevented the unionization of a plant. One of these involved Ford dealer Otto P. Graff, Inc., of Flint, Michigan. James Hoffa's Local 299 in Detroit informed the Graff Company that the local represented a majority of the company's salesmen. Company Vice-President Max Graff then approached George Kamenow, Shefferman's representative in Detroit, who agreed to represent Graff for $250 a month and $1,800 in entertainment expenses. Graff soon received a letter from Frank Kierdorf, the business agent of Teamster Local 332 in Flint, telling him that responsibility for organizing the company had been transferred from Local 299 to Local 332. Graff informed Kierdorf that he would be contacted by the firm's labor relations representative. No more was heard from the local, and the company remained unorganized. Kamenow subsequently charged Graff some $3,400 for the entertainment of union officials. Both Kamenow and Kierdorf invoked the Fifth Amendment before the Committee.

The Committee noted that four other firms in Flint had similar experiences with Kamenow and the Teamsters. "Despite their denials," the Committee said, "there can be no doubt that they all knew exactly what they were buying . . . They sought to avoid unionization and they found Mr. Kamenow a convenient conduit to make payments to union officials to leave them alone. The stories of these Flint businessmen that they did not know the purposes for which they were making payments to Kamenow are unworthy of belief."

The Committee described Shefferman's activities in general as "a shocking indictment" of the employers he dealt with. It also noted Shefferman's immunity from punishment. "Despite the fact that firms he represented had been involved in scores of unfair labor practices, Shefferman has never received even a slight reprimand, and the companies that he represents merely make a written statement that they will not do again what they have done. Shefferman moved from town to town, from State to State, with impunity, and the law as presently written is apparently powerless to deal with his activities."

16: The Carpenters,
the Operating Engineers
and the Sheet Metal Workers

The Carpenters

"The United Brotherhood of Carpenters and Joiners of America," the Committee observed, "is the Nation's oldest union, and one of the most respected." However, there were qualifications to be made.

Maurice A. Hutcheson, in the American labor movement's most prominent case of primogeniture in union office, became president of the Carpenters in 1952. His father, William L. Hutcheson, had led the union since 1913. "If the entrenchment of the Hutcheson dynasty has gone unquestioned," the Committee said, "so also has its management of the Carpenters . . . this has proved an expensive oversight for the more than 800,000 members of the union . . ."

In 1953 the Carpenters retained Maxwell C. Raddock, publisher of the bi-weekly *Trade Union Courier* and owner of a publishing house called the World Wide Press Syndicate, to write the biography of William Hutcheson. The *Courier* described itself as "America's leading labor newspaper," but the AFL-CIO took a sourer view, later describing the paper as "fraudulent, unfair, and deceptive as well as prejudicial and injurious to the public welfare . . ." Labor opposition to the *Courier* dated back at least to 1945, when AFL President William Green called it "an outlaw racket publication," warned all affiliated unions and Better Business Bureaus in the United States against patronizing it, and obtained an order from the Federal Trade Commission which prohibited the *Courier* from claiming any connection with the AFL. President George Meany of the AFL asked all affiliates to refrain from supporting the *Courier* and, as president of the AFL-CIO, ordered all state and local central bodies to cease patronizing such publications. However, neither the AFL-CIO nor the Federal Trade Commission nor various business organizations were able to change the *Courier's* ways. Hull Youngblood, Sr., a businessman in San Antonio, Texas, submitted to the Committee a tape recording of a telephone conversation he had recently had with *Courier* representative David Koota, a convicted swindler.

Koota: Youngblood, this is Dave Koota, with the *Courier,* the American Federation of Labor Unions . . . Anything we can do for you?

Youngblood: I don't think so; not that I know of.

Koota: Well, I say it for one reason, Mr. Youngblood, because we've always regarded you as a friend . . . Youngblood, you know we've had our big convention . . . one very important thing that came up that we are going to work on, and that is to get Communists out of organized labor.

Youngblood: Huh, Hmmm.

. . .

Koota: Definitely. I'll tell you this, Youngblood. It's gotten to a point now where not only did those Communists get into organized labor, they've gotten into our schools, our churches, and even into our State Department.

Youngblood: Uhuh.

Koota: And unless we do something, Youngblood, it's going to affect us all in a big way.

Now, Youngblood, we've always rated you as a friend . . . all our good friends in management, those we have always respected, are working along with us. They're taking space in our big convention paper to help us out with the expense, but I want you to know this, Hull, that if I ask you to take a little money out of your pocket, to help me, the time will come when I'll prove to you, Hull, that we've got darn big pockets ourselves . . . it's good to have friends in the right places. Do I make myself clear, Hull?

Youngblood: Yeah.

Koota was asked about the tape.

Q. That is your voice, is it not?
A. It sounds like it.
Q. Who are some of the big friends, the friends you had in the right places?
A. I wouldn't know, offhand.

. . .

Q. Are you a member of a union yourself?
A. Not now.

. . .

Q. Who is on your executive committee—"My executive committee is setting everything up"?
A. It is just an expression that I used. . . .
Q. Do you mean you sold with false representation?
A. No, sir . . . I don't know how to explain it. It is my way of selling.

The *Courier's* methods were successful. Its advertising revenue for the eight-year period studied by the Committee was $3,500,000, although its circulation was only 33,000. But by 1958 the paper was endorsed by only two central labor bodies, about seventy local unions, and one international union. The international union was the Carpenters, 346 of whose locals bought the paper.

Raddock agreed with Maurice Hutcheson to print 6,000 copies of the Hutcheson biography for $25,000 in time for the Carpenters' convention in November, 1954. No alternative authors were approached. "God and the elements willing," Raddock wrote to Hutcheson, "we feel confident the biography will be published ahead of the convention deadline . . . no more eloquent testimonial or memorial to the good name of the illustrious President of the United Brotherhood of Carpenters has ever been projected . . ." He received a check for $25,000 one month later. Shortly afterwards he asked for and received a further $25,000 for research.

The book was unfinished at the deadline. Nevertheless the Carpenters agreed to pay Raddock $200,000 to publish 50,000 copies of the book for distribution to libraries, schools, union officials and others. A New York printing executive told the Committee the order could have been met for a maximum cost of $75,000. By January, 1957, the Carpenters had paid Raddock $310,000 on an order for 68,000 volumes, only 8,100 of which had been printed. At the time of the hearings Raddock still owed 9,900 copies of the book.

Robert A. Christie, the author of an unauthorized history of the Carpenters, had been asked to review the biography for the *New Leader*.

Q. Did you then read the book?
A. I read it.
Q. What was your reaction?
A. It was like living a dream, something I had done before. I kept seeing myself in the pages. There were five or six thousand of my words stolen, plagiarized, borrowed, whatever you want to call it . . . As far as I can see, his only expenses for writing the book was a pair of scissors and a pot of glue.

Raddock had his own views on authorship.

Q. But you would not take someone else's material and copy it?
A. In a measure, I would . . . I have not read a single book that contains total originality from beginning to end, and there isn't a single new thought in this entire world that is not derived from God and the Bible.
Q. But Mr. Raddock, so I understand, you would then take somebody else's words and copy them, word for word, would you?
A. If it is good, I would borrow the thought, just like Jack Benny may borrow from Bing Crosby or somebody else.

The Carpenters also paid Raddock over $82,000 for publicity and related services in connection with the union's seventy-fifth anniversary celebrations. Hutcheson was questioned.

Q. Did you ask for any vouchers, any support for any of these bills?
A. No.

"The testimony clearly shows," the Committee stated, "that Maurice Hutcheson became involved with a shrewd confidence man in the person of Maxwell C. Raddock and turned over to him some $519,000 in Carpenters Union funds, with noticeably little return. Part of the money went to assist the *Trade Union Courier*—a pure and simple shakedown operated by Raddock . . . Another $310,000 went to Raddock for the production of a biography of Maurice Hutcheson's father . . . The facts clearly established that Raddock was overpaid some $20,000 for his work . . . had not the committee started its investigation into the Hutcheson book project, the United Brotherhood might not have fared as well as it did, for eighty percent of the books finally produced by Raddock were printed after the committee began its investigation."

There was evidence, Robert F. Kennedy told the Committee, that real estate worth $250,000 and originally owned by the Carpenters had become part of the private estate of William Hutcheson. Kennedy proposed impartial arbitration to determine whether the property should belong to the union or to William Hutcheson's heirs. The attorneys for the Carpenters replied that the property now belonged to the trustees of William Hutcheson's estate and that the probate court involved could not delegate its functions to an arbitrator. However, the issue of ownership was scheduled to be reviewed by Maurice Hutcheson and the Carpenters' executive board. There seems to be no public record of their action *.

Carpenters' funds were used in 1955 to pay the income tax debts of three incumbent or former officers of the union: former General Secretary Frank Duffy received $3,946.80, incumbent General Secretary A. E. Fisher received $376.61, and incumbent Treasurer S. P. Meadows got $1,552.25. No authorization of the gifts appeared in the union's records until after the Committee began its investigation of the Carpenters and raised the issue. The union later paid the expenses of General Secretary William O. Blaier's wife when she accompanied her husband on an official trip to Europe; the cost of the trip was $5,066 over and above Blaier's transportation and per diem allowance paid by the union and the $1,100 he received from the U.S. Government. Treasurer Frank Chapman went to Italy at the invitation of the Italian government, taking his wife with him at union expense; the trip —which Chapman extended to include a tour of Europe—cost the union $12,600.

In 1950 Carpenters' International Vice-President Charles Johnson be-

* I have been unable to obtain from the Carpenters any statement on the disposition of the property (Author).

came a mediator. A jurisdictional dispute had broken out at the Yonkers Raceway in Westchester County, New York. The contending unions were Local 456 of the Teamsters and Local 32E of the Building Service Employees. (The chief officer of each local—John Acropolis and Thomas Lewis respectively—were later murdered.) However, an agreement was reached through Johnson's offices, for which he demanded and received $30,000 from the employers. He was then retained by the raceway on a continuing basis, received another $7,000 in fees. According to one account, he later reported to the New York State Council of Carpenters that because of his training and experience in the labor movement "he was able to charge a high fee for representing the Yonkers Raceway, and he was proud of it . . ." Robert F. Kennedy read into the record a report of Johnson's speech. "Everybody in Westchester kidded me how lucky I was," Johnson said. "I did not think I was lucky. I thought I would get a whole lot more than I did." Apparently everyone then applauded.

Edward H. Weiss was a gasoline and oil jobber in Massachusetts. In 1949 he set up a new firm—Penn Products—in New York and retained Johnson "to see to it we were put on the invited list of bidders of these various contractors in the area . . ." For $250, Johnson's wife was given a twenty-five percent interest in the firm. From May, 1950, to November, 1957, Johnson's commissions on sales to nineteen companies totaled $96,-572. At the same time he was the Carpenter's representative in collective bargaining with seventeen of the firms involved.

"On the apparent theory that Carpenter officialdom represented an excellent ground school for the training of gas and oil salesmen," the Committee related "the Weiss enterprises also acquired the services of General Secretary Blaier and General Treasurer Chapman. Blaier received over $11,000 in commissions, although he made not a single sale. "I got the commissions," he told the Committee, ". . . out of the goodness of Mr. Johnson sharing with me his accounts, as an incentive. . . ."

William L. Streukens, a salesman for Christenson Oil, wondered why the Weiss firms were able to obtain contracts when their prices were higher than those of the competitive Christenson, and he questioned Emanuel Weiss, Edward's brother. "Manny Weiss told me," Streukens testified, "that he would go out to the construction site with a union official and talk to the boss on the job or the foreman about purchasing greases or gear oil from his firm. He said that if needed the union would apply the pressure on the company's labor relations with the union. I do not know what union officials were involved nor do I know to what union they belonged." Emanuel Weiss invoked the Fifth Amendment before the Committee.

In any event, the Weiss-Johnson alliance was prosperous. The Weiss brothers received a number of contracts from firms they had not hitherto been able to attract; some of the contracts merely required the Weiss brothers to act as intermediaries, collecting substantial sums for unnecessary paperwork on products supplied by other companies. Johnson evidently received commissions on some business agreements signed by the Weiss brothers whether or not he was involved in the negotiations. Johnson testified only briefly and inconclusively before the Committee, relying in part on the Fifth Amendment. He did not testify again, claiming ill health.

In 1956 Maurice Hutcheson, Blaier and Chapman bought some land in Lake County, Indiana, for $20,000. Some months later they resold the property—which lay along the route of a proposed interstate freeway—to the State of Indiana at a profit of $78,000. Part of the profit was allegedly paid by Chapman to an official in the state highway department. All three officials were convicted for conspiracy to bribe a public official, but the verdict was reversed on appeal. Hutcheson was also given a six-month sentence for contempt of Congress for refusing to tell the Committee whether union funds had been used in an attempt to fix the case, but the sentence was later reduced to six months' probation and a $500 fine.

The appearance and behavior of various Carpenters' officials before the McClellan Committee prompted Ronald H. Rowley, a business agent for Local 106 of the Carpenters in Des Moines, to appear voluntarily before the Committee. He had gone to the 1958 convention of the Carpenters as an elected delegate from his local union, he said, prepared to raise certain questions on the floor of the convention. Before he left Des Moines he was approached by Lew Farrell, a man described by the Committee as "an associate of the Capone mob, an identified racketeer . . . ," who had obtained from Rowley's assistant a copy of the questions Rowley intended to raise.

Q. What did Mr. Farrell say to you after examining the papers?
A. He told me that I should learn to keep my mouth shut and not write things down.
Q. What did you say?
A. I told him to stay out of the affairs of Local 106.
Q. What did Mr. Farrell have to do with the Carpenters at that time?
A. Not a thing.

. . .

Q. When you arrived [at the convention] in St. Louis, did you see Mr. Farrell there?
A. I saw him the next afternoon.

. . .

Q. Were you harassed at all while you were in St. Louis?

A. Yes, sir . . . I was accosted by a general representative of President Hutcheson's. His name was W. E. McDaniels . . . He threatened to kill me, exterminate me, and exterminate my local union.

Q. Was he with anyone at the time?

A. Yes, sir . . . There was a group around him . . . At least one had a gun and at least two had saps or blackjacks.

. . .

Q. What did you reply to this?

A. I didn't reply anything. I eased out the door. I was afraid.

. . .

Q. You tried to get into the convention; is that correct?

A. I tried to register on Saturday . . . Mr. Stevenson [an international representative] stepped forward just as my credential was passed to Mr. Hutcheson, and he picked it up and handed it to me, didn't even unfold . . . He said to President Hutcheson that this credential was no good—no damn good was his words . . . I asked him why, and he told me—he called me a son-of-a-b——— and said that "I will not speak to you" . . . I asked Mr. Hutcheson, "What about it?" And he said, "That goes for me, too."

Three other delegates from Local 106 were seated, including Rowley's assistant Robert Pepper, who had taken documents from Rowley's briefcase to show to Farrell. Pepper also allegedly informed Rowley that he would return to Des Moines "in a wooden overcoat."

Rowley was expelled from Local 106, evidently on orders from the international union, despite a vote of confidence in him passed by the local. An Iowa court enjoined his expulsion, ordering him and the union to come to terms. An agreement was reached whereby Rowley would retain his position as business agent until his term expired or a successor was elected, and would also keep his union card. The settlement was rejected by the international union. Rowley told the Committee he intended to ask for a permanent restraining order against the union, to remain in office until the next local union election, and to continue to fight for his rights. Replied Senator Ervin of North Carolina, "I think we should be grateful that there are some people in America who have a little courage."

The Operating Engineers

"Of all the unions subject to committee inquiry over the past year," the McClellan Committee declared, "none has proved more backward, more indifferent to the changing times, more incredibly feudal, than the International Union of Operating Engineers."

The Operating Engineers represented some 280,000 members, most of them skilled workers in the building trades. All IUOE members pay dues, but at the time of the investigation only forty-six percent of them were allowed to vote. Local union elections in some areas were held irregularly, in some places not at all. One-fifth of the total international union membership was in local unions under trusteeship. Seven locals had been in trusteeship for at least ten years, two locals for twenty-nine years.

"Literally millions of dollars," the Committee said, "have vanished from the IUOE treasury, often reappearing in the form of improved living standards for union bigwigs. In at least two locals, the rank and file have had to kick back five percent of their salaries over and above the dues they pay." Collusion with employers was apparently frequent, some contracts paying IUOE members one dollar an hour less than the contract rate. Some IUOE officials owned companies with which they negotiated as union representatives. The discipline of the union, the Committee alleged, was enforced by economic sanctions, intimidation, violence and apparently murder.

In 1924 William Maloney became, by appointment, a business representative of Chicago Local 569 of the IUOE. In 1929 he broke with his mentor, Local 569 President Edward Moore, and sided with IUOE President Arthur Huddell in a move to merge Local 569 with Local 42, also in Chicago. The members of Local 569 opposed the merger, supported Moore, and expelled Maloney by a vote of 400-1. Huddell then chartered a new Local 150 in Chicago and made Maloney its trustee. The local had no founding members, and began absorbing the members of Local 569 who, if they were slow in transferring, evidently lost their union death benefits. Local 150 stayed in trusteeship until the Committee's hearings.

Huddell died in 1930 after being shot, and was succeeded by John Possehl. Maloney remained in office. In 1934 Local 150 voted 268-1 to oust him, but was reprimanded by Possehl. At the time, Maloney was under indictment with several Chicago gangsters for extorting some $1,000,000 from building contractors, but he was acquitted. Then, according to the Committee, he allied himself with Teamster locals controlled by gangsters William J. ("Three-Fingered Jack") White and Charles Fiaschetti, Al Capone's cousin, to destroy Local 569 by armed violence. He also allegedly joined Michael Carrozzo of the Hod Carriers to extort money from contractors.

Dennis Ziegler was a leader of the anti-administration forces in Local 569. "The members of the organization," Ziegler wrote to AFL President William Green, "is sick and tired and disgusted with being classified as being dominated and controlled by the worst forms of racketeers, hoodlums, and murderers in America. We want and demand freedom from this stigma. . . ." Ziegler asked Green for an AFL charter. "I would strongly advise you against the action you are planning to take," Green replied. "It will serve no good purpose. If you have complaints against the administration of the officers of the existing organization of Operating Engineers, surely there is a way by which your complaint can be considered and adjusted."

"Do you have in mind," Ziegler wrote back to Green, "any method by which this can be done, or any tribunals to which we may go? We are not permitted to assemble in convention . . . Whole local unions are voted by supervisors appointed by the president of the International. Other local unions are bodily disenfranchised. The votes of other local unions are flagrantly miscounted . . . In the absence of a convention the only remaining tribunal is the officers themselves whom we charge with misconduct. Are they to be permitted to pass upon the propriety of their own acts? Are they to be judges of their own stewardship? What chance do we have . . . ?"

Green evidently did not reply. The exchange of letters took place in January, 1933, and the following month Ziegler was shot in the head on his way home. The correspondence was in his possession, as was a year-old memorandum dated a year and a day before his death, stating that he had been pursued one morning by Maloney and Maloney's assistant John T. Lynch, that Lynch had threatened him with death, and that he had escaped in a taxi. The exchange was confirmed by the driver of the taxi, who was interviewed after Ziegler's death. There were no arrests for the murder.

Philadelphia Local 542 of the Operating Engineers was under trusteeship—with Joseph Fay as trustee—from the early 1930's to 1948. In that year Roy Underwood was elected president and business agent of the local. He told the Committee that he could find no account of the spending of some $5,000,000 in local union funds from 1935 to 1948; the trustees had left no records, and all official books and documents had disappeared. Underwood also said, and Fay denied, that violence was commonly used to discipline restive members. The Committee questioned T. C. McCarty, a member of Local 542, who said he had once been warned by a business agent not to attend the next meeting.

A. And he says, "You," and he pointed to me, "Don't you be there." He says, "If you are there, we are going to have you carried out." . . . Apparently they knew what they were talking about, because they did it.

McCarty was set upon in an elevator.

A. So Frank Lentino, he went straight for the groin, the nice fellow that he is . . . the rest of the fellows worked above the belt . . . I was kicked and other things, and I took brass knuckles in the ear, I took them on the side of the jaw and on the nose. They tell me the elevator was going up and down while the fight was going on. I don't know where the elevator was going; I was busy. So finally they kicked me off at the sixth floor.

Q. Where did you go after they dumped you?

A. I went back in the union hall . . . I had something to say to them. Of course, at the time I was going to do it the old-style way, do everything the way they did it to me. But the body of men that was around, they talked me into taking things through court. . . . So we walked back out to the elevator . . . down to Wahnemann Hospital, and the nurse took care of me . . . she took care of everything above my belt. I didn't want to make too many complaints.

A local magistrate tried the case. "Well," he said, "this is nothing but a union brawl. Case dismissed." The district attorney's aid was enlisted and the case taken before another judge. Three of McCarty's assailants were convicted and fined. Their fines and legal fees were paid by Local 542, although the membership was not consulted on the matter. McCarty had to have all his teeth removed, and developed a cancerous tumor where he had been hurt in the side.

Maloney became president of the Operating Engineers upon the death of Possehl in 1940. The Committee investigated his subsequent relationship with Stephen A. Healy, the owner of one of the largest construction firms in the United States.

In 1943 Healy was involved in the trials of Fay and Bove. He denied before a grand jury that he had ever dealt with them, but admitted that he had paid Michael Carrozzo $125,000 to avoid labor troubles. Sometime afterwards he struck up a friendship with Maloney, becoming in 1950 his business partner in two oil-well investments together with Orville Soucie, a trustee for the Operating Engineers who later went to jail for extortion.

In 1951 Maloney ordered Underwood, Local 542 president and business agent, to send a number of striking members back to work for certain contractors without a labor agreement. Underwood refused. The following year Local 542 was seized by armed men and put back into trusteeship. The Committee questioned Underwood.

Q. You were talking about favoritism to contractors.

· · ·

A. The S. A. Healy Co. had a large project, Blue Ridge Summit, a government project, and we immediately began having difficulty with the company, attempting to induce them to comply with the area agreements . . . I contacted Mr. Healy . . . He told me I had better talk to Mr. Maloney before I insisted on anything . . . Mr. Maloney called me at our local union office in Philadelphia and he was very incensed over the fact that our agent up in the area had insisted that S. A. Healy comply with the terms of the existing collective bargaining agreement and told me to keep that agent away from him and to leave him alone . . . I said, "Why should he be treated any differently than any other employer in the area," and he said, "Because he is a friend of mine and that is all I should have to tell you . . ." I said, "I am sorry, Mr. Maloney, but we cannot do that."

Underwood was tried soon afterwards by a union board, suspended for six years and fined $3,500 for seeking a court injunction to cancel the trusteeship over Local 542. Not long after he testified before the Committee he committed suicide.

There was other testimony about preferential treatment. Clarence Donath, a member of Chicago Local 150, told the Committee that Healy received special consideration in Chicago, specifically that he was being allowed to pay straight time wages for overtime work.

> Q. Was it generally understood among the members of Local 150 that S. A. Healy got preferred treatment . . . that union conditions were not enforced?
> A. That is right.

In 1956 Donath presented a petition to Local 150 calling for the restoration of autonomy. It passed initially by a strong voice vote, but at a meeting a month later the international and local union officers were given a vote of confidence, the motion on autonomy being negated thereby. Donath said the meeting was packed with master mechanics. James Crane, the appointed president of Local 150, had a limited faith in autonomy. "Due to the ever-increasing expansion of heavy industry in the Chicago area," he wrote to Maloney, "in my opinion it is important that Local 150 have continuity of personnel in the administration of its officers . . . To subject this large local to periodic changes in management of its affairs by election of officers would not help the membership. It would bust it . . . The operation of this local union is not small business to be taken care of after working hours. It is big business."

Throughout this period Maloney was a prosperous man. Although he refused the Committee's request for an affidavit stating that he had reported all of his income, he did say that his total salary and expenses from the Operating Engineers from 1950 to 1956 was $388,758.13. In fact, his income from the union for that period was $742,228.20, or $353,650.07 more than he reported. The Committee deducted from the unreported sum what it considered to be $182,539.60 in legitimate income, leaving $171,-116.17 "for which no legitimacy whatever could be claimed."

The union also gave Maloney free use of a $35,000 yacht which was evidently never used on union business, met his racetrack and country club expenditures, and paid for a wide variety of his personal debts. Local 150 bought him a Cadillac every two years—one of which he sold, keeping the money—and paid for various personal expenses. On one occasion the international union gave him an advance of $10,000 to go to a conference of the International Labor Organization in Geneva for which the United States Government had already paid his expenses. "Maloney," the Committee found "developed to a high art the technique of extracting from various organizational sources double and often triple expenses for the self-same trips to meetings and conventions. From 1950 to 1956 . . . such duplicate outlays for Maloney totaled $69,100—over and above his expenses for hotels and entertainment . . . Maloney even pulled off the deft stunt of receiving payments and expenses for meetings at which he was not present."

There were abuses by others. Local 3 of the Operating Engineers in San Francisco had some 24,000 members, was the largest local union in the IUOE, and could claim the broadest territorial jurisdiction—including Northern California, Northern Nevada, Utah, the Hawaiian Islands and other Pacific possessions—of any local union in the United States. It had a net worth of some $3,000,000 with an annual income from dues and assessments of about $1,000,000 a year.

In 1955 Local 3 bought a parcel of land in Stockton, California. The price was $33,500. Ed Doran, a business agent for Local 3 in Stockton, received $4,000 of the purchase price. The land was resold in three parcels. The first parcel sold for $20,000, of which Doran received $9,884.76. The second parcel brought $24,900; the union received $10,858, the remainder apparently being split between Doran, Local 3 Business Manager Victor Swanson, and Local 3 President Pat Clancy. Swanson and Doran bought the third parcel for $15,150, then resold it to the local six months later for $35,000.

According to the Committee, the three officials made $44,805.76 on the transactions. Doran implicated other officials of the local, stating that another land scheme had been planned but was abandoned because of the Committee's pending investigation. Swanson denied that he received any money from the first two parcels, claiming in extenuation of the third transaction that if he and Doran had held on to the parcel for another month it would have been worth $70,000.

Local 3 also spent $120,000 on the purchase and maintenance of a yacht and airplane which were used mainly for the recreation of the local's officers. The purchase of the boat was disguised as payments to a building company. Clancy was questioned.

Q. Did you ever ride in the boat?

A. Three or four times . . .

Q. Who else has used the boat?

A. Swanson, the Swanson family. . . .

· ·

Q. The fact is that the boat was just used for the pleasure of the officers of the union?

A. That I couldn't say. I am an officer and it wasn't used for my pleasure . . . I got sick the first time. I didn't get no pleasure . . .

Clancy was a pilot. He flew his wife and various Local 3 officials to Mexico in the local's plane on several occasions, once crashing in San Francisco on return. The book value of the plane was $7,992.20, yet the repairs cost the union $32,252.28. On another occasion Swanson gave Clancy $10,000 in five equal checks to spend on internal union election campaigns. Clancy flew to Washington, Montana, South Dakota, Minnesota, Colorado and Nevada, cashing checks as he went.

Q. What was the purpose of the trip?

A. To campaign and to cash the checks, the money to be used in the campaign . . .

· · ·

Q. How many times did you go fishing?

A. I don't know. Not every day.

· · ·

Q. What did you do in Minneapolis?

A. In Minneapolis? Well, I went eighteen miles out of there and visited my mother, who is alive yet, thank God.

On his return Clancy handed over the remaining money to Swanson.

Q. You told me yesterday you turned over $9,500 . . . why did you say now you turned over $9,900?

A. I guess I got my nines mixed up, Bob.

· · ·

Q. Mr. Clancy, why did you participate in this fraud on your union?

A. What fraud?

Q. You do not see that there was a fraud on the union? You do not see that at all? That is, your taking these checks, this $10,000, and flying around the country in order to cash them, and make it appear to the membership that you were doing work in taking this money and cashing it?

A. I was just working there, Mr. Kennedy.

The local also had a defense fund to combat open shop and other restrictive legislation. The Committee was able to obtain an accounting for only $23,049.29 of a total disbursement from the fund of $79,399.29 from

1951 to 1957. Some of the money was used to employ Joseph Riley, an ex-convict, to investigate a rebel movement in the local. On one occasion Swanson intercepted a letter to Riley from the insurgents, inserted a death threat, and turned over the communication to the FBI. He was later fined $7,500 and put on two years' probation for giving false information.

Local 3 owned a cabin in Calaveras County, California. The cabin was used solely for the counting of election ballots. According to Edward Garrett, the underemployed accountant for Local 3, Swanson and two tally clerks once put the local's ballots in a car and drove to the cabin. Between 2,000 and 3,000 votes had been cast. Garrett described the count.

Q. How many votes did you count?
A. Either five or six hundred . . . That was all they wanted to count . . . it was decided that that was the trend of the election, and that was going to be it.

Swanson's opponents fared badly in the election, but he had an explanation.

Q. You felt . . . that under Maloney's direction, the other locals were stuffing the ballot boxes?
A. No; they were casting ballots that had not come in.

. . .

Q. . . . The only way to combat that, your group thought, was to stuff the ballot boxes, too?
A. That is correct . . . I don't see how else it could be.

William De Koning became business manager of IUOE Local 138 in Long Island in 1933. In 1949 he also assumed the presidency of the local. The following year his son became its financial secretary. In 1952 the elder De Koning retired and became president emeritus. The executive board of the local appointed his son to succeed him.

In 1953 both father and son were indicted on some one hundred counts for extortion and coercion. Both pleaded guilty and were convicted. The father received a short jail sentence; the son was placed on probation and ordered to refrain from union activities for a year. One Charles Britton was elected president of the local, but claimed ill health and resigned immediately upon the expiration of De Koning's probationary year. De Koning resumed the presidency.

"The testimony," the Committee recounted, "revealed a pattern of continued intimidation of union members and their subjugation through violence and undemocratic procedures." Local 138 had about 500 full members, of whom some 200 were evidently either supervisors or employers with whom the local negotiated. There were also two sub-locals. One consisted of about 400 apprentices, the other of some 300 branch shop and maintenance men and from 500 to 1,000 permit men; none of the sub-local members were allowed to vote in union elections. There was no right of transference to full membership. Garret Nagle, a member of one of the sub-locals, tried to obtain full membership; his application was rejected without explanation, whereupon he asked De Koning for an explanation. "You go———yourself," De Koning said. "My old man ran this local for twenty-five years the way it is now and I am not changing."

Further testimony indicated that the local's officers ignored the votes of the membership, and that dissenters were beaten up by professional thugs, suspended from the local and heavily fined for bringing disrepute on the organization. Two of the insurgents took their case to the executive board of the international union, which scaled down their fines but sustained their suspension. They then appealed to the union convention, but were turned down without a hearing.

A committee of Long Island ministers took an interest in Local 138. The Reverend John W. Van Zanten told the Committee of employer participation in local union affairs, political discrimination in hiring, and terror. "We have discovered in our community of Nassau County," he testified, "a great deal of fear . . . As some of the men have said to us when we discussed it with them, 'I have a wife and children. I can't stand up against this.' " Zanten had praise for the insurgents. "We therefore felt," he said, "that this group, this small group of men . . . are very brave men, and very strong men . . ."

Joseph Fay was released from jail in 1956. Local 825 in New Jersey voted him a pension, bought a building of which he was part owner, and helped to develop business for him as an automobile salesman. He had an exchange with the Committee.

Q. Did you have business interests in businesses that had contracts with the Operating Engineers?
A. Yes, sir, I did.

. . .

Q. Then you were indicted . . . and you were ultimately convicted of extorting $300,000 . . . $362,000?
A. Something like that.

. . .

Q. What about the union? Did they pay any legal bills . . . ?
A. In 1943, I believe they did.

Peter Weber had become business manager of Local 825 in 1953, having served many years under Fay. He evidently acquired some of his mentor's habits. He owned stock in companies with which the Operating Engineers had contractual relationships. One of the firms was Public Constructors, Inc.; from 1950 to 1957 the value of Weber's shares in the company rose from $761.75 to $108,677. He also signed, on behalf of Local 825, the contracts negotiated between the company and the local. Raymond S. Fisher, the head of Public Constructors and other firms in which Weber had an interest, and formerly employed by S. A. Healy, told the Committee that he usually dealt with Weber's subordinates, but that they, "of course, were mindful that he had an interest in the company."

By this time the AFL-CIO had promulgated a code of ethics which condemned the holding by any union official of a business interest which conflicted with his fiduciary duties as a union representative. Weber disagreed that he had engaged in any conflict-of-interest activities, claiming that the companies he had invested in were the first to agree to wage increases, and received no preferential treatment.

Q. Have you taken any steps to divest yourself of any of these companies in which you have an interest?
A. I have . . . since the newspapers got into it . . .
Q. Have you sold any of your interests in any of these companies?
A. No . . . I have been too busy.

Local 399 in Chicago was placed under trusteeship in December, 1929. It was still in trusteeship in 1957. Anton Imhahn and Andrew Leach, its appointed officers, claimed ill health and did not appear before the Committee. The local's records, however, showed that between 1950 and 1957 the two men spent $17,566.32 at a gourmet shop for a variety of purchases ranging from artichoke bottoms to champagne. One of the items was $9.40 for parrot liquor. "Although not sworn to under oath," the Committee commented, "the best information available to the committee staff was that parrot liquor is liquor poured over a stuffed parrot."

A further $10,000 was spent at the store, and the goods were picked up by an unidentified individual. Leach also spent $5,399.55 on monogrammed jewelry and other personal items. The local paid $1,031.11 from 1951 to 1953 for Leach's membership in the Wing and Fin Hunting and Fishing Club, and $3,823.26 for his membership in and purchases from the Tam O'Shanter Country Club. There were other expenditures for personal and household purposes, and one item of $8,258.39 for Leach's expenses at a hotel in Hot Springs, Arkansas, although no union meetings were held in the vicinity during the period in question. There was no evidence that the membership had been consulted about any of the above expenditures.

"It remained," the Committee said, "for Clarence Donath of Local 150, however, the veteran of thirty-five years' standing, to provide the most devastating, if oblique, commentary . . . As he ended his testimony, Donath requested—and received—a 'favor' of the committee: a statement by the Chairman that any attempts made to intimidate, coerce or threaten him in the wake of his committee testimony would be regarded as contempt of the United States Senate and a defiance of the authority of the United States Government."

The Sheet Metal Workers in Chicago

Arthur H. ("Harry") Cronin was the president of Local 73 of the Sheet Metal Workers International Association in the Chicago area. He was also the owner of a furnace fitting company and an air-conditioning company whose employees were members of the Sheet Metal Workers. Various witnesses alleged that Cronin had used his union position for private profit. One of these was Carl L. Burrows, an official of the Coleman Company of Wichita, Kansas.

The Coleman Company entered the air-conditioning and furnace field in 1950. For some twenty years the firm had been manufacturing heating equipment, and had maintained good relations with an independent union —the National Appliance Workers—in its home plant. Now it began to experience difficulty in getting members of the Sheet Metal Workers to handle its products. Burrows said he was told that $2,000 would settle the problem, and that on May 8, 1952, he gave that amount to Cronin on a street corner in Chicago.

Q. How much did you pay to Mr. Cronin?
A. We paid a total of $27,000; $5,000 of it was returned.

. . .

Q. Were you achieving the labor peace that you desired at this time?
A. I wouldn't say, sir, that we were using the proper approach, but yes, we were having no further trouble.

Warren A. Tapper, a non-union contractor in Des Plaines, Illinois, said he paid Cronin $250 one morning at breakfast.

Q. First, did you understand this was a general practice followed by all the contractors in the Chicago area?
A. As far as I know, nobody can open up a sheet-metal shop and hire union men without first paying off . . .

. . .

Q. Have you ever heard of the . . . Acme Furnace Co. that Mr. Cronin had an interest in . . . ?
A. Well, their salesman called on me from time to time and let us know it would be a good thing to buy their products; but I never bought any of their products.

. . .

Q. What basis did they give you as it being a good thing for you?

A. Well, that it is owned by Mr. Cronin and as long as we bought their products we would be on the good side.

. . .

Q. Mr. Tapper, will you look at the gentleman standing immediately behind you and state if you know him?

A. Yes, sir; that is Mr. Troutman [a Sheet Metal Workers' business agent].

Q. That is the man you have been talking about. . . . You couldn't be mistaken in the identity?

A. No, sir. I have known him for eight years.

. . .

Q. That is the man who told you to go see Mr. Cronin and straighten yourself out with the payment of the money?

A. Yes, sir.

Cecil L. Johnson, a ventilating contractor, told the Committee that Cronin had demanded $300 in cash for permission to enter the business in the Chicago area, and had told Johnson to clear all bids for jobs with him. One of the prohibited bids involved a county hospital.

Q. Did he call you from Florida . . . ? And he told you not to bid on the job?

A. Yes, sir.

Q. And did he tell you what would happen to you if you did bid on the job?

A. He would have a business agent at the door and they would rip [the employees' union cards] in half and I would be out of business.

Q. What about Narowetz [Louis Narowetz, a Chicago ventilating contractor]?

A. He took my partner and I out to lunch one time and told us that we should stick on the outer edge of town and try to develop those little factories that are going to grow into bigger factories some day and that the Loop [downtown Chicago] belonged to him and the other boys.

Other employer representatives testified that they had to make cash payments to officers of Local 73 for one purpose or another, and that the local even attempted to control the level of bids. Union witnesses uniformly denied engaging in extortionary activities or collaborating with employers to rig bids.

Senator McClellan declared that "there is considerable evidence or testimony of witnesses before this committee that is in irreconcilable conflict . . . There is no way to accept it as being honest differences of opinion, and there is definitely willful perjury present . . . the complete record will go to the Justice Department."

17: The Culinary Workers and the Coin Machine Operators

The Culinary Workers

The Chicago Restaurant Association was formed in 1914. "It probably was conceived," the Committee suggested, "in a spirit of lofty idealism . . ." Times had changed. The evidence, the Committee said, "establishes conclusively that [the Association] has functioned in recent years principally to defeat and destroy legitimate unionization and has callously used men with underworld connections to make collusive arrangements with dishonest union officials. There is additional undisputed testimony that gangsters and hoodlums were employed to handle the Association's labor relations; that Association members and individual restaurateurs outside the Association made deals that saved them large sums annually through the nonenforcement of contract terms, if contracts did in fact exist. Witness after witness told the Commiteee there were no written contracts, no negotiations of wages or working conditions, no evidence that employees ever wanted a union, and in many cases no knowledge on their part that they did hold membership in a union. It was in most instances a case of pay up 'or else.' "

The Committee also criticized the principal union involved, the HRE, accusing it of "indefensible indifference" about conditions in Chicago. The Committee noted that the union had acted promptly to put offending local unions into trusteeship after the Committee's disclosures, but accused it of tolerating an alleged long-time association between International Vice-President James V. Blakely and a number of Chicago's "leading hoodlums," some of whom had apparently obtained HRE charters under his sponsorship.

Virgil Peterson, the operating director of the Chicago Crime Commission, a voluntary organization, recounted to the Committee the intervention of Nitti and his associates in the affairs of the HRE and of Local 278 in particular. The local was put into receivership by a Chicago court subsequent to the submission of George McLane's affidavit. The master in chancery, Peterson said, "held that with the exception of those charges relating to fiscal irregularity, the original charges made by George V. McLane had been absolutely sustained." McLane had charged that the syndicate-sponsored Louis Romano had been in effective control since July, 1935, of both Local 278 and the HRE Joint Board in Chicago. A court-supervised election took place in Local 278 in January, 1941. Both McLane and Romano lost their elective jobs. Romano—who had twice been arrested in connection with a murder but acquitted when witnesses refused to testify —was hired shortly thereafter by the Chicago Restaurant Association as a labor relations consultant. Local 278 allegedly came again under syndicate influence after its trusteeship was dissolved. Romano was called to testify.

Q. You don't remember that, a half hour ago . . . you replied that you had been arrested about a dozen times . . .

. . .

A. Do you remember getting me all excited . . . How do you expect me to remember anything during an excitable conversation?

. . .

Q. Could you tell us what kind of work you were doing for the Restaurant Association?

A. Play it in another pitch. I can't sing the same tune. I decline to answer.

. . .

Q. According to the records that we have, on April 5, 1922, you shot Abe Rubin four times, and he was killed . . . also, you shot Isadore Suporr and Charles Hadesman.

A. Why don't you go and dig up all the dead ones out in the graveyard and ask me if I shot them, you Chinaman?

Romano, after listing a number of unlucrative jobs that he had held during most of his adult life, stated that he had been living in semi-retirement in Florida since 1953. For the previous four years he had declared an average income of $600. Senator Ervin suggested that Romano would be "one of the greatest public benefactors" if he told the Committee how to live in Florida on $600 a year.

A. Well, one reason is I buy very little food . . . I catch a lot of fish for food. And I can eat it six times a week. If you want any good hints how to cut down the high cost of living, there is a good one . . . If anybody wants any lessons, I will be glad to give them, free of charge.

A charter application for Local 450 was filed with the HRE on August 13, 1935, and granted the same day. Joseph Aiuppa, alias Joey O'Brien, was listed as secretary of the local. McLane was named as the organizer. Peterson testified that the dominant influence in Local 450 was Chicago gangster Claude Maddox. Maddox had a long record of arrests for burglary, larceny and other offenses. He was in early life a member of Egan's Rats, a prominent gang in St. Louis. He was also a prime suspect in the Valentine's Day Massacre of Capone's enemies in 1929, but was released on providing an alibi. During the 1930's he was closely associated with George ("Red") Barker and William ("Three-Finger Jack") White, who were allegedly influential in Chicago locals of the Teamsters and Operating Engineers. In 1943, according to Peterson, Maddox was "placed in charge of labor-union control" by Paul ("The Waiter") Ricca and Louis Campagna. He evidently remained active in union affairs until his death in 1958. "We received information in 1952," Peterson said, "to the effect . . . that Claude Maddox was allegedly receiving $10,000 a month from certain unions, including [Blakely's] local 593 . . ."

Abraham Teitelbaum, a former counsel for the Chicago Restaurant Association, refused to tell the Committee whether he knew Al Capone or a number of other leaders of the Chicago underworld.

> Q. Mr. Teitelbaum, when I was talking to you when you were not under oath in the office yesterday, you said that you did know Al Capone . . . you spoke very highly of him and said what a fine gentlemen he was. If he was such a fine gentleman, why would it incriminate you to say whether you knew him here under oath?
> A. The same answer . . .

Teitelbaum asked the Committee's permission to answer some questions but not others. The Committee declined to do so, in effect affirming the rule that once a witness answered any questions he must answer them all.

> A. Senator McClellan, there is an old proverb: "If you fool me once, shame on you. If you fool me twice, shame on me." I don't want to have that. I plead the Fifth Amendment to that.

Anthony V. Champagne took Teitelbaum's place in 1953. He was called to testify but refused to do so.

> Q. According . . . to the records we have here you were making some $8,000 or $9,000 a year in law practice, Mr. Champagne. At least, that is how much you were declaring . . . Then when you went to the Chicago Restaurant Association, you were given a retainer of $125,000 . . . settled the Marquis strike and then resigned on the basis you had to go back to your law practice, that it was taking up too much time . . . the reason that we have that you resigned was an argument that you got into with Tony Accardo, and he was going to have you killed at that time; that finally, through the intercession of some of your friends and relatives, that was prevented. Would you make any comment on that.
> A. I respectfully decline to answer . . .

Peterson told the Committee that Champagne had been representing prominent Chicago gangsters since 1945.

Q. Were you employed by this restaurant association by reason of the influence or the recommendation of a gangster, high in the crime operations
of the city of Chicago? . . . Did Anthony Accardo recommend you to
the restaurant association as a successor to Teitelbaum . . .
A. I respectfully decline to answer . . .

Donald Kiesau, executive vice president of the Association, told the
Committee that Teitelbaum was retained in 1938 or 1939 on the recommendation of a Mr. Toffenetti, who had been told that Teitelbaum might
be able to solve a strike then in process.

Q. Did you ever hear anybody state that he had any experience whatsoever in
labor-management relations?
A. Not that I recall.
Q. In 1942 or thereabouts, he retained to assist him Mr. Louis Romano. Did
you know anything about Mr. Romano's background?
A. Only what I read in the papers.

. . .

Q. You know Mr. Teitelbaum had participated in a bribe, extortion, or whatever it might be, back in 1949 and 1950 . . . Why didn't you take steps
to have him fired at that time?
A. Again . . . that was not my prerogative to do that.

The Association's board of directors was informed about Teitelbaum's
apparent deliquencies, but took no action.

Teitelbaum lost his job in 1953 when he failed to stop a strike by HRE
Local 593 against the Marquis chain of restaurants. Only about 150 of the
Association's members had any union members at all, but unionization was
not always opposed; sometimes an accommodation was reached. Leslie A.
Johnson, owner of the non-union Inglenook Cabin Restaurant in Chicago,
said that when a picket line suddenly appeared outside his establishment he
approached the Association. In Teitelbaum's absence he was referred to
Romano, who decided that Johnson should put six waitresses and two
kitchen helpers—only a portion of his work force—into HRE Local 394.
Johnson then paid the local the initiation fees and dues for ten employees
as a "running account." The identities of the employees was not a factor,
nor were any of them approached at all by Local 394. At one time Johnson was paying dues on a dead waitress and an employee who had left.

John McGann, part owner of the Beverly Woods and Lincoln Heights
Restaurants in Chicago, was general manager of Rupcich's Restaurant in
1950. At the suggestion of Local 394, McGann joined the Association,
then was picketed by the local. Teitelbaum arranged for one-third of
McGann's employees to be enrolled in Local 394. The new members were

not consulted, were not told they were now in the union, and received no improvements in wages, hours or working conditions. A similar procedure was followed when McGann opened the Beverly Woods Restaurant.

Q. They [the waitresses] have never agreed to it?
A. Not formally or written . . . They know that the situation exists.

. . .

Q. What you are actually doing, then, is collecting from these working people . . . and paying tribute to a union that is nothing but a shakedown racket. That is the truth about it, isn't it?
A. Yes, sir.

At the time, twenty-nine out of thirty waitresses at the Beverly Woods were being paid seventeen cents below the union scale of sixty-seven cents an hour, but were obliged to buy their own meals and uniforms. All the twenty-two miscellaneous employees were non-union, with eleven of them being paid below scale. All seven bartenders were paid at union scale, but only three of them belonged to the HRE. Union representatives never met with McGann after the initial agreement. The arrangement saved McGann some $21,300 a year.

Ellis Segal owned a restaurant in Chicago and in 1949 agreed with Secretary-Treasurer Frank Trungale of Local 394 that eight of his twenty-nine employees would become union members, with Segal paying twenty-four dollars a month in surrogate dues, and twenty-three of his employees being paid below union scale. Anthony DeSantis, the owner of the Martinique Restaurant in Evergreen Park, gave Trungale one hundred dollars and quantities of liquor on various occasions, and also gave money to Local 394 Business Agent James O'Connor. "I figured in my own common-sense," he testified, "the best thing to do was to give him a little cash . . . I tried to keep the peace . . ." Local 394 had once stated its intention to organize the Martinique, but did not do so.

The union seemed to act as little more than a job-referral agency. Merlin Griffith, formerly an organizer for the HRE Joint Board, testified about a contract settlement with the Nantucket Restaurant in South Chicago.

Q. What was the advantage, Mr. Griffith, for the employees for your making this arrangement . . . Was there any benefit as far as wages, hours, or conditions for the employee?
A. Well . . . No; there was none that I know of.
Q. Did they ever enforce their contract after they signed it?
A. Well, we got so busy with the strike that we never had time to enforce anything or follow up. I believe that some enforcement should have been done.

Q. . . . the fact that they may have signed up for sixty-seven cents an hour for wages does not mean necessarily that they had to pay it?

A. That is correct.

There was an incentive for organizing the workers, if none for enforcing their contract. Evidently the employer agreed to pay the initiation fees and dues of the steady employees. Griffith received half the initiation fees as compensation, but nothing of the dues.

It was a vigorous environment. Donald Strang operated a Howard Johnson restaurant in Niles, Illinois. In 1952, Local 450 wanted to bring his employees into the union without the ceremony of an election. Strang testified.

A. There was vandalism. There they put tacks all over the lot so that our customers would have punctures. They slashed our employees' tires, particularly at nighttime. They put sugar in the gasoline tank of our present manager. . . . They threw firecrackers after the employees as they would leave . . . Our employees were intimidated, they were followed home, run off the road . . . Girls going home late at night were followed and made fearful . . . We had a scavenger . . . he had his little boy in the seat with him, and they said, "If you think anything of that little boy, you will take that garbage back and put it where it was." He did. He couldn't take chances with his little boy.

Strang sought protection from the State police, but was told they had orders to lay off. The union withdrew its campaign after three weeks. Strang paid Teitelbaum $2,240 for what he thought were attorney's fees. Teitelbaum made the check over to Local 450 for the initiation fees and one year's dues for forty employees.

Beverly Sturdevant was a waitress at the Embassy Restaurant in Chicago. Daniel Leonardi of Local 450 allegedly told her and other waitresses to join the union or "there could be an accident down the stairs . . . whoever was pushed down the stairs would sue our employer and put him out of business . . . They told us there was no guaranty against any harm to the girls themselves."

Q. Why did the waitresses join the union?

A. We joined to protect our employer . . .

. . .

Q. Did you have any contract with the union after that?

A. No, sir.

. . .

Q. Did anybody speak to you about testifying before this committee?

A. Yes, sir . . . I was told not to come to Washington to testify . . . that I should get sick before coming down to Washington or be sicker when I got back.

"I think," counsel Kennedy said, "somebody as specifically threatened as this young lady has been, and who then comes and testifies anyway, is really doing something."

Leonardi refused to testify. Louis Madia, the secretary-treasurer of Local 450, also refused to testify when asked if he had attended lawn parties at Anthony Accardo's country estate and had associated with various underworld figures.

According to Lieutenant Joseph Morris of the Chicago Police Department, a witness, Teitelbaum was unpopular with the Association, the syndicate and various unions. James Weinberg and Paul ("Needlenose") Labriola, two relatively minor hoodlums, were given permission to organize a rival association for restaurant owners and another for tavern owners and liquor dealers.

> A. I had a man working for Weinberg . . . Teitelbaum was in bad graces with the syndicate powers . . . the union would not cooperate with Teitelbaum in his efforts to adjust labor difficulties . . . Weinberg said they had plans afoot to dispose of Teitelbaum . . . when Teitelbaum happened to be looking out of the window to enjoy the view of Lake Michigan, Labriola would give a little push . . .
>
> . . .
>
> Q. Was there any alternative suggestion made rather than killing him?
> A. Well, somebody mentioned they would push acid in his girl friend's face or something of that nature . . . we didn't know whether these plans were sincere . . . [but] Teitelbaum actually believed that they fully intended to kill him.

Morris said that the rival movement had the backing of the syndicate, that Accardo seemed to be the final authority, and that Sam ("Golf Bag") Hunt was the "real boss" of the restaurant situation. The plan was evidently to work with Blakely and the brothers John and Danny Lardino of Local 593, but because of police harassment it was abandoned.

Morris wrote a report of the case. "In conclusion," he said, "it might be well to note that it is quite evident that these associations were instigated by the underworld elements to act in collusion with the union and that the ultimate intention of these associations was to seize control of the liquor industry. . . . Once this was accomplished, it would then be possible to extort a certain percentage of every barrel and case of beer distributed in the State."

Weinberg and Labriola moved out to Elmhurst, where they formed another association.

Q. The same kind of operation?

A. That is right. They apparently had some kind of success. They became important enough to get killed.

Q. How were they killed?

A. They were poisoned. It is a new wrinkle in gang killing.

Fire was also a punishment. The Committee questioned John McFarland, an investigator for the State of Illinois.

Q. How long have you been working on arsons?

A. Probably the last ten years . . . in the last two or three years we have had a great increase in the number of fires in restaurants and cafes and taverns.

. . .

Q. Have you been able to solve any of these?

A. No; we have not.

. . .

Q. Could you tell us whether you received cooperation . . . from the owners of these restaurants and taverns in attempting to solve these fires?

A. That I will say we have not. They stand on the statement that they do not know why they should have such a fire, or what caused the fire . . . I think they are afraid to talk.

Anthony DeSantis of the Martinique Restaurant was asked about what the Committee had called "wholesale payoffs" to the underworld for protection against arson or stink-bombing.

Q. . . . You know that goes on, do you not?

A. I have heard that . . . I have never been approached. The reason for that is very, very simple. I don't have a 26 game * in my restaurant. I don't have a juke box in my restaurant. I don't have a cigarette girl in my restaurant. I don't have a girl that is trying to sell you a doll. I have one of the cleanest establishments in the entire country, let alone Chicago. And as long as I am clean, I believe they lay off me.

Q. You have heard it from other restaurant owners that they have to make payments?

A. I haven't heard that . . . I might have heard it hearsay. That I don't remember.

Q. What was your answer when I asked you or discussed this with you yesterday, Mr. DeSantis?

. . .

A. Gentlemen, I don't remember . . . I have been confused, and I am not a limelight guy. I am a fellow that works in a T-shirt all day, but if you tell me what I said, I will verify if I said that.

* A bar counter dice game.

Q. Do you remember about the fact that "You and I could sit down here for hours and hours and I would tell you the answers to these questions if I didn't have a family and didn't live at my restaurant"?

A. Yes, I remember saying that to you, Mr. Kennedy.

Senator Barry Goldwater asked a question.

Q. Do you know that some of these hoodlums that shake you down never worked in their lives?

A. I sense that.

Q. They live like big fat leeches. . . . What do you think we in the rest of the country think of your great city . . . don't you think you have some responsibility there?

A. I certainly do, Senator Goldwater . . . I have heard you speak up there before . . . but there's nothing a little guy like myself can do.

Senator McClellan concluded the exchange.

Q. Do you have some information that you would be willing to give us in an executive session?

A. No, Senator . . .

Q. . . . you have an apprehension about what might happen to you?

A. That is correct . . . I believe every restaurant owner in the city of Chicago feels the same way.

Private justice was one alternative. Arthur Eberhart owned the Flanders Tearoom in Chicago. For a time he paid dues to Local 593 on a quota of six employees, then stopped. He was threatened by a union official on a picket line.

A. Well . . . I said I wasn't going to join the union . . . I said if he broke my windows I would break his. I also said if he hurt my family I would hurt his . . . he left . . . I got nervous, as I am now, and, from trying to play safe, watching my car going home, trying to enter my home, I had a heart attack.

. . .

Q. What sort of safeguard were you taking for your own life after you had this fight?

A. Well, there is no place you can go . . . You have no friends. You are entirely on your own . . . you have to use whatever defense methods you have got, and mine was a shotgun.

All incumbent HRE officials summoned before the Committee resorted to the Fifth Amendment. Trungale and O'Connor resigned from office four days before appearing. John and Daniel Lardino resigned a few hours before being questioned; the Committee discovered that all Local 593's records for the years prior to 1955 had been destroyed, that John Lardino earned some $33,000 annually from the local and that he had $50,000 in cash and bonds in his safe deposit box. Leonardi and Madia resigned under pressure from the international union. Blakely declined to appear on grounds of ill-health and remained in office. Seven underworld figures sub-poenaed by the Committee—Accardo, Sam Battaglia, Marshal Caifano, Jack Cerone, Ross Prio, Gussie Alex and Joseph DiVarco (alias Joey Cae-sar)—refused to testify. The HRE placed all of its eleven Chicago locals into trusteeship. The Chicago Restaurant Association reported to the Com-mittee that "substantial progress" had been made in correcting abuses, and that steps were being taken to improve employer-employee relations in the industry.

"The Committee finds," it said, "that the mobster-dominated locals of the Hotel and Restaurant Employees Union in Chicago served only the purpose of giving a cloak of legitimacy to what was nothing more than a pure extortion racket . . . One restaurant owner had the employees vote by secret ballot on the question of whether they wanted to be represented by the union. The poll was overwhelmingly against it, but Danny Lardino, business agent for Local 593 told the proprietor, 'Line up the employees and tell them they're in the union. You deduct the dues from their wages. If any of them object, fire them, and we will furnish you help.' . . . The committee finds as an undisputed fact that restaurant operators who dealt with the union representatives in the manner heretofore described profited from the arrangement to the extent of thousands of dollars annually be-cause the union representatives, interested only in the flow of dues pay-ments into their hands, never made the slightest effort to enforce the pre-vailing minimum wage scale specified by the standard contract in the Chi-cago area."

The Committee noted, however, that while the HRE had moved "at least partially to clean its own house, the only response from the industry has been to heap abuse on the committee for looking into the matter in the first place . . . Instead of serving as the rallying point of resistance to iden-tifiable gangsters pursuing their policy of encroachment upon the industry, the Chicago Restaurant Association chose to make common cause with the enemy by functioning as a mere conduit for the appeasement of profes-sional racketeers. There is nothing in the record remotely suggesting bona fide collective bargaining."

The Coin Machine Operators

Coin-operated machines provide various services. "One-armed bandits" and other devices assuage the gambling instinct. Jukeboxes play the muse to other pleasures. Automatic vendors wash clothes, shine shoes, and sell all kinds of wares. The industry is substantial and growing. In 1957 the retail value of all machines sold was more than two billion dollars.

The entrepreneurs fall into four groups. The manufacturers are usually large corporations. Distributorships franchised by the manufacturers as exclusive agents in sales territories are mainly locally owned. Independent operators own from a few to several thousand machines, renting them to restaurants, taverns and other places of leisure in return for part of the income from the machines. The users, the location owners, seldom own the machines installed in their establishments. The Committee found no evidence of dubious practices among manufacturers, and little among others active in that segment of the industry which dealt with vending machines. The rest of the industry was less respectable.

"No matter where you go," Committee Investigator Arthur Kaplan testified, "you are almost certain to find that leading operators in various areas are hoodlums . . . they are people with racket connections . . . they are people with police records."

The Committee investigated the coin-machine industry in Cleveland, Chicago, Denver, Detroit, Los Angeles, Miami, New Orleans, Portland (Oregon), Seattle, and Youngstown (Ohio), finding "alarming examples of criminal domination of legitimate business achieved by using corrupt unions . . ." Many of the operators were organized into non-profit organizations for the declared purpose of "uplifting the ethics" of the industry. "Actually," the Committee said, "these associations function to restrain trade by allocating territories and customers, by fixing prices to the consumer, and by setting commission rates paid to location owners." They also boycotted the products of competitors, forced location owners to rent rather than buy machines, and policed their jurisdictions by whatever means necessary. Sometimes persuasion or economic sanctions were enough; sometimes unions were involved; sometimes violence was necessary, hard to resist. "You fight the Mafia," an unhappy location owner told the St. Louis police, "not me." At one remove or another the Committee encountered many of the major racketeers in the United States. "It appears no small coincidence," the Committee said, "that of the fifty-eight criminals at the notorious enclave of Apalachin * . . . more than a dozen . . . were connected with the coin-machine industry."

* On November 14, 1957, the New York State Police raided a meeting at Apalachin, in upstate New York, of fifty-eight alleged proconsuls of the American underworld. It was, the Committee said, "by far the biggest known assemblage of top racketeers." Industrially, those present represented the coin-machine, garment, grocery, restaurant, condiment, entertainment, waterfront, construction and general trucking and service trades. At least seven of them were past or present local union officials.

Connections were important. Milton J. Hammergren, a former vice president and general manager of the Rudolph Wurlitzer Company of Chicago, was asked how he improved a poor market.

A. Well, let's take Chicago. I had a very intimate friend named Goldberg . . . very aggressive and well connected . . . I used him as a sort of spearhead wherever I had trouble.

. . .

Q. He had connections, then, with the underworld element in the United States?
A. Yes, I would say so.

Hammergren had a number of friends—Jake ("Greasy Thumb") Guzik and Dennis ("The Duke") Cooney of the Capone organization in Chicago, Meyer Lansky in New York and Angelo Meli in Detroit, "Happy" Ruffa in East St. Louis and Sam Taran in St. Paul—all of whom had influence in the jukebox industry. It was not a gentle trade.

Q. Looking back, was there a considerable amount of violence in connection with the industry?
A. That was spotty. Yes, there was violence, such as blowing out the windows of the store or blowing up an automobile or something of that nature, or beat a fellow up . . . you would have to use some force . . . we didn't like it, but we still had to sell jukeboxes . . .
Q. Even if it became necessary that somebody was killed . . . ?
A. Well, that is pretty broad . . . I don't think we would condone that knowingly, no.
Q. I mean if somebody, just in the course of trying to get your boxes distributed, if somebody was killed, that was taken as part of the trade?
A. That is one of the liabilities of the business, I would say.

One of the reasons why the underworld was involved in the distribution of jukeboxes, Hammergren explained, was because "they were able to do things that the ordinary individual wasn't able to do in a big metropolitan area. They had unions and associations at their disposal."

Various inhabitants of the underworld were called to testify, but most were mute. The Committee questioned Frank Zito.

Q. Do you know a man by the name of De Rosa?
A. I decline to. It may incriminate myself.
Q. He was a pinball operator . . . in Illinois, during 1956–57 . . . until his headless body was found in a cornfield in Sangamon County . . . His body was found after a farm dog found the head and brought it to its master . . . He had worked for your brother and had set up a company in competition with your brother. Wasn't that one of the problems?
A. I decline to. It may incriminate myself.

Underworld infiltration, the Committee found, was widespread and increasing. Profits were high, at least for those using doctored game machines, and the business was a convenient cover for those active in gambling, narcotics and other rackets. On occasion the federal government was an unwitting ally; in some areas, jukebox operators were able to obtain licenses from the Federal Communications Commission for short-wave radio stations, used officially to direct service vehicles to jukebox locations but mainly to broadcast racing results for illegal bookmaking.

The business community was partly to blame. "Another and shocking reason for increasing industry control by the underworld was the willingness of ostensibly respectable business concerns to use criminals to increase sales," the Committee said. Legitimate unionism was virtually absent from the industry. "The history of every coin-machine union investigated," the Committee reported, "disclosed its formation, sustention, and direction by and for the employers . . . an astounding proportion of criminals was found in controlling roles in either—and sometimes both—union or employer groups . . . The gambling and jukebox segments reflected the deepest criminal permeation. However, underworld tentacles were evident in the game and vending machine operations."

Both local and international unions were created, at least on paper, to provide respectability and effective enforcement to operators and their associations. Competitive locations were picketed or boycotted. Independent operators were driven out of business. The union label, a time-honored *bona fide* of the products and services of union members, was used to restrict coin machine distribution and maintenance to collaborators and to make money for union officials who charged a price for the label. "Their obvious purpose," the Committee said of the so-called unions involved, "had no relations to legitimate labor objectives, and the committee could find no evidence that any one of the locals protected or improved the wages, working conditions, or standards of the industry's employees."

In New York, the jukebox field was dominated by the Music Operators of New York (MONY). The association had some 160 operators controlling 8,000 machines. Labor relations had some claim to legitimacy in the jukebox field, but none in the game machine industry. There the major employers' association was the Associated Amusement Machine Operators of New York (AAMONY). The chief local union—after a series of expulsions from various AFL and CIO unions—was Local 531 of a peculiar organization, the independent United Industrial Union. President Joseph LaRocco of the UIU became the first national union officer to refuse to testify before the McClellan Committee about his organization. The

Department of Labor produced records which showed that from 1950 to 1955 the national union had no receipts, disbursements, assets or liabilities of any kind. Local 531 received its charter in 1956 and began to raid jukebox locations. Phil ("Miami Phil") Corbisiero, an operator whose funeral in 1957 was attended by many underworld figures, successfully advised a number of tavern owners to avoid trouble by dealing with Local 531. The local did not appear to engage in any organizing activities, but concentrated instead on the sale of union labels to location owners. It had no bank account or records. Secretary Al Cohen paid all expenses himself by cash or personal check. There was a labor-management contract, but no grievance procedures and no enforcement. The general contract called for $1.50 an hour for a forty-hour week, or about $1.25 an hour less than the rate obtained by another jukebox union. The contract with Corbisiero called for only $1.25 a week. The general contract also required a payment by the employer of two percent of gross wages into a welfare fund, but there was no record of any such payments. In 1957, Local 1690 of the Retail Clerks International Association obtained a permanent injunction against Local 531, putting it out of business. "It is clear," the court said, "that the defendants do not constitute a *bona fide* union."

Another obscure institution, the Federated Service Workers Union, chartered a Local 19 which took the place of UIU Local 531 in both the game and jukebox businesses. Sidney Saul, an operator in both fields, was threatened with death by Ernest Filicomo, alias Ernie ("Kip") Kippy, unless he ceded one of his locations. He met Kippy and ex-convicts Anthony ("Dutch") Tuzio and Charles Panarella in a restaurant.

A. Tuzio went and put a coin in the jukebox . . . Kip took his coat off . . . started punching at me. They kept saying to each other, "This fellow is an actor," because I was pleading them to stop beating me . . . Tuzio kept saying, If you haven't got $500, give them $300. It is cheaper than buying a new set of false teeth . . . I was losing consciousness and slumping over the table . . . Before I had a chance to look up, Kip was back at me, and this time it was really heavy . . . I didn't cry . . . I was bleeding from both nostrils and my mouth . . . Kip didn't stop. He was like a wild man . . . I couldn't open my mouth at all, and my jaws felt as though they were locked at the end . . . Finally, out of desperation I said I would take them in as a partner . . . my nose was completely out of shape, and it was formed like a horseshoe, like a U . . . I couldn't chew food for almost three weeks . . .

. . .

Q. You have been under the protection of the district attorney's office since that time?

A. Yes, sir.

Q. You have had a police guard since that time?
A. Yes, sir.

According to other testimony, the notorious Gallo brothers of New York City gave their support to Local 19. Anthony Camerona, president of the local, had no previous trade union experience. John Amalfitano, the president of the FSWU, refused to testify about the union, about his association with the Gallo brothers or Carmine Lombardozzi—a jukebox operator present at the Apalachin meeting—or about the murder of Biago Latriano —an official of Local 19 who was shot eleven times through the head. The Music Operators of New York finally obtained an injunction against Local 19, and the local was succeeded in effect by Local 266 of the Teamsters. Against the opposition of Teamster International Organizer Thomas Hickey—later replaced by Hoffa—the Joint Council of Teamsters assigned jurisdiction to Local 266. The Gallo brothers and other coin-machine operators formed a new association, the United Coin Machine Operators of New York, and signed an agreement with Local 266. The game machine employers' group, the AAMONY, soon followed suit, afffiliating with the UCMONY.

The leader of Local 266 was Joseph DeGrandis, a man of various aliases and convictions, who refused to testify. He had been an officer of Local 413 of the Retail Clerks on Long Island. When the local's charter was revoked by the international union, the only effects found in its headquarter were a gun and a billy club. Brooklyn attorney Joseph A. Iovine, an uncle of the Gallo brothers, was vice president of Local 266, although he never paid dues and was thus ineligible for office under the international union's constitution; at the same time he was legal counsel for one of the operators. Local 266 operated out of DeGrandis' home. It was set up, according to the Committee, "strictly as a means of providing such fear and intimidation as is necessary to take over jukebox locations for the operators." Milton Green, an operator who wanted to put the AAMONY into voluntary bankruptcy to avoid contractual relations with Local 266, was followed home one night by the Gallo brothers and various of their allies in the UCOMONY and Local 266, and was beaten with a steel bar, receiving a skull fracture and other injuries from which he never completely recovered. "All this," in the Committee's view, "was a means toward achieving a monopoly in the business in the New York area, and was obviously done with the knowledge, consent, and approval of higher authorities in the Teamsters International, including James R. Hoffa."

Usury was a practice in the trade. Charles Bernoff was a vice president of MONY and president of the Regal Music Company—a jukebox and game machine business founded, according to the Committee, by a number of "top hoodlums, closely associated with the Lepke-Gurrah mob [Murder, Inc.] . . ." Bernoff lent money at rates of up to 198 percent to coin-machine operators, white slavers, gamblers, burglars, accused murderers and labor racketeers. The Committee heard testimony on some of the latter from Detective Thomas O'Brien of the New York City Police Department.

Q. What do we know of David Karpf . . . ?
A. He is actually a labor extortionist, and at the present time is serving a three-year sentence for extorting money from the union. He has been convicted with the business agent of the union while manager of local 102 of ILGWU . . . He has a brother Charles, who is a bookmaker . . . in 1958 he was kicked out of the AFL . . . He was connected with the Textile Workers Union and he used that union as a front for shakedowns in the jukebox industry . . . Little Augie [Lichtenstein] is another well-known labor racketeer . . . His association goes back to Murder, Incorporated . . that was terrorizing the garment industry in its day . . . he was part of the ring that extorted $2.5 million from the milk industry . . . with the connivance of some of the local officials of the Teamster Union.

Debt collection was brisk. Bernoff refused to testify, but the Committee produced letters he had written to his brother Jay, urging him not to forgive their debtors.

No. 4—Four. This one gets my goat . . . Nail him to the cross . . .
No. 5—Freddie Kaplan. Locate this swindler and needle him till he pays.
No. 6—Cuppy. This bum keeps ducking, let him borrow from his friends and pay up. Tell him any story, it's rough, etc., and we need it.
No. 9—Rosen. There's no reason in God's world why this dead beat won't pay you, of all people. He can certainly afford to pay $60,000 a week or more . . . This is one character I would like to see produce for you. . . . Are we going to let all this good money that we sweated blood for go to hell, not if I can help it. I'll do my share, you do yours. Pitch in, get in the ball game and let's hit a couple of homers and win a few ball games, it's about time . . . The Bible says, "Seek and ye shall find."

I almost left out our prize—B. Z.—don't take no more crap from him. He is playing cat and mouse with you. You be the cat and let him be the mouse. Let's see what 1951 brings and here's hoping Yonkey Doodle goes to town.

The Committee questioned Irving Mishel, one of Bernoff's employees, who had bridled at lending money to narcotics peddlers.

Q. So there was a direct tie-in between this operation which loaned money to these underworld figures and the jukebox operation that had been set up originally?

A. Yes, sir.

Q. And which, in turn, was set up by underworld figures, the jukebox operation itself being set up by these major underworld figures?

. . .

A. That is correct.

"In the Midwest," the Committee said, "the underworld is known as the 'Syndicate.' Its upper echelon still includes former Capone gang killers. It dominates the jukebox, game machine, and cigarette machine business."

The syndicate exacted over $200,000 a year from jukebox and game machine operators. The latter were forced to buy high-priced counterfeit records—copied records sold under forgeries of their original labels—from a syndicate shop. Businessmen were told to buy and promote the records of syndicate-owned singers. Legitimate operators were forced out of business or compelled to accept gangsters as non-contributing partners. "In each instance," the Committee asserted, "it seemed that law-enforcement agencies were ineffective . . . In each instance, Fred ("Jukebox") Smith, business representative of Local 134, International Brotherhood of Electrical Workers, [and] Joseph Paul Glimco, racketeer Teamster official, played a major role." *

Most Chicago jukebox operators belonged to an association, the Recorded Music Service Association. They and their employees also had to belong to Local 134 which, the Committee found, "served as the enforcement arm of the association." They were further required to belong to the Commercial Phonograph Survey, a private licensing agency, in order to do business; the agency was managed by one of Smith's protégés and three convicts—one of whom was a former assistant to Chicago gang leader Anthony Accardo. Smith and Glimco also frequently asked operators to buy the wares of the Lormar Distributing Company—said to be a gangster operation run by Charles English, a lieutenant of underworld chieftain Sam ("Mooney") Giancana; if the operators refused they lost their locations to the E. and E. Music Company, a "whip" company for Lormar. Lormar in time achieved a near-monopoly of sales in Chicago of both legitimate and counterfeit records. Smith took the Fifth Amendment when called to testify about his alleged extortions of and about his jukebox business partnership with Glimco. The IBEW tried to examine the books of the coin-machine division of Local 134, but Smith said there were none. The union expelled him. No action was taken by the Teamsters against Glimco.

In 1955 a group of amusement machine owners formed the Chicago Independent Amusement Machine Association, a non-profit corporation in-

* Joseph P. Glimco, president of Teamster Local 777 in Chicago.

tended to prevent location-jumping and competition among themselves. At Smith's suggestion they hired Hyman Larner to police the arrangement. Larner, using the name of Red Waterfall, then claimed to negotiate a contract with Local 134. Association dues were raised 600 percent to include the payment of employees' union dues. No contract in fact was signed, and no dues ever reached Local 134. The association's office, however, was equipped with rubber stamps, business cards and other paraphernalia belonging to Local 134. "These and other similar articles showed conclusively that the 'union' operated out of the offices of the employers' association," the Committee concluded.

After the alleged negotiation of the contract, the association advised all game machine operators in Chicago to join. Two professional thugs, Alex Ross and James Rini, wrecked twenty machines belonging to non-joiners with hatchets or sulphuric acid, receiving payments from Larner, association president Sam Greenburg, and from gangster Eddie ("Butch") Vogel —thought to be Smith's sponsor in union office. Larner, previously one of Vogel's employees, disappeared for nine months with the association's records. The Committee discovered that while for eight years he had declared an average annual income of $8,700, he had a home in Miami worth more than $55,000, an expensive apartment on Lake Shore Drive in Chicago, a Cadillac and several other cars, and a net worth of over $100,-000. When he was finally subpoenaed he invoked the Fifth Amendment. Vogel, allegedly the head of the coin-machine racket in Chicago, also refused to testify.

In 1951 John Testo organized an independent union of employees in the coin machine business in the city of Gary, Lake County, Indiana, just across the state line from Chicago. Two years later, the syndicate formed the Century Distributing Company, recruiting the aid of Rocco Schiralli, the deputy controller of Gary, for their operations in Lake County. Testo tried to organize the company, but was persuaded by Glimco—whom he met at Schiralli's suggestion—not to do so. Testo then began to have trouble with the law when he attempted to have union members service illegal pinball machines in Gary. He told the Committee of a conversation with Metro Holovachka, the Lake County prosecutor, on being summoned to the latter's office.

> A. . . . he told me I should behave myself, that I cause a lot of trouble . . . I say, "Listen, the other people is organized. Why not these people can be organized? And he told me, he said, 'listen, I am going to get something on you. I am going to put you in jail some of these days.' "

· · · ·

Q. And every time you made any effort to try to organize them . . . you would be subpoenaed . . . ?

Q. That is right . . .

The syndicate prevailed. Local police harried the locations of independent operators until the latter removed their pinball machines; in some cases the police themselves removed the machines. Syndicate machines were then installed, and left alone by the law. The independents, accusing Holovachka of framing tavern owners who supported his political opponents, appealed to the governor of Indiana for help, but with no result. The Indiana State Police later described law enforcement in Lake County as the worst in the state.*

Resistance was apparently futile. Walter Conroy, Holovachka's chief investigator, testified that he often confiscated pinball machines on instructions, without any evidence of illegal gambling being available. In no case was any legal action taken by or against the county prosecutor.

Q. These people lost their machines just on your say-so that there was gambling. Don't they have a right to go to court?

A. They go to the prosecuting attorney.

Holovachka's bank account showed deposits—many of them made in small bills—far in excess of expected savings. In 1957 and 1958 he reported income four times greater than his official salary. He refused to disclose the source of his non-official income.

Q. Do you think now, as a public official, that you owe it to the people of your community, in view of this public development, to let them know the truth about it?

A. About my private affairs . . . ? No, sir.

The independent union went out of business. "When they need a labor union," Robert F. Kennedy said of the underworld, "they set a labor organization up; when they feel it is more beneficial they put a labor organization out of existence."

"It appeared no coincidence," the Committee reported, "that the most extensive misuse of labor unions discovered in our coin-machine inquiry was in the personal bailiwick of Mr. James Hoffa. Indeed, he was responsible for the racketeer subversion of at least two locals in the Motor City."

* Holovachka had also apparently failed to press the case against Hutcheson, Blaier and Chapman of the Carpenters for alleged bribery of a public official, causing the indictment to take place in the neighbouring Marion County. Counsel Robert F. Kennedy contended that Maxwell C. Raddock had been employed by Hutcheson to prevent the indictment in Lake County and "fix this case." Holovachka declined to appear before the Committee to testify on the matter.

August Scholle, then president of the Michigan State CIO and later of the Michigan State AFL-CIO, told the Committee of a visit he received from two men who wanted a CIO charter for an employer-dominated local in the coin-machine business.

Q. Were they so-called gangster types, would you say?
A. Well, I would say that they certainly could have been put in that role in Hollywood . . . I advised them very carefully and very patiently that we didn't give out charters to employers . . . A fellow reached into his blue silk shirt pocket, rolled out a roll of bills wrapped up with a rubber band, and said, "Here is the downpayment" . . . they said that there would be ten grand in it for me . . . again I tried to carefully explain to them that we just didn't have CIO charters for sale . . . one fellow seemed seriously puzzled. He said, "Well, you are the boss, aren't you?" and I said, "Yes, I presume you would assume that. I am the highest authority of the organization in this area," and he said, "Well then, why can't I buy a charter?"

About a month later, evidently through Hoffa's efforts, a jukebox charter was issued by the Teamsters to Local 985. Scholle was asked about that.

A. Well, I know Jimmy. I have known him for a long time . . . I suppose he didn't care. I don't presume that he is as concerned, well, with trying to keep the organized labor movement's name clean and wholesome and appealing to people. I can't give you any other reason . . .

In 1945 the Michigan Automatic Phonograph Operators Association signed a "sweetheart" contract with AFL Federal Local 23814 headed by Eugene ("Jimmy") James. James also owned stock in two Detroit jukebox distributorships. Former MAPOA President Joseph Brilliant said that James and the Association got along very well.

Q. Were you pleased with the service that Mr. James was performing?
A. Very much . . . The association rendered him a Cadillac.

. . .

Q. Who was James representing, the union or the association?
A. Both.

One of the major investors in the Detroit coin machinery industry was Angelo Meli, once Detroit's Public Enemy No. 1. Associated with him in the Bilvin Distributing Company were John ("Papa John") Priziola, considered by the Federal Bureau of Narcotics to be one of the leading drug traffickers in the United States; and William Bufalino, the husband of Meli's niece.

James picketed some of the locations where the Bilvin Company's non-union jukeboxes were installed. A meeting was arranged between James's local and the employers. The Bilvin group was admitted into the association. Bufalino became James's assistant.

Morris Goldman, another former president of the association, told the Committee of a warning by the state liquor control commission that, unless the coin-machine industry was cleaned up, jukeboxes would be removed from all bars.

Q. Is cleaning up the industry bringing into your association this underworld group? . . . It meant complete capitulation on your part, did it not?
A. It did . . .

The AFL withdrew James's charter in 1947. Shortly afterwards he received the charter for Local 985 of the Teamsters. "The charter," the Committee said, "was fraudulently obtained by Hoffa personally for the use of Bufalino and his sponsors." The official jurisdiction of the local was over drivers and garage employees; the charter was granted on an application made in 1941; none of the original signatories to the application joined the local. Hoffa paid for the charter, its seal and stamp, and personally collected them for the local. James went off to Florida and other parts, finally becoming secretary-treasurer of the Laundry Workers, although he continued for some years to receive a salary as president of Local 985. Bufalino became business manager of the local. Brilliant told of a meeting with Hoffa.

A. We had one meeting. Mr. Hoffa brought us into his office and there were seven or eight members, and Mr. Bufalino, and myself. He told Mr. Bufalino to run a clean union and not to favor anybody. We thought it was a very nice speech.

. . .

Q. Did he tell Mr. Bufalino that he didn't want him to favor his relatives?
A. He sure did.

. . .

Q. Did Mr. Bufalino favor his relatives?
A. He sure did.

Local 985 signed a substandard contract with the association, agreeing to a wage scale less than that already being paid some jukebox operators in Detroit. The contract was not enforced, although employer opposition to Local 985 was sometimes followed by bombings.

Local 985 also represented carwash employees. The labor-management agreement provided for only the federal minimum wage. Members of the local paid dues of ten cents a day, but many of them were neither carried on the local's books nor reported for *per capita* tax purposes to the international union. In some cases, unionized carwash employees received $25 a week for seventy hours of work.

Local 985 did not organize various firms owned by Bufalino's relatives or allegedly controlled by the underworld. One unorganized firm belonged to Vincent Meli, Bufalino's brother-in-law, with whom Bufalino was a partner in the real estate business.

Brilliant told the Committee that several Teamster officials were in the jukebox business, "taking locations one at a time, from everybody."

Q. Were they difficult to compete with?
A. I should say they were . . . they just put in a new machine, and you were called to take yours out . . . It was impossible to compete with.

Three of the Teamster jukebox businessmen—Cecil Watts, Morris Coleman and Lawrence Welsh—were ex-convicts. Watts and Coleman were business agents for Local 337, headed by Hoffa's close associate Owen Bert Brennan. Welsh worked for Bufalino in Local 985. All three refused to testify.

Bufalino ran a separate business as a labor consultant, held interests in various coin machine firms, and managed real estate in partnership with a jukebox operator and the attorney for the employers' association. He also received legal fees or reimbursements from Teamster Locals 299 and 985 in connection with one or another of Hoffa's various trials, although he had been rejected three times for membership by the Michigan Bar Association. "Testimony established," the Committee said, "that Bufalino was closely associated in business with hoodlums and racketeers."

"[N]owhere in this hearing," Senator McClellan observed, "is there to be found one scintilla of evidence that Local 985 has done anything to help the wages and working conditions of its members in these industries. To the contrary . . . members of Mr. Bufalino's local had their wages drastically reduced after they became union members and their employers had signed contracts with Local 985 . . . we find a local in alliance with racketeers and which fails in any way to exercise the proper obligations of labor unionism toward its members and toward the community." Bufalino disclaimed any improper activities or relationships.

Carlos Marcello, according to the Committee, was the head of organized crime in Jefferson Parish, Louisiana. He came to the state in 1935 allegedly as a result of an agreement made by Frank Costello and Philip ("Dandy Phil") Kastel with Governor Huey Long to transfer some slot machine operators from New York to New Orleans. A former narcotics peddler, Marcello began a long-term residence in Jefferson Parish under the protection of Sheriff Frank ("King") Clancy. In 1956 Clancy was succeeded by "reform" candidate William S. Coci. Within a few weeks of his election, Coci and four senior associates called upon various bars and restaurants, removing jukeboxes and pinball machines and making it known that Marcello's equipment was available.

Coci declined to appear before the Committee. Marcello invoked the Fifth Amendment. Aaron M. Kohn, the managing director of the Metropolitan Crime Commission of New Orleans, described Marcello's inhibiting effect on trade unionism in the parish.

A. Our labor union organization has not yet caught up with the concentration of people and industry . . . in the jukebox-pinball area . . . many persons who might otherwise be interested in joining a union would think mighty, mighty long before identifying themselves with something which might, just might, displease the Carlos Marcello mob, who have a major interest in that industry . . . there have been two very timid attempts, one by the Electrical Workers [IBEW] some years ago, and then one by the Teamsters a couple of years ago. They made no real, aggressive effort to continue organization. There has not been, I might point out, violence of any kind or racketeering of any kind in the New Orleans area by the Teamsters . . .

. . .

Q. Because of this close tie-in that already exists between management, gangsters and certain public officials, there has been no need to try to bring in . . . a corrupt labor union . . . and honest labor unions have a difficult time moving in because of the fact that there is such control and domination of the area by these groups.

A. I would say that to be accurate . . .

Marcello, a Sicilian immigrant, was ordered deported in 1953. In 1968 he was still in business in Jefferson Parish.

Mr. X was a manufacturer of coin-operated radios in Los Angeles. In 1946 the Southern California Music Operators Association asked him to form a local union to protect its members from competition. X obtained a charter for Local 1052 of the IBEW.

Q. The primary purpose at that time was to protect the locations of the various operators . . . They had an agreement among themselves that they would not jump one another's location . . . The union was going to place a picket line in front of a tavern where a group which was not a member of the association, therefore not a member of the union, came in and tried to take a location . . . the association members and the union members were one and the same?

A. They were, sir.

In 1952 the Los Angeles Central Labor Council, AFL, refused to recognize Local 1052's pickets and the sale of union labels for machines was discontinued at the Council's request.

Prior to that, in 1950, Joseph ("Sugar Joe") Peskin had come to Los Angeles. Peskin won his nickname as the main supplier of sugar to Capone's bootlegging organization; he was also largely responsible for the enforcement system set up by the Illinois Phonograph Owners Association in cooperation with Local 134 of the IBEW. Peskin demanded membership in Local 1052; he insisted as well that the local's operator-members buy a set monthly quota of his machines, threatening violence if he was refused. Turned down, he went to see Frank Matula, the secretary-treasurer of Local 396 of the Teamsters in Los Angeles.

Matula began raiding IBEW coin machine locations. In response, Local 1052 picketed the main building of the Teamsters in Los Angeles, encountering both violence and infidelity. X testified.

> A. We put twenty-one men on the first day. The next day the Teamsters put an equal number in behind each one of our pickets with spikes in their shoes. They ripped our men's legs and sent most of them to the hospital. So we replaced them in a short time with girls. We put a lot of girls on. Then they dated the girls on and took them out to lunch until finally we ended up with ladies 55–60 . . . They didn't take them to lunch.

The uncourted pickets stayed on for nine months, until Local 1052 ran out of money. The Teamsters took over, while X developed other problems.

In 1952, X tried to organize the operators in San Diego. Frank Bompensiero, described by the Committee as a "notorious syndicate leader in Southern California," demanded fifty percent of the local's revenue. X refused and was punished.

> Q. . . . Would you relate that to the committee?
> A. That I would rather not relate to the committee . . . I registered at the Grand Hotel . . . I told Frank Bompensiero that he looked like a pretty smart man . . . We had to send *per capita* tax into the International, that we would go ahead with the organizing . . . The next day . . . several of the operators came up to the room in two's and three's, to talk to me . . . about 9:30 the last one left. Then about forty-five minutes later a rap came at the door and there was three big, I would say, Italians . . . there was a gun brought into evidence. I told them they wouldn't dare use a gun because it would be heard all over the hotel. So one of them pulled a knife . . . With that they manhandled me a little. They had a hammer, and they had a large object. They took my clothes off, inserted the object, and used the hammer and handle, at which time I passed out.

Q. This was a cucumber?

A. Yes, sir, it was.

Q. A large cucumber?

A. Yes, sir. And about 6:30 in the morning I came to. I was laying on the floor. I had lain there all night, in a pool of blood.

X was hospitalized. The IBEW ordered him not to return to San Diego and revoked Local 1052's charter. The Teamsters assumed jurisdiction in both Los Angeles and San Diego. X took up real estate.

In 1957 the two largest cigarette vending machine companies in Los Angeles—Rowe Service and Coast Cigarette Vendors—engaged in a location war. Thomas Vaughn, the president of a Rowe subsidiary in New Orleans, met with Los Angeles racketeer Mickey Cohen, who evidently said that gangster Fred Sica had been offered $20,000 by Coast Cigarette Vendors to take away Rowe Service locations. Vaughn and Rowe Service's Los Angeles manager George Seedman offered Cohen and Sica $5,000 each to stay neutral. Cohen turned the offer down, saying that only the day before he had been offered $50,000 "to put Mr. Seedman's lights out." Vaughn agreed to pay Cohen $10,000, and was asked about it.

Q. I have one question. What service did Mr. Cohen render for this $10,000?

A. No service whatsoever, sir.

"Here is a large company," Robert Kennedy told the Committee, "that is willing to pay $10,000 to him just to stay out of the company. There are large companies in the United States who want to be associated and who have become associated with gangsters in order to help their business . . . That is the reason that these kinds of people survive. They get payment from management . . . in order to take away stops, locations, business from their competitors . . . Management in the United States is willing to make these kinds of payoffs because these men have criminal and underworld connections."

Other testimony indicated that Cohen and Sica had in fact offered their services to Coast Cigarette Vendors, but had been turned down. Vaughn and Seedman paid the $10,000.

Sica took the Fifth Amendment. So did Cohen, although he had a special disclaimer when asked if he had in fact been offered $50,000 to put Seedman's lights out. "I got nothing to do," he said, "with electricity. . . ."

"For a decade," the Committee disclosed, "notorious hoodlums have manifested their interest in Miami coin-machine operations." One of these was evidently Joseph Massei, "a well-known gangster and suspected murderer from the Detroit area . . . a close associate of major Mafia criminals." Another was Joseph Mangone, who in 1950 combined with various other undesirables to form the Amusement Machine Operators Association to control competition in Miami. Anthony Randazzo, a former partner of the late Chicago gangster Joseph Embry (alias Vincent Ammerratti), was hired to police the arrangement. When a majority of the operators voted to fire Randazzo, Mangone and others seceded from the AMOA, formed the Automatic Music Guild and hired Randazzo.

Randazzo was assisted in his duties by ex-convict Charles Karpf, who presented himself to the operators as a business agent of Local 598 of the Upholsterers International Union. Karpf made the selling point that—unlike Local 359 of the IBEW in Miami, which was composed solely of employee technicians—Local 598 was composed mainly of employers, was interested solely in their security, and did not become involved in wages and working conditions. The Guild soon built a following and rejoined the AMOA, which then signed an agreement with Local 598.

Local 349 had been chartered to provide *bona fide* trade union competition for Local 598. On the representation of Leonard Baitler, an organizer for Local 349, President Sal Hoffman of the Upholsterers revoked the charter of Local 598. Karpf then conducted his business as a representative of Local 206 of the United Textile Workers of America, and was recognized by a majority of the operators. The IBEW cancelled the union membership of the seventy-five service men in Local 349, claiming racketeer infiltration of the industry as its reason. The disenfranchised members were thus forced into Karpf's organization.

The agreement between Local 206 and the operators provided for a weekly wage for employees of fifty dollars, with no other benefits or contractual protection. The wage was well below the industry average. The operators paid a monthly sum of $1,000 in dues to both the AMOA and Local 206. Operators who did not join the AMOA were picketed, beaten up, or stink-bombed. Robert Norman was one of the non-joiners, and his place of business was stink-bombed.

> Q. This was an attempt, was it not, to gain complete control of the industry in the Miami area . . . this collusive arrangement between certain employers and the union, and the union was dominated and controlled by gangsters and racketeers . . . ?
> A. Well, that was the general picture.
>
>   · · ·
>
> Q. I don't like to place on the record that your place still smells—
> A. It does on damp days.

Q. How long ago did this occur?

A. Approximately four years ago.

After the stink-bombing Norman was approached by Joseph ("Joe Scootch") Indellicato, an ex-convict associate of Massei and a former employee of Salvatore Falcone, one of the participants in the Apalachin conference. Indellicato offered to act as a mediator, but Norman turned him down. Indellicato refused to testify before the Committee and was reticent when asked how he could live in Miami on a declared annual income of between $1,500 and $2,500. Others' testimony suggested that he had been involved in shakedown activities with Teamster representative "Barney" Baker.*

Through the intervention of the Miami Crime Commission Karpf and some of his associates were convicted of extortion. Baitler organized a new local union which he led into the Teamsters, became disillusioned, and left for Japan. The Teamsters assumed jurisdiction over all coin-machine workers in Miami. The Committee said it was "surprised to learn that Sal Hoffman's disavowal of Karpf was the sole effective action against him by labor or government, even though the State acknowledged in May, 1955 that Karpf had not been licensed [as required by Florida law] as a business agent for the Upholsterers International Union. The Committee was not surprised to learn that Karpf subsequently attempted the same racket against the Miami window washing business nor that other hoodlums continued to prey upon coin-machine operators."

"The coin-operated machine industry of this Nation," the Committee observed, "is inherently a legitimate business . . . [but it] has been victimized by an astounding number of racketeers. During the past two decades, almost every infamous criminal in America has held interest in some segment of coin-machine operations . . . Racketeers have shown an increasing inclination to assume the role of labor leaders . . . the underworld has found an apparatus readymade to do its bidding. For many years employers had been acting in collusion with subservient union officials to enforce trade restraints to benefit favored employers and the corrupt labor officials . . . Criminals have used captive labor union locals as weapons to dominate various parts of the industry. They have had little trouble in obtaining racket locals for their own use. As honest labor leaders have withdrawn charters from locals perverted to non-trade union objectives, an increasing number of racket locals have taken over the field . . . No effort has been

* See pp. 246 ff. on Baker.

made to promote *bona fide* locals for industry employees. This has left a jurisdictional vacuum that has been filled almost completely by the Teamsters . . . In not a single area of its inquiry has the Committee found evidence of benefits obtained by coin-machine locals for the employees of the industry, with the fleeting exception of Mr. Baitler's unit of Local 349, IBEW, Miami . . . Management has knowingly used criminals to increase its sales . . . in some areas where small businessmen have sought to resist racketeers, they have received little help from local authorities, and have had to risk their entire resources and even their lives against well-financed and ruthless criminals. The Committee believes that such widespread lawlessness threatens the sovereignty of our democracy."

18: The Teamsters Here and There

The Committee spent a full two-thirds of its energies investigating the International Brotherhood of Teamsters, Chauffeurs, Warehousemen and Helpers of America—at that time, with some 1,600,000 members, the largest trade union in the United States. It turned first to the Western Conference of Teamsters, a regional body representing Teamsters in the eleven Western States.*

Frank Brewster was the chairman of the Western Conference. He liked horses, and owned a stable in partnership with George Newell, broker for the Western Conference's health and welfare funds. He made almost no investment in the stable, yet when the partnership broke up he took out a profit of $44,366.03. Newell lost $40,712.75. Brewster also owed Newell $40,000, but did not seem to consider it a pressing obligation.

Q. Do you think it is a proper transaction for the president [sic] of the Western Conference of Teamsters to allow himself to be owing the broker for the insurance fund $40,000?

A. I have known George Newell long before he brokered, all my life . . . I think it is all right. I am not taking advantage of the position.

Q. He makes from the Western Conference of Teamsters approximately $300,000 a year, does he not, net?

A. Yes. It is one of the lowest brokerage fees in the business.

      . . .

Q. You owe him $40,000.

A. And I intend to pay him.

Q. Have you written him any note?

A. There is still an argument about the books . . . they are not just exactly the way they were produced. There is a matter of a mare that he has that isn't on there that I sold him. That hasn't been deducted. It is a mare by the name of Whang Bang.

Q. Is this a kind of whang-bang transaction?

A. She was a whang-bang mare . . .

From 1951 to 1953 Newell also gave Brewster annual Christmas presents of stocks worth some $5,000, charging them to his brokerage company as commissions.

* The Teamsters are organized into four "conferences" or regions for administrative, organizational and bargaining purposes—the Western, Central States, Eastern and Southern Conferences.

229

Brewster was in the stable business with Teamster Organizer John J. Sweeney and Fred Galeno, a Seattle pinball machine and jukebox operator who had contractual relations with Local 353 of the Teamsters in Seattle.

> Q. Do you think it is a good idea, Mr. Brewster, for a president of the Western Conference of Teamsters to be having an interest in a company which does business with the Western Conference of Teamsters . . . you do not think there is any conflict there?
>
> A. I certainly do not.
>
> Q. What about having business with Mr. Galeno . . . Can you see there might be a problem if you did not have somebody with high principles . . . ?
>
> A. I am fortunate that Mr. Galeno has high principles.

Brewster was still president of his home Local 174 in Seattle. He could not account, however, for the expenditure of $99,999.65 from the local's "special fund," nor of $60,000 from the local's unemployment relief fund; neither fund had a bank account. Brewster was also president of the Seattle Joint Council of Teamsters, but he could not explain the disposition of $160,000 from the Council's convention fund. Committee investigators found that the first sixty-three pages of the convention fund's accounts—representing transactions up to February 1, 1953—had been torn out. They were never found.

The Committee charged that Brewster was involved in a conflict of interest with Newell; that Newell received excessive commissions for his services; that Brewster and General President Dave Beck of the Teamsters had a hidden ownership in a gas station next to the Teamsters' building in Seattle, profiting greatly from the station's sales to Teamster locals in "direct violation of their fiduciary responsibility"; that Brewster had filed false reports on the financial affairs of the Seattle Joint Council; that he had dissipated or improperly supervised the funds of the Western Conference of Teamsters; and that he had, in sum, "enriched himself at the expense of Teamster members."

Dave Beck was the founder and first chairman of the Western Conference of Teamsters, in his time a highly effective organizer and pacesetter for Teamster bargaining gains throughout much of the United States. He became president of the international union in 1952, he was a vice president of the AFL-CIO, a figure in the international labor movement, and by repute a millionaire. The Teamsters had helped.

Sometime in December, 1953, Beck evidently told Clark Mollenhoff of the Des Moines *Register* that "No union official can justify borrowing $10 or $10,000 through any employee pension or insurance fund, or from a union's petty cash . . . It is wrong and not in the best interest of the union members. I won't put up with it from the highest or the lowest union member." On the last day of the same month the building association of Joint Council 28 in Seattle had accounts receivable of $7,422.89. The following day the amount was $250,000 higher. The new loan was Beck's. Brewster said he knew nothing about it.

Brewster also could not account for the payment, during 1951 and 1952, of $146,678 by the Western Conference to a Seattle building contractor. The only construction performed for the Conference during that time was one small building costing about $35,000. The Committee was satisfied that the rest of the money had been used to build a swimming pool at Beck's home and houses for various relatives and Teamster associates in Sheridan Beach, a fashionable section of Seattle. Another $85,000 was sent to Nathan Shefferman, the strikebreaker, for personal items for Beck.

The exact amount that Beck "borrowed" from the Western Conference was never established. The Conference bookkeeper did not know how Beck had obtained the money. There was no evidence that Conference officials thought they might have authorized loans to Beck at any time. Conference records for the period in question disappeared before the Committee was able to examine them. However, by 1957 Beck had returned $370,000 to the Western Conference, although none of the money was repaid until after Beck had come under income tax investigation.

Beck was helped by the Fruehauf Trailer Company, one of the largest of its kind in the industry. In 1953 the company was involved in a proxy battle and asked Beck for assistance. The union loaned the company some $1,500,000. Soon afterwards the Internal Revenue Service showed an interest in Beck's finances. Beck then asked Roy Fruehauf, president of the company, for a loan of $200,000, apparently to help pay his debt to the Western Conference. Fruehauf arranged the loan through a complicated series of maneuvers involving several companies. He later tried to collect, but was unsuccessful until Beck sold his home to the Teamsters for $163,215; the check from the union was used in part payment on the loan. The home had originally been built with money Beck had "borrowed" from the Teamsters, was bought back by the General Executive Board of the union, then made available to Beck free of charge.

Fruehauf helped in other ways. He and Burt Seymour, president of Associated Transport and one of the movers in arranging Beck's $200,000 loan, invested $14,000 in a corporation formed to manufacture and promote the sale of toy trucks; the Teamsters also lent $20,000. The ostensible purpose of the venture was to improve the public relations of the trucking industry. Beck's role was to persuade Teamster locals to buy the toys. Teamster Joint Council 34 in St. Paul, Minnesota, did not do too well. Beck sent a telegram.

> The Minneapolis Joint Council has given splended cooperation. They have ordered 315 miniature trucks . . . We do not have a single purchase letter, wire or telephone call of any kind or character from the St. Paul's local union or the joint council, although we have had Hoffa and others trying to make contact. Please advise why we get no cooperation. If special meeting of council has not been called, please do so immediately and advise me by wire or telephone what is the matter in St. Paul.

Beck, his nephew Norman Gessert, and Shefferman were the sole financial beneficiaries of the toy truck corporation. None of them made any investment in the corporation, which was administered by Shefferman.

Fruehauf also obtained a boat for Dave Beck, Jr., at a twenty-five percent discount and shipped it to Seattle free; provided Beck himself with a car and chauffeur on a trip through France; made the Fruehauf company airplane available to Beck on various occasions; spent between $16,000 and $18,000 on a car and chauffeur for Beck's niece and her companions during a six-week tour of Europe; and lent Dave Beck, Jr., four trailers free of charge for use by a beer distributing firm in which the younger Beck had a financial interest. Fruehauf was questioned.

Q. Just why did you grant all these favors to Mr. Beck?
A. Well, I just considered it in the normal conduct of business. Mr. Beck had granted a considerable favor in saving our company.
Q. He had personally?
A. No, sir; the union.

Because of his own financial interest in the beer distributing company, together with the economic power of the Teamsters, Beck was able to have his son appointed to the presidency of the company. He also managed to win distribution rights for the company from several breweries with which the Teamsters had contractual relations—notably Anheuser-Busch, a firm in which Beck was known as "His Majesty, the wheel."

"Beck took, not borrowed," said the Committee, "more than $370,000 in union funds from the Western Conference of Teamsters Joint Council No. 28 Building Fund, and the public relations division of Joint Council No. 2." According to the Committee, Beck also received kickbacks from the placement of Teamster mortgages through a company in which he had a financial interest; received a kickback of $24,000 from the profits Shefferman had made on the sale of furniture and bookkeeping equipment to the Teamsters' international headquarters; gave union staff jobs to relatives, although they did almost no work; employed union accountants and attorneys on his own private business affairs; used his influence to obtain Teamster insurance business for a relative and for Donald Hedlund, a business associate; borrowed $270,000 at an unusually low rate of interest from Occidental Life Insurance Company, the Western Conference's chief insurer, and bought property anonymously through the company; and borrowed $100,000 at a low rate of interest from the Seattle First National Bank, where large Teamster accounts were kept. But probably the most distasteful transaction, perhaps a factor in his fall from office, followed upon the death of an old friend.

Ray Leheney was the public relations director for the Western Conference of Teamsters, a long-time Teamster official, and one of Beck's closest personal friends. Leheney died in 1956, whereupon Beck persuaded Teamster organizations throughout the country to contribute to a Leheney Memorial Fund to help the widow. Beck and Donald Hedlund used Teamster funds to buy a number of mortgages for $71,407.03. The mortgages were held for seven months, during which time their value declined. Beck and Hedlund then sold the mortgages to Mrs. Leheney at their par value of $71,607.32. Next they paid the union what the mortgages were actually worth, and shared the profit of $11,585.04 between themselves. "The committee feels," it said, "that if all points that it has elicited against Mr. Beck were written off the record, his handling of the trust fund of his best friend, Ray Leheney, would damn him in the eyes of all decent people. Even in the handling of a sacred trust from a lifelong friend Beck saw the chance for a profit and took it."

When president of the University of Washington, Beck had once condemned faculty members for resorting to the Fifth Amendment when questioned about their political activities. When questioned by the McClellan Committee, he invoked it himself.

"The fall of Dave Beck from a position of eminence in the labor union movement," the Committee noted, "is not without sadness. When named to head this rich and powerful union, he was given an opportunity to do much good for a great segment of American working men and women. But when temptation faced Dave Beck, he could not turn his back. His thievery in the final analysis became so petty that the committee must wonder at the penuriousness of the man. What would cause a man in such circumstance to succumb to the temptation of using union funds to pay for six pairs of knee drawers for $27.54, or a bow tie for $3.50? In Beck's case, the committee must conclude that he was motivated by an uncontrollable greed."

The UAW-AFL was formed in 1939, the product of internal dissension in the UAW-CIO. At first it was larger than the parent union, but was fast reduced and outpaced. By the 1950's it claimed only 80,000 members. Its standards had also declined.

The regional director for the union in the New York area during the early 1950's was racketeer Johnny Dio. He was also the business manager of Local 102. Some forty of his fellow officers were ex-convicts.

"It cannot be said," the Committee declared, "using the widest possible latitude, that John Dioguardi was ever interested in bettering the lot of the working-man." Most of the locals under Dio's influence operated essentially as rackets, extorting dues without providing services, concentrating on Negroes and Puerto Rican and other Spanish-speaking immigrants. One of Dio's organizers was "Benny the Bug" Ross. Samuel Zakmar, another UAW-AFL official, told the Committee about him.

> A. There is a fellow who did everything wrong and organized better than the rest of them . . . He would just walk into a shop and pull the switch and say, "Everybody out on strike." . . . Everybody thought he was crazy and they would walk out and the boss would sign a contract. It was as simple as that. I know it sounds unbelievable, but he organized many shops by the same method . . . He didn't believe in elections at that time.

Bargaining was less productive. The typical contract was never seen by the employees, provided for a wage rate below or just slightly above the federal minimum wage, offered no other benefits, and was unenforced. There were no union elections, no general meetings of the members, and employers usually attended the shop meetings that were held. There was no grievance process, and in many cases the union officials involved were unknown to the members. "These workers," the Committee stated, "were forced to join unions not of their own choosing or forced to work under sweatshop conditions in bitter cold and extreme heat, and are often passed around from one union to another, as the serfs of the Middle Ages were passed from one master to another."

In 1953–54, Dio and some of his associates were expelled from the UAW-AFL and the charters of several local unions were revoked. In 1955 Dio and the officers of five former UAW-AFL locals received charters for four Teamster local unions. These four locals, together with three other newly chartered organizations, were used in a Hoffa-supported move to gain control of New York Joint Council 16 of the Teamsters. As late as 1956, four of the locals had no members. "The officers and directors of these locals," the Committee reported, "read like a rogue's gallery of the New York labor movement. They include such convicted extortionists as

Joseph Cohen, Nathan Carmel, Aaron Kleinemann, Milton Levine, Dominic Santa Maria, Harry Davidoff, Sam Goldstein, and Max Chester. So phony were these locals that, in the mad dash which occurred in the Teamsters to get them chartered, officials were chosen who had never been members of the union, false addresses were given for the offices, and the stationery of five of the locals was jointly printed and kept under wraps in the offices of one of the locals." The ultimately successful move to oust the incumbent leadership of the Joint Council, the Committee said, was the "most concerted effort by the hoodlum and racketeer element to gain major power in the New York area . . ."

Hoffa had evidently dealt with Dio before. About 1953 he wanted to buy some eavesdropping devices. The Committee produced a recording of a telephone conversation he had with Dio.

Dio: I got a couple of those things.
Hoffa: Good.
Dio: So, ah, maybe— I'll have four of them tomorrow.
Hoffa: Fine.
Dio: They are the best; they work for the UN and everything else . . . and whenever you need 'em in any part of the country if you want to find out if they're your people let me know. You know what I mean?
Hoffa: Yup.

Hoffa was asked about the devices he bought.

Q. What did you do with the Minofons you purchased?
A. What did I do with them? Well, what did I do with them?

He said he could not remember.

Q. Mr. Hoffa . . . Did you in 1953 believe Dioguardi to be a man of good character and reputation?
A. . . . . I would have to say I judge people as I find them, and even though he has a conviction, it would not necessarily mean that he could not have rehabilitated himself and carried on an organization.

In 1957 Hoffa was indicted for illegally tapping the telephones of his Teamster subordinates in Detroit. The first trial ended in a hung jury, the second in acquittal. Hoffa was subsequently indicted on five counts of perjury, but the case was dropped. Meanwhile, Dio had left the Teamsters in 1954 to found Equitable Research Associates, a management consultant agency devoted, the Committee said, "to keeping employees non-union through the medium of payoffs." He later went to jail for extortion.

Abraham Gordon, rated by the Committee as one of Hoffa's chief supporters in New York, was vice president of Local 805 and the administrator of its welfare fund. Some of the officers of Local 805 had criminal backgrounds. Secretary-Treasurer Milton Holt, for example, was a confessed perjurer, and Trustee Henry DeRoma had been convicted of murder and trafficking in narcotics.

The administration of the welfare fund, according to a representative of the New York State Insurance Department, was "one of the worst" in the Department's experience. Gordon's voice on policy was final, and there was no appeal. He had sole discretion over investments, signed all checks, and fixed his own salary from the fund at between eight and ten percent of contributions, or some $20,000 a year, with two percent of contributions set aside for expenses. He also appointed himself administrator for life, although under pressure from the Insurance Department he reduced his term to fifteen years. The administrative costs of the fund were twenty-six cents on the dollar, far above average. In the eight and a half years prior to the hearings, Gordon received $26,561.95 in expenses, for which no vouchers were ever submitted. The Committee also traced the removal of $8,019.41 from the welfare fund to Gordon's personal bank accounts. "This is not a trust agreement," Senator Curtis observed, "it is a bequest." Gordon refused to testify.

The welfare fund bought a summer camp in the Catskill Mountains, at "a grossly inflated price," from Gordon's cousin Edward Robbins. Despite protests from other unions, the camp employed non-union help. Local 805 spent $250,000 on rental units at the camp, mainly for the use of officers of the local; the Committee estimated that the ordinary member of the local had a chance of staying at the camp once in every twenty years. The camp itself, however, was not much of an investment. Joseph P. Lloyd, the chairman of the county board of assessors, was asked about it.

Q. . . . The property itself was not the most valuable kind of land in that area; is that correct?

A. No, much of it was vertical; and what wasn't vertical was in a swamp.

Gordon himself preferred to stay at the nearby, expensive Concord Inn in Middletown, where he maintained a $100-a-week room the year round, but paid only his telephone bill. He did, however, pay the hotel bills for the brothers John and Thomas Dioguardi and their wives. Two of the hotel's labor advisers had criminal records. One of them, Carlo Gambino, was a delegate to the Apalachin conference.

Secretary-Treasurer Holt owned $191,000 worth of stock in companies with which Local 805 had contractual relations but refused to testify about it. Business Agent Bernard Blaustein, alias Bernard Barton or Lou Bernie, went to jail for using Local 805 as a base for narcotics traffic. Gordon had evidently retained while in union office an interest in his own firm, the Gordon Trucking Company, which had been non-union since 1946. Local 805 was strong in its support for Hoffa. In 1958 the local's executive board passed a resolution hailing Hoffa as a future "champion of the entire labor movement, for it is you and you alone who has had the courage to withstand the tremendous onslaught against labor, where weaker leaders have failed."

Anthony ("Tony Pro") Provenzano was the president of Local 560 of the Teamsters in Hoboken, New Jersey. He was, the Committee said, Hoffa's "chief henchman" in the New Jersey area, and also the associate of a "wide variety" of New York hoodlums, including Antonio ("Tony Ducks") Corallo, Carmine Tramunti, Sonny Campbell, and Anthony ("Tony Bender") Strollo.

Arthur Pitman, president of the Pitman Trucking Company, moved his business from New York City to Hoboken in 1952. He signed a contract with Local 560. The following year, he said, Provenzano demanded $5,000 from him, finally accepting $2,500.

Q. Had you been having labor trouble?
A. No . . .

. . .

Q. For what purpose was the payment made?
A. To stay in business, to stay out of trouble; that is all . . . I deducted on the trucking business as entertainment.

President Walter Dorn of the Dorn Transportation Company told the Committee that Provenzano had suggested he retain Michael Communale as a lawyer. He did so, paying Communale $200 a month, but Dorn never met or communicated with him or sought his advice.

Q. Is the reason you paid him $200 a month because you were told to do so by Tony Provenzano?
A. Yes . . . In order to avoid more labor trouble. I already had it.

Communale, who was also assistant prosecutor for Hudson County, testified.

Q. Doesn't it strike you as just a little bit peculiar, Mr. Communale, that you would be working for some five years and received some $200 a month and never be asked to do anything?
A. I had those thoughts; yes, sir. Do you want to know why I didn't do something about it?
Q. All right.
A. I felt that as long as this company was willing to pay me the sum of $200

a month on a retainer basis, and I had sufficient authority to accept it, I would continue so long as they wanted me. That is my answer.

Orestes Ciccarelli, an eighty-year-old disbarred lawyer who was a law clerk in Communale's office, was the middleman.

A. On occasions I would give him some money . . . He was not on my pay-roll, but he was there. After a while he got to be like the "Old Man and the Sea."
Q. What did you do with this money?
A. He entwined his legs about my neck one day when I fell asleep on the beach and he was with me until almost the time—
Q. A very visual picture . . .

Communale's job as assistant prosecutor evidently involved anti-labor rack-eteering activities.

Q. Do you think there is a good possibility that the reason you received the $200 a month was that you could perform, that the Teamster officials in the area would have a friend in the attorney general's office?
A. Well, sir, I beg your pardon. I would assume that would be begging the question, looking for the kind of answer you are looking for. But in all the ramifications of that question, particularly directed to me, it would be in-conceivable, it would be ridiculous, and it would be fantastic to think that anybody could obtain labor peace through me for any considerations. I am a lowly assistant in the prosecutor's office who does what he is told and follows orders. I do not make policy . . . It is very highly conjectural and to me appears almost fantastic. It is unreal.

William Jacobson had been the manager of the New York office of the now defunct L & H Transportation Company, during a time when the firm allegedly paid $300 a month in small bills to John Conlin, Provenzano's predecessor in Local 560, in return for labor peace.

Q. In late 1948, Mr. Jacobson, or early 1949, did you have some difficulty with Local 560 of the Teamsters . . . ?
A. I refuse to answer . . . I expect to be in this business for some years to come. There might be some retaliation . . .

· · ·

Q. Didn't you state when you talked to us downstairs, you said, "I am too scared of the situation; I want to go on breathing. I don't stick my neck out for nobody. I would rather be a live coward than a dead hero." . . . Didn't you say that?
A. Yes, sir; I said it a dozen times.

Provenzano declined to testify. He went on to become, with Hoffa's support, an international vice president of the Teamsters, and thence to jail in 1967 for extortion.

President Sam Goldstein of New York Local 239 of the Teamsters was convicted with Johnny Dio in 1957 for bribery and extortion, and in 1958 pleaded guilty to charges of attempted extortion, coercion and conspiracy. Hoffa stated in 1958 that Goldstein had been removed from office, but a Committee investigator found that as late as 1959 Goldstein was still on the local's payroll, receiving $400 a week in salary and expenses while in jail. The Committee subpoenaed Goldstein but he refused to testify.

The Committee claimed that the local was in fact controlled by Antonio ("Tony Ducks") Corallo, described by counsel Kennedy as "reasonably prominent" in the New York underworld. Corallo had been arrested many times on various charges but convicted only once for a narcotics offense; his nickname derived from his success in keeping out of jail. He entered the labor movement about 1951 as an organizer for Local 995 of the UAW-AFL, then became vice president of Local 239 when it was chartered in 1954. He maintained other interests, including a floating crap game. The Committee produced a police tape of a telephone conversation between Corallo and one Freddie, following a police raid of the game.

Corallo: Oi, yoi, yoi, yoi. They got Freddie? If they took Freddie they got the bankroll.
Freddie: Hello? Hello?
Corallo: Freddie?
Freddie: Yes.
Corallo: What happened?
Freddie: Oh, the same people . . . Not a penny they got . . . I had it in my shoe.
Corallo: O.K.
Freddie: O.K., boy?
Corallo: All right.
Freddie: I'm going to lay down for a while. O.K., Tony?

Corallo resigned from his vice presidency in 1958. The McClellan Committee spent no further time on him, but in 1961, after the demise of the Committee, the Senate authorized a further inquiry into Local 239 by the Permanent Subcommittee on Investigations of the Committee on Government Operations. Senator McClellan conducted the hearings.

"During the public hearings," the Subcommittee said, "it was conclusively established that Corallo controlled some six locals affiliated with var-

ious internationals, including 239, 875, 275 and 522 of the Teamsters . . .
The principal officers of each of these locals had criminal backgrounds.
One or more officers of five locals had been convicted of extortion committed while acting in their capacity as labor union officials. Obviously these
local labor unions were no more than an extension of Corallo's racket empire . . . More important, it was alleged that this control was with James
Hoffa's knowledge and acquiescence."

The New York police taped a telephone conversation between Corallo,
Secretary-Treasurer Bernard Stein of Local 239, and Mack Tane, the local's director of organization. Stein was apparently reporting a conversation
that day with Hoffa concerning the desirability of Goldstein leaving office
following his imprisonment.

> *Stein:* He says I don't give a —— what you do . . . Tony, the guy told me
> straight out, and I ain't making like my own words. I'm saying his words
> . . . you want to steal, you want to rob, go ahead, he says—don't get
> caught . . . let time go by a year, he can go back on the payroll . . .
> What's the difference . . . Don't you see, Tony? He was in a bad spot . . .
> The guy is, you know, fine. I mean he don't care one way.

Hoffa apparently argued that, with time off for good behavior, Goldstein
would be free in November and could return to Local 239.

> *Stein:* He says in November he goes on like a business agent for six months—
> a year—he then takes his office back, that's all. He says what do you think
> it's going to be like this winter? He says it's all forgotten. It's cold as the
> ice out in the street. He says it's all over. All the wind is gone. And this
> punk kid, here, Kennedy, he calls him punk kid. He's got his nose up
> everybody's ——. He'll be gone, too . . .

The trio on the telephone then discussed Hoffa's alleged proposal to
have Goldstein tried by the local's executive board and acquitted. Tane
also suggested that Corallo assume the presidency of the local. Corallo declined, and vetoed Goldstein's brother-in-law as either secretary-treasurer
or vice president.

The conversation satisfied the Subcommittee that Corallo continued to
control Local 239 from behind the scenes, and that Hoffa condoned his
control. Stein, Tane, and Corallo all invoked the Fifth Amendment. Hoffa
conceded that he had talked with Stein, but denied he had made the statements attributed to him. He said he could not recall having met Corallo,
and planned no investigation of Local 239. The Subcommittee had also
charged that officers of the local had misappropriated $31,000 by hiring
dummy organizers. Hoffa said that Tane had denied the charge.

Q. Would that satisfy you?

A. How else do you think that I would uncover that statement if they corroborated it? . . . Tell me how.

In 1954 Raymond Cohen was elected secretary-treasurer of Philadelphia Local 107 of the Teamsters. According to the McClellan Committee the election was rigged. Cohen supporters, including two Philadelphia racketeers and a strong-arm squad of ex-convicts, prevented the renomination of the incumbent, Edward Crumbock, secretary-treasurer for twenty years. Crumbock's supporters were beaten up. Union members were told to fold their ballots so as to show they had voted for Cohen. Funds for Cohen's election campaign evidently came from Local 107's treasury and another Teamster local. All Cohen supporters questioned by the Committee refused to testify. Dave Beck placed the local in trusteeship and ordered a new election. Cohen won overwhelmingly. Raymond J. Kelly, a business agent dismissed by Cohen, was asked why Cohen won.

A. Well, there was only one word for it. It was fear.

Cohen paid off his campaign debts, estimated at $85,344.98, and appointed a new set of business agents. One of them was Ben Lapensohn, a bondsman active in the Philadelphia numbers game, formerly dismissed by Crumbock for accepting a payoff from employers in a labor dispute. Another was Abraham Berman, also a numbers game operator. Cohen's opponents found it difficult to find work in the industry, and there was more violence. Vincent Minisci, a shop steward, told of an experience on the night shift.

A. I got down to the garage there . . . it was kind of dark . . . the first thing I knew somebody came up on the side of me . . . and hit me alongside of the head, the left side, with a pipe . . . I threw myself inside the cab of the truck, and someone opened the door on the right-hand side and hit me on the top of the head with a hammer . . . I still have a hole up there to prove my point.

Minisci lost his job, and was unable to get union clearance for another. The local's hiring hall was operated by two ex-convict supporters of Cohen, one of whom had helped to beat up Minisci in 1954.

Cohen at first promised to make his personal books and records available to the Committee, but later changed his mind and refused to testify. After its own investigation the Committee could not account for $9,523.72 in local union funds paid to Lapensohn, nor for Lapensohn's contribution to Cohen of $17,000 as part payment on a $24,000 yacht. Cohen credited $25,000 in union funds to lost time payments to members, but allegedly used the money for election expenses. The endorsements on four local union checks amounting to $3,850 were forgeries. Between 1954 and 1957, almost a quarter of a million dollars in union funds were charged to organizing and strike expenses without proper accounting; a number of members denied receiving the money credited to them. All Local 107's business agents refused to testify about the local's finances.

Cohen lived well. The local paid for an annual three-to-four month vacation in Florida for him and his family. From 1954 to 1957 Cohen spent $2,717.14 in union money on clothing and gifts, and another $2,032.25 on accessories. He also spent $8,000 on boats for himself, over $2,000 on boats for his two sons, and $15,471 on a new house. In all, Cohen made cash payments of over $58,000 which could not be accounted for. In the same period he increased his net worth—not counting real or personal property—by $46,051.02.

Lapensohn left for Europe, later dividing his time between Canada and the Bahamas, declining the Committee's invitation to testify. He had evidently been employed by Cohen as a general "fixer" at $200 a week, earning an additional $12,000 for "personal services," but he had other sources of income. From 1946 he had solicited advertising for the yearbook of the Pennsylvania State Federation of Labor, receiving sixty percent of the revenues. He allegedly used threats of labor trouble to persuade employers to buy space in the yearbook, even collecting checks after the yearbook ceased publication. Sometimes employers paid for advertisements which never appeared. In eight years Lapensohn received a total of $481,707.74 in advertising commissions; a Committee accountant estimated that Lapensohn's personal profit was $197,400.17. One of Lapensohn's agents, was a professional confidence man named Samuel Kirsch who had served five separate sentences in jail.

Lapensohn also solicited for the *New York Federationist,* published by the New York State Federation of Labor, and other labor publications in the state. His various solicitors, conducting their business by telephone, often used aliases for multiple soliciting from the same employer. Lapensohn received seventy-five percent of the advertising revenues; according to his office manager, much of the *Federationist's* share was never transmitted. The Committee estimated that Lapensohn diverted $156,422.03 and stole $39,105.51 from the State Federation. The Federation thanked the Committee for its information, and ceased using paid advertisements in its publications.

"The disposal of garbage," the Committee observed, "is not a matter on which the average citizen is inclined to dwell."

Inattention had its price. The Committee held hearings on the garbage disposal industry in the Los Angeles and New York metropolitan areas, encountering "revelations no more savory than the basic materials of the craft." The local unions involved, it said, served as enforcers for favored employers engaged in business wars, and ignored managerial violations of union rules; in return, employers forced union membership on their employees and made dubious financial contributions to the locals. In both cities the locals were Teamster affiliates.

In Los Angeles, the city fathers were responsible for the disposal of wet and non-combustible garbage. Private carters handled combustible rubbish, and the only civic regulation of consequence was that they must not spill garbage on the streets.

The garbage men—most of whom ran small operations—belonged to an employers' association which divided up jurisdictions like "pieces of pie," and could be fined by the State Rubbish Collectors Association for competing with each other. They also belonged to Local 396 of the Teamsters although, the Committee said, "the benefits they derived were invisible." The union policed the dump gates, turning away independents and jurisdictional poachers.

However, in agreement with the dump owners, Local 396 allowed non-union drivers for certain manufacturing and retail firms to ply the dumps. It also ignored the "stop-jumping" or raiding activities of a garbage-collecting company owned in part by attorney John C. ("Radio Speaker") Stevenson of Local 396 and Secretary-Treasurer John W. Filipoff of Local 208 in Los Angeles. John Andikian, an officer of the employers' state association, complained of this to Frank Matula, the secretary-treasurer of Local 396. According to Captain James E. Hamilton of the Los Angeles Police Department, Matula then told Andikian "that if he didn't keep his mouth shut, they would take more stops."

Industrial relations in the field were otherwise cordial. "Under this strange species of labor-management accord," the Committee found, "the union and the trade association operated to their own and each other's advantage with complete reciprocity, above all united in their belief that the customer came last." The customers complained, the Los Angeles police and the California State Assembly investigated, and the industry changed its rules to allow competition between employers. It was too late. The citizens of Los Angeles voted to place the entire garbage system under municipal ownership.

Matula's testimony before a committee of the Assembly brought him a conviction for perjury. Hoffa then appointed him to the Teamsters' board of trustees—traditionally known as the "conscience of the union." Matula was released temporarily from jail to help audit the books of the international union.

"Malodorous as the Los Angeles garbage situation has been," the Committee observed, "it seemed sweet-scented by comparison with conditions in the New York sector of the industry."

In 1949 the Yonkers (New York) Common Council voted to end the municipal garbage pickup service, prompting a rush by private operators to enter the field. Teamster Local 456 had jurisdiction in the area. However, New York City Local 17 signed a contract with the Westchester Carting Company, a garbage-collecting firm.

Joseph Parisi was the secretary-treasurer of Local 17. His background included eleven arrests, with indictments for coercion, homicide, felonious assault and armed robbery, and convictions for rape and disorderly conduct. He had also been tried and acquitted years before on a charge of conspiring with Luciano and Buchalter to extort money from drivers and manufacturers in the New York paperbox industry.

Alfred ("Nick") Ratteni was the president of the Westchester Carting Company, and had served time for burglary in Sing Sing. At the time of his indictment in 1953 for income tax evasion, he was described by United States Attorney General Herbert Brownell as one of the chief lieutenants of Frank Costello. He was also on the Federal Bureau of Narcotics' list of suspects. But he had a defender. "I would like the chairman and the committee to keep in mind," Teamster attorney David Shivitz testified, "that in the garbage industry we don't get Harvard alumni and Yale undergraduates . . ."

President John Acropolis of Local 456 refused to yield ground to Local 17, although he agreed to let the contract with the Westchester Carting Company stand provided Local 17 signed no others. However, the company increased its activities, and the territorial jurisdiction of Local 17 expanded. Violence broke out, Local 17 evidently threatening to picket storekeepers if they did not do business with Westchester Carting. Local 17 also obtained a charter from the international union for a subsidiary Local 813 to be based in Yonkers. Secretary-Treasurer Bernard Adelstein of Local 813 demanded that Local 456 surrender its jurisdiction. "You are not that tough," he told Acropolis, ". . . tougher guys than you have been taken care of . . ." Parisi offered a similar threat. Acropolis remained firm. Three weeks later he was shot in the head outside his home and killed. The following month Rex Carting, the principal firm under contract to Local 456, sold out to Westchester Carting. Relations between the latter firm and the Teamsters came to what the Committee described as "an amicable end." Local 813 was succeeded by a company union.

A new influence now arose in the garbage industry. Vincent ("Jimmy") Squillante was described during the hearings by an officer of the Federal Bureau of Narcotics as "a major source of supply for narcotics, as well as being a prominent racketeer." In 1953 the Greater New York Cartmen's Association—the principal employer group in the garbage trade—hired Squillante as its labor relations counsel at $10,000 a year. His sole prior work experience appeared to have been in gambling and waterfront racketeering, but he soon came to dominate the association.

The Committee, however, believed there was "a higher power behind the throne." It suspected C. Don Modica, a former convict and rumored Ph.D., who had served time for grand larceny and practising medicine without a license, but who claimed to have rehabilitated himself and taught philosophy at New York University and other institutions of learning. He had also been private tutor to the children of such underworld leaders as Joseph Adonis, Willie Moretti and Albert Anastasia. He went to work for Squillante as director of education and editor of a garbage industry publication called *The Hired Broom,* on whose masthead stood the aphorism: "Out of Garbage There Grows a Rose." He evidently labored for love; all he received in salary, he said, was a turkey at Christmas and an occasional ham.

Peter Parise, a former member of the Association, commented on Modica's status.

Q. What impression did you get about what his position was out there?
A. Well, I would say he was a watchdog . . . The newspapers are telling all of us that he was Anastasia's man.

Albert Anastasia was assassinated in a barber's chair in New York on October 25, 1957. Modica retired to his home in Hasbrouck Heights. He wanted, he said, to write on the three sicknesses of America: "Progressive education, delinquency, and subversive influences such as Communism."

Squillante remained in charge. No member was allowed to compete for the stops of another without permission, on penalty of a fine or expulsion from the association and raiding by other operators. General Sanitation, a "whip" company set up by Squillante and operating at low prices under non-union conditions, was used to undercut the business of uncooperative employers. Melville Wolpert, Bernie Adelstein's nephew and the auditor of the now independent Local 813's welfare fund, helped with the new company's books. The officers of Local 813 helped to persuade reluctant businessmen to switch from non-association garbage collectors to General Sanitation.

Both Squillante and Adelstein did well financially. When Squillante ran afoul of the Internal Revenue Service he set up a "Cartmen's Defense Fund," financed by the employers at $250 a truck. The official purpose of the Fund was to help cartmen in trouble and to contribute to "any charities, for the benefit of mankind." The Fund's resources reached $57,855. The sum of $14,215.99 was spent to pay Squillante's delinquent federal taxes. More than $12,000 was used to pay his state taxes and attorney's fees. Processed as loans, the contributions to Squillante were not subject to tax.

Adelstein received a salary of over $20,000 and expenses as the executive officer of a small local union of coopers. Four of his relatives worked for Local 813, whose welfare fund paid for his air-conditioned Cadillac and large quantities of liquor bought from a store owned by Adelstein himself. The Committee accused him of being an "abject tool" of Squillante, blinking at Squillante-favored non-union firms, and profiting "heavily" by spending union funds on himself.

Squillante went to jail for violating his tax probation. Both he and Adelstein were convicted for extortion. Both convictions were reversed on appeal, Hoffa announcing his support of Adelstein's appellate action. The New York garbage industry remained in private hands.

Robert ("Barney") Baker was one of the Teamsters' weightier recruits. He was, the Committee said, "a gargantuan individual who alternates between organizing for the Teamsters and staying in various health spas to lose weight." Depending on the circumstances, Baker weighed between 300 and 380 pounds.

Baker, a former longshoreman and professional boxer, was jailed in 1934 for stink-bombing New York theatres; one of his bombs allegedly killed Joe Penner's duck.* Thereafter he moved in underworld circles. He was associated on the waterfront with John ("Cockeye") Dunn, Don Gentile, Andrew ("Squint") Sheridan and Eddie McGrath. In the late 1930's he was shot at while in the company of waterfront racketeers Farmer Sullivan and Joe Butler.

Q. You never done anything to bring about this?
A. Fight Communism on the waterfront in New York.

· · ·

Q. Was anybody killed?
A. Mr. Joe Butler passed away.

· · ·

* Joe Penner was a vaudeville comedian active in the 1930's. His standard opening was to walk onstage with a duck and ask of the audience: "Wanna buy a duck?" He was very famous.

Q. The testimony we had yesterday is that there were two rival mobs causing all the difficulty and trouble on the waterfront, and you were a member of one, and this group shot you, and it had nothing to do with the Communists . . .

A. Mr. [Robert F.] Kennedy . . . believe me . . . I am proud of how I live . . . if I had to do it over again, this is the way I would live . . . I have lived a life, Mr. Chairman. It may not have been lily-white . . . What is the pay-off? Where is the penalty? When does it stop? Why don't they stop harassing people? . . . Excuse me, Mr. Chairman, for getting excited. I mean this is laying on my heart.

Baker worked for a time as a bouncer in a Florida gambling casino owned by leading racketeers Joe Adonis, Meyer Lansky, Frank Costello, Vincent ("Jimmy Blue Eyes") Alo, and others. Then he drove a truck in Washington, D.C., and in 1952 was elected to office in Teamster Local 730. He soon resigned, but was offered a job by Harold Gibbons, now an international vice president of the union, then and now the president of Local 688 in St. Louis. On his way to St. Louis he was arrested for carrying a gun. He lied to the police about the source of the weapon.

Q. May I ask a question here? . . . Do you feel that there is no compulsion upon you to tell the truth when you are not under oath?

A. Little white lies don't mean nothing, not when you are not under oath.

Baker became an organizer for the Central States Conference of Teamsters. He accrued a reputation for violence, especially for "belly-bumping," a specialized form of intimidation related to girth. Evidently he also had underworld connections. Hoffa was asked about that.

Q. Here was a business agent, rather prominent . . . Did you know in St. Louis he is a friend of Johnny Vitale, Joe Costello, Jack Joseph . . . Does that not disturb you at all . . . ?

A. It doesn't disturb me one iota.

In 1953, Bobby Greenlease, a six-year-old boy, was kidnapped in Kansas City, and found murdered in St. Louis. A ransom of $300,000 was paid but the boy was murdered. Baker's ex-wife testified that her husband told her that she should warn St. Louis gangster Joe Costello if ever she was questioned by police officers about the Greenlease case. Costello later tried to kill himself.

Q. Did Mr. Baker ever tell you why Joe Costello shot himself?

A. Do I have to answer that? . . . I don't want to answer it because I have to raise that little girl. I may get killed for telling. But I want to tell these people and all of you, and the whole United States . . . Baker told me, "Joe Costello got the Greenlease money," and that is why he tried to kill himself. I should never tell a soul, he said . . .

. . .

Q. Mrs. Baker . . . if you receive any threats . . . you will report that promptly to the committee. We will undertake to give you every protection within our power.

A. Thank you . . . this was the only thing I could do today, and if soldiers can die on the battlefront, I can die for what I did today . . . you can call me at any time.

Baker denied the statement attributed to him, but did concede that he once gave $1,500 to John Vitale to help him in business. Captain John Dougherty of the St. Louis Police Department testified.

Q. Did you find out anything more about Baker . . . ?

A. Yes . . . we found out he was a very close associate of Vitale's mob.

Q. Who is Vitale?

A. He is the head of the Italian syndicate in St. Louis . . . the top man.

. . .

Q. Do you find that any of these underworld figures were trying to move in on any of the other unions . . . ?

A. Well, it is a known fact that John Vitale is the boss of Local 110, Laborers' Union . . . Joe Gribler was the business agent, and George Meyers worked there . . . Both of them were killed . . . Shot in the head . . . Raymond Sarkus was appointed business agent . . . he was close to Vitale.

The Committee questioned Harold Gibbons about union members with criminal records.

Q. . . . How does it happen that in the Teamsters you seem to have so many members who either have criminal records or who have skirted the edge of it or fallen under the gangster class . . . ?

A. . . . you will probably find there is just as many in any other union with the exception of the higher skilled unions. There is no mystery . . . We happen to be in a heavily or largely unskilled area . . . One does not have to have too many talents to drive a truck . . . So it is easy to place them, and we probably have an undue amount of calls from parole agents, from priests, from ministers, who are working with people trying to rehabilitate them . . . I am very happy that unions are cooperating in this kind of work . . . otherwise we would be turning loose on society an awful lot of people who could only make their living by a gun.

In 1953 Local 688 was involved in a violent cab strike in St. Louis. Some of the local's members, including a number with criminal records, went to jail. Local 688 evidently paid their legal fees and took care of their families. Gibbons was accused of inviting his members to commit acts of violence.

A. No. That is an interpretation which you will have to take responsibility for . . . it is standard operating procedure in our organization . . . I will defend the right of workers to protect themselves against police, strike-breakers and thugs employed by the employers . . . Their instructions are to keep down violence and avoid any violence . . . there is bound to be violence now and again in areas of social conflict. There is no greater area of social conflict than a strike situation.

Gibbons specifically defended his right to provide financial assistance to his members in jail.

A. I was referring to the men who were unjustly arrested by the police department who hate our particular organization . . . I don't trust the police of St. Louis, in a labor dispute . . . they are not above framing individuals in the city of St. Louis.

In 1952–53 the Joint Council of Teamsters in St. Louis had a gangster problem. Beck put the council into trusteeship, making Gibbons trustee. Gibbons armed his staff.

A. You are as well acquainted as I am with the facts . . . There were people on the payroll of the joint council who were known as racketeers . . . I did not want it to be a deep-dark secret, either. I called in the editor of the *Post Dispatch* . . . I also called in a member of the St. Louis Police Board . . . Captain Dougherty assured me we did not have to carry guns, that all we had to do was "pick up the phone and call us." I told Captain Dougherty if he had been doing his job for twenty years, we would not be faced with this problem.

Gibbons argued that the nature of the industry made an occasional contact with marginal citizens inevitable. He had a nodding acquaintanceship or collective bargaining relationship with several St. Louis undesirables, and once had dealt with Johnny Dio when assigned by Beck to organize cab drivers in New York City. It was a brief encounter and Gibbons put it into perspective for the Committee. "I am friendly [with Dio]," Gibbons said, "at the point that Dulles and Eisenhower might be friendly with Ibn Saud."

Joseph P. Glimco was president of Chicago Local 777 of the Teamsters, composed largely of cab drivers. He had a record of thirty-six arrests for larceny, extortion, assault, robbery, attempted murder and murder, and had twice been denied citizenship on grounds of poor moral character. He numbered among his friends many of the leaders of Chicago's underworld, and was a frequent guest at their weddings and wakes.

Glimco came into the Teamsters during the 1930's, evidently at the behest of William Hanley, then the head of Produce Drivers Local 703. He was without previous trade union experience, and at first held no official position with Local 777, but from 1939 on he allegedly required various officers of the local to pay over to him their expenses and a portion of their salaries. The officials paid the income tax on the money they gave him. Glimco's monthly income from the local was about $3,000.

In 1952 Glimco was indicted for extortion from employers in the Fulton Street Poultry Market. He was said to have taken up to $60 a week from a scavenger company, $4,000 from a poultry firm when it changed hands, and another $4,000 from the successor company in connection with a sale of feathers to the Sumner Company. The latter company was allowed to operate with non-union drivers. Local 777 contributed $124,321.45 towards Glimco's trial expenses, although he still had no formal union position.

The local made other peculiar disbursements. From 1937 to 1958 it rebated varying percentages of membership dues to the two major taxicab companies in Chicago—Yellow Cab and Chequer Cab—ostensibly to help pay for the dues check-off system. The total rebate was $327,491.46. This practice was evidently unknown to the members, and was discontinued after the Committee brought it to light.

Glimco became president of Local 777 in 1958. He and Secretary-Treasurer George Marcie allegedly used their union influence to solicit business for the Best Sanitation and Deodorizing Company, in which Marcie, Mrs. Marcie and their stepson had financial interests. Glimco's son was also one of the company's employees. The company's offices were in Local 777's building, although the local's records showed no rent receipts. Marcie and his family also controlled Don Marcie, Inc., a cosmetics firm, which conducted business rent-free from the local's headquarters. Local 777 also paid a total of $10,611.69 for Marcie's membership in the Tam O'Shanter Country Club. Both Glimco and Marcie refused to testify.

Between 1952 and 1953 Glimco paid $83,325 to building contractor Frank V. Pantaleo for the addition of one or two rooms to the local's building. George Blum, a Chicago expert on building costs, told the Committee that the maximum possible real cost of all the improvements to the property from 1947 to 1957 was some $35,000.

In 1953 Pantaleo built a $44,000 house for Glimco in suburban Oak Park. Glimco obtained an $18,000 mortgage on the house, but there was no evidence that he paid Pantaleo the remaining $26,000. The Committee concluded that at least that amount was stolen from Local 777 to pay for the house. Pantaleo, a former business associate of the late Chicago gangster Charles ("Cherry Nose") Gioe, refused to testify. The Committee noted that Pantaleo had bought Glimco's children twenty shares of AT&T stock for $3,509.95; that he ran his business rent free from an office in

Local 777's building; and that in 1956 the local paid his expenses to attend a testimonial dinner for Hoffa in Detroit.

Glimco, by arrangement with the Occidental Life Insurance Company, was sole administrator of Local 777's welfare fund. The employers did not participate.

Louis Linzer, a cab driver, testified that he once tried to collect $180 in overdue health benefits from Glimco, but that Glimco refused to pay and instead arranged for Linzer to be fired by Chequer Cab. The benefits were finally paid after an investigation by the National Labor Relations Board.

Roy McDowell, a driver for Yellow Cab, told the Committee that he was fired for trying to collect three weeks' sick benefits. He complained to Glimco, who was unsympathetic.

Q. Would you repeat what he said again, please?
A. He said if I didn't stay away from there and behave myself and quit shooting my mouth off, I was going to be found in an alley with a hole in my head.

"Joseph Glimco," in the Committee's words, "possessed none of the qualifications of the bona fide labor leader . . . Glimco was shown to be a common thug and criminal who gained control of this union by violence and those strong-arm methods which are the stock-in-trade of the Chicago racketeer." The other officers, trustees and executive board members of the local, the Committee concluded, "were of similar ilk—parasites of organized labor." Among Glimco's underworld friends the Committee listed Anthony Accardo, Paul ("The Waiter") Ricca, Jake ("Greasy Thumb") Guzik, Louis ("Little New York") Campagna, Anthony ("Tough Tony") Capezio, Gussie Alex, and Murray ("The Camel") Humphreys.

The hearings brought discontent to the members of the local, who voted to leave the Teamsters and affiliate with the Seafarers International Union, AFL-CIO. Hoffa supported Glimco in the elections involved in the changeover, at one point embracing him in public.

Harland H. Maris was an insurance broker in Chicago. The Committee estimated that he was paid some $600,000 in excess commissions by the Occidental Life Insurance Company. Various welfare funds of the Teamsters and the HRE in Chicago accounted for some $415,000 of the overpayment.

Local 710 of the Teamsters paid the most. The Committee estimated that the local's secretary, International Vice-President John T. ("Sandy") O'Brien, together with former Local 777 President Frank Brown and International Vice-President James Blakely and Frank Vacey of the HRE, had a financial interest in the Dearborn Insurance Agency owned by Maris; and that they were mainly responsible for the excessive commissions.

Neither O'Brien nor his colleagues in Local 710 were pressed for income. The local had some 14,000 members. Dues were four dollars a month, ninety cents of which went into a commissions pool divided between the secretary-treasurer, the president and the vice president of the local. O'Brien received the largest share, forty-five percent. His total income from the local during the seven-year period 1952–58 was $471,-286.11 in salary, expenses, commissions and bonuses; at current rates of progression, the Committee estimated, O'Brien's income would surpass $100,000 in 1959 alone. The others received proportionate shares. From 1952 to 1958 the local's disbursements for the three officers were $1,-136,275.97. O'Brien was the only officer of the local to appear before the Committee, but he refused to testify.

The Committee found no satisfactory evidence that the members of Local 710 had sanctioned or even knew about the commission system. "[F]or sheer brazen plunder," the Committee commented, "the story of O'Brien and his companion officers . . . was unequalled in the Committee's experience."

"I submit," said Senator Frank Church of Idaho, ". . . that these men are not labor union leaders at all. They are capitalists, and they are the capitalists and exploiters in the same tradition as the robber barons of old."

19: Hoffa

But Hoffa was the main quarry. The Committee devoted more attention to him than to anyone or anything else. "Ignominy was piled on ignominy," the Committee declared. "Time and time again the committee has found Hoffa to be faithless to the members of his own union . . . Hoffa has consistently used union funds for his own benefit and that of his friends . . . Hoffa has consistently supported the interest of racketeer friends over those of his own members . . . Hoffa and his chief aides have consistently suppressed democratic rights within the union . . . Hoffa has connived and maneuvered union insurance to racketeer friends, bringing these friends gigantic profits . . . In the history of this country it would be hard to find a labor leader who has so shamelessly abused his trust."

James Riddle Hoffa was born in 1913 in Brazil, Indiana. His father was a coal miner who died when Hoffa was seven years old. His mother moved with her four children to Clinton, Indiana, where Hoffa started school. "Jimmy, running barefoot," a Teamster publication has recorded, "strung clam lines in the river for food, stole green apples and shot rabbits." In 1925 the family moved to Detroit. Hoffa left school at sixteen and went to work as a box-boy in a department store. The following year he took a job at the Kroger warehouse in Detroit, unloading box-cars for seventeen cents an hour. "You stayed as long as they wanted to keep you," he said. "But, you got paid only for the hours you actually worked. The rest of the time you just sat around waiting for more box-cars to come in."

Detroit was an open shop town, and jobs were scarce. "The depression in Detroit," Hoffa said, "it was knock down, drag out, starving people; it was murder, murder." Union talk was dangerous, but Hoffa got involved. "I got interested in unions," he recalled, "because we were getting kicked around. We started talking about it on the sly. We got four other people together who agreed to be leaders and we talked it up." Hoffa led his first strike at the age of eighteen, timing it with the arrival of a load of highly perishable strawberries. He won the strike and formed a local union. Six months later the AFL gave him a federal charter. Then he affiliated his local with the Teamsters, assuming before long the leadership of Detroit Local 299.

Organizing was hard. "In the early days," he stated, "every strike was a fight . . . I was in a lot of fights, got my head broke, got banged around.

253

My brother got shot. We had a business agent killed by a strikebreaker
. . . Our cars were bombed out . . . Cars would crowd us off the street
. . . They hired thugs who were out to get us, and Brother, your life was
in your hands every day. There was only one way to survive—fight back.
And we used to slug it out on the streets. They found we didn't scare . . .
The police were no help. The police would beat your brains out for even
talking union. The cops harassed us every day. If you went on strike, you
got your head broken . . . Once I was in jail eighteen times within twenty-four hours. That was the Crowley-Milner strike of 1939. Every time I
showed up on the picket line, I got thrown in jail. Every time they released
me, I went back on the picket line; eighteen times in one day, it happened.
But we stayed on the picket line for a year and a half, and we won the
strike."

The early years conditioned him for life. He was a fighting man, as
happy in the streets as at the bargaining table, suspicious of the world, determined on victory and careless of means, evidently without doubts or illu-
sions. "I know where I'm going," he once said. "I know what I'm going to
do. I've been around forty-three years and nobody's been leading me by
the hand . . . My friends in the labor business are mostly Teamsters. The
rest you gotta watch with both eyes . . . I learned a long time ago that
whatever you can do to me, I can do to you, only more . . . I'm no damn
angel . . ."

He married to a philosophy of the jungle a mastery of his trade, a personal asceticism, a great capacity for work, and a love of power. They
brought Hoffa to the top.

A major change in Teamster traditions took place in the 1930's. Until
then the leaders of the union had paid little attention to the strategically
placed long-haul drivers. Dan Tobin, president of the international union
from 1905, regarded them literally as trash, unworthy of membership in
the Brotherhood. Most of the union hierarchy seemed to agree. Then, in
1934, a group of Trotskyites under the leadership of Farrell Dobbs led a
successful Teamster general strike in Minneapolis. Thereafter they began
organizing the long-haul drivers, "leap-frogging" from terminal to terminal,
city to city, state to state; once the long-haul drivers were organized there
was new pressure available to organize in local cartage, warehouses and
other places of work. Dobbs and his associates eventually established the
Central States Drivers Council with jurisdiction in eleven states. The
Teamsters in the West, under the leadership of Dave Beck, formed the
Western Conference of Teamsters. In time the East and Southern Conferences of Teamsters were set up. The conference system, with organized

highway drivers its key source of strength, was spectacularly successful. The membership of the Teamsters increased more than tenfold in twenty years.

Dobbs resigned from office in 1939 to assume full-time duties with the Socialist Workers Party. Hoffa took his place as chairman of the Central States Drivers Council's negotiating committee. He had studied Dobbs, and learned his lesson well. "I don't care what kind of a strike you've got," he told a group of Teamsters. "Once you organize the road, the city, the warehouses, nobody can whip the Teamsters, nobody." Hoffa was elected vice president of the CSDC in 1940. In 1948 he organized the Michigan Conference of Teamsters, and was elected trustee of the international union. In 1952 he became an international vice president, in 1953 the chairman of the Central States Conference of Teamsters. Long in actual control in the Midwest, he also became the dominant informal influence in the Eastern and Southern Conferences of Teamsters. He was the most powerful man in the union.

Dan Tobin retired in 1952. Hoffa chose not to make a bid for the presidency, and Beck, who was also the executive vice president of the union, was elected. Beck reigned rather than ruled, strong only in small matters, aloof from the membership, given to resounding speeches and trips abroad. He once felt it necessary, indeed, to assert publicly that he and not Hoffa was the boss. "Dave Beck?" Hoffa said later. "Hell, I was running it while he was playing big shot. He never knew the score."

In 1957, after running afoul of the McClellan Committee, Beck decided or was persuaded not to run for re-election. Hoffa was also in trouble, but he had the votes, and was elected president of the Teamsters by a large majority.

During the next decade Hoffa showed that he was, beyond doubt, one of the ablest leaders ever produced by the American labor movement. He brought to his calling, first of all, a near-total concentration of effort. In personal habits he was something of a prude; he neither drank, nor smoked, nor enjoyed off-color stories, nor indulged in the after-hour relations of some traveling men. He had a passion for physical fitness—he sometimes carried gymnastic equipment with him from hotel to hotel, and once claimed he could do seven push-ups on the *finger-tips* of one hand—which equipped him for a working schedule beyond the capacity of the average Teamster. He read virtually nothing for pleasure, and almost never attended any public entertainment. He was known to hunt and fish, but neither activity was ever more than fitful. Presumably his business activities took up some time, but they were never more than marginal. There seemed to be nothing of importance to him, indeed, except the Teamsters and the family to which he was devoted.

He was also a natural captain, the undoubted chief of those he led. "A champion of champions," old Secretary-Treasurer John English called him at the 1966 convention, "a leader among men." There was some truth in the florid words. He had made his own way, owing little to patronage or seniority. He had always fought for control, was always in charge of his jurisdiction. Most important of all, great numbers of Teamsters saw themselves in him; they looked upon him as one of them, a grass-roots man, faithful to his origins and the members. For many in the union Dan Tobin was little more than a lobbyist, a Boston politician in Washington, distant and not very important in the decentralized union of his day. Dave Beck seemed even more of a stranger, greedy for eminence and famous company, a rich business agent hard to reach and out of touch. Hoffa was and was seen to be different, always eager to stop a truck and talk, accessible at work and in Washington and on the street corners to those who paid the dues. He knew his constituents exceedingly well, enjoyed their company, served them to widespread satisfaction, and persuaded most of them that he would stand against all authority on their behalf. The subsequent long and sometimes inquisitorial grilling by the McClellan Committee, the fervid Senatorial accusations of perfidy, the long string of trials and Hoffa's loud complaints of persecution, served mainly to sharpen the Teamsters' sense of solidarity, of a special self-identity, and of Hoffa as their hero in a hostile world. The loyalty he came to command, in some quarters at least, was close to fever point.

He added to an uncommon touch a first-rate intelligence. He did not have, to be sure, the most spacious of minds. "I figure we ought to settle our problems at home first," he told a group of Berkeley intellectuals in 1961, "then worry about things abroad." He was awkward and sometimes embarrassing on civil rights; only in later years did he begin to talk about politics as something more than a problem of buying votes; and on civil liberties his voice was muted until his own big problems with the courts. But if he was less than learned on most subjects, on the economics of trucking he approached omnicompetence. There developed a wide consensus in the industry, on both sides of the bargaining table, that he was the best there was.

His grasp of the subject was matched by his bargaining skills. He was a realist, seeking only what he believed the industry could pay or absorb; but he was also the great tactician—always probing for weaknesses, creating elaborate traps for the employers, pitting his adversaries against each other, intimidating the weak and undermining the strong, mapping strikes like a general at war, cajoling and bluffing and threatening as the occasion demanded—a master bargainer.

What did he achieve? Here too there were grounds for respect. Except in the Western States, the Teamsters' conference system was largely Hoffa's work. He was principal author of the greatly enlarged geographical scope of collective bargaining agreements, and thus of a growing uniformity in wages and working conditions for Teamsters throughout the country. He was the creator of an "open-ended" grievance procedure in the Central States—without arbitration and with freedom for the union to strike in the event of disagreement—which in effect made Hoffa the arbiter of most grievances. His personal impact on Teamster earnings was hard to measure; but Ralph and Estelle James, in the leading study of Hoffa's economic consequences, concluded that "most truck-freight workers have higher wages today because of Jimmy Hoffa." In the welfare fund field his reputation was not so secure. He bought insurance policies on a non-competitive basis from friends, and invested pension fund reserves in a series of precarious hotel and gambling operations. Nevertheless, the health benefit and pension levels he negotiated seemed to bear favorable comparison with those in other industries. Hoffa's *economic* record was hard to fault seriously.

But there was another side to the story. If he was long on achievements, he was short on principles and proprieties. Here, perhaps, it was unfair to expect too much in the way of the conventional virtues. The odds against an urbane Hoffa were high. The Detroit of his youth was not much of a finishing school. The trucking industry was not a breeding ground for scholars or gentle men. The Teamsters did not abound in social reformers or intellectuals. Representing truck drivers could be a rough occupation, fraught with physical risk and awkward friends and enemies. Hoffa was never a choir boy, nor a college man, nor fortunate enough when young to enjoy the guidance of more well-rounded men. He had a bad start, and it lasted a long time.

But he was not the only one to come up the hard way. Other union leaders had had it even harder, but showed more admirable qualities. Whatever the excuses or explanations, there was a black side to Hoffa.

He was, in some ways, a most unsavory individual. He commanded great loyalties, but treated many of his subordinates and followers with contempt and cruelty. He had brains and energy enough for his job, but owed too much to his fists and some gruesome friends. He was a violent man, an intimidator, a crippler by instinct, vicious in the clutch.

Hoffa was capable of pure venom. "I hear you have cancer, Sheridan," he said to the Department of Justice official, Walter Sheridan, in charge of his indictments. "How long does it take to work?" Sam Baron was one assistant who felt Hoffa's fists, and who was with Hoffa when the news came of the acid blinding of labor columnist Victor Reisel. "Hey, Baron," Hoffa allegedly said, "a friend of yours got it this morning . . . that son of a bitch Victor Reisel . . . too bad he didn't have it thrown on the hands he types with . . ." The Kennedy brothers, long critical of Hoffa, were among his hatreds. When President John F. Kennedy was shot, Teamster officials closed the union's Washington headquarters and sent a letter of condolence to Jacqueline Kennedy. Hoffa went into a rage, stormed against the letter, claimed that he at least was no hypocrite. He had another comment. "Now," he said, "Bobby Kennedy will be just another lawyer."

If he was capable of great enmity, he was also capable of friendships and tolerances repugnant to most of society. These, and a desire for money, brought him into trouble with the Congress. The interest in him was so great, the evidence against him so voluminous, and the power he came to wield so awesome, that he became the most investigated union official in American history. He dominated the McClellan Committee hearings on the Teamsters, making some eighteen appearances in all. Hoffa was not the most helpful of witnesses, particularly when questioned by the man who became his chief aversion, Committee Counsel Robert F. Kennedy. "I will have to stand on the answers I made in regards to my recollection," he said at one point, "and I cannot answer unless you give me some recollection other than I have answered . . . To the best of my recollection, I must recall on my memory, I cannot remember." Forgetfulness overcame him a hundred times, and there seemed to some in his audience a connection between the unsavoriness of the subject and the imperfections of his memory, prompting Senator Ives to observe that Hoffa had "the most convenient forgettery" he had ever encountered. But Hoffa never invoked the Fifth Amendment, nor was he always evasive. He talked, and talked a great deal.

Hoffa was a businessman of sorts. Sun Valley was a real estate development project in Florida sponsored by Joint Council 43 in Detroit, which Hoffa headed. It was to be a vacation and retirement resort for Teamsters, their families and friends, and was advertised as the "teamsters model city of tomorrow." Various Teamster officials acted as salesmen for the property, urging their members to buy lots. Land was also made available to the general public at higher prices to increase its value.

Henry Lower, a business agent for Teamster Local 376 in Detroit, was the administrator of the project. Hoffa persuaded a Detroit bank to lend

Lower $75,000 to help finance it. The Committee seemed persuaded that the bank, which held millions of dollars in Teamster pension funds, was told that if the loan were not granted the funds would be withdrawn. Hoffa also transferred $500,000 from Local 299 to the Florida National Bank in Orlando. Florida National then lent Lower $300,000 to finance improvements on the property. The Committee said that Lower took $144,000 for himself, diverting another $85,844.57 into two private ventures of his own in Detroit. Meanwhile, Hoffa and Owen Bert Brennan of Local 337 took out a personal option to buy almost half of Sun Valley at the original purchase price of $18.75 an acre.

There was a sequel. "The perplexing skein of James R. Hoffa's peculiar financial manipulations," the Committee said, ". . . more frequently than not reflected the shadowy image of a man named Benjamin Dranow . . ."

In 1953 the Retail Clerks struck the John W. Thomas Department Store in Minneapolis. Dranow was the manager of the store. The strike lasted four years, during which time Hoffa arranged for a loan of $200,000 to Dranow from Teamster funds. Hoffa helped to settle the strike, then lent Dranow a further $1,000,000. Dranow bought the store, which soon went bankrupt. "Dranow," the Committee disclosed, "then took off with more than $100,000 of the concern's funds, reflected in the books as a 'loan.' "

Dranow next became involved in the Sun Valley project. Directing its revival after an initial bankruptcy, he asked the Barnett National Bank of Cocoa, Florida, for a development loan, offering $1,000,000 in Teamster funds as security. He owned the Union Land and Home Company, a Florida corporation, which had bought the capital stock of Sun Valley. Union Land succeeded in borrowing $2,135,000 from the Central States, Southeast and Southwest area pension funds of the Teamsters during 1958 and 1959. In turn, Union Land lent $17,000 to Roy Williams, the head of Teamster Local 41 in Kansas City and a trustee of the funds.

The Sun Valley property was not in good condition. Irving Blum, a New York real estate developer, was asked by Dranow to buy the estate. He told the Committee that "it had been mishandled . . . Nothing had been done to put the property in shape. There were a few houses built there, and a short road of about 2,000 feet. But there was no possibility for the purchasers to get to their property. There was nothing there . . . Somebody got away with some of the funds . . . it just bogged down." Sun Valley was a failure. Hoffa and Brennan never exercised their options.

Dranow was also involved with Hoffa and Brennan in the purchase of uniform jackets for the members of Locals 299 and 337. About 1958 the two locals spent more than $325,000 on the purchase of some 26,000 jackets. Dranow was the middleman, earning about $75,000 in commissions and unrepaid loans. The Committee estimated that the jackets could have been bought for at least $50,000 less if Hoffa and Brennan had not dealt with Dranow. There was no evidence of competitive bidding. The markup on over half the jackets was more than one hundred percent. The markup on one-third of the jackets—bought from the open shop Union Local Supply Company in New York—was evidently over three hundred percent. Dranow refused to testify on this or any other of his dealings with Hoffa.

Commercial Carriers, a trucking firm in Michigan, decided after World War II to replace its largely driver-owned trailers with its own vehicles. The driver-owners, members of the Teamsters, struck the company. Hoffa intervened, arguing that the strike was illegal. The strikers went back to work on company-owned equipment.

The company later reverted to leased equipment. Test Fleet Corporation, a hauling company, was set up on the initiative of Commercial Carriers and transferred to the ownership of Mrs. Hoffa and Mrs. Owen Bert Brennan. Commercial Carriers provided the new company with a $50,000 loan and the free use of an attorney and accountant. The two ladies then leased equipment to Commercial Carriers, making a profit of some $125,-000 over a seven-year period on a total personal investment of $4,000. In 1955, the firm's name now changed to the Hobren Corporation, it bought property in Iron County, Michigan, which it leased to a non-profit hunting club run by Teamster officials from Detroit.

Q. Now, Mr. Hoffa . . . this money earned by your wife and Mrs. Brennan. Did you receive some of it or none of it?
A. We file a joint return, if that is what you mean . . .

He had a comment on conflict of interest.

A. I find nothing wrong with a labor leader having a business or his family having a business that may be in the same industry that that particular union has organized . . . . I have been around a long time, and I know my employers probably better than most people . . . I find nothing objectionable if an employer is going to lease equipment from a stranger, to lease it from somebody who is not a stranger, provided there is no strings attached . . . it is my firm belief as a labor leader that, if you know the business you are negotiating in, and if you have some touch of responsibility, you will be in a better position at the bargaining table to get more for your men . . . However, I notice that the [AFL–CIO] ethical practices committee has placed certain rules and regulations concerning investments and, as rapidly as possible, even though I don't agree, I am disposing of everything that I own except what I will earn from the union to comply with the ethical practices rulings.

Hoffa was active in still other enterprises. He had an interest in the J and H Sales Company, a trucking firm which after a series of disguised ownerships ended up in the names of Mrs. Hoffa and Mrs. Brennan, leasing equipment to the Baker Driveaway Company, a firm which had contractual relations with the Teamsters. Hoffa and Allen Dorfman, the broker for various Teamster welfare funds in the Midwest, were part owners of a real estate venture in North Dakota and of Joll Properties, a holiday resort in Wisconsin. Hoffa, Owen Bert Brennan, Paul Dorfman and Leo Perlman had investments in the Northwest Oil Company in North and South Dakota. Hoffa and Brennan also had an interest in the Columbus Trotting Association in Ohio, and once owned an obscure boxer named Embrell Davidson. Davidson spent much of his time on the Teamster payroll as a claims investigator for Local 337's welfare fund, but performed no services other than tending Brennan's horses and carrying feed out to the racetracks.

Hoffa was a borrower. He borrowed $25,000 from Harold Mark, the New York welfare fund consultant, who had recently received a $150,000 Teamster loan. He borrowed $11,000 from Teamster accountant Harold Grosberg, whose Marberry Construction Company—owned in partnership with Teamster lawyer George Fitzgerald—had received a $750,000 loan from the union. He borrowed $100,000 from a Chicago savings and loan company through the intercession of a New York agency which was part owner of Allen Dorfman's insurance firm; the money was used to buy bonds in the Fruehauf Trailer Company, itself a recipient of Teamster loans; some $76,000 was spent by Local 299 to help pay off the loan, although it was not clear from the records whether Hoffa borrowed the latter sum or sold the bonds to the local.

Hoffa also borrowed from a number of Teamster officials, estimating for the Committee that in one four-year period alone he borrowed $38,000 from fifteen Teamster officials. None of the officials seemed anxious to be repaid. This included Herman Kierdorf, who had been hired by Hoffa as a business agent for the Detroit Joint Council of Teamsters after serving time for armed robbery; he was released from jail and later from parole on Hoffa's intervention. Hoffa asked him for $2,000, which Kierdorf provided by forgoing a vacation in Florida with his wife. Hoffa subsequently approved a $1,500 loan from Local 299 to Kierdorf—who needed the money to help his son—but did not offer to repay the $2,000 he himself owed until the Committee began examining his borrowing habits.

In 1949 the Teamsters demanded a five-day week from the Detroit laundry industry. The employers refused, and asked labor relations consultant

Joseph Holtzman to settle the deadlock. Holtzman charged the employers $17,500 for evidently doing no more than arrange a meeting between Hoffa and the employers. A contract was then signed without the five-day week being granted. Hoffa subsequently borrowed $5,000 each from Holtzman and his partner Jack Bushkin, both of whom were consultants to Detroit supermarkets under contract to the Teamsters. There was no record kept of the loans, nor evidence other than his own testimony that Hoffa had repaid them. "I guess," he told the Committee, "you will have to take our word." His was the only one available. Holtzman was dead. Bushkin refused to testify.

Hoffa was also a lender. He helped to arrange a Teamster loan of between $40,000 and $50,000 to Michigan policy gambler John Bitonti; when Bitonti was visited by a Committee staff member he removed a picture of Hoffa from the wall of his study. Hoffa and Brennan engineered a loan of $50,000 to the Northville Downs race track, where Brennan kept a string of trotting horses. They arranged a loan of $281,000 to two former Detroit public officials to set up a private sanitarium, promising that the Teamsters would take over the establishment if it failed. Hoffa participated in the decision by the Michigan Conference of Teamsters to lend $1,-000,000 to the Winchester Village Land Company for property development, Teamster attorney George Fitzgerald allegedly receiving a finder's fee of $35,000 from the company; none of the principal on the loan had been repaid at the time of the Committee's investigation—almost three years after the loan was made; the Committee estimated that the union lost some $650,000 on the transaction.

Hoffa and Brennan also spent $149,317.79 in Detroit Teamster local union funds to buy a private home in Long Beach, Indiana, ostensibly for conversion into a school for Teamster business agents. The house belonged to Paul DeLucia, otherwise known as Paul ("The Waiter") Ricca, one of the most famous contemporary members of the Chicago underworld. Hoffa was asked about that.

Q. Do you know who Paul DeLucia is. Paul DeLucia is another name for Paul Ricca.
A. I don't believe it.

Ricca was uncommunicative.

Q. Isn't it a fact that you needed money at the time, as you were under investigation by the Internal Revenue Department, and you prevailed upon the Teamsters to purchase this property for the $150,000?
Q. I decline to answer.

. . .

Q. Now, was this also arranged not only by Mr. Brennan, but was it also arranged by Mr. Joey Glimco in Chicago?

A. I decline to answer . . .

The property sold to the Teamsters included all of the house, but only a part of the tennis court and a corner of the swimming pool. "[I]t was possible for a period of a year," the Committee observed, "for Teamster business agents to be dunking their feet in one end of the pool while Paul Ricca and his racketeer friends enjoyed the languid waters and the sunshine at the other end of the pool." The oversight was later remedied, but it did not seem to matter. The property was apparently never used for its stated purpose.

Hoffa was a gambler. On his income tax returns from 1948 to 1956 he listed as "collections" and "wagering" amounts ranging from $1,000 to $10,000. Brennan evidently was the expert. "My partner has some horses . . . and he places some bets and we are fortunate to win some money," Hoffa testified, ". . . I don't do the betting and I don't keep the records." Brennan was questioned.

Q. Mr. Hoffa says this money comes from gambling games. How can you continuously win at gambling games over a period of eight years, Mr. Brennan?

A. I respectfully decline to answer the question . . .

Brennan continued to invoke the Fifth Amendment, claiming through counsel that he was under investigation by the Internal Revenue Service. The Teamster accountant who handled Hoffa's income tax returns said he had to rely on Hoffa's memory for the winnings. Here, in an interesting change of form, the figures Hoffa usually gave were precise to the dollar. In 1956, for example, he told his accountant that he had won exactly $10,682 the previous year. "He has the most fabulous memory," counsel Kennedy said, "of anybody that ever lived." "I guess he has," the accountant replied.

Hoffa dealt in cash. He conceded to the Committee that he had $20,000 invested in a refinancing agency with Carney Matheson, a lawyer for trucking employers, but he said he had no records of the source of the money. Dealing in cash was a frequent habit. Kennedy suggested that it was "an interesting way to conduct your affairs as the head of a large union." Hoffa took a more patriotic view. "It is," he stated, "an American way."

He was evidently not without political connections. The Committee investigated a charge that high political influence had been brought to bear to terminate the 1953 investigation of Hoffa by a subcommittee of the House Committee on Education and Labor. Senator McClellan placed into the record an old clipping from the Detroit *Beacon.*

HOUSE LABOR RACKET PROBE DRAWING HEAT
PRESSURE ON TO SOFT-PEDAL INQUIRY INTO DETROIT CASE

DETROIT, November 28(AP)—In a copyrighted story the Detroit News said "terrific pressure" is being exerted on Congressmen to abandon their labor racketeering probe and dissolve the special subcommittee.

The News said two committee members and two staff members, in Detroit last week, confirmed that the heat was being applied to "soft-pedal or quit."

The story written by staff writer Robert S. Ball said the pressure is so strong from highly placed sources that members of the House Committee on Education and Labor feared to reveal their names for publication.

Representative Wint Smith (Republican, Kansas), the chairman of the subcommittee, was quoted as saying, "The pressure comes from way up there . . . and I just can't talk about it any more specifically than that." Republican Representative Clare Hoffman of Michigan gave names to the press but forbade their publication; he did say that powerful officials in Washington had told subcommittee members to "go easy, or get out." The Teamsters, meanwhile, had retained former Republican Governor Payne H. Ratner of Kansas for legal and other duties. Ratner conferred with Representative Smith on various matters. Hoffman prepared a contempt citation against Hoffa, which Smith refused to sign. "Wint told me today," Ratner wrote to Hoffa, "that he certainly got in bad with Hoffman and the staff for having gone along with me in his treatment of you Friday . . . He declared it is his best judgment that there will be no further effort to cite you." The hearings soon terminated, Smith claiming that the House subcommittee's work was finished.

The McClellan Committee observed that Hoffa's retention of Ratner to "ease his problems" with the subcommittee resembled his relations with "judges and prosecutors in the Michigan area." Sergeant Bernard Mullins of the Detroit Police Department told the Committee that Hoffa, angry with former Assistant Prosecutor Joseph Rashid's aggressive cross-examination of various Teamster officials, told Rashid "he would see to it that he never got anyplace politically . . . he said all he needed was to know who Mr. Rashid would go out with and who he would go with socially, and in a matter of ninety days he could frame him or any individual he wanted to frame."

"If I am elected president," Hoffa told the Committee just prior to his election in 1957, ". . . I intend to conduct myself with respectability . . . I will not be ashamed of it, I am sure . . . I have done as much good for the working man as any individual in the United States . . . am I going to run a good union? . . . Absolutely yes."

The Committee was skeptical. It accused him of "parlaying" his associations with the Detroit underworld into "equally close connections" with criminal elements in Illinois, New York, Ohio, Indiana, Nevada and elsewhere; of deliberately hiring ex-convicts for union work; of tolerating criminal activities on the part of incumbent officials and of rehiring those who had gone to jail on felony convictions.

Frank Kierdorf, Herman's nephew, was also an ex-convict. He was hired, evidently on Hoffa's recommendation, as a business agent by Teamster Local 332 in Flint, Michigan. Like his uncle, he had served time for armed robbery, and apparently had no previous union experience. He was soon accused of shaking down employers. Hoffa made his own kind of investigation.

Q. Did you investigate or look into that?

. . .

A. I discussed the matter with Frank, and he flatly denied it.
Q. Did you make any other investigation of it?
A. What other investigation could I possibly make?

Frank Kierdorf died the same day. He was fatally burned in trying to set fire to a cleaning and dyeing shop in Flint.

President Daniel Keating and Secretary-Treasurer Louis Linteau of Local 614 in Pontiac, Michigan, were indicted in 1953 for extortion. Beck put the local into trusteeship, appointing Hoffa as trustee. Hoffa reappointed Keating and Linteau to office. The Detroit Joint Council spent some $30,000 in the defense of Keating, Linteau and two other union officials. All four went to jail on reduced charges, the union paying out $85,489 in support of their families for nearly three years. Hoffa gave Linteau a job when he came out of jail.

Robert P. Scott, once a business agent for Local 614 and later secretary-treasurer of the Michigan State Federation of Labor, told the Committee that Hoffa had asked him to obtain a pardon for Pete Camponero, father-in-law of Detroit racketeer Pete Licavoli. He said that Hoffa also asked him to hide his brother William when the latter was a fugitive from justice, and that Local 614 paid William Hoffa's bills while he was in hiding. Scott testified that his life had been threatened twice just prior to his appearance before the Committee.

Zigmont ("Ziggy") Snyder, a man of various arrests who had served eleven years for armed robbery, became a business agent for the International Longshoremen's Association in Detroit. He was appointed in 1951 at a meeting in Hoffa's office, replacing a man who had allegedly displeased the ILA by asking the employers for too many wage increases and by calling too many strikes. Snyder changed sides when the AFL chartered the International Brotherhood of Longshoremen, but his local was soon put into trusteeship for "slipshod" administration. Snyder then transferred into Hoffa's Local 299, becoming a business agent for the local.

He became a businessman as well, setting up the Great Lakes Cargo Handling Corporation in Detroit, acting as both employer and union representative of some of the members of Local 299. Most of his employees, however, were hired casually off the street and were juveniles of fifteen and sixteen, as an investigation of the firm's high accident record showed. He also owned a non-union car washing service, paying his employees between seventy cents and $1.60 an hour. William Neff, manager of a Detroit garage, testified that he was asked by Lawrence Welsh, an official of Teamster Local 985, to transfer his auto wash business to Snyder's firm, and that his garage was picketed when he refused. Hoffa was asked about that.

Q. Did you ask Welsh about it?
A. Yes, sir, and Welsh said he didn't do it.
Q. Did you make any further investigation?
A. Where would I investigate?

Hoffa later conceded that the Committee was right, but that no action had been taken against Welsh.

"Hoffa," the Committee said, "runs a hoodlum empire, the members of which are steeped in iniquity and dedicated to the proposition that no thug need starve if there is a teamster payroll handy." The charge was absurd if applied to the entire union, but there were ex-felons in abundance. Jack Thompson, a business agent for Flint Local 332, had been convicted for arson, unlawful breaking and entry and armed robbery, and was accused in testimony of shaking down employers; he refused to testify. William ("Hard-of-Hearing Smitty") Smith of Nashville Local 327 had been convicted eleven times, most recently for conspiracy to assault with intent to kill, and was accused in testimony of five dynamitings; he refused to testify. Glenn Smith, president and business agent of Chattanooga Local 515, had served time for burglary, robbery and larceny; he refused to testify. President John McNamara of New York Local 295 was convicted with Dio for extortion; he refused to testify. Henry DeRoma, a trustee of New York Local 805, had been in prison for murder and selling heroin; he refused to testify. Al Reger, the secretary-treasurer of New York Local 522, had been convicted for extortion; he refused to testify.

In all, the Committee listed 141 Teamster officials "about whom testimony has been adduced relating to improper activities." Of these, fifty-four were no longer connected with the union, although in most cases the reason for separation was not specified. The Committee also listed seventy Teamster officials, past and present, who invoked the Fifth Amendment, and forty-seven "gangsters and racketeers about whom there is testimony regarding association with Teamster officials."

Senator McClellan questioned the propriety of allowing Teamster officials to stay on the payroll after they had been convicted. Edward Bennett Williams, the Teamsters' special counsel in the hearings and one of the nation's leading criminal lawyers, responded.

A. May I make this observation . . . as to whether an officer should be ousted immediately after conviction while he is pursuing his appeal at remedies . . . so far at least as I have been able to determine, never in the history of the United States has the Congress ousted a member immediately after conviction . . . Congress has always waited until the member has exhausted his appeal at remedies before taking summary action against him.

"Hoffa does not now have," the Committee said, "nor has he ever had, any intention of moving against his racketeer friends . . . he has never moved to exercise his powers even after convicted union officials have gone to jail and even though they continue to hold office and draw salaries and even Christmas bonuses while they languish in jail . . . The Committee is convinced that if Hoffa is unchecked he will successfully destroy the decent labor movement in the United States. Further than that, because of the tremendous economic power of the Teamsters, it will place the underworld in a position to dominate American economic life . . . The Committee finds that Hoffa, more than any other single individual, must bear the responsibility for specific provisions of the law that is now on the Nation's statute books. The decent elements of organized labor have hung a pariah's label on him".*

Hoffa had his own version of the evidence. "I say I stand here," he told the 1961 convention of the Teamsters, "and look you in the eye, each and

---

* The Congress had by now passed the Labor-Management Reporting and Disclosure Act, which provided for the detailed supervision of union internal affairs and for restrictions on union economic activities. The AFL–CIO had also expelled the Teamsters.

every one of you, and say I never sold out a worker in my life, never . . ."

He reflected later on his calling. "Money has no bearing on the question," he told a *Playboy* reporter. "If I couldn't draw a salary tomorrow morning, I would continue to do what I am doing and remain President of the Teamsters Union. If I had to get a job in the nighttime to carry on, I would do that, too. Money is no big deal in my life."

He dismissed the charge that he protected the guilty and consorted with racketeers. "Bobby Kennedy submitted a list of 107 names as being directly or indirectly aligned with the Teamsters Union and involved in some sort of illegal enterprises. I later submitted under oath to McClellan and Kennedy a breakdown of the 107 names, and out of those 107 names there was only sixteen people on the payroll of the Teamsters as of the day I testified, who had been involved in incidents of any great consequence in the courts. All of those incidents, by the way, were brought about by the occupation of being a labor leader . . . I would take each man on his own. The mere fact that he happened to know somebody would not necessarily stop me from hiring him even though the people he knew were so-called, alleged gangsters . . . I've saw too many alleged gangsters who, when you checked on the actual persons alleged to be gangsters, had no more to do with being a gangster than *you* are a gangster . . . I don't even know a syndicate exists, and I don't believe you do either . . . After all this malarkey about a Mafia, what have they really got? A new name for it: the Cosa Nostra."

He had two special antipathies. One was the press. "You talk about gangsters! Reporters are gangsters with a pencil instead of a gun. They distort, deceive, tell half-truths and complete lies . . . There is very few labor reporters in the United States that are free to write the truth about the Teamsters. Most of them are controlled by the anti-labor policies of their newspapers . . ."

The other was his chief interrogator on the McClellan Committee. "Now I regard Bobby Kennedy as a spoiled brat," he said. "He never had to work, wouldn't know how to work . . . He's just a brat that believes everybody is supposed to surrender and give in to whatever he wants, right or wrong . . . I question whether or not he has a single friend, and I question whether or not his associates are other than people who *have* to associate with him . . . As far as his associations are concerned, Bobby Kennedy should look in a mirror and find out whether or not he could stand an investigation like Hoffa has on his own personal life—and I say *personal* . . . I was reading a story about Bobby Kennedy which talked about the fact that Bobby was born to the silk and I was born to the burlap, and the author wondered what the difference would have been if I had been born to the silk and Kennedy to burlap.

"Well, you can't change life very easily and you can't go back, but I would venture to say that, knowing what I have did to get where I am at now and what it took to be part of building this union, that Bobby Kennedy would have found out that it is one thing to *make* people do things and another thing to get people to do things *without* making them. He would have found out that you do not always have a choice of who you deal with, who you associate with or what you do and the way you do it to be able to get a project completed successfully . . . Nobody lives alone."

He had no regrets. "I'll tell you about a public standard of morality. In my humble opinion there is none in the United States. Individuals are individuals, and each one grows up with the standards of the household he was born in and the society he's permitted to live in, based upon his economic position in life . . . Anybody that tells you that if he could relive his life, he wouldn't live it somewhat different than he did, must be a fool. If I made mistakes—and I'm not saying that I didn't—I would probably make the same mistakes if I had to do it over, being human, under the same circumstances. But I'm not ashamed of a single, solitary thing I ever did. Nothing."

Now Hoffa was in trouble with the law. A systematic investigation of his affairs, begun under the Eisenhower Administration, became under the Attorney Generalship of Robert F. Kennedy one of the most concentrated legal manhunts in American jurisprudence.

In 1957, in addition to his trial for wire tapping, Hoffa was indicted for the illegal possession of documents belonging to the McClellan Committee. The prosecution charged that he had bribed John Cye Cheasty, one of the Committee's employees, to steal the documents. The case was tried in Washington, D.C., before a predominantly Negro jury. Former heavyweight champion Joe Louis made several courtroom appearances to shake hands with the defendant. The trial ended in a hung jury.

Hoffa's involvement in the Sun Valley project led to an indictment in 1960 for using the United States mails to defraud Teamster members. The case was eventually abandoned, but the charge of fraud was revived when Hoffa and various associates were tried in 1964 for improperly obtaining $20,000,000 in loans from Teamster pension funds, allegedly diverting $1,700,000 to their own use. Hoffa was found guilty and sentenced to five years in jail. The case is still on appeal.

In 1962 Hoffa went on trial for violating a provision of the federal law which prohibits union representatives from demanding or receiving improper payments from employers. The federal government charged that Commercial Carriers, in setting up Test Fleet for Mrs. Hoffa and Mrs. Brennan, had in effect channeled more than one million dollars to Hoffa. The trial ended in a hung jury, but was followed by an indictment of Hoffa for attempting to bribe a juror. He was found guilty and sentenced to eight years in jail.

By this time the expensive federal effort to bring Hoffa down had prompted accusations—supported in quarters not normally friendly to Hoffa—of judicial persecution. The jury-tampering trial, in particular, brought allegations that illegal methods had been employed by the Department of Justice to get the needed evidence against Hoffa. The Supreme Court disagreed. On March 7, 1967, Hoffa entered a federal prison in Pennsylvania to serve his time for the jury-tampering conviction.

20: The Textile Workers, the Newspaper Drivers and the UAW

The Textile Workers

"Although puny by today's robust standards," the Committee noted, "the state of the UTWA's treasury has not rendered it immune against human temptation." The Committee had been investigating the financial affairs of the chief officers of the 50,000-member United Textile Workers of America.*

"As an open invitation to malfeasance," the Committee said, "the UTWA's financial procedures merit detailing." The governing body of the union was a twenty-two-member executive council elected in convention, and was composed of the president, the secretary-treasurer, and twenty vice presidents of the union. Salaries and expenses of all twenty-two officials were fixed by the president with the approval of the council. It was also the custom for executive council members to borrow money from the union without security or interest, the secretary-treasurer making provision for repayment "according to his best judgement." No comparable loan facilities were made available to the members of the union. Secretary-Treasurer Lloyd Klenert thought the practice was justifiable.

Q. I take it that this select circle of individuals entitled to interest-free loans without collateral did not include loans to union members who actually paid the dues to collect the funds . . .
A. No individual member has ever requested a loan from the international union . . . I think if I was asked for a loan from a worker, I think I would arrange to give it to him. Yes, I think I honestly would, sir.

A certified public accountant conducted periodic audits of the union's books. He told the Committee that while vouchers were complete enough for auditing purposes, some of them were short in detail. Other audits were carried out by three rank-and-file trustees of the union when summoned by the international officers. George Emerson, a maintenance worker who never finished high school and had no training in auditing, was one of the trustees. He described the procedure.

* Formerly of the AFL. Not to be confused with the Textile Workers Union of America, formerly of the CIO.

271

A. One of them takes the checks, and I take the stub, and the other takes the vouchers, and they call out the name of the check and the amount that is on it, and I check it against the stub . . . if the amount is correct, and there is no question about it, and if it is a routine thing, we go right on through.

. . .

Q. Do you ever ask the fellow what he was doing?

A. No; either someone on the board or someone in the office knows what the guy was there for. If it happens in the South, I am pretty well aware of where fellows are working.

Q. How about Mr. Klenert and [President Anthony] Valente themselves? They verify their own vouchers, do they?

A. Yes.

. . .

Q. What about Mr. Valente? Do you know if anybody checks to find out whether that is accurate?

A. No; they would have no reason to.

. . .

Q. Have you ever questioned Mr. Klenert about any of his expenses?

A. If we have, I don't recall any specific instance, but if we have we got the answer that was satisfactory.

In 1952 Valente and Klenert each bought a home in Maryland. The price for the two, purchased jointly, was $95,000. Three weeks later the UTWA executive council authorized the two officers to investigate the purchase of property by the union for office or investment purposes, giving Klenert permission to convert into cash $95,000 in defense bonds owned by the union. About the same time the UTWA accepted a splinter group from its CIO rival, the Textile Workers Union of America. As a precaution against possible TWUA reprisals, the UTWA executive council authorized the setting up of an organizing fund, the amount to be determined by Valente and Klenert. The sum they chose was $57,000, which equalled the amount they had recently paid down on their houses. The $57,000 was written off as organizational and allied expenses on such matters as "the Canadian situation" and "the North Carolina situation." Both Valente and Klenert conceded that union money had been used toward the purchase of their homes, but argued that it was a convenient way of concealing funds that the union might need in an emergency and wished to keep secret. Valente was questioned.

Q. . . . Would you recommend this character of transactions to another union?

A. Not in the normal operations, but we had a peculiar problem at the time . . . In a period of ten years we had 104 raids against our organization.

Out of a clear sky, these men—because they had an intra-union fight in the CIO Textile Union,—were coming into our union. A number of people were concerned of what was going to happen to our union . . . I felt I had a moral obligation to protect the future and the destiny of our union and these men.

Later in 1952, a further sum of $17,500 was drawn from the UTWA's treasury and charged to organizational expenses. About the same time Valente and Klenert spent large sums on furnishing their new houses. Klenert was asked to explain the expenditure of $8,500 in Canada. He said it was spent on an anti-Communist campaign, declaring that $7,500 went to a man named Jacques for "deputies" at the mill gates.

Q. Who introduced you to Jacques?
A. I received no personal introductions . . . he seemed to know quite a bit about it . . . he suggested this course of action and I accepted it.
Q. Did you try to check on him at all, on Jacques?
A. Did I ask any of the people about it? No.
Q. Do you know anybody in Canada that knows Jacques?
A. I don't know anybody in Canada.

The Committee's own investigations showed that another union had provided help free of charge at the mill gates in question, and that "Jacques" was unknown to officers of the Canadian labor movement in the area. No satisfactory explanation was given of the disposition of the remainder of the organizing funds.

In August, 1952, Valente and Klenert provided President George Meany of the AFL with a financial report he had requested as a condition of AFL financial aid to the UTWA. Meany rejected the report as unsatisfactory. Valente and Klenert thereafter borrowed money privately to pay off their debts to the union. "We decided," Valente testified, "that the device of the layaway was no longer necessary." The AFL then requested the appointment of a five-man UTWA committee to report on the financial activities of Valente and Klenert. Both men were exonerated by a committee appointed, in effect, by Valente himself. The AFL rejected the report. Valente and Klenert remained in office, although they returned the money they had used on their houses.

In 1954 both men came under investigation by the Internal Revenue Service. The same year the UTWA leadership authorized the destruction of all union records more than three years old, except those of a historical nature. Nonetheless, Valente and Klenert were jointly assessed over $12,-000 in penalties by the federal tax authorities for falsification of returns. The union paid some $2,000 on the debt, and raised the salaries and allowances of Valente and Klenert from $18,000 to $22,300, and from $17,935 to $21,300, respectively.

"Among the human frailties which have passed before the committee during the past twelve months," the Committee remarked, "one of the more recurrent has been the sheer greed of many of the individuals involved . . . As an unblushing exercise in avarice, the union careers of Anthony Valente and Lloyd Klenert can scarcely be matched . . . While much larger sums of union money may have been misused for personal profit and pleasure by other officials interrogated by the committee, in relative terms the peculations of Valente and Klenert were much more spectacular. The UTWA's wealth is comparatively small; its annual income is less than one million dollars. The funds misappropriated by its two top-ranking officers totaled $178,000 or about eighteen percent of the union's entire intake in any one year."

There were other culprits. The real estate transactions of Valente and Klenert were conducted in part with the help of Martin J. Quigley, president of the Mutual Title Company of Washington, D.C., who examined the titles and arranged the terms of settlement on the two houses purchased. "In a clear-cut abuse of his quasi-fiduciary function," the Committee said, "Quigley obligingly wrote letters, patently intended for the union auditor's eyes, which supported the fiction that union funds had gone for the purposes authorized by the UTWA and conveniently neglected all mention of the home-buying deal." The Committee also criticized Joseph Jacobs, the attorney for the union.* "Jacobs," the Committee said, "derived benefit from his union connection simultaneously as owner of a firm which leased cars to the UTWA. He was also a member of the UTWA subcommittee which supposedly 'investigated' the Valente-Klenert peculations and gave the two men a clean bill of health. Subsequently he was instrumental in having the union pay part of an assessment levied by the Internal Revenue Service on Valente and Klenert for faulty income tax returns."

The Newspaper Drivers

"The extent to which criminal and underworld elements have succeeded in infiltrating the management and labor ends of the newspaper and magazine wholesale and distribution business in the New York area," the Committee said, ". . . constitutes a potential threat to freedom of the press."

The Newspaper and Mail Deliverers Union represented some 4,500 drivers and helpers in the New York metropolitan area. It was an independent union, and had evidently long enjoyed a reputation for internal democracy. Local union officials were chosen in secret ballot elections supervised by

* Not of Chicago.

the Honest Ballot Association. All labor-management agreements were put to a direct vote of the membership, which often overturned the recommendations of the leadership.

Democracy was not enough. The McClellan Committee, hearing rumors of employer payoffs to union officials, conducted an investigation "in the face of unusual difficulties . . . It represented a singular instance where even in preliminary interviews both officials of management and officials of labor unions jointly refused to give any information . . . about the payment of bribes by management or the acceptance of bribes by officials of the union. It reached a stage where a special executive session was set in New York to put principal officers of each management concern and all the union officials on record. They all took the Fifth Amendment."

The union had bargaining agreements with five employer groups: the Newspaper Publishers Assocation, representing the major morning and evening newspapers; and the suburban Newsdealers Assocation, the Morning Wholesalers Group, the Evening Wholesalers Group, and the Magazine Wholesalers Group—all five representing thirty-seven wholesalers who bought newspapers and magazines from publishers for sale to retailers.

The Committee found that a number of the wholesalers made regular cash withdrawals from their bank deposits for which no credible accounting was given. It questioned thirteen wholesalers about the withdrawals; all refused to testify. It asked nineteen union officials if they knew anything about payoffs; only two—Joseph Baer and John McQuade, respectively the newly elected president and business representative of the union—did not resort to the Fifth Amendment. Both had a reputation for honesty; both denied they had received payments from employers; both disclaimed any knowledge of payoffs to others. McQuade was perplexed.

> Q. Does it disturb you at all, Mr. McQuade, that your fellow members of the executive board and fellow union officials . . . with the one exception of Mr. Baer, all appear before the committee and refuse to answer any questions regarding payoffs?
> A. I couldn't say, sir. I know most of these men and, believe me, I think most of them are good people . . . It puzzles me. I can't figure it out.

The Committee turned to the alleged monopolization of the wholesale business by racketeers. Irving Bitz was a vice president of the Bronx County News Company, a wholesale magazine distributorship. He had a record of eleven arrests and three jail sentences on narcotics and other charges, and supposedly was involved in the anti-union operations of Johnny Dio. The Committee questioned Theodore Thackrey, publisher and president of the now defunct *Daily Compass,* who had gone to Bitz for help in dealing with the union.

Q. Did you talk to some individuals who made some suggestions to you?

A. I talked to a number. Among them was James Gettleson, who had been circulation director at the time when I was the editor and associate editor of the *Post* in New York . . . He said he knew of a man who was reputed to have considerable influence with the union . . . He said his name was Irving Bitz.

. . .

Q. What did you know of his background?

A. I knew that he had been under arrest several times.

. . .

Q. And associated with the underworld; did you understand that?

A. It was my understanding.

. . .

Q. So he called you and you met with him . . . what happened at the meeting?

A. I told him our circumstances, and he said, "Well, I can deliver a contract for you." . . . I asked him how much it would be . . . he finally settled on a figure of $10,000, which he said was the minimum . . . to get a contract that would be satisfactory to us.

Thackrey said he paid Bitz $10,000, signed a contract with the union, and experienced no further labor trouble; but that Bitz was unhappy.

A. He said, "Well . . . I am not going to come out of this with any money . . . couldn't you get up at least $500 for me . . ."

. . .

Q. Did you regard this just as a shakedown payment . . . ?

A. Well, Senator, I have always had a hard time kidding myself . . . I regarded it as a shakedown, and I was very ashamed of my own part in it.

. . .

Q. What is your conclusion about whether you would have received a contract except that you made a payoff like that?

A. At that time, and under those circumstances, I don't think we would have received a contract we could have lived with.

There were other charges of racketeer influence and payoffs. As a result, a federal grand jury indicted six union officials and five employer representatives on anti-trust and extortion charges. A New York County grand jury indicted four union officials and two employer representatives on charges of conspiracy and extortion. Bitz was sentenced to five years in jail and $45,000 in fines.

Harold Gross was a convicted extortionist employed as a part-time platform worker for the Neo-Gravure Printing Company of Weehawken, New

Jersey. The company printed supplements for such publications as the *New York Times,* the *Mirror,* and the *Journal-American.*

Gross was a member of Inland Terminal Workers Local 1730 of the ILA, which represented the platform workers employed by Neo-Gravure. His employer paid him a formal weekly wage of $143, but also a monthly retainer of $460. These monthly payments, concealed from the rest of the company's employees, were for unspecified services. The Committee declared that they were "nothing more than a guarantee of labor peace."

Gross was not always present to collect his paychecks. In 1958 he became an official of Local 320 of the Teamsters in Miami Beach while remaining on Neo-Gravure's payroll. Charles E. Chenicek, a vice president of the company, explained.

Q. Is it true he is kept on the payroll at the present time because of his connections and contacts with certain labor officials?
A. Well, I would phrase it that he is kept on the payroll because the department does function harmoniously, it functions effectively, and on that basis his services are retained.

· · ·

Q. He is not there to personally supervise as a foreman should and would normally, is he?
A. That is correct.
Q. So he is off down in Florida running the Teamsters Union while he is on your payroll to keep labor peace; that is what it amounts to, isn't it?
A. Yes, sir.

Gross was not wholly a stranger. General Manager William H. Hillbrant confirmed that while Florida had been Gross's main headquarters for a year and a half, he maintained some contact with Neo-Gravure.

Q. He keeps in touch with your company by telephone, does he?
A. He does.

Miami Local 320 had thirty-two members, and cost the international union $3,000 in subsidies personally authorized by Hoffa. Miami Beach employers were sometimes asked to invest money in the local as a business venture, with unspecified prospects. Various hoodlums were said to be associated with the local's unspectacular organizing activities, and the international union was determined to do something about its reputation. Former United States Senator George H. Bender, appointed by Hoffa in 1958 as chairman of the Teamsters' new Anti-Racketeering Commission, wrote to the secretary-treasurer of Local 320 asking if there was any gangster or racketeering influence in the local. He received a prompt reply.

Dear Sir:

There are no cases of racketeering or gangster influence in this local union.

We will give you full cooperation on any investigation of this local union.

Very truly yours,
BERNARD DEROW
Secretary-Treasurer, Local 320

Bender was impressed.

Dear Mr. Derow:

Your letter of recent date in response to mine of October 24 has been received.

The fine report you give of your organization is most gratifying to the commission. The officials and members of your local are to be commended upon it.

Thank you sincerely for your fine spirit of cooperation . . .

Cordially yours,
GEORGE H. BENDER

Meanwhile, Gross had received special bonuses from Neo-Gravure in 1954 and 1955 in return for services connected with contract negotiations between the company and the ILA. His contribution was specific, as Chenicek testified.

A. Normally, the wage increase which would be realized by our platform workers in a new contract followed the pattern of wage increases that had been realized in the New York Teamsters contracts which came up shortly before our contract expired. In the case of this two-year contract, the wage increases which our platform workers realized were lesser than those realized by the New York Teamsters.
Q. He [Gross] was able to get you a better contract than you would ordinarily have gotten?
A. That is correct.
Q. At a lower wage rate for the employees?
A. That is correct.

Gross demanded and received $5,000 for his help in the negotiations; the fee was equal to the employer's savings in wage payments. Cornelius J. ("Connie") Noonan, the president of Local 1730, a former colleague of John ("Cockeye") Dunn and allegedly an intimate of assorted underworld figures, was in charge of negotiations for the ILA. He continued to receive from Neo-Gravure his annual Christmas present of $200 in cash.

Gross and Noonan had rendered other services to employers. In 1948 the Teamsters conducted an eight-day city-wide strike in New York. All newspaper deliveries were stopped. Gross and Noonan, however, were able to arrange the delivery of Sunday supplements to the *New York Times* and the *Mirror*. Their reward from Neo-Gravure was $47,750, or between $250 and $375 a truck. The newspapers footed the bill. A similar though less expensive transaction had taken place during a Teamster strike in 1946.

Gross also received money from the *American Weekly,* a Hearst publication, for assuring delivery of Sunday supplements despite a jurisdictional dispute between Local 807 of the Teamsters and the independent Newspaper and Mail Deliverers. "On the basis of incontrovertible evidence," the Committee stated, ". . . the American Weekly, in order to avoid threatened interruption of deliveries, was forced to pay $28,000 in tribute from 1952 to 1958 to Harold Gross, undoubtedly for further distribution to corrupt union officials." In addition, Gross and Noonan were on the payroll of the Associated Paper Company of Philadelphia, for whom they obtained a business contract with the Lily Tulip Cup Company of New York. Noonan represented the employees of Lily Tulip Cup for the ILA. Gross, Noonan and the Associated Paper Company shared the profits from the new arrangement.

Amory H. Bradford, then the business manager and a vice president of the *New York Times,* was asked about the payments to Gross and Noonan during the 1946 and 1948 strikes.

> A. I don't want to quibble about it, but . . . [the *Times*] certainly was aware that a man named Noonan said that for so much a truck these trucks could be moved . . . The payments were made. Certainly it is a fair deduction that the payments were made from Neo-Gravure to Noonan . . . I can say in the light of the circumstances that have developed since then . . . [we] would not today under any circumstances agree to reimburse any of its suppliers for payment to union officials. We would put the public interest against corruption in labor-management relations . . . all we can say is that we hope we have learned something from our own experience and that of others.

Gross and Noonan were indicted by a federal grand jury on charges of conspiracy. Gross was later convicted of income tax evasion, and resigned from his position with Miami Teamster Local 320.

"The hearings," the Committee declared, "as well as others, have served to convince the committee that one of the greatest contributing factors to corruption in the labor-management field is the lack of moral courage and sense of public responsibility on the part of the employers. To achieve a temporary economic advantage they have either submitted to payoff demands or actually sought out ways and means of 'fixing' a troublesome situation . . . Until such time as management realizes its responsibilities and resists these pressures, there is little possibility of stamping out the racketeer influence in this field."

The UAW

On April 5, 1954 the United Automobile Workers struck the Kohler Company of Sheboygan, Wisconsin. The strike lasted nine years. Essentially a demand for recognition of the union, it was one of the longest, harshest, and most violent labor disputes in American history. It divided families, the community, the union, and also the Committee. "Our hearings on the long, incredibly bitter UAW-Kohler strike," Robert F. Kennedy wrote later, "opened in March of 1958. Behind them lay a ten-month struggle within the staff and the Committee that almost caused its complete breakup."

The strike, which ended with a court order compelling the company to recognize the union, was investigated at one time or another by both a House committee and the National Labor Relations Board. Later, during the McClellan Committee's hearings on the Teamsters, the press reported rumors—authored, according to Robert F. Kennedy, by Republican Senator Karl Mundt of South Dakota—to the effect that the Committee was not investigating the strike or the UAW because counsel Robert Kennedy, Senator John Kennedy and other Democratic members of the Committee wanted to protect UAW President Walter Reuther. Robert Kennedy denied the stories and sent a staff representative, Vern Johnson, to Wisconsin to conduct a preliminary inquiry. Johnson reported that he had found nothing to suggest that a further investigation would add materially to the existing findings.

The Republican members of the Committee denied any dissatisfaction with the situation. "I'm as happy," Senator Barry Goldwater said, "as a squirrel in a little cage." "I too am perfectly happy," announced Senator Mundt, "and I'm as happy as a South Dakota pheasant in a South Dakota cornfield." But the rumors persisted, and Robert Kennedy assigned Jack McGovern—a staff member recently appointed at the request of Senator Goldwater—to conduct a formal investigation. Other staff members, Kennedy later said, were made available.

McGovern submitted a lengthy report. "We found," Robert Kennedy said, "that McGovern's report consisted largely of verbatim excerpts lifted from the National Labor Relations Board's Trial Examiner's hearings . . . there was nothing in his report unfavorable to the Kohler Company—this despite the fact that the NLRB examiner, though criticizing the union for mass picketing, had found that the company had refused to bargain in good faith and had been guilty of a number of unfair labor practices . . . If any other investigator had submitted such a report, based on someone else's work, I would have suggested to Senator McClellan that he be fired."

At the request of its Republican members, the Committee then conducted seven weeks of hearings on the Kohler strike, on another dispute between the UAW and the Perfect Circle Corporation in Indiana, and on charges of corruption within the union. The Democrats and Republicans on the Committee divided absolutely on party lines, reporting separately on every issue.

"The hearings on the UAW-Kohler dispute," the Democrats said, "were hearings quite different from others that have been held by the Committee. True, there were charges and countercharges of violence and intimidation as well as other bitter recriminations by both the UAW and Kohler Company. Beyond that, however, unlike other committee hearings, there were no charges of personal corruption or evidence presented of racketeering within the union. There was no testimony of misappropriation of union funds . . . " The Democrats made similar comments about the Perfect Circle strike of 1955.

The Republicans took a different view. They found in the Kohler strike "a clear pattern of crime and violence which has characterized and generally been associated with UAW strikes . . . We do not contend that the Kohler Company management was wholly blameless in this controversy, but it is clear that the violence which took place there was not in response to any company misconduct." They accused Robert Kennedy of indifference to the investigation, and the UAW of evasiveness in testimony. Finally, they claimed that their investigation of UAW International Vice-President Richard T. Gosser had brought out evidence of corruption within the UAW.

The Republicans were particularly interested in charges—presented to the international union some years before by three dissident members of Gosser's home Local 12 in Toledo, Ohio—that Gosser had forced the local to buy goods at exorbitant prices from a hardware store that he owned; that he had taken money from UAW members in kickbacks and improper fines; that he had appropriated for his own use the profits from the slot machines in the headquarters of Local 12; and that he had employed violence, expulsion and other punitive measures against his opponents. The UAW international executive board had dismissed the charges. Robert Kennedy dispatched two Committee staff members to re-examine the charges, later reporting that the only evidence of improper conduct was the fact that Gosser did in fact once have an interest in the Colonial Hardware Store which sold goods to Local 12, and that he was part owner of some land sold to the local. However, Kennedy said, most of the charges were originally made by a man of unsound mind; the other Local 12 members who had joined in making the charges now believed they were improperly advanced; and the two attorneys who had helped to broadcast the accusations admitted to the Committee's investigators that "these charges were all a fraud, that they couldn't sustain the charges." Walter Reuther told the Committee that Gosser had been asked to divest himself of his interest in the hardware store when the matter came to light and that he had done so; and that there had been no personal profit involved in the sale of land to Local 12. The Republicans on the Committee declared that the UAW's finding that Gosser made no personal profit from the sale of the land was "pure whitewash." The Democrats agreed with the union.

G.O.P. members were also interested in the UAW's "flower fund," an internal union account composed of contributions from full-time UAW officials. Some witnesses stated that contributions of five dollars a week or more were a *de facto* condition of employment by the union, and that paychecks were sometimes held up if payments became overdue. Reuther denied that there were any irregularities involved, saying that the fund was a purely internal operation "for the purpose of fighting the political fights of the union. This is how we finance the fight against the Communists. This is how we finance the fight to keep the racketeers from taking over the local union. We do not think it proper to finance internal political problems out of union dues . . ." Senator Carl T. Curtis (Republican, Nebraska) had a question.

> Q. How many anti-Reuther candidates for any office ever got any help out of the flower fund?
> A. . . . How many Democrats have ever gotten elected by the Republican Party? . . . Do you mean to tell me that a labor union can't internally . . . try to raise money voluntarily . . . to keep their union clean of Communism and corruption and to elect people to office who will do that? . . .

Reuther's testimony, the Republicans maintained, was "studded with misstatements of fact and outright falsehoods . . . these funds to re-elect Reuther and his slate of officers are nothing but salary kickbacks imposed as a condition of employment . . . Moreover, these kickbacks are always in cash; no records of them are maintained; and the contributors neither receive nor dare ask for accountings." The Democrats concluded that contributions to the flower fund were both a condition of employment and favored by a majority of the contributors. They found no fault with the administration of the fund as a whole, but did say that the bookkeeping practices in Gosser's Region 2-B flower fund left much to be desired.

The Republicans were unhappy with the Democrats. "We think," they said, "that Reuther and his UAW have much to hide and have hidden much from this committee. We express profound regret that this committee, constituted to investigate and expose management and union corruption wherever it exists, should be disinclined to follow the evidence because it leads to 'Solidarity House' in Detroit and to Walter Reuther, perhaps the most politically powerful labor leader in the United States."

The Democrats were unhappy with the Republicans. "The charges and allegations in this series of hearings," they said, "were substantially those which were discussed at length in the Toledo *Blade* during the period 1949–50 . . . the principal target of these charges was Richard T. Gosser." The Democrats dismissed the charges against Gosser, conceding only that he had acted improperly in selling goods to Local 12 from his own store, and that the flower fund in Region 2-B was poorly accounted. "Other allegations heard in the course of this series of hearings," they said, "do not appear to warrant individual mention, either because of their lack of documentation, or because of their lack of significance."

"As chairman of the committee," Senator McClellan declared, "I think it is proper for me to state that the foregoing UAW-Gosser hearing was conducted by the Republican members of the Committee and their counsel; also that the subsequent executive and public hearings were held at the request of Senator Curtis. All subpoenas for witnesses and documents requested by him were issued by the chairman . . . The witnesses, however, were not examined by the regular members of the staff, nor were the Democratic members of the Committee made acquainted by Senator Curtis, or other Republican members of the Committee, with the nature of the testimony that was to be presented. All documentary evidence which had been procured by Senator Curtis and by subpoenas issued by the Chair was withheld and kept secret from the Democratic members and the regular staff of this Committee until actually presented at the hearings." The UAW hearings, McClellan noted, took thirty-two days, involved 102 witnesses, and produced 2,572 printed pages of testimony. "We deeply regret," he said, ". . . that we are forced to the conclusion that some of the findings of the Republican members . . . transgress the nonpartisan spirit in which the chairman has endeavored to conduct the proceedings and report our findings and conclusions." The Republican charge that the Committee as a whole had failed to properly investigate the UAW, "wholly lacks foundation and credibility."

Senator John F. Kennedy offered his own opinion of the hearings on the UAW. "Since these hearings are coming to an end," he said, "I would like to remark for the record that I think they have been a monumental waste of time . . . investigations by congressional committees should be carried on in such a fashion that when hearings are held the materials and information exposed has at least some degree of authenticity to it . . . There has been nothing of consequence presented here that was not known to the UAW and to the reading public in 1949 and 1950 . . . I believe the good name of this committee has been used by some in their desire to indict a union whose political philosophy differs from theirs."

Gosser soon assumed an inactive status in the UAW, and later resigned. In 1964 he was convicted for attempting to steal Internal Revenue records pertaining to him.

The hearings on the UAW were the last conducted by the Committee. Robert Kennedy resigned as chief counsel, but then heard that Senator Goldwater had accused him of running out on the UAW investigation. He called Goldwater, he said, to confirm the charge and to ask if Goldwater thought there was anything further he could do.

"No, no," Goldwater said. "I want to get back to Arizona now. I don't want any more hearings."

"Then why did you say it?"

"That's politics."

Part V
Retribution and Retrospect

21: The Unions and the Corrupt: The AFL and the CIO

"The American Federation of Labor," Samuel Gompers declared in 1888, "avoids the fatal rock upon which all previous attempts to effect the unity of the working class have split, by leaving to each body or affiliated organization the complete management of its own affairs . . . each trade enjoys the most perfect liberty, while securing the advantages resulting from united action."

The autonomy of affiliated unions was a bedrock principle of the AFL, a condition of association. The federation was a truly voluntary organization, a gathering of sovereign bodies for limited ends. It was in fact a confederation, a creature of delegated and meager authority, more concerned with consensus than conformity. "The Federation has no powers," Gompers said, "except those which are authorized and conceded by the organizations which compose it . . . coercive methods are never employed . . . the AF of L has no power to enforce its judgment . . ." Suspension and expulsion were the only sanctions, something less than mortal for the vast majority of AFL affiliates, and almost never exercised. AFL unions were jealous of their independence, resentful of intrusions on their privacy. Gompers and William Green respected the sensitivities, seldom assayed more than circumspect advice, and always paid homage to autonomy. There were disputes to be solved, particularly over contesting claims of unions to men, work or territory, but arbitration was rare and victory most often the prerogative of the strong. The AFL was seldom more than a peacemaker, usually disclaiming the right to decide. Gompers, as he said, was "loath to give decisions in matters that arise between organizations, it seems to partake too much of dictatorship."

There were, of course, policies to be upheld. The violation of exclusive jurisdiction and the practice of dual unionism, both of them affronts to the theology of the AFL, always moved the federation to anger and occasionally to punishment. Neither Gompers nor Green were reluctant to scold when important principles were defied. The AFL did interfere with the internal affairs of unions in the pursuit of standards, although it seldom went beyond reproach.

In 1898 a member of the Retail Clerks National Protective Union registered charges with the AFL Executive Council of improper actions by his union. "All rights of complaining [local] unions," the Council said, "should first be exercised within their own national unions before coming to the AF of L with their complaints and grievances." Here, as throughout most of its history, the AFL insisted upon the exhaustion of internal remedies, however futile the prospect of justice, before taking action of its own. In this case, however, the Executive Council told the Retail Clerks that they should end the practices complained of and improve their internal grievance processes.

The same year the Council considered charges of fraud made against several international officers of the Hotel and Restaurant Employees. "Many charges of dishonesty," the Executive Council said, "were made against the officers of the organization; fraud was alleged in so many ways in such vital instances as to compel us to undertake an investigation. We have notified those who complained to the American Federation of Labor to help them save the national union from utter destruction to appear before us . . . and have furnished the officers of the organization, who are charged with holding office illegally and with the commission of these offenses, with copies of the complaints, inviting them to be present and give their version of the matters in question. The contending parties were represented at our session . . ." The HRE finally agreed to arbitration by the AFL, the offending officers of the union were removed, and the HRE given financial and advisory assistance by the federation. In Gompers' words, the AFL was determined, "to have the organization . . . rid . . . of an element which has tended to bring it into disrepute for personal and monetary reasons."

Strong action was also taken against the small American Agents Association in Ohio. The AFL Executive Council had received a report "that certain individuals with very shady reputations . . . have taken up the matter of trades unionism in this vicinity as a means of furthering their own selfish purposes financially and politically . . ." Gompers and two Executive Council members looked into the charges, concluded that the Association's bookkeeping practices were inadequate, and that in any event it was not a legitimate trade union. The federation revoked the Association's charter and advised its members to affiliate directly with the AFL.

Despite occasional reminders, the AFL took little further notice of corruption for a generation. "The trade union movement at large," said *Justice,* the journal of the ILGWU, of the revelations of the Lockwood Committee in New York City, "is still keeping silent over these disclosures. It apparently is still fearful of the dark powers of Brindellism. Sooner or later, however, this ostrich policy will have to be abandoned, and to save its reputation, its very existence, the labor movement will have to remove this cancer with the sharpest of instruments."

In 1928 the federation received a lecture. "I know the best of your great movement," the Reverend J. W. R. McGuire of St. Victor's College told the AFL convention, "and I also know all the worst of it . . . You have every reason to be proud of the honesty and fearlessness and the ability of your leadership. On the other hand—and I say this with sorrow—sometimes you do have men who betray the high and holy cause of labor by dishonesty, by graft, by crime, by corruption, yes, even by murder . . . I suggest that the finest thing the American Federation of Labor can do, allowing, of course, for the various laws and regulations of your different organizations, is to rigidly and immediately exclude from the ranks of organized labor all those who have been guilty of any kind of dishonesty . . . It is necessary that you shall come not only into the courts of equity and the courts of chancery but into [C]ongress and the legislatures of this land with clean hands . . ."

McGuire repeated his message at the 1930 convention, prompting a response from William Green. "There are some who masquerade as trade unionists," Green said. "They speak to us with the voice of Jacob, but they present the hand of Esau. We are endeavoring as best we can to drive out the racketeer and the traitor . . . if there is brought to my attention the racketeer moving under the garb of trades unionism, I will drive him from the movement if I can." Green then cited two cases—one in New York and one in Chicago—where AFL federal charters had been revoked and new ones issued after trouble with racketeers.

In 1931 the AFL Executive Council took up the charge that Theodore Brandle had accepted a $10,000 bribe from New Jersey employers, dividing the money among various officers of the Iron Workers. On instructions from the Council, Green asked President P. J. Morrin of the Iron Workers "to take such action as may seem necessary . . . to protect and safeguard the integrity, the good name and the standing of your own International Union, as well as the organized labor movement as represented by the American Federation of Labor."

Morrin evidently did nothing. Green wrote to him again, reminding him of the Council's duty to protect the honor of the federation by bringing the matter "forcibly to the attention of the proper officers for consideration and action . . ." but noting that "the Executive Council makes no charges. It has no authority to make charges . . . you have the power to deal with this case . . ." Brandle and four other Iron Workers' officials were later expelled from the union.

Green discussed with President John Possehl of the Operating Engineers the charges of misbehavior levelled against Vice-President Joseph Fay of that union, but was merely told that there was no widespread corruption in the union. He also wrote to Theatrical and Stage Employees President William C. Elliott about the corrupt activities of President Sam Kaplan of IATSE New York Local 306, stating that "the Executive Council appreciates fully its lack of authority to interfere in the internal affairs of a local union or of an International or National Organization . . . On the other hand, the Council is clothed with the authority to administer the affairs of the American Federation of Labor between conventions and to guard jealously the welfare of labor . . . the facts warrant decisive action on your part. Unpleasant as the duty may be, it seems that the duty cannot be evaded." No action was taken, although Kaplan went to jail for income tax evasion. Elliott soon retired unexpectedly, giving way to George Browne.

The next four conventions of the AFL warned against racketeering. In 1932 there was a protest against both exaggeration and invasion. "Altogether too often," the Executive Council reported to the convention, "do we find legitimate trade union activity described as racketeering by the unthinking or ill-disposed . . . That there is room here and there for improvement within the labor movement is not to be denied, but the greater danger is from without. More and more do we find those of criminal tendencies . . . endeavoring to gain control of our trade unions. . . . It is against this development we protest." The 1933 convention stated its opposition to "racketeering or gangsterism of all forms," urging its affiliates "to use every means within their power to prevent the entrance of any form of racketeering or gangsterism into any part of the movement, and to purge it of any taint of this menace." In 1934 Irving Matlin of Russian-Turkish Bath Workers and Rubbers Local 18702 offered a resolution stating that "in many Local Unions, affiliated National and International Unions, in various District Councils, Building Trades Councils and Central Labor Bodies, gangsterism and racketeering are rampant . . . Exposure by rank and file members in many instances [is] followed by reprisals organized by gangsters paid by corrupt officials out of union funds, in which union members are intimidated, terrorized, killed and maimed . . ." The resolution was undocumented, and altered before passage; but the convention had its say. "All that is uplifting and ennobling in our trade union movement," the convention said, "all that we have accomplished . . . is stained and besmirched when racketeering and gangsterism in any of its forms secures an entry. . . ."

The same year, President Dan Tobin of the Teamsters voiced a common trade union resentment against the press, charging that many journalists exaggerated the scale of corruption in unions and ignored the odds that unions faced in fighting corruption. "Our local unions in many different cities throughout the country," he wrote to one newspaperman, "are paying out each month thousands of dollars endeavoring to keep out gunmen and racketeers. Why didn't you tell in your story that men have been shot down like dogs, while trying to protect their unions. I dislike using the pronoun I, still I could say to you that my life has been endangered because I have tried to keep out wrongdoers."

The 1935 AFL convention passed another anti-racketeering resolution. Green also announced that a committee of the Executive Council had met with New York City District Attorney Thomas E. Dewey to offer the federation's help in fighting racketeers. The committee submitted a report to the Council, but it was evidently not made public.

Tobin returned to the attack in 1938 and 1940. He criticized Harold Seidman's book on trade union corruption, *Labor Czars,* saying that it was concerned only with the bad side of labor. "[T]hey do not mention the fact that the General President [Tobin] was beaten almost to a pulp in the City of New York while trying to clean out wrongdoers . . . that the General President in 1910 expelled from the International Union nearly ten thousand members in Chicago because of the fact that they had ten or twelve men representing their unions who, in the judgment of the General Executive Board, were dishonest, and that these unions were kept out of the International for a period of over twenty years, and that they were then only returned to membership after being approved by the State Attorney's office and on a request of the Mayor of Chicago. They do not mention the fact that out of eighteen hundred local unions, only two or three officers have gone wrong and that those have been put out of membership."

Westbrook Pegler had attacked the Teamsters. "[H]e lived in Chicago," Tobin wrote in the Teamsters' journal, "in the days when the membership in the International Brotherhood of Teamsters was being bought and sold by thieving employers and petty racketeering business agents, and he has seen the rank and file, through their officers, come up from the very bottom to positions of independence and safety in employment." Screening was a problem. "Because our work is considered unskilled," Tobin said, ". . . toughs and undesirables . . . get into membership in our union undercover, in disguise. Sometimes they drive a truck for a week or two, and after they once get in they begin to try to take control. Well, if we find that local has such people and will not get rid of them, I say to you it is the decision and expressed intention of the General Executive Board to get rid of that local union, and they can go where they please. The whole nation and press of this country are watching our membership and the calibre of men who run our organization, and we cannot make a home for those classes of so-called tough boys that want to get in and then mulct the membership and the employers . . . Get rid of any such individual. . . . If you do not, we will get rid of your charter."

By 1940 the internal problems of the IATSE and the Building Service Employees had come to a head. Scalise and Bioff were in jail, and George Browne—by now a vice president of the AFL—was embroiled in rumor. "Unfortunately," the AFL Executive Council told the 1940 convention, "we have found that men who have been influenced by criminal instincts have penetrated our movement and through a seizure of power have resorted to exploitation of hapless workers for purely selfish purposes. . . ." But autonomy still prevailed. While the Executive Council asked all affiliated unions to "exercise all care and diligence" in keeping out racketeers, it asserted that the AFL "could not confer upon . . . [its affiliates] . . . full and complete power to administer their own affairs and at the same time reserve to itself the right to exercise dictatorial control. Such attitude would be contradictory."

The ILGWU then offered a resolution proposing that the federation's authority over affiliates be strengthened. It recommended that the Executive Council or its agents assume "summary power" to order the dismissal of any union officer who used his position for private gain, and that all union constitutions should be amended to provide for adequate discipline against the corrupt. The Resolutions Committee of the convention, affirming the principle of autonomy, countered with the suggestion that affiliates merely be advised to make appropriate constitutional changes, and that the Executive Council merely "apply all its influence" to persuade unions into effective action against offenders. "The Foregoing," the Resolutions Committee added, "must not be construed as preventing any person from rehabilitating himself." The convention adopted the Committee's recommendations.

Browne was re-elected to the AFL Executive Council. Only the ILGWU voted against him, although other unions abstained. The ILGWU also refused to withdraw its resolution. President David Dubinsky of the ILGWU was then physically attacked by Joseph Fay of the Operating Engineers. Dubinsky asked for police protection for his family, declining Fay's later invitation to a friendly drink. Green was asked whether the altercation would be discussed by the convention. "Oh, no," he evidently said. "That's just personal. It has nothing to do with us."

There had been another test for the AFL. Jacob ("Jake the Bum") Wellner became business agent of Brooklyn Local 102 of the Painters in 1924, thereafter engaging in extortion from employers. Another business agent, Jacob Holtz, was appointed to Local 102 on the insistence of his brother Hymie Curley, a prominent Brooklyn hoodlum. In 1932 Curley disappeared and Holtz was then replaced by Oscar Amberg, a brother of racketeer Louis ("Pretty Boy") Amberg. "We was pretty square with Holtz," Wellner said. "The way he stood we didn't need to do nothing for him. But we gave him a thousand bucks and a car and told him to beat it."

Oscar Amberg became the sole business agent of the local in an election allegedly controlled by Buchalter and Shapiro. But Wellner made a trip to Chicago "and got it straightened out." Amberg resigned and became Wellner's assistant. In November, 1935 Louis Amberg was found nude in a blazing limousine; his wrists, ankles and throat had been wire-looped so that in his struggles he had strangled himself. Joseph Amberg, another brother, had been murdered the month before. Oscar Amberg disappeared.

Two months later Wellner went to jail for extortion. Meanwhile, 300 members of Local 102 had petitioned the AFL for relief. "We protest," they said, "against conditions in Local 102 and ask that you order the General Executive Board of the Brotherhood of Painters of America to have international officers investigate these conditions . . . We ask that legal action be instituted for the removal of present officers and ordering of a new election free from gangster methods . . . our union has become a nest of corruption, racketeering and gangsterism, preying on our membership, misusing our funds and collaborating with the employers to undermine union conditions and wages . . . We further demand that these business agents, Jake Wellner and Oscar Amberg, be immediately removed, together with the entire local administration and that a new election be held immediately for a one-year period for all officers, this election to be supervised by a reliable organization, friendly to the labor movement."

About the same time, Christian G. Norman, chairman of the board of governors of the local building trades employers' association, stated that in the presence of himself and President Lawrence P. Lindeloff of the Painters, Wellner had boasted of taking graft. "If it is true," Green wrote to Lindeloff, ". . . he ought to be removed from office immediately . . . I hope you will take action on this matter at once. It would have a wholesome effect. We cannot fail to act in cases of this kind because the name and honor of the labor movement are involved."

Members of Local 102 held a protest meeting. Lindeloff was invited but did not attend. According to an eyewitness, rebel members of the local were suppressed by force in the presence of police. Lindeloff publicly denied the statement attributed to Wellner, or that he had received any complaints of misconduct. No action was taken against the officers of Local 102. There was, it seemed, a constitutional obstacle. Lindeloff informed Green that "all requests for the services of either a general officer or organizer of the Brotherhood in this matter must come under the seal of the local union." Wellner controlled the seal.

Wellner served fifteen months in jail, worked at the trade for two years, then resumed his position as business agent for Local 102. New York District Council 18 of the Painters refused to recognize his reinstatement, whereupon the General Executive Board of the union threatened to revoke the Council's charter. The District Council appealed to the AFL. Matthew Woll of the Photoengravers then conducted an investigation on behalf of the AFL Executive Council. He found that the District Council had tried Wellner and removed him from office, had been overruled by the international union, then had appealed unsuccessfully to the courts. Woll recommended that the District Council take its case to the Painters' convention, stating that the policy statements of the 1940 AFL convention had not given the federation authority to intervene in internal union affairs. "The Federation has no compulsory or disciplinary power," he said. "The power delegated to it is that of the use of its influence." The AFL Executive Council left final consideration of the matter to Green, apparently without result.

"Each component part of our movement," the Executive Council told the 1941 AFL convention, "is autonomous . . ." However, the Council called for the punishment of any union officer convicted of a crime, noting that in the past year a number of affiliates had adopted new constitutional powers to deal more effectively with offenders and to make expulsion mandatory for those "found guilty of crime or wrong-doing which tends to bring dishonor on the union." The convention also instructed all state and local central bodies—themselves creatures of the federation—to eject or refuse to seat any delegate who had been convicted of wrongdoing reflecting dishonor on the labor movement.

There was a dissent on autonomy. "In spite of the fact that few trade unionists are prepared to surrender autonomy to a loosely constructed Federation of Labor Unions," the Brotherhood of Maintenance of Way Employees argued in 1941, "there must be some delegation of power to some group which could intelligently administer a policy of bringing to trial dishonest leaders, and if found guilty, to administer the proper punishment. If a group refused to be governed by such a law, they could be barred from associating with the general movement . . . Owing to the close association of all legitimate labor unions, it is not logical to argue that the acts of one group do not concern the other . . ."

There the matter rested until 1952. In that year the Executive Council appointed a committee to investigate the issuance of charters by unions to groups of employees outside of their formal jurisdictions. The committee obtained the withdrawal of three charters—two issued by the Jewelry Workers and one by the Distillery Workers—which had been used for "financial gain or to illegal ends."

The times had changed. The postwar Congressional investigations of corruption had produced new evidence, and also a stronger sensitivity within the labor movement to charges of wrongdoing. The AFL also had a new president. Green died in 1952 and was succeeded by AFL Secretary-Treasurer George Meany. Cradled in the traditions of the AFL, Meany nevertheless cared less for autonomy than for integrity. An obdurate man, he presided over a revolution in federation government.

He also had a special interest, aside from undoubted conviction, in curbing corruption in the AFL. With the death of Green and the passing of President Philip Murray of the CIO—both leading antagonists in the great schism of 1935—most obstacles to reunification had been removed. Neither Meany nor President Walter Reuther of the CIO had played prominent roles in the mid-thirties, and neither was yet burdened by nullifying animosities. Both men were anxious for unity. The jurisdictional battles of the previous twenty years had brought few gains to either side. The CIO, divided by the tensions between Reuther and President David J. McDonald of the Steelworkers, was a divided and unhappy organization. Meany, a man of wide interests, had little to lose and perhaps much to gain from the support of CIO unions against some of his more parochial colleagues. The labor movement itself—less popular than in the 1930's, a loser in recent legislative contests, and sluggish in growth—seemed in need of united resources. But there was a special barrier to partnership; the CIO had satisfied a long-standing complaint of the AFL by expelling its Communist-led affiliates in 1949. The AFL, on the other hand, had never taken strenuous action against the corrupt among its ranks, a frequent criticism of the CIO.

The AFL owed a move. As it happened, the turn of events on the New York waterfront presented Meany and the AFL with both a duty and an opportunity.

In January, 1953, the Executive Council of the AFL considered the findings of the New York State Crime Commission on the International Longshoremen's Association. The Council told ILA President Joseph Ryan that the hearings indicated "that these workers of the Port of New York are being exploited in every possible way . . . Your relationship with the American Federation of Labor demands that the democratic ideals, clean and wholesome free trade unionism must be immediately restored within your organization and all semblance of crime, dishonesty and racketeering be forthwith eliminated." In particular, the Executive Council demanded the reform of the shape-up and the dismissal of bribe-takers and officers with criminal records.

The Council restated its traditional position on autonomy, but added a codicil. "The founders of the American Federation of Labor," it said, "saw to it that there was no police power given to the central organization . . . However, no one should make the mistake of concluding that the American Federation of Labor will sit by and allow abuse of autonomy on the part of any of its affiliates to bring injury to the entire movement. The exercise of autonomy . . . presupposes the maintenance of minimum standards of trade union decency." An order was issued: "The Executive Council," it said, "will expect a report from you . . . on or before April 30, 1953."

Ryan submitted a long reply. He wrote that the Executive Council of the ILA had directed its New York locals to abolish the shape-up, but that the membership—in an election supervised by the Honest Ballot Association —had voted overwhelmingly to retain it. Nevertheless, he said, the ILA meant to replace the shape-up at the next negotiations with another system while retaining "the constructive hiring and priority features inherent in the present system of hiring through steady and regular gangs." Ryan also promised to put on trial any officers or members acting in violation of the ILA's constitution—particularly those who took bribes. Gifts were a different matter. "It is well known to us," Ryan said, ". . . that it is a commonplace occurrence for AFL union officials to both receive and make gifts to and from employers during the Christmas season and other holidays. These gifts may take the form of Thanksgiving turkeys, bottles of liquor or simple cash presents . . . we would not be justified in punishing an officer for acts which when committed were neither unlawful under the laws of the state where they took place nor a violation of the practices of the American Federation of Labor . . . As to the future, however, the situation is different . . . hereafter it shall be forbidden for any officer of the ILA or any Local to receive any gift or gratuity from any employer with whom the ILA does business."

Ryan agreed that criminals in office were undesirable, but opposed blanket condemnations. The ILA offered its help to the AFL in developing a code of practice in this matter, which should then be incorporated into the constitution of the AFL, after which the ILA would comply. At the same time Ryan modestly warned against the propitiation of enemies. "The AFL should not throw men and organizations to the wolves to justify journalistic hatchet men or ambitious politicians who seek to ride to power on the back of some outstanding labor leader. Yesterday the howling mob were after other labor leaders whose names are undoubtedly fresh in your minds.

Today it is Joseph P. Ryan . . . The AFL must be on guard against such a situation . . . The ILA and Joseph P. Ryan represent today a good case in which to apply the great principles of justice, law and equality for all!"

Ryan dismissed the suggestion that undemocratic practices had prevailed anywhere in the ILA after 1952, stating that the union had instituted its own internal reforms on the questions of admission to membership, financial records, and democratic procedures. The critics, Ryan said, were biased. The Crime Commission had used "triple-plated hearsay . . . notorious pro-Communist spokesmen—notorious criminals" to condemn the ILA, failing "to explore the alliance between organized crime and politics," using "sensational and headline-hunting tactics to make the ILA a scapegoat."

The AFL was unimpressed. It argued in its reply that there was no need to wait until the next negotiations to abolish the shape-up, that there was no evidence of any punitive action against bribe-takers or known associates of the underworld, and that there had been no actual implementation of democratic reforms. The AFL Executive Council offered the ILA a hearing in August, 1953, stipulating that there must be confirmation of compliance with its directives two weeks before that date. "You have to clean your own house," the Council told the ILA, "and, as an autonomous International Union having full power and authority to do so, should proceed to discipline under your own procedures. It is not the function of the American Federation of Labor to clean house for you." The ILA submitted a further report, claiming progress in all matters, and sent its officers and Executive Council to appear before the Executive Council of the AFL.

The latter was dissatisfied. "The ILA," it declared at the 1953 AFL convention, "has permitted gangsters, racketeers and thugs to fasten themselves to the body of its organizations, infecting it with corruption and destroying its integrity, its effectiveness and its trade-union character . . . For such, there is no place in the American Federation of Labor." The ILA was expelled by an almost unanimous vote.

The federation charted a new union, the International Brotherhood of Longshoremen. The leaders of the new union came from the ILA. "The only thing the [ILA] had to offer," they reported to the 1954 IBL convention, ". . . was a declaration of our intentions . . . We could not offer [the AFL] any evidence of having done anything concrete, nor evidence or intention of doing anything, except making promises." An AFL screening committee had compiled a list of seventeen ILA officials who should be brought up on charges by the ILA, but no trials were held. "Another [ILA] Executive Council meeting was held in the City of New

York," the IBL officers said, "which was a farce. We learned then that the top officers of the ILA had no intention of cleaning house." The ILA Executive Council discharged the screening and trial committees and resolved to take no reformative action until after negotiations with the New York Shipping Association late in 1953; its strategy was to accept expulsion, remain independent for a while, then apply for re-admission to the AFL "after six months, or after the whole affair had a chance to cool off." Seven vice presidents of the ILA then caucused and decided to ask for a new AFL charter as soon as the ILA was expelled.

The IBL met with some early success. All ILA locals on the Great Lakes and Pacific Coast, and scattered locals on the Atlantic and Gulf Coasts, voted quickly to affiliate with the new union. By mid-1964 the IBL claimed over 9,000 members, but New York was the test. The AFL appointed five trustees of the IBL—Meany, Dave Beck of the Teamsters, Secretary-Treasurer Paul Hall of the Atlantic and Gulf District of the Seafarers, President Albert J. Hayes of the Machinists, and President William Doherty of the Letter Carriers. Only Beck and Hall became involved in Brotherhood affairs to any extent, the Seafarers assuming virtually all of the burden of providing the IBL with manpower.

Ten ILA locals in New York now defected to the IBL. An alarmed ILA then tried to negotiate what the AFL called a "swift and sweetheart" contract with the shipowners. The AFL put pressure on the NYSA; the contract expired; and the ILA struck the port. President Eisenhower thereupon obtained an injunction against the strike under the national emergency provisions of the Taft-Hartley Act. The AFL then asked for a representational election among longshoremen in the Port of New York and vicinity —between 15,000 and 18,000 in number—and demanded that the ILA be excluded from the ballot on the grounds that it was not a *bona fide* union. The NYSA intervened with the National Labor Relations Board, the federal agency responsible for conducting representational elections, on behalf of the ILA; in particular, and in opposition to the AFL, the shipowners demanded that the longshore bargaining unit include cargo checkers, repairmen, carpenters and others considered less dissatisfied than working longshoremen and thus more likely to vote for the ILA.

The NLRB gave the ILA and the NYSA what they wanted, and with uncharacteristic speed scheduled the election for a week after its ruling. The decision angered the AFL—which wanted more time to organize—and was criticized by all New York City newspapers except the *Daily Worker*. It was alleged that the NYSA was engaged in the discriminatory firing of IBL supporters on the waterfront, and the AFL then instituted more than fifty legal actions against the employers. Tempers ran high. "There was," the IBL said later, "much violence and bloodshed." On election day, the IBL charged, longshoremen were forced into special buses by ILA hiring bosses and on the way to the polls were urged to vote for the ILA. The IBL polled 7,568 votes out of 21,128 and challenged 4,405 others. The ILA polled 9,060 votes, missing an absolute majority and losing its bargaining status.

The NLRB set aside the results and ordered a new election for May 26, 1954. More longshoremen signed up with the IBL, and some old ILA locals disintegrated. On March 5, 1954, allegedly with the support of the NYSA, the ILA struck the port again. The NLRB interpreted this as an attempt to influence the election and threatened to bar the ILA from the ballot. The ILA called off the strike.

But it won the election. The IBL polled sixteen percent more than its 1953 vote, receiving 8,791 votes to the ILA's 9,110 and challenging 1,797 votes. The NLRB disposed of the contested ballots and gave the ILA a majority of 263.

A promise to continue the battle was made by the AFL. "The new union tried hard to win the election," the Executive Council told the 1954 convention, "but the combined opposition of underworld forces, their threats and money actively assisted by the New York Shipping Association proved just strong enough to give the ILA a government certification as bargaining agent for the next two years . . . There is no doubt that their friends, the employers, will give them the union shop.* This means that AFL members and supporters will find it necessary to pay dues to the old ILA in order to get work and hold jobs . . . The American Federation of Labor will continue to render full assistance to this new international union until it succeeds . . . We warn, however, that state and local officials of New York and New Jersey must do their part in the administration of the public laws to prevent racketeers, bribers and thieves from again threatening, intimidating, beating and killing longshoremen . . ."

A third election was held in 1956, but it was foredoomed. The federation had continued its support of the IBL, but support from affiliates was waning. Early in the year, Hoffa had announced the Teamsters' readiness to lend the ILA up to $400,000 for organizational purposes. Meany objected. "As you know," he wrote to Beck, "the [ILA] was expelled from the American Federation of Labor . . . you supported this . . . As you know, the International Longshoremen's Association was expelled from the AF of L because of corrupt influence . . . To what extent the accord

---

* A union shop clause in a labor-management agreement requires employees in the bargaining unit to take out union membership as a condition of continued employment.

mentioned might make the Teamsters International Brotherhood an ally with the corrupt influence that still seems to dominate that Longshoremen's Union is a matter of concern . . . I would request you to advise me as early as possible as to the full details . . . whether such financial assistance has received your approval . . . . if the views purportedly expressed by Mr. Hoffa . . . accurately express your views and the views of the International Brotherhood of Teamsters." The Teamster-ILA pact was dropped, but damage had been done. Soon the Maritime Trades Department of the AFL-CIO declined to offer any further support to the IBL. Only the Seafarers pledged assistance. "Speaking for my own union," Paul Hall said, "we are going to furnish support to the fullest extent possible . . . even if it means mortgaging our union hall."

Beck had his own ideas. "I have worked very hard," he wrote to President Harry Bates of the Bricklayers, who was a member of the AFL-CIO Executive Council and one of Meany's closest friends, "to try to find a solution to the waterfront problem . . . there is no permanent solution . . . except that the Executive Council vest in the Teamsters International Union jurisdiction over this classification of employment . . . we will guarantee 100 percent clean-cut international wage, hour and condition procedure for every union affiliated with us under this jurisdiction . . . we cannot continue to have our jurisdiction and our working relations continually jeopardized by the present procedure . . . The [IBL] is but a paper organization, completely devoid of financial or physical resources . . . We would be ready to assimilate it, to play fair in every respect . . . I will be deeply appreciative of your personal support in this direction . . ."

Beck was wasting his time. He had presented his case at a meeting of the AFL Executive Council in May, 1955. Meany replied that there was nothing to indicate that the Teamsters could handle the New York waterfront problem. During the campaigns of 1953 and 1954, Meany said, the Teamster leadership in New York City had been "openly hostile" to both the AFL and their own international union, despite the fact that the latter had assured the AFL that it could "take care" of its New York affiliates. Meany expressed doubt that turning over the problem to the Teamsters would produce a favorable reaction for the AFL. In any event, he noted, the Teamsters were reported to have an organizing agreement with the ILA, and "if the Teamsters should get into an organizational campaign against the International Brotherhood of Longshoremen, AFL, what are the Teamsters going to do about that?"

Jurisdiction was not granted, but the damage had been done, many New York Longshoremen now believing that the interest of the Teamsters in the waterfront was essentially proprietary. Then in July, 1956 it was reported that the AFL-CIO now felt unable to contribute further to the IBL campaign. "We can't afford," one official said, "to put more money into what looks like a losing proposition." The ILA now had the union shop, had eliminated some of the more flagrant abuses, and had increased the average earnings of its members; there were even reports that ILA and IBL officials had recently been conferring, presumably about peace.

The ILA continued its supplication for affiliation with the AFL-CIO. In September, 1956 President William V. Bradley of the ILA met with Meany. It was an unfruitful encounter. Meany declared that he would not "even bother" to refer the ILA's request for affiliation to the AFL-CIO Executive Council. "It would be insulting to their intelligence," he said. "It is my opinion that the ILA officials have done nothing to rectify the conditions for which they were expelled . . . The matter is closed." The IBL had also filed for another election, and Meany called for support of the IBL, describing the ILA as "a disgrace to the good name of organized labor." Then, on the eve of the election, President Joseph Curran of the National Maritime Union—a major influence on the New York waterfront and a rival of the Seafarers International Union—announced his support of the ILA, suggesting that Meany do the same.

Meany was not amused. "I note with interest," he wrote to Curran, "your statement that you stand for honest, responsible, constructive trade unionism . . . I note you are aware of the shortcomings of the independent ILA and that your union has a prime interest in seeing that these faults and shortcomings are corrected forthwith . . . Did this realization of interest just become manifest to you on October 15, 1956? . . . just what have you done in this regard either in your capacity as President of the NMU, or as a member of the Executive Council of the AFL-CIO, or as a member for the past ten months of the AFL-CIO Ethical Practices Committee? I am unaware of any effort on your part . . . You wrote to me and transmitted the contents of your letter to the newspapers of New York City in the early evening of October 15 FOR ONE PURPOSE—AND ONLY ONE PURPOSE—TO ASSIST THE OLD ILA GANG TO RETAIN THEIR CONTROL OVER THE LONGSHOREMEN OF THE NEW YORK AREA . . . Under these circumstances, I have serious doubts as to any effective contribution you could make as a member of the Ethical Practices Committee . . ." *

The IBL lost by a margin of three to two. An absence of financial support from the AFL-CIO, the resentment against the jurisdictional ambitions of the Teamsters, the consolidation of the ILA through the union shop and other bargaining gains, and no doubt the last-minute intervention

---

* Emphasis in original.

of the NMU, all contributed to the IBL's defeat. Only the Seafarers had consistently rendered aid. "It was Paul Hall and the SIU," IBL President Larry Long told the 1957 IBL convention, "that made it possible for us to stay in business . . . They were the people who kept the IBL ship afloat and helped us over the rough spots." He reported that the IBL had suffered raids from the ILA, the Teamsters, the West Coast International Longshoremen's and Warehousemen's Union, and the catch-all District 50 of the United Mine Workers, but vowed that the IBL would persevere. "We're going to harass them, beat them and pound them until we get control of New York," he said. "I think we can do it in 1959." Hall, by now president of the Seafarers, said that the SIU would stick with the IBL "all the way . . . We'll put up whatever money is required for an organization drive, if we have to fight the ILA, the ILWU, or anyone else else who sticks their noses into our affairs . . ." The following year Hall appealed for another campaign against the ILA, lauding Meany's efforts to reform the waterfront, but noting that the SIU had underwritten the cost of the last election and expressing contempt for "all those high and mighty in the labor movement who deserted" the IBL in the 1956 election.

But there were no more elections. The IBL ran no more campaigns, and gradually withdrew from the New York waterfront. In January, 1959 the ILA appealed again for admission into the AFL-CIO. Meany appointed a committee of the Executive Council to examine the application. The committee recommended that affiliation be granted, dependent on an approved arrangement with the IBL, the submission of the ILA to any order issued by Meany, the provision of any reports the federation required, the right of Meany to attend all meetings of the ILA Executive Council, and the right of the AFL-CIO to impose any appropriate discipline. "The [AFL-CIO] Executive Council believes," it said, ". . . that the ILA is now in substantial compliance with the principles and standards established by the AFL-CIO. It further believes . . . that additional progress is desirable and that this additional progress can be aided and accelerated by the affiliation of the ILA with the AFL-CIO."

"I happen to know a good deal about this union," Meany told the 1959 AFL-CIO convention. "[I]n 1952 I made a public statement . . . that there was nothing there that even resembled a trade union . . . but the situation did change . . . The average take-home pay . . . went from $52 to $102.50 in 1957 due to the elimination of this so-called casual labor that was representing the outside racketeer . . . Bookkeeping is now the order of the day. They now have officers for their union . . . we did some good when we kicked them out and we are now ready to take them back . . . we spent a million dollars, as I told you, in order to give their membership an opportunity to leave the ILA . . . We failed by a very few votes. And we failed because of the support of the membership of that union . . . you had to admire some of those old members . . . I had one case where I knew the people quite well, two boys and a father. The boys voted AFL; the father voted ILA. He said, 'It may be a bad union, some bad people in it, but I have memories and it is still my union.' That was the sentiment that beat us there."

The ILA was admitted to the AFL-CIO and subsequently absorbed the IBL. "It is encouraging," Meany stated, "because now we have developed an element inside the ILA that is just as much interested in fighting corruption and fighting for decent unionism as we were when we put them out in 1953."

The AFL had also taken up the matter of welfare fund administration. In 1953 it announced its opposition to existing federal regulation of welfare funds, but the House and Senate investigations caused it to change its mind. "The American Federation of Labor," the Executive Council reported to the 1954 convention, "is deeply concerned about recent reports and disclosures of abuses and violations of trust on the part of some individuals holding positions of responsibility in the operation of health and welfare funds established for the benefit of trade union members. There can be no excuse for or defense of the actions of any trade union officer who becomes a party to such abuses, or who takes advantage of his position for the purpose of self-enrichment . . . Such individuals are traitors to labor and deserve only condemnation and expulsion." The federation promised to "cooperate fully" with any "objective and impartial" investigation, although not with "a political maneuver operating in the disguise of an investigation . . ."

Dave Beck added his support. "I say to you," he told the convention, "and I say it to my own people, and you can carry it into every nook and cranny of this country and into every labor union, that if there is associated with the Teamsters, in my opinion, any man who would racketeer on a welfare or insurance program of any kind, or pensions or anything where he is handling the trust of men and women that put him in those offices, he is lower than the belly of a snake." He was applauded, perhaps for the last time.

The AFL affirmed its support of fair investigations at its 1955 convention, adding that welfare plans unilaterally administered by employers—by far the greatest majority of all plans—should be regulated as thoroughly as jointly administered plans. It then adopted a series of guidelines for the administration of welfare funds, urging its affiliated unions to take "every step

. . . against any official guilty of abuses," and to amend their constitutions where necessary to provide for adequate disciplines. The guidelines proposed that union officials should receive no extra payment for welfare fund duties, should be free of any compromising ties, and should be removed from office for improper activities. The federation also recommended a body of rules for the solicitation of insurance policies and for the actual administration of welfare plans. The Executive Council noted that the Laundry Workers' welfare fund had been criticized by the Senate Committee on Labor and Public Welfare, and that it had urged the president of that union to take appropriate corrective action. An AFL representative had been sent to advise the union at its own request, and had made recommendations for "far-reaching" reforms.

The CIO took note of the problem of corruption at its 1951 convention. "We in the CIO," it said, "have been constantly vigilant to purge our ranks of subversives and corruption . . . There is no place in the CIO for racketeers, for agents of racketeering interests, or for any criminal elements . . . We call upon other elements in our American society to move with equal vigor against the racketeering and dishonest elements in American life."

CIO President Philip Murray observed that the constitutions of all CIO affiliates made provisions for the disciplining of the corrupt, and that the UAW had imposed penalties in the "few isolated situations" where corruption had occurred in that union. He had a shaft for the AFL. "There are other labor organizations," he noted, "that evidently have not had the foresight to meet up with propositions of this description like the CIO . . ."

The 1952 and 1953 conventions of the CIO reaffirmed its policy on corruption. A specific case arose in 1954. Hearings before the New York State Insurance Board disclosed welfare fund irregularities among some local affiliates of the Retail, Wholesale and Department Store Union. Walter Reuther wrote to RWDSU President Max Greenberg saying he expected "a full report of the corrective actions taken by your union against the individuals named in these hearings and any others against whom there is a legitimate charge of racketeering or maladministration." Greenberg later reported to the CIO Executive Board that five New York locals had been disciplined. Three locals had submitted to trusteeship; in a fourth case "we had to take physical possession of the local offices . . . the fifth local union was expelled from RWDSU for refusing to accede to the suspension."

The convention recommended Reuther's "prompt and effective" action and the remedial efforts of the RWDSU, and sanctioned the creation of a CIO Standing Committee on Ethical Practices to investigate alleged cases of corruption and to recommend corrective legislation where necessary.

The convention concluded that new welfare fund legislation was required, and adopted a model "Employee Welfare Plan Disclosure Act" for recommendation to the Congress.

The 1955 conventions of the AFL and CIO, both held in New York City on December 1 and 2, were their last solo performances. On December 5 the two organizations met, and merged. The new federation, the American Federation of Labor and Congress of Industrial Organizations, adopted special measures against corruption.

The AFL-CIO constitution declared one of the purposes of the federation to be the protection of the labor movement "from any and all corrupt influences." The Executive Council was empowered to conduct investigations of any unions suspected of corrupt activities, to make recommendations or give directions to the unions concerned, and to suspend affiliates who refused to reform. The powers were new. Neither the AFL nor the CIO had previously had any specific authority to act against corrupt organizations.

The AFL-CIO constitution also authorized the appointment of a Committee on Ethical Practices "vested with the duty and responsibility to assist the Executive Council in carrying out the constitutional determination of the Federation to keep the Federation free from any taint of corruption." In time, on the Committee's recommendations, the AFL-CIO adopted six Codes of Ethical Practices covering the issuance of local union charters, the adoption of proper accounting procedures, the disciplining of wayward union officials, the avoidance of conflicts of interest, the administration of union funds, and internal union democracy.

In general, the posture now taken by the AFL-CIO, the powers it assumed and the rules it recommended, represented a radical departure from custom and constitutional theory. Deference was made to autonomy, but now it was differently conceived. Now there was a higher law. It was soon invoked.

22: The Trade Unions and the Corrupt: The AFL-CIO

In June, 1956, the AFL-CIO Executive Council ordered its Committee on Ethical Practices * to investigate charges of corrupt practices in various unions and to make appropriate reports and recommendations. The Committee turned its attentions to the Distillery Workers.

The Senate Subcommittee on Welfare and Pension funds chaired by Senator Douglas had conducted hearings on the Distillery Workers in 1954, leading President Joseph O'Neill of the union to prefer charges against International Secretary-Treasurer Sol Cilento, accusing him of "willful neglect . . . disregard of your duty . . . gross negligence . . . and conduct unbecoming an officer." The Distillery Workers' General Executive Board suspended Cilento from office as secretary-treasurer and trustee of the union's welfare fund. Cilento thereupon resigned, although he retained his position as executive vice president of the large Local 2 in New York. "So far as is known," an AFL-CIO staff group reported to the Committee on Ethical Practices, "neither the international union nor the local union has made any effort to remove him from this key local union position."

A New York grand jury indicted Cilento on February 2, 1955 on charges of bribery and conspiracy in connection with the union's welfare fund. Cilento's co-defendants were former Building Service Employees' President George Scalise, and Anthony ("Little Augie Pisano") Carfano —a former bootlegger in the Capone organization. Louis Saperstein, the broker for the welfare fund already sentenced to five years in jail for embezzling Laundry Workers' welfare fund money, turned state's evidence. He was forced, he testified, to turn over fifty percent of his commissions— some $540,000 in all—to the three defendants, Cilento receiving more than $100,000. The defendants were acquitted on the technical ground that, as the court said, "a trustee of a union welfare fund, except that he commits larceny, is not chargeable with a crime for violating his trust, even

* The chairman of the Committee was President Albert J. Hayes of the Machinists. The other members of the Committee were President George M. Harrison of the Railway Clerks, President David Dubinsky of the ILGWU, President Joseph Curran of the NMU, and President Jacob Potofsky of the Amalgamated Clothing Workers.

though he simultaneously be an officer of the union. A trustee can only be sued in a civil court to make him account for his unlawful acts."

But the Distillery Workers had refused in any case to cooperate with the civil authorities; it was not, the union's counsel said, "in the best interest of the international union and its membership to volunteer any examination of the international books and records by an outside agency." Soon afterwards the union claimed that all of its financial records had been stolen by three gunmen. New York District Attorney Frank S. Hogan called the statement a fake, a "bizarre conclusion" to the union's efforts to use "every trick, dodge and device" to impede his inquiry. O'Neill refused to go to New York to testify before the grand jury, but was finally arrested in Miami Beach as a material witness. The uncooperative attitude of the union, the AFL-CIO staff group reported, "has had the obvious effect of shielding Cilento from effective prosecution."

Cilento was indicted again on June 12, 1956, on charges of conspiracy and grand larceny in the theft of $16,125 from Local 2. The money represented "wages" paid by him to a woman clerk who, in four and a half years of ostensible employment with the local, evidently visited the union office only twice to attend Christmas parties. The Distillery Workers again refused to cooperate with Hogan. "[U]nion books," the General Executive Board said, "should not be made available to the fishing expeditions of a district attorney who was interested primarily in publicity and was not friendly to labor".*

The AFL-CIO Executive Council directed the Distillery Workers to "show cause" why they should not be suspended from the federation. "We have made it clear," Meany said, "that union autonomy may not be used as a cloak for corruption."

"I desire to assure the Executive [Council] and you personally," O'Neill wired Meany, "that upon evidence that the Distillery Workers International Union has not conformed in any respect to the principles and policies of the AFL-CIO Constitution I will take immediate and necessary action . . ." The Committee on Ethical Practices held a hearing on the union in October, 1956. Union witnesses denied any knowledge of Cilento's alleged relationships with Saperstein, Scalise or Carfano, but agreed to follow the federation's recommendations in any action against him once his trial was over. O'Neill said that he personally saw no impropriety in paying union officials or trustees for welfare fund duties, but that he would stop such payments immediately.

Cilento himself appeared before the Committee at a later hearing, saying

* Hogan usually received the support of the New York City labor movement at election time.

that he wanted to clear his name with the AFL-CIO because "this is my home." He denied receiving any improper payments. "I hold in my hands," he said, "photostatic copies of every one of the checks which make up [the $107,000 paid by Security Mutual] . . . The endorsements on these checks clearly show that the moneys were deposited in the bank account of the International Union . . . not one penny of the moneys was diverted by me or anyone else . . . I never received a penny from Louis Saperstein." Cilento conceded that he had been involved with Saperstein in a real estate transaction, but denied that it influenced his conduct of union business. He denied knowing Scalise and having any business dealings with Carfano, whom he said he knew only slightly.

However, the Committee concluded that corrupt conduct in the union had been proven but not eliminated. It said that the Distillery Workers had deliberately violated the AFL guidelines for the administration of welfare funds in making payments to union officials. "When an employer trustee questioned the payments in view of then AFL standards," the Committee said, "President O'Neill declared that President Meany had changed his views. There is no other explanation possible for this but deliberate misrepresentation for the sole purpose of keeping these payments in effect." The Committee also charged that Saperstein was chosen as the welfare fund's broker because of his willingness to make kickbacks to union officials, and that welfare fund representatives were selected on the basis of O'Neill's personal and political preferences.

The union, the Committee contended, had simply "not done enough to clean up its Social Security Fund. The abuses are so outrageous that anyone occupying key positions . . . must necessarily be suspect . . . The time involved is too long, six to eight years; the money involved is too great, hundreds of thousands of dollars; the number of abuses is too many, including high commissions, kickbacks, special payments, nepotism, failure to inquire about dividends and other aspects of the union welfare program and lack of any effective check on union finances. It seems inexcusable that all these who were involved have not been replaced or disciplined . . . the Committee believes that there is no real understanding on the part of this Union of the spirit of ethical union practices . . . The Union has assumed no real initiative in unearthing and correcting abuses. It is even now offering explanations for not taking obvious second steps. It has no proposals for eliminating all traces of past corruption and no programs for insuring that AFL-CIO standards will be rigorously maintained in the future . . ."

On February 6, 1957, the Executive Council ordered the Distillery Workers to clean house within ninety days or "stand suspended and face expulsion from the AFL-CIO." The union held a special convention the following month. O'Neill reported to Meany that the convention had approved his recommendation that Melvin Dykes, Cilento's nephew, be removed as manager of the Social Security Fund and that Local 2 be placed in receivership for not disciplining Cilento—although the local quickly reverted to autonomous status when Cilento resigned from office.

O'Neill described the mood of the convention. "The delegates," he wrote to Meany, "were disturbed by the lack of particulars in the charges preferred . . . [by] the apparent reliance of the Ethical Practices Committee upon the hearsay reports of the Douglas Committee . . . the Executive Board and I have always felt that the proposed action of the AFL-CIO Executive Council was unjustified . . . we still feel that way . . . We are now doubly sure . . . that any basis, baseless as it was, for our intended expulsion has now been removed."

The Executive Council thought otherwise. It declared that the Distillery Workers would be suspended unless they accepted probationary status for a year and the appointment of a monitor to supervise their affairs. The union agreed. Meany appointed Peter M. McGavin, his administrative assistant, as monitor.

McGavin wrote to George Oneto, the acting secretary-treasurer of the union, stating that the delegates to the February convention had not been provided with copies of the AFL-CIO's report on the union, nor informed what the specific charges against the union were. He called for a second special convention to discuss the charges, and recommended that all incumbent officers should resign and run for re-election. On October 15, O'Neill removed Oneto from office. Five days later the General Executive Board removed O'Neill, barring him permanently from office and appointing Oneto as acting president. O'Neill refused to recognize the action of the Board. McGavin then called a meeting of the Board "to dispel all the confusion . . ." He obtained the resignations of all incumbent officers and an agreement to hold the special convention on November 25.

This convention, according to the *New York Times,* was "a near riot of cursing and name-calling." McGavin, in the chair, ordered a secret ballot for new officers, whereupon O'Neill and some of his supporters stormed the platform, shouting "Hitlerism" and other expletives. McGavin adjourned the convention and left, followed by a number of delegates. The rest, representing about two-thirds of the union's membership, remained and re-elected O'Neill and Oneto to their previous posts. "The undemocratic tactics employed by Brother McGavin," O'Neill and Oneto wrote to Meany, ". . . naturally provoked the delegates into a demonstration . . . Indeed, admirable restraint was exercised by the delegates . . ."

Further conversations were held, and the Distillery Workers agreed to hold a further special convention chaired by an AFL-CIO representative, and to conduct elections by secret ballot. "Under these circumstances," Meany told the 1957 AFL-CIO convention, "the Council decided to go along with this Union to see if they straighten themselves out."

The convention was held on April 12, 1958. The officers—the same roster as before—reported that the Social Security Fund had become self-insuring, thus achieving considerable savings and an increase in benefits. The convention adopted the AFL-CIO Code of Ethics on financial practices, and submitted the Social Security Fund's books for auditing by the AFL-CIO. "Your trustees are happy to report," they told the convention, "that our Fund in every respect is in complete compliance with the AFL-CIO Codes of Ethical Practices."

Yet a doubt remained. "The President's office," Meany told the 1959 AFL-CIO convention, "is investigating certain conditions in this union . . ." Four weeks earlier Meany had received a memorandum from McClellan Committee Counsel Robert F. Kennedy. "It appears," Kennedy wrote, "that some of the matters we have uncovered in the course of our investigation of the [Distillery Workers] are as serious as those uncovered in the Textile workers." Kennedy indicated that Oneto, together with President Mortimer Brandenburg and one Max Drexler, of Local 2, received weekly expense allowances from their local unions, yet billed the international union for their expenses; that these three and O'Neill had made a practice of taking extended vacations with their wives at union expense; that a secret payment of $12,000 a year was being made to O'Neill—who had retired from international office shortly after the 1958 convention, assuming the presidency of Local 62 in Chicago—for advisory services; and that Local 2 had paid Max Drexler's son Edward a salary while he was in college and military service, had excused him from paying the local's initiation fee of $1,000, and had given him a wedding present of $1,000.

Local union stipends were evidently generous too. Local 2 had only 1,-650 members, but in 1958 Brandenburg received salary and expenses of $51,264.50. Max Drexler received $66,430.49, while Joseph Matranga— another official of Local 2—got $57,264.50. Edward Drexler was paid $23,367. Cilento was on a pension of $20,000 a year. Financial reports on these matters were evidently not submitted to the members of the local. For fifteen years, also, the executive officers of the local had each received payments of eight to ten weeks' salary in lieu of vacations, and Christmas presents of ten to twenty weeks' salary. Oneto, the president of New York Local 1, received some $50,000 a year in salary and expenses, while his expense vouchers were unsupported. Four of O'Neill's sons were on the payrolls of various local unions in Chicago. An AFL-CIO auditing committee appointed by Meany seemed to confirm the additional charge that Brandenburg, Oneto and Max Drexler had submitted, and were reimbursed for, unsupported expense claims upon the international union.

Brandenburg, now president of the international union, wrote to Meany in response to Kennedy's charges. O'Neill's "secret retainer," he said, was approved as a matter of record by the General Executive Board. There was no reason to suppose that O'Neill's sons "do not earn the compensation paid them or that they are not fully qualified for their positions." All other payments listed by Kennedy, Brandenburg said, were authorized and legitimate; in particular, expense claims submitted to the international union were always itemized—although a much more stringent accounting system was introduced in 1959. Further, he said, the wives of union officials were not taken on vacations at union expense. Indeed, Brandenburg argued, the McClellan Committee's criticism came "in poor grace" when the Congress so often authorized millions of dollars in expenses for the President of the United States for which no accounting was required.

Local union salaries, Brandenburg continued, were all approved by local union executive boards in accordance with the provisions of the international union's constitution. If they were high, they reflected the high average earnings of the members—some of whom made as much as $50,000 a year.

Then there was the sensitive matter of status at the bargaining table. "The officials of the employers who negotiate with the officials of these local unions," Brandenburg said, "also receive compensation in high surtax brackets and, needless to say, the interests of the locals are not disserved by having union officials on a comparable prestige and remuneration level."

There was also a patriotic by-product. "The Federal Internal Revenue," Brandenburg asserted, "has been a principal beneficiary of the salary situation. For example, Dr. Drexler paid over $25,000 in Federal taxes on his 1958 compensation and in the past five years has paid some $65,000 in taxes, and Mr. Brandenburg more than $67,000. . . ."

Finally, inflation was a leveller. "If the officers' compensation is computed on the basis of an inflated forty-five cent dollar after taxes, the notion of excessiveness is rapidly dissipated," Brandenburg concluded. All was well and proper. However, if the AFL-CIO had any reservations about the union's conduct of its affairs, the union would "continue its cooperation with the monitor of the AFL-CIO and immediately comply with all its constructive recommendations and suggestions."

It evidently did. The federation issued no more reports on the Distillery Workers, and seemed in time to be satisfied. "I do want to . . . record," McGavin wrote to Brandenburg, "my satisfaction with the substantial progress being made by your International Union . . . every mandate of the 1958 convention has been filled to the letter . . . in a spirit that conforms to the highest ethical standards of the AFL-CIO. . . . Why this [McClellan Committee] investigation took place—and what it had hoped to accomplish—are puzzlers to me. No one can deny, of course, that there were certain aspects of the operations of your International Union in the past which could be criticized . . . All the McClellan Committee did, in effect, was to take the report of the AFL-CIO Committee on Ethical Practices—which dealt only with past practices—and pass it along as current practices. The result was the kind of distorted picture against which the AFL-CIO has protested and which prompted the AFL-CIO convention this week to castigate the Committee . . . An objective reading . . . can lead to no other conclusion than that the Distillery Workers' Union has irrevocably committed itself in practice to the AFL-CIO codes . . ."

That was all. The AFL-CIO dissolved the Distillery Workers' monitorship and probationary status in January, 1961, and restored the union to full standing in the federation.

Johnny Dio became prominent in the affairs of the UAW-AFL in the early 1950's. Meany, hearing rumors, asked UAW-AFL President Lester Washburn for an explanation.

"First of all," Washburn replied, "I believe I should explain the extent to which we have been involved with the two individuals Paul Dorfman and Sam Berger . . ." Dorfman and Berger—the business manager for the garment drivers' Local 102 of the ILGWU and a partner with Dio in a flower shop—had persuaded Washburn and Anthony Doria to grant them a charter for UAW-AFL Local 102 in New York. "I would like to make it clear," Washburn continued, "that John Dio was in no manner involved at the time the original charter was issued nor was John Dio known to any officer of our organization. To make this even clearer, John Dio was not among the first eighteen charter applicants." However, at the 1951 convention of the union, despite the fact that he had never been employed in the industries organized by the UAW-AFL, Dio was appointed acting president of Local 102. "The situation," Washburn related, "required that competent leadership be established for this local . . ."

The appointment was criticized by various newspapers. Washburn had his own accusations to make. "We have made our own investigation," he wrote, "and have found no proof . . . we are satisfied that there is some evidence of what might be considered an unholy alliance between members of CIO organizations working with individuals in comparatively high positions in the AFL to cooperate in placing every possible organizational obstacle in the path of our organizational activity in New York City." There was not "even the flimsiest type of evidence that individuals connected with our local union 102, are guilty of . . . undesirable or illegal activities."

In July, 1952, the New York City Anti-Crime Committee and District Attorney Hogan accused UAW-AFL Locals 102 and 227—Dio was associated with both—of various wrongdoings. The following February the AFL Executive Council ordered the union to revoke the charter of Local 102. Dio was indicted and convicted about this time for state income tax evasion. After a further threat of action by Meany, Local 102 was dissolved. In April, 1954, Washburn expelled Dio from the union and lifted the charters of six locals allegedly dominated by Dio, but the Executive Board of the UAW-AFL reinstated Dio and the charters of three of the locals. Washburn resigned in protest, and was succeeded by Earl Heaton. Three months later the Executive Board took notice of various charges against Dio, but concluded that "by all New York standards our operations were clean." Dio appeared before the Board to defend himself, and was judged innocent of any improper activities.

Nevertheless he resigned. "I have recognized for a long time," he wrote to Heaton, "that the attacks made against me, although untrue, not supported by proof, and in instances not even related to my union activities have provided enemies of our Union with a basis for attack against the Union itself." Heaton replied that "the New York Crime Committee advised us that it had no evidence of improper activities on your part . . . the attacks upon you were based on events which occurred long before you were elected to your present position." The events in question presumably were Dio's five arrests for vagrancy, coercion, extortion and possession of an unregistered liquor still, and one jail sentence from 1932 to 1934 for extortion.

Dio's departure gave the union a respite from unfavorable publicity until 1955, when the Douglas Subcommittee investigated Chicago Local 286. One of the local's members was an unhappy refugee from New York.

"Dear Mr. Meany," he wrote, "I am a good union member and still believe in the principles of the AFL, and so, I hope you will act on this story . . . While living in New York, I was employed in a plant where the union is the AFL Auto Workers . . . The union is run by an ex-convict John Dio and his henchmen. I tried to protest a contract sellout at a meeting and was called at home by these thugs and told if I loved my children to shut up . . . I'm no hero, so I did . . . We moved to Chicago and I got a job . . . where the UAW-AFL is the union. This was worse than before. A local hoodlum, Angelo Inciso, runs this union . . . I was told to keep my mouth shut or I would be thrown down the steps . . . This is no crackpot letter . . . I do not sign my name as such action might bring swift reprisal on my family. Hence, I used a pseudonym . . . Hoping you can clean up this menace to all American unionism."

Inciso also had his troubles. His criminal record dated back to 1930 when he went to jail for stealing automobile tires. In subsequent years he was convicted for grand larceny, shoplifting, and violation of federal liquor laws, serving two jail sentences. In 1953 he was shot and wounded by an unknown assailant. In 1955 the offices of Local 286 were bombed. In December, 1955, Inciso appeared at the Douglas Subcommittee hearings with two bodyguards evidently provided by the Chicago Police Department since 1953 and who had accompanied him on some of his travels at home and abroad. "During this period," the Chicago Crime Commission noted, "the police department complained of its shortage of personnel. It would appear that the services of those two detectives could have been better utilized than as nursemaids to a pal of Tony Accardo."

The Executive Board of the UAW-AFL revoked the charter of Local 286 on February 1, 1956. The following day it rescinded its action on the advice of legal counsel, who argued that complicated legal proceedings might ensue. The Board then allowed Inciso to disaffiliate Local 286 from the union and to take with him assets equal to one-fifth of those of the entire international union, on the condition that he would appeal neither to the courts nor to the next UAW-AFL convention. Meantime, the union had changed its name to the Allied Industrial Workers of America.

"As a result of our preliminary inquiry," the AFL Committee on Ethical Practices reported in August, 1956, ". . . the Committee without prejudging the matter, concludes that the published reports provide a sufficient reason to believe that the Allied Industrial Workers of America may be dominated, controlled or substantially influenced in the conduct of its affairs by corrupt influences . . ." Heaton protested to the Committee that he was unaware of any charges against the AIW before the Committee, and that no hearings had been held. "In spite of all this," he said, "press smears continue to be made against our International Union . . . We hope . . . to be permitted to face our accusers."

They were. The Committee held a hearing on October 3, 1956, and issued a report. It concluded that the AIW "does not meet the standards for ethical union practices set forth in the AFL-CIO Constitution . . . corrupt conduct has been amply proved and was not promptly and effectively cleaned up by the International Union . . ." The Committee observed that while Dio had had no connection with the industries in which the UAW-AFL was active, he had contributed his personal funds to the operation of at least one local. "As practical trade unionists," the Committee said, "the Committee does not believe Dio was a philanthropist." The union itself had violated federation principles in issuing paper charters and "hunting licenses" to Dio; it had investigated him, but found him innocent of any charges; it did not expel him, but rather accepted his resignation because he was causing adverse publicity. "The Union apparently would not have separated itself from Dio," the Committee said, "if left to its own values and standards . . ."

On Inciso, the evidence was "shocking." The facts, the Committee held, were not in dispute. Welfare and general union funds were commingled. The members of Local 286 were kept ignorant of financial transactions. Inciso used union funds for personal purposes. Inciso himself "had not the slightest inkling of appropriate union conduct. He saw nothing wrong with what he did . . . Inciso was not tried or expelled . . . The International voluntarily consented to the departure of a Local with a treasury of approximately $300,000 and with 4,200 union members . . . This voluntary self-infliction of major surgery is extraordinary . . . completely at odds with normal, healthy union policy." Further, Inciso's departure was prompted by the Douglas Subcommittee's investigation, not by the application of internal union standards. Indeed, the Committee reported, the AIW had defended many of Inciso's activities, apparently considering them consistent with ethical union standards.

Anthony Doria—secretary-treasurer of both the international union and Local 286—came in for criticism. He knew, the Committee said, that Dio used his own money to support a local; he knew that Inciso was subject to underworld influences; and he was responsible for the accounting procedures which permitted Inciso's corruption of Local 286. "The entire method of record keeping in this case," the Committee noted, "was almost an invitation to corruption and virtually a device for covering it up." Doria, in sum, was not a "wholly innocent bystander."

"A union official," the Committee stated, "had a most solemn obligation. He must always put first the interests of his members. He must guard against the fact or even the appearance of putting personal benefit or gratification before the Union welfare. There seems to be no such spirit in the administration of the affairs of this Union." The Executive Council ordered the AIW to accept a monitorship, and to eliminate all corrupt influences within ninety days or "stand suspended and face expulsion from the AFL-CIO."

The union moved to comply. Four New York locals were expelled. The AIW Executive Board revised its policies on the chartering and financial procedures of local unions, ruled that any violations of the AFL-CIO Codes of Ethical Practices would be cause for expulsion, and also asked

Doria to resign. Doria demanded severance pay of $150,000 and a car as the price of resignation. The Board, meeting in Miami, agreed. One of the Board members then threatened to hold a press conference to denounce the arrangement, whereupon the Board quickly reconvened, cancelled its previous action, and voted to give Doria only $50,000 and a car to settle all his claims against the union. Heaton reported to McGavin that Doria had resigned, but evidently did not mention the financial arrangement; then he allegedly signed a personal agreement with Doria—without informing the Board—to pay him $80,000 over a period of two years. McGavin heard of the agreement "by way of rumor and unsigned letters." Heaton said afterwards he did not think McGavin would be interested in the matter.

Meany summoned Heaton and the entire Board to a meeting. The arrangement with Doria was dropped and the AIW held a special convention in August, 1957, at which Heaton was replaced as president by Carl W. Griepentrog. The convention also set new limits to the power of the international president, formally adopted the Codes of Ethical Practices, introduced annual audits for local unions, and voted to move its headquarters from Beverly Hills back to the Midwest.* It also commended Meany and the AFL-CIO Executive Council "for their forthright action and leadership in fighting this small cancerous element of corruption which foisted itself on the labor movement . . ."

"I note with satisfaction," Meany wrote to Griepentrog, "the progress that your International Union has made . . ." In October, 1957, the Executive Council terminated the AIW's probationary status; the AIW, the Executive Council reported to the AFL-CIO convention later in the year, was the only one of several unions disciplined by the federation to accept in full the Council's recommendations on reform. The monitorship remained in force for a few months, McGavin continuing to advise the officers of the AIW; it was ended in May, 1958, since the AIW, according to Meany, "had done an outstanding job in rebuilding the international union . . ."

"To make a long story short," Secretary-Treasurer Lloyd Klenert of the United Textile Workers of America wrote to AFL President Meany in 1952, "we have just about reached the end of our rope. This week no salaries will be paid starting from [President Anthony] Valente and myself all the way down the line . . ."

---

* The large majority of the AIW's membership was concentrated in the East and Midwest. The UAW–AFL's headquarters had once been in Milwaukee, but in recent years had been located in Beverly Hills, California, where the union had virtually no members at all.

The UTWA was in process of weaning a dissident group away from the CIO Textile Workers Union of America, and expenses for this and other activities were said to be heavy. Klenert asked Meany for a loan. "I was somewhat surprised at this," Meany revealed later, "because the campaign had been going only six or seven weeks . . ." He asked Klenert for a financial report, which upon receipt he condemned as a "phony." Rumors were now circulating that Valente and Klenert were using union funds to buy houses and other personal goods. Meany told the two officers that they could appear before the AFL Executive Council in support of their loan application, on the understanding that they would be questioned further about the financial report. Valente and Klenert refused the invitation. "They now felt," Meany thought, "that the question of financial assistance to the United Textile Workers was of no importance compared to the question of their integrity."

Valente and Klenert then met with Meany, confessing that the report was "a complete fabrication," designed to conceal their union's assets from their CIO rival. Meany told them he thought its purpose was to deceive the AFL. "We built this organization," Meany declared before the AFL Executive Council, "by the expenditure of thousands and thousands of dollars . . . For a number of years . . . the American Federation of Labor paid the salary and expenses of the organizing staff of the United Textile Workers, including the salaries and expenses of the present President . . . and Secretary-Treasurer . . . I feel that the American Federation of Labor should take immediate action to protect the interests of the 90,000 members of the United Textile Workers." William Green appointed a committee consisting of Meany, President William Doherty of the Letter Carriers and President Dan Tracy of the Brotherhood of Electrical Workers. The committee met in New York with the Executive Board of the UTWA.

> *Valente:* Before we start, we thought you wanted an opportunity to address our Council, and we have no objection to that . . . However, I don't think we should have the record kept . . . we are not on trial; we are not going to have cross-examination. I think this is a family matter.
>
> *Meany:* Well, this man [the stenographer] is taking a record for the American Federation of Labor.
>
> *Valente:* Well, our counsel [Joseph Jacobs] objects to it.
>
> *Meany:* Your counsel objects to it?
>
> *Valente:* Yes.
>
> *Meany:* Well, so far as I am concerned, that is the end of the meeting.

The meeting proceeded with the reporter present. The discussion covered the complex financial transactions of Valente and Klenert in buying real estate, listing unusual organizing expenses, and other matters.

Members of the UTWA Board admitted they knew the report was fraudulent, but argued that it was done for a legitimate purpose.

> *Meany:* And you think as a Board and as officers running this union that you had a right to hide the organization's money to protect your own particular future interests in case of a split of some kind? Do you think you had the right to do that?
>
> . . .
>
> *Jacobs:* We were protecting the organization, Brother Meany . . .
>
> *Meany:* All I can say is you are going to have a great opportunity from now on to protect . . . because God knows it will need protection. O.K. Let's go.

Meany reported the matter to the AFL Executive Council. The Council referred it back to the UTWA Executive Board, which cleared Valente and Klenert. Apparently no further action was taken by the AFL.

The AFL-CIO Committee on Ethical Practices held a hearing on the UTWA in August, 1957, after the union had been investigated by the McClellan Committee. Valente, Klenert and Jacobs were present. The UTWA officers conceded again that the 1952 report was false, but argued that the incident was five years old and thus not a proper subject for the Ethical Practices Committee's attention.

The Committee asserted its jurisdiction and studied the records available. It concluded that the real purpose of the report was to conceal the attempted use of union funds by Valente and Klenert to buy two houses, and that "but for Mr. Meany's intervention in 1952 the Union might well have sustained a loss from that transaction . . . devious means were used in an attempt to cover up that transaction, including the falsification of Union records . . . Klenert and Valente had financial dealings with employers under contract to the Union and with a supplier to the Union . . . Klenert extensively used Union money for personal purposes and . . . none of this money has been repaid. . . . Jacobs engaged in a transaction clearly conflicting with his Union position . . . the practices and procedures of the Union were so loose as to permit these and other irregularities to develop . . . Valente as the President and principal officer, and Klenert as the chief financial officer of the Union, must be held responsible . . . the United Textile Workers does not meet the standards for ethical practices set forth in the AFL-CIO Constitution."

In a series of communications the Executive Council ordered the UTWA to eliminate various abuses and to dismiss Valente, Klenert and Jacobs from office. On December 4, 1957, the Council concluded that the union had not complied in good faith and declared its suspension from the AFL-

CIO, stating that the Council would recommend expulsion if prompt and effective steps were not taken by the union. A committee of UTWA Executive Board members then met with McGavin and agreed to hold a special convention within ninety days; to elect all delegates and officers by secret ballot; to bar Valente, Klenert and Jacobs permanently from office; to distribute copies of the Committee on Ethical Practices' report to convention delegates; to formally adopt all of the Codes; and to submit periodic reports to the Executive Council of the AFL-CIO.

"The record on this union," Meany told the 1957 AFL-CIO convention, ". . . would make fantastic reading . . . we asked this [UTWA] Committee . . . if [Klenert] had now resigned. They said, 'Oh, yes, he is out.' . . . 'Have there been any financial arrangements made with him?' . . . They said, 'Oh, yes, we are paying him $100 a week.' 'For how long?' it was asked. 'Oh, for twenty years . . .' They made a simple arrangement when he resigned to pay him $100 a week as a reward for stealing the Union's money to the extent of well over a quarter of a million dollars . . . That action was rescinded. We got the resignation of the president . . ."

The UTWA was placed under monitorship, and held a special convention on March 15, 1958. George Baldanzi—who had led the breakaway movement from the CIO textile union in 1952 but soon resigned from the UTWA to work for the Teamsters—became president. Francis M. Schaufenbil, a former member of the Executive Board and a member of the negotiating committee which finally accepted the AFL-CIO's terms, was elected secretary-treasurer. Two weeks later Baldanzi reported to Meany that further reforms had been instituted, including the prohibition of personal loans to officers, the tightening of financial safeguards, the bonding of officers, and a number of other steps recommended by McGavin at the convention.

"It is my opinion," Meany told the AFL-CIO Executive Council on May 1, 1958, "that the United Textile Workers of America . . . has made substantial progress . . . [but] much remains to be done." He demanded the removal from office of UTWA Vice-President Burton Hyman, who evidently had been expelled from the CIO union for irregular handling of unions funds. Meany also proposed the continued probation of the union, and its suspension if it did not expel Hyman within eight days. Hyman resigned, but was retained on the union's payroll as an international representative since he was in very poor health and had no prospects of employment elsewhere.

McGavin continued as monitor for another year. In December, 1959, the Executive Council reported to the AFL-CIO convention that the leaders of the UTWA had "earnestly and successfully brought the organization to a position of good standing in the trade-union movement." McGavin recommended the following month that the monitorship be terminated. "I have no hesitation in saying," he wrote to Meany, "that in my opinion the United Textile Workers under its present leadership is conducting its affairs in keeping with the best trade union traditions . . . in complete compliance with the directives of Executive Council and the Ethical Practices Codes." The Executive Council ended the UTWA's probation on February 16, 1960.

"I want to make it perfectly clear to you," Secretary-Treasurer Curtis E. Sims of the Bakery and Confectionery Workers told his General Executive Board on March 7, 1957, ". . . that I do not, by appearing here today, concede the jurisdiction or competence of this body to determine the charges against me . . . most of my judges are employed by my accuser, and all of them are subject to economic gain or loss by his favor or displeasure . . . you have already prejudged me . . ."

The tables had been turned. Four days before, Sims had formally charged President James G. Cross and Vice-President George Stuart of the Bakers with misusing the union's funds and bringing the organization into disrepute. The Board cleared Cross and Stuart, whereupon Cross filed charges against Sims, accusing him of revealing his charges against Cross to the press and injuring the reputation of the union, and of causing the union "unwarranted and unnecessary expense" by requiring the convening of a special meeting of the Board to hear his complaints against Cross and Stuart. The Board suspended Sims from office. Stuart resigned. The incident received considerable publicity, and prompted the investigation of the Bakers by the McClellan Committee.

Meany placed the matter before the Committee on Ethical Practices. The Bakers' legal counsel urged the Committee to postpone its deliberations because the McClellan Committee "may well turn up evidence that would be most embarrassing to you." Further, the union's counsel said, this was "really an intra-union fight" in which a dissident, minority faction was trying to undermine the leadership in a "masterpiece of a hatchet job." The AFL-CIO Committee rejected his advice, stating that it had no intention of intervening in internal disputes, but did have jurisdiction over matters which might be brought to light by intra-union frictions. It then conducted a series of hearings at which both Cross and Sims, as well as their allies or representatives, testified.

The Committee concluded that "certain unethical practices" had been proved, and that the Bakers did not meet the standards of the AFL-CIO Constitution. The facts of the financial relationships between Cross and employer Martin Philipsborn of Zion Industries, the Committee said, were "not in serious dispute." Cross had borrowed some $96,700 from Philipsborn on exceptionally favorable terms, indicating "a relationship of special trust and confidence . . . plainly contrary to the basic ethical principle of the trade union movement . . . [that] no responsible trade union official should have a personal financial interest which conflicts with the full performance of his fiduciary duties as a worker's representative." The funds of Local 100 in Chicago, under Stuart's trusteeship, were depleted by $13,-100.18—ostensibly to finance a cooperative organizing drive with the Detroit Joint Council of Teamsters but in fact to pay for two Cadillacs bought by the Joint Council for Cross and Stuart. In general the Committee found a commingling of union and personal funds, a failure to account for cash advances for expenses, and the expenditure of union funds on such personal items as air conditioners, luggage, camera supplies, Christmas gifts and candy. Other expenditures were dubious, the Committee finding it "impossible to determine from the Union's records whether particular expenditures were for a proper purpose . . . Clearly, the Bakery Workers' Union's practices with respect to accounting and financial controls require careful re-examination . . ." The Committee was particularly critical of the Bakers for not expelling Stuart for his misuse of the funds of Locals 100 and 149 and recovering the money. "While certain corrective measures have been taken," the Committee concluded, ". . . these measures have not been sufficient . . ."

"I have answered fully and frankly all questions of the McClellan Committee," Cross wrote to all the Bakers' members, "about my actions as President of our Union . . . a hostile and anti-labor press twisted, distorted and mangled my testimony. They were supported by a propaganda machine illegally financed by unaccounted Union funds, run by a self-styled 'integrity committee.' This group still accepts union pay while neglecting their union duties . . . the actual charges leveled against me as your President were inconsequential . . . I was blamed for excessive expenditures in 1956 . . . a period of major activities . . . I was charged with unorthodox methods of organizing by hiring a special woman organizer . . . I was falsely charged with making personal loans from an employer in exchange made . . . there was no such sellout as my enemies have recklessly accused for favors . . . My borrowings are fully repaid, were openly and honestly . . . I was again falsely charged with participating in an alleged armed assault and kidnapping at the San Francisco convention . . . I was not indicted, despite the lying testimony of the six who made the police complaint . . . After more than twenty years of service to our Union, the expressions of confidence from the membership have sustained me against the bitter and vicious and personal attack on my character and reputation. I thank God and all of you, my fellow members, for myself and my family, for your trust and loyalty, your confidence and support and the privilege of serving each and every one of you."

However, the AFL-CIO Executive Council ordered the Bakers to correct the abuses outlined by the Committee on Ethical Practices, and to bar from office those responsible for the abuses. The Bakers tried both defiance and accommodation. "Our union will not leave the AFL-CIO," the Bakers' Executive Board declared. "President Cross will remain at this post as head of the union . . . To assure our continued affiliation . . . we are going far beyond any recommendations of the Ethical Practices Committee." Peter H. Olson, the acting secretary-treasurer, wrote to Meany submitting "evidence of substantial compliance" with the Executive Council's directive. Cross had demanded Stuart's resignation, the return of a Cadillac and a refund of $4,287.34 to Local 100. Financial relationships with employers were now forbidden. New financial controls had been introduced, following the recommendations of Professor David S. Brown of George Washington University. "We are confident," Olson said, ". . . that total compliance will be forthcoming with reasonable dispatch." The Executive Council was less certain, and gave the Bakers three weeks to agree to reinstate Sims, requiring also that the union hold a special convention within ninety days to take whatever further steps might be necessary to eliminate corrupt practices.

The Bakers' Executive Board agreed to call a convention, but refused to reinstate Sims or to get rid of Cross. On November 15, 1957, Meany announced the suspension of the union.

There were other troubles for the Bakers. The "Committee to Preserve Integrity," an internal group in the Bakers headed by Vice-President Daniel Conway, claimed the support of 150 of the union's 250 locals in its efforts to ensure full compliance with the AFL-CIO's demands. Charges were filed with the federation to the effect that Cross had retaliated against the "Integrity" Committee by firing eight full-time representatives, by transferring members from rebel to loyal locals, and by plotting to get rid of four international vice presidents who supported the anti-Cross move. The Baltimore local of the Bakers filed suit against Cross for an accounting and restitution of the money he had allegedly misspent. The Bakers' Executive Board asked for a meeting with Meany. He agreed, "with the understanding that this committee will not include in its membership the President of your organization." The meeting was held, but nothing was achieved.

The AFL-CIO convention met on December 5, 1957, in Atlantic City. Cross said he was told that the Bakers could remain in the federation if he stepped down. "I'm the whipping boy now," he told the convention, "the scapegoat . . ." President Emeritus Herman Winter of the Bakers, a member of the Executive Council, intervened in the debate. "This is an internal trouble that we have," he said. "There is a lot of jealousy involved in it . . . Whatever waste Jimmie Cross has been responsible for, so has Bill Schnitzler.* There is no question about it; I can prove it . . . Schnitzler had no use for Cross and neither did Curtis Sims . . . All three of them are good trade unionists . . . There is nothing wrong with this fellow James Cross that can't be straightened out." Nonetheless, the Appeals Committee of the convention recommended that the Bakers be expelled unless full compliance was achieved by March 15, 1958.

"I find myself after listening to Brother Cross," Meany told the convention, "in the position of wondering whether or not the Appeals Committee should have taken more summary action . . . there is every evidence right at this minute that there is no intention to comply . . . this [Cross] is a remarkable guy. But I have seen both sides of him, and I can tell you frankly that this union is in a bad way if he continues to run its affairs, whether he runs them from one of his two homes in Palm Beach or whether he runs them from his other mansion, or whether he runs them in conjunction with the Employers' Association or with George Stuart . . . This is a workers' organization. . . Let's keep it that way."

The convention authorized the expulsion of the Bakers by a roll call vote of seven to one. Meany invited the members of the union's Executive Board to meet with him, but they refused. He gave the union until the end of the convention to make some accommodation, but no action was taken. The Bakery and Confectionery Workers were expelled and the AFL-CIO chartered a new union, the American Bakery and Confectionery Workers.

"Trade Union history," Cross and his supporters wrote to their members, "records no greater crime than that of 'dual unionism' . . . yet this is precisely what a small group of desperate and discredited officials of your International have done, while voting for their personal gain. In this criminal act they were aided and abetted by George Meany acting out of his own personal hatred of one man . . . [history] will record the failure of this attempt to destroy our seventy-year-old International." The old union held a special convention in March, 1958, ratifying various internal reforms and instructing its officers to seek ways to comply with the directives of the AFL-CIO; but deference was absent. "You know," Cross told the convention, "we are in changing times. If the Government keeps going, and if the AFL-CIO leaders keep staying as dumb as they are, there is liable to

* Secretary-Treasurer William F. Schnitzler of the AFL–CIO was Cross's predecessor as president of the Bakers, and retained an active interest in the union's affairs.

be more unions outside the AFL-CIO than there is inside." He had an ally in another expatriate. The union had recently signed a joint mutual assistance with the Teamsters—also now expelled—and invited Hoffa to address the convention. Hoffa promised the full cooperation of the Teamsters "in any dispute . . . with any employer or with anybody else who tries to destroy this International Union."

But the old union's fortunes declined. By mid-1959 the new organization claimed more than half of 150,000 organized bakers in the United States. During the same year, the Department of Labor conducted an investigation of the Bakery and Confectionery Workers, obtaining a court order directing the reinstatement of a group of officials Cross had removed for supporting reunification with the AFL-CIO union. The internal pressure for Cross' departure increased. In January, 1961, he agreed to resign on the receipt of $250,000 in severance pay and a promise to meet the cost of any future litigation against him. The union then elected new officers at its 1962 convention, rejected a proposal to merge with the Teamsters and voted to seek re-admission to the AFL-CIO, although it also voted to oppose a merger with the AFL-CIO Bakers. Sometime later Cross, Olson and four former vice presidents of the old Bakers were convicted of embezzling union funds since the time of expulsion. In 1962 both the old and new unions entered into peace negotiations with the active assistance of Meany.

"We understand," James B. Carey wrote to Albert J. Hayes in 1956, "that in 1952 an AFL committee looked into allegations of corrupt practices in the International Jewelry Workers Union and particularly its largest local union, Local 222 . . . there is some doubt whether Local 222 and the International Union have succeeded in freeing themselves from corrupt influences. The general reputation of the Union is not good . . ." Carey was secretary-treasurer of the Industrial Union Department of AFL-CIO.* The Jewelry Workers had applied for affiliation, and Carey wanted the advice of the Committee on Ethical Practices on the matter.

A committee of the AFL—composed of Meany, Dubinsky and McFetridge—had investigated the Jewelry Workers in 1952, reporting to the AFL convention that the union had agreed to withdraw a charter issued

---

* The Industrial Union Department of the AFL–CIO is composed mainly of former CIO unions. Carey was the first and only secretary-treasurer the CIO ever had, and upon the merger of the AFL and CIO became the secretary-treasurer of the federation's IUD. He was also president of the International Union of Electrical Workers, formerly of the CIO. He lost both offices in 1965 when his re-election as president of his union was overturned by the courts on grounds of ballot-rigging by one or more of Carey's supporters.

outside its jurisdiction; action on another local was postponed because of current court proceedings. Under pressure from the committee, IJWU Secretary-Treasurer Hyman Powell suspended the officers of New York Local 222 after the arrest of Business Agent George ("Muscles") Futterman for the attempted intimidation and coercion of a major witness in the case of the murder of William Lurye, an organizer for the ILGWU. Bernard Rifkin, an IJWU international representative, became trustee of Local 222. He discharged one business agent for attempting to extort $5,000 from an employer in the Bronx, cut the salaries of the local officers, and arranged for a Congregationalist minister to participate in all contract negotiations. The officers of the local then removed all records, whereupon Powell expelled the local. It tried unsuccessfully to obtain a charter from the Retail Clerks, affiliated briefly with the United Textile Workers until public criticism caused the latter to withdraw the local's charter, then returned to the Jewlery Workers in 1953 after agreeing to discharge Futterman and five other ex-convicts on the staff.

The 1953 IJWU convention amended its constitution to require all candidates for international or local union office to sign a sworn statement attesting to whether or not they had criminal records. Three of them were former officials of Local 32B of the Building Service Employees. Isidore Schwartz, who became head of Local 222 when it was expelled from the union, was the same "Izzy" Schwartz who turned state's evidence in 1940 against George Scalise; he now "lost interest" in Local 222 and left. Frank Gold, now of IJWU Local 8, had been convicted in 1941 of extortion from employers. Powell himself, formerly of Local 32B and once known as Palatnik, was indicted in 1940 for extortion from Wall Street employers; the indictment was apparently dropped when he agreed to leave the local.

There matters stood until 1957. In that year an AFL-CIO group, the Committee to End Exploitation of Puerto Rican and Other Minority Workers, reported to Meany that a number of members of IJWU Local 122 had revolted, left the union and negotiated a satisfactory contract. Al Nash, a reputable UAW official, became administrator of the local by consent of the parties, but left after three weeks with the statement that "under present conditions it is impossible to clean up this local." Another group of 300 members tried to break with Local 222, after which the Minority Workers' committee met with the officers of the local. "[N]othing," the Committee reported to Meany, "has been accomplished . . . The case of [these] workers can be duplicated over and over again in the shops of the two locals of the International Jewelry Workers. . . ."

The two locals represented nearly half of the IJWU's 23,000 members. In most shops the weekly wage varied between forty and forty-four dollars.

Employers usually appointed the shop stewards. The union seldom processed grievances, and employees sometimes lost their jobs—without protest from the union—for filing them. Appeals procedures were virtually non-existent. Union representatives met with employers rather than with members on their rare visits to the shops. Local union meetings seldom occurred more than once a year. Officials were often elected by a show of hands. Local union executive boards rarely included rank and file members; they appointed convention delegates and set their own salaries, allegedly exorbitant. Officers negotiated agreements with employers without the participation or ratification of members, seldom providing the latter with copies of the contracts. Accounting methods were casual.

The welfare fund of the international union was a family affair. Mrs. Powell, wife of the secretary-treasurer, was a business partner of the fund's broker, Simon Tripani, and shared with him the brokerage fees on the fund's insurance policies. Stanley Rubenzahl, Powell's nephew, was both administrator of the fund and a broker for the bond business of the fund. W. C. Eitelberg, Mrs. Powell's brother, was once attorney for the fund; he was succeeded by Fred Deutch, another brother. The trustees of the fund—one of whom was Local 8 official Frank Gold's brother-in-law —received salaries for which they allegedly performed no services. Tripani and Mrs. Powell received commissions of eleven percent—reduced to six percent after an investigation by the New York State Insurance Commission—on the welfare fund's insurance business. They also handled the fire, burglary and miscellaneous insurance for the international union.

In April, 1957, the IJWU General Executive Board set up a Fair Practices Committee to investigate the complaints against the union and to take disciplinary action where necessary. The Board retained James D. Walsh, the former executive director of the defunct New York City Anti-Crime Committee, to supervise the investigation. It revoked the charters of six locals and appointed Al Nash administrator over Local 122; he left Local 222 earlier in the year, the Board said, merely to conserve his regular job with the UAW. Indeed, the Board concluded, Local 122's contracts were now comparable to those in related industries; the problem was policing, which had improved. Regular meetings now took place, rank and file members presently comprised a majority of the local's executive board, and officers paid regular visits to the shops to handle grievances, the Board said. "Whatever derelictions Local 122 has, therefore, been guilty of in the past," IJWU President Joseph Morris and Powell jointly wrote to Meany, "the situation is being rapidly corrected." They reported similar improvements in Local 222; in particular, the minimum wage was now forty-four dollars a week for a completely inexperienced woman and forty-eight dollars a week for a completely inexperienced man; some members even earned as much as seventy dollars a week. Further, Morris and Powell were "rather amazed" that the Minority Workers' committee knew of fifty-three complaints against the union, because they themselves had received only five. Finally, they denied any knowledge of improprieties in the administration of the welfare fund.

Morris and Powell met with the Minority Workers' committee. Morris stated that he knew of only one complaint against the union, and Powell contended that complaints submitted to him by the Association of Catholic Trade Unionists "were found to be 100 percent wrong." They nevertheless agreed to institute a series of reforms, including the adoption of the Codes of Ethical Practices and the disciplining of erring officials. But as the Minority Worker's committee later reported to Meany, no progress had been made.

Meany asked the Committee on Ethical Practices to investigate the union. Its findings were adverse. Numerous financial and accounting procedures "violated the letter and spirit of the Ethical Practices Code, as well as the Union's own constitution." Morris and Powell had allowed the use of union money in "unauthorized ways." Corrupt elements still controlled some of the locals. The union had made collusive agreements with employers. Locals 122 and 222 had been allowed to disaffiliate without any action by the union. Other locals were negotiating for affiliation with the Teamsters and the ILA. The union "had become thoroughly demoralized . . . it was on the verge of moral and financial bankruptcy . . . the executive board was unable to function effectively . . . the union was rapidly disintegrating . . ."

Powell defended himself before the Committee and denied, as had been charged, that he had ever taken salary kickbacks from IJWU officials; and that he had ever asked Bernard Rifkin to steal an election, to pad expenses, or to use violence against anyone. Nor, he said in response to one charge, had he ever used his entertainment allowance carelessly. "I can assure this Committee," testified Powell, "that I did not see 'My Fair Lady' twenty-three separate times." He had used his union airline credit card to pay for trips abroad for his wife and daughter in 1956, fully intending to repay, but "the matter escaped my attention . . ." He took his wife to conventions at union expense, he said, but so did other IJWU officials. If anything was wrong with the union's financial controls, he declared, it was Morris' fault.

Morris charged that Powell had taken kickbacks and misappropriated union money. He had suspended Powell from office, but the Board overruled him. "He seeks to save his own skin," Powell told the Committee, "by making false charges against me . . . As experienced union leaders, the members of the Ethical Practices Committee will, I am sure, recognize an internal political attack when they see one . . ."

There was another view. IJWU Vice-President Andrew Leredu told the Commmittee that "both Brothers Morris and Powell were able to spend monies without indicating the specific purpose of these expenditures except in the most vague and general of terms." They allowed Locals 122 and 222 to secede by paying $5,000 in back per capita taxes to the international union instead of the $52,000 owed, and had refused to take any further action. Morris had relinquished his constitutional obligation to countersign checks. Both Morris and Powell were delinquent in filing financial reports with the Executive Board. "Morris," Leredu stated, "in effect abdicated all of his powers and prerogatives to the tender mercies of Hyman Powell . . . who made a shambles of our organization—flaunting its every law . . . That Brother Powell must be dealt with summarily goes without saying . . . [he] could not, however, have taken the IJWU for the ride he did had brother Morris attended to his duties even on a minimum basis . . . Powell and Morris must go."

"Under the circumstances," Meany wrote to Morris and Powell, "I have no other course of action except to direct you to end these practices forthwith and to take whatever steps are necessary, including the expulsion of all officers who refuse to abide by the Code of Ethics set up by the AFL-CIO and . . . to end exploitation of any of the workers in any of your shops in your jurisdiction." Meany met with the IJWU's General Executive Board, which asked the AFL-CIO to assume full powers over the organization, and Meany appointed Charles Hasenmeyer monitor over the union. Morris and Powell, who had resigned to become employees of the union, now lost their jobs. The union held a convention in 1959 under Hasenmeyer's supervision to elect new officers, and in other ways satisfied the AFL-CIO. "Thus this union," the Executive Council said, "is on its way to rehabilitation . . ." There were no more reports, and the monitorship over the union was lifted before its 1962 convention.

"It is the sincere desire and firm intention of the Laundry Workers' International Union," LWIU President Sam J. Byers wrote to AFL President Meany in 1955, "to take such action with respect to its welfare fund as it may find to be necessary, appropriate and legally proper . . . I request the assistance of the American Federation of Labor." The Douglas Subcommittee had just reported on the union.

Meany promised his help and sent Nelson Cruikshank, director of the

AFL Department of Social Security, to the headquarters of the LWIU. Cruikshank recommended separating the California Life Insurance Company from the welfare fund, seeking more beneficial insurance policies on a competitive basis, discontinuing the employment of union officials as welfare fund "deputies," eliminating all conflicts of interest in union investments, and replacing the entire board of trustees.

Meany urged prompt action by the union. "I am sure that you recognize," he wrote to Byers, "that to take the position that no action by the union is called for until action is instituted by the Department of Justice or by a State, and finally determined by the Courts, would be tantamount to an abdication of the responsibility of a trade union to protect the interests of its members. It is a firm and cherished principle of the American Federation of Labor that our unions are capable of exercising their own discipline . . . Any failure to measure up to this responsibility . . . would put in jeopardy the freedom from control of the internal affairs of all unions." Byers referred the matter to the welfare fund trustees.

An AFL-CIO staff report, prepared at Meany's request in 1956, said that some reforms had been undertaken by the LWIU welfare fund trustees, but that their effectiveness had not yet been assessed, and that Eugene C. ("Jimmy") James—accused with broker Louis Saperstein of diverting large sums from the welfare fund—was still secretary-treasurer of the union. The AFL-CIO Executive Council ordered a full investigation by the Committee on Ethical Practices.

Byers appeared before the Committee. The welfare fund deputy system, he reported, no longer existed. For himself, he denied that he was a trustee of Chicago Local 46's welfare fund, that he had put any of his own money into the purchase of California Life, or that he knew anything about the manipulations of James and Saperstein. He had relied in all welfare fund matters he said, on the advice of others, and had seen nothing amiss. LWIU members, he argued, had suffered not at all from the diversion of funds, since legitimate claims had always been paid by either Saperstein or the carrier. The union had taken no action against James pending the outcome of trial proceedings against him; indeed, Byers said, the union did not have enough evidence to sustain any charges against James. However, Byers agreed to recommend James's dismissal as international secretary-treasurer at the next Executive Board meeting.

James, it appeared, was not like other international secretary-treasurers. He did not have an office at the LWIU's headquarters, and rarely went there. "He gets to Headquarters," LWIU Counsel Herbert S. Thatcher wrote to the Committee, "for one day at invervals of every six months . . .

He doesn't operate as a usual International Secretary-Treasurer." Byers told the Committee that he had been performing James's duties for some time, although the latter still received his salary for the position.

Soon afterwards Byers and James became "gravely ill" and "very seriously ill" respectively, unable to carry out their duties. The LWIU General Executive Board suspended James indefinitely as secretary-treasurer, but allowed him to retain office in Local 46. The local, Thatcher declared, did not control the international union; nor had James done any harm to the local itself. "For this Committee," Thatcher said, "to ask the International at this time to take action at the local level as well would hardly seem to be justified." For the rest, he said, the union had taken "every possible step" to repair itself. Security Mutual, not the union, lost $900,000 as a result of Saperstein's peculations; the union did lose rate credits or dividends, but the $150,000 recovered from Security Mutual probably more than covered the loss. "Surely, given the facts," he wrote, ". . . neither the general public nor anyone in the trade union movement could reasonably conclude that the Laundry Workers International Union is presently conducting its affairs in other than an honest and efficient manner."

The Committee disagreed. The minutes of the LWIU Board meetings, it said, showed "that the Union was most reluctant to take any action whatever . . . there was no recognition of grievous wrongdoing . . . [or] a determination that nothing similar would happen in the future." Contrary to Byers' testimony, the Committee contended, James had in fact been performing the duties of his office; welfare fund malpractices continued to the present time; union officials apparently still received payment for welfare fund work; and the welfare fund deputy system was still in force. "The explanation of innocent ignorance," the Committee declared, ". . . cannot be accepted. These abuses involved over $1,000,000. They continued for over five years. They included a whole variety of evil practices—exceedingly high commissions, kickbacks, special expense payments, payment of premiums to someone other than the insurance carrier, failure to enquire about dividends, or about the receipt of claims checks from other than the carrier, or about a host of other irregularities. The Committee finds it incredible that such abuse could be carried on . . . there is no real understanding on the part of the Union of the spirit of ethical trade union practices . . . the plain fact is that a dollar which went down the drain of excessive commissions or plain graft is a dollar which otherwise would necessarily have been expended either for improved benefits or for increased dividends or other cost savings. The members lost the value of that dollar . . ."

The Committee found no excuse for the union's inaction against James. It declared that James's denials of guilt were refuted by the public record;

in particular, Byers had accepted James's denial that he kept a separate bank account, yet did nothing when informed by the bank manager in question that the account existed. "There is no investigation even at this point," the Committee said, ". . . no outburst of indignation at what is evidently a barefaced falsehood . . ." The union did not have to wait for the law. "Guilt under criminal law is simply a different question from guilt under ethical and union standards," the Committee claimed. The obligation of a union official was "much more than the bare requirement of keeping inside the boundaries of the criminal law . . . The failure of public prosecutors to move is obviously not an underwriting of the quality of the conduct involved." Action should have been taken, the Committee said, at both the international and local union levels.

"Serious abuses are still evident," was the Committee's conclusion. "Even now, the Union is offering excuses and explanations for not taking obvious steps. It has no proposals for eliminating all traces of past corruption. It has no program for insuring that AFL-CIO standards will be rigorously maintained in the future . . . [it] does not meet the standards for ethical trade union practices set forth in the AFL-CIO Constitution."

The Laundry Workers held a convention in May, 1957. Now there were rebels at work. "We have our campaign to unseat a few undesirables," Russell Crowell of Oakland (California) Local 23 wrote to McGavin, ". . . well under way . . . Our biggest job will be to find a slate of officers to run against the incumbents. It's too bad we are forced to wait until the Convention is actually under way to find out who will be willing to make the fight." Crowell was the sole delegate at the convention to speak against the granting of a full-salary pension of $18,000 to Byers as president emeritus, and to urge compliance with the AFL-CIO Codes. "This is a low paid industry, probably the lowest paid in the United States," he told the delegates, "and can you tell your members . . . that you agree that a man is worth $18,000 just to get rid of him? Byers should either be running for president or he is entitled to not one red cent." Crowell ran for vice president, but was openly endorsed by only two other delegates and lost overwhelmingly.

Byers got his pension and retired. He was succeeded by Ralph T. Fagan of James's Local 46. "Fagan is clean, honest and has integrity," James announced. "I know him well. He is my employee."

James also retired, but there was no further concession to the AFL-CIO. The rebels distributed copies of the Committee on Ethical Practices' report on the union, but it was not read to the delegates; the newly elected General Executive Board members later claimed they knew nothing about it until after they took office. The following month, after receiving a further report on the LWIU, the AFL-CIO Executive Council directed that the union "stand suspended and face expulsion from the AFL-CIO."

Fagan wrote to Meany shortly before the 1957 AFL-CIO convention. He said that James now had no connection with the union, that all the old welfare fund trustees had been replaced, that the welfare fund was now being administered according to Cruikshank's recommendations and under the supervision of a university professor, and that Byers had been removed as president emeritus and chairman of the welfare fund trustees—although he still received an annual pension of $18,000. Fagan told Meany that— aside from holding the special convention demanded by the federation, which he said would be too costly—the union was now in compliance with the standards of the AFL-CIO.

Meany countered with a last offer, proposing that the LWIU hold within ninety days a special convention presided over by an AFL-CIO representative, require all incumbent officers to submit themselves for re-election, read the AFL-CIO report on the union to the delegates and print it in the union's convention proceedings, and start court action against James.

The union rejected Meany's proposals, offered only to hold a regular convention at the proper time with Meany attending as an observer, and appealed to the AFL-CIO convention. The Appeals Committee of the convention noted that the union had refused to hold a special convention, now claiming that such an action would be unconstitutional; that neither Fagan nor the union had tried to get an accounting or recovery from James of the money he had misappropriated; and that no legal action against James had been taken. On the contrary, the Committee said, James had attended the last LWIU convention, held Executive Board meetings in his hotel room, and had "obviously dictated the election of a new president and secretary-treasurer."

"[O]ur rank and file," Fagan told the federation convention, "has shown complete satisfaction with the results reached at our convention . . . we have not received a single letter, or even a post card, from any member of our International criticizing our action in this regard."

Meany had received a letter. "Dear Mr. Meany," an LWIU laundress had recently written, "I would like to know *Why* our laundry only starts with 65¢ an hour . . . every year you get a nickel raise till the amounts come to a *Dollar*. That is a Union Ha Ha Ha . . . No contract on wall or Labor law hung up in shop so that we can see what we should know . . . when we have our meetings some of the girls have to say some things to the other girls and they are told to shut there mouth and to sit down or do not attend any more meetings or be fined 5 dollars . . . we work like horses and I mean horses . . . Our Boss said that our Union is nothing and is not worth the paper it is wrote on . . . they make you pay the full month dues when you are sick and that is 2.50 a month the books say 35¢ a month and they wrote the contract that way . . . Well all I have to say is I do hope you will help us out and get us a good Union in . . . send some one down to help us PLEASE PLEASE."

"He looks like a very reasonable person," Meany said of Fagan at the AFL-CIO convention. "I know absolutely nothing detrimental to his character. There has been no request that he eliminate himself from this picture. . . . However, I think I must fill in a little bit . . ." Fagan had spent most of his working life as an employer, undergoing a "rapid transition" to vice president of James's local. "He said it was like a bolt from the blue; he had no idea the mantle was going to fall on him," Meany said of Fagan's rise to the presidency of the union. "[W]e now hear that everything has been running right. They have a professor—these professors come in handy at times—who is going to guide them . . . Now, this man looks all right and his remarks make me wonder why it is he could not accept our proposal . . . We feel there is every reason to believe that up until this present moment the same forces that controlled this Union may still be in control . . . Has Mr. Fagan any further comment?" Fagan was silent. The convention expelled the Laundry Workers by a vote of over fourteen to one.

The rebels now were stronger, and received a charter from the federation as the AFL-CIO Laundry and Dry Cleaning International Union. Winfield Chasmar of New Jersey, a member of the original executive board, became the new union's first president. In 1962 he gave way to Russell Crowell, the first of the open rebels. The new union now claimed some one-third of the old union's original membership. The LWIU affiliated with the Teamsters.

"I have nothing to fear," Dave Beck said after his appearance before the McClellan Committee. "My record is an open book. I make this fight for others, not for myself." Beck, who reportedly had threatened to "blow the lid right off the Senate" when he testified, instead invoked the Fifth Amendment over 200 times. Meany declared that any union official who refused to testify on the handling of union funds had no right to hold office. Beck took his case to the AFL-CIO Executive council, saying that he would not remove any union officer for exercising his constitutional rights. "I know all the things you're not going to do," Meany said. "What I want to know is what you are going to do to clean things up." The Executive Council suspended Beck from membership in the Council and ordered an investigation of the Teamsters.

Beck announced that the Teamsters would spend a million dollars to counter the unfavorable publicity incurred by the union. But Teamster Secretary-Treasurer John F. English refused to sign the checks and the union's General Executive Board approved only "reasonable" expenditures, none of them to be for Beck's personal defense. Anti-Beck demonstrations broke out in Teamster locals in various parts of the country; he was hung in effigy in his home state; and pressure from his colleagues for his resignation increased. However, the Teamster Board criticized Beck's suspension, and authorized him to appoint a committee to meet and discuss the matter with the AFL-CIO Executive Council.

"I wish to point out," Meany wrote to Beck, "that membership on the Executive Council is a personal matter. Members of the Council do not sit on the Council as representatives of any particular Union but are required to act in the interests of the general membership of the entire trade union movement. The action of the Council in suspending you as a member was based on your personal actions and not on any actions take by the Teamsters Brotherhood as such . . . I will, however, convey your request [for a meeting] to the Executive Council . . ." The Council heard Beck's claim that his suspension was a nullity, expelled him, and appointed English in his place.

"We are going to wash our own dirty linen," English told the Executive Council. "American labor is going to be proud of us again." The sixty-seven-year-old English, respected in both the Teamsters and the AFL-CIO, was looked upon as an influence for integrity in the Teamsters; but pride was delayed. The Teamsters' General Executive Board affirmed the right of any Teamster official to use the Fifth Amendment under Congressional questioning, and at first refused to participate in the hearings of the federation's Committee on Ethical Practices. Vice-President John T. O'Brien of Chicago announced his candidacy for the presidency of the Teamsters, but soon made it clear that he would run only with Hoffa's blessing. Hoffa, who had just been indicted on the charge of illegally wiretapping the telephones of his Teamster colleagues in Detroit, then entered the race. English threw his support to Hoffa. Beck, after repeated assertions that he would run again, withdrew. Meany announced that Hoffa was unacceptable to the AFL-CIO.

"We find," the Committee on Ethical Practices reported at this time, "that President Beck, Vice-President Brewster, and Vice-President Hoffa extensively used Union funds for personal purposes . . . Beck used Union funds as if they were his private funds . . . no records were kept of the transactions and no instruments of indebtedness were signed by him . . . all of the evidence indicates that there was initially no intention to repay

. . . Brewster treated Union funds in exactly the same way . . . the only difference between the two situations is in the amount of money involved."

"Hoffa violated standards of ethical conduct in borrowing money directly and indirectly from local unions under his control . . . Hoffa was engaged in improper activities relating to health and welfare funds . . . There is no dispute that Vice-President Hoffa has had dealings with John Dio since 1952 . . . Hoffa stated that he dealt with Dio because of the mutual interest of the Teamsters and Dio's union in the taxicab drivers in New York City. We reject that defense completely . . . There is testimony that . . . Hoffa was a strong advocate of bringing Dio into the Teamsters Union . . . The plain fact is that Johnny Dio was a well-known labor racketeer. His career has run the gamut from breaking strikes as an employer's representative to making 'sweetheart' contracts as a Union representative. He was known throughout the labor movement as an undesirable character. We reject completely Vice-President Hoffa's defense that he was naive as to the character of Dio . . . Hoffa even worked against his own Union's organizing efforts because of his relationship with Dio. The New York taxicab situation . . . was a clear-cut situation where Hoffa was sabotaging the Teamster Union's efforts to organize the drivers in order to promote Dio's efforts to bring himself and his practices directly into the Teamsters' Union . . . Indeed, the list of many of Hoffa's proteges and friends reads like a rogue's gallery . . . We do not accept Hoffa's explanation that these associations were an attempt to rehabilitate juvenile delinquents."

When the Teamsters eventually appeared before the Committee they argued that the merger of the AFL and CIO did not dilute the principle of autonomy; that only local instances of corruption in the Teamsters had been charged; that they would take no action against any official while he was being investigated by government agencies, nor question his use of the Fifth Amendment, nor discuss any charges of corruption with the Committee without an assurance that the proceedings would not be subject to a subpoena; and that in any event the Teamsters' constitution prevented the union from taking action against those accused of corrupt practices.

"We think," the Committee replied, "that the position taken by the Union is untenable in its entirety . . . The autonomous rights of international unions within the Federation do not embrace the right of a union to be dominated or influenced by corrupt influences . . . It is incredible that the Union chooses to characterize [the] evidence as 'isolated' instances of corruption . . . The Teamsters' constitution . . . contains ample provisions to correct the abuses which have been charged . . . We think the Teamster Union position as stated to this Committee completely ignored the constitutional obligation imposed upon the Union to keep its house clean of corrupt influences . . . the unrefuted and unanswered evidence shows that the Teamsters Union has been and continues to be dominated or substantially influenced by corrupt influences . . ."

The Executive Council ordered the Teamsters to eliminate such elements and report to the satisfaction of the Council on October 24, 1957, a month thence. Only English voted against the motion, although Council members reported that all of his own proposals for fiscal reform in the Teamsters had been regularly and overwhelmingly defeated in recent sessions of the Teamsters' General Executive Board.

The Teamsters met in convention in Miami the following week. Hoffa now led the field of candidates, claiming that he would receive seventy-five percent of the votes. O'Brien had withdrawn and thrown his support of Hoffa. Congressman John F. Shelley, a former Teamster official, had entered the contest in symbolic protest, but finally dropped out. Thomas L. ("Honest Tom") Hickey, an international vice president from New York long known for his opposition to racketeering, withdrew on the day of the election and endorsed Vice-President William A. Lee of Chicago. Lee and Thomas J. Haggerty, also of Chicago, completed the race, failing to form a unity ticket. Hoffa, sure of a comfortable victory, happily conceded contested delegates and won by a two to one margin.

He commanded the convention from the start, openly—with Beck still in the chair—semaphoring from the wings of the platform the responses he wanted from his supporters. He arranged the amendment of the Teamsters' constitution to increase his control over collective bargaining, overwhelmingly defeated a move to compel his resignation upon conviction of a crime, and elected his own slate to the General Executive Board. He read to the delegates his statement in a hearing before the Committee on Ethical Practices, asserting innocence of all charges against him. He claimed to value affiliation with the AFL-CIO, but suggested that the Teamsters might "tell the AFL-CIO to go to hell." His supporters derided a reading of the report on the Teamsters by the Committee on Ethical Practices. "The charges contained in this report are serious charges," Delegate Jeffery Cohelan from Oakland said. "If this convention is foolish enough to sweep this from the record . . . we will stand before this country, and in the labor movement particularly, indicted . . ." The pro-Hoffa majority ignored him and expunged the report from the record. In a final accolade, they raised Hoffa's salary from $50,000 to $75,000 a year, making him perhaps the most highly paid union president in the world.

Beck made his farewell. "God never created me," he stated, "in the crucible of infallibility . . . undoubtedly I have made mistakes . . . I only ask you . . . to see if you can't find something that I have done that is perhaps just a little bit over on the credit side—just a little." The delegates saw enough in him to vote him the $50,000 a year pension Meany had recently declared Beck did not deserve, but denied him Tobin's old status of president emeritus. "I sincerely hope and trust," Beck said, "that in some manner in domestic and foreign fields I will from time to time have the opportunity to represent and assist this International Union. I want to remain associated with you . . ." He was not called back.

The AFL-CIO Executive Council suspended the Teamsters on October 24, stipulating that the suspension would be lifted if the Teamsters agreed to bar from office those criticized in the report, and to accept the directives on further reforms from a committee of the Council; otherwise the Council would recommend the expulsion of the Teamsters at the AFL-CIO convention in December, 1957. Four members of the Council—Hutcheson of the Carpenters, Herman Winter of the Bakers, William C. Doherty of the Letter Carriers, and English—voted against the Council's action. "The drastic action of suspension and recommended expulsion," Beck wrote to Schnitzler, "is entirely and grossly discriminatory . . . refusing the reasonable request for a period of time in which to seek out, review and modify those practices and situations which might require adjustment. . . ."

There was time for adjustment in at least one case, but the remedy was less than perfect. A Teamster committee appointed by Beck recommended that the officers of the six New York locals allegedly controlled by Dio and Corallo be dismissed. The report was not published, but Beck appointed a trustee over the locals. The condemned officials remained in office. Shortly afterwards Beck announced that the Teamsters had given up trying to reform five of the locals and had withdrawn their charters.

"We are not condemning the Teamsters," Alex Rose told the AFL-CIO convention, ". . . nor are we condemning the thousands of local officers of the Teamsters Union. We are condemning a system . . . which . . . does not work to the benefit of that organization, but to the benefit of Dave Beck and Jimmy Hoffa . . . All we are doing . . . is denying Mr. Hoffa the right to represent the AFL-CIO. We deny him that honor because there is enough evidence to prove that he does not deserve that honor." The convention Appeals Committee heard out the Teamsters, declared their case to be without merit, and recommended their expulsion.

"It's all right," English replied. "You will weep before we will . . ." He reminded the delegates of the debts to the Teamsters, and asked for a year to reform. "Beck is gone," he said, "Brewster is gone, Sidney Brennan is gone. There is only one man—Jimmy Hoffa. And Jimmy Hoffa has done more for our International Union than anybody connected with it, including myself. How in the hell can we kick him out? . . . Oh, it makes my blood run cold. I am coming near to the end of my days. I never thought I would see this . . . the Teamsters will get along . . . We won't forget our friends . . . As far as our enemies are concerned, they can all go straight to hell . . ."

Meany wound up the debate. He noted that the Teamsters' constitution provided for the disciplining or expulsion of any member convicted of a crime, or who engaged in racketeering, or who brought dishonor on the union, but that no action of importance had yet been taken. "The Teamsters," he said, "have made no move . . . to live up to their own Constitution in regard to these crimes against the trade union movement . . . Their convention took up this matter not at all . . . they read the Ethical Practices Report in an atmosphere of hilarity. They had a nice time doing it . . . they didn't do anything, they didn't investigate anything . . ." Meany had agreed several times through an intermediary to meet with Hoffa, but on each occasion Hoffa had cancelled the appointment. "I have the door open," Meany stated, "it was open until eleven o'clock last night; it will be open after you finish voting . . . But we have got to give these members a chance . . . when you vote for this committee's report you are voting to free the Teamsters from the dictatorship of these men." The convention expelled the Teamsters by a vote of just over four to one.

However, the AFL-CIO did not charter a new Teamsters' union. In the instances of the Bakers and the Laundry Workers, large dissident groups had actively sought new charters. "[W]hen we expelled the Bakers," Meany told the 1959 AFL-CIO convention, ". . . there were sitting in the balcony all during that session 1,200 representatives of the Bakers Union . . . waiting for a charter . . . In the Laundry Workers . . . there again we had about thirty-five percent of that organization that immediately left and took an AFL-CIO charter."

The Teamsters were a different matter, something of a clan, the only trade unionists in America to refer to their own organization as a "movement," and now under special control. Further, the intercity and interstate movement of truck drivers—their essential interdependence—made the survival of any minority rebels a hazardous affair. "It would not be possible for them," Meany said, "to go to another city in complete control of the Hoffa forces and deliver their goods . . . they would have to be sacrificed." Teamster defections to the AFL-CIO were minor, all local in character, insufficient for a rebellion.

Invasion brought violence faced by only a few. The Seafarers, on behalf of the AFL-CIO, organized a group of truck drivers in Puerto Rico. "[W]e took to the field," Paul Hall told the convention, ". . . there were those of our members who had everything from their legs broken to being stabbed . . . the fight lines were drawn and the blood flowed . . . Many of these people who made such glorious speeches on the floor . . . were conspicuous by their absence . . . we should call the roll of the speechmakers and see how many have been down on the line."

The federation's door was open for the Teamsters, but not for Hoffa. "As the matter now stands," Schnitzler wrote in 1961 to an AFL-CIO official in Wisconsin, "the door of the AFL-CIO is open for the Teamsters to return and take their rightful place in the ranks of the trade union movement . . . the Teamsters must, of course, meet the conditions laid down by the AFL-CIO Executive Council under their Constitution. This means, among other things, the elimination of Jimmy Hoffa as an officer of the international union."

Hoffa himself made few concessions to acceptability. He evidently divested himself of his business interests, and repeatedly announced his desire to take the Teamsters back into the AFL-CIO; but otherwise he went his own way, largely without reprisal. He maintained a range of organizational alliances with various AFL-CIO affiliates. In 1958 he formed the Conference on Transportation Unity with the NMU and the ILA, later developing a joint bargaining alliance with the ILWU and the Mine, Mill and Smelter Workers—both expelled from the CIO for alleged Communist affinities. In 1962 he officially broadened the jurisdiction of the Teamsters to include all unorganized workers, and raided some AFL-CIO unions. He expanded his authority in the Teamsters, personally conducting negotiations for regional and national agreements which supplanted local agreements in hands other than his. He maintained some old and dubious friendships, disciplined few officials for error, and engineered Teamster loans for gambling and related enterprises. The Teamsters' raids on other unions often failed, but they seldom lost what they already had. Only the Seafarers fought them in the streets, taking over Teamster taxicab drivers' locals in Chicago, Detroit and St. Louis, and other locals elsewhere. For the rest, Hoffa claimed that the Teamsters had gained substantially in membership since their expulsion.

Now and again there were demands for the readmission of the Teamsters into the AFL-CIO. "We have," President Michael Quill of the Transport Workers told the 1961 AFL-CIO convention, "an army of hypocrites among us . . . under the table every one of them has made a secret deal with Hoffa to protect their lines . . . His Holiness, Pope John XXIII," Quill said, "is changing Vatican precedent. He visits the prisons and hospitals . . . The first time I ever heard of any labor leader making a pilgrimage to a jail was yourself, Mr. Meany, to comfort a convicted racketeer in Sing Sing many years ago . . . You have amongst yourselves on the Executive Council a man who is already convicted of a crime . . . But a man who hasn't been convicted, Hoffa, you keep out . . . I for one am not afraid of Bobby Kennedy. He said that if Hoffa wasn't sent to jail he would jump out of the window of the Capitol. Let him jump. We have a labor movement to protect . . ."

More influential voices were heard. "Hoffa," Paul Hall declared, ". . . is a fink from his very heart. He always has been and always will be . . . our organization has wholeheartedly supported this program. We paid for it the hard way . . . we are not going to shine anybody's shoes to get out from any of that heat . . . act like men all the way instead of going outside and putting the raps on this organization and then coming in here and trying to pretend these are matters of a personality nature, when in fact they are . . . basic trade union issues."

"[T]here is no personality involved here," Meany stated. "I scarcely know this man [Hoffa] . . . I did not write this [AFL-CIO] Constitution . . . But as long as it is there, it is the Bible so far as I am concerned."

Secretary of Labor Arthur J. Goldberg added his views. "[L]aw or no law," he said, "the trade union movement itself has an old and eternal obligation to exercise vigilance against those who would corrupt it and use it for their personal gain . . . I think it was the finest hour of the trade union movement in America when you took the action that you did." A resolution calling for a membership referendum on the readmission of the Teamsters was defeated.

In time there were murmurs of dissent among Teamster leaders. After the altercation over sending condolences to Jacqueline Kennedy at the time of President Kennedy's assassination, there were rumors that the Teamsters' General Executive Board was moving to depose Hoffa. In July, 1964, International Vice-President John Backhus announced that he would ask Hoffa to resign because "he's done too much damage to the union's reputation." The request was premature. "Jack's a little ahead of the rest of us," another Board member stated. "I think the general inclination would be to wait and see what happens to Jimmy on his appeals in these convictions . . . as of today I don't think [Backhus would] have a majority with him—even though a majority of the board agrees with the feeling." Relationships were strained. The atmosphere around Hoffa, according to Ralph and Estelle James, became "saturated with suspicion, acrimony and intrigue." Hoffa's temper, always formidable, became increasingly explosive with the tightening of the legal net around him. His subordinates, bearing the brunt of his outbreaks, stayed wary of contact with him. Members of the General Executive Board, once accustomed to fraternization at the conclusion of business, now tended to go their separate ways. There was unrest in the field. "We're getting hurt in organizing," a Teamster official reported. "Every time we get into a campaign, the employer hits us with Hoffa's trials and convictions."

But Hoffa stayed in control. There were none to match his ability, none to challenge his authority. Indeed, as the pressures of the law upon him mounted, there was a silencing of internal criticism, an upsurge of union testimonials to him, a growing sense of persecution in the union and a tightening of loyalties to the constitutional chief Teamster. At Hoffa's last convention, in July of 1966, there was a proliferation of praise, a salary increase to $100,000 a year, and a constitutional amendment to provide for an acting president in the event of Hoffa's incarceration. When he went to jail, his long-time assistant and loyal supporter, Frank S. Fitzsimmons of Detroit Local 299, stood substitute for him. Absence was risky politics, but there was no doubt about Hoffa's own intentions. "Those who think Jimmy Hoffa is out of the picture," he wrote to his members just before going to jail, "don't know what kind of stuff a Teamster is made of. I'll be back . . ."

The Committee on Ethical Practices conducted one more inquiry—an informal investigation of the Operating Engineers in 1958—recommending that no formal action be taken if the union complied with the Committee's suggestions for reform, which were not published. Evidently all went well. "The union has agreed to abide by the committee's recommendations," the AFL-CIO Executive Council reported to the 1959 convention, "and it has periodically reported to President Meany the progress which has been made. President Meany, in turn, has kept the Executive Council informed of these developments." President Maloney of the Engineers retired, International Vice-President Swanson was dismissed. Presumably other actions were taken. There were no more reports.

President Maurice Hutcheson of the Carpenters was convicted in 1963 for bribing a state official in order to obtain advance information on routes for new roads in Marion County, Indiana, but the conviction was reversed, a higher court holding that the trial records were devoid of facts establishing a conspiracy to bribe. Hutcheson also received a six-month jail sentence for contempt of Congress after refusing to tell the McClellan Committee whether he had used union funds in an attempt to fix the bribery charge against him. The court later reduced the sentence to two years' probation and a $500 fine. Meany supported the plea for probation. No disciplinary actions were taken against Hutcheson or, evidently, any other officials of the Carpenters.

Other unions criticized by the McClellan Committee were left alone. Presumably their problems were resolved, or diminished, or judged to be less serious than charged.

23: The Law and the Corrupt

For most of its history, the American labor movement has had to live with a hostile law. Until well into the nineteenth century a trade union was a criminal conspiracy. Not until 1914 was the labor of a human being declared by Congress not to be an article of commerce, and thus exempt from the antitrust provisions of the federal law; not until 1932 was an effective curb placed on the easy use of the injunction by anti-union employers; and not until 1935 was trade unionism and collective bargaining given the formal support of the federal law.

But if the law was usually unfriendly, it was concerned overwhelmingly with the economic relations between unions and employers. There was no legislative intervention in internal union affairs, no public supervision of the morals of the parties to the collective bargaining process. Prior to 1934, there was no federal or state legislation directed specifically at the problem of corruption in trade unions and labor-management relations. In 1933, however, the investigation of racketeering in industrial relations by the Copeland Committee of the Senate brought about the passage of the Coleman Act, which made the exaction of money or "other valuable considerations" by violence or coercion a felony.

The Act had some effect. Bioff and Browne were convicted under it; so were those underworld figures—Campagna, Ricca, D'Andrea, Gioe and others—implicated by Bioff. In 1941, also, International Vice-President John P. Nick of the IATSE and Clyde Weston of the IATSE motion picture projectionists' local in St. Louis were convicted for extorting money from employers; they had evidently organized a sound equipment "service" agency to which various exhibitors felt obliged to subscribe. Other convictions were few and minor. Then, in 1942, the Supreme Court rendered a decision which seemed to many to seriously weaken the Act. New York Local 807 of the Teamsters had made a practice of imposing a levy on out-of-state trucks entering the city in order to compensate its members for "lost" work. Violence was involved, and the local was convicted of extortion under the Coleman Act. An appellate court, however, held that the levy amounted to the collection of *bona fide* wages and that no felony was involved.

The Congress was concerned, and in 1945 passed the Hobbs Act. The Act provided that anyone who "obstructs, delays or affects . . . commerce,

342

by robbery or extortion . . . shall be fined not more than $10,000 or imprisoned for not more than twenty years, or both. . . ." Unlike the Coleman Act, the Hobbs Act did not exempt the collection of wages from its prohibitions.

Only three minor cases were processed under the Hobbs Act until 1954, when the number of prosecutions turned upwards. Carl Bianchi of St. Louis Local 513 of the Operating Engineers was convicted for demanding three cents a foot on outside piping in return for labor peace. Paul H. Hulahan of Hod Carriers' Local 42 in Missouri received a twelve-year sentence for demanding $2,000 a month from a construction firm; "they're all paying it," he told one of his victims. Evan Dale, a business representative of the Hod Carriers and Common Laborers in Southern Illinois received a fifteen-year sentence for demanding a one percent commission on a $130,-000,000 atomic energy construction project; when Dale's demand was refused he embarked on a series of strikes, slowdowns and acts of sabotage which added an estimated $51,000,000 to the cost of construction. Anthony Provenzano, an international vice president of the Teamsters, was convicted for extorting $17,000 from a trucking company; his conviction was sustained by the Supreme Court, after which he was re-elected to local union office by a large majority. In all, there have been some one hundred convictions under the Hobbs Act.

The Taft-Hartley Act, passed in 1947 after a postwar wave of strikes, was designed primarily to circumscribe some of the traditional economic tactics of unions, not to regulate the process of union government or the morals of labor-management relations. It did, however, forbid the bribery of a union official by an employer, and made it an unfair labor practice to exact a payment for which no services were performed. The latter provision was directed mainly at featherbedding, but has had little history or effect. There have been some seventy convictions under the Act, most of them for bribery. Meantime, none of the States have had any laws dealing specifically with extortion or bribery in labor-management relations, although eleven of them have required the filing of union financial reports, with mild reprisals for violations of the law.

In sum, the federal law was concerned essentially with extortion from employers and bribery by them, and until the 1950's was only lightly enforced. The States showed little concern, and then only with accounting procedures. There was no major governmental intervention in either union government or the morals of labor-management relations. The crisis on the New York waterfront brought a change of pace.

On August 12, 1953, President Eisenhower signed into law a bi-state compact between New York and New Jersey—the Waterfront Commission Act—authorizing the establishment of the Waterfront Commission of New York Harbor.

The Act empowered the Commission to register longshoremen, checkers, port watchmen, pier superintendents, hiring agents and stevedores for work on the waterfront; to deny registration and thus employment on grounds of various felony and high misdemeanor convictions; to abolish public loading and transfer its functions to shippers, pier operators and stevedores; and to regularize waterfront employment through the operation of employment information centers throughout the harbor. It also enabled the effective disbarment of ex-convicts from elective office in ILA longshore locals—some thirty percent of the total in 1952—by making it a misdemeanor for such persons to collect dues or other moneys from registered longshoremen.

The Commission has registered all active workers covered by the Act, and has liberally exercised its power to deny or revoke the registration of some 5,000 longshoremen it considered undesirable. Once lost, registration is extremely hard to regain. In particular, ex-convicts must receive a certificate of good conduct from a parole board. These are often difficult to obtain, and in any event the Commission rejects applications for registration or re-registration if it has any doubts about the respectability of the applicants. Only a few hundred of those barred from the waterfront have been re-registered, usually under the sponsorship of a religious or community organization.

Waterfront employment has become a far less casual affair. Twice a year the Commission removes from the register all longshoremen who have not applied for work on at least eight days a month during five of the preceding six months. Registration and some hirings are administered through fifteen employment information centers. Permanent employees are hired through the centers or upon application to the Commission by employers. Regular gangs or employees report daily in most cases directly to the place of work by prearrangement between the employers, hiring agents and the Commission. About ninety percent of all longshoremen are so hired, knowing at least a day in advance if work will be available. The Commission reserves the right to cancel any arrangement if the numbers of employees or gangs requested is excessive.

The Commission has also imposed a seniority system on the industry. In 1957 the ILA and the NYSA, now more sensitive to the issue, negotiated a formal seniority agreement, but repeatedly ignored its provisions; in 1963 the Commission wrote a seniority system into its own regulations. All longshoremen are now classified into A, B, C and Casual categories, depending on their seniority. Even the Casuals have a form of seniority; they are divided into D-Men (those with two years' seniority), Medical Men (those with less than two years' seniority but who are physically acceptable for work), and the rest. Most gangs and individual longshoremen are identified with and enjoy seniority on particular piers.

The Commission has imposed other disciplines. It requires stevedoring companies to itemize disbursements and expenses and to submit to quarterly audits by the Commission. About twenty-five stevedoring firms have undergone major ownership changes, while nine—including some of the largest companies—have either sold out or dissolved. The audits, intended primarily to keep watch on dubious payments to shipping companies and union officials, showed a fifty-five percent decline in unsubstantiated cash outlays up to 1965. Further, a screening program has weeded out many of the older or less competent port watchmen; remaining and new watchmen are required to take qualifying examinations and triennial refresher courses. The Commission also conducts between 4,000 and 5,000 investigations a year of pilferage, gambling and loansharking, and engages in extensive litigation in furtherance of the purposes of the Act.

"Substantial progress," Waterfront Commissioner David C. Thompson testified at a legislative hearing in 1961, "has been made since 1953. . . . Unlawful 'quickie' strikes, commonly used for extortion by labor racketeers, have been reduced to a minimum. Violence as a means of determining the outcome of labor-management disputes appears to be a thing of the past. Swift and firm enforcement of the law has substantially reduced crime and corruption in all its forms and has resulted in a more general respect for law and order. The Commission has repressed and cut deeply into the profits of such waterfront racketeering as wage kickbacks, gambling, loansharking and pilferage. Commercial bribery by stevedores to employees and agents of steamship companies for procuring business and to union officials for labor peace has virtually disappeared. Particular progress has been made in reducing criminal influence in waterfront unions through the use of Section 8 [of the Act] to keep felons from union office . . . a longshoreman no longer has to wear a toothpick on his ear to show his willingness to pay a kickback to the hiring agent. . . . The pier head 'shape' is abolished."

The waterfront was a better place, but hardly a paradise. Pilferage, both casual and organized, continued at the rate of some $5,000,000 a year. Registered and licensed personnel continued to engage in loansharking and narcotics trafficking. The hiring of "phantoms" still went on. Port security was imperfect; the Commission required watchmen to keep log books of traffic on the piers, but many of the watchmen continued to play the old waterfront game of "D 'n' D" (deaf and dumb), not reporting all they saw. The employers, resentful of past revelations and the obligation to pay the costs of the Commission, opposed the keeping of log books and other records on the grounds that it was "an unnecessary clutter of paper"; they progressively reduced the number of watchmen employed as the ILA negotiated wage increases for them, actually spending $400,000 less on watchmen's wages in 1963 than in 1954. "It is regrettable," the Commission said, "that . . . elementary security standards must be established by government action of the Commission rather than industry initiative."

The ILA, in turn, was something less than a model union. It was almost wholly uncooperative with the Commission, initiating a long series of court actions designed to invalidate the Act or limit the powers of the Commission. ILA officials and gang foremen continued to appear in loansharking cases processed by the Commission. The union seemed to show little interest in financial or administrative propriety. It permitted local unions to cheat on their *per capita* taxes to the international union, and did not require financial reports from them, although it had the constitutional power to do so. It was even unable, when asked by the Commission, to provide a financial report on the *ILA Longshore News,* the international union's paper.

In 1958 the ILA made what it called a "serious attempt at centralization," claiming that it would issue membership books itself, insist on numbered receipts for dues paid, and require a uniform bookkeeping system of all local unions; but two and a half years later the rules were still unenforced. It evidently continued to issue local union charters without checking on the personal history or even the union membership of the applicants, and could provide no record of disciplinary action against any affiliates, some of which still held few or no meetings and submitted no financial reports to their members. It was evidently still a tolerant organization. "I do not know," Executive Director Myles Ambrose of the Waterfront Commission testified at its hearings in 1961, "of one corrective step taken by the leadership of the ILA. . . . The fact is that the leadership of the ILA had done nothing and will do nothing unless compelled by the law."

In 1960 the Commission had issued a special report, declaring that the aim of the States of New York and New Jersey to eliminate "criminal domination and control . . . has not been fully accomplished."

The report concentrated on the apparent sins of the ILA. Chenangoes —men who load and unload railroad lighters—were not covered by the Act, although they traditionally belonged to a number of ILA locals whose other members were covered. In 1955 the ILA chartered a separate local, Local 1826, for chenangoes. Two of the petitioners for the charter, Douglas Rago and James Vanderwyde, had criminal records. Rago had only recently come out of jail. Vanderwyde had just been released from parole, and together with Frank Gagliardi—who become business agent of the local—had been denied registration as a longshoreman. Four of the five officers of the new local had criminal records. George Barone, the president of the local, allegedly forced the *ILA Longshore News* to give jobs to waterfront hoodlums John ("Baseball Bat") Scanlon and Daniel St. John. Local 1826 also employed as a clerk one Edmund Flynn, an ex-convict and an alleged associate of major underworld figures Carlos Marciello and Ray Patriarca.

Freight packers, organized into Local 205, were also exempt from the Act. Barone was president of Local 205 as well. From 1953 to 1958, with one exception, all the principal officers of the Local had "serious criminal records." Three of them were eventually convicted for using their union positions to extort money from the employers.

Prior to 1957, pier and ship maintenance workers—all members of Local 1277—were not covered by the Act. In that year the law was amended to include pier maintenance workers. Battista Balsamo, a business agent of Local 1277, thus became ineligible for union office because of his long criminal record. The ILA then chartered a new Local 1277-1 for pier maintenance workers. Battista was thus able to continue as business agent for Local 1277. The separation of the locals was evidently a sham. They shared common headquarters and held joint meetings presided over by the president of Local 1277. The same secretary-treasurer served both locals. The recording secretary for Local 1277 kept the minutes for both organizations, and indeed when questioned by the Commission claimed that he did not know of the separation until six months after it took place. Anthony Miascana, the nominal president of Local 1277-1, was not even present at the meeting of the local when he was elected. When the Waterfront Commission examined the books of both locals a total of $16,000 was missing.

Two New Jersey affiliates of the ILA, Local 1823 and Local 1478, represented warehouse workers not covered by the Act. Frank ("Machine Gun") Campbell, allegedly a former member of the Arsenal Mob and "one of the most notorious mobsters on the New York waterfront scene," was said to have controlled Local 1478 from 1956 and Local 1823 from 1958. He was president and business agent of Local 1478, although he was ineligible for registration as a longshoreman because of his convictions for assault, robbery, and using dangerous weapons. He refused to testify at a New Jersey legislative hearing in 1960 on his relationship with Local 1823. Lucy Panzini, a Hoboken tavern owner who was not a member of the ILA, was listed as the president of Local 1478 but did not know it. Other individuals, not members of the local, were also listed as holding office. With the advent of the 1960 hearings the books of both locals disappeared.

In September, 1959, President William E. Bradley of the ILA appointed Anthony ("Tony Cheese") Marchitto as trustee of both locals. Marchitto, Bradley said, was "the last guy I would have put any place, but I had no-body else." Marchitto refused to testify on his activities in the two locals, and was indicted three times for non-compliance with subpoenas. Campbell continued his association with Local 1478, sharing with Vice-President Joseph ("Heels") Murphy of Local 1823 the sole right to draw on the bank deposits of the latter organization. Both men refused to explain at the hearings the withdrawals they had made.

Ex-convicts were ineligible for elective office in locals covered by the Act, but could accept appointive jobs. Five of the six appointed investigators for the NYSA-ILA welfare fund had served time in jail. Ex-convicts allegedly controlled the welfare fund of Local 205. John Keefe resigned his elective vice presidency of "Pistol Local" 824 in Manhattan, but returned as a clerk at the highest salary paid by the local. George DeVeau evidently resigned as secretary-treasurer of Local 1346 under threat of prosecution, but came back as a custodian and clerk; the secretary-treasurership remained open. In all, some twenty-two enforced retirees found other work in the ILA.

"It is vain to hope," the Commission reported, "that mere exposure of these conditions will impel the International to clean up its own house . . . the International has been and continues to be either unable or unwilling to eliminate criminal influence in the ILA . . . [it] has aided and abetted criminals to control and dominate locals outside the purview of Section 8 . . . [it] has completely failed in its legal and moral obligations to supervise the procedures and finances of its locals." The Commission asked the legislatures of New York and New Jersey to extend the coverage of Section 8 to include all welfare fund personnel and employees as well as officers of the ILA; to add certain misdemeanors as grounds for disbarment from registration; to require the registration of chenangoes; and to prohibit interference "with the duties of licensed or registered personnel without justification in law."

The ILA opposed the requested changes. It introduced a resolution at the 1961 convention of the AFL-CIO, describing the Waterfront Commission Act as harsh and discriminatory, accusing the Commission of denying jobs to hundreds of deserving longshoremen and acting as a strikebreaking agency, and recommending that Congress withdraw its consent to the Act. The convention referred the resolution to the Executive Council without approving it. At the 1963 convention, the ILA proposed that New York and New Jersey be asked either to abolish the Commission or to return hiring on the waterfront to the joint control of labor and management. The Resolutions Committee of the convention expressed its general sympathy, but recommended that the matter be referred to the Executive Council "for appropriate action to correct the undesirable situation."

Meanwhile, the federation had opposed two bills introduced in the New York and New Jersey State legislatures to give effect to the Commission's recommendations, on the grounds that the bills "would present the specter of imprisonment each time workers and their unions engaged in an economic struggle to secure better wages and improved working conditions." There was also resentment at the fact that restrictions on members and officers of the ILA were not applied to employers. "I suggest to you," Paul Hall said at the 1961 hearings, "that management could not meet these requirements . . . there are people in high places in management in this industry who could not even work as an office boy for the ILA. . . ." Nonetheless, New York and New Jersey expanded the Commission's powers substantially as requested. Murphy, Rago, Vanderwyde, Gagliardi and others lost their jobs with the ILA.

Conditions continued to improve. The longshore work force was reduced from 51,000 in 1953 to some 22,000 in 1967. Regularity in employment was now the rule, with New York something of an exemplar. "New York," the United States Bureau of Labor Statistics reported, "is the only port on the Atlantic and Gulf Coasts to have achieved a relative stability in longshore employment." Casual workers—those hired for less than 700 hours a year—constituted from a third to a half of the work force in other ports, but only seven percent in New York. The average annual earnings of longshoremen and checkers rose from $2,356 in 1953 to over $7,000 in 1967, with fifteen percent earning more than $10,000.

The ILA itself improved. Its collective bargaining became more aggressive, accounting for some twenty-five percent of increased earnings. Most of the undesirables were gone from office, the remainder showed a new solicitude for the grievances of their members. Union fiscal administration became a more systematic and careful affair, the "cookie jar" treasury of the past now replaced in many cases by computers. Emboldened by job security and the presence of the Commission, ILA members attended meetings in greater numbers than before, often criticizing and even abusing their officers, sometimes even changing policies and supporting opposition candidates. Given the past record, the improvements were substantial.

The Commission has not been immune to criticism. Its rule, the critics say, is too strict, smacking of police-state methods. Every longshoreman charged with or arrested for any crime under federal or state law—except for traffic offenses—must notify the Commission within twenty days. He must then appear for an interview, and if he refuses to testify he is suspended until the court charges are disposed of. The punishment is severe for working longshoremen, and can be irrelevant to waterfront employment: one man was suspended for fighting a taxi driver far from the docks, another for beating his wife. Critics also charge that the Commission is prosecutor, judge and jury rolled into one, for it employs its own hearing officers, and sometimes overrules them when it thinks their decisions are too lenient. Longshoremen can appeal only to the courts—an impractical resource for most of them. The Commission has consistently opposed proposals for an independent board of review.

The ILA has accused the Commission of strikebreaking by issuing temporary registrations to white-collar and supervisory employees, allowing them to carry baggage and perform other manual tasks during work stoppages. It also charges that the Commission undermines the cohesion and bargaining strength of the union by refusing to close the register in spite of a surplus of longshoremen, thus encouraging a constant influx of inexperienced and uncommitted workmen. The NYSA, after years of opposition to the ILA on this point, now supports the closing of the register. The Commission concedes that there is an occasional surplus of labor, but contends that it is necessary for dirty work. On the other hand, the ILA and the NYSA have negotiated an agreement which permits the rotation of men in unpleasant jobs in return for a guarantee of continuous work, and the U.S. Department of Labor has explicitly recommended closing the register or otherwise reducing the inflow of new applicants. The Commission claims it has no power to close the register; but when the NYSA tried to close it in effect by denying medical clearance to new applicants, the Commission obtained a court restraining order against the shipping companies.

Incompetence is another issue. Few of the Commission's staff have had previous waterfront experience, and there is a considerable turnover. Some critics charge that the Commission is a sanctuary for political hacks, for politicians and lawyers between campaign or jobs, and that in general it is insensitive to the problems and folkways of longshoremen, more concerned with control than understanding, more involved with petty delinquencies than the root causes of major corruption. "Only a few of the centers are doing their job," a director of one of the employment information centers told writer Budd Schulberg. "We're supposed to *help* the men, not police them. Too many of the center directors are men of lower caliber who got there through their political connections. . . . An investigator catches a man stealing a bottle. Well, hell. That isn't the biggest crime on the waterfront. . . . Too many of these investigators are retired detectives who have the small-mind-cop mentality. . . . In this center we've got the confidence of the men and they come to us with their problems. We loan them a deuce or a pound if things are slow. They don't go to their union delegates with their beefs because they don't trust them. You won't find any of this in the Waterfront Commission charter. We play it by ear, in an area where the shipping companies have never felt any responsibility to their employees and where the union is still tainted with the same old tough-guy psychology . . . I think the trouble with Park Row [the Commission's headquarters] is that they're in an ivory tower. They never drop in and see what's really going on. That's one reason they don't realize how unpopular the Commission really is. . . . They've got to stop harassing these men individually, concentrate more on the criminal element that's either back or trying to get back in. . . ."

There is another grievance. Public loading is gone, but old problems remain. Traffic congestion is still severe despite large expenditures on port rehabilitation. The only change, according to Schulberg, has been from centralized graft to a "democratic shakedown." "Hell," said Hugh Sheridan, the head of a trucking association, "I wish we had the public loaders back. . . . The loader used to work by the tonnage, pieceload. Now the stevedores charge us by the hour, and the longshoremen they pick are the bottom of the barrel. Guys with pressed pants and their shoes polished. . . . It takes four hours just to get onto the docks. . . . We used to get two loads a day out of the trucks. Now it sometimes takes as long as two days to get rid of just a single load. . . . You tip the pier boss to get a higher priority number to get your rig onto the pier. If you want a hi-lo [forklift] driver to get you out first, you slip him a pound. You have to get the checker to your truck at the same time, so you slip the checker a deuce or a pound.* And so it goes, day in and day out all around the harbor. If it was ever added up, I think the shakedown runs us higher than before. . . . And the Waterfront Commission hasn't done a damn thing about it. . . . Why don't they get busy and move in on this racket?" The Commission had an answer. "We've been urging them to report the shakedowns," legal counsel William P. Sirignano told Schulberg. "The only way we can help them is if they tell us what's going on under the table. They complain about it to you, but they don't report it to me."

The old ways of the waterfront die hard. It is a better place, but habit, self-interest and lasting circumstances are powerful factors. The logistical shortcomings of the harbor are still an inducement to graft. The ILA and the NYSA are less than perfect allies of the Commission. Men

* A deuce is two dollars, a pound is five.

barred from longshoring return to the waterfront in ancillary trades, ready to resume their former depredations. Pilferage, loansharking and extortion still go on. Racketeers are still a power in some places; according to one observer they "run most Jersey docks as if the Waterfront Commission never existed." They linger around the waterfront, taking what they can, awaiting a relaxation of the law. "Actually," New York Port Authority Director Austin J. Tobin said, "the hoodlums never went away."

The ILA wants the Commission abolished, but the union's own credentials are in doubt. "If [the ILA] . . . had proven that it could responsibly protect the employment rights of bona fide longshoremen," one of the most experienced observers of the waterfront has written, "it would be in a different position." The ILA has few allies. The AFL-CIO accepted the ILA back as an affiliate probably more from a fear that the ILA would join the Teamsters than from a conviction that it was fully redeemed as a union, and may have lingering doubts; the federation has sympathized strongly with the ILA's grievances against the Commission, but has stopped short of recommending that the Commission should go. The NYSA has attacked and obstructed the Commission on various grounds and occasions, but draws the line at full condemnation. "Our overall position with respect to the Waterfront Commission remains unchanged," one of its representatives wrote, "namely that as long as the conditions which brought the Commission into existence prevail it should be continued as a regulatory body." Unpopular on the waterfront but strong in public esteem, imperfect in performance but valued in service, the Commission can probably look forward to a long life.

Fear of reversion is the key. "I haven't the slightest doubt," Tobin said, "but that, without the Commission, the situation would revert immediately to the jungle it was before."

"God save labor," Samuel Gompers once said, "from the courts." His view, born of long experience with the bench, was shared by most of those who accompanied or came after him in the labor movement. None held it more strongly than Hoffa, yet he was party to a unique legal arrangement —what Justice Felix Frankfurter called "a most unusual manifestation of the equity powers" of a court: the supervision of the affairs of the Teamsters by a court-appointed and court-governed Board of Monitors.

The seventeenth convention of the Teamsters was scheduled to take place in September, 1957, not long after the McClellan Committee had begun its investigation of the union. Beck was under a heavy cloud, and his departure from office seemed certain. Hoffa was in the lead to succeed him, and was evidently bent on ignoring the directive of the AFL-CIO to eliminate corrupt elements from the union. Shortly before the convention was due to open, thirteen rank and file Teamsters from New York City petitioned for a court injunction to prohibit the holding of the convention; they charged that many of the delegates had been improperly elected, and asked for the appointment by the court of a master or receiver to supervise the election of delegates to a new convention and to correct "constitutional abuses and corrupt practices" in the union.

Judge F. Dickinson Letts of the Washington, D.C., federal district court enjoined the convention. The appellate court reversed the injunction; the convention was held; and Hoffa was elected president of the Teamsters. The thirteen dissidents went back to Letts and obtained an injunction barring Hoffa and other officers-elect from taking office. After a long and highly complex series of legal moves and negotiations, the union and the dissidents agreed to a consent order by Judge Letts which allowed the elected officers to assume their positions temporarily and set up a Board of Monitors whose duty—under the direction of the court—was to "counsel with" and make "recommendations" to the Teamsters on the financial and governmental procedures of the union. The Monitors were also instructed to draft a model set of local union bylaws, and were given permission to suggest changes in the Teamsters' constitution. There were to be three Monitors —one chosen by the dissidents, one by the union, and one mutually agreed upon by the parties; the union was to bear all the costs. The Monitors were to stay in office until a new convention could be held. The new convention could be called by the Teamsters' General Executive Board anytime after the expiration of one year from the date of the consent order.

Relations between the Teamsters and the Monitors were harmonious for some time. The chairman of the Monitors, retired Judge Nathan Cayton of the District of Columbia bench, resigned after four months but spoke of the "enlightened cooperation" of the union. On the other hand Godfrey P. Schmidt, attorney for the dissidents and their representative on the Board of Monitors, thought that the Monitors were too lenient with the provisional officers of the union and should act more like receivers. Martin O'Donoghue, who had represented the Teamsters in the early litigation, now became chairman of the Monitors, but quickly confounded expectations. He held that the Monitors had mandatory powers, and with Schmidt's support began issuing "Orders of Recommendation" [sic] with the intent of reforming the union and ousting Hoffa from the presidency. Judge Letts ruled that the union would be subject to judicial sanctions if it did not obey the Orders, but the appellate court found that the Monitors had only advisory powers; their orders were legally enforceable only if the district court ordered their adoption.

Meanwhile, Judge Letts had unilaterally amended the consent order by transferring to the Monitors the right given to the General Executive Board to call a convention. O'Donoghue continued his attempts to remove Hoffa from office; but the General Executive Board, the only body with the power to try Hoffa, refused to do so. O'Donoghue asked the federal district court to try the Teamster president, but Letts refused. Relations between the Teamsters and the Monitors continued to worsen. The union accused the Monitors of improperly interfering in its affairs. The Monitors complained that the union was harrying them with trivial correspondence, by delaying payment of expenses, and by refusing to cooperate even in minor matters. The friction produced thirty-five appeals from district court decisions, several petitions to the United States Supreme Court, and a "nightmarish deluge" of procedural actions in court. O'Donoghue failed in his major objectives and resigned as chairman of the Monitors in July, 1960. Bad relations and tortuous legal actions continued. Judge Letts finally ordered the Monitors to take a vacation while he studied the materials. In January, 1961 he agreed to let the Teamsters hold another election and thus brought the monitorship to an end.

The Monitors did have some laudable effect. The Teamsters adopted their suggestions for changes in the union's trial and appellate procedure and in the union's bookkeeping system, although a professional accountant's survey of that system had found little to criticize. They also accepted new rules for local elections and took back several expelled members.

Otherwise, the Teamsters went their own way. They "approved" the Monitors' recommendations on local union bylaws, but left their implementation up to the local unions themselves. They did not accept the Monitors' suggestions for constitutional changes. Some progress was made in releasing local unions from trusteeship, but the process came almost to a halt during O'Donoghue's chairmanship. There were a few resignations and trials of suspect officials, but most suspects went untroubled.

The McClellan Committee was now disbanded, but a subcommittee of the Senate Committee on Government Operations—also under the chairmanship of Senator McClellan—conducted its own investigation of the monitorship in 1961. O'Donoghue was the chief witness. He reported some progress in election and auditing procedures, but little in eliminating corrupt officials. "In my opinion," he said, ". . . the defendant provisional officers have not taken proper remedial action against those union members, particularly officers, guilty of violating fiduciary standards and their obligations [under] . . . the international constitution. . . . The board of monitors' recommendations concerning these individuals have met with stiff resistance. . . ."

O'Donoghue cited Frank Matula as an example. Matula was given six months' imprisonment and five years' probation with a $2,500 fine for perjury as a result of the McClellan Committee's investigation into the garbage industry. Hoffa appointed him trustee of the international union after the sentence but before the disposition of Matula's appeal. The appellate court sustained the sentence and Matula went to jail in October, 1959. In January, 1960, he was released temporarily on petition of the Teamsters to audit the union's books, then returned to jail. He remained as trustee during and after his imprisonment.

There were others, according to O'Donoghue, who went unpunished by the union. John McNamara, president of New York Local 295 and secretary-treasurer of Local 808, was convicted of extortion. Hoffa then appointed him a general organizer for aviation freight carriers, promised later to take action against him, but did not. "He has done absolutely nothing," O'Donoghue said, "and that fellow is a scoundrel. He shouldn't be in charge of any local union. . . ." In another instance, the Monitors found that Anthony Provenzano, president of Hoboken Local 560 and Teamsters' Joint Council 73 in Newark, New Jersey, had demanded and received money from two employers under contract to Local 560 to maintain labor peace. They recommended that the Teamsters remove Provenzano temporarily from office and bring charges against him. Instead, Hoffa made him an international vice president of the union. Provenzano was later convicted of extortion, then re-elected to all his offices while under conviction.

The Monitors found that Joseph Glimco of Chicago Local 777 had failed to provide a bond on his services as required by the Teamsters' constitution and the law, had received kickbacks, and had engaged in extortion. They recommended that Local 777 be placed in trusteeship, but Hoffa refused. He said he would prefer charges against Glimco, but did not.

Harold Gross, formerly of New York Local 138 of the Teamsters and New Local 1730 of the ILA, became president of Teamster Local 320 in Miami after being involved in shakedown activities against the Neo-Gravure Printing Company of New York. The Monitors recommended that Gross be temporarily removed from office and put on trial. In support of their recommendation they cited Article XVIII, Section 13(a) of the Teamsters' constitution, which provided that any member of the Teamsters convicted of a crime or serious wrongdoing tending to bring dishonor on the union should be expelled. No action was taken by the union until Gross was convicted of an income tax violation arising out of the Neo-Gravure case. He was then allowed to resign and given an honorable withdrawal card. Article XVIII, Section 13(a) was expunged from the Teamsters' constitution at the 1961 convention.

Raymond Cohen, president of Philadelphia Local 107 of the Teamsters and a trustee of the international union, was accused in testimony before the McClellan Committee of involvement in the squandering of more than $200,000 in local union funds. The Monitors recommended an investigation by the international union. "Mr. O'Donoghue," Teamster Secretary-Treasurer John F. English evidently said, "I think it [local 107] should be put into trusteeship. It is a bad situation." A firm of accountants submitted a report to Hoffa apparently substantiating most of the charges made against Local 107 by a group of rank and file members; among the exhibits were a number of local union checks with forged endorsements. Hoffa appointed an investigating panel of two union officials and an outside member. The accountants' report was not given to the panel. Rank and file complainants were not allowed legal counsel. Cohen was not called as a witness, since he and five other officials of Local 107 had been indicted in a Philadelphia court on charges of forgery, conspiracy, and misappropriation of funds. Hoffa told the Committee that Cohen had told him that he was innocent of any wrongdoing. "I had no reason to disbelieve Cohen," Hoffa said. No action was taken against Cohen by the international union. The Government Operations subcommittee concluded "that Hoffa has used every means available to thwart bona fide attempts on the part of the U.S. district court-appointed monitors to accomplish a clean-up of corrupt and criminal elements within the Teamster movement."

The achievements of the Monitors were meager, and very expensive for the Teamsters. By the end of 1960 they had cost the union $634,026 in direct expenses and probably over $1,000,000 in legal fees.

There were several reasons for the failure of the Monitors. Their powers were never clear; the courts disagreed on the matter, and there were frequent squabbles among the Monitors themselves over what they could or could not do. There was obvious and very strong resistance by the Teamsters to the encroachments of the Monitors, and a massive counter-attack by the union in the courts. The union never agreed that the Monitors had mandatory powers, nor did it agree with the view of Letts and O'Donoghue that the acceptance by the Teamsters of the consent order implied an admission of guilt. There was a frequent change in the personnel of the Monitors accompanied by a steadily increasing acrimony in relationships; in particular, there was a sharp feud between Hoffa and O'Donoghue, no doubt exacerbated by the fact that O'Donoghue was a former Teamster lawyer.

The unity of the Teamsters' resistance to the Monitors was encouraged by the apparent liaison between Robert F. Kennedy and those Monitors antagonistic to Hoffa. The credibility of the Monitors was damaged by the finding of an appellate court that Godfrey Schmidt engaged in conflict of interest activities while he was a Monitor by representing various employers in negotiations with the Teamsters; he was obliged to resign from the Board of Monitors, but was allowed to designate his successor.

The law was weak and the Teamsters were strong. The Board of Monitors was essentially a failure. The last indication of its futility came when, after deciding that each delegate to the next Teamsters' convention should receive a full report on the Board's activities, it could not agree on a final text. "The monitorship," Sam Romer said, ". . . must be laid to rest without even an obituary." But if the experiment was futile, it was also an alarming one. The unilateral amendment of the consent order by Judge Letts, which destroyed the logic of the arrangement, was an ominous precedent. Monitorship was not destined for popularity.

"There is almost complete unanimity in labor and management circles," the McClellan Committee said, "that . . . [welfare] funds should be subject to some federal regulation and control." The sentiment was shared by Congress; only six states had laws requiring the disclosure and regulation of welfare fund operations, and except for the minimal stipulations of the Taft-Hartley Act there was no federal law on the matter at all.

There was agreement in principle, but not in detail. The Senate passed a relatively strong bill in 1958. Virtually all health and pension plans were covered, including those administered unilaterally by employers as well as those run jointly by unions and employers or run by unions alone; only those plans with less than one hundred members were to be exempted. All plans were to file annual reports with the Secretary of Labor while making them available to beneficiaries and other interested persons. The Secretary would be empowered to make regulations affecting the preparation and submission of reports, to conduct investigations of health and pension plans, and to institute court actions against those seeming to break the law. Violations of the new law were to be punishable by imprisonment for up to five years and a fine of not more than $5,000. Embezzlement of funds would be punishable by five years in jail and a fine of $10,000.

The House passed a much milder bill. It required only sketchy reporting and gave the Secretary of Labor only custodial authority over the documents; it denied him the power to issue regulations or to initiate investigations and court actions, directing him merely to make the reports available for inspection in the public documents room of the Department of Labor. Plans with fewer than twenty-five beneficiaries were exempted. The maximum jail sentence for violating such requirements as the bill provided was to be six months, with a maximum fine of $1,000; there was no penalty for embezzlement. Enforcement of the law was the duty of the beneficiaries of the plan.

The Welfare and Pension Plans Disclosure bill finally adopted by the Congress—with minor concessions to the Senate—was essentially the House bill. Plans covering not more than twenty-five persons were exempted, and deliberate misrepresentation in reports was made punishable by five years in jail and a fine of $10,000. Otherwise, the House version prevailed.

The bill was modest in aim. It was, according to Representative Lee Metcalf of Montana, an "attempt at self-policing of pension and welfare funds by the employers and employees without establishing a centralized investigative agency and complex reporting, accounting and registration procedures in addition to the disclosure." Plan descriptions and annual reports were to be submitted to the Secretary of Labor, but all he could do was to make them available for scrutiny by interested parties. Beneficiaries were entitled to reports on request, but only in summary form. The Secretary was empowered to prepare forms for use in making reports, but their adoption was optional. Enforcement was left entirely to beneficiaries and participants in welfare fund administration. Beneficiaries could sue administrators for non-compliance with requests for reports, and if successful could collect fifty dollars for each day of non-compliance, together with costs and reasonable attorney's fees; they could also seek injunctions to restrain the violation of the disclosure provisions of the bill. Violations were punishable by six months in jail and a fine of $1,000. The Secretary of Labor had no role in enforcement at all.

President Eisenhower reluctantly signed the bill into law. He signed it, he said, only because "it establishes a precedent of Federal responsibility in this area. It does little else. . . . If the bill is to be at all effective, it will require extensive amendment at the next session of Congress."

The Act was both inadequate and ignored. It went into force on the first day of 1959. By March, Secretary of Labor James P. Mitchell was complaining that many plans were simply not complying with the duty to report; the following year he asked, without success, for enforcement powers to deal with kickbacks, embezzlement, and other abuses. In 1961, Secretary of Labor Arthur J. Goldberg said that some 27,000 union welfare and pension plans out of a total of 152,000 were delinquent in their reports, that the Department had no means of checking the accuracy of the information given, and that the requirement of only summary information was an incentive to deception.

The notion of self-policing, Goldberg told the Congress, was "the ultimate in unreality. . . . Experience has shown that employee suits, if provided as a means of enforcement, are seldom pursued. . . . Individual employees, lacking financial resources, can easily be intimidated, subjected to reprisals, and discouraged from taking effective action. To the best of our knowledge, only one beneficiary suit has been instituted under the Disclosure Act."

Congress amended the Act in 1962. The amendments were supported by the AFL-CIO, although not by the National Association of Manufacturers or the United States Chamber of Commerce.

The amended Act requires the submission of plan descriptions and annual reports in the form prescribed by the Secretary of Labor, and stipulates in detail the kind of information to be provided. The Secretary is authorized to issue written and binding interpretations of the Act. All administrators, officers and employees of welfare funds must take out fidelity bonds under rules prescribed by the Secretary, who is also empowered to conduct investigations of plans where he believes violations of the law might have occurred, to command testimony, and to initiate injunction proceedings; criminal proceedings are referred to the Department of Justice. Embezzlement, theft and misrepresentation in reporting are punishable by five years in jail and a fine of $10,000; the offering or acceptance of bribes or kickbacks is punishable by three years in jail and a fine of $10,000.

The Act is administered by the Office of Labor-Management and Welfare-Pension Reports (OLMWPR) of the Department of Labor. The enforcement powers granted by the amended Act, the OLMWPR has stated, have been concentrated on securing "voluntary compliance with the reporting provisions of the Act." An overwhelming majority of actions by the Office are concerned with overdue or deficient plan descriptions and annual reports; almost all actions are resolved by voluntary action. The Office also receives a large number of requests for help in collecting benefits allegedly due to the correspondents from one fund or another; but the letters rarely allege violations of the Act, which does not in any case permit the Secretary to assist individuals in the collection of benefits. There are some 170,000 active health and pension plans covered by the Act, representing assets of perhaps $80,000,000,000. The OLMWPR disposes of between 500 and 1,000 cases a year. Less than one hundred have been referred to the Department of Justice since 1962 for criminal prosecution.

The amended Act, indeed, seems to have had a most uncontroversial life. There appear to be no important criticisms of its administration, nor any strong demand for its amendment.

"God save us," George Meany told a Senate Subcommittee, "from our friends." Senator John F. Kennedy had asked him if he would support various proposals for labor reform legislation made by academicians reputedly friendly to organized labor. Meany, always suspicious of the academic embrace, was in any case skeptical of further attempts to regulate trade union affairs. The AFL-CIO had supported the passage of the Welfare and Pension Plans Disclosure Act and its amendments, promulgated its own codes of ethical behavior, completed most of its own disciplining of corrupt elements, and moreover had become very critical—particularly since the investigation of the Kohler strike—of the motives and activities of the McClellan Committee.

The federation was especially fearful of punitive legislation irrelevant to corruption. "The AFL-CIO favors and will support," the Executive Council said, "such other legislative measures as may be needed to protect trade unions and their members from those, whether within the ranks of labor or management or outside, who seek to despoil or exploit unions or union members. Such legislation should be directed to meet specific disclosed abuses which cannot be adequately dealt with without Government help; and undue and unnecessary legislation should be avoided. . . . The AFL-CIO will resist to the utmost any and every proposal which, under the guise of seeking to protect workers from corruption or improper activities, seeks instead to destroy honest, decent American trade unions, or to weaken their ability to fulfill their responsibilities. . . ."

However, it was clear that the Congress intended to enact new labor legislation of one kind or another, and the AFL-CIO soon endorsed legislation requiring detailed union reports on finances, trusteeships and elections; it also asked for amendments to the Taft-Hartley Act which would loosen existing restrictions on picketing, boycotting and striking activities. John Kennedy conducted hearings on labor reform legislation, and together with Senator Irving M. Ives of New York introduced a bill in 1958 which proposed secret ballot elections for local union officials; detailed reports on union finances, conflicts of interest, trusteeships, and employer payments to consultants; the adoption of codes of ethical practices by both labor and management; and various ameliorative changes in the economic provisions of the Taft-Hartley Act. The AFL-CIO supported the bill, which passed the Senate by a large majority.

Trouble developed in the House of Representatives. Conservatives said the bill was not strong enough. Business lobbyists, little interested in legislation on internal union affairs, campaigned almost exclusively for stronger restrictions on union economic activities. Some labor lobbyists, formally in support of the bill, allegedly worked quietly against it. The AFL-CIO, busy with other legislative problems, did not fight strongly for the bill. Despite a personal intervention by Speaker Sam Rayburn to bring the matter to a vote, the bill died in committee.

The 1958 Congressional elections were a landslide for the Democrats, bringing the defeat of a number of conservative Republicans who had opposed the AFL-CIO's legislative program. There were now large and evidently invincible majorities for the Democrats in both houses, and clear, pro-labor majorities on both the Senate and House labor committees. "America," said Republican Postmaster-General Arthur Summerfield, "teeters on the precipice of a labor-bossed Congress. . . ." Several Democratic presidential aspirants were now in the field, anxious to court the AFL-CIO and the labor vote. The AFL-CIO, in turn, had expended great energies on the election of Democratic friends, and expected a return. The portents were favorable for a labor reform law that the AFL-CIO could support. As it happened, the federation lost the battle.

The new Congress assembled in January, 1959. Ives, a liberal Republican, had retired. Democrat Kennedy was unable to find another Republican co-sponsor, and finally joined with Senator Sam J. Ervin of North Carolina—a conservative Democrat—in introducing a bill very similar to the Kennedy-Ives original proposal. Republican Senator Barry Goldwater of Arizona introduced the Eisenhower Administration's bill, which provided for stricter penalties than the Kennedy-Ives bill, and also proposed new restrictions on picketing and boycotting. Senator McClellan, a Democrat, introduced a "Bill of Rights" for union members to be attached to the Kennedy-Ives bill; the amendment provided for equal rights for all union members, freedom of speech and assembly on union matters, freedom from arbitrary union assessments and penalties, and for the right of union members to inspect membership lists and sue a union. The AFL-CIO opposed the McClellan amendment on the grounds that it might produce a welter of nuisance legislation.

The Senate passed the Kennedy-Ervin bill almost as it was introduced; only Senator Goldwater voted against it. But the Senate also accepted the McClellan amendment after an emotional appeal by its author, although it later softened the measure after Southern Senators evidently realized that it might be used to open up union membership to Negroes and to justify greater federal intervention in the field of civil rights. The bill now went to the House, with the announced opposition of the AFL-CIO.

The House Committee on Education and Labor reported out a bill, sponsored by Representative Carl Elliott of Alabama, which even when amended was more lenient to labor than the Kennedy-Ervin bill. Nevertheless, the AFL-CIO refused to endorse it, and supported a still milder measure submitted by Representative John F. Shelley of San Francisco, a former Teamster official who enjoyed AFL-CIO support. Meanwhile, Democratic Representative Philip M. Landrum of Georgia and Republican Representative Robert P. Griffin of Michigan had introduced a bill which provided for severe penalties for various offenses and incorporated a number of restrictions on union economic activities. President Eisenhower endorsed it, as did most conservatives and moderates on both sides of the House. Business groups, pleased with the economic provisions of the bill, mounted a publicity drive for its adoption allegedly more highly organized and financed than any political campaign "ever undertaken by business in the past."

Labor was divided. The AFL-CIO remained officially in favor of the Shelley bill, but not all unions supported it strongly. Various railroad and building trades unions lobbied for economic protections of their own, neglecting other issues. The United Mine Workers and the Teamsters opposed any labor reform legislation at all. Hundreds of labor lobbyists, officials and members descended on Capitol Hill; but they came on many missions, contributing, by one account, "much to the bedlam but little to the cause of labor." The Shelley bill was defeated, leaving only a choice between the Elliott and Landrum-Griffin bills. Elliott, an influential moderate, was absent during the crucial votes on the floor of the House. President Eisenhower, in a nationwide radio and television broadcast, called for passage of the Landrum-Griffin bill. The Senate-House conference softened some of the bill's economic restrictions—offering special union security protections to unions in the construction and garment trades, relaxing some restrictions on picketing, and allowing economic strikers to vote in union representation elections—but the bill was still unpalatable to the AFL-CIO. The bill, as amended, passed the House and Senate by overwhelming majorities, and President Eisenhower signed it into law.

The Labor-Management Reporting and Disclosure Act of 1959—or Landrum-Griffin Act as it is popularly called—is an ambitious attempt so to regulate the government of unions and the relations between labor and management as to greatly reduce the opportunities and increase the dangers of corruption.

The "Bill of Rights"—Title I of the Act—protects the rights of union members to nominate candidates, to vote in union elections and referendums, and to participate fully in union meetings subject only to reasonable rules and regulations. It guarantees the right of free speech and free assembly in union affairs, again subject only to reasonable rules of conduct. It prohibits the raising of dues and levying of assessments except by secret ballot in local unions, or by proper action of executive boards, convention delegates or secret ballot referendums of the membership in the case of national unions. It protects the right of a member to sue his union, provided only that he may first be required to exhaust available internal remedies for a maximum period of four months, and that no employer or employers' association may support a member's legal action against his union. A union member may not be disciplined, except for non-payment of dues, unless he has been served with written charges, given time to prepare his defense, and afforded a "full and fair hearing." (Elsewhere the Act provides that no member may be disciplined for exercising his rights under it, and makes it a crime to "restrain, coerce, or intimidate" any member trying to do so.) Unions must provide their members with copies of collective bargaining agreements upon request, and inform them of the provisions of the Act. Title I is enforceable, not only by aggrieved individuals, but by the Secretary of Labor, who may petition the courts for relief if he believes that anyone has violated or is about to violate it.

Title II of the Act outlines the reporting requirements of the Act. All labor organizations, except state and local central bodies, must file annual reports with the Secretary of Labor, reporting on such matters as dues, fees, assessments, insurance contributions, salaries, loans and other disbursements. They must also report on qualifications for union membership, procedures for the calling of meetings and the holding of elections, disciplinary provisions and actions, bargaining activities, strike votes and contract approvals, and the issuance of work permits. All union officers and employees, other than clerical and custodial employees, must report any financial benefit they or members of their close families have received from any employer whose employees are represented by the union in question, or from any labor consultant to such an employer. Employers must report certain types of payments, made or promised, to union representatives, union members or labor consultants. The Act adds to the prohibitions of the Taft-Hartley Act by making it illegal for an employer to make or agree to make loans to union officials, employees and members under certain conditions, or for union representatives to demand or receive such loans. Violations of Title II are punishable by both criminal and civil sanctions.

Reports on trusteeships, required under Title III, must be filed with the Secretary of Labor within thirty days of imposition, and semiannually thereafter. Reasons must be given for a trusteeship, which is permissible only "for the purpose of correcting corruption or financial malpractice, assuring the performance of collective bargaining agreements or other duties of a bargaining representative, restoring democratic procedures, or otherwise carrying out the legitimate objects" of a union. It is unlawful to count the votes of a trusteed local in a union convention unless the delegates from the local have been chosen by secret ballot in an election in which all members in good standing were able to participate; it is also illegal to transfer to a national union from a trusteed local any monies save the normal *per capita* taxes and assessments levied on all affiliates.

The Secretary of Labor must investigate any complaint he receives to the effect that the law on trusteeships has been violated. If he finds probable cause to believe that the complaint is justified he must—without disclosing the identity of the complainant—bring a civil action in the courts for relief; so may any member or subordinate body of the union involved. In any case, a trusteeship properly established under the law and union rules is presumed valid for only a year and a half. After that it is presumed invalid, and may be continued only upon evidence satisfactory to the Secretary that it is necessary for a purpose allowed by the law.

Title IV deals with union elections. All national labor organizations, with the exception of the AFL-CIO itself and its subordinate state and local bodies, must elect their officers at least once every five years either by secret ballot referendum of the membership or by convention delegates elected by secret ballot. Intermediate labor bodies, such as regions or districts of a national union, must hold elections at least every four years by secret ballot referendum or by open ballot among delegates elected by secret ballot. Local unions must elect officials at least every three years by secret ballot. Unions must also comply with "all reasonable requests" by candidates for help in distributing campaign literature among the membership at the candidates' expense, or under conditions applicable to all candidates. Candidates have the right to inspect membership lists and to post observers at the polls and at the counting of the ballots. All union members in good standing are eligible for election, subject only to "reasonable qualifications uniformly imposed" and to a prohibition—under Title V—against Communists and felons holding office within five years of party membership or incarceration. Election notices must be mailed to union members at their last known addresses not less than fifteen days before an election. Members who pay their dues under a check-off system may not be declared ineligible to vote because of an alleged delay or default in the payment of dues. Union funds may not be used to promote the candidacy of anyone for union office; employer contributions are similarly proscribed. Finally, if the

Secretary finds on complaint of a union member that no adequate means exist for the removal of an elected officer guilty of serious misconduct, that officer may be removed by secret ballot vote of the members in good standing under rules prescribed by the Secretary.

Title V of the Act declares that a union official is in effect a trustee of his organization and must conduct himself in accordance with standards traditionally applicable to trustees. He must hold the money and property of the union solely for its benefit and that of its members; he may not be relieved of such responsibility by the union, and is open to suit by union members for proper accounting or other appropriate relief. He may not engage in conflict of interest activities, and must report to his union whatever income he makes from activities conducted on behalf of the union. Specifically, the law makes it a crime—punishable by a maximum jail sentence of five years and a fine of $10,000—for a union official or employee to embezzle, steal, or improperly convert to private use the assets of a labor organization.

Every union official must be bonded for the faithful performance of his duties, and there must be no conflict of interest between the bonded person and the bonding company; the latter must be approved by the Secretary of Labor. Unions may not make loans in excess of $2,000 to any officer or employee. Both unions and employers are forbidden to pay, directly or indirectly, the fines of any officer or employee convicted of a wilful violation of the Act.

Title V also bars from elective or appointive union office anyone who has been convicted or imprisoned within five years for any one of a number of felonies; these are robbery, bribery, extortion, embezzlement, grand larceny, burglary, arson, violations of the narcotics laws, assault with intent to kill or resulting in grievous bodily injury, violations of Titles I or II of the Act, or conspiracy to commit any of the listed offenses. As already noted, Communists are similarly banned from office. The Title V prohibitions do not extend to clerical or custodial employees of unions, but do include labor relations consultants and representatives of employer groups active in labor-management relations.

Title VI of the Act is composed of miscellaneous provisions. It authorizes the Secretary of Labor to make investigations, with access to union records, whenever he deems such action necessary to determine whether anyone has violated or is about to violate the Act. It prohibits picketing "for the personal profit or enrichment of any individual," and makes this punishable by a prison sentence of twenty years and a fine of $10,000 or both. It makes it unlawful to discipline a union member for exercising his rights under the Act, or to prevent the exercise of any such right by violence or intimidation; the latter offense is punishable by a year's imprisonment and a fine of $1,000.

The last Title of the Act—Title VII—is almost wholly concerned with the economic activities of unions. One neutral provision attempts to clarify federal-state relationships in labor law; others deal with procedural matters. Two provisions, welcomed by the AFL-CIO, permit economic strikers to vote in representation elections, and allow unions in the garment and construction trades to enter into pre-hire agreements with employers—thus virtually ensuring closed shop conditions. Other sections, however, impose new restrictions on trade union economic activities. The Act prohibits picketing to gain union recognition when the employer has already recognized another union, or when a valid representation election has been held within a year, or when a petition for an election has not been filed by the picketing union within thirty days. Extortionary picketing, already banned by the Hobbs Act, the Taft-Hartley Act and Title VI, is banned anew, presumably for good measure. Other provisions are intended to eliminate the secondary boycotting and hot cargo activities of unions. In the first case, unions are forbidden to induce individuals to cease work when the object is to injure another firm which is in dispute with the union, or to "threaten, coerce or restrain" anyone engaged in commerce in order to persuade him not to do business with another firm. In the second case, unions and employers are forbidden to negotiate agreements in which the union has the right to refuse to handle goods from a struck firm.

The economic provisions of Title VII bear no readily discernible relationship to the central purpose of the Landrum-Griffin Act: the reduction of corrupt practices through the regulation of union government and the ethics of labor-management relations. The record is virtually devoid of instances where secondary boycotts or hot cargo agreements have been used for extortionary or other dishonest purposes. They are, of course, aspects of union power and thus susceptible of abuse; but their inclusion in the Act was hardly germane to its purpose, and only specious argument seems to have been offered in justification. The AFL-CIO unintentionally invited this intrusion by insisting that the economic amendments to the existing law be included in the Landrum-Griffin Act. Employers and their legislative allies evidently recognized an opportunity. "The method by which the provisions of Title VII of the LMRDA were enacted," Benjamin Aaron has written, "justify the most extreme cynicism toward the legislative process. Quite simply, the purposes of the various amendments were consistently and deliberately misrepresented to the general public. . . . Organized industry exploited the popular concern over dishonesty in labor-management relations and lack of democracy in internal union affairs, and rallied support for amendments having little or no relevance to those issues. . . ."

The Secretary of Labor is formally responsible for the administration and enforcement of the Landrum-Griffin Act, except for Titles I and VII. Title I is enforced by civil action on the part of aggrieved union members. Title VII is administered by the National Labor Relations Board. Until 1963 the Bureau of Labor-Management Reports (BLMR) of the Department of Labor administered Titles II-VI. In that year the Bureau merged with the Office of Welfare and Pension Plans, which administered the Welfare and Pension Plans Disclosure Act. Both Acts—with the exception of the two sections noted above—are now administered by the Office of Labor-Management and Welfare-Pension Reports (OLMWPR). However, the Department of Labor has delegated to the Department of Justice the responsibility for investigating certain criminal violations of the Landrum-Griffin Act, such as the embezzlement of union funds, extortionary picketing, the deprivation of rights under the Act by force and violence, and illegal payments of various kinds to employers.

The duties of the Secretary in administering the Landrum-Griffin Act have been described as those of "watchdog, evangelist, and researcher." Acting through the Commissioner of the OLMWPR, the Secretary supervises the preparation and submission of financial and organizational reports by almost 53,000 labor organizations, making them available for public inspection; conducts advisory and auditing activities through five regional and twenty-four city offices; launches investigations—upon his own volition or after the receipt of complaints—to determine whether violations of the Act have taken place; establishes minimum procedural standards for the internal government of unions; and supervises new elections after irregularities have been discovered. The OLMWPR also conducts a nationwide "technical assistance" program for unions and employers, designed to encourage effective voluntary compliance; and encourages research activities by private and public bodies on matters related to the Act.

Both the BLMR and the OLMWPR have taken particular pains to understand the administrative problems presented to unions by the Act, to explain the meaning of the Act to union officials, and to seek the voluntary rather than the compulsory solution to violations of the law. "The major highlight of the administration of the Act," the BLMR reported in 1962, "continues to be the excellent cooperation received by the BLMR from the vast majority of union members and officers." The OLMWPR processes thousands of complaints or alleged violations of the law every year; well over ninety percent of these are found to be without foundation, or are settled by voluntary compliance after discussions with OLMWPR officials. The technical assistance program, according to one observer, "has been popular with unions, and it has helped to make the BLMR's relations with Congressional appropriations committees unusually smooth." The House Committee on Appropriations itself noted in 1964, in approving the OLMWPR entire budgetary request, that "Since the Committee has received no complaints that the job is not being well done, it can only conclude that the administration of the program is in capable hands."

What has been the effect of the Act? It seems at least to be enforced. The courts, traditionally reluctant to interfere in the government of private institutions, have nevertheless upheld the letter and intent of Title I of the Act, and also the investigative and subpoena powers of the Secretary of Labor. In criminal matters, particularly embezzlement, indictments continue at a rate of some seventy or more a year throughout the country, indicating a productive supervision of union financial and other administrative affairs. In the field of union elections, the OLMWPR has supervised a number of court-ordered elections, and has helped to police international elections in which the incumbent presidents—David J. McDonald of the Steelworkers and James B. Carey of the International Union of Electrical Workers—were defeated. Some fifty-four unions have amended their consitutions to comply with the electoral requirements of the Act. Precise figures are unavailable, but there seems to have been an appreciably greater membership participation in elections, and a greater turnover of officers, since the passage of the Act. "There is abundant evidence," the BLMR reported as early as 1961, two years after enactment, "that the minimum election safeguards required by the Act are universally popular with the rank and file."

Trusteeships have declined drastically. There were nearly five hundred of them in force when the Act went into effect in September, 1959; all but a handful of those have been terminated. Some 130 new trusteeships are established every year; the number in existence at any given time averages about 200, all subject after eighteen months to the approval of the Secretary of Labor. "The malpractices [in trusteeships] disclosed by the McClellan Committee," Secretary of Labor Arthur J. Goldberg reported in 1962, "are no longer found to exist to any significant extent. . . . Many national union constitutions have been amended to provide greater safeguards against unnecessary suspension of autonomy. . . . With few exceptions since passage of the Act, parent labor unions have imposed trusteeships sparingly and only as a last resort. . . . The trade union movement has cooperated in voluntarily correcting violations of the trusteeship provisions. . . ." The Secretary of Labor has had to take legal action only twice to have trusteeships removed. There have been no complaints from the AFL-CIO on this score.

The federation has been virtually uncritical of the OLMWPR and its predecessors, but has complained about other matters. It objected from the outset to the costly bonding provisions of the Act, until they were ameliorated by a federation-sponsored bill which the Congress passed in 1965. It also complained in 1963 about the "frivolous, unwarranted, costly and harassing litigation" arising out of Title I. Several unwelcome decisions had been handed down. One national union had to appeal in order to establish its right to discipline a local union for striking without permission of the national organization. Another appealed to vindicate its authority to raise minimum local union dues by convention action. One appeals court held that a union could not discipline a member for libeling the union's officers because this would be a violation of free speech. Another court held that a union had no authority to pay the costs of defending an officer charged with injuring the union, even though the charge was as yet unproved. The AFL-CIO noted at the same time, however, that litigation under Title I continued "at a relatively slow pace, further confirming the 1959 view of the AFL-CIO that this was an unnecessary part of the Act." The results rather than the volume of litigation seemed to be the chief complaint. By 1965 the AFL-CIO could report in convention that the first Landrum-Griffin cases had reached the United States Supreme Court, producing "a string of labor triumphs," principally on matters affecting the conduct of union elections and conventions. Early in the year Meany was reported to have accused the Department of Labor of adopting investigatory policies which went "far beyond" the requirements of the law, amounting in some cases to "witch-hunting and harassment of unions"; but the convention took no formal action on the charge, concentrating its attacks—as it always had done—on the economic provisions of Title VII. In 1967 the Maritime Trades Department of the AFL-CIO prepared a report on the administrative and judicial history of the Landrum-Griffin Act, arguing that its ambiguities permitted the courts and the Department of Labor to erode the internal disciplinary processes of unions and thus their ability to bargain responsibly with employers; but no action was taken by the AFL-CIO convention. It appears unlikely, after ten years of operation in essentially its original form, that the Act will undergo any major transformation in the future.

The general effect of the Act is hard to measure; much of the evidence is imprecise; judgment is largely a matter of impression. But there are grounds for assessment. In the first place, there are some things the Act was not designed to do. The Southern bloc in Congress made certain that the notion of freedom did not embrace the right of a qualified Negro to join a union; there is no reference whatever in the Act to ethnic minorities. Further, the sponsors of the Act were greatly concerned with union democracy, but they did not properly address themselves to the problem of justice in union disciplinary actions. Most unions probably conduct their trials with reasonable due process, but almost none of them has an independent judiciary. Union members are accorded the right to sue their unions after the exhaustion of internal remedies, and may in fact sue before exhaustion if the outcome seems prejudged; but for most working people, court action is a financially unfeasible resort. For racial minorities and poor men the pretensions of the Act exceed its imperatives.

Yet it is hardly open to doubt that the Act has been generally beneficial. The "Bill of Rights" provides needed protections, and has not produced the flood of nuisance litigation the labor movement feared. It is said that the bureaucracy created by the Act, and in particular the paperwork imposed by its reporting requirements, have deterred many members from running for union office; but resignations are hardly endemic, and the fiscal supervision the Act provides is surely wholesome. It would be foolish to argue that union democracy has been born again of the Act; there is little evidence to suggest that—quantitatively at least—membership participation in internal union affairs has appreciably increased. But there are signs of new life among the active. Union members seem readier to criticize their leaders, to reject negotiated agreements, and to throw out unsatisfactory incumbents. Indeed, there are those on both sides of the bargaining table who look back with nostalgia on the days when an agreement between leaders was the last word in the matter. On their part, it can quite properly be argued that the sense of freedom engendered by the Act has, on some occasions at least, made collective bargaining less responsible. Militancy is not a perfect substitute for experienced judgment.

Nevertheless, a greater freedom is now available to union members; there are few signs of serious abuse; instinct approves the change. Perhaps it is fair to say that the Act has given needed protection to the commonalty, and more freedom to the interested, against those who have become careless of rights and duties. Whether it has brought adequate and lasting protection against those who work outside the law is another matter.

24: The Anatomy of Corruption

Why did it all take place?

Business unionism is a common target, a favorite devil of the critics. The charge is that it is a narrow creed, a child of the acquisitive society and tolerant of its manifestations, a handmaiden of corruption. The charge is suspect, not least since the term itself is often misunderstood.

Business unionism is the pursuit of improvements in wages, hours and working conditions primarily through collective bargaining. At its best it is a perfectly honorable if modest pursuit, and indeed dominates the conduct of many union leaders formally dedicated to a more expansive view of their calling; the first priority of most union officials, whatever the content of their major policy statements, is the servicing of their members at the workplace. It is not a venal idea at all, giving no sanction to peculation; it is worth noting that most unions distinguished for their commitment to business unionism—notably the United Mine Workers of America, the International Typographical Union, and the railroad brotherhoods—have remained virtually free of fiscal scandal. It is not a lazy view of trade unionism, and most business unionists have contributed as much in time, risk and fidelity to their unions as have their more cosmic-minded counterparts. The average business unionist has served his constituents honestly and well.

Yet a doubt remains. It may be, as Philip Taft has suggested, that the only requirement is simple honesty; but honesty is nowhere an absolute; the ideal is perhaps less reliable alone than when supported by other convictions. Business unionism is not a mercenary creed, but neither is it much of a discipline. It does not sanction the pursuit of collateral interests, but neither does it forbid them. It is short on imperatives. For some it is indeed a dedication, demanding in time and propriety, exclusive of other gainful activities. For some it is a worthy way of life, a form of service, but not prohibitive of other sources of income. For a few it is indeed a business— perhaps with a special rhetoric and appeal, but still a business. Even so defined, it is not a license for theft. But the commodity conception of trade unionism is a poor guide to ethics; the narrowness of its vision leaves too much to the imagination of the acquisitive and the weak.

It does seem from the record that a contrast, however meager in validity, can be drawn between the behavior of the business unionists and those now called social unionists—those of the larger view, committed to the notion of trade unionism as a moral cause broad in social jurisdiction, demanding in standards and hopefully exemplary in behavior. The transition in the leadership of the ILGWU from the conservatives to the social democrats brought with it a stronger resistance to corruption. The business and the social unionists in the Hatters reacted differently to the intrusions of the underworld. Opposition in the IATSE to Browne and Bioff was led largely by men who could qualify as social unionists. Hugo Ernst of the Hotel and Restaurant Employees and Charles Hardy of the Building Service Employees, and many of those who followed them, were men of the broader gauge. In general, the CIO was always more sensitive to charges of corruption than the pre-Meany AFL. There were special reasons why this was so; there was less corruption in the industries organized by the CIO, and the more compact distribution of CIO members in the basic industries made them less vulnerable to intimidation than the more geographically scattered craft unionists. But there was also an element of ideology involved; the litany of trade unionism, in the CIO, always had a more prescriptive quality to it than in the AFL. The older organization, before 1952, often seemed too prone to tolerate, too seldom ready to cure. It is hard to avoid the impression that, throughout the history of American labor, the most effective opposition to corruption has come from those for whom the labor movement was more than a service agency.

But there is no precision here. There was no necessary causative relationship between business unionism and corruption, only a negative connection at worst. Perhaps it should be argued that in the presence of temptation or error the so-called business unionists could have used a stronger creed. On the other hand, behavior was unpredictable; craft unions led by business unionists remained free of corruption, while industrial unions led by men of high pretensions went astray. In any event there were always minimum standards, applicable to all regardless of philosophical commitment. Theft was always one of the basest of trade union crimes, as well as a felony. "I am kind of old-fashioned," George Meany said of the comment by the Committee on Ethical Practices that James G. Cross's worst offense was to indulge in business activities with employers. "I think the stealing of the members' money was the worst thing."

Further, the distinction between philosophical types has been hazy for a generation, and in modern times is misleading. Business unionism was always an inexact term, covering a multitude of styles, and is seldom used today. Social unionism is a relatively recent label, also vague in content, virtually without circulation except among intellectuals. The conventional posture of the labor movement, in fact, has long rejected the notion of a parochial trade unionism committed to limited ends; the broad and the narrow, the wise and the dull, the noble and the selfish, the honest and the corrupt—almost all pay tribute to the idea of a labor movement deeply involved in human affairs, high in purpose, complex in method and global in jurisdiction. There are corollary standards of behavior, prohibitive of cheating and disloyalty, long a part of the folklore and are now formalized in the AFL-CIO codes. Ignorance of the rules, for a generation, has been a poor excuse for delinquency. At the same time, a fine philosophy has never been a guarantee of good behavior. It might reasonably be said that the American labor movement, like all human institutions, has attracted its quota of the greedy, the hypocritical, and the frail. Some needed no special temptation to steal. Others did. The circumstances deserve consideration.

Union government is an issue. American unions are sometimes charged with a high frequency of autocracy. The common assumption is that autocracy is a cause of corruption, and that the imposition of democracy by the law will eliminate the corrupt. It hardly seems necessary to state that democratic unions are less likely to be corrupt than undemocratic ones, but there are other points to consider.

A trade union is by proper origin and nature a voluntary organization, a natural response to indignity and arbitrary authority. If it is faithful to its credentials, it should negate by example the evils it was founded to resist. At its best, it is a democracy of intelligent grievances, servant in purpose and careful of rights.

But perfection is an imperfect counsel. No institution shows at birth or maturity all the virtues it might claim. Athenian democracy is a poor model for most working organizations, and there have been special strains on the ability of American unions to emulate the early Greeks. Violence was the midwife of many unions and a companion of their lives; very few other Western labor movements have had to deal over so long a period with such opposition—both political and physical—to the elementary right to exist. Survival or effective performance have therefore sometimes seemed to require special disciplines, not always gently imposed. Loyalty is a natural principle of trade union organization, always necessary in some form, but sometimes invoked to crush dissent. Orthodoxy is a great temptation, particularly in dangerous times; even among the most sedulously democratic of unions there are deviations under pressure from high constitutional principles. Then age and habit beget oligarchy, lightly resisted when the essential functions are performed, resentful of challenge or discomfort.

But strong rule is not a necessary cause of corruption. John L. Lewis dominated the United Mine Workers for forty years without a murmur of financial scandal about him. In fact, in some cases the authority of union leaders has been stretched to eliminate rather than entrench the corrupt. For a generation the president of the International Ladies Garment Workers Union has had the power to require of every elected or appointed official a signed, undated letter of resignation, requiring only a majority vote of the union's executive board and the president's date-stamp to make it effective; the practice dates back to the 1920's when the internal struggle against both racketeers and Communists threatened to destroy the union; however undesirable in principle, it seemed justified at the time to men committed to democratic trade unionism, and has been retained in part to fight lingering corruption. The extraordinary powers given to former President James C. Petrillo of the Musicians—enabling him to interpret the union's constitution virtually at will—might not have been unrelated to the attempts of the Capone organization to annex the union's affiliates in Chicago. The nature of the opposition in the AFL's battle against the ILA in the 1950's, as well as the traditional ebullience of the waterfront, did not encourage the observance of Queensberry rules.

What might without facetiousness be termed the responsible abuse of power—the imaginative interpretation of union constitutions, the insistence on orthodoxy in times of trouble, the individual approach to parliamentary procedure, the selective processing of grievances, the response in kind to the methods of the enemy—has seemed to some from time to time to be a necessary resort. Sometimes the odds do not permit of both survival and the elementary courtesies. Anyone familiar with the folklore of the principal trade union victories over the underworld has leave to doubt whether it would always have been better to observe all the rules.

American unions are imperfectly governed, but what of it? Autocracy is observable in other private institutions—in churches as in business, and not least in other labor movements—without the conspicuous accompaniment of theft. It might be argued, on something less than conclusive evidence, that American unions are more autocratic than their foreign counterparts; but it can also be argued, on ample evidence, that the great majority of American unions conduct their affairs to the general satisfaction of their members. Indeed, a strong case can be made for the proposition that the indifference of satisfied union members is a stronger inducement to corruption than the heavy-handedness of union leaders. One of the more disturbing lessons of American trade unionism is that morally dubious activities on the part of economically effective leaders is so seldom a cause of membership revolt. "I've got mine," a Teamster said in Detroit. "Why shouldn't Hoffa get his?"

This is not to elevate autocracy, or to deny its role in corruption; it was almost always a precursor or a companion. Parks, Madden, Brindell, Brandle, Commerford, Fay, Scalise, Browne, Bioff, Ryan and most of the latter-day delinquents were destroyers of union democracy. Corruption in democratic unions is a much rarer event than the innocence of satrapies. The benefit of small doubt lies with the free union. Congress was right to intervene.

It is proper to ask, in turn, whether everything feasible has been done to encourage trade union democracy. New ideas do not proliferate. Rather there is a sense of saturation. Supervision of internal union affairs by the law is probably more detailed in the United States than in any other Western society. The law requires detailed reports of union finances, proscribes special misdemeanors and felonies for which union officials can be punished, regulates the financial relationships between unions and officials and members, awards formidable investigative and reporting powers to the Secretary of Labor, requires the bonding of union officials, reinforces the common law on conflict of interests, protects the right of the union member to speak on and participate in the affairs of his union, supervises the internal judicial processes of unions, restrains the use of trusteeships, oversees the electoral process within unions, and other things besides. Further, the courts generally interpret the law to favor individual rights. If American unions are to be in any sense free and self-governing, the limit to governmental intervention in their affairs cannot be too far away. It is only fair to report, also, that even before the passage of the Landrum-Griffin Act the internal justice available to union members might well have been much better than the well-aired evidence of imperfection implied. "The rights of members and their protection," wrote Philip Taft in 1954 after making a survey of union disciplinary practices, "seem on the whole adequate. . . . Whatever evidence one turns to, whether it is the disciplinary penalties in unions or the number of cases in the courts, one must conclude that the unions are handling the problem with reasonable satisfaction. . . ." The Courts, also, were apparently more effective than commonly supposed. "Judicial remedies," Clyde W. Summers wrote of the legal protection of aggrieved union members before the Landrum-Griffin Act had any effect, "are as effective as any the law knows."

Yet the record permits no doubt of serious flaws in trade union government, and no institution is beyond improvement. If the justice of the courts is salutary, it is also slow and expensive, beyond the resources of most union members. For most of the aggrieved the union is the only resort; but if the appellate processes of most unions provide reasonable redress, there is an inherent deficiency in a system in which the final judge can be the accused himself. This anachronism has led one major union to provide a new ingredient in its own appellate procedures: an independent judiciary.

"The UAW is both democratic and clean," Walter Reuther told the union's 1957 convention, "and we intend to keep it that way. For some time, however, we have been giving consideration to providing a new step in the Union's internal trial machinery . . ." The UAW's concern was no doubt heightened by the early findings of the McClellan Committee, but predated the formation of the Committee by at least two years. The steps the union took are without effective parallel in the American—and perhaps any other —labor movement.

The UAW International Executive Board made two recommendations to the 1957 convention. Both were adopted as constitutional amendments. The first provided for the selection of local union trial committees by lottery at membership meetings rather than by election; the purpose was to remove the trial process as far as possible from local union politics. The second amendment provided for the establishment of an external, independent Public Review Board available to UAW members unhappy with the disposition of their grievances by the union.

The Board was set up in the same year. It is composed of seven prominent citizens—presently three clergymen, two judges, and two university professors—who must be "impartial persons of good repute"; the Board also has an executive director, again from outside the UAW. Board members are appointed for two-year terms by the president of the UAW, subject to the approval of the International Executive Board and ratification by the biennial convention. Vacancies on the Public Review Board are filled by a similar process from a list of names provided by the Review Board. The Board's offices are in Detroit, but physically distant from the international headquarters of the UAW; the Review Board has never met with the Executive Board, and has only minimal personal contact with the officers of the UAW. Members of the Review Board set their own compensation; the UAW routinely pays all costs without question. The current annual cost of this Board is some $55,000.

Under previous circumstances, any member of the UAW who had a grievance against the union, or who had been found guilty by a local union trial committee of an offense against the UAW's constitution, could appeal to the International Executive Board for redress; if he was unsatisfied with the IEB's decision, he could make a final appeal to the UAW convention. This procedure is characteristic of most unions.

The Public Review Board is an alternative to the UAW convention as a source of final appeal. However, there are rules affecting the Board's jurisdiction and procedures. The Board hears appeals from decisions of the IEB on actions allegedly violating the rights of UAW members or the provisions of the AFL-CIO Codes of Ethical Practices; the appeals may be made by either individuals or subordinate bodies of the UAW. The Board may also, on its own initiative, review the decisions of the IEB on charges of violating the Codes. The IEB, in turn, may by majority vote submit complaints of Code violations to the Board. Appellants are normally required to exhaust the internal appeals procedures of the UAW before making a final appeal to either the Review Board or the convention; they may not appeal to both. The decision of either body is final and binding, unless fraud or error of law or other cause would permit reversal by the courts. The Board may not hear cases involving the collective bargaining policies of the UAW, and in grievance cases may pass judgment only on charges of fraud, discrimination, or collusion with the employer. It can dismiss an appeal without a hearing if its initial inquiries indicate that the appeal is insubstantial, and is empowered to levy a fine of $500 on those who submit complaints "in bad faith or with malicious intent." All Board hearings are public; all appellants are entitled to counsel; and all expenses are borne by the Board. Appeals dismissed by the Board for lack of jurisdiction may be taken to the convention for its decision.

The Board makes some ten formal decisions a year, and has reversed the IEB in about twenty-five percent of them—far more than the convention has reversed. It has even reprimanded the UAW for delay in processing cases, and on one occasion accused the IEB of violating the UAW's constitution. The Board also deals with some sixty cases a year brought informally to it by aggrieved members; depending on the nature of the complaint, the Board will either offer informal advice or suggest that the grievant go through the normal procedures of the union.

How effective has it been? It has rendered decisions on a wide range of issues, sometimes causing consternation in the union; but it has concentrated on procedural matters, seldom challenging the IEB on the merits of a case. Nevertheless, it has not hesitated to criticize the Executive Board or to reverse it. Its concern with due process has caused the Board and other bodies in the UAW to exercise great care in the processing of appeals, and in one instance has prompted an amendment to the UAW constitution to conform with its ruling. It is evidently both independent and significant in a special way. "I want to say again publicly," the late Board Chairman Rabbi Morris Adler said in 1964, "that the UAW has kept its promise of guaranteeing the complete independence of the Public Review Board." Adler was also concerned to show that the existence and continued activities of the Review Board were not evidence of "irresponsibility or corruption" in the UAW, but "rather of a continuing refinement of procedure and practice, so that even the subtlest nuance of the democratic idea may not be stilled by the bigness and the influence and the power which the UAW enjoys." It is an open question whether the Board is fully understood or used by the membership of the UAW; but it is used to substantial effect, and by its very existence creates a climate of justice. It is also a popular institution. Every UAW convention must vote on whether to continue the Board, and every vote for continuation has been virtually unanimous.

Only three other unions have shown active interest in public review. The Upholsterers International Union set up a Public Appeal Board in 1953. The Board may hear appeals only on disciplinary matters. In addition, the union uses professional hearing officers, not union officials, at the trial stages; these officers are legally trained and wholly independent of the union. Perhaps because of the smallness of the union—some 55,000 members compared with the UAW's 1,400,000—and the expertise applied in the early stages of the trial process, only one case has ever reached the Public Appeal Board.

In 1959 the United Packinghouse Workers of America set up a committee, composed of members of the union's executive board, to seek out violations of the AFL-CIO Codes of Ethical Practices and to report its findings and recommendations to the board. However, to "review the good faith" of the board's actions in the matter of unethical practices, the UPWA also set up a Public Advisory Review Commission composed of three university professors and two clergymen. Very few problems have been submitted to the Commission for its opinion. No reports on either the committee or the Commission have been issued. Another AFL-CIO affiliate, the American Federation of Teachers, recently voted to adopt an appeals system comparable to the UAW's.

The principle of independent review and judgment has been applied, and in one case at least has worked frequently and effectively. On the other hand, there has been no rush to embrace it. The irony is that all four unions which have accepted it have excellent records of internal democracy. Whether or not there is a general need for independent review, those unions most in need of it are the least likely to adopt it.

The secret ballot is another agency of union democracy which has not, perhaps, been sufficiently used. The Landrum-Griffin Act requires the election of local union officers by secret ballot, and the election of national officers either by secret ballot membership referendum or by open ballot in convention on the part of delegates themselves elected locally by secret ballot. The question raised here is whether a secret ballot convention vote on elections might be desirable, and should be made by law the sole alternative to the referendum.

Trade union conventions, like all conventions, respond to political realities. Conventions of labor federations are democratic enough, with only the normal political instincts inhibiting dissent; the independence of affiliated unions is a guarantee of free debate. The conventions of individual unions are more restrictive. There is always the formal right to dissent, and in most cases there is real debate of the issues. But there can be formidable discouragements to rebellion against the incumbents. The deportment of a convention is a litmus test of the control of an administration. Strong disagreement on large issues betokens weak leadership and a divided union, not least to the interested employer. The instinct for loyal behavior is strong. The essentially unitary system of government in virtually all unions provides ready penalties for the rebel; he can be isolated both politically and personally, and if necessary undermined in his home base. Appointed union officials serve at the pleasure of the administration; as convention delegates—and their numbers have been appreciable—they are captive voters when the roll is called. In general, the advent of age and the proliferation of pension plans for union officials ensure the silence of many who would prefer other leaders and policies; most union officials love their jobs, and few have anywhere else to go. There is a great deal of unease that goes unrecorded, well understood and well controlled by incumbents who understand the deterrence of the open vote. It is reasonable to suspect that secret ballot convention elections might produce a greater turnover of unpopular leaders, or at least make them more sensitive to discontent.

The arguments against such a step are familiar: that a convention is the high forum of a union, and should be open in all things; that delegacy is an inalienable function, and that local unions properly insist on knowing how their delegates vote; that the secret ballot puts a premium on political cowardice and duplicity, weakening the democratic process, and should be used neither on issues nor on elections. It is a matter of choice. It is hard enough to vote against incumbents on issues; but most such votes are voice votes, unitemized and unpunished; there may be a case for secret ballot roll-call votes, if that is not taking shelter too far. But it is in elections that defiance is most crucial, the pressure to conform the strongest, the risks the highest, the decision the most fundamental; the absence of a recorded vote does not seem too high a price to pay for a free vote. In any case it is very likely that, in the privacy of the booth, the average delegate will vote as expected by those who know and elect him, and quite unlikely that he will vote against his better judgment. Convention delegates are usually the activists of the union, by and large its most experienced men, probably surer in judgment than most rank and file members. Perhaps they deserve more strength. If they do not, there is always the alternative of the referendum.

There must be some appeal in a secret ballot convention vote. By order of the federation, all local central labor councils affiliated with the AFL-CIO—and they are delegate bodies, composed of representatives of local unions—must elect their officers by secret ballot. A substantial number of AFL-CIO unions—among them the Communication Workers, the Laundry and Dry Cleaning International Union, the American Federation of Teachers, the American Federation of State, County and Municipal Employees, the IATSE and other various unions in the entertainment field, and all the affiliated operating railroad brotherhoods—elect by secret ballot in convention. The laundry workers and the IATSE had the memory of former sorrows to recommend the secret ballot. As it happens, none of the other unions cited above has been troubled with corrupt practices.

But democratic forms are not the only issue, nor internal reforms the only need. All unions are *pro forma* democracies, but constitutional provisions are seldom self-enforcing. No union can be a perfect democracy, and departures from the Athenian ideal are not unusual, unnatural, or always wholly undesirable. Democratic control over wayward officers can never be complete, and even when at a peak is not a guarantee of purity. The New York news vendors' local was a freely functioning organization, but not a showpiece of propriety. The generally democratic traditions and constitutions of the Meat Cutters, the Hotel and Restaurant Employees, the Bakers, the Teamsters and other unions did not prevent the emergence of national or local redoubts of corruption. The expectations for democracy should not be too high. It is not a cure-all. Sometimes more powerful factors are at work.

The market is one, perhaps the strongest of all. Trade union corruption has been most flagrant and enduring in industries of shared characteristics. It has been most obvious, it seems, in the building, garment, longshoring, service and road transportation industries. All these industries are notable in some degree for small business units, high proportional labor costs, small profit margins, intensive competition, and a considerable rate of business failures. At least in the past the battle for survival was severe, with ethics an early casualty. Wages were a natural point of attack by employers who, alone or in concert, sought cheapness and stability by whatever means were available—coercion, bribery, or collaboration. Union officials used their economic power to private advantage against employers especially vulnerable to the strike. The frequent chaos of these industries was a strong temptation to the professional marauder, the professional and violent stabilizer. Corruption in law and politics took their toll. Union members and the public paid the price.

There were special circumstances. In the building trades the rigors of competition, sharpened by the practice of subcontracting, the absence of extra-local competition, the need for an early return on investment, the penalty clause, the relative autonomy of local unions, the power of the business agent and the ethically tolerant politics of the cities, all encouraged the development of bribery and extortion; the inevitable growth of collusion diminished the ravages of competition, but it was seldom all-inclusive, and for a long time did little to dull the appetites of the greedy and dishonest on both sides. The jobbing system and the uncertainties of fashion brought a special competitiveness to the garment trades, most of all in the ladies' garment industry, while the high proportion of recent immigrants and female employees made the work force particularly vulnerable to intimidation. In longshoring the physical characteristics of the New York waterfront, the proliferation of immigrants, the criminal invasion, the dishonesty of the employers, the collusion of the police and the corruption of the social environment, made easier the work of the predator. The hotel and restaurant industries were natural extensions of underworld jurisdiction with the advent of Prohibition. Both longshoring and road transportation, because of the relatively low demands on skill, were favorite job markets for ex-convicts and the criminally inclined. In the theatrical industry, the stink-bomb was the simplest and most crippling of weapons for the extortionists.

There were reasons, too, why other unions remained virtually free of corrupt influences. The job printing industry is highly competitive among generally small firms; but the printing trades unions have been fortunate in always having had a highly trained labor force of above average intelligence, strong in self-discipline and pride of craft, an occupational community governed by long traditions of propriety and democracy. Other industries, such as the railroads and public utilities, are internally uncompetitive and subject to a high degree of public regulation. The white-collar and professional unions—the Teachers, the Airline Pilots, the Architects and Engineers—can probably claim the relative sophistication of their members and the public visibility of their trades, in addition to the simple shortage of opportunities for theft or extortion in teaching or commercial flying, as reasons for their respectability. In particular, the circumstances of the mass production industries have always been a hindrance to trade union corruption. These industries are large, highly centralized, stable, not savagely competitive, very much in the public eye, too big for the racketeers. The mass production unions—the UAW, the Steelworkers, the Rubber Workers —are organized typically into substantial locals; their members are grouped together in large numbers and close contact, better equipped to watch over the affairs of the union and to resist intimidation, and in any case subject to strong national union discipline growing out of both ethical tradition and nation-wide bargaining patterns. The industrial unionists, in sum, were generally both more inclined and better prepared to resist corrupt influences than their counterparts in the more competitive industries and fragmentized unions. The industrial environment had much to do with both the propensity and the opportunity to steal.

Given the inducement, the transgressors were two in kind: the amateurs and the professionals. The amateurs were in the majority, at home in their industries and up from the shops, trade unionists with a flaw, poorly prepared for the temptations of office, often brutal but seldom lethal, usually entitled to some claim of legitimacy and service, and not too hard to frighten into virtue once the odds had changed. The philosophical, industrial and social conditions which encouraged the amateurs had much to do with the success of the professionals, but there was a special quality about the latter. Whether they came into the labor movement as mercenaries, enforcers, parasites, businessmen or simple captors, they came armed with a terrible reputation and power. They were the proconsuls of the American underworld—a criminal system which, particularly from the 1920's, enjoyed a prestige and power unique in the civilized world, which worked largely in disdain of the law, and whose justice could be swift, terminal, and unrequited. Neither the labor movement nor the law was prepared for effective response.

Terror was the note. Resistance to the amateurs could be physically uncomfortable and economically disastrous, but it seldom involved mortal consequences. The rebel against the racketeers, however, faced not only the resentment of his more pliable brethren but also the private remedies of the underworld. Some union officials—not to speak of employers and public officials with a vested interest in criminal ways—stood aside from greed or indifference; but they all had cause enough for fear. The open threats and anonymous telephone calls, the revolver on the negotiating table, the warning treatments in the alleys, the ineffectiveness of the law, the natural care for life and especially for dependents, the well-known roll of the union dead—the deterrents to resistance were ample. The alternative to surrender, it seemed to many trade unionists of good disposition, was a high chance of death. It was a hard choice for all but the rarest of men.

All were victims of a social condition. Crime is an expected feature of any new society, but it has shown a special strength and endurance in the United States. Far into the twentieth century the heritage of frontier justice, the contempt of the pioneer for the law, a restless population, an individualistic culture, an entrenched philosophy of acquisition, an admiration for the sharp transaction, a tolerance of the fix, and a legacy of politics viewed as a business have brought to American criminal behavior a boldness, and to law enforcement a capriciousness, foreign to most civilized societies. The gangs received early recognition, became part of the political and industrial folkways, and were thrust to unparalleled eminence by the scofflaws of Prohibition. There is no satisfactory explanation of the professional corruption of American unions which does not give a prime place to the Great Experiment and its aftermath.

The business community also made a contribution to lawlessness. It held a privileged place in the law. The tolerable ruses of the employer were often the crimes of the employee. The rich found it easier than the poor to claim innocence of criminal intent before the courts. The legal doctrine of the corporation sheltered the criminal acts of an individual partner. The civil prosecution of criminal conspiracies under the antitrust laws removed from errant businessmen the stigma of crime and made collusion a matter of light concern. Corporation lawyers protected their clients by formidable opposition to reform of the criminal law. Business crime was an institution, defiant of law enforcement, a major phenomenon in a tolerant society. "The financial loss of white-collar crime," E. H. Sutherland has written, "is probably several times as great as the financial loss of all the crimes which are customarily regarded as the 'crime problem.'" It was encouraged by philosophy and usage, and lightly punished. "The one thing on which all authorities seem to agree," Sutherland also wrote, "is that white-collar crime . . . [has] a low vulnerability to official action."

Business standards were a model for the envious, affecting the morals of politics and the law, adding ambition to the activities of major and minor criminals, a contributory cause to the peculiar scale of American crime. "Both crime and racketeering today," Harry Elmer Barnes told a committee of the United States Senate in 1934, "have derived their ideals and methods from the business and financial practices of the last generation . . . the younger generation looked with envy, not at the bowed backs and wrinkled brows of their parents, but rather at the financial achievements of the American financial buccaneers who had made away with their millions, with little or no service to society."

The same standards conditioned the response of the business community to corruption in trade unions and labor-management relations. Extortion was usually acceptable if it meant a softening of union demands or led to a cooperative control of the market; the mistreatment of employees seldom occasioned much protest if the costs were light; the condition of business was the yardstick. Not in the building trades, nor in the garment industry, nor on the New York waterfront, nor in the service trades, nor in the entertainment industry, nor in trucking, nor in any other seriously affected industry is there a public record of substantial employer opposition to the works of the corrupt in the labor-management field. In most cases there was only collaboration or silence. The way of the reformers, in or out of the labor movement, was always harder than it might have been.

Crime grew on fertile soil. The long wave of immigration to the United States during the Gilded Age brought to the mercenary a pool of exploitable ignorance and to city life a legacy of ethnic hatreds. Immigrant groups lived in enclaves, resented by and resenting other races, suspicious of the law and the dominant Anglo-Saxons, resistant to the communal pursuit of lawful ways. The racial discrimination which created the Irish, Jewish and Italian ghettoes thwarted the occupational ambitions of their native-born generations, and some individuals took the criminal road to status and wealth. Ethnic gangs came into being, protected from the law by the clan. Racial discrimination was a source of crime, ethnic isolation one of its main supports.

The gangs multiplied and prospered, becoming a worldwide symbol of American civilization. Indignation grew with time, but reforms were uneven in effect. The solitary common criminal, short on political strength and private resources, was a relatively easy target; but the criminal working out of an organization, wise to power and skilled in evasions, sought refuge in his political friends and the criminal law. The law was a complex instrument, a child of Anglo-Saxon tradition but noted for features alien to its parent. The anxiety of bygone American legislatures to protect the innocent against hasty or prejudiced justice brought to the criminal law a procedural complexity unknown elsewhere, multiplying the obstacles to acceptable proof or effective decision, a boon to the innocent and guilty alike. Law and politics were often allies, leading to discretionary arrests by the police, the convenient loss of records, the purchased alternatives in pleading, the arranged neglect to prosecute, and the building of civic sanctuaries for the underworld. Poor justice was in part a matter of obsolete jurisdictions, inadequate intelligence on criminal matters, and public indifference to police administration; but it was also a matter of political influence, private income and advocative ingenuity. The underworld knew the law, and was well protected in times of trouble. It became literally true that a powerful criminal figure, with enough money and connections, could get away with murder. "There is," criminologist Walter C. Reckless wrote in 1955, "no direct legal attack on racketeering . . . local ordinances are powerless to get at the operations of racketeers. So are the ordinary state laws. So are the federal laws. . . . Professional and organized crime have always had the advantage of the American police through fixing and political pressure. . . . Under the American system of law enforcement and prosecution, racketeers are practically immune."

The culture was tainted, the law was unreliable, the public was tolerant, the witnesses were silent, and the racketeers were safe. Few institutions escaped the consequences. The labor movement was one of the victims.

How well did it do? The record is uneven. The vast majority of unions, of course, were untroubled by the problem of corruption. Others, like the Retail Clerks and the International Union of Electrical Workers, were touched by it in minor and local fashion, and dealt with it in rapid and salutary fashion.

But where the problem was serious the response was usually less effective. Corruption in the New York and Chicago building trades during the worst days was generally of the amateur variety, the least risky kind to challenge; yet internal resistance to it at any level was only occasional, and sometimes quite lethargic. At virtually no time was strong disciplinary or retaliatory action taken by either national or local building trades organizations, at least until embarrassment was intolerable or the membership took charge. Perhaps the relative harmlessness of the amateur grafter helps to explain the inaction. He was not usually a stranger, nor a simple marauder; he stole and extorted, but not too much from his members; he was a crook, but his criminality was often combined with genuine service to his union. Since, also, he was almost always an official with some internal political power, he was usually left alone. This last fact, indeed, helps to explain the poor disciplinary records of a number of individual unions both within and without the building industry. The corrupt were always in authority. They controlled or influenced the disciplinary procedures which should have been used against them. They controlled or influenced the election of those who might have moved to punish them. They were hard to dislodge.

Resistance to the professionals, of course, was a much more dangerous matter. One of the irritating elements in the criticism of corruption in American unions is the failure or refusal of the critics to recognize the odds sometimes faced by the honest. There is an element of bad grace in the florid denunciations—not least by contemporary members of the Congress —of the "cowardice" of those whose dangers they do not share. There are immunities usually enjoyed by Congressmen which are denied, for example, to working longshoremen. Underworld reprisals, ranging from the lost job to death in a lime-pit, are romantic morbidities to some critics but morbid realities to the threatened. The fact is that in many cases the victim has had nowhere to turn for help. If—again as in the case of the New York waterfront—the union was corrupt, virtually in the hands of racketeers, in collusion with the employers, and protected by venal politicians, judges and policemen, it was not hard for the average dock worker to conclude that, for the breadwinner of his family, silence was preferable to valor.

There were like circumstances in other industries. Thus effective resistance to the racketeers was all the more impressive when it came about. It is hard to withhold high respect from those men in the garment trades who have fought a long and complex war with the underworld: from Hugo Ernst and his supporters in their successful resistance to the Capone organization; from Charles Hardy for the rare creation of a redoubt within a union to defy a Capone-sponsored assumption of power; from Russell Crowell for his lonely defiance of long odds; from Paul Hall and the Seafarers for the protection they have given—not only to their own, but to longshoremen and to many men in other industries—against the terrors of the gangs; and from the legion of individual union officers and members who have taken their lives and livelihoods in their hands for the sake of their unions. They all confronted the deadliest of opponents, with all too rare assistance from the public authorities. It is a pity, but hardly a surprise, that the history of the wars is not more minutely recorded.

The AFL-CIO also played a remarkable role. Individual unions are, in a trade union sense, sovereign bodies, with great power to act against internal enemies once the decision has been made. That has never been as true of trade union federations in the United States. The AFL was a highly permissive organization, a confederation, powerless to give orders except to the weakest of its affiliates. Neither Gompers nor Green, as a matter of personal inclination, was given to strong intervention in the internal affairs of affiliated unions; neither of them, as a matter of political reality, could be much more than a conciliator.

The CIO was a more strongly governed body. The enormous ability and prestige of John L. Lewis, and the dependency of many young CIO unions on the financial help of the United Mine Workers and the personal guidance of the miners' president, gave Lewis a great influence in the affairs of many unions. But Lewis left the CIO after only five years, and even before his departure had ceased to dominate all but the smallest of organizations. His two successors, Philip Murray of the Steelworkers and Walter Reuther of the UAW, had to rule with a lighter hand. The expulsion of the Communist-led unions from the CIO in 1949 was a major act of self-discipline, but it was plainly made easier, if not imperative, by the state of national opinion.

Much the same, no doubt, could be said of the AFL-CIO's actions against corruption in its affiliates. The findings of the McClellan Committee were sensational, and the federation's leaders probably felt that to leave the malefactors alone or unhurt would incur a great danger of punitive legislation. The new federation was also better placed than either the AFL or the CIO alone to impose strong disciplinary action. It was a new aggregation of power. The affairs of both the AFL and the CIO tended to be dominated by a few large unions—the Teamsters and the Carpenters in the AFL, the UAW and the Steelworkers in the CIO. Both the Teamsters and the Carpenters were led during the twentieth century by assertive men who between them strongly affected the decisions of the AFL, acting as a roadblock to anything that Green or Gompers might want to do against their will. The Steelworkers and the UAW accounted for about half of the membership of the CIO, and the tension between them after Murray's death in 1952 decreased the strength and effectiveness of the organization. The merger of the AFL and CIO, however, diluted the influence of the giants by increasing their number; no single union or pair of unions now had a veto. Furthermore, the merger brought together a number of unions which, long separate in affiliation, thought similarly enough on important issues to be ready for united action on a matter of major consequence to the welfare of the labor movement.

But if the disciplines imposed by the AFL-CIO were generated largely by a combination of principle, apprehension and size, it does seem that much was due to the personal influence of Meany. The record strongly suggests that he dominated the process of reform.

George Meany was accustomed to prevailing from the day in 1952 when he became president of the AFL. On that day he nominated President William F. Schnitzler of the Bakers to succeed him as secretary-treasurer of the federation. President Daniel J. Tobin of the Teamsters objected. That, according to the custom of a generation, should have been sufficient to quash the nomination. Green had never defied Tobin, who only recently had boasted that he controlled half of the votes on the Executive Council. Meany, much to Tobin's surprise, pushed the matter to a vote of the Council. Schnitzler was elected.

The precedent became a practice. Meany was the prime mover for the expulsion of the ILA from the AFL in 1953, although no strong AFL affiliate had ever been disciplined for corruption. In the same year he defied President Emeritus William Hutcheson of the Carpenters. The Carpenters were the second largest AFL Union after the Teamsters, and were the biggest of the powerful building trades group. Hutcheson, long a member of the Executive Council and one of the most influential men in the AFL, had never suffered the restraining hand of Green. On this occasion he threatened in a meeting of the Council to resign and withdraw from the AFL if he did not have his way on jurisdictional policies. Green, in such crisis, was evidently wont to lay a friendly hand on Hutcheson and make some gentle promise of accommodation. Hutcheson waited for the traditional act of conciliation, but Meany merely offered the observation that "when a vacancy occurs, all vice presidents move up one seat. Do I hear a resolution to that effect?" In a brief moment Hutcheson was without a place on the Council and the Carpenters were out of the AFL. The federation's jurisdictional policies remained unchanged, and three weeks later the Carpenters made a sheepish re-entry into the AFL. Hutcheson never regained his seat on the Executive Council.

Meany showed the same habits as president of the AFL-CIO. In the early days of the federation he opposed an alliance between the Teamsters and the outlawed ILA, forcing the Teamsters to postpone action on a proposed mutual assistance agreement with the ILA, then to cancel a $400,-000 loan to the Longshoremen, and finally to drop the joint organizing plan which was the heart of the agreement. In other matters—removing obstacles to the merging of state and local bodies of the AFL and CIO, in settling jurisdictional disputes, and in formulating AFL-CIO policies on both domestic and foreign issues—he has shown similar strength.

He was most obdurate when dealing with corruption in member unions. No doubt the presidency of the AFL-CIO vested him with a special authority, psychological as well as constitutional; no doubt, since the incidence of corruption was confined almost wholly to former AFL unions, the chief critic had to come from the AFL; and no doubt Meany had the urging and support of powerful men. Nevertheless, the actions taken by the AFL-CIO were not precisely dictated by circumstance. Several alternatives were always available; there were face-saving substitutes for the drastic and unpopular measures of expulsion and monitorship. It is clear that the firmest hand was that of Meany, and questionable whether—in the absence of such manifest personal influence as his—the federation could have survived such draconian self-discipline.

What more could the federation have done? It took action against almost every union criticized by the McClellan Committee. It expelled three organizations, losing some ten percent of its income and an unmeasurable degree of political and economic strength in the departure of the Teamsters. In a step without real precedent it established virtual trusteeship over those unions who preferred the ignominy of tutelage to the loneliness of disaffiliation. It might have kept out the ILA, or imposed stricter conditions of reaffiliation; but there was always the danger of the Teamster embrace, and in any event the ILA was under the most exacting public supervision of any union in American history. The AFL-CIO declared its standards clearly and imposed them with a vigor unknown in Western trade unionism. It espoused, and practiced in fact, a doctrine of revolutionary intervention in the internal affairs of its affiliates. "The autonomous rights of international unions," the federation's Committee on Ethical Practices said, "do not include the right of a union to be dominated or influenced by corrupt influences." No doubt intervention was related to feasibility; the Teamsters were a different proposition from the smaller unions. In one case, also, the cost of action might have loomed too large after the loss of the Teamsters; evidently no steps were taken against the officials of the Carpenters who engaged in dubious activities. In other cases probably no action was needed. The McClellan Committee congratulated the Meat Cutters on their prompt disciplinary moves. The Hotel and Restaurant Employees moved against their errant Chicago affiliates. Almost all the remaining charges of corruption were confined to isolated local incidences, perhaps too remote or minor for the federation's attention.

But where discipline was imposed it was a major break with tradition. The grounds for the expulsions were unprecedented, except in the case of the ILA. In the matter of monitorship, the erosion of autonomy could go little further. It was surprising enough that such a doctrine was advanced at all; it was even more surprising that it was accepted to the extent that it could be applied. The submissive were taken over. The recalcitrant were expelled. There was little more that the federation could have done.

What should be the verdict? Like Israel, as John L. Lewis once said, labor has many sorrows. The labor movement in America, like other social and economic movements, has suffered the privations of an unfriendly environment and the arrows of armies and critics; like many such movements, it has struggled for years with the problems of growth and influence in a time when prosperity, technological change and the skill of the opposition present the prospect of decline; its problems are universal. But corruption has been a special sorrow. Alone among its peers, the American labor movement has been accused of corruption in intolerable degree. The charges, and various versions of the facts, have become a currency of international conversation, and have left a mark at home.

The need is perspective. Corruption there was, prominent and irrefutable; but it was never as widespread as the public seemed, or was often urged, to believe; in terms of undoubted culprits, it was very small in scale. Tolerance there was, a disparity between language and action which persisted for over half a century; but the labor movement was not an agency of the law—itself most imperfect—and finally demonstrated a capacity for self-expurgation probably without parallel in the world of free trade unions. Culpable the labor movement was, but so was the nation; such corruption as existed sprang as much from the sicknesses of American society as from the imperfections of the labor movement. Terrible the corruption was, to the awful damage to the reputation of American trade unionism; but one wonders what inquisitions elsewhere would reveal. It is not enough, to be sure, to point to the faults of other institutions by way of excuse; the nature of trade unionism should demand its own standards. But no organization lives alone. The American labor movement bears the mark of errors other than its own.

What are the prospects? There are occasional reminders of the weaknesses of the flesh. There have been recent charges of corruption in New York and Northern California locals of the Painters, revolving in the latter case around the murder of two union officials. The New York waterfront is a continuing if subdued source of criminal behavior, while convictions under the Landrum-Griffin Act continue at a slow but steady pace. Senator McClellan talks darkly of misdeeds in the welfare and pension fund field.

But in general the issue is quiescent, a rare topic of public or private debate. Corruption has not been officially discussed by the AFL-CIO for years, and the Committee on Ethical Practices never meets. The unions reformed by fiat of the federation invoke no comment. The old and new bakers' unions—the former purged of undesirables—merged in 1969 and affiliated with the AFL-CIO. The laundry workers' unions still compete, but the wars are mild and interspersed with talk of reconciliation. Hoffa, the great symbol, is still serving time, and the not unlikely upholding by the courts of his second conviction—involving, as the first one did not, an offense under the Landrum-Griffin Act—may well banish him permanently from high union office. The Teamsters are still outside, now joined in odd political marriage with a self-exiled UAW; but the law and self-interest have made them one of the most carefully governed unions in the United States, and they no longer generate the criticisms of the past.

Meanwhile there has been an elevation of the moral standards and performance of the American labor movement, partly voluntary and partly induced, but surely permanent. A higher code of behavior is now part of the spirit and law of the movement; the warnings of experience and the presence of the law will probably keep it there. Whatever the effects of time, habit and carelessness, the amateur offender is probably in permanent retreat as a serious problem for American trade unionism.

The professional might be a different matter. There has been an acceleration in recent years in activity against the underworld. There are new laws against racketeering. Since 1960 there has been at least a fourfold expansion in federal personnel dealing with organized crime, and a manifold increase in both indictments and convictions. But the empires of crime remain, and optimism is limited. "We have made significant progress," Attorney General Robert F. Kennedy reported to his brother in 1963, ". . . however . . . no one believes the tide of battle has turned." Early in 1967 the President's Commission on Law Enforcement and Administration of Justice declared that organized crime was in many ways "the most sinister kind of crime in America . . . a national problem of the highest priority." The Commission said that the Cosa Nostra, the leadership of organized crime, was now powerful enough in legitimate businesses to manipulate the stock market and the price of bread; that it operated in big cities across the nation, corrupting local officials, controlling nation-wide manufacturing and services industries of outward respectability; and that money for its "respectable" activities came from its illegal or marginal activities—from six to seven billion dollars a year in gambling alone—which included labor racketeering. The professional is thus still at hand, lingering at the edges, unwelcome but resourceful, afraid of the law but greedy for opportunity, respectful of law enforcers but dangerous to private opponents. He is an outlaw with protection, the hunted beneficiary of sectional interests and an apathetic public, capable in more casual days of terrible damage. Not all the good intentions and vigilance of the labor movement can entirely eliminate the threat he represents.

Only time and social change can heal. The leveling of crime to tolerable proportions in the United States will depend upon many developments—among them the reform of the criminal law, the raising of business and political ethics, the recession of racial intolerance, the decline of want, and a sharpening of the public sensitivities. They will not come soon in proper measure; but until they do, the American labor movement will continue to suffer the attentions of the enemy outside.

Notes and Comments

The manuscript for this book was originally written with footnotes in full view throughout the text. They were such a burden on the eye that I decided to put them out of sight at the end of the book. This is not the easiest nor even the most natural way to handle bibliographical notes and marginal comments, but not everybody is interested in them. Those who are will perhaps excuse the deficiencies in style and the extra work imposed.

The Prologue

The Hoxie quotation is from Robert Franklin Hoxie, *Trade Unionism in the United States,* New York: Appleton and Company, 1922, p. 45. For the Rockefeller statement see Ralph Henry Gabriel, *The Course of American Democratic Thought,* New York: The Ronald Press Company, 1940, p. 149; the later quote is on p. 232. The Huntington and Bryan statements are in Richard Hofstadter, *The American Political Tradition,* New York: Alfred A. Knopf, 1951, pp. 163, 187.

Court decisions during the last quarter of the nineteenth century unfavorable to labor included *Wallace v. George C. and N. Ry. Co.,* 94 Ga. 732(1894); *Godcharles and Others v. Wigeman,* 113 Pa. St. 431(1886); *Frorer v. People,* 141 Ill. 171(1892); *State and Fire Creek Coal and Coke Co.,* 33 W.Va. 188(1889); *in re Morgan,* 26 Colo. 415(1889); *Gillespie v. People,* 188 Ill. 176(1890); and *State v. Julow,* 129 Mo. 163(1895).

Strasser's comments were in testimony before the Senate Committee on Education and Labor. See *Report of the Committee of the Senate Upon the Relations Between Capital and Labor* (Washington, D.C.: U.S. Government Printing Office, 1885), Vol. I, p. 460. On the history of the AFL and the issue of business unionism, see Selig Perlman and Philip Taft, *History of Labor in the United States,* New York: The Macmillan Company, 1935, pp. 3–12. See also Philip Taft, "On the Origins of Business Unionism," *Industrial and Labor Relations Review,* October, 1963. On the growth of national union authority see Lloyd Ulman, *The Rise of the National Union,* Cambridge: Harvard University Press, 1955, particularly pp. 43–44.

Chapter 1

The Landis quotation is from Royal Montgomery, *Industrial Relations in the Chicago Building Trades,* Chicago: University of Chicago Press, 1927, p. 247. See also William Haber, *Industrial Relations in the Building Industry,* Cambridge: Harvard University Press, 1930.

See James Lynch, "The First Walking Delegate," *American Federationist,* September, 1901, p. 347. On the same subject see "The Business Agent," *Iron Molders' Journal,* November, 1900, p. 651; Franklin Clarkin, "The Daily Walk of the Walking Delegate," *The Century Magazine,* December, 1903; and Luke Grant, "The Walking Delegate," *The Outlook,* November 10, 1906. Gompers' complaint against the press treatment of business agents is in Gompers, *Labor and the Employer,* New York: E. P. Dutton and Company, 1920, pp. 10–11.

Austin F. MacDonald's comments on corruption in local government are in his *American City Government and Administration,* New York: Thomas Y. Crowell and Company, 1936, pp. 65–66.

Chapter 2

See Steffens, *The Shame of the Cities,* New York: Sagamore Press, 1957, pp. 203, 205.

The quotations from the Mazet Committee's report are in New York State Legislature, Special Committee of the Assembly Appointed to Investigate the Public Officers and Departments of the City of New York and of the Counties Therein Included, *Final Report,* Assembly Document No. 26, 1900, pp. 6–7, 19, 21. For the Lexow

Committee see New York State Legislature, Special Committee Appointed to Investigate the Police Department of the City of New York, *Report,* Senate Document No. 25 (Albany: 1895), pp. 15, 24.

The comment on the Manhattan market is in *Real Estate Record and Builders' Guide* (New York City), August 8, 1903, p. 244. The first comment on the Iron Workers is from Luke Grant, *The National Erectors' Association and the International Association of Bridge and Structural Ironworkers,* Washington: United States Industrial Relations Commission, 1915, p. 8. See John R. Commons, "The New York Building Trades," in *Trade Unionism and Labor Problems,* New York: Ginn and Company, 1905, p. 86. Parks's prowess as a pugilist is described in the Clarkin article cited in Chapter 1. Jerome's comments are in *New York Times,* June 9, 1903. The quotation on the relations between the Board of Delegates and the major employers is from William English Walling, "The Building Trades Employers and the Unions," *The World's Work,* August, 1903, pp. 3790–91. For Commons on the Fuller Company see *op. cit.,* pp. 69–70. The second comment on the Fuller Company is in Ray Stannard Baker, "The Trust's New Tool—The Labor Boss," *McClure's Magazine,* November, 1903, p. 40. The Board delegate's second statement on the Fuller Company is in Walling, *loc. cit.* See Commons, *op. cit.,* p. 9, on the painters' issue and the Board of Delegates. Further on Jerome see *New York Times,* June 10, 1903. On Parks see Harold Seidman, *Labor Czars—A History of Labor Racketeering,* New York: Liveright Publishing Corporation, 1938, pp. 16–17. On Parks and Loebel-Andrews, Tiffany, and the Murphy trial see *New York Times,* June 10, 1903; August 13, 1903; and August 1, 1903.

On the authority of the BTEA see Commons, *op. cit.,* p. 73. On the BTEA's dual union policy, see the testimony of Otto M. Eidlitz of the BTEA before the United States Commission on Industrial Relations, in *Final Report and Testimony,* Senate Document No. 415, 64th Cong., 1st sess. (Washington: 1916), Vol. II, p. 1585. Eidlitz said it was found necessary to form dual unions in "less than a third" of the crafts involved.

On the absorption of the IDU into the Carpenters and the expulsion of the Iron Workers from the AFL, see *Proceedings, New York State Federation of Labor Convention,* 1914, and *AFL Convention,* 1916, *passim.*

Reports of renewed corruption in the New York building trades appeared in the *New York Times,* October 22 and 30, 1920. The Lockwood Committee quotations are in New York State Legislature, Joint Legislative Committee on Housing of New York State, *Intermediate Report,* Legislative Document No. 60 (Albany: 1922), pp. 56, 65, 79–80; and Legislative Committee . . . , *Final Report,* Legislative Document No. 28 (Albany: 1923), p. 23. The "piker" comment on Brindell is in Seidman, *op. cit.,* p. 78. The BTEA's charge of "inquisition" is in Seidman, p. 82. For the Industrial Survey Commission's comment see New York State Legislature, Special Joint Committee, *Report,* Legislative Document No. 69 (Albany: 1927), p. 15.

For the threats to Owen Tierney and Mrs. John Irwin see Seidman, *op. cit.,* p. 158. See *Commerford v. U.S.* 64 F2d 28, 289 US 759, 53 SCt 792(1933). Christian Norman's offer was reported by Edward Levinson, "Business Prefers Racketeers," *New Republic,* November 27, 1935. On Commerford's expulsion from Mine, Mill see *Proceedings,* International Union of Mine, Mill and Smelter Workers, 1937, p. 46. Acting Governor Richard's praise of Fay is in Seidman, *op. cit.,* p. 162. On Norman Redwood see Seidman, p. 162, also "Sandhog's Death Gets a Pair of Bosses in Hot

Water," *Newsweek,* March 6, 1937. On the Green-Possehl exchange see Philip Taft, *The AFL From the Death of Gompers to the Merger,* New York: Harper and Brothers, 1959, p. 423. Fay's comment to District Attorney Hogan is in Malcolm Johnson, *Crime on the Labor Front,* New York: McGraw-Hill, 1950, p. 59. See *Fay v. New York* (also *Bove v. New York*), 270 App. Div. 261, 59 NYS. 2d 127, 296 NY 510, 68 NE 2d 453, 332 US 261, 68 SCt 66(1945). On Fay's "labor relations deal" see Johnson, *op. cit.,* p. 61.

Chapter 3

The best single source on the Hague machine is Dayton David McKean, *The Boss—The Hague Machine in Action,* Boston: Houghton Mifflin Company, 1940. For "I am the law" see pp. 224, 270. The episode on Frank, Jr., is on p. 81. For "politics is a business" see p. 268.

The investigation of Hague's income is reported in *New York Times,* June 25, 1929. McKean's comparison with fascist regimes is in McKean, *op. cit.,* p. xv.

For Hague on dissenters see *Frank Hague et al. v. The Committee for Industrial Organization et al.,* 307 US 500(1939), transcript p. 1146, cited in McKean, *op. cit.,* p. 228. Also *Report of the Committee on Civil Rights of the Junior Bar Conference of the American Bar Association,* Chicago: American Bar Association, 1938, pp. 16–17.

The Chamber of Commerce's statement on the open shop is in McKean, *op. cit.,* p. 184. Brandle's comment on serving both sides is in Seidman, *Labor Czars,* p. 149; see p. 150 for Brandle's political support of Hague. On Hague's tax troubles see *New York Times,* March 18, 19, 24, 27 and 28, 1931.

For the exchange between Green and Morrin see Taft, *The AFL in the Time of Gompers,* p. 423. On the Pulaski Highway strike and Hague's intent to "disorganize" the labor movement see McKean, *op. cit.,* p. 187. The comment on "gorilla labor leaders" is in Seidman, *op. cit.,* p. 156. The New Jersey Disorderly Persons Act is in N.J. Stats. Ann. (1953), 2A; 170, sec. 1. The last two quotations from McKean are on pp. 191 and 197. See also Alfred H. Hirsch, "Scab City," *Nation,* October 31, 1934. The CIO and ACLU case is cited above.

Chapter 4

See Steffens, *The Shame of the Cities, op. cit.,* pp. 162, 164–65. The "mosaic" quotation is from Ray Ginger, *Altgeld's America,* New York: Funk and Wagnall's Company, 1958, p. 96. The comments of Kipley and Harrison are in Franklin Matthews, "Wide-Open Chicago," *Harper's Weekly,* January 22, 1898. The second Harrison quotation is from his autobiography, *The Stormy Years,* Indianapolis: Bobbs-Merrill Company, 1955, p. 80.

See Eugene Staley, *History of the Illinois State Federation of Labor,* Chicago: University of Chicago Press, 1930, pp. 87–88; the comment on Pomeroy is on p. 89. See also *Rights of Labor,* December 17, 1892. The despondent letter to Gompers was from Lee M. Hart, quoted in Philip S. Foner, *History of the Labor Movement in the United States,* New York: International Publishers, 1936, Vol. II, p. 290n. On Madden's rule "by gun and blackjack" see Seidman, *op. cit.,* pp. 26–30.

On the 1900 lockout see United States Industrial Commission, *Report on the*

Chicago Dispute of 1900, Washington: U.S. Government Printing Office, 1901, Vol. VIII, p. XII. The Montgomery quotations are from Royal Montgomery, *Industrial Relations in the Chicago Building Trades,* Chicago: University of Chicago Press, 1927, pp. 38, 115, 116.

For the establishment of the Illinois joint legislative commission see Illinois General Assembly, Committee Appointed Under Senate Joint Resolution No. 9 of the Fifty-Second General Assembly of the State of Illinois, *Report,* Journal of the Senate, 1921, particularly p. 1664. On the findings of the Commission see Illinois Building Investigation Commission (Dailey Commission), *Report to His Excellency Len Small, Governor, and the Fifty-Third General Assembly,* Springfield, 1923; the quotations shown in the text here are on pages 3 (twice), 44–45, 45–46, 47 and 85.

Michael ("Umbrella Mike") Boyle was one of the more colorful figures of the period. He earned his nickname from his alleged practice of hanging an umbrella on the rail of his favorite saloon, wherein could be deposited the offerings of grateful employers. Boyle was said to hold that this voluntary act absolved him from any charges of bribery or extortion. At his first trial for extortion the prosecution introduced evidence alleging that Boyle was personally worth some $500,000. See "Gigantic Network of Blackmail in Chicago," *The Iron Trade Review,* July 30, 1914; "Umbrella Mike—Chicago Labor Organizer on the Job," *Literary Digest,* August 7, 1920; Arthur M. Evans, " 'Umbrella Mike' Pulls 'One Man' Strike," *The Open Shop Review,* August, 1920.

On the Citizens' Committee to Enforce the Landis Award, see Alexander M. Bing, "The Posse Comitatus in Industry," *The Survey,* January 15, 1923. On the attendant violence see *New York Times,* May 11, 1922.

Chapter 5

See Austin F. MacDonald, *American City Government and Administration,* New York: Thomas Y. Crowell and Company, 1936, p. 349. On the use of mercenaries in industrial disputes see *Violations of Free Speech and Rights of Labor,* U.S. House Committee on Education and Labor, Report No. 6, 76th Cong., 1st sess. (Washington: 1939), Part I.

For the text of the Volstead Act see U.S. Statutes at Large, XLI, p. 1, 305–323. The aspirations of the Anti-Saloon League are reported in Herbert Asbury, *The Great Illusion,* New York: Doubleday and Company, 1950, pp. 154–55. John F. Kramer is quoted in Frederick Lewis Allen, *Only Yesterday,* New York: Harper and Brothers, 1931, p. 248. On the climb in alcoholic consumption after the Volstead Act see Millard E. Tydings, *Before and After Prohibition,* New York: The Macmillan Company, 1930, *passim.* On the private production of alcohol see John T. Flynn, "Home, Sweet Home-Brew," *Colliers,* September 1, 1928. See John McConaughy, *From Cain to Capone—Racketeering Down the Ages,* New York: Brentano, 1931, p. 263. Colonel William Baker's statement is in Asbury, *op. cit.,* p. 161. President Harding's statement is in the same book, pp. 179–80.

See John Landesco, "Prohibition and Crime," *Annals of the American Academy of Political and Social Science,* September, 1932. The figures on malfeasance in federal office are in Preston William Slosson, *The Great Crusade and After,* New York: The Macmillan Company, 1931, p. 114; also Asbury, *op. cit.,* p. 183, and Tydings, *op. cit.,* pp. 72–73. On the political corruption of law enforcement see

Frank Tannenbaum, *Crime and the Community,* New York: Columbia University Press, 1951. General Butler's comment is in Asbury, *op. cit.,* p. 186. See *Report on Enforcement of the Prohibition Laws of the United States,* National Committee on Law Observance and Enforcement (Washington: 1931), pp. 37, 44.

Chapter 6

Collinson Owen, *King Crime,* London: Ernest Benn Limited, 1931, p. 28. On the gangs and Tammany Hall see Herbert Asbury, *The Gangs of New York,* Garden City: Garden City Publishing Company, 1927, pp. 268–69. See Burton B. Turkus, *Murder, Inc.,* New York: Farrar, Straus and Young, 1951, p. 334. See Benjamin Stolberg, *Tailor's Progress,* New York: Doubleday Doran, 1944, pp. 235, 252. Beveridge's remark is reported in *New York Times,* April 13, 1915.

Norman Thomas and Paul Blanchard, *What's the Matter With New York?,* New York: The Macmillan Company, 1932, p. 44. On the Meyer Committee see *Report,* New York State Joint Legislative Committee to Investigate the Affairs of the City of New York, Legislative Document No. 107 (Albany: 1922). See John Dewey, *New York and the Seabury Investigation,* New York: The City Affairs Committee of New York, 1933; and Raymond Moley, *Tribunes of the People,* New Haven: Yale University Press, 1932. McGoldrick's estimate is in Thomas and Blanchard, *op. cit.,* pp. 24–25.

See *Report on Lawlessness and Law Enforcement,* National Committee on Law Observance and Law Enforcement (Wickersham Commission), Report No. 2 (Washington: 1931), p. 86; also *Report on the Enforcement of the Prohibition Laws of the United States,* Report No. 4, p. 43. Seabury's comment is in William B. and John B. Northrup, *The Insolence of Office,* New York: G. P. Putnam's Sons, 1932, p. 117.

Daniel Bell, *The End of Ideology,* Glencoe: The Free Press, 1960, pp. 118–19. On Rothstein as the underworld banker see Craig Thompson and Allen Raymond, *Gang Rule in New York,* New York: The Dial Press, 1940, p. 55. The *World* estimate is cited in Louis Adamic, "Racketeers," *The New Republic,* January 7, 1931. See Benjamin Stolberg, *Tailor's Progress,* New York: Doubleday Doran, 1944, pp. 252–55.

On the careers of Buchalter and Shapiro see, in particular, *Federal Bureau of Investigation,* Report I.C. #60-151; also Turkus, *op. cit., passim.* Hogan's statement is in *Report of the District Attorney,* County of New York, 1944, p. 31. On cases, see *People v. Buchalter,* 44 NYS 2d 449(1940); 289 NY 181, 45 NE 2d 225(1942); 289 NY 244, 45 NE 2d 425(1942).

The Murtagh statement is in John M. Murtagh, "Gambling and Police Corruption," *Atlantic Monthly,* November, 1960. On the nether side of New York in the years after World War II see Ed Reid, *The Shame of New York,* New York: Random House, 1953; Norton Mockridge and Robert H. Prall, *The Big Fix,* New York: Henry Holt and Company, 1954; William J. Keating with Richard Carter, *The Man Who Rocked the Boat,* New York: Harper and Brothers, 1956; *The Kefauver Committee Report on Organized Crime,* New York: Didier, n.d.; Richard H. Rovere, "Father Hogan's Place," *New Yorker,* August 16, 1947; Fred J. Cook and Gene Gleason, "The Shame of New York," *Nation,* October 31, 1959; H. H. Martin, "New York's Finest—Their Greatest Ordeal," *Saturday Evening Post,* December 10,

1960; "New York Police Exposé," *Scholastic,* May 21, 1952; "Gangs of New York," *Newsweek,* September 14, 1957; Julius Horwitz; "The Lady Fights Back," *Look,* October 4, 1966.

Chapter 7

Joel Seidman, *The Needle Trades,* New York: Farrar and Rinehart, Inc., 1942, p. 189.

See "Labor Violence and Corruption," *Business Week,* August 31, 1957. The Dewey statement is in the same article. The Amalgamated's denial is in *New York Times,* December 21, 1922; I am indebted to Professor Philip Taft for this reference. For Potofsky's letter see *Business Week,* September 28, 1957.

On Buchalter's control of the New York Jewish gangs see *Federal Bureau of Investigation,* Report I.C. #60-1501; also *New York Times,* August 10, 1937 and January 17, 1940.

On Hillman's statement see *Advance,* June 26, 1931. On the Local 4 episode in general see Matthew Josephson, *Sidney Hillman—Statesman of American Labor,* New York: Doubleday and Company, 1952, Ch. 14. The second quotation from Hillman was reported in *New York Times,* June 26, 1931; so was the statement by Mayor Walker. See New York *Herald-Tribune,* August 2, 1931. On the trial see the affidavits by Sidney Hillman, Joseph Schlossberg, Irving Weinzweig and Samuel Bilus, in *Kluft v. Hillman,* New York County Court House, Index #28488-1931. The action against the other locals is reported in Schlossberg's affidavit and in *Advance,* July 10 and September 4, 1931.

See *Proceedings,* 13th Biennial Convention of the Amalgamated Clothing Workers of America, 1940, in *Documentary History,* ACWA, 1938–40, New York: Amalgamated Clothing Workers of America, 1940, pp. 380–82.

THE FUR INDUSTRY

See *Fortune,* January, 1936. The NRA statement is in *Report of the Special Commission on Wages and Hours in the Fur Manufacturing Industry,* National Recovery Administration, Division of Review, Work Materials No. 6 (Washington: 1936), p. 13. See Victor Fuchs, *The Economics of the Fur Industry,* New York: Columbia University Press, 1957, p. 82.

There is no scholarly history of trade unionism and industrial relations in the New York fur industry. The principal work in the field, voluminous but very biased, is Philip S. Foner, *The Fur and Leather Workers Union,* Newark: Nordan Press, 1950. See also Seidman, *op. cit.,* and Benjamin Gitlow, *I Confess,* New York: E. P. Dutton, 1939, Ch. 10. For another pro-Communist account similar to Foner's see Jack Hardy, *The Clothing Workers,* New York: International Publishers, 1935. On Communist policy in the needle trades and other areas see John Hutchinson, "Trade Unionism and the Communists—American and International Experiences," in William Petersen (ed.), *The Realities of World Communism,* New York: Prentice-Hall, 1953, and Reprint No. 215, Institute of Industrial Relations, University of California, Berkeley, 1963.

For the second Foner quotation see *op. cit.,* p. 45. See *New York Times,* June 23 and August 1, 1912. Foner, *op. cit.,* pp. 83–84. Gitlow, *op. cit.,* pp. 343–44. Judge Mancuso's statement is reported in *New York Times,* April 6, 1926. The AFL report is in *New York Times,* January 14, 1927. For Woll's testimony see *New York Times,*

April 7, 1927. Malkin's testimony is reported in *New York Times,* October 14, 1939. On violence in the fur industry see *Investigation of Communist Infiltration into the Fur Industry,* Hearings before a Special Subcommittee of the House Committee on Education and Labor, 80th Cong., 2d sess. (Washington: 1948). A Communist version of racketeering in the industry is given by Ben Gold, *ibid.,* p. 307. On Gold's acquittal see *New York Times,* April 12, 1927 *et. seq.*

On the activities of Buchalter and Shapiro in the fur industry see *Federal Bureau of Investigation,* Report I.C. #60-1501, pp. 9–10. Beckerman's statement to the FBI is in *New York Times,* October 28, 1936. On later developments see *New York Times,* October 30, 1936, and November 12, 1933. On the FDFC indictment see *New York Times,* November 7, 1933. On the NTWIU case see *New York Times,* December 17, 1937.

THE HEADWEAR INDUSTRY

On the history of trade unionism in the headwear industry see Charles H. Green, *The Headwear Workers—A Century of Trade Unionism,* New York: The United Hatters, Cap and Millinery Workers International Union, 1944; Donald B. Robinson, *Spotlight on a Union—The Story of the United Hatters, Cap and Millinery Workers International Union,* New York: The Dial Press, 1948; and Joel Seidman, *The Needle Trades,* esp. Ch. 7.

See "Anarchy in the Hat Business," *Fortune,* September, 1938. On Orgen's murder see Burton B. Turkus, *Murder, Inc.,* New York: Farrar, Straus and Young, 1951, pp. 336–37. See Green, *op. cit.,* p. 117. The Hat Makers' letter to Crain is in Robinson, *op. cit.,* p. 165. The full text of the Seabury report is in *New York Times,* September 1, 1931; see also Seidman, *op. cit.,* pp. 194–96. Zaritsky's statements are in Robinson, *op. cit.,* p. 169 and *New York Times,* March 21, 1932. For an additional account of the union's campaign see *Proceedings,* United Cloth Cap and Hat Makers Convention, 1933, pp. 17–18. Mendolowitz's statement is in Robinson, *op. cit.,* p. 174.

THE LADIES' GARMENT INDUSTRY

On the history of the ILGWU see Seidman, *op. cit.,* especially Chapter 5; and Stolberg, *op. cit., passim.*

On the ILGWU's "New Program" see *Report of an Investigation,* Governor's Advisory Commission, Cloak, Suit and Skirt Industry (New York: 1925); and *Final Recommendations,* Governor's Advisory Commission, Cloak, Suit and Skirt Industry (New York: 1926).

On Max Sulkes and the indictment of the five ILGWU officials see Stolberg, *op. cit.,* pp. 93–94. Gitlow's statement is in *I Confess,* p. 339. Zimmerman's statement was made to the author in an interview, September 27, 1961. See Melech Epstein, *Jewish Labor in U.S.A.—1914 to 1952,* New York: Trade Union Sponsoring Committee, 1953, p. 187. And Stolberg, "The Collapse of the Needle Trades," *Nation,* May 4, 1927, and *Tailor's Progress,* pp. 138–39, on the role of Rothstein. The report on District Attorney Banton is in *New York Times,* November 24, 1928. See also Epstein, *op. cit.,* pp. 149–51. The quotation "look well on the books" is in Stolberg's article "Collapse of the Needle Trades." See Max Danish, *The World of David Dubinsky,* New York: The World Publishing Company, 1957, p. 71, on the non-observance of contracts, and p. 70 for Dubinsky's statement in 1932 on the state of the ILGWU. For the ILGWU's statement about employer bribes see *New York Times,* July 17, 1930.

On the NRA and the ladies' garment industry see *Report of the Commission for the Coat and Suit Industry,* National Recovery Administration, Division of Review, Work Materials No. 10 (Washington: 1935); *The Dress Manufacturing Industry,* National Recovery Administration, Division of Review, Evidence Study No. 9 (Washington: 1935); *The Cotton Garment Industry,* National Recovery Administration, Division of Review, Evidence Study No. 8 (Washington: 1935); *The Children's Wear Industry,* National Recovery Administration, Division of Review, Evidence Study No. 20 (Washington: 1953).

Daniel Bell, *The End of Ideology,* Glencoe: The Free Press, 1960, p. 119. For the charge by the general counsel of the NRA's Dress Code Authority see *Federal Bureau of Investigation,* Report I.C. #60-1501, pp. 30–31. On the 1944 suits against the employers see *U.S. v. Cloak and Suit Industry Trucking Association, Inc.,* Case 824, and *U.S. v. Affiliated Ladies Apparel Carriers' Association of the Eastern Area,* Case 812, in *The Federal Anti-Trust Laws,* New York: Commerce Clearing House, 1945. On the 1951 suits see *U.S. v. Cloak and Suit Trucking Association,* Case 1078, and *U.S. v. Garment Truckmen's Association of New Jersey, Inc.,* Case 1079, in *The Federal Anti-Trust Laws,* New York: Commerce Clearing House, 1952.

The ILGWU's charge of an increase in racketeering is reported and discussed in *New York Times,* September 22 and 26, 1948. For Hogan's statement see *Report of the District Attorney,* County of New York, 1949–54 (New York: 1954), p. 130. See New York *Herald-Tribune,* June 22 and July 1, 1958. The second Hogan statement is in the July 1 issue, as is the Dubinsky statement on striking. On the ILGWU's internal problems see *New York Times,* April 5, June 22 and July 16, 1957; also *Proceedings,* ILGWU Convention, 1956, pp. 22–23, 271. The statement on the union's attitude to Local 102 is based on an interview by the author with David Dubinsky, September 27, 1961; see also "The Ghost of Lepke," *Fortune,* September, 1952. For additional commentary see Lester Velie, "Gangsters in the Dress Business," *Reader's Digest,* July, 1955. See *New York Times,* August 2, 1957, for a charge that Dubinsky had used Dioguardi as an agent about 1950; and *Justice,* August 15, 1957, the ILGWU's newspaper, for Dubinsky's affidavited denial of the charge before the McClellan Committee. For the final comment on Dubinsky see *New York Times,* July 22, 1958.

Chapter 8

The New York waterfront is probably the best-documented case of corruption in labor-management relations. I have relied for this account principally on Charles P. Larrowe, *Shape-Up and Hiring Hall,* Berkeley: University of California Press, 1955; Daniel Bell, "The Racket-Ridden Longshoremen," in *The End of Ideology,* Glencoe: The Free Press, 1960; Malcolm Johnson, *Crime on the Labor Front,* New York: McGraw-Hill Book Co., 1950; Allen Raymond, *Waterfront Priest,* New York: Henry Holt and Company, 1955; New York State Crime Commission, *Fourth Report (and Hearings)* (Albany: 1953); Charles B. Barnes, *The Longshoremen,* New York: Survey Associates, Inc., 1915; Edward E. Swanstrom, *The Waterfront Labor Problem,* New York: Fordham University Press, 1938. Among public documents see *Industrial Relations,* Report of the Commission on Industrial Relations of the United States Senate, 64th Cong., 1st sess., Sen. Doc. 415 (Washington: 1916); *Labor Conditions Affecting Waterfront Employment,* Mayor's Joint Committee on Port Industry, Report of Subcommittee No. 5 (New York: 1951); *Final Report to the Industrial*

Commissioner, New York State Board of Inquiry on Longshore Industry Work Stoppage (New York: 1952); *Investigation of Preparedness Program,* Subcommittee on Preparedness of the U.S. Senate Committee on the Armed Services, 83rd Cong., 1st sess., Committee Report No. 44 (Washington: 1953); *Mobilization of Shipping Resources,* Subcommittee on War Mobilization of the U.S. Senate Committee on Military Affairs, 78th Cong., 1st sess., Committee Report No. 3 (Washington: 1943). A good bibliography on waterfront problems can be found in Larrowe, *op. cit.*

An indication of the social status of the longshoremen was the fact that banks and finance companies normally do not make personal loans to longshoremen, nor were the latter usually accepted as good financial risks even in low-income housing projects.

See Bell, *op. cit.,* p. 174. Barnes, *op. cit.,* p. 6. Richard Butler and Joseph Driscoll, *Dock Walloper,* New York: G. P. Putnam's and Sons, 1933, pp. 65, 67, 221.

Ryan's reputation as a bargainer was unenviable. He was known throughout the waterfront as a devotee of the ceremonial annual "Woolworth" raise of five or ten cents an hour, seldom accompanied by other benefits. "We call Ryan in once a year or so," a prominent stevedore said, "and say, 'Joe, how much of a raise do you need to keep the boys in line?'" Ryan's demands were seldom discomfiting to the employers. See Larrowe, *op. cit.,* p. 64; and *The New York Waterfront,* Citizens' Waterfront Committee (New York: 1930), p. 13.

See Larrowe, *op. cit.,* p. 15. The allusion to "Chinese warlords" is in Bell, *op. cit.,* p. 165.

The ILA had two "Jim Crow" locals, composed mainly of Negro longshoremen refused membership in other locals. Uniquely among ILA locals, they did not have exclusive jurisdiction over any pier, but dispatched their members from the union hall to whatever jobs might be available. In 1949, ILA officials were said to have urged their members to oppose the institution of a hiring hall system on the grounds that it would "break the morale of the union through the wholesale hiring of Negro longshoremen"; see Larrowe, *op. cit.,* pp. 72–73. Racial discrimination was not confined to Negroes. Depending on the dominant ethnic group at a given pier, Irish or Italian longshoremen were given first preference in jobs. Manhattan is traditional Irish territory. Brooklyn is Italian.

On the Frank Savio case see Johnson, *op. cit.,* p. 114. The quotation from Dominick Genova is in Johnson, New York *Sun,* November 9, 1948. See *Final Report to the Industrial Commissioner,* New York State Board of Inquiry, p. 28. The quotation on employer preference for ex-convicts is from Bell, *op. cit.,* "The Last of the Business Rackets." The statement on Ackalitis is in Richard Carter, "Behind the Waterfront Rackets," *Compass,* December 3, 1951. George Cable Wright's statement is in the *New York Times,* January 4, 1953. Ryan's comment on parolees is in Mary Heaton Vorse, "The Pirate's Nest in New York," *Harper's Magazine,* April, 1952. The following quotation from Bell, *op. cit.,* is in his chapter on "The Racket-Ridden Longshoremen." See *New York Times,* February 1, 1953. Larrowe, *op. cit.,* p. 16. *Amending the Merchant Marine Act of 1936,* U.S. Senate Committee on Commerce and the Committee on Education and Labor, *Hearings,* 75th Cong., 3d sess. (Washington: 1938), p. 1201. Keating's statement is in Johnson, *op. cit.,* p. 166. On Keating's role in the prosecution of waterfront criminals see William J. Keating and Richard Carter, *The Man Who Rocked the Boat,* New York: Harper and Brothers, 1936, Chs. 7–19.

In 1941 Dunn assaulted Edward J. Kelly, a hiring boss in Pier 51, for refusing to cooperate, then struck the pier, causing two British ships to miss a convoy. He went to jail for the assault in January, 1942, was paroled on the intercession of the then New York City Councilman Adam Clayton Powell, but was recommitted for violation of parole. The United States Army then tried to obtain his release because of his proven effectiveness in handling "labor disturbances" on the piers. Mayor LaGuardia protested to Secretary of War Henry L. Stimson, who ordered the Army's request withdrawn. See New York *Sun,* November 23, 1948.

On the New Jersey waterfront see *Investigation of the Preparedness Program,* Senate Committee on the Armed Services, Subcommittee on Preparedness, Report No. 44 (Washington: 1953), p. 16. The Hogan statement is in Bell, *op. cit.,* "The Racket-Ridden Longshoremen."

The NYSA-ILA statement is in Mayor's Joint Committee on Port Industry, *op. cit.,* p. 6.

Up to 1945 the standard work-week on the waterfront was forty-four hours, with time-and-a-half premium pay for evening and Sunday work. Most longshoremen did not regard the premium pay as true overtime pay, but rather as a special rate based essentially on the danger of night work. In 1940, the federal Wage and Hour Law specified a forty-hour week in interstate commerce, with overtime at time-and-a-half beginning immediately thereafter. In 1941 a group of ILA members filed suit to have overtime pay as well as premium pay. The suit was upheld by the United States Supreme Court. The ILA and the employers then successfully sponsored a bill which, from 1949, exempted the longshore industry from the provisions of the Wage and Hour Law and destroying all claims for back pay for the years 1940–48.

See New York State Board of Inquiry, *op. cit.,* pp. 3–4. Mayor's Joint Committee, *op. cit.,* p. 38. All subsequent quotations in this chapter are from the New York State Crime Commission's report and hearings, *op. cit.* The hearings are indexed. The quotations from the Commission's report, *seriatim,* are from pp. 26, 29, 44, 45, 45, 7 and 67.

Chapter 9

Virgil Peterson, *Barbarians in Our Midst,* Boston: Little, Brown, 1952, pp. 34, 42. The quotation from Stead is on p. 64, the report on the Chicago Civil Service Commission on pp. 90–91. The Peterson book is one of the best histories of crime and politics in an American city.

Chicago Vice Commission, *The Social Evil in Chicago,* Chicago: Gunthrop-Warren Printing Company, 1911. *Report of the Chicago City Council Committee on Crime,* Chicago: Adair, 1915, pp. 10, 184. For a more tolerant view of Chicago's morals see Charles E. Merriam, *Chicago—A More Intimate View of Urban Politics,* New York: Macmillan, 1936, p. 19.

Lloyd Wendt and Herman Kogan, *Big Bill of Chicago,* New York: Bobbs-Merrill, 1953, p. 1. Peterson, *op. cit.,* p. 107; the Fitzmorris statement is on p. 11; the following quotation is taken from pp. 107, 110, 120. Thompson's "ninety days" statement is in Wendt and Kogan, *op. cit.,* p. 276.

The Illinois Crime Survey, Chicago: The Illinois Association for Criminal Justice, 1929, p. 1091, 326, 326–7, 329, 219, 418–19, 359, and 366–67. Citizen's Police Committee, *Chicago Police Problems,* Chicago: University of Chicago Press, 1931, pp. 1, 3. On the question of underworld involvement in Cermak's assassination, see John H. Lyle, *The Dry and Lawless Years,* Englewood Cliffs: Prentice-Hall, 1960, pp. 266–68. Harold Gosnell, *Machine Politics—Chicago Model,* Chicago: University of Chicago Press, 1939, pp. 90, 78. See also Gosnell, "Fighting Corruption in Chicago," *Polity,* July–August, 1935; Raymond Moley, *Politics and Criminal Prosecution,* New York: J. J. Little and Ives, 1929.

For an account of violence and corruption in Chicago elections see Carroll Hill Wooddy, *The Chicago Primary of 1926—A Study in Election Methods,* Chicago: University of Chicago Press, 1926, esp. Ch. 6. See also D. M. Maynard, "Fraud and Error in Chicago Referendum Returns," *National Municipal Review,* March, 1930. On Chicago as a sanctuary for criminals see Peterson, *op. cit.,* p. 171; on graft to public officials, pp. 193–94, 165. On the county clerk's testimony see Peterson, "Chicago's Crime Problem," *Journal of Criminal Law and Criminology,* May–June, 1944. On crime in Chicago during this period see also Allison J. Smith, *Syndicate City,* Chicago: Henry Regnery, 1954. Peterson's comment on Capone is in *Barbarians in our Midst,* p. 133. See also Fred Pasley, *Al Capone—The Biography of a Self-Made Man,* New York: Ives Washburn, 1930. The estimate of Capone's income is in Lyle, *op. cit.,* p. 84.

Capone's offer to police Chicago was reported in a letter from Loesch to U.S. Senator William Borah. The offer was allegedly made by a Capone representative to Justice John P. McGoorty, the Chief Justice of the Chicago Municipal Court. See *New York Times,* March 25, 1932.

Hostetter's letter was addressed to members of the Employers' Association of Chicago, and is quoted in Frank Dalton O'Sullivan, *Enemies of Industry,* Chicago: The O'Sullivan Publishing House, 1933, p. 34. The Association's reports are in Gordon L. Hostetter and Thomas Quinn Beasley, *It's a Racket!* Chicago: Les Quin Books, 1929, pp. 9–11. See also Hostetter, "Gangsterized Industry," *The Survey,* January, 1933. See *Illinois Crime Survey,* p. 639. See also Loesch, "Crime and Your Balance Sheet," *The Magazine of Business,* April, 1929.

Chicago *Tribune,* April 20, 1930. For individual cases see Harold Seidman, *Labor Czars,* New York: Liveright, 1936, Ch. 8; Fred Pasley, *Muscling In,* New York: Ives Washburn, 1931; Elmer L. Irey, *The Tax Dodgers,* New York: Greenberg, 1948; and Louis Adamic, *Dynamite,* New York: Viking Press, 1934, pp. 325–50. Capone's "former underworld enemy" was Roger Tuohy. After serving a long prison sentence for what he claimed was a framed kidnapping charge, he wrote a book leveling various charges at the Capone organization. See Tuohy with Ray Brennan, *The Stolen Years,* Cleveland: The Pennington Press, 1959, esp. Ch. 7. Shortly after the book was published he was assassinated.

Loesch's estimate of Capone's control over the Chicago labor movement was reported in *New York Times,* March 25, 1932. The estimate of AFL officials is in Seidman, *op. cit.,* p. 116.

Chapter 10

The Sullivan statement is in Matthew Josephson, *Union House—Union Bar,* New York: Random House, 1956, p. 130. See also Jay Rubin and M. J. Obermeier, *Growth of a Union—The Life and Times of Edward Flore,* New York: The Union Historical Association, Inc., 1943, pp. 153–56.

On the conversion of bartenders' locals into speakeasies, see *Report of International Vice-President Hugo Ernst,* in "Mixer and Server," June 15, 1923; also *Proceedings,* AFL Convention, 1932, p. 224. The statement on the loyalty of bartenders is in Rubin and Obermeier, *op. cit.,* p. 182. Flore's statement on his meeting with Obergfell is in Josephson, *op. cit.,* p. 212; see also pp. 215, 218.

The Dewey statement is in Stanley Walker, *Dewey—An American of This Century,* New York: Whittlesey House, 1944, p. 208. The rank and file protest is in Josephson, *op. cit.,* pp. 218–19, Kearney's testimony on p. 220. On the charges against Coulcher see Morris A. Horowitz, *The New York Hotel Industry,* Cambridge: Harvard University Press, 1960, p. 27. For Coulcher's trial see *People v. Coulcher,* 255 AD 954, 8 NYS 2d 162(1938). Also Rupert Hughes, *Attorney for the People,* Boston: Houghton Mifflin Company, 1940; Edward Levinson, "Business Prefers Racketeers," *New Republic,* November 27, 1935; and Victor Weybright, "Unions and the Rackets," *Survey-Graphic,* May, 1937. The threat to Gottesman is reported in Josephson, *op. cit.,* p. 235. See also Hughes, *op. cit.,* pp. 128ff; and *New York Times,* January 30 and November 1, 1937. On Coulcher's sentencing see *New York Times,* March 26, 1937.

On McLane's experiences before the 1938 convention and his affidavit see *Chicago Times,* March 21 and December 4, 1940. On the convention see *Proceedings,* HRE Convention, 1938, *passim,* and San Francisco *Chronicle,* August 15, 1938ff. Staggenburg's nomination speech is in *Proceedings,* p. 139. The exchange between Ernst and Parker is in Rubin, *op. cit.,* p. 300 and Josephson, *op. cit.,* pp. 256–57. It is not reported in the convention proceedings.

Chapter 11

See James J. Bambrick, *The Building Service Story,* New York: The Labor History Press, n.d., for Bambrick's account of his troubles. The "throw the crumbs a crust" line is on p. 21.

Bambrick's apology to Sullivan and Sullivan's reply are reported in a letter from Sullivan to the author, January 31, 1962.

On Scalise's appointment as international representative and subsequent election as an international vice president see *Proceedings,* BSEIU Convention, 1935, in *Public Safety,* June, 1935, pp. 14, 28–29. On the threats to Bambrick's life see Bambrick, *op. cit.,* p. 43.

Scalise's elevation to the presidency of the BSEIU is commented on in *New York Times,* April 27, 1940; see also Peterson, *Barbarians in Our Midst,* Boston: Little, Brown, 1952, pp. 173ff. Bambrick's discharge of criminals is reported in *op. cit.,* p. 57. Dewey's comment on Bambrick's conviction is in Malcolm Johnson, *Crime on the Labor Front,* New York: McGraw-Hill, 1950, p. 49. On the history of Local 32B see *Going Up!* New York: Building Service Employees International Union, 1955, p. 49.

Charles Hardy's advice to Scalise is reported in *Proceedings,* BSEIU Convention, 1942, p. 131. For the suit against Hardy see *Theodore Canavaro et al. v. Theatre and Amusement Janitors Local #9,* Superior Court File No. 292428, San Francisco, 1940. Burke had been accused of collaborating with the Chicago underworld. For Scalise's appeal see 15 Cal. 2d 495(1940). The note on Hardy's trial and exoneration is based on a conversation between the author and San Francisco Superior Judge Francis

McCarty, in 1940 the counsel for Hardy. On Altschuler's testimony see *New York Times,* August 29, 1940.

McFetridge's statement is in *People v. Scalise,* Papers on Appeal, Court of Appeals of the State of New York (New York: 1941), Vol. II, p. 1229. See also *People v. Scalise,* 263 App. Div. 704, 31 NYS 2d 664(1941); 228 NY 220, 42 NE 2d 494, mod'g 263 AD 704(1942). Also *Annual Report of the Chief Clerk to the District Attorney,* County of New York (New York: 1940), pp. 27–29. *Newsweek,* April 29, 1940. *Time,* May 6, 1940. *Life,* May 6, 1940.

Horan's denial of underworld infiltration is reported in *New York Times,* March 1 and 8, 1936. See also Edward Dean Sullivan, *This Labor Union Racket,* New York: Hillman-Curl, 1936, pp. 115–18. On the activities of Scalise and Carfano see *New York Times,* October 8, 1948. Matthew Taylor's affidavit is discussed in Chicago *Herald-American,* September 7, 1940. Scalise's self-defense is in "Report and Statement of George Scalise," *Proceedings,* BSEIU Convention, 1940, p. 27. The proceedings note the fact but not the volume or source of applause at the end of Scalise's report. The "Hardy Clan" was composed of Charles Hardy and his two sons, George and Charles, Jr. Both sons were active in BSEIU affairs from the onset of its activities in San Francisco. On Charles Hardy's death in 1948 he was succeeded in his vice presidency by George Hardy.

McFetridge's final statement is in *Proceedings,* BSEIU Convention, 1960, p. 16. Scalise's last conviction is reported in *New York Times,* April 9, 1957.

Chapter 12

For a short general survey of labor-management relations in the motion picture industry see Hugh Lovell and Tasile Carter, *Collective Bargaining in the Motion Picture Industry,* Berkeley: University of California Press, 1955. On jurisdictional problems see *Jurisdictional Disputes in the Motion Picture Industry,* Hearings before a Special Subcommittee of the House Committee on Education and Labor, 80th Cong., 1st sess. (Washington: 1948). On corruption in the IATSE see Malcolm Johnson, *Crime on the Labor Front,* New York: McGraw-Hill, 1950, Ch. 2; Virgil Peterson, *Barbarians in Our Midst,* Boston: Little, Brown and Company, 1952, pp. 230–35; and Elmer L. Irey, *The Tax Dodgers,* New York: Greenberg, 1948, Ch. 14. On Bioff's police record see Chicago *Tribune,* July 19, 1935; and *IA Progressive Bulletin,* mimeo, December 22, 1937.

The accession of Browne to the presidency was the first time corrupt elements had gained power at the national level of the IATSE, but corruption was not unknown at the local level. From 1926 to 1931 Samuel Kaplan was the chief officer of Motion Picture Operators Local 306 in New York City. He received a salary of $21,800 a year, and during his years in office collected some $55,000 in "gifts" from employers. A large number of projectionists worked not as union members but as "permit" men, paying an initiation fee of $500 and refunding twenty percent of their salaries to Kaplan. Members of the local who asked for an accounting of local union funds were beaten up by the three bodyguards retained by Kaplan at the union's expense. Kaplan was also the owner of the Kaplan Supply Company, a non-union motion picture projector manufacturing firm; a Kaplan company truck once crossed a Local 306 picket line to deliver supplies to a theatre in the Bronx. Kaplan was indicted in December, 1931, for conspiracy and extortion and was later expelled from IATSE. He was succeeded in office by Harry Sherman, a motion picture publicist, who held office for a year and a half. On May 18, 1936, Sherman was indicted for stealing $150,961.75 from the local's funds; the prosecution stated that none of the $1,322,279 collected and spent by the local during Sherman's term of office was properly accounted for. The indictment failed when members of the local failed to testify. *New York Times,* September 9, 1932, and May 18, 1936. See also Harold Seidman, "Labor Racketeering," *Nation,* August 16, 1933, and *Labor Czars,* New York: Liveright Publishing Corporation, 1938, pp. 177–84.

Thomas Maloy, a former chauffeur for racketeer Mossy Enright, was for many years the head of Motion Picture Operators Local 110 in Chicago. Four of his opponents were murdered during his time in office. The permit system in Local 110 was widespread, permit men often receiving the best jobs in preference to IATSE members in return for a remittance of ten percent of wages and a bribe of $450 to $1,000. In his early career Maloy threw stink bombs in theatres, then sold to owners his own deodorizer—which cost seventy cents a quart to make—at $22.50 a quart. Maloy also collected bribes for his brother Joseph Maloy who, as Assistant Commissioner for Gas and Electricity in Chicago, had control over the issuance of departmental licenses to theatre owners. Maloy was indicted in 1935 for non-payment of $81,059 in taxes; federal authorities estimated that Maloy's income between 1929 and 1933 was $350,939, and that in 1932 alone he received $124,300 from unidentified sources. The case never came to trial. Maloy was at odds with Browne and Bioff, wishing to retain independent control over Local 110. In February, 1935, he was shot dead in a Chicago street. His successor, appointed by Browne, was Nicholas Circella. See Seidman, *Labor Czars,* pp. 171–77; Walter Chambers, *Labor Unions and the Public,* New York: Howard-McCann Inc., 1936, pp. 114–236.

The success of Browne and Bioff with the Chicago Exhibitors' Association prompted the syndicate to raise its share of the proceeds from a half to two-thirds. *New York Times,* October 8, 1943. When asked by a grand jury in 1943 whether it was necessary to have two projectionists in every booth, Bioff replied: "To be honest with you, I never was inside a booth. I wouldn't know . . ." *New York Times,* November 1, 1943.

Bioff's exchange with Schenck is in *Time,* October 18, 1943. There was never any doubt that Bioff was the senior partner. The public treatment that Browne received at Bioff's hands was often humiliating, and his resort to the comforts of alcohol—always impressive—assumed epic proportions. There was a wide but undocumented belief that he could drink one hundred bottles of beer a day. On one occasion, at least, he was seen to drink seventy-two bottles in one sitting. (Interview by the author with an eyewitness.)

On the trial of Browne and Bioff see *U.S. v. Bioff,* 40 Fed. Supp. 497(1941). Also Lovell and Carter, *op. cit.,* p. 21; and George H. Dunne, S.J., *Hollywood Labor Dispute—A Study in Immorality* (mimeo, n.d.).

See *Proceedings,* IATSE Convention, 1936, pp. 73–74, 211–14, 59, 128. And *Proceedings,* IATSE Convention, 1938, pp. 48, 62, 10, 16, 75, 128–30.

On Local 37, see Carey McWilliams, "Racketeers and Movie Magnates" *New Republic,* October 27, 1941. I am unable to trace a copy of the report by the California Assembly Committee on Capital and Labor. On the second report see H. R. Philbrick, *Legislative Investigation Report,* Sacramento: Edwin N. Atherton and Associates, 1938, Part II, pp. 25–39. Bioff's trip to South America is reported in Los Angeles *Times,* October 22, 1940.

Pegler's distaste was not confined to Browne and Bioff. "I remind you," he wrote years later, "that throughout their reign in collusion with the vermin who ran the business there these evil objects never were exposed by any of the payolas in the hire of chains and syndicates of newspapers and radio. I am not convinced whether these persons were on the take, cowards or fawning slobs who enjoyed the social life of the vilest aristocracy since the Louis' and Henry VIII." Letter to the author, n.d.

On the charges and counter-charges between factions in the Hollywood locals see *IATSE Facts,* and the *IATSE Progressive Bulletin, passim.* For Schenck's trial see *U.S. v. Schenck,* 162 F2d 702, 40 Fed. Supp. 56; also *Moskowitz v. U.S.,* 62 SCt 1309, 316 US 705, 86 LEd 1773. *New York Times,* June 6 and 13, 1940. The IATSE Board's tribute to Bioff is in *Proceedings,* IATSE Convention, 1940, pp. 61–62; for the flood of telegrams and other tributes see *ibid.,* pp. 40, 87–95. Compagna's threat to Bioff is in Irey, *op. cit.,* p. 285. On Bioff's return to the IATSE payroll, the later sentencing of Bioff, Browne and Schenck, and the postmortem on Browne and Bioff see *Proceedings,* IATSE Convention, 1942, pp. 97, 285–86, 68–69, and 117–18. See also *New York Times,* November 11, 1941.

Testimony was offered at the 1943 investigation that Browne and Bioff received money regularly from the employers in return for a no-strike pledge; that in 1936, in return for a ten percent wage increase, the Hollywood employers were allowed to adopt hiring practices that eliminated overtime; and that on one occasion Joseph Schenck told Bioff that the IATSE "had to win" a contested NLRB election in the Hollywood studios. *New York Times,* December 1 and 12, 1943.

On Estelle Carey's murder see John Bartlow Martin, "Who Killed Estelle Carey?" *Harper's,* June, 1944. Bioff's testimony is reported in *New York Times,* October 7, 8, 9 and December 2, 1943. On the indictment of Nitti and others, and the subsequent history of the case, see *U.S. v. Compagna et al.,* 146 F2d 524; 65 SCt 912, 324 US 867, 89 LEd 1422; 65 SCt 1084, 325 US 892, 89 LEd 2004. Also *Kaufman v. U.S.,* 65 SCt 913, 324 US 867, 89 LEd 1422. See Peterson, *op. cit.,* p. 289. The memorandum from the federal prosecutor to the U.S. Attorney General is in *ibid.,* p. 236. For the Congressional investigation of the matter see *Investigation into the Manner in Which the United States Board of Parole is Operating and as to Whether There is a Necessity for a Change in Either the Procedure or Basic Law,* House Committee on Expenditures in the Executive Departments, Report No. 2441 and Hearings, 80th Cong., 2d sess. (Washington: 1948). For the IATSE Board's 1946 statement see *Proceedings,* IATSE Convention, 1946, pp. 183–84.

Chapter 13

See *Report of the Committee of the Senate Upon the Relations Between Labor and Capital, and Testimony Before the Committee,* Senate Committee on Education and Labor, Report No. 1262, Vols. I–IV, 48th Cong., 2d sess. (Washington: 1885). The excerpts used here are from Vol. I only, pp. 810–12.

Reports, United States Industrial Commission, Vols. I–XIX (Washington: 1900–02). The excerpts here are taken from Vols. VII, VIII, and IX. The *Reports* are indexed.

United States Commission on Industrial Relations, *Final Report* (Washington: 1915). The *Report* is indexed. The italics in the statement on the strikebreaker and the attitude of the state toward him are in the original.

"Investigation of So-Called Rackets," *Hearings,* Subcommittee of the Senate Committee on Commerce, 73d Cong., 2d sess. (Washington: 1934), Vols. I and II. The hearings are indexed, as are all Congressional hearings hereinafter cited.

"Crime and Criminal Practices," *Report,* No. 1189, Senate Committee on Commerce, 75th Cong., 1st sess. (Washington: 1937). The report is indexed. The amendment to the Packers and Stockyards Act is in *Public Law* 272 (1937). The law on public contracts is in *Public Law* 324 (1937). The Committee sent a questionnaire to some 1,000 businessmen and business organizations, asking the question: "Do racketeering and cutthroat competition go hand in hand?" Among the respondents, 190 said yes, 25 said no, 54 said "not in all cases" (*Report,* p. 7). The Committee also estimated that the total cost of crime in the United States was $12,933,000,000 a year including the cost of law enforcement—amounting to six times the cost of education, ten times the cost of the Army and Navy, four times the cost of normal operations of the federal government, more than the annual intake of all federal, state and local taxes, and equal to about one-fourth of the national income (*Report,* p. 13).

"Violations of Free Speech and Assembly and Interference with the Rights of Labor," *Hearings,* Subcommittee of the Senate Committee on Labor and Public Welfare, LaFollette Committee), 74th Cong., 2d sess. (Washington: 1936). "Violations of Free Speech and the Rights of Labor," *Report,* Senate Committee on Labor and Public Welfare, Parts I–IV, 76th Cong., 1st sess. (Washington: 1939–41), Part VII, 77th Cong., 1st sess. (Washington: 1941). See in particular *Report,* No. 6, "Strikebreaking Services," 76th Cong., 1st sess. (Washington: 1939); "Industrial Espionage," *Report,* No. 6, 75th Cong., 2d sess. (Washington: 1937); "Industrial Munitions," *Report,* No. 6, 76th Cong., 1st sess. (Washington: 1939); "Employers' Associations and Collective Bargaining in California," *Report,* No. 398, 78th Cong., 1st sess. (Washington: 1943). The law prohibiting the use of detective agencies by the federal government and the District of Columbia is in 27 *Stat.* 591; the law prohibiting the interstate transportation of strikebreakers is in 52 *Stat.* 1242.

"Investigation of the Effectiveness of the Hobbs Amendment in Suppressing Racketeering," *Hearings and First Intermediate Report,* House Committee on Expenditures in the Executive Department, 80th Cong., 1st sess. (Washington: 1947). On the poultry industry see "Labor Practices in the Food Industry," *Hearings,* Special Subcommittee of the House Committee on Education and Labor, 80th Cong., 1st sess. (Washington: 1947).

"Union Democracy," *Hearings,* Special Subcommittee of the House Committee on Education and Labor, 81st Cong., 1st and 2d sess. (Washington: 1950).

"Strikes and Racketeering in the Kansas City Area," *Hearings,* Special Subcommittee of the House Committees on Education and Labor, and Government Operations, 83d Cong., 1st sess. (Washington: 1953).

"Investigation of Racketeering," *Hearings,* Special Subcommittee of the House Committees on Education and Labor, and Government Operations, 83d Cong., 1st sess. (Washington: 1953). "Jimmy James" was Eugene C. James, who left Detroit to become secretary-treasurer of Local 2 of the Laundry Workers International Union in Chicago. He later became secretary-treasurer of the international union. He was subsequently indicted and convicted for complicity in embezzling some $900,000 from the LWIU's welfare fund.

Chapter 14

On welfare funds in general see Margaret C. Klem and Margaret F. McKiever, *Management and Union Health and Medical Programs,* Washington: Department of Health, Education and Welfare, 1953; Franz Goldmann, *Voluntary Medical Care Insurance in the United States,* New York: Columbia University Press, 1948. For more recent comments see Joseph W. Garbarino, *Health Plans and Collective Bargaining,* Berkeley: University of California Press, 1960; and Herman M. and Ann R. Somers, *Doctors, Patients and Health Insurance,* Washington: The Brookings Institution, 1961.

The Taft-Hartley Act is in 61 *U.S.,* Ch. 120, pp. 136–62. The federal court decision noted was *Inland Steel Company v. National Labor Relations Board,* 170 F2d, 247; 60 SCt. 887; 336 US 960(1949). The 1869 decision was *Paul v. Virginia,* 79 US (8 Wall), 168(1869). The 1944 decision was *United States v. Southeastern Underwriters Association,* 322 US 533.

The statement by the Treasury official is in "Welfare and Pension Plans Investigation," *Hearings,* Subcommittee on Welfare and Pension Funds of the Senate Committee on Labor and Public Welfare, 84th Cong., 2d sess. (Washington: 1956), Part 3, p. 838. On the 1953 House investigation see "Investigation of Welfare and Pension Funds," *Hearings* and *Interim Report,* Special Subcommittee of the House Committee on Education and Labor, 83d Cong., 1st sess. (Washington: 1954). The quotations from the interim report are on pp. 5, 7, 10 and 12. See also "Investigation of Welfare Funds and Racketeering," *Hearings,* Special Subcommittee of the House Committee on Education and Labor, 83d Cong., 1st sess. (Washington: 1953).

See "Welfare and Pension Plans Investigation," *Interim Report,* Senate Committee on Labor and Public Welfare, Subcommittee on Welfare and Pension Funds, 84th Cong., 1st sess. (Washington: 1955), p. 9.

A survey reported by the Subcommittee of 79 companies accounting for 95 percent of all group insurance business in the United States in 1952 showed the following:

Claims paid:	79.5 percent of premium income
Dividends to policyholders:	8.0 percent of premium income
Retentions:	12.5 percent of premium income
a. Commissions:	3.4 percent of premium income
b. Service fees:	0.9 percent of premium income
c. Carrier retentions:	8.2 percent of premium income

See "Welfare and Pension Plans Investigation," *Final Report,* Senate Committee on Labor and Public Welfare, Subcommittee on Welfare and Pension Funds, 84th Cong., 2d sess. (Washington: 1956).

Also *Hearings,* 84th Cong., 1st and 2d sess. (Washington: 1955 and 1956), Parts 1–3. Inciso's questioner on his travels was Senator Paul H. Douglas of Illinois, the chairman of the Subcommittee.

The second interim report is in *Interim Report: Panel Discussion,* 84th Cong., 1st sess. (Washington: 1955). The LWIU case is in Part 2 of the hearings. The Distillery Workers' hearings are in Part 3.

On Sidney Brennan's conviction see *U.S. v. Brennan,* 134 Fed. Supp. 42, 137 Fed. Supp. 888. On Saperstein see *People v. Saperstein,* 140 NE 2d 252, 2 NY 2d 210, 159 NYS 2d 160; *Saperstein v. People of New York,* 77 SCt 25, 353 US 946 (denied certiorari). On James see *U.S. v. James,* 273 F2d 5, 366 US 213, 81 SCt 1052. A civil suit filed by the Laundry Workers against James and Saperstein was settled out of court for $247,136.

For the charges against Cilento see *New York Times,* March 11, 1956.

The Welfare and Pension Plans Disclosure Act is Public Law 836, 85th Cong., 2d sess. (1958).

See "Violation or Nonenforcement of Government Laws and Regulations in the Labor Union Field," *Hearings,* Senate Committee on Government Operations, Permanent Subcommittee on Investigations, 85th Cong., 1st sess. (Washington: 1957). McClellan's comment is on p. 254.

Chapter 15

Chapters 15–20 inclusive are based mainly on the hearings and reports of the McClellan Committee. The hearings are extremely well indexed. I have noted page numbers for the reports.

On the Meat Cutters in general see McClellan Committee, *Second Interim Report,* Report No. 621, 86th Cong., 1st sess. (Washington: 1959), pp. 208–375; also *Hearings,* Parts 29 and 30, 85th Cong., 2d sess. (Washington: 1958).

An unfair labor practice is an act barred to employers or unions by the National Labor Relations Act, as interpreted and amplified by the National Labor Relations Board (NLRB), which administers the relevant sections of the Act. The NLRB also conducts "representational" elections among groups of employees, after a union has produced cards signed by thirty percent of the employees in question, to determine whether a majority wish to be represented by the union in negotiations with the employer. If a majority so votes, the employer is bound by law to recognize the union and bargain in good faith with it.

Testimony at the hearings indicated that the Block brothers originally obtained a charter from the Meat Cutters in 1934 through the intervention of George Scalise of the BSEIU. Anthony ("Little Augie Pisano") Carfano was said to have been involved in the proceedings. The international union denied the charges.

The Committee's concluding statement on the Block family is in *Interim Report,* p. 391 and pp. 370–71.

On the Bakers see *Interim Report,* Report No. 1417, 85th Cong., 2d sess. (Washington: 1958). The first three quotations in this section are in *ibid.,* pp. 106–08. See also *Hearings,* Part 8, 85th Cong., 1st sess. (Washington: 1957). On the matter of falsified expense accounts, the Committee said that in 1956 Cross's expenses amounted to $39,682.55, of which $30,015.16 was unaccounted for. *Interim Report,* p. 120. For other statements of the Committee on the Bakers see *Interim Report,* pp. 122, 126, 131.

On Shefferman see *Interim Report,* pp. 255–300, and *Hearings,* Part 15, 85th Cong., 1st sess. (Washington: 1957). His personal account of his career is in Shefferman, *The Man in the Middle,* New York: Doubleday, 1961.

Chapter 16

On the Carpenters see McClellan Committee, *Second Interim Report,* Report No. 621, Part 2, 86th Cong., 1st sess. (Washington: 1959). Also *Hearings,* Parts 31 and 44, 85th Cong., 2d sess. (Washington: 1958).

For the AFL's condemnation of racket labor-press operations see *Proceedings,* AFL Convention, 1954, pp. 87–88.

Christie's book on the Carpenters is *Empire in Wood,* Ithaca: Cornell University Press, 1956.

Max Raddock's defense of borrowing is in *Hearings,* Part 31, p. 12003. There appears to be no public evidence that Mr. Benny ever borrowed material from Mr. Crosby.

In the Marion County indictment, Hutcheson, Blaier and Chapman were found guilty of bribing a public official. *New York Times,* October 29, 1960. Hutcheson was also convicted of contempt of Congress, failing in an appeal to the U.S. Supreme Court. *New York Times,* April 12, 1960 and April 15, 1962.

The opening statement on the Operating Engineers is in McClellan Committee, *First Interim Report,* Report No. 1417, 85th Cong., 2d sess. (Washington: 1958), p. 371; the second is on p. 372.

Both Huddell and Frank E. Langdon, the editor of the IUOE's newspaper, were shot. Huddell died ten days later of pneumonia. Various sources suggested that the shooting was a plot by Maloney and Possehl to get rid of Huddell and Langdon. The Washington *Herald* stated that one George MacScullen of Chicago had admitted that he had been hired by Maloney and Possehl to kill the two victims. *Herald,* May 23, 1931. Dave Evans, the secretary-treasurer of the IUOE, later convicted of embezzling some $68,000 of IUOE funds, was also implicated. *Herald, loc. cit.;* Washington *Evening Star,* May 27, 1931; letter from General Secretary-Treasurer Frank A. Fitzgerald to Vice-President William L. Welsh, August 13, 1931—all cited in Garth L. Mangum, *The Operating Engineers: The Operating History of a Trade Union,* Cambridge: Harvard University Press, 1964, p. 326 n. Mangum doubts the story, pointing out that Possehl was in Huddell's company during the shooting and evidently enjoyed affectionate relations with him, and also that the attempted killing might well have originated with any one of the many dissident groups then active in the IUOE. The matter is unresolved. MacScullen was arrested for the shooting the following year and indicted, but died in jail without confessing. See Mangum, *op. cit.,* pp. 129–30. Also *First Interim Report,* p. 373.

For the testimony on the IUOE see McClellan Committee, *Hearings,* Parts 19 and 20, 85th Cong., 2d sess. (Washington: 1958).

It was clear at the time of the Ziegler case that there was no effective appeals procedure in the IUOE. Further, the international union held no conventions from 1928 to 1940.

On Maloney's accounts see *Interim Report,* p. 379. On the DeKoning family see *ibid.,* pp. 404ff.

The Committee's finding on parrot liquor is reported in *Interim Report,* p. 436. The final comment on Donath is on p. 437.

On the Sheet Metal Workers in Chicago see McClellan Committee, *Final Report,* Report No. 1139, Part I, 86th Cong., 2d sess. (Washington: 1960).

James J. Tracy, the secretary-treasurer of Local 73, told the Committee that he was president of a building company and also a stockholder in a sign-erecting company. Like Cronin, he denied accepting bribes.

Chapter 17

On the Chicago restaurant industry see McClellan Committee, *Second Interim Report,* Report No. 621, Part 2, 86th Cong., 1st sess. (Washington: 1959). Also *Hearings,* Parts 33 and 34, 85th Cong., 2d sess. (Washington: 1958).

At the time of the hearings, Blakely was a vice president of the international union from Chicago. In 1960, labor columnist Victor Riesel wrote that "At one moment recently there were fifty officials with police records" in the Chicago group of HRE locals. Cincinnati *Enquirer,* February 10, 1960. At the 1960 HRE convention, Blakely was attacked by President John Cooper of the Los Angeles Local Joint Executive Board of the HRE on grounds of alleged racketeer connections. The charges were evidently not processed in formal hearings, but neither were they sustained. Cooper's organization was placed in trusteeship by the international union and Cooper himself turned out of office.

The Committee said that Danny Lardino had "long been an associate of some of the principal syndicate leaders," that his police record showed an arrest in 1927 for robbery, and that the evidence suggested that he was one of Chicago gang leader Anthony Accardo's "chief lieutenants." *Second Interim Report,* pp. 594–96.

On the matter of Joseph Aiuppa and/or Joey O'Brien, members of the American underworld have the occasional habit, confusing to students of the ethnic and cultural aspects of crime, of adopting aliases or *noms de guerre* of an ethnic origin different from their own. The practice seems to be most frequent among criminals of Central and Southern European extraction.

On more recent corruption in the Chicago Police Department see Robert Bendiner, "A Tale of Cops, Robbers, and the Visiting Professor," *Reporter,* September 15, 1960. Also, and more particularly, Virgil W. Peterson, *A Report on Chicago Crime for 1960,* Chicago: Chicago Crime Commission, 1961, pp. 3–21. The problem was the protection of a Chicago burglary ring by a number of policemen who, in return for their services, shared in the loot. The scandal led to a major reorganization of the Chicago Police Department. The annual reports by Peterson for the Chicago Crime Commission are the best source known to the author of current events in urban crime.

On February 14, 1952, the Chicago City Council set up an Emergency Crime Committee, colloquially known as the "Big 9," to discover what links might exist between police, politicians and criminals in Chicago. Various reports submitted to the Emergency Crime Committee charged that such links did exist. In a "tentative" final report, six members of the Emergency Crime Committee said that no evidence had been found that such was the case, but accused the Chicago Police Department of laxity in investigating the behavior of policemen. The minority held that there was an alliance between crime and politics in Chicago, and that gambling was protected. The report was made public on December 19, 1960. On January 18, 1961, the City Council ordered the Committee disbanded and sealed its records in the city clerk's vaults. See Chicago *Sun-Times,* February 14, 1960.

On the coin machine industry see McClellan Committee, *Final Report,* Report No. 1139, Part IV, 86th Cong., 2d sess. (Washington: 1960). Also *Hearings,* Part 46, 85th Cong., 2d sess. and 86th Cong., 1st sess. (Washington: 1959).

During William Bufalino's term of office, Local 985 sent out a notice which stated that "All members of the union *and their employees* are urgently requested to attend a meeting of the union." *Hearings,* p. 17654 (author's italics).

Chapter 18

On the Western Conference of Teamsters see McClellan Committee, *Interim Report,* Report No. 1417, 85th Cong., 2d sess. (Washington: 1958). Also *Hearings,* Parts 4 and 7, 85th Cong., 1st sess. (Washington: 1957).

Beck's statement on borrowing by union officials appeared in the Des Moines (Iowa) *Register* on December 11, 1953. It was reproduced in the *Oregon Labor Press* on April 5, 1957, and in *Hearings,* p. 1372.

On the UAW-AFL see McClellan Committee, *Interim Report,* Report No. 1417, 85th Cong., 2d sess. (Washington: 1958). Also *Hearings,* Parts 10–14, 85th Cong., 1st sess. (Washington: 1957).

The postwar membership of the UAW-AFL was concentrated in the East and Midwest. It had almost no members in the West. In 1954, however, the union established its national headquarters in Beverly Hills, California. Secretary-Treasurer Anthony Doria told the Committee that the move was made to enable more intensive organizing in the West. The union's old headquarters in Milwaukee were sold to Doria's business partner, Spiros Kallas, for $80,000 in March, 1955. Three weeks later Kallas sold the property for $115,000. See *Hearings,* pp. 4380ff.

On Abraham Gordon see *Hearings,* Part 55, and *Final Report,* Report No. 1139, Part 3, 86th Cong., 1st sess. (Washington: 1960).

On Anthony Provenzano and Local 560 see *Hearings,* Part 55, 86th Cong., 1st sess. (Washington: 1959).

On Corallo and Local 239 see *Hearings,* Part 12, 85th Cong., 1st sess. (Washington: 1957).

For the second investigation of Teamster Local 239 see "James R. Hoffa and Continued Underworld Control of New York Teamster Local 239," Senate Committee on Government Operations, Permanent Subcommittee on Investigations, Report No. 1784, 87th Cong., 2d sess. (Washington: 1962). Also *Hearings,* 87th Cong., 1st sess. (Washington: 1961).

On Raymond Cohen and Local 107 see *Hearings,* Part 27, 85th Cong., 1st and 2nd sess. (Washington: 1958).

On the garbage industry see McClellan Committee, *Interim Report,* Report No. 1417, 85th Cong., 2d sess. (Washington: 1958); *Second Interim Report,* Report No. 621, Part 2, 86th Cong., 1st sess. (Washington: 1959); and *Hearings,* Part 17, 85th Cong., 1st sess. (Washington: 1957).

For more on Modica's hams and turkeys, his newspaper and his literary ambitions, see Murray Kempton, *America Comes of Middle Age,* Boston: Little, Brown, 1963, pp. 54–55.

On Barney Baker see McClellan Committee, *Second Interim Report,* Report No.

621, Part 1, 86th Cong., 1st sess. (Washington: 1959); and *Hearings,* Parts 37, 39 and 40, 85th Cong., 2d sess. (Washington: 1958). Gibbons' comments on the hiring of ex-convicts are in *Hearings,* Part 39.

"It fractured the nation," Irving Bernstein has said of Joe Penner's introduction. "It pulled us through the depression." (Interview with the author, April 21, 1965.)

Gibbons' rise to prominence in the Teamsters was by an unusual route. A sometime college student, socialist, WPA employee and labor educator, he became active in the labor movement on a full-time basis through the CIO Textile Workers Organizing Committee. He subsequently joined the CIO Retail, Wholesale and Department Store Union (RWDSU), becoming its staff director in St. Louis. After the war the St. Louis locals of the RWDSU merged into one, and in 1948, after a dispute with the national union, disaffiliated. A few months later the amalgamated local, composed almost wholly of retail store and warehouse employees, joined Local 688 of the Teamsters, a small local. Gibbons became president of the local, which under his leadership became widely regarded as something of a model local, frequently visited by foreign trade unionists. Gibbons was also at one time or another an international vice president of the American Federation of Teachers and a national board member of Americans for Democratic Action. In time he also became one of Hoffa's closest associates, and was often referred to as the "Teamsters' longhair." Gibbons became an international vice president of the Teamsters after Hoffa was elected president, subsequently being appointed executive vice president. He resigned the latter position when Hoffa castigated him for closing the Teamsters' Washington office and sending a message of condolence to Jacqueline Kennedy on the assassination of President John F. Kennedy.

On Glimco see McClellan Committee, *Final Report,* Report No. 1139, Part 3, 86th Cong., 1st sess. (Washington: 1960), and *Hearings,* Parts 33 and 39, 85th Cong., 1st sess. (Washington: 1958), and 85th Cong., 2d sess. and 86th Cong., 1st sess. (Washington: 1959). Also Chicago Crime Commission, *Report on Chicago Crime,* 1956, 1958, 1959, 1960, 1961, 1962.

The purpose of the testimonial dinner for Hoffa, aside from celebrating the guest of honor, was to raise money for a children's home in Israel. Some 2600 representatives from labor and management paid $100 a plate to attend. The funds were used to build, in Hoffa's name, a children's home in Ein Kerem, Jerusalem. The home has been in operation since 1959 and is run by Mish'an, the Social Welfare Fund of Histadrut—the Israeli labor federation—in conjunction with the municipality of Jerusalem. (Letter to the author from the Embassy of Israel, May 17, 1965.)

On Occidental Life and IBT Local 710 see *Final Report,* and *Hearings,* Part 49. On Paul Dorfman see *Second Interim Report,* Part 1, and *Hearings,* Part 13, 85th Cong., 1st sess. (Washington: 1959), and Parts 40 and 43. On Dorfman's expulsion from the AFL-CIO see *Proceedings,* AFL-CIO Convention, 1957, Vol. I, pp. 560–83.

Chapter 19

There have been two worthwhile biographies of Hoffa. By far the best study of him and his stewardship of the Teamsters is Ralph and Estelle James, *Hoffa and the Teamsters,* Princeton: Van Nostrand, 1965. A more personal and journalistic account is Clark R. Mollenhoff, *The Tentacles of Power,* Cleveland: World Publishing Company, 1966. A brief and light description of Hoffa's problems is in James Bartlow Martin, *Jimmy Hoffa's Hot,* Greenwich, Conn.: Fawcett Publications, 1959.

See McClellan Committee *Second Interim Report,* Report No. 621, Part 1, 86th Cong., 1st sess. (Washington: 1959), pp. 109–10 for the opening comments on Hoffa in this chapter.

The Teamster publication is *The Name Is Hoffa,* Washington: International Brotherhood of Teamsters, n.d. "I know where I'm going . . . I'm no damn angel" is from Paul Jacobs, "The World of Jimmy Hoffa," *Reporter,* Parts I and II, January 24 and February 7, 1957, and Martin, *op. cit.*

On the growth of the conference system see James and James, *op. cit.,* also Robert D. Leiter, *The Teamsters Union: A Study of Its Economic Impact,* New York: Bookman Associates, 1957.

Hoffa's comment on Dave Beck is in William Gomberg, "Hoffa: A Study in Power," *Nation,* June 17, 1961.

On the Sun Valley operation see McClellan Committee, *Interim Report,* Report No. 1417, 85th Cong., 2d sess. (Washington: 1958). Also *Hearings,* Part 40, 85th Cong. 2d sess. (Washington: 1958), and Part 54, 86th Cong., 1st sess. (Washington: 1959). On Hoffa's relationship with Benjamin Dranow see *Final Report,* Report No. 1139, Part 3, 86th Cong., 2d sess. (Washington: 1960).

On the Test Fleet case and the James jukebox local see *Hearings,* Part 13, 85th Cong., 1st sess. (Washington: 1957). On Embrell Davidson see *Hearings,* Part 36, 85th Cong., 2d sess. (Washington: 1958), on Herman Kierdorf see *Hearings,* Part 14, 85th Cong., 1st sess. (Washington: 1957).

On the Detroit laundry industry see *Second Interim Report,* Report No. 621, 86th Cong., 1st sess. (Washington: 1959), and *Hearings,* Part 36, 85th Cong., 2d sess. (Washington: 1958). Payments to facilitate negotiations were evidently not unique in the Detroit laundry industry. Balkwill and John Charles Meissner, the secretary-treasurer of the Institute, admitted paying $16,000 to the late John Paris of the Detroit Laundry Workers for that purpose.

The episode involving Paul ("The Waiter") Ricca is in *Hearings,* Part 13, 85th Cong. 1st sess. (Washington: 1957), Part 36, and *Second Interim Report.* Hoffa's gambling activities are also discussed in *Hearings,* Part 36, and Part 56, 86th Cong., 1st sess. (Washington: 1959).

The report on the Hoffman investigations is in *Hearings,* Part 39, 85th Cong., 2d sess. (Washington: 1958). The exchange with Payne Ratner is in *Hearings,* Part 37, 85th Cong., 2d sess. (Washington: 1958). The Committee's comment on it is in *Second Interim Report.* Mullins' comment about Judge Rashid is in *Hearings,* Part 40, 85th Cong., 2d sess. (Washington: 1958), as is Hoffa's promise to run a good union. The Committee rejoinder is in *Interim Report.* The exchanges on the Kierdorfs are in *Hearings,* Part 36, as is the evidence on Daniel Keating, Clinteau, Robert P. Scott and Gerald Connelly.

On Zigmont Snyder see *Interim Report,* and *Hearings,* Part 14. Hoffa's interrogation of Welsh is reported in *Hearings,* Part 36.

The Committee's comment on Hoffa's "hoodlum empire" is in *Interim Report.* See also *Hearings,* Part 40. The colloquy on Hoffa's courage is in *Hearings,* Part 36, as is the observation of Edward Bennett Williams. For the Committee's final comments see *Second Interim Report,* and *Final Report,* Part 3. Except for the statement to the

1961 Teamsters' convention, for which see *Proceedings,* p. 40, the remaining quotations are from "James Hoffa: A Candid Interview with the Contentious Kingpin of the Teamster Union," *Playboy,* November, 1963. Despite the title and source, this is one of the most informative recorded interviews with Hoffa.

Chapter 20

On the United Textile Workers see McClellan Committee, *Interim Report,* Report No. 1417, 85th Cong., 2d sess. (Washington: 1958). Also *Hearings,* Part 9, 85th Cong., 1st sess. (Washington: 1957).

On the Newspaper and Mail Deliverers Union see McClellan Committee, *Final Report,* Report No. 1139, Part I, 86th Cong., 2d sess. (Washington: 1960). Also *Hearings,* Part 51, 86th Cong., 1st sess. (Washington: 1959). The Gross and Noonan episode is reported in the same volumes. I am unable to obtain any reports of the Bender Commission.

See Robert F. Kennedy, *The Enemy Within,* New York: Harper and Brothers, 1960, pp. 266, 268.

The investigation of the Kohler strike is reported in McClellan Committee, *Final Report,* Report No. 1139, Part 2, 86th Cong., 2d sess. (Washington: 1960), and in *Hearings,* Part 58, 86th Cong., 1st sess. (Washington: 1959).

The happiness of Senators Goldwater and Mundt is noted in Kennedy, *op. cit.,* p. 268. The comment on the McGovern report is in *ibid.,* p. 271.

The exchange between Senator Curtis and Walter Reuther is in *Hearings,* Part 25, 85th Cong., 2d sess. (Washington: 1958).

On Gosser's trial and conviction see *New York Times,* November 30 and December 8, 1962, and December 9, 1964.

In 1962 the Permanent Subcommittee of the Senate Committee on Government Operations, also under the chairmanship of Senator McClellan, investigated the American Guild of Variety Artists (AGVA), an affiliate of the AFL-CIO. AGVA has jurisdiction over performers in cabarets, ice shows, circuses and others of the lighter theatrical pursuits. Most of its active members work in night clubs, a large number of these as exotic dancers—more accurately known as strippers. Various former and current members of the union charged that AGVA had failed to provide reasonable working conditions for female performers in night clubs; that some AGVA officials collaborated with club owners—some of them underworld figures—in maintaining below-scale wage payments and other violations of the basic AGVA collective bargaining agreement; and that, as a condition of employment, many dancers were forced to act as B-girls, soliciting overcharged drinks from customers and sometimes providing sexual services.

B-girl activity is prohibited by law in a number of states, as well as by Clause 6 of the AGVA agreement. The clause was evidently poorly enforced; the Subcommittee found no evidence that AGVA had struck or otherwise reproached any night club for violating the clause. See Permanent Subcommittee on Investigations, Senate Committee on Government Operations, *Hearings,* Vols. I and II, 87th Cong., 2d sess. (Washington: 1962). There was no report.

The telephone conversation between Senator Goldwater and Robert F. Kennedy is in Kennedy, *op. cit.,* p. 298.

Chapter 21

The opening Gompers' statement on autonomy was made on March 8, 1888, and is quoted in Philip Taft, *The A. F. of L. in the Time of Gompers,* New York: Harper and Brothers, 1957, p. 40. The second statement is in Gompers, *The American Labor Movement,* Washington: The American Federation of Labor, 1914(?), pp. 7–9. His remark on dictatorship was made on May 11, 1888, and is in Taft, *op. cit.,* pp. 163–64.

The Retail Clerks' case and the Executive Council pronouncement are in Taft, *op. cit.,* p. 167. On the HRE case see *Proceedings,* AFL Convention, 1898, p. 54, and Taft, *op. cit.,* p. 167. The American Agents Association case is reported in Taft, *loc. cit.* Taft's materials on these three cases are taken from the AFL Executive Council minutes.

See *Justice,* December 4, 1920. The quotation from the first McGuire address is in *Proceedings,* AFL Convention, 1928, pp. 246–47. Green's response to his second address is in *Proceedings,* 1929, p. 189.

See Bricklayers, Masons and Plasterers International Union of America, *Sixth Biennial and Fifty-Eighth Report of the President and Secretary* (1930), pp. XII–XIII.

The correspondence between Green and Morrin is taken from the AFL Executive Council minutes and reported in Taft, *op. cit.,* p. 423. The exchange with Elliott is in Taft, p. 424.

See *Proceedings,* AFL Convention, 1932, pp. 397–98; 1933, p. 523; 1934, pp. 251–52, 628–29; 1935, p. 589. Tobin's statements are in *The International Teamster,* June, 1934, June, 1938, March, 1940 and May, 1940.

See *Proceedings,* AFL Convention, 1940, pp. 64–65, 504–506 for the Executive Council's report and the ILGWU resolution. For the convention debate on the powers of the federation see *ibid.,* pp. 446ff. On the Fay-Dubinsky incident and Green's comment see *New York Times,* November 21 and 22, 1940, and *Newsweek,* December 2, 1940.

On Wellner and Local 102 of the Painters see Edward Dean Sullivan, *This Labor Union Racket,* New York: Hillman-Curl, 1936, pp. 38ff. Woll's statement is in Taft, *op. cit.,* p. 427. The succeeding comments of the AFL Executive Council are in *Proceedings,* AFL Convention, 1941, pp. 28, 542, 69, 542, 69 *seriatim.* See "Just Some Thoughts," *Brotherhood of Maintenance of Way Employees Journal,* November, 1941. On the 1952 action against the Jewelry Workers and the Distillery Workers see *Proceedings,* AFL Convention, 1952, p. 401.

On the actions against the ILA see *Proceedings,* AFL Convention, 1953, pp. 54–68, 487. See *Proceedings,* IBL Convention, 1954, pp. 7–8. The AFL's condemnation of the ILA's "swift and sweetheart" contract is in the 1954 *Proceedings,* p. 52.

Charges were made from time to time that the Communists were helping the ILA. The International Longshoremen's and Warehousemen's Union (ILWU), expelled from the CIO in 1949 on grounds of Communist domination, did send in emissaries from time to time, and at one point made a small loan to the ILA. See *New York Times,* June 19, 1957. On the "violence and bloodshed" see *Proceedings,* IBL Convention, 1954, p. 9. The AFL Executive Council report on the second AFL-ILA election is in *Proceedings,* AFL Convention, 1954, p. 534.

The correspondence between Meany and Beck and Bates, and Meany and Curran, are taken by the author from the AFL-CIO archives. Meany to Beck, February 29, 1956. Beck to Bates, April 22, 1955. Meany to Curran, October 23, 1956. Paul Hall's pledge of support to the IBL is in *New York Times,* June 30, 1956. Meany's comments to the Executive Council in Beck's presence are taken from the AFL-CIO Executive Council *Minutes* (AFL-CIO files). On subsequent developments see *New York Times,* July 20, 1956, September 10, 1956, and September 22, 1956. Larry Long's tribute to the SIU is in *Proceedings,* IBL Convention, 1957, p. 14; see also pp. 4–5, 15. Hall's appeal for another campaign against the ILA is in *New York Times,* November 14, 1957. Meany's final comments on the ILA are in *Proceedings,* AFL-CIO Convention, 1959, pp. 421, 430, 430–31.

The AFL's 1953 statement on welfare fund administration is in *Proceedings,* AFL Convention, 1953, pp. 144–45. The Executive Council's 1954 statement and Beck's declaration are in *Proceedings,* 1954 Convention, pp. 563–64, 567. See the 1955 *Proceedings,* pp. 243, 248, and *Guides for Administration of Health and Welfare Funds,* Washington: American Federation of Labor, 1955.

Proceedings, CIO Convention, 1951, pp. 321, 332; 1954, pp. 434, 470; 1955, pp. 231–32.

AFL-CIO Constitution, Article II, Section 10; AFL Constitution, Article IX, Section 5(1955); CIO Constitution, Article VI, Section 10(1955); AFL-CIO Constitution, Article XIII, Section 1(d); and AFL-CIO Codes of Ethical Practices, Washington: AFL-CIO, 1957. The texts of all three constitutions can be found in the appropriate convention proceedings.

Chapter 22

"Report of Ethical Practices Committee on Distillery, Rectifying and Wine Workers' International Union," *Proceedings,* AFL-CIO Convention, 1957, Vol. II, pp. 448–66. Also "Staff Report Relating to the Distillery, Rectifying and Wine Workers' International Union" (AFL-CIO files, n.d.).

The comments of the Distillery Workers' GEB on Hogan are in "Report . . . ," p. 459.

Meany's statement on autonomy is in *AFL-CIO News,* September 1, 1956.

O'Neill to Meany, August 30, 1956 (AFL-CIO files). *Hearing,* Committee on Ethical Practices, October 2, 1956, *passim* (AFL-CIO files). The second hearing was on December 17, 1956, and is reported separately (AFL-CIO files).

O'Neill to Meany, April 11, 1957 (AFL-CIO files). See also *Proceedings,* Special Convention of the Distillery, Rectifying, Wine and Allied Workers' International Union of America, March 21–22, 1957 (mimeo) (AFL-CIO files).

McGavin to Oneto, September 18, 1957. McGavin to General Executive Board, October 23, 1957. (Both in AFL-CIO files.) *The New York Times* report on the November convention is in November 27, 1957.

O'Neill to Meany, November 27, 1957 (AFL-CIO files).

The 1958 Distillery Workers' report on compliance with the Codes is in their *Report of Labor Trustees of the Social Security Fund,* April 18, 1958 (AFL-CIO files).

See *Proceedings,* AFL-CIO Convention, 1959, Vol. II, p. 375 for Meany's comment on his investigation of the Distillery Workers. Kennedy to Meany, August 11, 1959 (AFL-CIO files). The finances of Locals 1 and 2 are reported on in "International Union Matters," *Staff Report,* August 19, 1959 (mimeo) (AFL-CIO files). Brandenburg's report is in *Comments with Respect to the Investigative Staff Memorandum of the McClellan Committee Concerning the Distillery, Rectifying and Wine Workers' International Union and Several of its Locals* n.d. (mimeo) (AFL-CIO files). McGavin to Brandenburg, September 23, 1959 (AFL-CIO files). See *Proceedings,* AFL-CIO Convention, 1961, Vol. II, p. 44, for the restoration of the Distillery Workers to good standing in the AFL-CIO.

Washburn to Meany, September 7, 1952 (AFL-CIO files). On the UAW-AFL's investigation of Dio see *Minutes,* UAW-AFL International Executive Board, August 5–9, 1954, and *Memorandum,* Heaton to AIW officials and locals, September 7, 1954 (AFL-CIO files).

Dioguardi to Heaton, September 3, 1954. Heaton to Dioguardi, September 7, 1954 (Both in AFL-CIO files.)

The items on Dioguardi's police record are from a mimeographed memorandum in the AFL-CIO files, n.d.

Letter to Meany, n.d. (AFL-CIO files).

The comment on Inciso's police escorts is in Virgil Peterson, *A Report on Chicago Crime for 1956,* Chicago: Chicago Crime Commission, 1957, p. 21.

On Inciso's disaffiliation see *Minutes,* AIW International Executive Board, February 1, 1956 (AFL-CIO files). The statement by the Committee on Ethical Practices is taken from an AFL-CIO press release, August 27, 1956. Heaton to A. J. Hayes, September 6, 1956 (AFL-CIO files).

See "Regarding the Allied Industrial Workers of America, International Union," *Report of the AFL-CIO Ethical Practices Committee to the AFL-CIO Executive Council,* January 28, 1957 (AFL-CIO files). See also *AFL-CIO Staff Report Relating to Allied Industrial Workers of America, International Union,* n.d. (AFL-CIO files). On the AFL-CIO order to the AIW see *New York Times,* February 6, 1957. And on the reform measures taken by the AIW see *Report to the AFL-CIO . . . Regarding Efforts of the International Union to Meet the Ethical Practices Codes,* Allied Industrial Workers, March 5, 1957 (AFL-CIO files).

On the arrangement between Doria and Heaton see *Memorandum,* May 9, 1957 (AFL-CIO files). Meany summoned Heaton and the AIW Board in a letter to Heaton, May 10, 1957 (AFL-CIO files). Griepentrog reported the actions of the special convention in a letter to Meany, September 20, 1957 (AFL-CIO files). Meany's response is in two letters to Griepentrog, October 8 and 29, 1957 (AFL-CIO files). See also *Proceedings,* AFL-CIO Convention, 1957, Vol. II, p. 69; and *ibid.,* 1959, Vol. II, p. 58.

Klenert to Meany, July 18, 1952 (AFL-CIO files). On Meany's subsequent communications with Valente and Klenert and his meeting with the Executive Board of the UTWA, see *Report,* Meeting of a Sub-Committee of the Executive Council of the American Federation of Labor and the Executive Board of the United Textile Workers of America, September 24, 1952, *passim.* See also *New York Times,* July 23, 1957. On the report of the Committee on Ethical Practices see *Regarding the United Textile Workers of America,* Report of the AFL-CIO Ethical Practices Committee to the AFL-CIO Executive Council, September 16, 1957, pp. 25–26. See also *Brief and Exhibits . . . ,* United Textile Workers of America, n.d. (AFL-CIO files).

On the disciplinary action of the AFL-CIO Executive Council, see *Resolutions of the AFL-CIO Executive Council,* September 24 and October 25, 1957 (AFL-CIO files). Schnitzler to Valente, October 29, 1957. McGavin to Schaufenbil, November 18, 1957. Meany to Schaufenbil, December 5, 1957 (AFL-CIO files). Also *Proceedings,* AFL-CIO Convention, 1957, Vol. I, pp. 485–86, 461. And *United Textile Workers of America,* Transcript of Hearing, Appeals Committee, December 9, 1957 (AFL-CIO files).

Baldanzi to Meany, March 27, 1958 (AFL-CIO files). Meany's subsequent comment on the UTWA is in *Resolution,* AFL-CIO Executive Council, May 1, 1958 (AFL-CIO files). On the Executive Council's report see *Proceedings,* AFL-CIO Convention, 1959, Vol. I, p. 58. McGavin to Meany, January 6, 1960. See also McGavin to Meany, November 6, 1958; Baldanzi to Meany, August 11 and 25, 1958, and February 26, 1960. The UTWA's probation was ended in a letter from Meany to Baldanzi. (All in AFL-CIO files.)

Statement of Secretary-Treasurer Curtis R. Sims, before the Bakers' General Executive Board, in defense of charges bought against him by Cross, n.d. (AFL-CIO files). See also charges against Cross by Sims, March 6, 1957 (AFL-CIO files).

Regarding the Bakery and Confectionery Workers International Union of America, Report of the Ethical Practices Committee to the AFL-CIO Executive Council, September 16, 1957, *passim* (AFL-CIO files).

Cross to members, July 1, 1957. "Our Union and the AFL-CIO," Statement by the General Executive Board, October 4, 1957. Olson to Meany, October 21, 1957. See also "Statement by David S. Brown, Ph.D.," September 24, 1957. (Both in AFL-CIO files.)

On the Bakers' refusal to reinstate Sims or remove Cross, see *Statement of Policy and Resolution of the General Executive Board . . . ,* n.d. (AFL-CIO files). For the federation's actions against the Bakers, see *Proceedings,* AFL-CIO Convention, 1957, Vols. I and II, *passim.*

Meany's agreement to meet with the Bakers' GEB is in a letter to Olson, November 25, 1957 (AFL-CIO files). On the convention comments of Cross and Winter see *Proceedings,* Vol. I, pp. 221–40.

Cross *et al.* to members, December 13, 1957 (AFL-CIO files). *Proceedings,* BCW Special Convention, 1958, Third Day, p. 77, Second Day p. 41. On the convictions of Cross and others see *New York Times,* April 11, 1963. On the affairs of the ABC, see *Proceedings,* ABC Conventions, 1958 and 1962.

Carey to Hayes, July 6, 1956 (AFL-CIO files). On the AFL investigation of the IJWU see *Proceedings,* AFL Convention, 1952, pp. 94–95. See also *New York Times,* May 22, July 3 and October 2, 1952; April 27, May 27 and July 13, 1953; and March 4, 1956.

On the Minority Workers' committee see James C. Quinn and Morris Iushewitz to Meany, September 21, 1957 (AFL-CIO files). See also *Résumé of Complaints Involving the International Jewelry Workers Union,* n.d. (AFL-CIO files).

Morris and Powell to Meany, November 18, 1957. Minutes of Minority Workers committee, November 20, 1957 (AFL-CIO files).

For the findings of the Committee on Ethical Practices on the Jewelry Workers see *Proceedings,* AFL-CIO Convention, 1959, Vol. II, pp. 53–54. See also Staff Report for the Committee on Ethical Practices, April 14, 1958 (mimeo). Also *Supplemental Comments to Committee on Ethical Practices,* November 20, 1958, and *Comments on Supplemental Staff Report,* n.d., by Hyman Powell (mimeo); *Comments on Supplemental Staff Report,* n.d., by Joseph Morris (mimeo); and *Comments on Staff*

Report and Supplemental Staff Report, n.d., by Andrew Leredu (mimeo). (All in AFL-CIO files.)

Meany to Morris and Powell, November 15, 1957 (AFL-CIO files). The Executive Council's report is in *Proceedings,* AFL-CIO Convention, 1959, Vol. II, p. 56.

Byers to Meany, August 10, 1955. Meany to Byers, September 29, 1955. See also *Memorandum,* Cruikshank to Byers, September 28 1955. (All in AFL-CIO files.) *Staff Report* (mimeo, n.d.) and *Preliminary Report* (typescript, n.d.). (Both in AFL-CIO files.) See also *Proceedings,* AFL-CIO Convention, 1957, Vol. II, pp. 432–33.

On Byers' testimony see *Hearings before the Ethical Practices Committee . . . Concerning Laundry Workers International Union,* October 4, 1956 (mimeo), pp. 85–86, 116. Thatcher to Meany, December 7, 1957 (AFL-CIO files). On the report of the Committee on Ethical Practices see *Proceedings,* AFL-CIO Convention, 1957, Vol. II, pp. 423–46.

Crowell to McGavin, April 16 and 29, 1957 (AFL-CIO files). *Proceedings,* LWIU Convention, 1957, pp. 190–91. The statement by James on Fagan is in a typescript memorandum, May 15, 1957, in the AFL-CIO files. On the LWIU's suspension see *Proceedings,* AFL-CIO Convention, 1957, Vol. II, p. 447. For the debate on the LWIU's proposed expulsion see *Proceedings,* Vol. I, pp. 518–43. See also *Before the Appeals Committee,* Hearing, December 5, 1957 (mimeo); laundress to Meany, June 10, 1957; Fagan to McGavin, December 10, 1957. (All in AFL-CIO files.)

For the initial statements of Beck and Meany, and English's opposition to Beck, see *New York Times,* March 29, April 3 and April 17, 1957. Beck was under investigation at this time by the Internal Revenue Service for suspected income tax evasion.

Meany to Beck, April 25, 1957 (AFL-CIO files). English's statement on "dirty linen" is in *New York Times,* May 22, 1957. For the report of the Committee on Ethical Practices on the Teamsters see *Proceedings,* AFL-CIO Convention, 1957, Vol. II, pp. 469–505. See also *Staff Reports* (with Supplements) (mimeo) (AFL-CIO files). Hoffa's invitation to the AFL-CIO to "go to hell" is reported in *New York Times,* October 3, 1957. For Cohelan's statement to the Teamsters' convention see *Proceedings,* pp. 315–16; on Beck, see pp. 21–22, 711–12.

Beck to Schnitzler, November 1, 1957 (AFL-CIO files). On the trusteeship of the New York locals see *New York Times,* September 5, November 13 and 14, 1957.

For the debate on the expulsion of the Teamsters see *Proceedings,* AFL-CIO Convention, 1957, Vol. I, pp. 55–105. See also *Before the Appeals Committee,* Hearing, December 4, 1957 (mimeo) (AFL-CIO files). Brewster and Sidney L. Brennan lost their vice presidencies at the Teamsters' convention. English resigned from the AFL-CIO Executive Council.

Paul Hall's statement on resistance to the Teamsters is in *Proceedings,* AFL-CIO Convention, 1959, Vol. I, pp. 464–69.

Schnitzler to Walter Jeske, February 15, 1961 (AFL-CIO files).

See *Proceedings,* AFL-CIO Convention, 1961, Vol. I, pp. 216–18, 221–22, 224–25, 110–11. Hoffa's post-assassination comment on Robert Kennedy is in *New York Times,* December 13, 1963. On Backhus see *Wall Street Journal,* July 30, 1964. The quotation on "suspicion, acrimony and intrigue" is in Ralph and Estelle James, *Hoffa and the Teamsters,* Princeton: Van Nostrand, 1965, p. 10. The latter-day habits of the Teamsters' Board were described to the author by a Teamster official. The statement on organizing problems is in *Wall Street Journal, op. cit.*

On the Operating Engineers see *Proceedings,* AFL-CIO Convention, 1959, Vol.

I, p. 53. On Hutcheson see *New York Times,* May 15, 1962; June 28, 1963; February 14, 1964.

Chapter 23

On the history of the Coleman and Hobbs Acts, see Peter Megargee Brown and Richard S. Peer, "The Anti-Racketeering Act: Labor and Management Weapon Against Labor Racketeering," *New York University Law Review,* May, 1957. See also Joseph A. Padway, "The Hobbs Act—How Does It Affect Labor?" *American Federationist,* September, 1946, and *Union Reporting Requirements in State Law,* U.S. Department of Labor (Washington: 1958).

See New York Laws 1953, c.882 (McK. Unconsol. Laws #6700–aa and following); New Jersey Laws 1953, c.203 (N.J.S.A. 32:23–1 and following; Congressional Act of August 12, 1953, c.407. On the activities of the Waterfront Commission see *Annual Reports,* Waterfront Commission of New York Harbor, 1953–54, *et. seq.* The David C. Thompson quotation is taken from *Public Hearings Before Assembly Committee on Labor and Industrial Relations,* New Jersey, April 28, 1961 (mimeo), pp. 8–10. The NYSA comment on "paper work" is in *New York Times,* November 1, 1959. The Commission's comment on port security is in *Annual Report,* 1962–63, p. 10. For the Ambrose testimony see *Public Hearings,* p. 36. See *Special Report to the Governors and the Legislatures of the States of New York and New Jersey,* December, 1960, *passim.* On the AFL-CIO's actions see *Proceedings,* AFL-CIO Convention, 1961, Vol. I, pp. 557–58, and *ibid.,* 1963, Vol. I, pp. 507–8. The federation's opposition to the two bills introduced in New York and New Jersey was transmitted by telegram from Meany to Governor Nelson Rockefeller of New York on February 27, 1961 (AFL-CIO files). Paul Hall's comments are in *Public Hearings,* p. 39A. The BLS comment is in *Manpower Utilization—Job Security in the Longshore Industry: Port of New York,* United States Department of Labor (Washington: 1964). On the issue of closing the register, see *New York Times,* July 3, 1964, and April 9, 1965. Budd Schulberg's comments are in his article "The Waterfront Revisited," *Saturday Evening Post,* September 7, 1963. The adverse comment on the ILA in the last paragraph of this section is from Vernon Jensen, *Hiring of Dock Workers,* Cambridge: Harvard University Press, 1964, p. 117. This is by far the best discussion in print of prevailing conditions on the New York waterfront. See also T. Johnson, "The Waterfront Commission of New York Harbor: A Case Study of a Bi-State Regulatory Agency," Columbia University: Dissertation Abstract, December, 1963. The NYSA policy was conveyed by letter from Edward P. Tastrom to Lester Rosenthal on March 10, 1965 (author's files). The final Tobin comment is in Schulberg, *op. cit.*

The quotation from Gompers on the courts is in United States Commission on Industrial Relations, *Final Report* (Washington: 1915), p. 54.

There is an enormous list of court cases on the Teamster monitorship; it seems unnecessary to reproduce it here. Those interested should consult Leonard B. Mandelbaum, "The Teamster Monitorship: A Lesson for the Future," *Federal Bar Journal,* Spring, 1960; and "Monitors: A New Equitable Remedy," in *Note, Yale Law Journal,* November, 1960.

The quotation from Frankfurter is in William Goffen, "Monitors vs. the Teamsters," *Nation,* April 9, 1960. The "nightmarish deluge" quotation is from the *Note* in the *Yale Law Journal.*

On the Senate investigation of the monitorship see "James R. Hoffa and Continued Underworld Control of New York Teamster Local 239," *Report No. 1784,* Permanent Subcommittee on Investigations of the Senate Committee on Government Operations, 87th Cong., 2d sess. (Washington: 1962), and *Hearings,* 87th Cong., 1st sess. (Washington: 1961).

The late Sam Romer was labor editor for the Minneapolis *Tribune* and an authority on the Teamsters. See his "The Teamster Monitors and the Administration of the International Union," *Labor Law Journal,* July, 1961. On the alleged activities of the McClellan Committee and Robert F. Kennedy in the Monitors' case see Paul Jacobs, "Extracurricular Activities of the McClellan Committee," *California Law Review,* May, 1963.

On the history and content of the Welfare and Pension Plans Disclosure Act see "Legislative History of the Welfare and Pension Plans Disclosure Act of 1958, as amended by Public Law 87–420 of 1962," U.S. Department of Labor, (Washington: 1962); *Federal-State Regulation of Welfare Funds.* Bureau of National Affairs, (Washington, 1958); *New Disclosure Requirements,* Chicago: Commerce Clearing House, 1958; William J. Isaacson, "Employee Welfare and Pension Plans: Regulation and Protection of Employee Rights," *Columbia Law Review,* January, 1959; G. Robert Blakey, "The Welfare and Pension Plans Disclosure Act," *Notre Dame Lawyer,* April, 1963; Anthony Abato, Jr., "The Welfare and Pension Plans Disclosure Act—Its History, Operation and Amendment," *George Washington Law Review,* April, 1962. The full text of President Eisenhower's statement is in *Federal-State Regulation . . . ,* p. 26. Goldberg was testifying on bills being studied by the House Committee on Education and Labor; see *Hearings,* 87th Cong., 1st sess. (Washington: 1961), p. 14. On the administrative history of the Act see the annual reports of the Secretary of Labor, also *Reports to Congress,* OLMWPR, 1963ff. On state disclosure acts see Abato, *op. cit.* The National Association of Insurance Commissioners has adopted a code of ethical practices; however, it applies only to the ten percent of welfare plans represented by those administered jointly by labor and management or by labor alone. See *Welfare and Pension Plans Disclosure Act,* Report No. 1440, Senate Committee on Labor and Public Welfare, 85th Cong., 2d sess. (Washington: 1958), p. 11. The amended Act exempts from coverage those plans administered by agencies of the federal and state governments, those maintained solely for the purpose of complying with workmen's compensation laws, those administered by tax-exempt organizations and those covering less than twenty-five persons.

Unless otherwise noted, all the quotations in this section, and the best single record of the Landrum-Griffin debates, may be found in *Legislative History of the Labor-Management Reporting and Disclosure Act,* United States Department of Labor (Washington: 1964). On the AFL-CIO's statement on prospective legislation, see *New York Times,* December 11, 1957. Summerfield's statement is in *New York Times,* December 6, 1958. The quotation on the business publicity campaign for Landrum-Griffin is from Bernard Nossiter, Washington *Post,* September 10, 1959. The criticism on labor lobbying is from Sar Levitan, "Labor Lobbyists' Contribution to Tough Labor Legislation," *Labor Law Journal,* October, 1959. The citation and text of the LMRDA are in *Legislative History . . .* Benjamin Aaron's comment is in Aaron, "The Labor-Management Reporting and Disclosure Act of 1959," *Harvard Law Review,* March and April, 1960. Other comments by Aaron on the history of the LMRDA are found in "The Union Member's 'Bill of Rights': The First Two

Years," *Industrial Relations,* February, 1962, and "Internal Relations Between Unions and Their Members: United States Report," *Rutgers Law Review,* Winter, 1964. The "watchdog" quote is from John D. Stewart, "The Bureau of Labor-Management Reports," in Martin Estey *et al., Regulating Union Government,* New York: Harper and Row, 1964, p. 66. For the BLMR's report see *Summary of Operations,* Bureau of Labor-Management Reports (Washington: 1962), p. 2. The comment on the technical assistance program is from Stewart, *op. cit.,* p. 82; that on the House Committee on Appropriations from Stewart, *op. cit.,* p. 88. The Estey volume is a study of the legislative and administrative history of the LMRDA. The statement on election safeguards is from John Holcombe, "Union Democracy and the LMRDA," *Labor Law Journal,* July, 1961. The Goldberg statement on trusteeships is in a special report, *Union Trusteeships,* U.S. Department of Labor (Washington: 1962), p. 5. For the AFL-CIO's comments on the LMRDA, see *Proceedings,* AFL-CIO Convention, 1963, Vol. I, p. 293, Vol. II, p. 190, and *ibid.,* 1965, Vol. II, p. 167. For indictments under various laws see the annual reports of the Attorney-General of the United States. For Meany's comment on "witch-hunting" see *New York Times,* May 21, 1965; see also *Seafarers Log,* January 20 and February 17, 1967, and *A Report After Eight Years of the Landrum-Griffin Act,* Maritime Trades Department, AFL-CIO (Washington: 1967).

Chapter 24

There is not much of a theoretical literature on the subject of trade union corruption. For probably the earliest attempt at categorization see Robert F. Hoxie, *Trade Unionism in the United States,* New York: Appleton and Company, 1922, esp. pp. 50–51. The best comment on the subject in general is Philip Taft, *Corruption and Racketeering in the Labor Movement,* Ithaca: New York State School of Industrial and Labor Relations, Bulletin No. 38, 1958. See also David J. Saposs, "Labor Racketeering: Evolution and Solutions," *Social Research,* Autumn, 1958. The best causative analysis of a single case of corruption is Daniel Bell, "The Racket-Ridden Longshoremen," in his *The End of Ideology,* Glencoe: The Free Press, 1960. There is no scholarly history of trade union corruption in existence. For journalistic treatment of the subject see Harold Seidman, *Labor Czars—A History of Labor Racketeering,* New York: Liveright Publishing Corporation, 1938, and Malcolm Johnson, *Crime on the Labor Front,* New York: McGraw-Hill Book Co., 1950. For a brief historical account see my "Corruption in American Trade Unions," *Political Quarterly* (London), July, 1957.

For two attempts at an economic analysis of trade union corruption see Simon Rottenberg, "A Theory of Corruption in Trade Unions," National Institute of Social and Behavioral Sciences, Series Studies in Social and Economic Sciences, Symposia Studies Series No. 3, Washington: 1960, and Paul A. Weinstein, "Racketeering and Labor: an Economic Analysis," *Industrial and Labor Relations Review,* April, 1966. The first concludes *inter alia* that corruption is most likely to be found in industries where there is no easy substitute for the labor class involved or for the product (not true of the trucking, culinary, longshoring and building service industries), or where the demand for labor is relatively inelastic because the labor cost factor is small (the labor cost factor in the needle trades is high), or where the supply of labor is relatively inelastic because of the higher skill involved (not true of truck-driving, some of the culinary labor categories, and building services, and most longshore employment). The second article argues that "The larger the number of firms or the more difficult the control of entry [into an industry] the less likely is racket organization because of its expense." This cannot be reconciled with the experience in the garment, trucking, culinary, entertainment, longshoring, construction and building service industries.

On the sources of labor racketeering in general see Louis Adamic, "Racketeers and Organized Labor," *Harper's Monthly,* September, 1930; Lewis W. Hunt, "The Rise of a Racketeer," *The Outlook,* December, 1930; Burdette G. Lewis, "How Racketeering Began," *Review of Reviews,* July, 1932; Walter Lippmann, "The Underworld, Our Secret Servant," *Forum,* January, 1931; Copal Mintz, "Trade Union Abuses," *St. John's Law Review,* May, 1932; Gordon L. Hostetter and Thomas Q. Beesley, "The Rising Tide of Racketeering," *The Political Quarterly,* Vol. 4, 1933; "Legal Implications of Racketeering," *Columbia Law Review,* Vol. 37, 1937; William F. Whyte, "The Social Structure of Racketeering," in *Cities and Society,* Glencoe: The Free Press, 1957; and Virgil W. Peterson, "Rackets in America," *Journal of Criminal Law, Criminology and Police Science,* April, 1959.

On business unionism see Philip Taft, "The Origins of Business Unionism," *Industrial and Labor Relations Review,* October, 1963. The point on "simple honesty" is in his *Corruption and Racketeering in the Labor Movement.*

The Meany statement on Cross is in *Proceedings,* AFL-CIO Convention, 1957, Vol. I, p. 233. The Detroit Teamster's comment was in a private interview with the author, but it is hardly original; there are many versions of it about.

The quotation from Taft is in his *The Structure and Government of Labor Unions,* Cambridge: Harvard University Press, 1954, p. 245. The Summers statement is in his "The Law of Union Discipline: What the Courts Do in Fact," *Yale Law Review,* December, 1960.

On the UAW Public Review Board in general see Jack Stieber, Walter E. Oberer and Michael Harrington, *Democracy and Public Review: An Analysis of the UAW Public Review Board,* Santa Barbara: Center for the Study of Democratic Institutions, 1960. See also Jerome H. Brooks, "Impartial Review of Internal Union Disputes: Experiment in Democratic Self-Discipline," *Ohio State Law Journal,* Winter, 1960.

The Reuther statement is taken from a UAW press release of March 24, 1957. See the UAW convention proceedings for the proposals and debate on public review, *passim.* Rabbi Adler's statement is in *Proceedings,* 1964, p. 303. The UAW publishes an annual report on the Board. There has been very little literature on the subject.

For the efforts of the Packinghouse Workers and the Upholsterers see Brooks, *op. cit.* I am indebted to the Brooks article for the point that the mere existence of the UAW Public Review Board has had a salutary effect.

Shortly after the onset of the McClellan Committee hearings, two proposals were made for the improvement of union trial procedures. President Louis Hollander of the then unmerged New York State CIO suggested the establishment of a "supreme court" of distinguished citizens and senior labor officials to pronounce on charges of corruption against individual union representatives. He said it was unfair to "throw the rank and file of unions to the wolves because their officers were corrupt . . . The constitution of the AFL-CIO should be amended to permit a top-level court to root out the crooks without penalizing the entire membership." *New York Times,* April 2,

1957. A few weeks later Professor Walter Gellhorn of the Columbia University Law School proposed the creation of a centralized grievance machinery within the labor movement to which individual union members could appeal against the misdeeds of their officers. *New York Times,* May 1, 1957. Both proposals, of course, would involve the assumption by the AFL-CIO of substantial sovereignty over the affairs of every affiliated union. Neither proposal received any important attention.

See E. H. Sutherland, "White Collar Criminality," *American Sociological Review,* February, 1940, and his *White Collar Crime,* New York: Dryden, 1949, p. 223. Also Harry Elmer Barnes in "Crime and Crime Control: Digest of Hearings before a Subcommittee of the Senate Committee on Commerce" (Washington: 1934), p. 710. The Reckless quotation is in his *The Crime Problem,* New York: Appleton Century-Crofts, 1955, p. 189.

On immigration and crime see *Report on Crime and the Foreign Born,* National Committee on Law Observance and Enforcement, Washington: USGPO, 1931. Discontent came mainly with the second and succeeding generations. The Committee reported that the foreign-born "commit considerably fewer crimes than the native born." *Op. cit.,* p. 195.

Meany's jousts with Tobin and Hutcheson are reported in A. H. Raskin, "New Task for the Blunt Meany," *New York Times Magazine,* February 20, 1955.

There is a large and growing literature on corrupt practices in American business. In general see Mabel E. Elliott, *Crime in Modern Society,* New York: Harper, 1952. For the point that American business would be uncomfortable operating under the principles expected of American labor see Frederic Meyers, "Dual Standard for Corruption," *Nation,* March 1, 1958.

Robert F. Kennedy's statement is in "Report to the President from the Attorney General on the Fight Against Organized Crime," January 10, 1963, mimeo. See also *Wall Street Journal,* January 29, 1964. On the President's Commission on Law Enforcement and Administration of Justice see *New York Times,* February 19, 1967.

Appendixes

Appendixes

AFL-CIO CONSTITUTION ON ETHICAL PRACTICES

Article II, Section 10:

The objects and principles of this Federation are:

. . . To protect the labor movement from any and all corrupt influences and from the undermining efforts of Communist agencies and all others who are opposed to the basic principles of our democracy and free and democratic unionism.

• • •

Article VII, Section 7:

It is a basic principle of this Federation that it must be and remain free from any and all corrupt influences and from the undermining efforts of Communist, Fascist or other totalitarian agencies who are opposed to the basic principles of our democracy and of free and democratic trade unionism. The Executive Council, when requested to do so by the President or by any other member of the Executive Council, shall have the power to conduct an investigation, directly or through an appropriate standing or special committee appointed by the President, of any situation in which there is reason to believe that any affiliate is dominated, controlled or substantially influenced in the conduct of its affairs by any corrupt influence, or that the policies or activities of any affiliate are consistently directed toward the advocacy, support, advancement or achievement of the program or of the purposes of the Communist party, any Fascist organization or other totalitarian movement. Upon the completion of such an investigation, including a hearing if requested, the Executive Council shall have the authority to make recommendations or give directions to the affiliate involved and shall have the further authority, upon a two-thirds vote, to suspend any affiliate found guilty of a violation of this section. Any action of the Executive Council under this section may be appealed to the convention, provided, however, that such action shall be effective when taken and shall remain in full force and affect pending any appeal.

Article XIII, Section 1 (d):

The Committee on Ethical Practices shall be vested with the duty and responsibility to assist the Executive Council in carrying out the constitutional determination of the Federation to keep the Federation free from any taint of corruption or Communism, in accordance with the provisions of this constitution.

AFL-CIO RESOLUTION ON ETHICAL PRACTICES
(Adopted by the AFL-CIO Convention, December, 1955)

The democratic institutions of the United States of America were established on the foundation of honesty, integrity, responsibility. The free and democratic labor movement of our country similarly rests upon the foundations of brotherhood, honesty and integrity.

Any departure from the most exacting ethical principles is harmful not only to the people directly affected but to the whole fabric of our civilization.

The American labor movement has ever been quick in its denunciation of public officials who betray their trust. We have been equally critical of businessmen who have used corrupt methods and bribery to gain their selfish, acquisitive ends. We must be equally quick to recognize and condemn those instances of racketeering, corruption, and disregard for ethical standards when they occur inside our labor movement.

The vast majority of labor union officials accept their responsibility and trust. They endeavor honestly to carry out the democratic will of their members and to discharge the duties of their office. Yet the reputations of the vast majority are imperiled by the dishonest, corrupt, unethical practices of the few who betray their trust and who look upon the trade union movement not as a brotherhood to serve the general welfare, but as a means to advance their own selfish purposes or to forward the aim of groups or organizations who would destroy our democratic institutions. By the adoption of the Constitution of the American Federation of Labor and Congress of Industrial Organizations, the American labor movement has clearly accepted the responsibility for keeping its own house in order and to protect the movement "from any and all corrupt influences and from the undermining efforts of Communist agencies and all others who are opposed to the basic principles of our democracy and free and democratic unionism." Only by their whole-hearted dedication to this constitutional objective can labor unions meet their obligations to their memberships. Failure to meet these responsibilities can only result in governmental assumption of what are properly trade union functions. Reliance on the agencies of government for keeping our movement free from the infiltration of racketeers, crooks, Communists, Fascists and other enemies of free democratic unionism would constitute a threat to the independence and freedom of the entire movement;

Now, therefore, be it resolved:

1. The First Constitutional Convention of the AFL-CIO calls upon all its affiliated national and international unions to take whatever steps are necessary within their own organizations to effect the policies and ethical standards set forth in the constitution of the AFL-CIO. When constitutional amendments or changes in internal administrative procedures are necessary for the affiliated organizations to carry out the responsibilities incumbent upon autonomous organizations, such amendments and changes should be undertaken at the earliest practicable time.

2. This First Constitutional Convention of the AFL-CIO pledges its full support,

good offices, and staff facilities of the AFL-CIO Committee on Ethical Practices to all national and international unions in their efforts to carry out and put into practice the constitutional mandate to keep our organization "free from any taint of corruption or Communism."

AFL-CIO RESOLUTION ON PROCEDURES
(Adopted by AFL-CIO Executive Council, June, 1956)

WHEREAS, Article II, Section 10 and Article VIII, Section 7, of the AFL-CIO Constitution provide that it is a basic principle of this Federation that it must be and remain free from any and all corrupt influences; and

WHEREAS, Article VIII, Section 7, authorizes the Executive Council, upon the request of the President or any other member of the Executive Council, "to conduct an investigation directly or through an appropriate standing committee or special committee appointed by the President, of any situation in which there is reason to believe that any affiliate is dominated, controlled or substantially influenced in the conduct of its affairs by any corrupt influence . . ."; and

WHEREAS, Article XIII, Section 1 (d) provides for a Committee on Ethical Practices which shall be vested with the duty and responsibility to assist the Executive Council in carrying out the above constitutional principles, and such committee has been appointed by the President with the approval of the Executive Council; now, therefore, be it

RESOLVED by the Executive Council of the American Federation of Labor and Congress of Industrial Organizations:

1. That the Committee on Ethical Practices is vested with the authority of the Council to conduct formal investigations, including a hearing if requested, on behalf of the Council, into any situation in which there is reason to believe an affiliate is dominated, controlled or substantially influenced in the conduct of its affairs by any corrupt influence and in which such formal investigation is requested by the President or any member of the Executive Council. The Committee shall report to the Executive Council the results of any such investigation with such recommendations to the Council as the Committee deems appropriate.

2. The Committee is authorized, upon its own motion or upon the request of the President, to make such preliminary inquiries as it deems appropriate in order to ascertain whether any situations exist which require formal investigation. The Committee will report to the Executive Council as to any situations in which it believes that formal investigation is required or desirable and shall undertake such formal investigation as provided in paragraph 1 of this resolution.

3. The Committee is directed to develop a set of principles and guides for adoption by the AFL-CIO in order to implement the constitutional determination that the AFL-CIO shall be and remain free from all corrupt influences. Upon the development of such recommended guides and principles, they shall be submitted by the Committee to the Executive Council for appropriate action.

AFL-CIO STATEMENT REGARDING COOPERATION
WITH ALL APPROPRIATE PUBLIC AGENCIES
INVESTIGATING RACKETEERING
(Adopted by the AFL-CIO Executive Council, January 28, 1957)

The American Federation of Labor and Congress of Industrial Organizations is pledged both by its constitution and by fundamental principles of trade union morality to keep the labor movement free from any taint of corruption.

While the AFL-CIO has its own responsibility for keeping its house in order and is attempting to meet this obligation to the best of its ability, this does not in any sense mean that appropriate agencies of government and the public do not have rights, obligations and responsibilities in eliminating racketeering and corruption from all segments of American life, including the labor movement.

No institution or agency, whether labor or business, public or private, enjoys special immunity from the equal application of the laws, from appropriate investigation by duly constituted legislative committees and from scrutiny of its operations by the members of the press or the general public.

Investigations by fair and objective legislative comittees in the field of labor-management relations have been of tremendous help in eliminating abuses in this area.

The investigation conducted by the LaFollette Committee exposing as it did, unsavory and illegal practices on the part of important business interests, contributed greatly to the enactment of the Wagner Act and to the elimination of employer practices which prevented union organization and caused strife and violence in labor-management relations. The recent investigation by the Douglas subcommittee of the Senate Labor Committee, exposing as it did, instances of corruption and improper conduct by labor officials and others in the handling of health and welfare funds, has provided for the public and the labor movement invaluable information which has laid the foundation for proposed disclosure legislation in this field, endorsed by the AFL-CIO, and which in addition, has enabled the AFL-CIO and its affiliates to do a better job of keeping their house in order. Both law enforcement agencies, in the interest of enforcing law, and legislative committees in the interest of enacting corrective legislation, by reason of their power and authority to subpoena witnesses and to place them under oath, as well as their superior investigatorial facilities, have means beyond those of the labor movement to expose and bring to light corrupt influences.

It goes almost without saying that law enforcement agencies, legislative committees, and the labor movement itself share the common responsibility of conducting investigations fairly and objectively, without fear or favor and in keeping with due process concepts firmly imbedded in the tradition and constitution of our great country. It is a firm policy of the AFL-CIO that the highest ethical standards be observed and vigorously followed by all officials of the AFL-CIO and its affiliates in the conduct of their offices, in the handling of trade union and welfare funds, and in the administration of trade union affairs. Trade union and welfare funds are the common property of the members of our unions and must, therefore, be administered as a high and sacred trust for their benefit.

The AFL-CIO is detemined that any remaining vestiges of racketeering or corruption in unions shall be completely eradicated. We believe that Congress, in the interest of enacting corrective legislation, if the same be deemed and found necessary, has the right, through proper committees, to investigate corruption wherever it exists, whether in labor, industry or anywhere else.

It is the firm policy of the AFL-CIO to cooperate fully with all proper legislative committees, law enforcement agencies and other public bodies seeking fairly and objectively to keep the labor movement or any other segment of our society free from any and all corrupt influences. This means that all officials of the AFL-CIO and its affiliates should freely and without reservation answer all relevant questions asked by proper law enforcement agencies, legislative committees and other public bodies, seeking fairly and objectively to keep the labor movement free from corruption. We recognize that any person is entitled, in the exercise of his individual conscience, to the protection afforded by the Fifth Amendment and we reaffirm our conviction that this historical right must not be abridged. It is the policy of the AFL-CIO, however, that if a trade union official decides to invoke the Fifth Amendment for his personal protection and to avoid scrutiny by proper legislative committees, law enforcement agencies or other public bodies into alleged corruption on his part, he has no right to continue to hold office in his union. Otherwise, it becomes possible for a union official who may be guilty of corruption to create the impression that the trade union movement sanctions the use of the Fifth Amendment, not as a matter of individual conscience, but as a shield against proper scrutiny into corrupt influences in the labor movement.

THE AFL-CIO CODES OF ETHICAL PRACTICES
CODE I: LOCAL UNION CHARTERS
(Approved by the AFL-CIO Executive Council, August 29, 1956)

The AFL-CIO, as one of its specific objectives, has a constitutional mandate "to protect the labor movement from any and all corrupt influences . . ."

The Committee on Ethical Practices has been vested by the AFL-CIO constitution with the "duty and responsibility" to assist the Executive Council in its determination to keep the AFL-CIO "free from any taint or corruption . . ."

As the Statement on Ethical Practices adopted unanimously by our First Constitutional Convention pointed out, "The vast majority of labor union officials accept their responsibility and trust. . . . Yet the reputations of the vast majority are imperiled by the dishonest, corrupt, unethical practices of the few who betray their trust and who look upon the trade union movement not as a brotherhood to serve the general welfare, but as a means to advance their own selfish purposes. . . ."

The statement of our constitutional convention specifically called upon our affiliated national and international unions "to take whatever steps are necessary within their own organizations to effect the policies and ethical standards set forth in the constitution of the AFL-CIO." The same resolution pledged the "full support, good offices and staff facilities" of the Ethical Practices Committee to our affiliated national and international unions in "their efforts to carry out and put into practice the constitutional mandate" to keep our organization free of corruption.

At its June, 1956, meeting the Executive Council directed the Committee on Ethical Practices "to develop a set of principles and guides for adoption by the AFL-CIO in order to implement the constitutional determination that the AFL-CIO shall be and remain free from all corrupt influences" and directed that such recommended guides and principles be submitted to the Council.

In accordance with these constitutional responsibilities and mandates, the Committee on Ethical Practices, in the period since its formal creation, undertook an analysis of the issuance of local union charters as it relates to the problem of corruption. The code recomended in this report is the first in a series which the Committee plans to develop in accordance with the Executive Council's direction.

The Committee found that in this area, as in the field of union welfare funds, the instances of corruption are relatively rare. The vast majority of local union charters are issued by the affiliated national and international unions of the AFL-CIO for legitimate trade union purposes and without any taint or possibility of corruption. In a few instances, however, local union charters have fallen in the hands of corrupt individuals who have used these charters for their own illicit purposes instead of legitimate trade union objectives.

The possession of charters covering "paper locals" has enabled such racketeers to victimize individual workers, employers and the general public, while giving a black eye to the labor movement. They have used these charters to enter into conspiracies with corrupt employers to prevent, for a price, the genuine organization of workers into legitimate unions, thus depriving these workers of the benefit of honest collective bargaining agreements. These racketeers also use a charter as a basis to falsely

437

invoke the collective strength of the trade union movement for their illegitimate ends, thus demeaning the trade union's historic respect for the legitimate picket line, and injuring honest businessmen in the conduct of their affairs. A local union charter, improperly issued, can be used to control a local union unit vote, which negates the legitimate unit vote of bona fide local unions and thus subverts the democratic process within the trade union movement at various levels. A racketeer treats a charter as a "hunting license" to invade the jurisdictions of other national or international unions, in the interests only of corruption and dishonest gain, and to cloak with a respectable name a whole range of nefarious and corrupt activities.

Such corrupt practices are not widespread. But even the few instances in which local union charters have been corruptly used are too many. The name of the AFL-CIO, and of the national and international unions affiliated with it, must always be a hallmark of ethical trade union practices.

Scrupulous adherence, the Committee believes, to certain traditional practices and principles of the trade union movement with reference to the issuance of local union charters will serve to prevent and to eliminate the specific evils in this area.

The basic principle with reference to the issuance of a local union charter is that the charter is, in all unions, a solemn instrument establishing a subordinate or affiliated body of the international union, composed of organized workers in a particular subdivision of the union. The Committee has made a study of the practices and constitutions of a great number of national and international unions with respect to the issuance of local union charters. In the vast majority of cases, the Committee found, there is a constitutional prohibition against the issuance of charters in the absence of application by a minimum number of bona fide employees, eligible for membership in the union, within the jurisdiction covered by the charter.

The specific rules governing the issuance of charters necessarily vary greatly from union to union. And each national and international union, as part of its autonomous right, has complete authority to prescribe the particular procedures governing the issuance of local union charters. But whatever the particular procedures, each autonomous union has the duty to see to it that the purpose of issuing local union charters is to promote the general welfare of workers. The constitution of the AFL-CIO makes it clear that no affiliate has an autonomous right to permit corrupt or unethical practices which endanger the good name of the trade union movement.

The Committee believes that implementation and enforcement of the basic principle that local union charters are to be issued only to give recognition to workers joining together in a subordinate or affiliated body of a national or international union, which is in fact expressed in the vast majority of union constitutions, will provide an effective method of preventing the kind of evils described in this statement.

Therefore, the Ethical Practices Committee, under the authority vested in it by the constitution of the AFL-CIO and pursuant to the mandate of the First Constitutional Convention of the AFL-CIO, recommends that the Executive Council of the AFL-CIO adopt the following policies to safeguard the good name of the AFL-CIO and its affiliated unions and to prevent any taint or possibility of corruption in the issuance of local union charters:

1. A local union charter, whether issued by the AFL-CIO or by a national or international union affiliated with the AFL-CIO, should be a solemn instrument establishing a subordinate or affiliated body. To assure this, the AFL-CIO and each national and international union, by constitution or administrative regulation, should

require, for issuance of a local union charter, application by a group of bona fide employees, eligible for membership in the union, within the jurisdiction covered by the charter.

2. The purpose of issuing such charters should be to promote the general welfare of workers and to give recognition to their joining together in a subordinate or affiliated body.

3. A charter should never be issued to any person or persons who seek to use it as a "hunting license" for the improper invasion of the jurisdictions of other affiliated unions.

4. A charter should never be issued or permitted to continue in effect for a "paper local" not existing or functioning as a genuine local union of employees.

5. A charter should never be issued to persons who are known to traffic in local union charters for illicit or improper purposes.

6. The provision of the AFL-CIO constitution prohibiting the AFL-CIO and any affiliated national or international union from recognizing any subordinate organization that has been suspended or expelled by the AFL-CIO or any national or international union plainly includes and prohibits the issuance of a local union charter by the AFL-CIO or any affiliated national or international union to any group of individuals or any individuals suspended or expelled from the AFL-CIO or any affiliated national or international union for corruption or unethical practices.

7. The AFL-CIO and each national and international union shall take prompt action to eliminate any loop-holes through which local union charters have been or can be issued or permitted to continue in effect contrary to these policies.

8. The AFL-CIO and each national and international union shall take prompt action to insure the forthwith withdrawal of local union charters which have been issued and are now outstanding in violation of these policies.

CODE II: HEALTH AND WELFARE FUNDS
(Approved by the AFL-CIO Executive Council, January 31, 1957)

At its June, 1956 meeting the Executive Council directed the Committee on Ethical Practices "to develop a set of principles and guides for adoption by the AFL-CIO in order to implement the constitutional determination that the AFL-CIO shall be and remain free from all corrupt influences" and directed that such recommended guides and principles be submitted to the Council. In accordance with this direction, and its constitutional responsibilities, the Committee on Ethical Practices submitted to the Executive Council at its August, 1956 meeting the first of a proposed series of recommended codes. This code covering the issuance of local union charters was unanimously adopted by the Council.

This report, and the recommended code contained in it, is the second in the series which the Committee, in accordance with the Council's direction, is developing to implement the constitutional mandate that the AFL-CIO shall be and remain free from any and all corrupt influences and the determination of the first Constitutional Convention of the AFL-CIO that the reputations of the vast majority of labor union officials, who accept their responsibilities and trust, are "imperiled by the dishonest, corrupt, unethical practices of the few who betray their trust and who look upon the trade union movement not as a brotherhood to serve the general welfare, but as a means to advance their own selfish purposes. . . ."

Both the American Federation of Labor and the Congress of Industrial Organizations prior to the merger of these two organizations into the AFL-CIO gave thorough consideration to the subject of Health and Welfare Funds. This subject was also considered by and dealt with by the First Constitutional Convention of the AFL-CIO and a resolution dealing with this subject matter was adopted by that convention.

As stated in the resolution adopted by the First Constitutional Convention of the AFL-CIO, the task of administering and operating health and welfare programs which have been developed through collective bargaining has placed heavy new responsibilities upon the shoulders of trade union officials. The funds involved are paid for through the labor of the workers covered by the plans. They must be administered, therefore, as a high trust for the benefit only of those workers.

Most trade union officials have been faithful to the high trust which has been imposed upon them because of the development of health and welfare funds. The malfeasances of a few, however, have served to bring into disrepute not only the officials of the particular unions involved, but also the good name of the entire American labor movement. For this reason, it is imperative that the AFL-CIO and each of the national and international unions affiliated with it rigorously adhere to the highest ethical standards in dealing with the subject of health and welfare funds.

For these reasons, the Ethical Practices Committee, under the authority vested in it by the Constitution of the AFL-CIO and pursuant to the mandate of the First Constitutional Convention of the AFL-CIO, recommends that the Executive Council of the AFL-CIO adopt the following policies to safeguard the good name of the AFL-CIO and its affiliated unions:

1. No union official who already receives full-time pay from his union shall receive fees or salaries of any kind from a fund established for the provision of a health, welfare or retirement program. Where a salaried union official serves as employee representative or trustee in the administration of such programs, such service should be regarded as one of the functions expected to be performed by him in the normal course of his duties and not as an extra function requiring further compensation from the welfare fund.

2. No union official, employee or other person acting as agent or representative of a union, who exercises responsibilities or influence in the administration of welfare programs or the placement of insurance contracts, should have any compromising personal ties, direct or indirect, with outside agencies such as insurance carriers, brokers, or consultants doing business with the welfare plan. Such ties cannot be reconciled with the duty of a union official to be guided solely by the best interests of the membership in any transactions with such agencies. Any union official found to have such ties to his own personal advantage or to have accepted fees, inducements, benefits or favors of any kind from any such outside agency, should be removed. This principle, of course, does not prevent the existence of a relationship between a union officer or employee and an outside agency where

(a) No substantial personal advantage is derived from the relationship, and

(b) the outside agency is one in the management of which the union participates, as a union, for the benefit of its members.

3. Complete records of the financial operations of all welfare funds and programs

should be maintained in accordance with the best accounting practice. Each such fund should be audited regularly by internal auditors. In addition, each such fund should be audited at least once each year, and preferably semi-annually, by certified public or other independent accountants of unquestioned professional integrity, who should certify that the audits fully and comprehensively show the financial condition of the fund and the results of the operation of the fund.

4. All audit reports should be available to the membership of the union and the affected employees.

5. The trustees or administrators of welfare funds should make a full disclosure and report to the beneficiaries at least once each year. Such reports should set forth, in detail, the receipts and expenses of the fund; all salaries and fees paid by the fund, with a statement of the persons to whom paid; the amount paid and the service or purpose for which paid; a breakdown of insurance premiums paid, if a commercial insurance carrier is involved, showing, insofar as possible, the premiums paid, dividends, commissions, claims paid, retentions and service charges; a statement of the person to whom any commissions or fees of any kind were paid; a financial statement on the part of the insuring or service agency, if an agency other than a commercial insurance carrier is employed; and a detailed account of the manner in which the reserves held by the fund are invested.

6. Where health and welfare benefits are provided through the use of a commercial insurance carrier, the carrier should be selected though competitive bids solicited from a substantial number of reliable companies, on the basis of the lowest net cost for the given benefits submitted by a responsible carrier, taking into consideration such factors as comparative retention rates, financial responsibility, facilities for and promptness in servicing claims, and the past record of the carrier, including its record in dealing with trade unions representing its employees.

The trustees of the fund should be required to include in reporting to the membership the specific reasons for the selection of the carrier finally chosen. The carrier should be required to warrant that no fee or other remuneration of any kind has been paid directly or indirectly to any representative of the parties in connection with the business of the fund.

7. Where a union or union trustees participate in the administration of the investment of welfare fund reserves, the union or its trustees should make every effort to prohibit the investment of welfare fund reserves in the business of any contributing employer, insurance carrier or agency doing business with the fund, or in any enterprise in which any trustee, officer or employee of the fund has a personal financial interest of such a nature as to be affected by the fund's investment or disinvestment.

(This is not to be construed as preventing investment in an enterprise in which a union official is engaged by virtue of his office, provided (i) no substantial personal advantage is derived from the relationship, and (ii) the concern or enterprise is one in the management of which the union participates for the benefit of its members.)

8. Where any trustee, agent, fiduciary or employee of a health or welfare program is found to have received an unethical payment, the union should insist upon his removal and should take appropriate legal steps against both the party receiving and the party making the payment. Where health and welfare funds are negotiated or

administered by local unions or by other organizations subordinate to or affiliated with a national or international union, provision should be made to give the national or international union the authority to audit such funds and to apply remedies where there is evidence of a violation of ethical standards.

9. Every welfare program should provide redress against the arbitrary or unjust denial of claims so as to afford the individual member prompt and effective relief where his claim for benefits has been improperly rejected. Every program should provide for the keeping of complete records of the claims experience so that a constant check can be maintained on the relationship between claims and premiums and dividends, and on the utilization of the various benefits.

10. The duty of policing and enforcing these standards is shared by every union member, as well as by local, national and international officials. The best safeguard against abuses lies in the hands of a vigilant, informal and active membership, jealous of their rights and interests in the operation of health and welfare programs, as well as any other trade union program. As a fundamental part of any approach to the problem of policing health and welfare funds, affiliated unions, through education, publicity and discussion programs, should seek to develop the widest possible degree of active and informed interest in all phases of these programs on the part of the membership at large. International unions should, wherever possible, have expert advice available for the negotiation, establishment and administration of health and welfare plans, and should provide training for union representatives in the techniques and standards of proper administration of welfare plans.

11. Where constitutional amendments or changes in internal administrative procedure are necessary to comply with the standards herein set forth, such amendments and changes should be undertaken at the earliest practicable time.

CODE III: RACKETEERS, CROOKS, COMMUNISTS AND FASCISTS
(Approved by the AFL-CIO Executive Council, January 31, 1957)

This is the third in a series of recommended codes which the Committee on Ethical Practices has developed in accordance with the direction of the Executive Council that it should "develop a set of principles and guides for adoption by the AFL-CIO in order to implement the constitutional determination that the AFL-CIO shall be and remain free from all corrupt influences."

Article VIII, Section 7 of the Constitution of the AFL-CIO establishes that "it is a basic principle of this Federation that it must be and remain free from any and all corrupt influences and from the undermining efforts of Communist, Fascist or other totalitarian agencies who are opposed to the basic principles of our democracy and of free and democratic trade unionism." Under this constitutional provision there is no room within the Federation or any of its affiliated unions for any person in a position of leadership or responsibility who is a crook, a racketeer, a Communist or a Fascist. And it is the obligation of every union affiliated with the AFL-CIO to take appropriate steps to ensure that this principle is complied with.

To be sure, neither the AFL-CIO nor its affiliated unions are law-enforcing agencies. It is not within the purview or authority of a trade union to convict its members of a violation of statutory law. But it is the duty and responsibility of each national and international union affiliated with the federation to see to it that it is free of all corrupt, Communist or Fascist influences. Consequently, a trade union need not wait upon a criminal conviction to bar from office corrupt, Communist or Fascist influences. The responsibility of each union to see to it that it is free of such influences is not a responsibility placed upon our unions by law. It is a responsibility which rests upon our unions by the AFL-CIO Constitution and by the moral principles that govern the trade union movement. Eternal vigilance in this area is the price of an honest democratic trade union movement.

It is not possible, nor is it desirable, to set down rigid rules to determine whether a particular individual in a position of responsibility or leadership in the trade union movement is a crook, a racketeer, a Communist, or a Fascist. Obviously, if a person has been convicted of a crime involving moral turpitude offensive to trade union morality, he should be barred from office or responsible position in the labor movement. Obviously also, a person commonly known to be a crook or racketeer, should not enjoy immunity to prey upon the trade union movement because he has somehow managed to escape conviction. In the same manner, the fact that a person has refrained from formally becoming a member of the Communist party or a Fascist organization should not permit him to hold or retain a position of responsibility or leadership in the trade union movement if, regardless of formal membership, he consistently supports or actively participates in the activities of the Communist party or any Fascist or totalitarian organization.

In this area, as in all others, determinations must be made as a matter of common sense and with due regard to the rights of the labor unions and the individuals involved.

On the basis of these considerations, the Ethical Practices Committee, under the authority vested in it by the Constitution of the AFL-CIO, pursuant to the mandate of the First Constitutional Convention of the AFL-CIO, recommends that the Executive Council of the AFL-CIO adopt the following policies to safeguard the good name of the AFL-CIO and its affiliated unions:

1. The AFL-CIO and each of its affiliated unions should undertake the obligation, through appropriate constitutional or administrative measures and orderly procedures, to insure that no persons who constitute corrupt influences or practices or who represent or support Communist, Fascist or totalitarian agencies should hold office of any kind in such trade unions or organizations.

2. No person should hold or retain office or appointed position in the AFL-CIO or any of its affiliated national or international unions or subordinate bodies thereof who has been convicted of any crime involving moral turpitude offensive to trade union morality.

3. No person should hold or retain office or appointed position in the AFL-CIO or any of its affiliated national or international unions or subordinate bodies thereof who is commonly known to be a crook or racketeer preying on the labor movement and its good name for corrupt purposes, whether or not previously convicted for such nefarious activities.

4. No person should hold or retain office or appointed position in the AFL-CIO or any of its affiliated national or international unions or subordinate bodies thereof who is a member, consistent supporter or who actively participates in the activities of the Communist party or of any Fascist or other totalitarian organization which opposes the democratic principles to which our country and the American trade union movement are dedicated.

CODE IV: INVESTMENTS AND BUSINESS INTERESTS
OF UNION OFFICIALS
(Approved by the AFL-CIO Executive Council, January 31, 1957)

This is the fourth in a series of recommended codes which the Committee on
Ethical Practices has developed in accordance with the direction of the Executive
Council that it should "develop a set of principles and guides for adoption by the
AFL-CIO in order to implement the constitutional determination that the AFL-CIO
shall be and remain free from all corrupt influences." Prior codes have dealt with
the issuance of local union charters; welfare funds; racketeers, crooks and Communists. The code herein recommended deals with conflicts of interest in the investment and business interests of union officials.

It is too plain for extended discussion that a basic ethical principle in the conduct of trade union affairs is that no responsible trade union official should have a
personal financial interest which conflicts with the full performance of his fiduciary
duties as a workers' representative.

Obviously an irreconcilable conflict of interest would be present if a trade union
official, clothed with responsibility and discretion in conducting the representation
of workers, simultaneously maintains a substantial interest in the profits of the
employer of the workers whom he is charged with representing. Even though, in a
particular instance, there may be no actual malfeasance in the representation of
the employees involved, the opportunity for personal gain at the expense of the
welfare of the employees whom the union official represents obviously exists.

Such a simple case, however, does not fully present the problems which exist,
or may exist, in this area. There may be cases in which the conflict of interests
is not so clear, but nevertheless exists. There are, on the other hand, forms of
private investment which seem wholly devoid of any possibility of corruption or
dereliction in trade union responsibility. It will be the purpose of this report to
discuss some of the varying situations which may arise in this area and, on the
basis of such discussion, to present a recommended code of minimum standards
to which the Committee believes all trade union officials should adhere in their
investment and business interests.

The problems in this area, of course, could all be eliminated by adoption of the
simple principle that no trade union official should, under any circumstances, use his
own personal funds or property in any form of business enterprise or investment.
But the Committee feels that it is both unnecessary and unwise to establish such a
rigid standard for trade union officials; union officers and agents should not be
prohibited from investing their personal funds in their own way in the American
free enterprise system so long as they are scrupulously careful to avoid any actual
or potential conflict of interest. The American trade union movement does not
accept the principle that either its members or its leaders should own no property.
Both union leaders and members have the right to set aside their own personal
reserves for themselves and their families, and to invest and use those reserves
in legitimate ways.

But the trade union leader does have certain special responsibilities which he must
assume and respect because he serves as a leader in the trade union movement. And
those responsibilities, the Committee believes, necessarily imply certain restraints upon

his right to engage in personal investment, even with his own funds and on his own time. In a sense, a trade union official holds a position comparable to that of a public servant. Like a public servant, he has a high fiduciary duty not only to serve the members of his union honestly and faithfully, but also to avoid personal economic interest which may conflict or appear to conflict with the full performance of his responsibility to those whom he serves.

Like public servants, trade union leaders ought to be paid compensation commensurate with their services. But, like public servants, trade union leaders must accept certain limitations upon their private activities which result from the nature of their services. Indeed, the nature of the trade union movement and the responsibilities which necessarily must be accepted by its leaders, make the strictest standards with respect to any possible conflict of interest properly applicable.

It is plain, as already stated, that a responsible trade union official should not be the owner in whole or in part of a business enterprise with which his union bargains collectively on behalf of its employees. The conflict in such a case is clear.

It is almost equally clear, the Committee believes, that a trade union official should not be the owner of a business enterprise which sells to, buys from or in other ways deals, to any significant degree, with the enterprise with which he conducts collective bargaining. Again, the possibility that the trade union official may be given special favors or contracts by the employer in return for less than discharge of his obligations as a trade union leader, exists.

Somewhat different considerations, however, apply to the ownership, through purchase on the open market or other legitimate means, of publicly traded securities. Employee ownership of stock is certainly a fairly common practice in American life. Often, indeed, there are special stock purchase plans designed to stimulate such employee investments.

On the other hand, ownership, even of publicly traded securities, in sufficient amounts to influence the course of management decision seems to the Committee incompatible with the proper representation of the employees by a trade union official.

The Committee believes, therefore, that the minimum standards of ethical conduct in this area should not forbid all investments by a trade union official in the corporate securities of companies employing the workers he represents. Such investment by a trade union official, however, should always be subject to the restriction that it is not acquired in an illegitimate or unethical manner, that it is limited to securities which are publicly traded, and that his interest should never be large enough so as to permit him to exercise any individual influence on the course of corporate decision.

There is nothing in the essential ethical principles of the trade union movement which should prevent a trade union official, at any level, from investing personal funds in the publicly traded securities of corporate enterprises unrelated to the industry or area in which the official has a particular trade union responsibility. Such securities offer a wide choice of investment and are, generally speaking, so far removed from individual stockholder control or influence that with the exceptions above noted, there is no reason to bar investment by trade union officials.

The same principles apply with respect to privately owned or closely held businesses which are completely unrelated to the industrial area in which the trade union leader serves.

On the basis of these considerations, the Ethical Practices Committee, under the authority vested in it by the Constitution of the AFL-CIO and pursuant to the mandate of the First Constitutional Convention of the AFL-CIO, recommends that the Executive Council of the AFL-CIO adopt the following policies to safeguard the good name of the AFL-CIO and its affiliated unions:

1. No responsible trade union official should have a personal financial interest which conflicts with the full performance of his fiduciary duties as a workers' representative.

2. No responsible trade union official should own or have a substantial business interest in any business enterprise with which his union bargains collectively, or in any business enterprise which is in competition with any other business enterprise with which his union bargains collectively.

3. No responsible trade union official should own or have a substantial business interest in a business enterprise a substantial part of which consists of buying from, selling to, or otherwise dealing with the business enterprise with which his union bargains collectively.

4. The provisions of paragraphs 2 and 3 above do not apply in the case of an investment in the publicly traded securities of widely held corporations which investment does not constitute a substantial enough holding to affect or influence the course of corporate decision.

5. No responsible trade union official should accept "kickbacks," under-the-table payments, gifts of other than nominal value, or any personal payment of any kind other than regular pay and benefits for work performed as an employee from an employer or business enterprise with which his union bargains collectively.

6. The policies herein set forth apply to: (a) all officers of the AFL-CIO and all officers of national and international unions affiliated with the AFL-CIO, (b) all elected or appointed staff representatives and business agents of such organizations, and (c) all officers of subordinate bodies of such organizations who have any degree of discretion or responsibility in the negotiation of collective bargaining agreements or their administration.

7. The principles herein set forth apply not only where investments are made by union officials, but also where third persons are used as blinds or covers to conceal the financial interests of union officials.

CODE V: FINANCIAL PRACTICES AND PROPRIETARY ACTIVITIES OF UNIONS
(Approved by the AFL-CIO Executive Council, May 22, 1957)

This is the fifth in a series of recommended codes which the Committee on Ethical Practices has developed in accordance with the direction of the Executive Council that it should "develop a set of principles and guides for adoption by the AFL-CIO in order to implement the constitutional determination that the AFL-CIO shall be and remain free from all corrupt influences." On August 29, 1956, the Council approved a code dealing with the issuance of local union charters; on January 31, 1957, the Executive Council approved codes dealing with health and welfare funds, racketeering, crooks and Communists, and investment and business interests of union officials.

There are principles inherent in the conception of a free, honest, and democratic trade union movement, which, the Committee believes, virtually dictate the outlines of any Code of Ethical Practices dealing with union finances. The first of these principles hardly requires statement. It is simply that a labor union is an organization whose primary function is to improve the wages, hours and working conditions of the employees it represents, through the processes of collective bargaining with employers. It is not a business enterprise or an investment company. Unions, of course, must have funds with which to operate and it is clearly desirable that they should maintain reserves to cover contingencies which may arise in the course of the performance of their functions as workers' representatives. But, equally clearly, the accumulation of funds *per se* is not the objective for which the union exists. A union is not a profit-making institution but a democratic organization with definite social aims and principles. Union funds are held in trust for the benefit of the membership. But a union, unlike a bank, a trustee, or other fiduciaries, is not primarily a manager of funds vested with the duty of enhancing their value and making distributions. Increasing the value of the union's funds should never become an objective of such magnitude that it in any way interferes with or obscures the basic function of the union, which is to devote its resources to representing its members, honestly and faithfully.

A second basic principle which dictates the terms of a Code of Ethical Practices with respect to the handling of union funds is again simple. It is that unions are democratic organizations. The fact that a union is a democratic organization plainly implies that the members of the union are entitled to assurance that the union's funds, which are their funds, are not dissipated. They are also entitled to be reasonably informed as to how the funds of the organization are being used or invested. Finally, their delegated representatives in the union's governing body and conventions should have the power and responsibility to oversee the expenditure of the union's monies so that the members can be guaranteed that funds are expended solely for the purposes for which the organization exists.

A final fundamental principle, the Committee believes, is involved. That principle is that each national or international union affiliated with the AFL-CIO, in the words of the Resolution on Ethical Practices which was unanimously adopted by the founding Convention of the AFL-CIO in December, 1955, "has clearly accepted the responsibility for keeping its own house in order and to protect the movement 'from any and all corrupt influences and from the undermining efforts of Communist agencies and all others who are opposed to the basic principles of our democracy and free and democratic unionism.' "

From these three basic principles, the Committee believes that certain conclusions necessarily follow. Since a union holds its funds for the benefit of its membership and to further their interests it should comply with standards generally applicable to fiduciaries or trustees with respect to the manner in which it keeps its records and accounts. Regular audits should be made and there should be appropriate distribution of summaries of such audits so that the membership and the public are adequately apprised of the state of the organization's finances.

In this connection, a Committee of Secretary-Treasurers of AFL-CIO affiliates has drawn up a suggested set of minimum accounting and financial controls for affiliates of the AFL-CIO. This set of controls represents, the Committee believes, the minimum with which any affiliated organization should comply in order to fulfill the constitutional mandate that the labor movement should be kept free from any taint of corruption. Almost all unions, the Committee believes, today comply with the minimum controls set forth in the recommendation of the Secretary-Treasurers. Many, indeed, have much stricter controls. The minimum controls suggested by the Secretary-Treasurers, therefore, should not be regarded as an optimum. Unions are to be commended and encouraged to establish and maintain even more stringent accounting and financial controls.

In addition to accounting and financial procedures necessary to conform to the controls applicable generally to well-run business organizations and fiduciaries, the Committee believes that certain other rules follow from the basic principles set forth above. Because a union is a union, not a business organization or a trust company, the rules which guide its use and investment of funds are necessarily different. For example, investments by business organizations in other businesses from which they buy or sell, so that the investing business may get favored treatment in its sales or purchases, may be an acceptable business practice; similar investment by a labor union in business enterprises with which it bargains collectively presents serious problems. Such investment is not good practice for a union.

The fact that the basic objective in the management of trade union funds is not the maximizing of profit, but to further the objectives of the members' joining together in a union leads to additional conclusions.

A business organization has one function: to make money for its stockholders. A fiduciary's primary obligation is to preserve and, within limits defined by the necessity for safety, to augment the funds which the trustee is charged with holding for the benefit of the beneficiaries.

Since these are not a union's primary functions, a union's investment policy may properly be governed by different considerations. For example, business institutions and corporate trustees might question today the propriety of investing all of their reserves in government bonds because of their comparatively low yield. Yet, for a trade union, one of whose fundamental objects is "to protect and strengthen our democratic institutions," such an investment policy is to be commended. Similarly, since another object of a trade union is to aid and assist other unions and "to promote the organization of the unorganized into unions of their own choosing," loans and grants for mutual aid and assistance are part of the proud tradition of the labor movement even though foreign to the business community and not justified by any considerations of financial gain or even security.

Similarly, the business community may not regard it to be a bad business practice for a business enterprise to buy or sell from firms in which the officers of the business have a financial interest. Nor may the business community regard it as bad practice for a business organization to lend money, on adequate security, to members of the organization. Because the funds of a labor union are both held in trust for the benefit of its members and are held to further legitimate trade union purposes, practices which may be acceptable in business organizations, the Committee believes, should be limited if not completely eliminated among labor organizations.

All of these considerations lead to this ultimate conclusion. With respect to accounting and financial controls and the expenditure of its funds for proprietary (housekeeping) functions the labor movement, it goes almost without saying, should follow the strictest rules applicable to all well-run institutions. With respect to the policies governing its financial and proprietary decisions, a higher obligation rests upon the trade union movement: to conduct its affairs and to expend and invest its funds, not for profit, but for the benefit of its membership and the great purposes for which they have joined together in the fraternity of the labor movement.

On the basis of these considerations the Committee on Ethical Practices, under the authority vested in it by the Constitution of the AFL-CIO and pursuant to the mandate of the First Constitutional Convention of the AFL-CIO and of the Executive Council, recommends that the Executive Council of the AFL-CIO adopt the following policies to safeguard the good name of the AFL-CIO and its affiliated unions:

1. The AFL-CIO and all affiliated national and international unions should comply with the minimum accounting and financial controls suggested by the Committee of Secretary-Treasurers and approved by the Executive Council, which is annexed hereto.

2. The AFL-CIO and all affiliated national and international unions should conduct their proprietary functions, including all contracts for purchase or sale or for the rendition of housekeeping services, in accordance with the practices of well-run institutions, including the securing of competitive bids for all major contracts.

3. Neither the AFL-CIO nor any national or international union affiliated with the AFL-CIO should permit any of its funds to be loaned, invested, or otherwise dealt with in a manner which inures to the personal profit or advantage of any officer, representative or employee of the union.

4. Neither the AFL-CIO nor any national or international union affiliated with the AFL-CIO should enter into any contracts of purchase or sale or for the rendition of services which will inure to or result in the personal profit or advantage, including gifts of more than nominal value, other than his regular salary or compensation, of any officer, representative or employee of the union.

5. Neither the AFL-CIO nor any national or international union affiliated with the AFL-CIO should invest in or make loans to any business enterprise with which it bargains collectively.

6. The provisions of paragraph 5 shall not be construed as prohibiting investment by unions in the publicly traded securities of widely held corporations which investment does not constitute a substantial enough holding to affect or influence the course of corporate decision; the provisions of paragraphs 3 and 4 shall not be construed as applying to the profit that may result from a proper investment by a union officer, representative or employee. Nor shall such provisions be construed as preventing investment in a business or enterprise in which an official of an affiliate is engaged by virtue of his office, provided (a) no substantial personal advantage is derived from the relationship, and (b) the business or enterprise is one in the management of which the affiliate participates for the benefit of its members. The provisions of such paragraphs, however, shall apply wherever third persons are used as blinds or covers to conceal the personal profit or advantage of union officials.

7. Neither the AFL-CIO nor any national or international union affiliated with the AFL-CIO should make personal loans to its officers, representatives, employees, or members, or members of their families, for the purpose of financing the private business or investment of such persons.

8. Each national or international union affiliated with the AFL-CIO should promptly take whatever internal steps are needed to ensure that the standards set forth in this Code are made applicable to itself and each of its locals and other subordinate or affiliated bodies. Wherever constitutional amendments or changes in internal administrative procedures are necessary to fully comply with those standards, such amendments and changes should be undertaken by the affiliates at the earliest practicable opportunity.

Supplemental Code

MINIMUM ACCOUNTING & FINANCIAL CONTROLS

(Drafted by Special Committee of Union Secretary-Treasurers;
Approved by Executive Council, May 22, 1957)

A. Detailed and accurate records of accounts, in conformity with generally recognized and accepted principles of accounting, should be currently maintained by all affiliates of the AFL-CIO. These records should include, as a minimum need, a cash receipt record, a cash disbursements record, a general ledger, a dues or per capita tax record, an investment record, and a payroll record.

B. All receipts should be duly recorded and currently deposited. No disbursements of any nature should be made from undeposited cash receipts.

C. All expenditures should be approved by proper authority under constitutional provision and be recorded and supported by vouchers, providing an adequate description of the nature and purpose of the expenditure sufficient for a reasonable audit by internal and independent auditors. Disbursements should be made only by check, with the exception of disbursements from petty cash, in which situation, an imprest petty cash fund should be established.

D. Salaries of elected officials should be established only by constitutional provision. Compensation to non-salaried elected officials, and to other officials, representatives and employees, if not fixed by constitutional provision, should be established and paid in strict conformity with such authority as is provided by the constitution and in accordance with its applicable provisions.

E. Reimbursement of expenses, including per diem expenses, should be made only where such expenses have been duly authorized and are supported in a manner that will permit a reasonable audit.

F. Every precaution should be taken to ensure the soundness and safety of investments and that investments are made only by persons duly authorized to act for and on behalf of the affiliate. Investments in securities should either be restricted to the type of securities which legally qualify for trust fund investments in the domicile state or a person or persons authorized to invest funds of an affiliate should, in making such investment, be required to exercise the judgment and care under the circumstances then prevailing which men of prudence, discretion and intelligence exercise in the management of their own affairs, not in regard to speculation but in regard to the permanent disposition of their funds, considering probable safety of their capital as well as probable income. No investment should be made by an affiliate in a business or enterprise in which any officer of that affiliate has a direct or indirect personal financial interest of such a nature as to be affected by the affiliate's investment or withdrawal of investment. (This last stated provision is not to be construed as preventing investment in a business or enterprise in which an official of an affiliate is engaged by virtue of his office, provided (a) no substantial personal advantage is derived from the relationship, and (b) the business or enterprise is one in the management of which the affiliate participates for the benefit of its members.) Securities owned by the affiliate should be under dual officer control and held by a bank or a trust company as agent or if that is not feasible, such securities should be placed in a safety deposit vault. All investments and legal title to all assets of an affiliate should be in the name of the affiliate or its duly designated agent or trustee.

G. Periodic, but not less than semi-annual, detailed financial reports should be prepared in accordance with generally recognized and accepted standards of financial reporting. These reports should be prepared and submitted by the elected financial office of the affiliate to the executive body of such affiliate for its study and such action as may be required.

H. A record of each meeting of the executive body of an affiliate should be made and maintained. These records should note all official actions taken by that body, in relation to accounting and financial matters.

I. Adequate fidelity bond coverage should be required by an affiliate for all officers, representatives and employees of that affiliate in positions of trust, including officers and employees of subordinate bodies of such affiliate.

J. Affiliates and their subordinate bodies should be subject to a system of internal audits made by auditors or by other competent persons in accordance with generally accepted standards of auditing so as to maintain current vigilance over all financial transactions.

K. At least annually, an audit of the accounts of each affiliate, except directly affiliated local unions of the AFL-CIO, should be made by independent certified public accountants. A summary of such audit approved by such independent certified public accountants should be made available to the membership of the affiliate and the public.

Each such affiliate should require, at least annually, that an audit be made of the accounts of its subordinate bodies by competent persons. A summary of such audit approved by such competent persons should be made available to the membership of such subordinate body.

An annual audit of the accounts of directly affiliated local unions should be made by authorized competent representatives of the AFL-CIO designated by the Secretary-Treasurer of the AFL-CIO. A summary of such audit, approved by such representative, shall be made available to the membership of such directly affiliated local unions.

L. All financial and accounting records of affiliates and their subordinate bodies, and all supporting vouchers and documents, or microfilm copies thereof, should be preserved for a period of time not less than that prescribed by applicable statutes of limitations.

M. Neither the AFL-CIO nor any national or international union affiliated with the AFL-CIO should make personal loans to its officers, representatives, employees, or members, or members of their families, for the purpose of financing the private business or investment of such persons.

N. No "kickbacks" or any other improper payments should be accepted or made, directly or indirectly, by any officer, representative or employee of an affiliate in connection with any financial transaction of such affiliate.

O. Affiliates should take every precaution necessary to insure their full compliance with all properly authorized and applicable requirements of state or federal law pertaining to financial and accounting matters and to reporting.

P. In order to protect and safeguard the good name and reputation of the AFL-CIO and its affiliates, the financial and accounting controls set forth herein are made applicable to itself and each of the affiliates of the AFL-CIO and their subordinate bodies and to all their funds of whatever nature.

Q. Where constitutional amendments or changes in internal administrative procedure are necessary to a full compliance with the standards set forth herein, such amendments and changes should be undertaken by affiliates at the earliest practicable opportunity.

CODE VI: UNION DEMOCRATIC PROCESSES
(Approved by the AFL-CIO Executive Council, May 23, 1957)

This is the sixth in a series of recommended codes developed by the AFL-CIO Committee on Ethical Practices. The prior codes have dealt, primarily, with the questions related to corruption and conflicts of interest. The present code has been developed by the Committee pursuant to the mandate contained in Article II, Sections 10 and 11, of the Constitution of the AFL-CIO which sets forth the basic objectives of the Federation to protect the labor movement not only from corrupt influences and Communist agencies but also from "all others who are opposed to the basic principles of our democracy and free and democratic unionism," and "to safeguard the democratic character of the labor movement."

These constitutional provisions of the AFL-CIO give effect to the democratic tradition upon which the entire labor movement is based. Freedom and democracy are the essential attributes of our movement. Labor organizations lacking these attributes, like Hitler's Labor Front, Franco's syndicates, and Moscow's captive unions, are unions in name only. Authoritarian control, whether from within the labor movement or imposed from without by government, is contrary to the spirit, the tradition and the principles which should always guide and govern our movement.

We are proud of our record. Just as the Constitution of the AFL-CIO proclaims its dedication to the concepts of freedom and democracy and contains machinery for their implementation in the Federation's operations, so also do the constitutions of its affiliates. Almost without exception, they provide for the basic elements of union democracy: the right of full and equal participation by each member in the affairs and processes of union self-government, in accordance with the principles of representative democracy, and the necessity for protecting the rights of individual members.

The record of union democracy, like the record of our nation's democracy, is not perfect. A few unions do not adequately, in their constitutions, provide for these basic elements of democratic practice. A few unions do not practice or implement the principles set forth in their constitutions. Finally, while the overwhelming majority of American unions both preach and practice the principles of democracy, in all too many instances the membership by apathy and indifference have forfeited their rights of union citizenship.

The provisions of the Taft-Hartley Act have substantially frustrated previously successful efforts by unions to ensure maximum attendance and participation by the membership in union meetings and affairs. The real corrective in this area is not so much the establishment of new principles as the exercise of rights presently recognized and accorded. Just as eternal vigilance is the price of liberty, so is the constant exercise of the rights of union citizenship the price of union democracy.

It is valuable, nevertheless, to restate the principles which should govern all free and democratic unions and to rededicate the labor movement to the preservation of these principles.

The Committee on Ethical Practices has attempted to formulate in the following code the basic and elementary principles which any affiliated union should achieve if it is to comply with the basic principles and objects of the AFL-CIO Constitution. Necessarily, since each union has grown up in its own tradition and with its own background, forms and procedures may differ widely. Unions should be free to determine their own governmental structure and to regulate their own affairs. But, whatever the form, the basic democratic rights set forth in the code should be guaranteed.

1. Each member of a union should have the right to full and free participation in union self-government. This should include the right (a) to vote periodically for his local and national officers, either directly by referendum vote or through delegate bodies, (b) to honest elections, (c) to stand for and to hold office, subject only to fair qualifications uniformly imposed, (d) to voice his views as to the method in which the union's affairs should be conducted.

2. Each member of a union should have the right to fair treatment in the application of union rules and law. The general principle applicable to union disciplinary procedures is that such procedures should contain all the elements of fair play. No particular formality is required. No lawyers need be used. The essential requirements of due process, however—notice, hearing, and judgment on the basis of the evidence—should be observed. A method of appeal to a higher body should be provided to ensure that judgment at the local level is not the result of prejudice or bias.

3. Each member of a union has the responsibility (a) fully to exercise his rights of union citizenship and (b) loyally to support his union. The right of an individual member to criticize the policies and personalities of his union officers does not include the right to undermine the union as an institution, to advocate dual unionism, to destroy or weaken the union as a collective bargaining agency, or to carry on slander and libel.

4. To safeguard the rights of the individual members and to safeguard its democratic character, the AFL-CIO and each affiliated national or international union should hold regular conventions at stated intervals, which should be not more than four years. The convention should be the supreme governing body of the union.

5. Officers of the AFL-CIO and of each affiliated national or international union should be elected, either by referendum vote or by the vote of delegate bodies. Whichever method is used, election should be free, fair and honest and adequate internal safeguards should be provided to ensure the achievement of that objective.

6. All general conventions of the AFL-CIO and of affiliated national or international unions should be open to the public, except for necessary executive sessions. Convention proceedings or an accurate summary thereof should be published and be available to the membership.

7. The appropriate officials of the union and such bodies which are given authority to govern a union's affairs between conventions should be elected, whether from the membership at large or by appropriate divisions, either by referendum vote or by the vote of delegate bodies. Such bodies shall abide by and enforce the provisions of the union's constitution and carry out the decisions of the convention.

8. Membership meetings of local unions should be held periodically with proper notice of time and place.

9. Elections of local union officers should be democratic, conducted either by referendum or by vote of a delegate body which is itself elected by referendum or at union meetings.

10. The term of office of all union officials should be stated in the organization's constitution or by-laws and should be for a reasonable period, not to exceed four years.

11. To ensure democratic, responsible, and honest administration of its locals and other subordinate bodies, the AFL-CIO and affiliated national and international unions should have the power to institute disciplinary and corrective proceedings with respect to local unions and other subordinate bodies, including the power to establish trusteeships where necessary. Such powers should be exercised sparingly and only in accordance with the provisions of the union's constitution, and autonomy should be restored promptly upon correction of the abuses requiring trusteeship.

12. Where constitutional amendments or changes in internal administrative procedures are necessary to comply with the standards herein set forth, such amendments and changes should be undertaken at the earliest practicable time.

Index